To Eddy
learn to live & grow
in God's love for you
Fr. B Bonell

THE JERUSALEM BIBLE
NEW TESTAMENT

General Editor
ALEXANDER JONES
L.S.S., S.T.L., I.C.B.

THE JERUSALEM BIBLE

NEW TESTAMENT

HODDER AND STOUGHTON
LONDON SYDNEY AUCKLAND TORONTO

CONTENTS

CONTENTS

INTRODUCTION TO
THE SYNOPTIC GOSPELS

The first three gospels are called synoptic ('with the same eye') because their narratives are all built on the same events in the life of Jesus and indeed many passages from all three of them can be placed side by side as evident parallels. From the earliest times, Matthew, Mark and Luke respectively have been named as the writers of them.

According to a tradition dating from the 2nd century, St Matthew was the first to write a gospel and he wrote 'in the Hebrew tongue'. Our Greek 'Gospel according to St Matthew' is not identified with this early Aramaic book, which is lost, though there are times when it appears to represent a more primitive text than Mark.

Some parts of the gospel story assumed a fixed and stereotyped pattern in the oral tradition founded on the preaching of the apostles; the similarity of the Passion in all four gospels suggests a common oral tradition very firmly fixed. But the relationships between the three synoptic gospels are too close and too complex to be explained by a common oral tradition underlying all of them. It is clear that Luke depends on Mark, and although it was held for a long time that Mark depends on Matthew, a number of indications now suggest the reverse. Luke and Matthew also have a number of non-Marcan passages common to both, and these probably have a common source or sources; in addition, each of these gospels includes episodes and sayings not found in the other.

Mark, said to have been Peter's interpreter, is mentioned in St Paul's letters as one of his companions, and described in Acts as a disciple from Jerusalem. Luke is also mentioned in St Paul's letters and when writing Acts incorporated parts of a first-person travel diary. Mark's gospel can be dated before A.D. 70, perhaps about 64. Our Greek Matthew and Luke are later and probably date from 70 to 80.

The arrangement and presentation of the historical facts in the synoptic gospels are dictated by the purposes of a written gospel: to convert, to edify, to infuse faith, to enlighten it and defend it against its opponents.

Mark

The shortest of the gospels, it is not concerned with elaborating Christ's teaching and it records few of his sayings; the real point of its message is *the manifestation of the crucified Messiah*. While on the one hand Jesus is seen by the writer as the Son of God, acknowledged by the Father and vindicating his power and his mission by miracles, on the other hand he chooses to appear to the world under the mysterious title 'Son of Man', and the gospel puts great emphasis on his apparent frustration and rejection by the people. The 'messianic secret' is a basic idea of Mark's gospel.

Matthew

This gospel is divided into five books, each consisting of a discourse introduced by painstakingly selected narrative matter which follows the same broad outline as in Mark. These are preceded by the story of the Infancy and followed by that of the Passion. The fact that this gospel reports Christ's teaching much more fully than Mark and stresses especially the theme of the 'kingdom of heaven' makes it *a dramatic account in seven acts of the coming of the kingdom*. Matthew, writing for Jewish Christians, makes a special point of demonstrating, by the use of Old Testament quotations, that *the scriptures are fulfilled* in the person and work of Jesus.

Luke

The plan of this gospel follows Mark's outline as a rule, but the narrative is controlled and edited to bring in much teaching, including the longer parables, and to omit episodes that would not interest Luke's non-Jewish readers. The originality of Luke is in *his religious mentality*: he is the faithful recorder of Christ's lovingkindness, he emphasises the necessity for prayer and he is the only one of the synoptic authors to give the Holy Spirit the prominence which we find in Paul and in Acts.

Greek style

Mark's Greek is rough, strongly Aramaic and often faulty, but it is fresh and frank. Matthew's Greek is also rather Aramaic but smoother and more correct than Mark's, though less picturesque. Luke's style is variable: excellent when he is writing independently but at other times incorporating the peculiarities of his sources; as in Acts he suits the style to the subject and occasionally he goes out of his way to give a good imitation of Septuagint Greek.

THE GOSPEL

ACCORDING TO

SAINT MATTHEW

I. THE BIRTH AND INFANCY OF JESUS

The ancestry of Jesus

1 A genealogy of Jesus Christ, son of David, son of Abraham:[a]
2 Abraham was the father of Isaac,
Isaac the father of Jacob,
Jacob the father of Judah and his brothers,
3 Judah was the father of Perez and Zerah, Tamar being their mother,
Perez was the father of Hezron,
Hezron the father of Ram,
4 Ram was the father of Amminadab,
Amminadab the father of Nahshon,
Nahshon the father of Salmon,
5 Salmon was the father of Boaz, Rahab being his mother,
Boaz was the father of Obed, Ruth being his mother,
Obed was the father of Jesse;
6 and Jesse was the father of King David.

David was the father of Solomon, whose mother had been Uriah's wife,
7 Solomon was the father of Rehoboam,
Rehoboam the father of Abijah,
Abijah the father of Asa,
8 Asa was the father of Jehoshaphat,
Jehoshaphat the father of Joram,
Joram the father of Azariah,
9 Azariah was the father of Jotham,
Jotham the father of Ahaz,
Ahaz the father of Hezekiah,

1 a. Showing the descent of Joseph, legally the father of Jesus, from Abraham and David, to whom the messianic promises were made.

10 Hezekiah was the father of Manasseh,
Manasseh the father of Amon,
Amon the father of Josiah;
11 and Josiah was the father of Jechoniah and his brothers.
Then the deportation to Babylon took place.

12 After the deportation to Babylon:
Jechoniah was the father of Shealtiel,
Shealtiel the father of Zerubbabel,
13 Zerubbabel was the father of Abiud,
Abiud the father of Eliakim,
Eliakim the father of Azor,
14 Azor was the father of Zadok,
Zadok was the father of Achim,
Achim the father of Eliud,
15 Eliud was the father of Eleazar,
Eleazar the father of Matthan,
Matthan the father of Jacob;
16 and Jacob was the father of Joseph the husband of Mary;
of her was born Jesus who is called Christ.

17   The sum of generations is therefore: fourteen from Abraham to David; fourteen from David to the Babylonian deportation; and fourteen from the Babylonian deportation to Christ.

The virginal conception of Christ

18   This is how Jesus Christ came to be born. His mother Mary was betrothed to Joseph;[b] but before they came to live together she was found to be with child through the Holy
19 Spirit. ·Her husband Joseph, being a man of honour and wanting to spare her publicity, decided to divorce her
20 informally. ·He had made up his mind to do this when the angel of the Lord appeared to him in a dream and said, 'Joseph son of David, do not be afraid to take Mary home as your wife, because she has conceived what is in her by the
21 Holy Spirit. ·She will give birth to a son and you must name him Jesus, because he is the one who is to save[c] his people
22 from their sins.' ·Now all this took place to fulfil the words spoken by the Lord through the prophet:

23   *The virgin will conceive and give birth to a son*
         and they will call him Immanuel,[d]

24 a name which means 'God-is-with-us'. ·When Joseph woke up he did what the angel of the Lord had told him to do: he

25 took his wife to his home ·and, though he had not had intercourse with her, she gave birth to a son; and he named him Jesus.

The visit of the Magi

2 After Jesus had been born at Bethlehem in Judaea during the reign of King Herod,[a] some wise men came to Jerusalem
2 from the east. ·'Where is the infant king of the Jews?' they asked. 'We saw his star as it rose[b] and have come to do him
3 homage.' ·When King Herod heard this he was perturbed,
4 and so was the whole of Jerusalem. ·He called together all the chief priests and the scribes of the people, and enquired of
5 them where the Christ was to be born. ·'At Bethlehem in Judaea,' they told him 'for this is what the prophet wrote:

6 *And you, Bethlehem, in the land of Judah,*
*   you are by no means least among the leaders of Judah,*
*   for out of you will come a leader*
*   who will shepherd my people Israel'.*[c]

7 Then Herod summoned the wise men to see him privately. He asked them the exact date on which the star had appeared,
8 and sent them on to Bethlehem. 'Go and find out all about the child,' he said 'and when you have found him, let me
9 know, so that I too may go and do him homage.' ·Having listened to what the king had to say, they set out. And there in front of them was the star they had seen rising; it went forward and halted over the place where the child was.
10
11 The sight of the star filled them with delight, ·and going into the house they saw the child with his mother Mary, and falling to their knees they did him homage. Then, opening their treasures, they offered him gifts of gold and frankin-
12 cense and myrrh.[d] ·But they were warned in a dream not to go back to Herod, and returned to their own country by a different way.

The flight into Egypt. The massacre of the Innocents

13 After they had left, the angel of the Lord appeared to Joseph in a dream and said, 'Get up, take the child and his

b. In a Jewish betrothal the man was already called the 'husband' of the woman, and he could release himself from the engagement only by an act of repudiation, v. 19. c. 'Jesus' (Hebr. Yehoshua) means 'Yahweh saves'. d. Is 7:14
2 a. About 5 or 4 B.C. Herod was king of Judaea, Idumaea and Samaria from 37 to 4 B.C. b. 'In the east' is an alternative translation, here and in v. 9. c. Mi 5:1 d. The wealth and perfumes of Arabia.

mother with you, and escape into Egypt, and stay there until I tell you, because Herod intends to search for the child and
14 do away with him'. ·So Joseph got up and, taking the child and his mother with him, left that night for Egypt,
15 where he stayed until Herod was dead. This was to fulfil what the Lord had spoken through the prophet:

I called my son out of Egypt,[e]

16   Herod was furious when he realised that he had been outwitted by the wise men, and in Bethlehem and its surrounding district he had all the male children killed who were two years old or under, reckoning by the date he had been
17 careful to ask the wise men. ·It was then that the words spoken through the prophet Jeremiah were fulfilled:

18
> *A voice was heard in Ramah,*
> *sobbing and loudly lamenting:*
> *it was Rachel weeping for her children,*
> *refusing to be comforted*
> *because they were no more.*[f]

From Egypt to Nazareth

19   After Herod's death, the angel of the Lord appeared in a
20 dream to Joseph in Egypt ·and said, 'Get up, take the child and his mother with you and go back to the land of Israel, for
21 those who wanted to kill the child are dead'. ·So Joseph got up and, taking the child and his mother with him, went back
22 to the land of Israel. But when he learnt that Archelaus[g] had succeeded his father Herod as ruler of Judaea he was afraid to go there, and being warned in a dream he left for the
23 region of Galilee.[h] ·There he settled in a town called Nazareth. In this way the words spoken through the prophets were to be fulfilled:

He will be called a Nazarene

II. THE KINGDOM OF HEAVEN PROCLAIMED

A. NARRATIVE SECTION

The preaching of John the Baptist

3   In due course John the Baptist appeared; he preached in
2 the wilderness of Judaea and this was his message:
3 'Repent, for the kingdom of heaven[a] is close at hand'.

3 This was the man the prophet Isaiah spoke of when he said:

> *A voice cries in the wilderness:*
> *Prepare a way for the Lord,*
> *make his paths straight.*[b]

4 This man John wore a garment made of camel-hair with a leather belt round his waist, and his food was locusts and
5 wild honey. ·Then Jerusalem and all Judaea and the whole
6 Jordan district made their way to him, ·and as they were baptised by him in the river Jordan they confessed their sins.
7 But when he saw a number of Pharisees and Sadducees[c]
8 coming for baptism he said to them, ·"Brood of vipers, who warned you to fly from the retribution that is coming? But if
9 you are repentant, produce the appropriate fruit, ·and do not presume to tell yourselves, "We have Abraham for our father", because, I tell you, God can raise children for
10 Abraham from these stones. ·Even now the axe is laid to the roots of the trees, so that any tree which fails to produce good
11 fruit will be cut down and thrown on the fire. ·I baptise you in water for repentance, but the one who follows me is more powerful than I am, and I am not fit to carry his sandals; he
12 will baptise you with the Holy Spirit and fire. ·His winnowing-fan is in his hand; he will clear his threshing-floor and gather his wheat into the barn; but the chaff he will burn in a fire that will never go out.'

Jesus is baptised

13 Then Jesus appeared: he came from Galilee to the Jordan
14 to be baptised by John. ·John tried to dissuade him. 'It is I who need baptism from you' he said 'and yet you come to
15 me!' ·But Jesus replied, 'Leave it like this for the time being; it is fitting that we should, in this way, do all that righteousness demands'. At this, John gave in to him.
16 As soon as Jesus was baptised he came up from the water, and suddenly the heavens opened and he saw the Spirit of God
17 descending like a dove and coming down on him. ·And

e. Ho 11:1 f. Jr 31:15 g. Ethnarch of Judaea, 4 B.C. to A.D. 6. h. The territory of Herod Antipas.
3 a. 'kingdom of God'; Mt's phrase reflects the Jewish scruple against using the name of God. b. Is 40:3 c. Pharisees: members of a Jewish sect known for its strict observance of the Law as it was interpreted and developed by their rabbis. Sadducees: conservatives who observed the written form of the Law in the scriptures.

a voice spoke from heaven, 'This is my Son, the Beloved;
my favour rests on him'.

Temptation in the wilderness

4 Then Jesus was led by the Spirit out into the wilderness to
2 be tempted by the devil. ·He fasted for forty days and forty
3 nights, after which he was very hungry, ·and the tempter
came and said to him, 'If you are the Son of God, tell these
4 stones to turn into loaves'. ·But he replied, 'Scripture says:

> *Man does not live on bread alone*
> *but on every word that comes from the mouth of God'.ᵃ*

5 The devil then took him to the holy city and made him stand
6 on the parapet of the Temple. ·'If you are the Son of God' he
said 'throw yourself down; for scripture says:

> *He will put you in his angels' charge,*
> *and they will support you on their hands*
> *in case you hurt your foot against a stone'.ᵇ*

7 Jesus said to him, 'Scripture also says:

> *You must not put the Lord your God to the test'.ᶜ*

8 Next, taking him to a very high mountain, the devil showed
9 him all the kingdoms of the world and their splendour. ·'I will
give you all these' he said, 'if you fall at my feet and worship
10 me.' ·Then Jesus replied, 'Be off, Satan! For scripture says:

> *You must worship the Lord your God,*
> *and serve him alone.'ᵈ*

11 Then the devil left him, and angels appeared and looked
after him.

Return to Galilee

12 Hearing that John had been arrested he went back to
13 Galilee, ·and leaving Nazareth he went and settled in
Capernaum, a lakeside town on the borders of Zebulun and
14 Naphtali. ·In this way the prophecy of Isaiah was to be
fulfilled:

15 > *Land of Zebulun! Land of Naphtali!*
> *Way of the sea on the far side of Jordan,*
> *Galilee of the nations!*
16 > *The people that lived in darkness*
> *has seen a great light;*
> *on those who dwell in the land and shadow of death*
> *a light has dawned.ᵉ*

17 From that moment Jesus began his preaching with the message, 'Repent, for the kingdom of heaven is close at hand'.

The first four disciples are called

18 As he was walking by the Sea of Galilee he saw two brothers, Simon, who was called Peter, and his brother Andrew; they were making a cast in the lake with their net,
19 for they were fishermen. ·And he said to them, 'Follow me
20 and I will make you fishers of men'. ·And they left their nets at once and followed him.
21 Going on from there he saw another pair of brothers, James son of Zebedee and his brother John; they were in their boat with their father Zebedee, mending their nets, and
22 he called them. ·At once, leaving the boat and their father, they followed him.

Jesus preaches and heals the sick

23 He went round the whole of Galilee teaching in their synagogues, proclaiming the Good News of the kingdom and curing all kinds of diseases and sickness among the people.
24 His fame spread throughout Syria,[f] and those who were suffering from diseases and painful complaints of one kind or another, the possessed, epileptics, the paralysed, were all
25 brought to him, and he cured them. ·Large crowds followed him, coming from Galilee, the Decapolis,[g] Jerusalem, Judaea and Transjordania.

B. THE SERMON ON THE MOUNT[a]

The Beatitudes

5 Seeing the crowds, he went up the hill. There he sat down
2 and was joined by his disciples. ·Then he began to speak. This is what he taught them:

3 'How happy are the poor in spirit;
theirs is the kingdom of heaven.
4 Happy *the gentle:*[b]
they shall have the earth for their heritage.

---

4 a. Dt 8:3 **b.** Ps 91:11–12 **c.** Dt 6:16 **d.** Dt 6:13 **e.** Is 8:23–9:1 **f.** I.e. Galilee and the districts listed in v. 25. **g.** The 'ten towns', a region south-east of Galilee.
5 a. In this discourse, which occupies three ch. of this gospel, Mt has included sayings which probably originated on other occasions (cf. their parallels in Lk). **b.** Or 'the lowly'; the word comes from the Greek version of Ps 37.

5 Happy those who mourn:
  they shall be comforted.
6 Happy those who hunger and thirst for what is right:
  they shall be satisfied.
7 Happy the merciful:
  they shall have mercy shown them.
8 Happy the pure in heart:
  they shall see God.
9 Happy the peacemakers:
  they shall be called sons of God.
10 Happy those who are persecuted in the cause of right:
  theirs is the kingdom of heaven.
11 'Happy are you when people abuse you and persecute you
  and speak all kinds of calumny against you on my account.
12 Rejoice and be glad, for your reward will be great in
  heaven; this is how they persecuted the prophets before you.

Salt of the earth and light of the world

13 'You are the salt of the earth. But if salt becomes tasteless,
  what can make it salty again? It is good for nothing, and can
  only be thrown out to be trampled underfoot by men.
14 'You are the light of the world. A city built on a hill-top
15 cannot be hidden. ·No one lights a lamp to put it under a tub;
  they put it on the lamp-stand where it shines for everyone in
16 the house. ·In the same way your light must shine in the sight
  of men, so that, seeing your good works, they may give the
  praise to your Father in heaven.

The fulfilment of the Law

17 'Do not imagine that I have come to abolish the Law or
  the Prophets. I have come not to abolish but to complete
18 them. ·I tell you solemnly, till heaven and earth disappear,
  not one dot, not one little stroke, shall disappear from the
19 Law until its purpose is achieved. ·Therefore, the man who
  infringes even one of the least of these commandments and
  teaches others to do the same will be considered the least in
  the kingdom of heaven; but the man who keeps them and
  teaches them will be considered great in the kingdom of
  heaven.

The new standard higher than the old

20 'For I tell you, if your virtue goes no deeper than that of
  the scribes and Pharisees, you will never get into the kingdom
  of heaven.

21 'You have learnt how it was said to our ancestors: *You must not kill;*[c] and if anyone does kill he must answer for it
22 before the court. ·But I say this to you: anyone who is angry with his brother will answer for it before the court; if a man calls his brother "Fool"[d] he will answer for it before the Sanhedrin;[e] and if a man calls him
23 "Renegade"[f] he will answer for it in hell fire. ·So then, if you are bringing your offering to the altar and there remember
24 that your brother has something against you, ·leave your offering there before the altar, go and be reconciled with your brother first, and then come back and present your offering.
25 Come to terms with your opponent in good time while you are still on the way to the court with him, or he may hand you over to the judge and the judge to the officer, and you will be
26 thrown into prison. ·I tell you solemnly, you will not get out till you have paid the last penny.

27 'You have learnt how it was said: *You must not commit*
28 *adultery.*[g] ·But I say this to you: if a man looks at a woman lustfully, he has already committed adultery with her in his
29 heart. ·If your right eye should cause you to sin, tear it out and throw it away; for it will do you less harm to lose one part of you than to have your whole body thrown into hell.
30 And if your right hand should cause you to sin, cut it off and throw it away; for it will do you less harm to lose one part of you than to have your whole body go to hell.

31 'It has also been said: *Anyone who divorces his wife must*
32 *give her a writ of dismissal.*[h] ·But I say this to you: everyone who divorces his wife, except for the case of fornication, makes her an adulteress; and anyone who marries a divorced woman commits adultery.

33 'Again, you have learnt how it was said to our ancestors: *You must not break your oath, but must fulfil your oaths to the*
34 *Lord.*[i] ·But I say this to you: do not swear at all, either by
35 *heaven*, since that is God's throne; ·or by *the earth*, since that is *his footstool;* or by Jerusalem, since that is *the city of the*
36 *great king.* ·Do not swear by your own head either, since you
37 cannot turn a single hair white or black. ·All you need say is "Yes" if you mean yes, "No" if you mean no; anything more than this comes from the evil one.

38 'You have learnt how it was said: *Eye for eye and tooth for*
39 *tooth.*[j] ·But I say this to you: offer the wicked man no resist-

c. Ex 20:13 d. Translating an Aramaic term of contempt. e. The High Court at Jerusalem. f. Apostasy was the most repulsive of all sins. g. Ex 20:14 h. Dt 24:1 i. Ex 20:7 j. Ex 21:24

ance. On the contrary, if anyone hits you on the right cheek,
40 offer him the other as well; ·if a man takes you to law and
would have your tunic, let him have your cloak as well.
41 And if anyone orders you to go one mile, go two miles with
42 him. ·Give to anyone who asks, and if anyone wants to
borrow, do not turn away.

43 'You have learnt how it was said: *You must love your*
44 *neighbour* and hate your enemy.[k] ·But I say this to you: love
45 your enemies, and pray for those who persecute you; ·in this
way you will be sons of your Father in heaven, for he causes
his sun to rise on bad men as well as good, and his rain to fall
46 on honest and dishonest men alike. ·For if you love those
who love you, what right have you to claim any credit? Even
47 the tax collectors[l] do as much, do they not? ·And if you save
your greetings for your brothers, are you doing anything
exceptional? Even the pagans do as much, do they not?
48 You must therefore be perfect just as your heavenly Father is
perfect.

Almsgiving in secret

6 'Be careful not to parade your good deeds before men to
attract their notice; by doing this you will lose all reward
2 from your Father in heaven. ·So when you give alms, do not
have it trumpeted before you; this is what the hypocrites do
in the synagogues and in the streets to win men's admiration.
3 I tell you solemnly, they have had their reward. ·But when
you give alms, your left hand must not know what your right
4 is doing; ·your almsgiving must be secret, and your Father
who sees all that is done in secret will reward you.

Prayer in secret

5 'And when you pray, do not imitate the hypocrites: they
love to say their prayers standing up in the synagogues and at
the street corners for people to see them. I tell you solemnly,
6 they have had their reward. ·But when you pray, *go to your*
private room and, when you have shut your door, pray[a] to your
Father who is in that secret place, and your Father who sees
all that is done in secret will reward you.

How to pray. The Lord's Prayer

7 'In your prayers do not babble as the pagans do, for they
think that by using many words they will make themselves
8 heard. ·Do not be like them; your Father knows what

9 you need before you ask him. ·So you should pray like this:

> 'Our Father in heaven,
> may your name be held holy,
10   your kingdom come,
> your will be done,
> on earth as in heaven.
11   Give us today our daily bread.
12   And forgive us our debts,
> as we have forgiven those who are in debt to us.
13   And do not put us to the test,
> but save us from the evil one.

14 Yes, if you forgive others their failings, your heavenly Father
15 will forgive you yours; ·but if you do not forgive others, your Father will not forgive your failings either.

Fasting in secret

16 'When you fast do not put on a gloomy look as the hypocrites do: they pull long faces to let men know they are fasting. I tell you solemnly, they have had their reward.
17 But when you fast, put oil on your head and wash your face,
18 so that no one will know you are fasting except your Father who sees all that is done in secret; and your Father who sees all that is done in secret will reward you.

True treasures

19 'Do not store up treasures for yourselves on earth, where moths and woodworms destroy them and thieves can break
20 in and steal. ·But store up treasures for yourselves in heaven, where neither moth nor woodworms destroy them and
21 thieves cannot break in and steal. ·For where your treasure is, there will your heart be also.

The eye, the lamp of the body

22 'The lamp of the body is the eye. It follows that if your eye
23 is sound, your whole body will be filled with light. ·But if your eye is diseased, your whole body will be all darkness. If

---

k. The quotation is from Lv 19:18; the second part of this commandment, not in the written Law, is an Aramaic way of saying 'You do not have to love your enemy'. **l.** They were employed by the occupying power and this earned them popular contempt.
6 a. Not a direct quotation but an allusion to the practice common in the O.T., see 2 K 4:33.

then, the light inside you is darkness, what darkness that will be!

God and money

24 'No one can be the slave of two masters: he will either hate the first and love the second, or treat the first with respect and the second with scorn. You cannot be the slave both of God and of money.

Trust in Providence

25 'That is why I am telling you not to worry about your life and what you are to eat, nor about your body and how you are to clothe it. Surely life means more than food, and the
26 body more than clothing! ·Look at the birds in the sky. They do not sow or reap or gather into barns; yet your heavenly Father feeds them. Are you not worth much more than they
27 are? ·Can any of you, for all his worrying, add one single
28 cubit to his span of life? ·And why worry about clothing? Think of the flowers growing in the fields; they never have to
29 work or spin; ·yet I assure you that not even Solomon in all
30 his regalia was robed like one of these. ·Now if that is how God clothes the grass in the field which is there today and thrown into the furnace tomorrow, will he not much more
31 look after you, you men of little faith? ·So do not worry; do not say, "What are we to eat? What are we to drink? How are
32 we to be clothed?" ·It is the pagans who set their hearts on all these things. Your heavenly Father knows you need them all.
33 Set your hearts on his kingdom first, and on his righteousness, and all these other things will be given you as well.
34 So do not worry about tomorrow: tomorrow will take care of itself. Each day has enough trouble of its own.

Do not judge

7 'Do not judge, and you will not be judged; ·because the judgements you give are the judgements you will get, and the amount you measure out is the amount you will be given.
3 Why do you observe the splinter in your brother's eye and
4 never notice the plank in your own? ·How dare you say to your brother, "Let me take the splinter out of your eye",
5 when all the time there is a plank in your own? ·Hypocrite! Take the plank out of your own eye first, and then you will see clearly enough to take the splinter out of your brother's eye.

Do not profane sacred things

6   'Do not give dogs what is holy;[a] and do not throw your pearls in front of pigs, or they may trample them and then turn on you and tear you to pieces.

Effective prayer

7   'Ask, and it will be given to you; search, and you will find;
8 knock, and the door will be opened to you. ·For the one who asks always receives; the one who searches always finds; the one who knocks will always have the door opened to him.
9 Is there a man among you who would hand his son a stone
10 when he asked for bread? ·Or would hand him a snake when
11 he asked for a fish? ·If you, then, who are evil, know how to give your children what is good, how much more will your Father in heaven give good things to those who ask him!

The golden rule

12   'So always treat others as you would like them to treat you; that is the meaning of the Law and the Prophets.

The two ways

13   'Enter by the narrow gate, since the road that leads to
14 perdition is wide and spacious, and many take it; ·but it is a narrow gate and a hard road that leads to life, and only a few find it.

False prophets

15   'Beware of false prophets[b] who come to you disguised as
16 sheep but underneath are ravenous wolves. ·You will be able to tell them by their fruits. Can people pick grapes from
17 thorns, or figs from thistles? ·In the same way, a sound tree
18 produces good fruit but a rotten tree bad fruit. ·A sound tree
19 cannot bear bad fruit, nor a rotten tree bear good fruit. ·Any tree that does not produce good fruit is cut down and thrown
20 on the fire. ·I repeat, you will be able to tell them by their fruits.

The true disciple

21   'It is not those who say to me, "Lord, Lord", who will enter the kingdom of heaven, but the person who does the will of
22 my Father in heaven. ·When the day[c] comes many will say to

---

7 **a.** The meat of animals which have been offered in sacrifice in the Temple; the application is to the parading of holy beliefs and practices in front of those who cannot understand them. **b.** Lying teachers of religion. **c.** The day of Judgement.

me, "Lord, Lord, did we not prophesy in your name, cast out
demons in your name, work many miracles in your name?"
23 Then I shall tell them to their faces: I have never known you;
away from me, you evil men!

24   'Therefore, everyone who listens to these words of mine
and acts on them will be like a sensible man who built his
25 house on rock. ·Rain came down, floods rose, gales blew and
hurled themselves against that house, and it did not fall: it
26 was founded on rock. ·But everyone who listens to these
words of mine and does not act on them will be like a stupid
27 man who built his house on sand. ·Rain came down, floods
rose, gales blew and struck that house, and it fell; and what a
fall it had!'

The amazement of the crowds

28   Jesus had now finished what he wanted to say, and his
29 teaching made a deep impression on the people ·because he
taught them with authority, and not like their own scribes.[d]

III. THE KINGDOM OF HEAVEN IS
PREACHED

A. NARRATIVE SECTION: TEN MIRACLES

Cure of a leper

8   After he had come down from the mountain large crowds
2 followed him. ·A leper now came up and bowed low in front
of him. 'Sir,' he said 'if you want to, you can cure me.'
3 Jesus stretched out his hand, touched him and said, 'Of
course I want to! Be cured!' And his leprosy was cured at once.
4 Then Jesus said to him, 'Mind you do not tell anyone, but go
and show yourself to the priest and make the offering
prescribed by Moses, as evidence for them'.

Cure of the centurion's servant

5   When he went into Capernaum a centurion came up and
6 pleaded with him. ·'Sir,' he said 'my servant is lying at home
7 paralysed, and in great pain.' ·'I will come myself and cure
8 him' said Jesus. ·The centurion replied, 'Sir, I am not worthy
to have you under my roof; just give the word and my servant
9 will be cured. ·For I am under authority myself, and have
soldiers under me; and I say to one man: Go, and he goes; to
another: Come here, and he comes; to my servant: Do this,
10 and he does it.' ·When Jesus heard this he was astonished and

said to those following him, 'I tell you solemnly, nowhere in
11 Israel have I found faith like this. ·And I tell you that many
will come from east and west to take their places with Abraham and Isaac and Jacob at the feast in the kingdom of
12 heaven; ·but the subjects of the kingdom[a] will be turned out
into the dark, where there will be weeping and grinding of
13 teeth.' ·And to the centurion Jesus said, 'Go back, then; you
have believed, so let this be done for you'. And the servant
was cured at that moment.

Cure of Peter's mother-in-law

14 And going into Peter's house Jesus found Peter's mother-
15 in-law in bed with fever. ·He touched her hand and the
fever left her, and she got up and began to wait on him.

A number of cures

16 That evening they brought him many who were possessed
by devils. He cast out the spirits with a word and cured all
17 who were sick. ·This was to fulfil the prophecy of Isaiah:

He took our sicknesses away and carried our diseases for us.[b]

Hardships of the apostolic calling

18 When Jesus saw the great crowds all about him he gave
19 orders to leave for the other side.[c] ·One of the scribes then
came up and said to him, 'Master, I will follow you wherever
20 you go'. ·Jesus replied, 'Foxes have holes and the birds of the
air have nests, but the Son of Man has nowhere to lay his
head'.
21 Another man, one of his disciples, said to him, 'Sir, let me
22 go and bury my father first'. ·But Jesus replied, 'Follow me,
and leave the dead to bury their dead'.

The calming of the storm

23 Then he got into the boat followed by his disciples.
24 Without warning a storm broke over the lake, so violent that
the waves were breaking right over the boat. But he was
25 asleep. ·So they went to him and woke him saying, 'Save us,
26 Lord, we are going down!' ·And he said to them, 'Why are
you so frightened, you men of little faith?' And with that he
stood up and rebuked the winds and the sea; and all was

d. Doctors of the law, who buttressed their teaching by quotation from
the scriptures and traditions.
8 a. The Jews, natural heirs of the promises. **b.** Is 53:4 **c.** The E.
bank of Lake Tiberias.

27 calm again. ·The men were astounded and said, 'Whatever kind of man is this? Even the winds and the sea obey him.'

The demoniacs of Gadara

28 When he reached the country of the Gadarenes on the other side, two demoniacs came towards him out of the tombs—creatures so fierce that no one could pass that way.
29 They stood there shouting, 'What do you want with us, Son of God? Have you come here to torture us before the time?'[d]
30 Now some distance away there was a large herd of pigs
31 feeding, ·and the devils pleaded with Jesus, 'If you cast us out,
32 send us into the herd of pigs'. ·And he said to them, 'Go then', and they came out and made for the pigs; and at that the whole herd charged down the cliff into the lake and perished
33 in the water. ·The swineherds ran off and made for the town, where they told the whole story, including what had hap-
34 pened to the demoniacs. ·At this the whole town set out to meet Jesus; and as soon as they saw him they implored him to leave the neighbourhood.

Cure of a paralytic

9 He got back in the boat, crossed the water and came to his
2 own town.[a] ·Then some people appeared, bringing him a paralytic stretched out on a bed. Seeing their faith, Jesus said to the paralytic, 'Courage, my child, your sins are forgiven'.
3 And at this some scribes said to themselves, 'This man is
4 blaspheming'. ·Knowing what was in their minds Jesus said, 'Why do you have such wicked thoughts in your hearts?
5 Now, which of these is easier: to say, "Your sins are for-
6 given", or to say, "Get up and walk"? ·But to prove to you that the Son of Man has authority on earth to forgive sins,'— he said to the paralytic—'get up, and pick up your bed and
7 go off home'. ·And the man got up and went home. ·A
8 feeling of awe came over the crowd when they saw this, and they praised God for giving such power to men.

The call of Matthew

9 As Jesus was walking on from there he saw a man named Matthew[b] sitting by the customs house, and he said to him, 'Follow me'. And he got up and followed him.

Eating with sinners

10 While he was at dinner in the house it happened that a number of tax collectors and sinners[c] came to sit at the table
11 with Jesus and his disciples. ·When the Pharisees saw this,

they said to his disciples, 'Why does your master eat with tax
12 collectors and sinners?' ·When he heard this he replied, 'It is
13 not the healthy who need the doctor, but the sick. ·Go and
learn the meaning of the words: *What I want is mercy, not
sacrifice.*[d] And indeed I did not come to call the virtuous, but
sinners.'

A discussion on fasting

14   Then John's[e] disciples came to him and said, 'Why is it
that we and the Pharisees fast, but your disciples do not?'
15 Jesus replied, 'Surely the bridegroom's attendants would
never think of mourning as long as the bridegroom is still
with them? But the time will come for the bridegroom to be
16 taken away from them, and then they will fast. ·No one puts
a piece of unshrunken cloth on to an old cloak, because the
17 patch pulls away from the cloak and the tear gets worse. ·Nor
do people put new wine into old wineskins; if they do, the
skins burst, the wine runs out, and the skins are lost. No;
they put new wine into fresh skins and both are preserved.'[f]

Cure of the woman with a haemorrhage. The official's daughter raised to life

18   While he was speaking to them, up came one of the
officials, who bowed low in front of him and said, 'My
daughter has just died, but come and lay your hand on her
19 and her life will be saved'. ·Jesus rose and, with his disciples,
followed him.
20   Then from behind him came a woman, who had suffered
from a haemorrhage for twelve years, and she touched the
21 fringe of his cloak, ·for she said to herself, 'If I can only touch
22 his cloak I shall be well again'. ·Jesus turned round and saw
her; and he said to her, 'Courage, my daughter, your faith has
restored you to health'. And from that moment the woman
was well again.
23   When Jesus reached the official's house and saw the flute-
players, with the crowd making a commotion[g] he said,
24 'Get out of here; the little girl is not dead, she is asleep'. And
25 they laughed at him. ·But when the people had been turned

d. The day of Judgement, when the reign of God would banish all
demons.
9 a. Capernaum, cf. 4:13. **b.** Called Levi by Mk and Lk. **c.** Social
outcasts, made 'unclean' by breaking religious laws or following a
disreputable profession. **d.** Ho 6:6 **e.** John the Baptist. **f.** New de-
votional exercises, like those which John and the Pharisees add to the
religion of the old order, will not preserve it. **g.** The loud wailing of
the oriental mourner.

out he went inside and took the little girl by the hand; and she
26 stood up. ·And the news spread all round the countryside.

Cure of two blind men

27   As Jesus went on his way two blind men followed him
28 shouting, 'Take pity on us, Son of David'. ·And when Jesus
reached the house the blind men came up with him and he
said to them, 'Do you believe I can do this?' They said, 'Sir,
29 we do'. ·Then he touched their eyes saying, 'Your faith
30 deserves it, so let this be done for you'. ·And their sight
returned. Then Jesus sternly warned them, 'Take care that no
31 one learns about this'. ·But when they had gone, they talked
about him all over the countryside.

Cure of a dumb demoniac

32   They had only just left when a man was brought to him, a
33 dumb demoniac. ·And when the devil was cast out, the dumb
man spoke and the people were amazed. 'Nothing like this
34 has ever been seen in Israel' they said. ·But the Pharisees said,
'It is through the prince of devils that he casts out devils'.

The distress of the crowds

35   Jesus made a tour through all the towns and villages,
teaching in their synagogues, proclaiming the Good News of
the kingdom and curing all kinds of diseases and sickness.
36   And when he saw the crowds he felt sorry for them because
they were harassed and dejected, like sheep without a shep-
37 herd. ·Then he said to his disciples, 'The harvest is rich but
the labourers are few, so ask the Lord of the harvest to send
labourers to his harvest'.

B. THE INSTRUCTION OF THE APOSTLES

The mission of the Twelve

10   He summoned his twelve disciples, and gave them authority over unclean spirits with power to cast them out and to
cure all kinds of diseases and sickness.
2   These are the names of the twelve apostles: first, Simon
who is called Peter, and his brother Andrew; James the son
3 of Zebedee, and his brother John; ·Philip and Bartholomew;
Thomas, and Matthew the tax collector; James the son of
4 Alphaeus, and Thaddaeus; ·Simon the Zealot and Judas
5 Iscariot, the one who was to betray him. ·These twelve Jesus
sent out, instructing them as follows:
'Do not turn your steps to pagan territory, and do not enter

6 any Samaritan town; ·go rather to the lost sheep of the House
7 of Israel. ·And as you go, proclaim that the kingdom of
8 heaven is close at hand. ·Cure the sick, raise the dead, cleanse
the lepers, cast out devils. You received without charge, give
9 without charge. ·Provide yourselves with no gold or silver,
10 not even with a few coppers for your purses, ·with no haversack for the journey or spare tunic or footwear or a staff, for
the workman deserves his keep.
11   'Whatever town or village you go into, ask for someone
12 trustworthy and stay with him until you leave. ·As you enter
13 his house, salute it, ·and if the house deserves it, let your peace
descend upon it; if it does not, let your peace come back to
14 you. ·And if anyone does not welcome you or listen to what
you have to say, as you walk out of the house or town shake
15 the dust from your feet. ·I tell you solemnly, on the day of
Judgement it will not go as hard with the land of Sodom and
16 Gomorrah as with that town. ·Remember, I am sending you
out like sheep among wolves; so be cunning as serpents and
yet as harmless as doves.

The missionaries will be persecuted[a]

17   'Beware of men: they will hand you over to sanhedrins and
18 scourge you in their synagogues. ·You will be dragged before
governors and kings for my sake, to bear witness before them
19 and the pagans. ·But when they hand you over, do not worry
about how to speak or what to say; what you are to say will
20 be given to you when the time comes; ·because it is not you
who will be speaking; the Spirit of your Father will be
speaking in you.
21   'Brother will betray brother to death, and the father his
child; children will rise against their parents and have them
22 put to death. ·You will be hated by all men on account of my
name; but the man who stands firm to the end will be saved.
23 If they persecute you in one town, take refuge in the next;
and if they persecute you in that, take refuge in another. I tell
you solemnly, you will not have gone the round of the towns
of Israel before the Son of Man comes.
24   'The disciple is not superior to his teacher, nor the slave to
25 his master. ·It is enough for the disciple that he should grow
to be like his teacher, and the slave like his master. If they
have called the master of the house Beelzebul, what will they
not say of his household?

10 a. The conditions described in vv. 17–39 are those of a later time
than this first mission of the Twelve.

Open and fearless speech

26 'Do not be afraid of them therefore. For everything that is now covered will be uncovered, and everything now hidden
27 will be made clear. ·What I say to you in the dark, tell in the daylight; what you hear in whispers, proclaim from the housetops.
28 'Do not be afraid of those who kill the body but cannot kill the soul; fear him rather who can destroy both body and soul
29 in hell. ·Can you not buy two sparrows for a penny? And yet not one falls to the ground without your Father knowing.
30 Why, every hair on your head has been counted. ·So there is
31 no need to be afraid; you are worth more than hundreds of sparrows.
32 'So if anyone declares himself for me in the presence of men, I will declare myself for him in the presence of my
33 Father in heaven. ·But the one who disowns me in the presence of men, I will disown in the presence of my Father in heaven.

Jesus, the cause of dissension

34 'Do not suppose that I have come to bring peace to the
35 earth: it is not peace I have come to bring, but a sword. ·For I have come to set *a man against his father*, *a daughter against her mother*, *a daughter-in-law against her mother-in-law.*
36 *A man's enemies will be those of his own household.*[b]

Renouncing self to follow Jesus

37 'Anyone who prefers father or mother to me is not worthy of me. Anyone who prefers son or daughter to me is not
38 worthy of me. ·Anyone who does not take his cross and fol-
39 low in my footsteps is not worthy of me. ·Anyone who finds his life will lose it; anyone who loses his life for my sake will find it.

Conclusion

40 'Anyone who welcomes you welcomes me; and those who welcome me welcome the one who sent me.
41 'Anyone who welcomes a prophet because he is a prophet will have a prophet's reward; and anyone who welcomes a holy man because he is a holy man will have a holy man's reward.
42 'If anyone gives so much as a cup of cold water to one of these little ones because he is a disciple, then I tell you solemnly, he will most certainly not lose his reward.'

IV. THE MYSTERY OF THE KINGDOM OF HEAVEN

A. NARRATIVE SECTION

11   When Jesus had finished instructing his twelve disciples he moved on from there to teach and preach in their towns.[a]

The Baptist's question. Jesus commends him

2   Now John in his prison had heard what Christ was doing
3 and he sent his disciples to ask him, ·'Are you the one who is
4 to come, or have we got to wait for someone else?' ·Jesus answered, 'Go back and tell John what you hear and see;
5 the blind see again, and the lame walk, lepers are cleansed, and the deaf hear, and the dead are raised to life and the
6 Good News is proclaimed to the poor;[b] ·and happy is the man who does not lose faith in me'.

7   As the messengers were leaving, Jesus began to talk to the people about John: 'What did you go out into the wilderness
8 to see? A reed swaying in the breeze? No? ·Then what did you go out to see? A man wearing fine clothes? Oh no, those
9 who wear fine clothes are to be found in palaces. Then what did you go out for? To see a prophet? Yes, I tell you, and
10 much more than a prophet: ·he is the one of whom scripture says:

> Look, I am going to send my messenger before you;
> he will prepare your way before you.[c]

11   'I tell you solemnly, of all the children born of women, a greater than John the Baptist has never been seen; yet the
12 least in the kingdom of heaven is greater than he is. ·Since John the Baptist came, up to this present time, the kingdom of heaven has been subjected to violence and the violent are
13 taking it by storm. ·Because it was towards John that all the
14 prophecies of the prophets of the Law were leading; ·and he, if you will believe me, is the Elijah who was to return.[d]
15 If anyone has ears to hear, let him listen!

b. Mi 7:6
11 a. I.e. the Jews' towns. b. These are signs of the messianic age in the prophecies of Isaiah. c. Ml 3:1 d. According to the last of the prophets, Ml 3:23.

Jesus condemns his contemporaries

16 'What description can I find for this generation? It is like children shouting to each other as they sit in the market place:

17
"We played the pipes for you,
and you wouldn't dance;
we sang dirges,
and you wouldn't be mourners".

18 'For John came, neither eating nor drinking, and they say,
19 "He is possessed". ·The Son of Man came, eating and drinking, and they say, "Look, a glutton and a drunkard, a friend of tax collectors and sinners". Yet wisdom has been proved right by her actions.'

Lament over the lake-towns

20 Then he began to reproach the towns in which most of his miracles had been worked, because they refused to repent.
21 'Alas for you, Chorazin! Alas for you, Bethsaida! For if the miracles done in you had been done in Tyre and Sidon, they would have repented long ago in sackcloth and ashes.
22 And still, I tell you that it will not go as hard on Judgement
23 day with Tyre and Sidon as with you. ·And as for you, Capernaum, did you want to be exalted as high as heaven? *You shall be thrown down to hell.*[e] For if the miracles done in you had been done in Sodom, it would have been standing
24 yet. ·And still, I tell you that it will not go as hard with the land of Sodom on Judgement day as with you.'

The Good News revealed to the simple. The Father and the Son

25 At that time Jesus exclaimed, 'I bless you, Father, Lord of heaven and of earth, for hiding these things from the learned
26 and the clever and revealing them to mere children. ·Yes,
27 Father, for that is what it pleased you to do. ·Everything has been entrusted to me by my Father; and no one knows the Son except the Father, just as no one knows the Father except the Son and those to whom the Son chooses to reveal him.

The gentle mastery of Christ

28 'Come to me, all you who labour and are overburdened,
29 and I will give you rest. ·Shoulder my yoke and learn from me, for I am gentle and humble in heart, *and you will find*

30 *rest for your souls.*[f] ·Yes, my yoke is easy and my burden light.'

Picking corn on the sabbath

12 At that time Jesus took a walk one sabbath day through the cornfields. His disciples were hungry and began to pick
2 ears of corn and eat them. ·The Pharisees noticed it and said to him, 'Look, your disciples are doing something that is
3 forbidden on the sabbath'. ·But he said to them, 'Have you not read what David did when he and his followers were
4 hungry—·how he went into the house of God and how they ate the loaves of offering which neither he nor his followers were allowed to eat, but which were for the priests alone?
5 Or again, have you not read in the Law that on the sabbath day the Temple priests break the sabbath without being
6 blamed for it? ·Now here, I tell you, is something greater
7 than the Temple. ·And if you had understood the meaning of the words: *What I want is mercy, not sacrifice*, you would not
8 have condemned the blameless. ·For the Son of Man is master of the sabbath.'

Cure of the man with a withered hand

9 He moved on from there and went to their synagogue,
10 and a man was there at the time who had a withered hand. They asked him, 'Is it against the law to cure a man on the sabbath day?' hoping for something to use against him.
11 But he said to them, 'If any one of you here had only one sheep and it fell down a hole on the sabbath day, would he not
12 get hold of it and lift it out? ·Now a man is far more important than a sheep, so it follows that it is permitted to do good
13 on the sabbath day.' ·Then he said to the man, 'Stretch out your hand'. He stretched it out and his hand was better, as
14 sound as the other one. ·At this the Pharisees went out and began to plot against him, discussing how to destroy him.

Jesus the 'servant of Yahweh'

15 Jesus knew this and withdrew from the district. Many
16 followed him and he cured them all, ·but warned them not to
17 make him known. ·This was to fulfil the prophecy of Isaiah:

18 > *Here is my servant whom I have chosen,*
> *my beloved, the favourite of my soul.*
> *I will endow him with my spirit,*
> *and he will proclaim the true faith to the nations.*

e. Is 14 f. Jr 6:16

19   *He will not brawl or shout,*
        nor will anyone hear his voice in the streets.
20   *He will not break the crushed reed,*
        nor put out the smouldering wick
        till he has led the truth to victory:
21   *in his name the nations will put their hope.*^a

Jesus and Beelzebul

22   Then they brought to him a blind and dumb demoniac;
and he cured him, so that the dumb man could speak and
23 see. ·All the people were astounded and said, 'Can this be the
24 Son of David?' ·But when the Pharisees heard this they said,
'The man casts out devils only through Beelzebul,^b the prince
of devils'.

25   Knowing what was in their minds he said to them, 'Every
kingdom divided against itself is heading for ruin; and no
26 town, no household divided against itself can stand. ·Now if
Satan casts out Satan, he is divided against himself; so how
27 can his kingdom stand? ·And if it is through Beelzebul that I
cast out devils, through whom do your own experts cast
28 them out? Let them be your judges, then. ·But if it is through
the Spirit of God that I cast devils out, then know that the
kingdom of God has overtaken you.

29   'Or again, how can anyone make his way into a strong
man's house and burgle his property unless he has tied up the
strong man first? Only then can he burgle his house.

30   'He who is not with me is against me, and he who does not
31 gather with me scatters. ·And so I tell you, every one of men's
sins and blasphemies will be forgiven, but blasphemy
32 against the Spirit will not be forgiven. ·And anyone who says
a word against the Son of Man will be forgiven; but let
anyone speak against the Holy Spirit and he will not be
forgiven either in this world or in the next.

Words betray the heart

33   'Make a tree sound and its fruit will be sound; make a tree
rotten and its fruit will be rotten. For the tree can be told by
34 its fruit. ·Brood of vipers, how can your speech be good when
you are evil? For a man's words flow out of what fills his
35 heart. ·A good man draws good things from his store of
goodness; a bad man draws bad things from his store of
36 badness. ·So I tell you this, that for every unfounded word
37 men utter they will answer on Judgement day, ·since it is by
your words you will be acquitted, and by your words
condemned.'

The sign of Jonah

38   Then some of the scribes and Pharisees spoke up. 'Master,'
39 they said 'we should like to see a sign[c] from you.' ·He replied,
'It is an evil and unfaithful generation that asks for a sign!
The only sign it will be given is the sign of the prophet Jonah.
40 For as Jonah *was in the belly of the sea-monster for three days
and three nights,[d]* so will the Son of Man be in the heart of the
41 earth for three days and three nights. ·On Judgement day the
men of Nineveh will stand up with this generation and condemn it, because when Jonah preached they repented; and
42 there is something greater than Jonah here. ·On Judgement
day the Queen of the South will rise up with this generation
and condemn it, because she came from the ends of the earth
to hear the wisdom of Solomon; and there is something
greater than Solomon here.

The return of the unclean spirit

43   'When an unclean spirit goes out of a man it wanders
through waterless country looking for a place to rest, and
44 cannot find one. ·Then it says, "I will return to the home I
came from". But on arrival, finding it unoccupied, swept and
45 tidied, ·it then goes off and collects seven other spirits more
evil than itself, and they go in and set up house there, so that
the man ends up by being worse than he was before. That is
what will happen to this evil generation.'

The true kinsmen of Jesus

46   He was still speaking to the crowds when his mother and
his brothers[e] appeared; they were standing outside and were
48 anxious to have a word with him. ·But to the man who told
him this Jesus replied, 'Who is my mother? Who are my
49 brothers?' ·And stretching out his hand towards his disciples
50 he said, 'Here are my mother and my brothers. ·Anyone who
does the will of my Father in heaven, he is my brother and
sister and mother.'

12 a. Is 42:1–4 **b.** 'prince Baal' often contemptuously changed (e.g. 2
K 1:2f) to 'Beelzebub' 'Lord of the flies'. **c.** A miracle to prove his
authority. **d.** Jon 2:1 **e.** In Hebr. and Aramaic (and many other
languages), 'brothers' is the word used for cousins or even more distant
relations of the same generation.

B. THE SERMON OF PARABLES

Introduction

13 That same day, Jesus left the house and sat by the lakeside,
2 but such crowds gathered round him that he got into a boat
3 and sat there. The people all stood on the beach, ·and he told
them many things in parables.

Parable of the sower

4 He said, 'Imagine a sower going out to sow. ·As he sowed,
some seeds fell on the edge of the path, and the birds came
5 and ate them up. ·Others fell on patches of rock where they
found little soil and sprang up straight away, because there
6 was no depth of earth; ·but as soon as the sun came up they
were scorched and, not having any roots, they withered away.
7 Others fell among thorns, and the thorns grew up and choked
8 them. ·Others fell on rich soil and produced their crop, some a
9 hundredfold, some sixty, some thirty. ·Listen, anyone who has
ears!'

Why Jesus speaks in parables

10 Then the disciples went up to him and asked, 'Why do you
11 talk to them in parables?' ·'Because' he replied 'the mysteries
of the kingdom of heaven are revealed to you, but they are
12 not revealed to them. ·For anyone who has will be given
more, and he will have more than enough; but from anyone
13 who has not, even what he has will be taken away. ·The
reason I talk to them in parables is that they look without
14 seeing and listen without hearing or understanding. ·So in
their case this prophecy of Isaiah is being fulfilled:

You will listen and listen again, but not understand,
see and see again, but not perceive.
15 *For the heart of this nation has grown coarse,*
their ears are dull of hearing, and they have shut their eyes,
for fear they should see with their eyes,
hear with their ears,
understand with their heart,
and be converted
and be healed by me.^a

16 'But happy are your eyes because they see, your ears
17 because they hear! ·I tell you solemnly, many prophets and
holy men longed to see what you see, and never saw it; to
hear what you hear, and never heard it.

The parable of the sower explained

18 'You, therefore, are to hear the parable of the sower.
19 When anyone hears the word of the kingdom without understanding, the evil one comes and carries off what was sown in
his heart: this is the man who received the seed on the edge of
20 the path. ·The one who received it on patches of rock is the
man who hears the word and welcomes it at once with joy.
21 But he has no root in him, he does not last; let some trial
come, or some persecution on account of the word, and he
22 falls away at once. ·The one who received the seed in thorns
is the man who hears the word, but the worries of this world
and the lure of riches choke the word and so he produces
23 nothing. ·And the one who received the seed in rich soil is the
man who hears the word and understands it; he is the one
who yields a harvest and produces now a hundredfold, now
sixty, now thirty.'

Parable of the darnel

24 He put another parable before them, 'The kingdom of
heaven may be compared to a man who sowed good seed in
25 his field. ·While everybody was asleep his enemy came,
26 sowed darnel all among the wheat, and made off. ·When the
new wheat sprouted and ripened, the darnel appeared as well.
27 The owner's servants went to him and said, "Sir, was it not
good seed that you sowed in your field? If so, where does the
28 darnel come from?" ·"Some enemy has done this" he
answered. And the servants said, "Do you want us to go and
29 weed it out?" ·But he said, "No, because when you weed out
30 the darnel you might pull up the wheat with it. ·Let them
both grow till the harvest; and at harvest time I shall say to
the reapers: First collect the darnel and tie it in bundles to be
burnt, then gather the wheat into my barn." '

Parable of the mustard seed

31 He put another parable before them, 'The kingdom of
heaven is like a mustard seed which a man took and sowed in
32 his field. ·It is the smallest of all the seeds, but when it has
grown it is the biggest shrub of all and becomes a tree so that
the birds of the air come and shelter in its branches.'

13 a. Is 6:9–10

Parable of the yeast

33　He told them another parable, 'The kingdom of heaven is like the yeast a woman took and mixed in with three measures of flour till it was leavened all through'.

The people are taught only in parables

34　In all this Jesus spoke to the crowds in parables; indeed, he
35　would never speak to them except in parables. ·This was to fulfil the prophecy:

I will speak to you in parables
and expound things hidden since the foundation of the world.[b]

The parable of the darnel explained

36　Then, leaving the crowds, he went to the house; and his disciples came to him and said, 'Explain the parable about
37　the darnel in the field to us'. ·He said in reply, 'The sower of
38　the good seed is the Son of Man. ·The field is the world; the good seed is the subjects of the kingdom; the darnel, the
39　subjects of the evil one; ·the enemy who sowed them, the devil; the harvest is the end of the world; the reapers are the
40　angels. ·Well then, just as the darnel is gathered up and burnt
41　in the fire, so it will be at the end of time. ·The Son of Man will send his angels and they will gather out of his kingdom
42　all things that provoke offences and all who do evil, ·and throw them into the blazing furnace, where there will be
43　weeping and grinding of teeth. ·Then the virtuous will shine like the sun in the kingdom of their Father.[c] Listen, anyone who has ears!

Parables of the treasure and of the pearl

44　'The kingdom of heaven is like treasure hidden in a field which someone has found; he hides it again, goes off happy, sells everything he owns and buys the field.
45　'Again, the kingdom of heaven is like a merchant looking
46　for fine pearls; ·when he finds one of great value he goes and sells everything he owns and buys it.

Parable of the dragnet

47　'Again, the kingdom of heaven is like a dragnet cast into
48　the sea that brings in a haul of all kinds. ·When it is full, the fishermen haul it ashore; then, sitting down, they collect the good ones in a basket and throw away those that are no use.
49　This is how it will be at the end of time: the angels will

50 appear and separate the wicked from the just ·to throw them into the blazing furnace where there will be weeping and grinding of teeth.

Conclusion

51 'Have you understood all this?' They said, 'Yes'. ·And
52 he said to them, 'Well then, every scribe who becomes a disciple of the kingdom of heaven is like a householder who brings out from his storeroom things both new and old'.*d*

V. THE CHURCH, FIRST-FRUITS
OF THE KINGDOM OF HEAVEN

·A. NARRATIVE SECTION

A visit to Nazareth

53 When Jesus had finished these parables he left the district;
54 and, coming to his home town,*e* he taught the people in their synagogue in such a way that they were astonished and said, 'Where did the man get this wisdom and these miraculous
55 powers?' ·This is the carpenter's son, surely? Is not his mother the woman called Mary, and his brothers James and
56 Joseph and Simon and Jude? ·His sisters, too, are they not all
57 here with us? So where did the man get it all?' ·And they would not accept him. But Jesus said to them, A prophet is only despised in his own country and in his own house',
58 and he did not work many miracles there because of their lack of faith.

Herod and Jesus

14 At that time Herod the tetrarch heard about the reputation
2 of Jesus, ·and said to his court, 'This is John the Baptist himself; he has risen from the dead, and that is why miraculous powers are at work in him'.

John the Baptist beheaded

3 Now it was Herod who had arrested John, chained him up and put him in prison because of Herodias, his brother
4 Philip's*a* wife. ·For John had told him, 'It is against the Law
5 for you to have her'. ·He had wanted to kill him but was

---

b. Ps 78:2 c. The kingdom of the Son, v. 41, is succeeded by the kingdom of the Father. d. Perhaps a saying of particular significance to Mt, a 'scribe who became a disciple'. e. Nazareth, see 2:23.
14 a. Philip, Herod's half-brother, was still alive.

6 afraid of the people, who regarded John as a prophet. ·Then, during the celebrations for Herod's birthday, the daughter of Herodias[b] danced before the company, and so delighted
7 Herod ·that he promised on oath to give her anything she
8 asked. ·Prompted by her mother she said, 'Give me John the
9 Baptist's head, here, on a dish'. ·The king was distressed but, thinking of the oaths he had sworn and of his guests, he
10 ordered it to be given her, ·and sent and had John beheaded
11 in the prison. ·The head was brought in on a dish and given
12 to the girl who took it to her mother. ·John's disciples came and took the body and buried it; then they went off to tell Jesus.

First miracle of the loaves

13 When Jesus received this news he withdrew by boat to a lonely place where they could be by themselves. But the people heard of this and, leaving the towns, went after him
14 on foot. ·So as he stepped ashore he saw a large crowd; and he took pity on them and healed their sick.
15 When evening came, the disciples went to him and said, 'This is a lonely place, and the time has slipped by; so send the people away, and they can go to the villages to buy them-
16 selves some food'. ·Jesus replied, 'There is no need for them
17 to go: give them something to eat yourselves'. ·But they answered, 'All we have with us is five loaves and two fish'.
18
19 'Bring them here to me' he said. ·He gave orders that the people were to sit down on the grass; then he took the five loaves and the two fish, raised his eyes to heaven and said the blessing. And breaking the loaves he handed them to his
20 disciples who gave them to the crowds. ·They all ate as much as they wanted, and they collected the scraps remaining,
21 twelve baskets full. ·Those who ate numbered about five thousand men, to say nothing of women and children.

Jesus walks on the water and, with him, Peter

22 Directly after this he made the disciples get into the boat and go on ahead to the other side while he would send the
23 crowds away. ·After sending the crowds away he went up into the hills by himself to pray. When evening came, he was
24 there alone, ·while the boat, by now far out on the lake, was
25 battling with a heavy sea, for there was a head-wind. ·In the fourth watch of the night[c] he went towards them, walking
26 on the lake, ·and when the disciples saw him walking on the lake they were terrified. 'It is a ghost' they said, and cried out in
27 fear. ·But at once Jesus called out to them, saying, 'Courage! It

28 is I! Do not be afraid.' ·It was Peter who answered. 'Lord,' he
said 'if it is you, tell me to come to you across the water.'
29 'Come' said Jesus. Then Peter got out of the boat and started
30 walking towards Jesus across the water, ·but as soon as he
felt the force of the wind, he took fright and began to sink.
31 'Lord! Save me!' he cried. ·Jesus put out his hand at once and
held him. 'Man of little faith,' he said, 'why did you doubt?'
32 And as they got into the boat the wind dropped. ·The men in
the boat bowed down before him and said, 'Truly, you are
the Son of God'.

Cures at Gennesaret

34 Having made the crossing, they came to land at Gennes-
35 aret. ·When the local people recognised him they spread the
news through the whole neighbourhood and took all that
36 were sick to him, ·begging him just to let them touch the
fringe of his cloak. And all those who touched it were
completely cured.

The traditions of the Pharisees

15 Pharisees and scribes from Jerusalem then came to Jesus
2 and said, "Why do your disciples break away from the tradition of the elders?*a* They do not wash their hands when they
3 eat food.' ·'And why do you' he answered 'break away from
the commandment of God for the sake of your tradition?
4 For God said: *Do your duty to*b *your father and mother* and:
*Anyone who curses father or mother must be put to death.*c
5 But you say, "If anyone says to his father or mother: Anything I have that I might have used to help you is dedicated to
6 God", ·he is rid of his duty to father or mother.*d* In this way
you have made God's word null and void by means of your
7 tradition. ·Hypocrites! It was you Isaiah meant when he so
rightly prophesied:

8 *This people honours me only with lip-service,*
while their hearts are far from me,
9 *The worship they offer me is worthless;*
*the doctrines they teach are only human regulations.'*e

---

b. According to Josephus, the girl's name was Salome. **c.** 3 to 6 a.m.
15 a. The traditional teaching, including many additions to and ex-
tensions of the Law. **b.** Often translated 'honour', but the word implies
a respect expressed in practical ways, Ex 20:12. **c.** Lv 20:9 **d.** Property
dedicated in this way could not be passed to another person. **e.** Is 29:13.

On clean and unclean

10　He called the people to him and said, 'Listen, and under-
11　stand. ·What goes into the mouth does not make a man
unclean; it is what comes out of the mouth that makes him
unclean.'

12　Then the disciples came to him and said, 'Do you know
that the Pharisees were shocked when they heard what you
13　said?' ·He replied, 'Any plant my heavenly Father has not
14　planted will be pulled up by the roots. ·Leave them alone.
They are blind men leading blind men; and if one blind man
leads another, both will fall into a pit.'

15　At this, Peter said to him, 'Explain the parable for us'.
16
17　Jesus replied, 'Do even you not yet understand? ·Can you not
see that whatever goes into the mouth passes through the
18　stomach and is discharged into the sewer? ·But the things
that come out of the mouth come from the heart, and it is
19　these that make a man unclean. ·For from the heart come
evil intentions: murder, adultery, fornication, theft, perjury,
20　slander. ·These are the things that make a man unclean. But
to eat with unwashed hands does not make a man unclean.'

The daughter of the Canaanite woman healed

21　Jesus left that place and withdrew to the region of Tyre and
22　Sidon. ·Then out came a Canaanite woman from that district,
and started shouting, 'Sir, Son of David, take pity on me. My
23　daughter is tormented by a devil.' ·But he answered her not a
word. And his disciples went and pleaded with him. 'Give her
what she wants,' they said 'because she is shouting after us.'
24　He said in reply, 'I was sent only to the lost sheep of the
25　House of Israel'. ·But the woman had come up and was
26　kneeling at his feet. 'Lord,' she said 'help me.' ·He replied, 'It
is not fair to take the children's food and throw it to the
27　house-dogs'. ·She retorted, 'Ah yes, sir; but even house-dogs
28　can eat the scraps that fall from their master's table'. ·Then
Jesus answered her, 'Woman, you have great faith. Let your
wish be granted.' And from that moment her daughter was
well again.

Cures near the lake

29　Jesus went on from there and reached the shores of the Sea
30　of Galilee, and he went up into the hills. He sat there, ·and
large crowds came to him bringing the lame, the crippled, the
blind, the dumb and many others; these they put down at his
31　feet, and he cured them. ·The crowds were astonished to see

the dumb speaking, the cripples whole again, the lame walking and the blind with their sight, and they praised the God
of Israel.

Second miracle of the loaves

32 But Jesus called his disciples to him and said, 'I feel sorry
for all these people; they have been with me for three days
now and have nothing to eat. I do not want to send them off
33 hungry, they might collapse on the way.' ·The disciples said
to him, 'Where could we get enough bread in this deserted
34 place to feed such a crowd?' ·Jesus said to them, 'How many
loaves have you?' 'Seven' they said 'and a few small fish.'
35 Then he instructed the crowd to sit down on the ground,
36 and he took the seven loaves and the fish, and he gave thanks
and broke them and handed them to the disciples who gave
37 them to the crowds. ·They all ate as much as they wanted,
and they collected what was left of the scraps, seven baskets
38 full. ·Now four thousand men had eaten, to say nothing of
39 women and children. ·And when he had sent the crowds away
he got into the boat and went to the district of Magadan.

The Pharisees ask for a sign from heaven

16 The Pharisees and Sadducees came, and to test him they
asked if he would show them a sign from heaven. ·He replied,
2 'In the evening you say, "It will be fine; there is a red sky",
3 and in the morning, "Stormy weather today; the sky is red
and overcast". You know how to read the face of the sky, but
4 you cannot read the signs of the times. ·It is an evil and
unfaithful generation that asks for a sign! The only sign it
will be given is the sign of Jonah.' And leaving them standing
there, he went away.

The yeast of the Pharisees and Sadducees

5 The disciples, having crossed to the other shore, had for-
6 gotten to take any food. ·Jesus said to them, 'Keep your eyes
open, and be on your guard against the yeast of the Pharisees
7 and Sadducees.' ·And they said to themselves, 'It is because
8 we have not brought any bread'. ·Jesus knew it, and he said,
'Men of little faith, why are you talking among yourselves
9 about having no bread? ·Do you not yet understand? Do you
not remember the five loaves for the five thousand and the
10 number of baskets you collected? ·Or the seven loaves for
the four thousand and the number of baskets you collected?
11 How could you fail to understand that I was not talking
about bread? What I said was: Beware of the yeast of the

12 Pharisees and Sadducees.' ·Then they understood that he was telling them to be on their guard, not against the yeast for making bread, but against the teaching of the Pharisees and Sadducees.*a*

Peter's profession of faith; his pre-eminence

13 When Jesus came to the region of Caesarea Philippi he put this question to his disciples, 'Who do people say the Son of
14 Man is?' ·And they said, 'Some say he is John the Baptist, some Elijah, and others Jeremiah or one of the prophets'.
15
16 'But you,' he said 'who do you say I am? ·Then Simon Peter spoke up, 'You are the Christ,' he said 'the Son of the living
17 God'. ·Jesus replied, 'Simon son of Jonah, you are a happy man! Because it was not flesh and blood that revealed this to
18 you but my Father in heaven. ·So I now say to you: You are Peter*b* and on this rock I will build my Church. And the gates
19 of the underworld*c* can never hold out against it. ·I will give you the keys of the kingdom of heaven: whatever you bind on earth shall be considered bound in heaven; whatever you
20 loose on earth shall be considered loosed in heaven.'*d* ·Then he gave the disciples strict orders not to tell anyone that he was the Christ.

First prophecy of the Passion

21 From that time Jesus began to make it clear to his disciples that he was destined to go to Jerusalem and suffer grievously at the hands of the elders and chief priests and scribes, to be
22 put to death and to be raised up on the third day. ·Then, taking him aside, Peter started to remonstrate with him. 'Heaven preserve you, Lord;' he said 'this must not happen
23 to you'. ·But he turned and said to Peter, 'Get behind me, Satan! You are an obstacle in my path, because the way you think is not God's way but man's.'

The condition of following Christ

24 Then Jesus said to his disciples, 'If anyone wants to be a follower of mine, let him renounce himself and take up his
25 cross and follow me. ·For anyone who wants to save his life will lose it; but anyone who loses his life for my sake will find
26 it. ·What, then, will a man gain if he wins the whole world and ruins his life? Or what has a man to offer in exchange for his life?
27 'For the Son of Man is going to come in the glory of his Father with his angels, and, when he does, he will reward
28 each one according to his behaviour. ·I tell you solemnly,

there are some of these standing here who will not taste death before they see the Son of Man coming with his kingdom.'*e*

The transfiguration

17 Six days later, Jesus took with him Peter and James and his brother John and led them up a high mountain where they
2 could be alone. ·There in their presence he was transfigured: his face shone like the sun and his clothes became as white as
3 the light. ·Suddenly Moses and Elijah*a* appeared to them;
4 they were talking with him. ·Then Peter spoke to Jesus. 'Lord,' he said 'it is wonderful for us to be here; if you wish, I will make three tents here, one for you, one for Moses and one for
5 Elijah.' ·He was still speaking when suddenly a bright cloud covered them with shadow, and from the cloud there came a voice which said, 'This is my Son, the Beloved; he enjoys my
6 favour. Listen to him.' ·When they heard this, the disciples
7 fell on their faces, overcome with fear. ·But Jesus came up and touched them. 'Stand up,' he said 'do not be afraid.'
8 And when they raised their eyes they saw no one but only Jesus.

The question about Elijah

9 As they came down from the mountain Jesus gave them this order, 'Tell no one about the vision until the Son of Man
10 has risen from the dead'. ·And the disciples put this question to him, 'Why do the scribes say then that Elijah has to come
11 first?' ·'True;' he replied 'Elijah is to come to see that every-
12 thing is once more as it should be; ·however, I tell you that Elijah has come already and they did not recognise him but treated him as they pleased; and the Son of Man will suffer
13 similarly at their hands.' ·The disciples understood then that he had been speaking of John the Baptist.

The epileptic demoniac

14 As they were rejoining the crowd a man came up to him
15 and went down on his knees before him. ·'Lord,' he said 'take

16 a. Yeast, here, is regarded as adulterating pure flour. **b.** Not, until now, a proper name: Greek *petros* (as in Engl. saltpetre) represents Aramaic *kepha*, rock. **c.** The gates symbolise the power of the underworld to hold captives. **d.** The keys have become the traditional insignia of Peter. **e.** In vv. 27–28, two different sayings have been combined because both refer to the coming of the kingdom; but the first is about Judgement day, and the second is about the destruction of Jerusalem, the sign of 'the last days'.
17 a. Representing the Law and the prophets.

pity on my son: he is a lunatic and in a wretched state; he is
16 always falling into the fire or into the water. ·I took him to
17 your disciples and they were unable to cure him.' ·'Faithless
and perverse generation!' Jesus said in reply 'How much
longer must I be with you? How much longer must I put up
18 with you? Bring him here to me.' ·And when Jesus rebuked it
the devil came out of the boy who was cured from that
moment.

19   Then the disciples came privately to Jesus. 'Why were we
20 unable to cast it out?' they asked. ·He answered, 'Because
you have little faith. I tell you solemnly, if your faith were the
size of a mustard seed you could say to this mountain,
"Move from here to there", and it would move; nothing
would be impossible for you.'

Second prophecy of the Passion

22   One day when they were together in Galilee, Jesus said to
them, 'The Son of Man is going to be handed over into the
23 power of men; ·they will put him to death, and on the third
day he will be raised to life again'. And a great sadness came
over them.

The Temple tax paid by Jesus and Peter

24   When they reached Capernaum, the collectors of the half-
shekel[b] came to Peter and said, 'Does your master not pay
25 the half-shekel?' ·'Oh yes' he replied, and went into the
house. But before he could speak, Jesus said, 'Simon, what is
your opinion? From whom do the kings of the earth take toll
26 or tribute? From their sons or from foreigners?' ·And when
he replied, 'From foreigners', Jesus said, 'Well then, the sons
27 are exempt. ·However, so as not to offend these people, go to
the lake and cast a hook; take the first fish that bites, open its
mouth and there you will find a shekel; take it and give it to
them for me and for you.'

B. THE DISCOURSE ON THE CHURCH

Who is the greatest?

18   At this time the disciples came to Jesus and said, 'Who is
2 the greatest in the kingdom of heaven?' ·So he called a little
3 child to him and set the child in front of them. ·Then he said,
'I tell you solemnly, unless you change and become like little
4 children you will never enter the kingdom of heaven. ·And
so, the one who makes himself as little as this little child is the
greatest in the kingdom of heaven.

On leading others astray

5 'Anyone who welcomes a little child like this in my name
6 welcomes me. ·But anyone who is an obstacle to bring down
one of these little ones who have faith in me would be better
drowned in the depths of the sea with a great millstone round
7 his neck. ·Alas for the world that there should be such
obstacles! Obstacles indeed there must be, but alas for the
man who provides them!
8 'If your hand or your foot should cause you to sin, cut it
off and throw it away: it is better for you to enter into life
crippled or lame, than to have two hands or two feet and be
9 thrown into eternal fire. ·And if your eye should cause you to
sin, tear it out and throw it away: it is better for you to enter
into life with one eye, than to have two eyes and be thrown
into the hell of fire.
10 'See that you never despise any of these little ones, for I tell
you that their angels in heaven are continually in the presence
of my Father in heaven.ª

The lost sheep

12 'Tell me. Suppose a man has a hundred sheep and one of
them strays; will he not leave the ninety-nine on the hillside
13 and go in search of the stray? ·I tell you solemnly, if he finds
it, it gives him more joy than do the ninety-nine that did not
14 stray at all. ·Similarly, it is never the will of your Father in
heaven that one of these little ones should be lost.

Brotherly correction

15 'If your brother does something wrong, go and have it out
with him alone, between your two selves. If he listens to you,
16 you have won back your brother. ·If he does not listen, take
one or two others along with you: *the evidence of two or three*
17 *witnesses is required to sustain any charge.* ·But if he refuses to
listen to these, report it to the community;ᵇ and if he refuses
to listen to the community, treat him like a pagan or a tax
collector.
18 'I tell you solemnly, whatever you bind on earth shall be
considered bound in heaven; whatever you loose on earth
shall be considered loosed in heaven.

b. A tax for the upkeep of the Temple.
18 a. V. 11, at the time when verse numbers were added, consisted of a
sentence which is not now accepted as part of the original text. b. The
community of the brothers (the Church).

Prayer in common

19   'I tell you solemnly once again, if two of you on earth agree to ask anything at all, it will be granted to you by my Father
20 in heaven. ·For where two or three meet in my name, I shall be there with them.'

Forgiveness of injuries

21   Then Peter went up to him and said, 'Lord, how often must I forgive my brother if he wrongs me? As often as
22 seven times?' ·Jesus answered, 'Not seven, I tell you, but seventy-seven times.

Parable of the unforgiving debtor

23   'And so the kingdom of heaven may be compared to a king
24 who decided to settle his accounts with his servants. ·When the reckoning began, they brought him a man who owed ten
25 thousand talents;ᵉ ·but he had no means of paying, so his master gave orders that he should be sold, together with his wife and children and all his possessions, to meet the debt.
26 At this, the servant threw himself down at his master's feet.
27 "Give me time" he said "and I will pay the whole sum." ·And the servant's master felt so sorry for him that he let him go
28 and cancelled the debt. ·Now as this servant went out, he happened to meet a fellow servant who owed him one hundred denarii;ᵈ and he seized him by the throat and began to
29 throttle him. "Pay what you owe me" he said. ·His fellow servant fell at his feet and implored him, saying, "Give me
30 time and I will pay you". ·But the other would not agree; on the contrary, he had him thrown into prison till he should
31 pay the debt. ·His fellow servants were deeply distressed when they saw what had happened, and they went to their master
32 and reported the whole affair to him. ·Then the master sent for him. "You wicked servant," he said "I cancelled all that
33 debt of yours when you appealed to me. ·Were you not bound, then, to have pity on your fellow servant just as I had
34 pity on you?" ·And in his anger the master handed him over
35 to the torturers till he should pay all his debt. ·And that is how my heavenly Father will deal with you unless you each forgive your brother from your heart.'

VI. THE APPROACHING ADVENT
OF THE KINGDOM OF HEAVEN

A. NARRATIVE SECTION

The question about divorce

19   Jesus had now finished what he wanted to say, and he left
Galilee and came into the part of Judaea which is on the far
2 side of the Jordan. ·Large crowds followed him and he healed
them there.

3   Some Pharisees approached him, and to test him they said,
'Is it against the Law for a man to divorce his wife on any
4 pretext whatever?' ·He answered, 'Have you not read that
the creator from the beginning *made them male and female*
5 and that he said: *This is why a man must leave father and
mother, and cling to his wife, and the two become one body*?
6 They are no longer two, therefore, but one body. So then,
what God has united, man must not divide.'

7   They said to him, 'Then why did Moses command that a
8 writ of dismissal should be given in cases of divorce?' ·'It was
because you were so unteachable' he said 'that Moses allowed
you to divorce your wives, but it was not like this from the
9 beginning. ·Now I say this to you: the man who divorces his
wife—I am not speaking of fornication—and marries another, is guilty of adultery.'

Continence

10   The disciples said to him, 'If that is how things are between
11 husband and wife, it is not advisable to marry'. ·But he
replied, 'It is not everyone who can accept what I have said,
12 but only those to whom it is granted. ·There are eunuchs born
that way from their mother's womb, there are eunuchs made
so by men and there are eunuchs who have made themselves
that way for the sake of the kingdom of heaven. Let anyone
accept this who can.'

Jesus and the children

13   People brought little children to him, for him to lay his
hands on them and say a prayer. The disciples turned them
14 away, ·but Jesus said, 'Let the little children alone, and do
not stop them coming to me; for it is to such as these that the
15 kingdom of heaven belongs'. ·Then he laid his hands on
them and went on his way.

c. 'Millions of pounds'—about £3,000,000. d. Under £5.

The rich young man

16 And there was a man who came to him and asked, 'Master, what good deed must I do to possess eternal life?'
17 Jesus said to him, 'Why do you ask me about what is good? There is one alone who is good. But if you wish to enter into
18 life, keep the commandments.' ·He said, 'Which?' 'These:' Jesus replied '*You must not kill. You must not commit adultery. You must not steal. You must not bring false witness.*
19 *Honour your father and mother*, and: *you must love your*
20 *neighbour as yourself.*'ᵃ ·The young man said to him, 'I have
21 kept all these. What more do I need to do?' ·Jesus said, 'If you wish to be perfect, go and sell what you own and give the money to the poor, and you will have treasure in heaven;
22 then come, follow me'. ·But when the young man heard these words he went away sad, for he was a man of great wealth.

The danger of riches

23 Then Jesus said to his disciples, 'I tell you solemnly, it will be hard for a rich man to enter the kingdom of heaven.
24 Yes, I tell you again, it is easier for a camel to pass through the eye of a needle than for a rich man to enter the kingdom
25 of heaven.' ·When the disciples heard this they were aston-
26 ished. 'Who can be saved, then?' they said. ·Jesus gazed at them. 'For men' he told them 'this is impossible; for God everything is possible.'

The reward of renunciation

27 Then Peter spoke. 'What about us?' he said to him 'We have left everything and followed you. What are we to have,
28 then?' ·Jesus said to him, 'I tell you solemnly, when all is made new and the Son of Man sits on his throne of glory, you will yourselves sit on twelve thrones to judgeᵇ the twelve
29 tribes of Israel. ·And everyone who has left houses, brothers, sisters, father, mother, children or land for the sake of my name will be repaid a hundred times over, and also inherit eternal life.
30 'Many who are first will be last, and the last, first.

Parable of the vineyard labourers

20 'Now the kingdom of heaven is like a landowner going out
2 at daybreak to hire workers for his vineyard. ·He made an agreement with the workers for one denarius a day, and sent
3 them to his vineyard. ·Going out at about the third hour he
4 saw others standing idle in the market place ·and said to

them, "You go to my vineyard too and I will give you a fair
5 wage". ·So they went. At about the sixth hour and again at
6 about the ninth hour, he went out and did the same. ·Then at
about the eleventh hour he went out and found more men
standing round, and he said to them, "Why have you been
7 standing here idle all day?" ·"Because no one has hired us"
they answered. He said to them, "You go into my vineyard too".
8 In the evening, the owner of the vineyard said to his bailiff,
"Call the workers and pay them their wages, starting with the
9 last arrivals and ending with the first". ·So those who were
hired at about the eleventh hour came forward and received
10 one denarius each. ·When the first came, they expected to get
11 more, but they too received one denarius each. ·They took it,
12 but grumbled at the landowner. ·"The men who came last"
they said "have done only one hour, and you have treated
them the same as us, though we have done a heavy day's
13 work in all the heat." ·He answered one of them and said,
"My friend, I am not being unjust to you; did we not agree
14 on one denarius? ·Take your earnings and go. I choose to
15 pay the last-comer as much as I pay you. ·Have I no right to
do what I like with my own? Why be envious because I am
16 generous?" ·Thus the last will be first, and the first, last.'

Third prophecy of the Passion

17   Jesus was going up to Jerusalem, and on the way he took
18 the Twelve to one side and said to them, ·'Now we are going
up to Jerusalem, and the Son of Man is about to be handed
over to the chief priests and scribes. They will condemn him
19 to death ·and will hand him over to the pagans to be mocked
and scourged and crucified; and on the third day he will rise
again.'

The mother of Zebedee's sons makes her request

20   Then the mother of Zebedee's sons came with her sons to
21 make a request of him, and bowed low; ·and he said to her,
'What is it you want?' She said to him, 'Promise that these
two sons of mine may sit one at your right hand and the
22 other at your left in your kingdom'. ·'You do not know what
you are asking' Jesus answered. 'Can you drink the cup that
23 I am going to drink?' They replied, 'We can'. ·'Very well,' he
said 'you shall drink my cup,[a] but as for seats at my right

19 a. Ex 20:12–16; Dt 5:16–20 b. I.e. to govern.
20 a. Perhaps a prophecy of the martyrdom of James and John;
James was certainly put to death by Herod Agrippa about 44 A.D., Ac
12:2.

hand and my left, these are not mine to grant; they belong to those to whom they have been allotted by my Father.'

Leadership with service

24 When the other ten heard this they were indignant with the
25 two brothers. ·But Jesus called them to him and said, 'You know that among the pagans the rulers lord it over them, and
26 their great men make their authority felt. ·This is not to happen among you. No; anyone who wants to be great
27 among you must be your servant, ·and anyone who wants to
28 be first among you must be your slave, ·just as the Son of Man came not to be served but to serve, and to give his life as a ransom for many.'

The two blind men of Jericho

29
30 As they left Jericho a large crowd followed him. ·Now there were two blind men sitting at the side of the road. When they heard that it was Jesus who was passing by, they
31 shouted, 'Lord! Have pity on us, Son of David.' ·And the crowd scolded them and told them to keep quiet, but they only shouted more loudly, 'Lord! Have pity on us, Son of
32 David.' ·Jesus stopped, called them over and said, 'What do
33 you want me to do for you?' ·They said to him, 'Lord, let us
34 have our sight back'. ·Jesus felt pity for them and touched their eyes, and immediately their sight returned and they followed him.

The Messiah enters Jerusalem

21 When they were near Jerusalem and had come in sight of Bethphage on the Mount of Olives, Jesus sent two disciples,
2 saying to them, 'Go to the village facing you, and you will immediately find a tethered donkey and a colt with her. Untie
3 them and bring them to me. ·If anyone says anything to you, you are to say, "The Master needs them and will send them
4 back directly".' ·This took place to fulfil the prophecy:

5   *Say to the daughter of Zion:*
       Look, your king comes to you;
       he is humble, he rides on a donkey
       and on a colt, the foal of a beast of burden.[a]

6 So the disciples went out and did as Jesus had told them.
7 They brought the donkey and the colt, then they laid their
8 cloaks on their backs and he sat on them. ·Great crowds of people spread their cloaks on the road, while others were cutting branches from the trees and spreading them in his

9 path. ·The crowds who went in front of him and those who followed were all shouting:

> '*Hosanna*[b] to the Son of David!
> *Blessings on him who comes in the name of the Lord!*[c]
> *Hosanna* in the highest heavens!'

10 And when he entered Jerusalem, the whole city was in
11 turmoil. 'Who is this?' people asked, ·and the crowds answered, 'This is the prophet Jesus from Nazareth in Galilee'.

The expulsion of the dealers from the Temple

12 Jesus then went into the Temple and drove out all those who were selling and buying there; he upset the tables of the money changers and the chairs of those who were selling
13 pigeons.[d] ·'According to scripture' he said '*my house will be called a house of prayer;*[e] but you are turning it into a
14 *robbers' den.*'[f] ·There were also blind and lame people who
15 came to him in the Temple, and he cured them. ·At the sight of the wonderful things he did and of the children shouting, 'Hosanna to the Son of David' in the Temple, the chief
16 priests and the scribes were indignant. ·'Do you hear what they are saying?' they said to him. 'Yes,' Jesus answered 'have you never read this:

> *By the mouths of children, babes in arms,*
> *you have made sure of praise?*'[g]

17 With that he left them and went out of the city to Bethany where he spent the night.

The barren fig tree withers. Faith and prayer

18 As he was returning to the city in the early morning, he felt
19 hungry. ·Seeing a fig tree by the road, he went up to it and found nothing on it but leaves. And he said to it, 'May you never bear fruit again'; and at that instant the fig tree
20 withered. ·The disciples were amazed when they saw it. 'What happened to the tree' they said 'that it withered there
21 and then?' ·Jesus answered, 'I tell you solemnly, if you have faith and do not doubt at all, not only will you do what I have done to the fig tree, but even if you say to this mountain, "Get up and throw yourself into the sea", it will be done.

21 a. Is 62:11; Zc 9:9 b. Conventional shout of acclaim, like a cheer. c. Ps 118:26 d. Money changers provided Temple currency, and the traders the animals, for making sacrificial offerings. e. Is 56:7 f. Jr 7:11 g. Ps 8:2 (LXX); Ws 10:21

22 And if you have faith, everything you ask for in prayer you will receive.'

The authority of Jesus is questioned

23 He had gone into the Temple and was teaching, when the chief priests and the elders of the people came to him and said, 'What authority have you for acting like this? And who
24 gave you this authority?' ·'And I' replied Jesus 'will ask you a question, only one; if you tell me the answer to it, I will then
25 tell you my authority for acting like this. ·John's baptism: where did it come from : heaven or man?' And they argued it out this way among themselves, 'If we say from heaven, he will
26 retort, "Then why did you refuse to believe him?"; ·but if we say from man, we have the people to fear, for they all hold
27 that John was a prophet'. ·So their reply to Jesus was, 'We do not know'. And he retorted, 'Nor will I tell you my authority for acting like this.

Parable of the two sons

28 'What is your opinion? A man had two sons. He went and said to the first, "My boy, you go and work in the vineyard
29 today". ·He answered, "I will not go", but afterwards thought
30 better of it and went. ·The man then went and said the same thing to the second who answered, "Certainly, sir", but did
31 not go. ·Which of the two did the father's will?' 'The first' they said. Jesus said to them, 'I tell you solemnly, tax collectors and prostitutes are making their way into the kingdom
32 of God before you. ·For John came to you, a pattern of true righteousness, but you did not believe him, and yet the tax collectors and prostitutes did. Even after seeing that, you refused to think better of it and believe in him.

Parable of the wicked husbandmen

33 'Listen to another parable. There was a man, a landowner, who planted a vineyard; he fenced it round, dug a winepress in it and built a tower; then he leased it to tenants and went
34 abroad. ·When vintage time drew near he sent his servants to
35 the tenants to collect his produce. ·But the tenants seized his servants, thrashed one, killed another and stoned a third.
36 Next he sent some more servants, this time a larger number,
37 and they dealt with them in the same way. ·Finally he sent his
38 son to them. "They will respect my son" he said. ·But when the tenants saw the son, they said to each other, "This is the heir. Come on, let us kill him and take over his inheritance."
39 So they seized him and threw him out of the vineyard and

40 killed him. ·Now when the owner of the vineyard comes,
41 what will he do to those tenants?' ·They answered, 'He will
bring those wretches to a wretched end and lease the vineyard to other tenants who will deliver the produce to him
42 when the season arrives'. ·Jesus said to them, 'Have you
never read in the scriptures:

> *It was the stone rejected by the builders*
> *that became the keystone.*
> *This was the Lord's doing*
> *and it is wonderful to see?*[h]

43 I tell you, then, that the kingdom of God will be taken from
you and given to a people who will produce its fruit.'

45   When they heard his parables, the chief priests and the
46 scribes realised he was speaking about them, ·but though
they would have liked to arrest him they were afraid of the
crowds, who looked on him as a prophet.

Parable of the wedding feast

22   Jesus began to speak to them in parables once again, ·'The
kingdom of heaven may be compared to a king who gave a
3 feast for his son's wedding. ·He sent his servants to call those
4 who had been invited, but they would not come. ·Next he
sent some more servants. "Tell those who have been invited"
he said "that I have my banquet all prepared, my oxen and
fattened cattle have been slaughtered, everything is ready.
5 Come to the wedding." ·But they were not interested: one
6 went off to his farm, another to his business, ·and the rest
7 seized his servants, maltreated them and killed them. ·The
king was furious. He despatched his troops, destroyed those
8 murderers and burnt their town. ·Then he said to his servants, "The wedding is ready; but as those who were invited
9 proved to be unworthy, ·go to the crossroads in the town and
10 invite everyone you can find to the wedding". ·So these
servants went out on to the roads and collected together
everyone they could find, bad and good alike; and the
11 wedding hall was filled with guests. ·When the king came in
to look at the guests he noticed one man who was not wearing
12 a wedding garment, ·and said to him, "How did you get in
here, my friend, without a wedding garment?" And the man
13 was silent. ·Then the king said to the attendants, "Bind him
hand and foot and throw him out into the dark, where there
14 will be weeping and grinding of teeth". ·For many are
called, but few are chosen.'

h. Ps 118:22–23

On tribute to Caesar

15   Then the Pharisees went away to work out between them
16 how to trap him in what he said. ·And they sent their disciples
to him, together with the Herodians,[a] to say, 'Master, we
know that you are an honest man and teach the way of God
in an honest way, and that you are not afraid of anyone,
17 because a man's rank means nothing to you. ·Tell us your
opinion, then. Is it permissible to pay taxes to Caesar or not?'
18 But Jesus was aware of their malice and replied, 'You hypo-
19 crites! Why do you set this trap for me? ·Let me see the
money you pay the tax with.' They handed him a denarius,
20 and he said, 'Whose head is this? Whose name?' ·'Caesar's'
21 they replied. He then said to them, 'Very well, give back to
Caesar what belongs to Caesar—and to God what belongs to
22 God'. ·This reply took them by surprise, and they left him
alone and went away.

The resurrection of the dead

23   That day some Sadducees—who deny that there is a resurrection—approached him and they put this question to him,
24 'Master, Moses said that if a man dies childless, his brother is
to marry the widow, his sister-in-law, to raise children for his
25 brother. ·Now we had a case involving seven brothers; the
first married and then died without children, leaving his wife
26 to his brother; ·the same thing happened with the second and
27 third and so on to the seventh, ·and then last of all the
28 woman herself died. ·Now at the resurrection to which of
those seven will she be wife, since she had been married to
29 them all?' ·Jesus answered them, 'You are wrong, because
you understand neither the scriptures nor the power of God.
30 For at the resurrection men and women do not marry; no,
31 they are like the angels in heaven. ·And as for the resurrection of the dead, have you never read what God himself said
32 to you: *I am the God of Abraham, the God of Isaac and the
God of Jacob?*[b] God is God, not of the dead, but of the
33 living.' ·And his teaching made a deep impression on the
people who heard it.

The greatest commandment of all

34   But when the Pharisees heard that he had silenced the
35 Sadducees they got together ·and, to disconcert him, one of
36 them put a question, ·'Master, which is the greatest com-
37 mandment of the Law?' ·Jesus said, *'You must love the Lord
your God with all your heart, with all your soul,* and with all

38 your mind. ·This is the greatest and the first commandment.
39 The second resembles it: *You must love your neighbour as*
40 *yourself.* ·On these two commandments hang the whole Law,
and the Prophets also.'

Christ not only son but also Lord of David

41 　While the Pharisees were gathered round, Jesus put to
42 them this question, ·'What is your opinion about the Christ?
43 Whose son is he?' 'David's' they told him. ·'Then how is it'
he said 'that David, moved by the Spirit, calls him Lord,
where he says:

44 　　　　　*The Lord said to my Lord:*
　　　　　Sit at my right hand
　　　　　and I will put your enemies
　　　　　under your feet?[c]

45 'If David can call him Lord, then how can he be his son?'
46 Not one could think of anything to say in reply, and from
that day no one dared to ask him any further questions.

The scribes and Pharisees: their hypocrisy and vanity

23　Then addressing the people and his disciples Jesus said,
2 'The scribes and the Pharisees occupy the chair of Moses.
3 You must therefore do what they tell you and listen to what
they say; but do not be guided by what they do; since they do
4 not practise what they preach. ·They tie up heavy burdens
and lay them on men's shoulders, but will they lift a finger to
5 move them? Not they! ·Everything they do is done to attract
attention, like wearing broader phylacteries and longer tassels,[a]
6 like wanting to take the place of honour at banquets and the
7 front seats in the synagogues, ·being greeted obsequiously
in the market squares and having people call them Rabbi.
8 　'You, however, must not allow yourselves to be called
Rabbi, since you have only one Master, and you are all
9 brothers. ·You must call no one on earth your father, since
10 you only have one Father, and he is in heaven. ·Nor must you
allow yourselves to be called teachers, for you have only one
11 Teacher, the Christ. ·The greatest among you must be your
12 servant. ·Anyone who exalts himself will be humbled, and
anyone who humbles himself will be exalted.

22 **a.** Supporters of the ruling family, hoping to find a cause for de-
nouncing Jesus to the Romans. **b.** Ex 3:6 **c.** Ps 110:1
23 **a.** Phylacteries: containers for short texts taken from the Law; they
were worn on the arm or the forehead in obedience to Ex 13:9, 16 and
Dt 6:8. The tassels were sewn to the corners of the cloak.

The sevenfold indictment of the scribes and Pharisees

13   'Alas for you, scribes and Pharisees, you hypocrites! You who shut up the kingdom of heaven in men's faces, neither going in yourselves nor allowing others to go in[b] who want to.

15   'Alas for you, scribes and Pharisees, you hypocrites! You who travel over sea and land to make a single proselyte, and when you have him you make him twice as fit for hell as you are.

16   'Alas for you, blind guides! You who say, "If a man swears by the Temple, it has no force; but if a man swears by the 17 gold of the Temple, he is bound". ·Fools and blind! For which is of greater worth, the gold or the Temple that makes 18 the gold sacred? ·Or else, "If a man swears by the altar it has no force; but if a man swears by the offering that is on the 19 altar, he is bound". ·You blind men! For which is of greater worth, the offering or the altar that makes the offering 20 sacred? ·Therefore, when a man swears by the altar he is 21 swearing by that and by everything on it. ·And when a man swears by the Temple he is swearing by that and by the One 22 who dwells in it. ·And when a man swears by heaven he is swearing by the throne of God and by the One who is seated there.

23   'Alas for you, scribes and Pharisees, you hypocrites! You who pay your tithe of mint and dill and cummin[c] and have neglected the weightier matters of the Law—justice, mercy, good faith! These you should have practised, without neglect-24 ing the others. ·You blind guides! Straining out gnats and swallowing camels!

25   'Alas for you, scribes and Pharisees, you hypocrites! You who clean the outside of cup and dish and leave the inside full 26 of extortion and intemperance. ·Blind Pharisee! Clean the inside of cup and dish first so that the outside may become clean as well.

27   'Alas for you, scribes and Pharisees, you hypocrites! You who are like whitewashed tombs that look handsome on the outside, but inside are full of dead men's bones and every 28 kind of corruption. ·In the same way you appear to people from the outside like good honest men, but inside you are full of hypocrisy and lawlessness.

29   'Alas for you, scribes and Pharisees, you hypocrites! You who build the sepulchres of the prophets and decorate the 30 tombs of holy men, ·saying, "We would never have joined in shedding the blood of the prophets, had we lived in our 31 fathers' day". ·So! Your own evidence tells against you! You

32 are the sons of those who murdered the prophets! ·Very well then, finish off the work that your fathers began.

Their crimes and approaching punishment

33 'Serpents, brood of vipers, how can you escape being con-
34 demned to hell? ·This is why, in my turn, I am sending you prophets and wise men and scribes: some you will slaughter and crucify, some you will scourge in your synagogues and
35 hunt from town to town; ·and so you will draw down on yourselves the blood of every holy man that has been shed on earth, from the blood of Abel the Holy to the blood of Zechariah son of Barachiah*d* whom you murdered between the
36 sanctuary and the altar. ·I tell you solemnly, all of this will recoil on this generation.

Jerusalem admonished

37 'Jerusalem, Jerusalem, you that kill the prophets and stone those who are sent to you! How often have I longed to gather your children, as a hen gathers her chicks under her wings,
38 and you refused! ·So be it! Your house will be left to you
39 desolate, ·for, I promise, you shall not see me any more until you say:

*Blessings on him who comes in the name of the Lord!'*e

B. THE SERMON ON THE END

Introduction

24 Jesus left the Temple, and as he was going away his disciples came up to draw his attention to the Temple build-
2 ings. ·He said to them in reply, 'You see all these? I tell you solemnly, not a single stone here will be left on another:
3 everything will be destroyed.' ·And when he was sitting on the Mount of Olives the disciples came and asked him privately, 'Tell us, when is this going to happen, and what will be the sign of your coming and of the end of the world?'

The beginning of sorrows

4 And Jesus answered them, 'Take care that no one deceives
5 you; ·because many will come using my name and saying, "I
6 am the Christ", and they will deceive many. ·You will hear of wars and rumours of wars; do not be alarmed, for this is

b. By interpreting the Law so strictly that nobody could obey all of it.
c. The law of paying tithes on crops was extended to include herbs and plants grown for flavouring. d. Possibly Zechariah, the last of the prophets to be killed, according to the Jewish scriptures (2 Ch 24:20–22). e. Ps 118:26

something that must happen, but the end will not be yet.

7 For nation will fight against nation, and kingdom against kingdom. There will be famines and earthquakes here and

8 there. ·All this is only the beginning of the birthpangs.

9 'Then they will hand you over to be tortured and put to death; and you will be hated by all the nations on account of

10 my name. ·And then many will fall away; men will betray one

11 another and hate one another. ·Many false prophets will

12 arise; they will deceive many, ·and with the increase of law-

13 lessness, love in most men will grow cold; ·but the man who stands firm to the end will be saved.

14 'This Good News of the kingdom will be proclaimed to the whole world[a] as a witness to all the nations. And then the end[b] will come.

The great tribulation of Jerusalem

15 'So when you see *the disastrous abomination*, of which the prophet Daniel spoke, set up in the Holy Place (let the reader

16 understand), ·then those in Judaea must escape to the

17 mountains; ·if a man is on the housetop, he must not come

18 down to collect his belongings; ·if a man is in the fields, he

19 must not turn back to fetch his cloak. ·Alas for those with child, or with babies at the breast, when those days come!

20 Pray that you will not have to escape in winter or on a sabbath.

21 For then there will be *great distress such as, until now, since* the world began, there never *has been*, nor ever will be again.

22 And if that time had not been shortened, no one would have survived; but shortened that time shall be, for the sake of those who are chosen.

23 'If anyone says to you then, "Look, here is the Christ" or,

24 "He is there", do not believe it; ·for false Christs and false prophets will arise and produce great signs and portents, enough to deceive even the chosen, if that were possible.

25 There; I have forewarned you.

The coming of the Son of Man will be evident

26 'If, then, they say to you, "Look, he is in the desert", do not go up there; "Look, he is in some hiding place", do not

27 believe it; ·because the coming of the Son of Man will be like lightning striking in the east and flashing far into the west.

28 Wherever the corpse is, there will the vultures gather.

The universal significance of this coming

29 'Immediately after the distress of those days[c] the sun will be darkened, the moon will lose its brightness, the stars will fall

30 from the sky and the powers of heaven will be shaken. ·And
then the sign of the Son of Man will appear in heaven; then
too all the peoples of the earth will beat their breasts; and
they will see the Son of Man coming on the clouds of heaven
31 with power and great glory.*ᵈ* ·And he will send his angels with
a loud trumpet to gather his chosen from the four winds,
from one end of heaven to the other.

The time of this coming

32 'Take the fig tree as a parable: as soon as its twigs grow
supple and its leaves come out, you know that summer is
33 near. ·So with you when you see all these things: know that
34 he is near, at the very gates. ·I tell you solemnly, before this
generation has passed away all these things will have taken
35 place.*ᵉ* ·Heaven and earth will pass away, but my words will
36 never pass away. ·But as for that day and hour, nobody
knows it, neither the angels of heaven, nor the Son, no one
but the Father only.

Be on the alert

37 'As it was in Noah's day, so will it be when the Son of Man
38 comes. ·For in those days before the Flood people were
eating, drinking, taking wives, taking husbands, right up to
39 the day Noah went into the ark, ·and they suspected nothing
till the Flood came and swept all away. It will be like this
40 when the Son of Man comes. ·Then of two men in the fields
41 one is taken, one left; ·of two women at the millstone
grinding, one is taken, one left.
42 'So stay awake, because you do not know the day when
43 your master is coming. ·You may be quite sure of this that if
the householder had known at what time of night the burglar
would come, he would have stayed awake and would not
have allowed anyone to break through the wall of his house.
44 Therefore, you too must stand ready because the Son of Man
is coming at an hour you do not expect.

Parable of the conscientious steward

45 'What sort of servant, then, is faithful and wise enough for
the master to place him over his household to give them their
46 food at the proper time? ·Happy that servant if his master's

24 a. The 'inhabited world' as it was known. **b.** The fall and destruction of Jerusalem. A prophecy of this is combined, in this discourse, with descriptions of the 'last days'. **c.** Join with v. 22. Vv. 23–28 are a digression. **d.** As foretold in Dn 7:14. **e.** Meaning the fall and destruction of Jerusalem.

47 arrival finds him at this employment. ·I tell you solemnly, he
48 will place him over everything he owns. ·But as for the
dishonest servant who says to himself, "My master is taking
49 his time", ·and sets about beating his fellow servants and
50 eating and drinking with drunkards, ·his master will come on
a day he does not expect and at an hour he does not know.
51 The master will cut him off and send him to the same fate as
the hypocrites, where there will be weeping and grinding of
teeth.

Parable of the ten bridesmaids

25   'Then the kingdom of heaven will be like this: Ten bridesmaids took their lamps and went to meet the bridegroom.
$\frac{2}{3}$ Five of them were foolish and five were sensible: ·the foolish
4 ones did take their lamps, but they brought no oil, ·whereas
5 the sensible ones took flasks of oil as well as their lamps. ·The
bridegroom was late, and they all grew drowsy and fell
6 asleep. ·But at midnight there was a cry, "The bridegroom is
7 here! Go out and meet him." ·At this, all those bridesmaids
8 woke up and trimmed their lamps, ·and the foolish ones said
to the sensible ones, "Give us some of your oil: our lamps are
9 going out". ·But they replied, "There may not be enough for
us and for you; you had better go to those who sell it and buy
10 some for yourselves". ·They had gone off to buy it when the
bridegroom arrived. Those who were ready went in with him
11 to the wedding hall and the door was closed. ·The other
bridesmaids arrived later. "Lord, Lord," they said "open the
12 door for us." ·But he replied, "I tell you solemnly, I do not
13 know you". ·So stay awake, because you do not know either
the day or the hour.

Parable of the talents

14   'It is like a man on his way abroad who summoned his
15 servants and entrusted his property to them. ·To one he gave
five talents, to another two, to a third one; each in proportion
16 to his ability. Then he set out. ·The man who had received the
five talents promptly went and traded with them and made
17 five more. ·The man who had received two made two more in
18 the same way. ·But the man who had received one went off
and dug a hole in the ground and hid his master's money.
19 Now a long time after, the master of those servants came
20 back and went through his accounts with them. ·The man
who had received the five talents came forward bringing five
more. "Sir," he said "you entrusted me with five talents; here
21 are five more that I have made." ·His master said to him,

"Well done, good and faithful servant; you have shown you
can be faithful in small things, I will trust you with greater;
22 come and join in your master's happiness". ·Next the man
with the two talents came forward. "Sir," he said "you
entrusted me with two talents; here are two more that I have
23 made." ·His master said to him, "Well done, good and faithful servant; you have shown you can be faithful in small
things, I will trust you with greater; come and join in your
24 master's happiness". ·Last came forward the man who had
the one talent. "Sir," said he "I had heard you were a hard
man, reaping where you have not sown and gathering where
25 you have not scattered; ·so I was afraid, and I went off and
hid your talent in the ground. Here it is; it was yours, you
26 have it back." ·But his master answered him, "You wicked
and lazy servant! So you knew that I reap where I have not
27 sown and gather where I have not scattered? ·Well then, you
should have deposited my money with the bankers, and on
my return I would have recovered my capital with interest.
28 So now, take the talent from him and give it to the man who
29 has five talents. ·For to everyone who has will be given more,
and he will have more than enough; but from the man who
30 has not, even what he has will be taken away. ·As for this
good-for-nothing servant, throw him out into the dark, where
there will be weeping and grinding of teeth."

The Last Judgement

31 'When the son of man comes in his glory. escorted by all
the angels, then he will take his seat on his throne of glory.
32 All the nations will be assembled before him and he will
separate men one from another as the shepherd separates
33 sheep from goats. ·He will place the sheep on his right hand
34 and the goats on his left. ·Then the King will say to those on
his right hand, "Come, you whom my Father has blessed,
take for your heritage the kingdom prepared for you since
35 the foundation of the world. ·For I was hungry and you gave
me food; I was thirsty and you gave me drink; I was a
36 stranger and you made me welcome; ·naked and you clothed
me, sick and you visited me, in prison and you came to see
37 me." ·Then the virtuous will say to him in reply, "Lord, when
did we see you hungry and feed you; or thirsty and give you
38 drink?·When did we see you a stranger and make you welcome;
39 naked and clothe you; ·sick or in prison and go to see you?"
40 And the King will answer, "I tell you solemnly, in so far as you
did this to one of the least of these brothers of mine, you did it
41 to me". ·Next he will say to those on his left hand, "Go away

from me, with your curse upon you, to the eternal fire pre-
42 pared for the devil and his angels. ·For I was hungry and
you never gave me food; I was thirsty and you never gave me
43 anything to drink; ·I was a stranger and you never made me
welcome, naked and you never clothed me, sick and in
44 prison and you never visited me." ·Then it will be their turn
to ask, "Lord, when did we see you hungry or thirsty, a
stranger or naked, sick or in prison, and did not come to
45 your help?" ·Then he will answer, 'I tell you solemnly, in so
far as you neglected to do this to one of the least of these, you
46 neglected to do it to me". ·And they will go away to eternal
punishment, and the virtuous to eternal life.'

VII. PASSION AND RESURRECTION

The conspiracy against Jesus

26   Jesus had now finished all he wanted to say, and he told his
2 disciples, ·'It will be Passover, as you know, in two days'
time, and the Son of Man will be handed over to be crucified'.
3   Then the chief priests and the elders of the people assembled in the palace of the high priest, whose name was
4 Caiaphas, ·and made plans to arrest Jesus by some trick and
5 have him put to death. ·They said, however, 'It must not be
during the festivities; there must be no disturbance among
the people'.

The anointing at Bethany

6   Jesus was at Bethany in the house of Simon the leper, when
7 a woman came to him with an alabaster jar of the most
expensive ointment, and poured it on his head as he was at
8 table. ·When they saw this, the disciples were indignant; 'Why
9 this waste?' they said. ·'This could have been sold at a high
10 price and the money given to the poor.' ·Jesus noticed this.
'Why are you upsetting the woman?' he said to them. 'What
she has done for me is one of the good works[a] indeed!
11 You have the poor with you always, but you will not always
12 have me. ·When she poured this ointment on my body, she
13 did it to prepare me for burial. ·I tell you solemnly, wherever
in all the world this Good News is proclaimed, what she has
done will be told also, in remembrance of her.'

Judas betrays Jesus

14   Then one of the Twelve, the man called Judas Iscariot,
15 went to the chief priests and said, 'What are you prepared to
16 give me if I hand him over to you?' ·They paid him thirty

silver pieces,[b] and from that moment he looked for an opportunity to betray him.

Preparations for the Passover supper

17 Now on the first day of Unleavened Bread[c] the disciples came to Jesus to say, 'Where do you want us to make the
18 preparations for you to eat the passover?' ·'Go to so-and-so in the city' he replied 'and say to him, "The Master says: My time is near. It is at your house that I am keeping Passover
19 with my disciples."' ·The disciples did what Jesus told them and prepared the Passover.

The treachery of Judas foretold

20 When evening came he was at table with the twelve dis-
21 ciples. ·And while they were eating he said, 'I tell you
22 solemnly, one of you is about to betray me'. ·They were greatly distressed and started asking him in turn, 'Not I,
23 Lord, surely?' ·He answered, 'Someone who has dipped his
24 hand into the dish with me, will betray me. ·The Son of Man is going to his fate, as the scriptures say he will, but alas for that man by whom the Son of Man is betrayed! Better for
25 that man if he had never been born!' ·Judas, who was to betray him, asked in his turn, 'Not I, Rabbi, surely?' 'They are your own words' answered Jesus.

The institution of the Eucharist

26 Now as they were eating,[d] Jesus took some bread, and when he had said the blessing he broke it and gave it to the
27 disciples. 'Take it and eat;' he said 'this is my body.' ·Then he took a cup, and when he had returned thanks he gave it to
28 them. 'Drink all of you from this,' he said ·'for this is my blood, the blood of the covenant, which is to be poured out for
29 many for the forgiveness of sins. ·From now on, I tell you, I shall not drink wine until the day I drink the new wine with you in the kingdom of my Father.'

26 a. As 'good works', charitable deeds were reckoned superior to almsgiving. **b.** 30 shekels, the price fixed for a slave's life, Ex 21:32. **c.** Unleavened bread was normally to be eaten during the seven days which followed the Passover supper; here the writer appears to mean the first day of the whole Passover celebration. **d.** The Passover supper itself, for which exact rules for the blessing of bread and wine were laid down. The 'eating' of v. 21 is the first course, which came before the Passover itself.

Peter's denial foretold

30 After psalms had been sung^e they left for the Mount of
31 Olives. ·Then Jesus said to them, 'You will all lose faith in
me this night,^f for the scripture says: *I shall strike the shep-*
32 *herd and the sheep of the flock will be scattered,*^g ·but after my
33 resurrection I shall go before you to Galilee'. ·At this, Peter
said, 'Though all lose faith in you, I will never lose faith'.
34 Jesus answered him, 'I tell you solemnly, this very night,
before the cock crows, you will have disowned me three
35 times'. ·Peter said to him, 'Even if I have to die with you,
I will never disown you'. And all the disciples said the same.

Gethsemane

36 Then Jesus came with them to a small estate called Gethsemane; and he said to his disciples, 'Stay here while I go
37 over there to pray'. ·He took Peter and the two sons of
Zebedee with him. And sadness came over him, and great
38 distress. ·Then he said to them, 'My soul is sorrowful to the
39 point of death. Wait here and keep awake with me.' ·And
going on a little further he fell on his face and prayed. 'My
Father,' he said 'if it is possible, let this cup pass me by.
40 Nevertheless, let it be as you, not I, would have it.' ·He came
back to the disciples and found them sleeping, and he said to
Peter, 'So you had not the strength to keep awake with me
41 one hour? ·You should be awake, and praying not to be put
42 to the test. The spirit is willing, but the flesh is weak.' ·Again,
a second time, he went away and prayed: 'My father,' he
said 'if this cup cannot pass by without my drinking it, your
43 will be done!' ·And he came back again and found them
44 sleeping, their eyes were so heavy. ·Leaving them there, he
went away again and prayed for the third time, repeating the
45 same words. ·Then he came back to the disciples and said to
them, 'You can sleep on now and take your rest. Now the hour
has come when the Son of Man is to be betrayed into the
46 hands of sinners. ·Get up! Let us go! My betrayer is already
close at hand.'

The arrest

47 He was still speaking when Judas, one of the Twelve,
appeared, and with him a large number of men armed with
swords and clubs, sent by the chief priests and elders of the
48 people. ·Now the traitor had arranged a sign with them. 'The
one I kiss,' he had said 'he is the man. Take him in charge.'
49 So he went straight up to Jesus and said, 'Greetings, Rabbi',

50 and kissed him. ·Jesus said to him, 'My friend, do what you are here for'. Then they came forward, seized Jesus and took
51 him in charge. ·At that, one of the followers of Jesus grasped his sword and drew it; he struck out at the high priest's
52 servant, and cut off his ear. ·Jesus then said, 'Put your sword
53 back, for all who draw the sword will die by the sword. ·Or do you think that I cannot appeal to my Father who would promptly send more than twelve legions of angels to my
54 defence? ·But then, how would the scriptures be fulfilled that
55 say this is the way it must be?' ·It was at this time that Jesus said to the crowds, 'Am I a brigand, that you had to set out to capture me with swords and clubs? I sat teaching in the
56 Temple day after day and you never laid hands on me.' ·Now all this happened to fulfil the prophecies in scripture. Then all the disciples deserted him and ran away.

Jesus before the Sanhedrin

57   The men who had arrested Jesus led him off to Caiaphas the high priest, where the scribes and the elders were
58 assembled. ·Peter followed him at a distance, and when he reached the high priest's palace, he went in and sat down with the attendants to see what the end would be.
59   The chief priests and the whole Sanhedrin were looking for evidence against Jesus, however false, on which they might
60 pass the death-sentence. ·But they could not find any, though several lying witnesses came forward. Eventually two stepped
61 forward ·and made a statement, 'This man said, "I have power to destroy the Temple of God and in three days build
62 it up"'. ·The high priest then stood up and said to him, 'Have you no answer to that? What is this evidence these men are
63 bringing against you?' ·But Jesus was silent. And the high priest said to him, 'I put you on oath by the living God to tell
64 us if you are the Christ, the Son of God'. ·'The words are your own' answered Jesus. 'Moreover, I tell you that from this time onward you will see the *Son of Man seated at the right hand of the Power* and *coming on the clouds of heaven*.'
65 At this, the high priest tore his clothes and said, 'He has blasphemed. What need of witnesses have we now? There!
66 You have just heard the blasphemy. ·What is your opinion?' They answered, 'He deserves to die'.
67   Then they spat in his face and hit him with their fists;

e. The psalms of praise which end the Passover supper. f. 'be brought down': the regular expression for the losing of faith through a difficulty or blow to it. g. Zc 13:7

68 others said as they struck him, ·'Play the prophet, Christ! Who hit you then?'

Peter's denials

69 Meanwhile Peter was sitting outside in the courtyard, and a servant-girl came up to him and said, 'You too were with
70 Jesus the Galilean'. ·But he denied it in front of them all. 'I
71 do not know what you are talking about' he said. ·When he went out to the gateway another servant-girl saw him and said to the people there, 'This man was with Jesus the
72 Nazarene'. ·And again, with an oath, he denied it, 'I do not
73 know the man'. ·A little later the bystanders came up and said to Peter, 'You are one of them for sure! Why, your
74 accent gives you away.' ·Then he started calling down curses on himself and swearing, 'I do not know the man'. At that
75 moment the cock crew, ·and Peter remembered what Jesus had said, 'Before the cock crows you will have disowned me three times'. And he went outside and wept bitterly.

Jesus is taken before Pilate

27 When morning came, all the chief priests and the elders of the people met in council to bring about the death of Jesus.
2 They had him bound, and led him away to hand him over to Pilate,[a] the governor.

The death of Judas

3 When he found that Jesus had been condemned, Judas his betrayer was filled with remorse and took the thirty silver
4 pieces back to the chief priests and elders. ·'I have sinned;' he said 'I have betrayed innocent blood.' 'What is that to us?'
5 they replied 'That is your concern.' ·And flinging down the silver pieces in the sanctuary he made off, and went and
6 hanged himself. ·The chief priests picked up the silver pieces and said, 'It is against the Law to put this into the treasury; it
7 is blood-money'. ·So they discussed the matter and bought
8 the potter's field with it as a graveyard for foreigners, ·and this is why the field is called the Field of Blood today.
9 The words of the prophet Jeremiah[b] were then fulfilled: *And they took the thirty silver pieces, the sum at which the precious*
10 *One was priced by children of Israel, ·and they gave them for the potter's field, just as the Lord directed me.*

Jesus before Pilate

11 Jesus, then, was brought before the governor, and the governor put to him this question, 'Are you the king of the

12 Jews?' Jesus replied, 'It is you who say it'. ·But when he was
accused by the chief priests and the elders he refused to
13 answer at all. ·Pilate then said to him, 'Do you not hear how
14 many charges they have brought against you?' ·But to the
governor's complete amazement, he offered no reply to any
of the charges.

15   At festival time it was the governor's practice to release a
16 prisoner for the people, anyone they chose. ·Now there was
at that time a notorious prisoner whose name was Barabbas.
17 So when the crowd gathered, Pilate said to them, 'Which do
you want me to release for you: Barabbas, or Jesus who is
18 called Christ?' ·For Pilate knew it was out of jealousy that
they had handed him over.

19   Now as he was seated in the chair of judgement, his wife
sent him a message, 'Have nothing to do with that man; I
have been upset all day by a dream I had about him'.

20   The chief priests and the elders, however, had persuaded
the crowd to demand the release of Barabbas and the execu-
21 tion of Jesus. ·So when the governor spoke and asked them,
'Which of the two do you want me to release for you?' they
22 said, 'Barabbas'. ·'But in that case,' Pilate said to them 'what
am I to do with Jesus who is called Christ?' They all said,
23 'Let him be crucified!' ·'Why?' he asked 'What harm has he
done?' But they shouted all the louder, 'Let him be crucified!'
24 Then Pilate saw that he was making no impression, that in
fact a riot was imminent. So he took some water, washed his
hands in front of the crowd and said, 'I am innocent of this
25 man's blood. It is your concern.' ·And the people, to a man,
shouted back, 'His blood be on us and on our children!'
26 Then he released Barabbas for them. He ordered Jesus to be
first scourged[c] and then handed over to be crucified.

Jesus is crowned with thorns

27   The governor's soldiers took Jesus with them into the
28 Praetorium and collected the whole cohort round him. ·Then
they stripped him and made him wear a scarlet cloak,
29 and having twisted some thorns into a crown they put this
on his head and placed a reed in his right hand. To make fun
of him they knelt to him saying, 'Hail, king of the Jews!'
30 And they spat on him and took the reed and struck him on
31 the head with it. ·And when they had finished making fun of

27 a. The Jews had to approach the Roman governor for confirmation
and execution of any sentence of death. b. Actually a free quotation
from Zc 11 : 12–13. c. The normal prelude to crucifixion.

him, they took off the cloak and dressed him in his own clothes and led him away to crucify him.

The crucifixion

32 On their way out, they came across a man from Cyrene,
33 Simon by name, and enlisted him to carry his cross. ·When they had reached a place called Golgotha,^d that is, the place
34 of the skull, ·they gave him wine to drink mixed with gall,
35 which he tasted but refused to drink. ·When they had finished crucifying him they shared out his clothing by casting lots,
36 and then sat down and stayed there keeping guard over him.
37 Above his head was placed the charge against him; it read:
38 'This is Jesus, the King of the Jews'. ·At the same time two robbers were crucified with him, one on the right and one on the left.

The crucified Christ is mocked

39 The passers-by jeered at him; they shook their heads
40 and said, 'So you would destroy the Temple and rebuild it in three days! Then save yourself! If you are God's son, come
41 down from the cross!' ·The chief priests with the scribes and
42 elders mocked him in the same way. ·'He saved others;' they said 'he cannot save himself. He is the king of Israel; let him come down from the cross now, and we will believe in him.
43 He puts his trust in God; now let God rescue him if he wants
44 him. For he did say, "I am the son of God".' ·Even the robbers who were crucified with him taunted him in the same way.

The death of Jesus

45 From the sixth hour there was darkness over all the land
46 until the ninth hour.^e ·And about the ninth hour, Jesus cried out in a loud voice, 'Eli, Eli, lama sabachthani?' that is, '*My*
47 *God, my God, why have you deserted me?*'^f. ·When some of those who stood there heard this, they said, 'The man is
48 calling on Elijah', ·and one of them quickly ran to get a sponge which he dipped in vinegar^g and, putting it on a reed,
49 gave it him to drink. ·'Wait!' said the rest of them 'and see if
50 Elijah will come to save him.' ·But Jesus, again crying out in a loud voice, yielded up his spirit.
51 At that, the veil of the Temple^h was torn in two from top to
52 bottom; the earth quaked; the rocks were split; ·the tombs opened and the bodies of many holymen rose from the dead,
53 and these, after his resurrection, came out of the tombs, entered the Holy City and appeared to a number of people.

54 Meanwhile the centurion, together with the others guarding Jesus, had seen the earthquake and all that was taking place, and they were terrified and said, 'In truth this was a son of God.'

55 And many women were there, watching from a distance, the same women who had followed Jesus from Galilee and

56 looked after him. ·Among them were Mary of Magdala, Mary the mother of James and Joseph, and the mother of Zebedee's sons.

The burial

57 When it was evening, there came a rich man of Arimathaea, called Joseph, who had himself become a disciple of

58 Jesus. ·This man went to Pilate and asked for the body of

59 Jesus. Pilate thereupon ordered it to be handed over. ·So

60 Joseph took the body, wrapped it in a clean shroud ·and put it in his own new tomb which he had hewn out of the rock. He then rolled a large stone across the entrance of the tomb

61 and went away. ·Now Mary of Magdala and the other Mary were there, sitting opposite the sepulchre.

The guard at the tomb

62 Next day, that is, when Preparation Day[i] was over, the

63 chief priests and the Pharisees went in a body to Pilate ·and said to him, 'Your Excellency, we recall that this impostor said, while he was still alive, "After three days I shall rise

64 again". ·Therefore give the order to have the sepulchre kept secure until the third day, for fear his disciples come and steal him away and tell the people, "He has risen from the dead". This last piece of fraud would be worse than what went

65 before.' ·'You may have your guard' said Pilate to them. 'Go

66 and make all as secure as you know how.' ·So they went and made the sepulchre secure, putting seals on the stone and mounting a guard.

The empty tomb. The angel's message

28 After the sabbath, and towards dawn on the first day of the week, Mary of Magdala and the other Mary went to visit the

2 sepulchre. ·And all at once there was a violent earthquake, for the angel of the Lord, descending from heaven, came and

d. The Aramaic form of the name of which Calvary is the more familiar Latin equivalent. **e.** From mid-day to 3 p.m. **f.** Ps 22:1 **g.** The rough wine drunk by Roman soldiers. **h.** There were two curtains in the Temple; most probably this was the inner curtain which guarded the Most Holy Place. **i.** The day before the sabbath.

3 rolled away the stone and sat on it. ·His face was like light-
4 ning, his robe white as snow. ·The guards were so shaken, so
5 frightened of him, that they were like dead men. ·But the
angel spoke; and he said to the women, 'There is no need for
you to be afraid. I know you are looking for Jesus, who was
6 crucified. ·He is not here, for he has risen, as he said he
7 would. Come and see the place where he lay, ·then go quickly
and tell his disciples, "He has risen from the dead and now he
is going before you to Galilee; it is there you will see him".
8 Now I have told you.' ·Filled with awe and great joy the
women came quickly away from the tomb and ran to tell the
disciples.

Appearance to the women

9　　And there, coming to meet them, was Jesus. 'Greetings' he
said. And the women came up to him and, falling down be-
10 fore him, clasped his feet. ·Then Jesus said to them, 'Do not
be afraid; go and tell my brothers that they must leave for
Galilee; they will see me there'.

Precautions taken by the leaders of the people

11　　While they were on their way, some of the guard went off
into the city to tell the chief priests all that had happened.
12 These held a meeting with the elders and, after some discussion, handed a considerable sum of money to the soldiers
13 with these instructions, 'This is what you must say, "His
disciples came during the night and stole him away while we
14 were asleep". ·And should the governor come to hear of this,
we undertake to put things right with him ourselves and to
15 see that you do not get into trouble.' ·The soldiers took the
money and carried out their instructions, and to this day that
is the story among the Jews.

Appearance in Galilee. The mission to the world

16　　Meanwhile the eleven disciples set out for Galilee, to the
17 mountain where Jesus had arranged to meet them. ·When
they saw him they fell down before him, though some hesi-
18 tated. ·Jesus came up and spoke to them. He said, 'All
19 authority in heaven and earth has been given to me. ·Go,
therefore, make disciples of all the nations; baptise them in
the name of the Father and of the Son and of the Holy Spirit,[a]
20 and teach them to observe all the commands I gave you. And
know that I am with you always; yes, to the end of time.'

28 a. This formula is perhaps a reflection of the liturgical usage of the
writer's own time.

THE GOSPEL

ACCORDING TO

SAINT MARK

I. PRELUDE TO THE PUBLIC MINISTRY OF JESUS

The preaching of John the Baptist

1 The beginning of the Good News about Jesus Christ, the
2 son of God. ·It is written in the book of the prophet Isaiah:

> *Look, I am going to send my messenger before you;*
> *he will prepare your way.*
3 *A voice cries in the wilderness:*
> *Prepare a way for the Lord,*
> *make his paths straight,*[a]

4 and so it was that John the Baptist appeared in the wilderness,
proclaiming a baptism of repentance for the forgiveness of
5 sins. ·All Judaea and all the people of Jerusalem made their
way to him, and as they were baptised by him in the river
6 Jordan they confessed their sins. ·John wore a garment of
7 camel-skin, and he lived on locusts and wild honey. ·In the
course of his preaching he said, 'Someone is following me,
someone who is more powerful than I am, and I am not fit to
8 kneel down and undo the strap of his sandals. ·I have baptised you with water, but he will baptise you with the Holy
Spirit.'

Jesus is baptised

9 It was at this time that Jesus came from Nazareth in
10 Galilee and was baptised in the Jordan by John. ·No sooner
had he come up out of the water than he saw the heavens
torn apart and the Spirit, like a dove, descending on him.
11 And a voice came from heaven, 'You are my Son, the
Beloved; my favour rests on you'.

1 a. Is 40:3

Temptation in the wilderness

12 Immediately afterwards the Spirit drove him out into the
13 wilderness ·and he remained there for forty days, and was
tempted by Satan. He was with the wild beasts, and the
angels looked after him.

II. THE GALILEAN MINISTRY

Jesus begins to preach

14 After John had been arrested, Jesus went into Galilee.
15 There he proclaimed the Good News from God. ·'The time
has come' he said 'and the kingdom of God is close at hand.
Repent, and believe the Good News.'

The first four disciples are called

16 As he was walking along by the Sea of Galilee he saw
Simon and his brother Andrew casting a net in the lake—for
17 they were fishermen. ·And Jesus said to them, 'Follow me and
18 I will make you into fishers of men'. ·And at once they left
their nets and followed him.
19 Going on a little further, he saw James son of Zebedee and
his brother John; they too were in their boat, mending their
20 nets. He called them at once ·and, leaving their father
Zebedee in the boat with the men he employed, they went
after him.

Jesus teaches in Capernaum and cures a demoniac

21 They went as far as Capernaum, and as soon as the sab-
22 bath came he went to the synagogue and began to teach. ·And
his teaching made a deep impression on them because, unlike
the scribes, he taught them with authority.
23 In their synagogue just then there was a man possessed by
24 an unclean spirit, and it shouted, ·'What do you want with
us, Jesus of Nazareth? Have you come to destroy us? I know
25 who you are: the Holy One of God.' ·But Jesus said sharply,
26 'Be quiet! Come out of him!' ·And the unclean spirit threw
the man into convulsions and with a loud cry went out of
27 him. ·The people were so astonished that they started asking
each other what it all meant. 'Here is a teaching that is new'
they said 'and with authority behind it: he gives orders even
28 to unclean spirits and they obey him.' ·And his reputation
rapidly spread everywhere, through all the surrounding
Galilean countryside.

Cure of Simon's mother-in-law

29 On leaving the synagogue, he went with James and John
30 straight to the house of Simon and Andrew. ·Now Simon's
mother-in-law had gone to bed with fever, and they told him
31 about her straightaway. ·He went to her, took her by the
hand and helped her up. And the fever left her and she began
to wait on them.

A number of cures

32 That evening, after sunset, they brought to him all who
33 were sick and those who were possessed by devils. ·The
34 whole town came crowding round the door, and he cured
many who were suffering from diseases of one kind or
another; he also cast out many devils, but he would not allow
them to speak, because they knew who he was.[b]

Jesus quietly leaves Capernaum and travels through Galilee

35 In the morning, long before dawn, he got up and left the
house, and went off to a lonely place and prayed there.
36 Simon and his companions set out in search of him, ·and
37 when they found him they said, 'Everybody is looking for
38 you'. ·He answered, 'Let us go elsewhere, to the neighbouring
country towns, so that I can preach there too, because that is
39 why I came'. ·And he went all through Galilee, preaching in
their synagogues and casting out devils.

Cure of a leper

40 A leper came to him and pleaded on his knees: 'If you
41 want to' he said 'you can cure me'. ·Feeling sorry for him,
Jesus stretched out his hand and touched him. 'Of course I
42 want to!' he said. 'Be cured!' ·And the leprosy left him at
43 once and he was cured. ·Jesus immediately sent him away
44 and sternly ordered him, ·'Mind you say nothing to anyone,
but go and show yourself to the priest, and make the offering
for your healing prescribed by Moses as evidence of your
45 recovery'. ·The man went away, but then started talking
about it freely and telling the story everywhere, so that Jesus
could no longer go openly into any town, but had to stay
outside in places where nobody lived. Even so, people from
all around would come to him.

b. Throughout this gospel, Jesus never explicitly claims to be the
Messiah and he forbids others to speak of the fact.

Cure of a paralytic

2   When he returned to Capernaum some time later, word
2 went round that he was back; ·and so many people collected
that there was no room left, even in front of the door. He was
3 preaching the word to them ·when some people came bring-
4 ing him a paralytic carried by four men, ·but as the crowd
made it impossible to get the man to him, they stripped the
roof over the place where Jesus was; and when they had
made an opening, they lowered the stretcher on which the
5 paralytic lay. ·Seeing their faith, Jesus said to the paralytic,
6 'My child, your sins are forgiven'. ·Now some scribes were
7 sitting there, and they thought to themselves, ·'How can this
man talk like that? He is blaspheming. Who can forgive sins
8 but God?' ·Jesus, inwardly aware that this was what they
were thinking, said to them, 'Why do you have these thoughts
9 in your hearts? ·Which of these is easier: to say to the paralytic, "Your sins are forgiven" or to say, "Get up, pick up
10 your stretcher and walk"? ·But to prove to you that the Son
11 of Man has authority on earth to forgive sins,'—he said to
the paralytic—'I order you: get up, pick up your stretcher,
12 and go off home.' ·And the man got up, picked up his
stretcher at once and walked out in front of everyone, so that
they were all astounded and praised God saying, 'We have
never seen anything like this'.

The call of Levi

13   He went out again to the shore of the lake;[a] and all the
14 people came to him, and he taught them. ·As he was walking
on he saw Levi the son of Alphaeus, sitting by the customs
house, and he said to him, 'Follow me'. And he got up and
followed him.

Eating with sinners

15   When Jesus was at dinner in his house, a number of tax
collectors and sinners were also sitting at the table with Jesus
and his disciples; for there were many of them among his
16 followers. ·When the scribes of the Pharisee party saw him
eating with sinners and tax collectors, they said to his disciples, 'Why does he eat with tax collectors and sinners?'
17 When Jesus heard this he said to them, 'It is not the healthy
who need the doctor, but the sick. I did not come to call the
virtuous, but sinners.'

A discussion on fasting

18 One day when John's disciples and the Pharisees were
fasting, some people came and said to him, 'Why is it that
John's disciples and the disciples of the Pharisees fast, but
19 your disciples do not?' ·Jesus replied, 'Surely the bridegroom's attendants would never think of fasting while the
bridegroom is still with them? As long as they have the
20 bridegroom with them, they could not think of fasting. ·But
the time will come for the bridegroom to be taken away from
21 them, and then, on that day, they will fast. ·No one sews a
piece of unshrunken cloth on an old cloak; if he does, the
patch pulls away from it, the new from the old, and the tear
22 gets worse. ·And nobody puts new wine into old wineskins;
if he does, the wine will burst the skins, and the wine is lost
and the skins too. No! New wine, fresh skins!'

Picking corn on the sabbath

23 One sabbath day he happened to be taking a walk through
the cornfields, and his disciples began to pick ears of corn as
24 they went along. ·And the Pharisees said to him, 'Look, why
are they doing something on the sabbath day that is for-
25 bidden?' ·And he replied, 'Did you never read what David
did in his time of need when he and his followers were hungry
26 —·how he went into the house of God when Abiathar[b] was
high priest, and ate the loaves of offering which only the
priests are allowed to eat, and how he also gave some to the
men with him?'
27 And he said to them, 'The sabbath was made for man, not
28 man for the sabbath; ·so the Son of Man is master even of the
sabbath'.

Cure of the man with a withered hand

3 He went again into a synagogue, and there was a man there
2 who had a withered hand. ·And they were watching him to
see if he would cure him on the sabbath day, hoping for
3 something to use against him. ·He said to the man with the
4 withered hand, 'Stand up out in the middle!' ·Then he said to
them, 'Is it against the law on the sabbath day to do good, or
5 to do evil; to save life, or to kill?' But they said nothing. ·Then,
grieved to find them so obstinate, he looked angrily round at
them, and said to the man, 'Stretch out your hand'. He

---

2 a. Tiberias, the 'Sea of Galilee'. **b.** See 1 S 21:1–7. Abiathar was
the better known as high priest in David's reign, but Ahimelech is
named in this source.

6 stretched it out and his hand was better. ·The Pharisees went out and at once began to plot with the Herodians against him, discussing how to destroy him.

The crowds follow Jesus

7 Jesus withdrew with his disciples to the lakeside, and great
8 crowds from Galilee followed him. From Judaea, ·Jerusalem, Idumaea, Transjordania and the region of Tyre and Sidon, great numbers who had heard of all he was doing came to
9 him. ·And he asked his disciples to have a boat ready for him
10 because of the crowd, to keep him from being crushed. ·For he had cured so many that all who were afflicted in any way
11 were crowding forward to touch him. ·And the unclean spirits, whenever they saw him, would fall down before him
12 and shout, 'You are the Son of God!' ·But he warned them strongly not to make him known.

The appointment of the Twelve

13 He now went up into the hills and summoned those he
14 wanted. So they came to him ·and he appointed twelve; they
15 were to be his companions and to be sent out to preach, ·with
16 power to cast out devils. ·And so he appointed the Twelve:
17 Simon to whom he gave the name Peter, ·James the son of Zebedee and John the brother of James, to whom he gave the
18 name Boanerges or 'Sons of Thunder'; ·then Andrew, Philip, Bartholomew, Matthew, Thomas, James the son of Al-
19 phaeus, Thaddaeus, Simon the Zealot ·and Judas Iscariot, the man who was to betray him.

His relatives are concerned about Jesus

20 He went home again, and once more such a crowd collected
21 that they could not even have a meal. ·When his relatives heard of this, they set out to take charge of him, convinced he was out of his mind.

Allegations of the scribes

22 The scribes who had come down from Jerusalem were saying, 'Beelzebul is in him' and, 'It is through the prince of
23 devils that he casts devils out'. ·So he called them to him and spoke to them in parables, 'How can Satan cast out Satan?
24 If a kingdom is divided against itself, that kingdom cannot
25 last. ·And if a household is divided against itself, that house-
26 hold can never stand. ·Now if Satan has rebelled against himself and is divided, he cannot stand either—it is the end of
27 him. ·But no one can make his way into a strong man's house

and burgle his property unless he has tied up the strong man first. Only then can he burgle his house.

28 'I tell you solemnly, all men's sins will be forgiven, and all
29 their blasphemies; ·but let anyone blaspheme against the Holy Spirit and he will never have forgiveness: he is guilty of
30 an eternal sin.' ·This was because they were saying, 'An unclean spirit is in him'.

The true kinsmen of Jesus

31 His mother and brothers now arrived and, standing out-
32 side, sent in a message asking for him. ·A crowd was sitting round him at the time the message was passed to him, 'Your mother and brothers and sisters are outside asking for you'.
33
34 He replied, 'Who are my mother and my brothers?' ·And looking round at those sitting in a circle about him, he said,
35 'Here are my mother and my brothers. ·Anyone who does the will of God, that person is my brother and sister and mother.'

Parable of the sower

4 Again he began to teach by the lakeside, but such a huge crowd gathered round him that he got into a boat on the lake and sat there. The people were all along the shore, at the
2 water's edge. ·He taught them many things in parables, and
3 in the course of his teaching he said to them, ·'Listen!
4 Imagine a sower going out to sow. ·Now it happened that, as he sowed, some of the seed fell on the edge of the path, and
5 the birds came and ate it up. ·Some seed fell on rocky ground where it found little soil and sprang up straightaway, because
6 there was no depth of earth; ·and when the sun came up it was scorched and, not having any roots, it withered away.
7 Some seed fell into thorns, and the thorns grew up and
8 choked it, and it produced no crop. ·And some seeds fell into rich soil and, growing tall and strong, produced crop; and
9 yielded thirty, sixty, even a hundredfold.' ·And he said, 'Listen, anyone who has ears to hear!'

Why Jesus speaks in parables

10 When he was alone, the Twelve, together with the others
11 who formed his company, asked what the parables meant. ·He told them, 'The secret of the kingdom of God is given to you, but to those who are outside everything comes in parables,
12 so that *they may see and see again, but not perceive; may hear and hear again, but not understand; otherwise they might be converted and be forgiven*.[a]

4 a. Is 6:9–10

The parable of the sower explained

13 He said to them, 'Do you not understand this parable?
14 Then how will you understand any of the parables? ·What
15 the sower is sowing is the word. ·Those on the edge of the
path where the word is sown are people who have no sooner
heard it than Satan comes and carries away the word that was
16 sown in them. ·Similarly, those who receive the seed on
patches of rock are people who, when first they hear the
17 word, welcome it at once with joy. ·But they have no root in
them, they do not last; should some trial come, or some
persecution on account of the word, they fall away at once.
18 Then there are others who receive the seed in thorns. These
19 have heard the word, ·but the worries of this world, the lure
of riches and all the other passions come in to choke the
20 word, and so it produces nothing. ·And there are those who
have received the seed in rich soil: they hear the word and
accept it and yield a harvest, thirty and sixty and a hundred
fold.'

Parable of the lamp

21 He also said to them, 'Would you bring in a lamp to put it
under a tub or under the bed? Surely you will put it on the
22 lamp-stand? ·For there is nothing hidden but it must be
23 disclosed, nothing kept secret except to be brought to light. ·If
anyone has ears to hear, let him listen to this.'

Parable of the measure

24 He also said to them, 'Take notice of what you are hearing. The amount you measure out is the amount you will be
25 given—and more besides; ·for the man who has will be given
more; from the man who has not, even what he has will be
taken away.'

Parable of the seed growing by itself

26 He also said, 'This is what the kingdom of God is like. A
27 man throws seed on the land. ·Night and day, while he sleeps,
when he is awake, the seed is sprouting and growing; how,
28 he does not know. ·Of its own accord the land produces first
29 the shoot, then the ear, then the full grain in the ear. ·And
when the crop is ready, he loses no time: he starts to reap
because the harvest has come.'

Parable of the mustard seed

30 He also said, 'What can we say the kingdom of God is like?
31 What parable can we find for it? ·It is like a mustard seed

which at the time of its sowing in the soil is the smallest of all
32 the seeds on earth; ·yet once it is sown it grows into the
biggest shrub of them all and puts out big branches so that
the birds of the air can shelter in its shade.'

The use of parables

33   Using many parables like these, he spoke to them, so far
34 as they were capable of understanding it. ·He would not
speak to them except in parables, but he explained everything
to his disciples when they were alone.

The calming of the storm

35   With the coming of evening that same day, he said to them,
36 'Let us cross over to the other side'. ·And leaving the crowd
behind they took him, just as he was, in the boat; and there
37 were other boats with him. ·Then it began to blow a gale and
the waves were breaking into the boat so that it was almost
38 swamped. ·But he was in the stern, his head on the cushion,
39 asleep. ·They woke him and said to him, 'Master, do you not
care? We are going down!' And he woke up and rebuked the
wind and said to the sea, 'Quiet now! Be calm!' And the wind
40 dropped, and all was calm again. ·Then he said to them, 'Why
are you so frightened? How is it that you have no faith?'
41 They were filled with awe and said to one another, 'Who can
this be? Even the wind and the sea obey him.'

The Gerasene demoniac

5   They reached the country of the Gerasenes[a] on the other
2 side of the lake, ·and no sooner had he left the boat than a
man with an unclean spirit came out from the tombs towards
3 him. ·The man lived in the tombs and no one could secure
4 him any more, even with a chain; ·because he had often been
secured with fetters and chains but had snapped the chains
and broken the fetters, and no one had the strength to control
5 him. ·All night and all day, among the tombs and in the
mountains, he would howl and gash himself with stones.
6 Catching sight of Jesus from a distance, he ran up and fell at
7 his feet ·and shouted at the top of his voice, 'What do you
want with me, Jesus, son of the Most High God? Swear by
8 God you will not torture me!'—For Jesus had been saying to
9 him, 'Come out of the man, unclean spirit'. ·'What is your
name?' Jesus asked. 'My name is legion,' he answered 'for
10 there are many of us.' ·And he begged him earnestly not to

5 a. 'Gadarenes' in some versions.

11 send them out of the district. ·Now there was there on the
12 mountainside a great herd of pigs feeding, ·and the unclean
spirits begged him, 'Send us to the pigs, let us go into them'.
13 So he gave them leave. With that, the unclean spirits came out
and went into the pigs, and the herd of about two thousand
pigs charged down the cliff into the lake, and there they
14 were drowned. ·The swineherds ran off and told their story in
the town and in the country round about; and the people
15 came to see what had really happened. ·They came to Jesus
and saw the demoniac sitting there, clothed and in his full
senses—the very man who had had the legion in him before—
16 and they were afraid. ·And those who had witnessed it
reported what had happened to the demoniac and what had
17 become of the pigs. ·Then they began to implore Jesus to
18 leave the neighbourhood. ·As he was getting into the boat,
the man who had been possessed begged to be allowed to
19 stay with him. ·Jesus would not let him but said to him, 'Go
home to your people and tell them all that the Lord in his
20 mercy has done for you'. ·So the man went off and proceeded
to spread throughout the Decapolis all that Jesus had done
for him. And everyone was amazed.

**Cure of the woman with a haemorrhage. The daughter of
Jairus raised to life**

21   When Jesus had crossed again in the boat to the other side,
a large crowd gathered round him and he stayed by the
22 lakeside. ·Then one of the synagogue officials came up, Jairus
23 by name, and seeing him, fell at his feet ·and pleaded with
him earnestly, saying, 'My little daughter is desperately sick.
Do come and lay your hands on her to make her better and
24 save her life.' ·Jesus went with him and a large crowd followed
him; they were pressing all round him.
25   Now there was a woman who had suffered from a
26 haemorrhage for twelve years; ·after long and painful treatment under various doctors, she had spent all she had
without being any the better for it, in fact, she was getting
27 worse. ·She had heard about Jesus, and she came up behind
28 him through the crowd and touched his cloak. ·'If I can
touch even his clothes,' she had told herself 'I shall be well
29 again.' ·And the source of the bleeding dried up instantly,
and she felt in herself that she was cured of her complaint.
30 Immediately aware that power had gone out from him, Jesus
turned round in the crowd and said, 'Who touched my
31 clothes?' ·His disciples said to him, 'You see how the crowd
is pressing round you and yet you say, "Who touched me?"'

32 But he continued to look all round to see who had done it.
33 Then the woman came forward, frightened and trembling[b] because she knew what had happened to her, and she fell at
34 his feet and told him the whole truth. ·'My daughter,' he said 'your faith has restored you to health; go in peace and be free from your complaint.'

35 While he was still speaking some people arrived from the house of the synagogue official to say, 'Your daughter is
36 dead: why put the Master to any further trouble?' ·But Jesus had overheard this remark of theirs and he said to the official,
37 'Do not be afraid; only have faith'. ·And he allowed no one to go with him except Peter and James and John the brother of
38 James. ·So they came to the official's house and Jesus noticed all the commotion, with people weeping and wailing un-
39 restrainedly. ·He went in and said to them, 'Why all this commotion and crying? The child is not dead, but asleep.'
40 But they laughed at him. So he turned them all out and, taking with him the child's father and mother and his own companions, he went into the place where the child lay.
41 And taking the child by the hand he said to her, 'Talitha,
42 kum!' which means, 'Little girl, I tell you to get up'. ·The little girl got up at once and began to walk about, for she was twelve years old. At this they were overcome with astonish-
43 ment, ·and he ordered them strictly not to let anyone know about it, and told them to give her something to eat.

A visit to Nazareth

6 Going from that district, he went to his home town and his
2 disciples accompanied him. ·With the coming of the sabbath he began teaching in the synagogue and most of them were astonished when they heard him. They said, 'Where did the man get all this? What is this wisdom that has been granted
3 him, and these miracles that are worked through him? ·This is the carpenter, surely, the son of Mary, the brother of James and Joset and Jude and Simon? His sisters, too, are
4 they not here with us?' And they would not accept him. ·And Jesus said to them, 'A prophet is only despised in his own country, among his own relations and in his own house';
5 and he could work no miracle there, though he cured a few
6 sick people by laying his hands on them. ·He was amazed at their lack of faith.

b. According to the Law, she was unclean, and to be touched by her would be defilement.

The mission of the Twelve

7 He made a tour round the villages, teaching. ·Then he summoned the Twelve and began to send them out in pairs 8 giving them authority over the unclean spirits. ·And he instructed them to take nothing for the journey except a staff—no bread, no haversack, no coppers for their purses. 9 They were to wear sandals but, he added, 'Do not take a 10 spare tunic'. ·And he said to them, 'If you enter a house 11 anywhere, stay there until you leave the district. ·And if any place does not welcome you and people refuse to listen to you, as you walk away shake off the dust from under your 12 feet as a sign to them.' ·So they set off to preach repentance; 13 and they cast out many devils, and anointed many sick people with oil and cured them.

Herod and Jesus

14 Meanwhile King Herod had heard about him, since by now his name was well-known. Some were saying, 'John the Baptist has risen from the dead, and that is why miraculous 15 powers are at work in him'. ·Others said, 'He is Elijah'; others again, 'He is a prophet, like the prophets we used to 16 have'. ·But when Herod heard this he said, 'It is John whose head I cut off; he has risen from the dead'.

John the Baptist beheaded

17 Now it was this same Herod who had sent to have John arrested, and had him chained up in prison because of Herodias, his brother Philip's wife whom he had married. 18 For John had told Herod, 'It is against the law for you to 19 have your brother's wife'. ·As for Herodias, she was furious with him and wanted to kill him; but she was not able to, 20 because Herod was afraid of John, knowing him to be a good and holy man, and gave him his protection. When he had heard him speak he was greatly perplexed, and yet he liked to listen to him.

21 An opportunity came on Herod's birthday when he gave a banquet for the nobles of his court, for his army officers and 22 for the leading figures in Galilee. ·When the daughter of this same Herodias came in and danced, she delighted Herod and his guests; so the king said to the girl, 'Ask me anything you 23 like and I will give it you'. ·And he swore her an oath, 'I will 24 give you anything you ask, even half my kingdom'. ·She went out and said to her mother, 'What shall I ask for?' She 25 replied, 'The head of John the Baptist'. ·The girl hurried

straight back to the king and made her request, 'I want you
to give me John the Baptist's head, here and now, on a dish'.
26 The king was deeply distressed but, thinking of the oaths he
had sworn and of his guests, he was reluctant to break his
27 word to her. ·So the king at once sent one of the bodyguard
28 with orders to bring John's head. ·The man went off and
beheaded him in prison; then he brought the head on a dish
and gave it to the girl, and the girl gave it to her mother.
29 When John's disciples heard about this, they came and took
his body and laid it in a tomb.

First miracle of the loaves

30   The apostles rejoined Jesus and told him all they had done
31 and taught. ·Then he said to them, 'You must come away to
some lonely place all by yourselves and rest for a while'; for
there were so many coming and going that the apostles had
32 no time even to eat. ·So they went off in a boat to a lonely
33 place where they could be by themselves. ·But people saw
them going, and many could guess where; and from every
town they all hurried to the place on foot and reached it before
34 them. ·So as he stepped ashore he saw a large crowd; and he
took pity on them because they were like sheep without a
35 shepherd, and he set himself to teach them at some length. ·By
now it was getting very late, and his disciples came up to him
36 and said, 'This is a lonely place and it is getting very late, ·so
send them away, and they can go to the farms and villages
37 round about, to buy themselves something to eat'. ·He replied, 'Give them something to eat yourselves'. They
answered, 'Are we to go and spend two hundred denarii on
38 bread for them to eat?' ·'How many loaves have you?' he
asked 'Go and see.' And when they had found out they said,
39 'Five, and two fish'. ·Then he ordered them to get all the
40 people together in groups on the green grass, ·and they sat
41 down on the ground in squares of hundreds and fifties. ·Then
he took the five loaves and the two fish, raised his eyes to
heaven and said the blessing; then he broke the loaves and
handed them to his disciples to distribute among the people.
42 He also shared out the two fish among them all. ·They all ate
43 as much as they wanted. ·They collected twelve basketfuls of
44 scraps of bread and pieces of fish. ·Those who had eaten the
loaves numbered five thousand men.

Jesus walks on the water

45   Directly after this he made his disciples get into the boat
and go on ahead to Bethsaida, while he himself sent the

46 crowd away. ·After saying good-bye to them he went off into
47 the hills to pray. ·When evening came, the boat was far out
48 on the lake, and he was alone on the land. ·He could see they
were worn out with rowing, for the wind was against them;
and about the fourth watch of the night he came towards
49 them, walking on the lake. He was going to pass them by, but
when they saw him walking on the lake they thought it was a
50 ghost and cried out; ·for they had all seen him and were
terrified. But he at once spoke to them, and said, 'Courage!
51 It is I! Do not be afraid.' ·Then he got into the boat with
them, and the wind dropped. They were utterly and com-
52 pletely dumbfounded, ·because they had not seen what the
miracle of the loaves meant; their minds were closed.

Cures at Gennesaret

53 Having made the crossing, they came to land at Genne-
54 saret and tied up. ·No sooner had they stepped out of the
55 boat than people recognised him, ·and started hurrying all
through the countryside and brought the sick on stretchers to
56 wherever they heard he was. ·And wherever he went, to
village, or town, or farm, they laid down the sick in the open
spaces, begging him to let them touch even the fringe of his
cloak. And all those who touched him were cured.

The traditions of the Pharisees

7 The Pharisees and some of the scribes who had come from
2 Jerusalem gathered round him, ·and they noticed that some
of his disciples were eating with unclean hands, that is,
3 without washing them. ·For the Pharisees, and the Jews in
general, follow the tradition of the elders and never eat
4 without washing their arms as far as the elbow; ·and on
returning from the market place they never eat without first
sprinkling themselves. There are also many other observances which have been handed down to them concerning the
5 washing of cups and pots and bronze dishes. ·So these
Pharisees and scribes asked him, 'Why do your disciples not
respect the tradition of the elders but eat their food with
6 unclean hands?' ·He answered, 'It was of you hypocrites that
Isaiah so rightly prophesied in this passage of scripture:

> *This people honours me only with lip-service,*
> *while their hearts are far from me.*
7 > *The worship they offer me is worthless,*
> *the doctrines they teach are only human regulations.*[a]

8 You put aside the commandment of God to cling to human

9 traditions.' ·And he said to them, 'How ingeniously you get round the commandment of God in order to preserve your
10 own tradition! ·For Moses said: *Do your duty to your father and your mother,* and, *Anyone who curses father or mother*
11 *must be put to death.* ·But you say, "If a man says to his father or mother: Anything I have that I might have used to
12 help you is Corban[b] (that is, dedicated to God), ·then he is forbidden from that moment to do anything for his father or
13 mother". ·In this way you make God's word null and void for the sake of your tradition which you have handed down. And you do many other things like this.'

On clean and unclean

14 He called the people to him again and said, 'Listen to me,
15 all of you, and understand. ·Nothing that goes into a man from outside can make him unclean; it is the things that
16 come out of a man that make him unclean. ·If anyone has ears to hear, let him listen to this.'
17 When he had gone back into the house, away from the
18 crowd, his disciples questioned him about the parable. ·He said to them, 'Do you not understand either? Can you not see that whatever goes into a man from outside cannot make
19 him unclean, ·because it does not go into his heart but through his stomach and passes out into the sewer?' (Thus he
20 pronounced all foods clean.) ·And he went on, 'It is what
21 comes out of a man that makes him unclean. ·For it is from within, from men's hearts, that evil intentions emerge: forni-
22 cation, theft, murder, adultery, ·avarice, malice, deceit,
23 indecency, envy, slander, pride, folly. ·All these evil things come from within and make a man unclean.'

III. JOURNEYS OUTSIDE GALILEE

The daughter of the Syrophoenician woman healed

24 He left that place and set out for the territory of Tyre. There he went into a house and did not want anyone to
25 know he was there, but he could not pass unrecognised. ·A woman whose little daughter had an unclean spirit heard about him straightaway and came and fell at his feet.
26 Now the woman was a pagan, by birth a Syrophoenician, and she begged him to cast the devil out of her daughter.
27 And he said to her, 'The children should be fed first, because it is not fair to take the children's food and throw it to the
28 house-dogs'. ·But she spoke up: 'Ah yes, sir,' she replied, 'but

7 **a.** Is 29:13 **b.** See note on Mt 15:6.

the house-dogs under the table can eat the children's scraps'.
29 And he said to her, 'For saying this, you may go home
30 happy: the devil has gone out of your daughter'. ·So she
went off to her home and found the child lying on the bed and
the devil gone.

Healing of the deaf man

31   Returning from the district of Tyre, he went by way of
Sidon towards the Sea of Galilee, right through the Deca-
32 polis region. ·And they brought him a deaf man who had an
impediment in his speech; and they asked him to lay his hand
33 on him. ·He took him aside in private, away from the crowd,
put his fingers into the man's ears and touched his tongue
34 with spittle. ·Then looking up to heaven he sighed; and he
35 said to him, 'Ephphatha', that is, 'Be opened'. ·And his ears
were opened, and the ligament of his tongue was loosened
36 and he spoke clearly. ·And Jesus ordered them to tell no one
about it, but the more he insisted, the more widely they
37 published it. ·Their admiration was unbounded. 'He has
done all things well,' they said 'he makes the deaf hear and
the dumb speak.'

Second miracle of the loaves

8   And now once again a great crowd had gathered, and they
had nothing to eat. So he called his disciples to him and said to
2 them, ·'I feel sorry for all these people; they have been with
3 me for three days now and have nothing to eat. ·If I send
them off home hungry they will collapse on the way; some
4 have come a great distance.' ·His disciples replied, 'Where
could anyone get bread to feed these people in a deserted
5 place like this?' ·He asked them, 'How many loaves have
6 you?' 'Seven' they said. ·Then he instructed the crowd to sit
down on the ground, and he took the seven loaves, and after
giving thanks he broke them and handed them to his disciples
to distribute; and they distributed them among the crowd.
7 They had a few small fish as well, and over these he said a
8 blessing and ordered them to be distributed also. ·They ate as
much as they wanted, and they collected seven basketfuls of
9 the scraps left over. ·Now there had been about four thousand
10 people. He sent them away ·and immediately, getting into the
boat with his disciples, went to the region of Dalmanutha.

The Pharisees ask for a sign from heaven

11   The Pharisees came up and started a discussion with him;
12 they demanded of him a sign from heaven, to test him. ·And

with a sigh that came straight from the heart he said, 'Why does this generation demand a sign? I tell you solemnly, no
13 sign shall be given to this generation.' ·And leaving them again and re-embarking he went away to the opposite shore.

The yeast of the Pharisees and of Herod

14 The disciples had forgotten to take any food and they had
15 only one loaf with them in the boat. ·Then he gave them this warning, 'Keep your eyes open; be on your guard against the
16 yeast of the Pharisees and the yeast of Herod'. ·And they said
17 to one another, 'It is because we have no bread'. ·And Jesus knew it, and he said to them, 'Why are you talking about having no bread? Do you not yet understand? Have you no
18 perception? Are your minds closed? ·Have you *eyes that do not see, ears that do not hear*?[a] Or do you not remember?
19 When I broke the five loaves among the five thousand, how many baskets full of scraps did you collect?' They answered,
20 'Twelve'. ·'And when I broke the seven loaves for the four thousand, how many baskets full of scraps did you collect?'
21 And they answered, 'Seven'. ·Then he said to them, 'Are you still without perception?'

Cure of a blind man at Bethsaida

22 They came to Bethsaida, and some people brought to him
23 a blind man whom they begged him to touch. ·He took the blind man by the hand and led him outside the village. Then putting spittle on his eyes and laying his hands on him, he
24 asked, 'Can you see anything?' ·The man, who was beginning to see, replied, 'I can see people; they look like trees to me,
25 but they are walking about'. ·Then he laid his hands on the man's eyes again and he saw clearly; he was cured, and he
26 could see everything plainly and distinctly. ·And Jesus sent him home, saying, 'Do not even go into the village'.

Peter's profession of faith

27 Jesus and his disciples left for the villages round Caesarea Philippi. On the way he put this question to his disciples,
28 'Who do people say I am?' ·And they told him. 'John the Baptist,' they said 'others Elijah; others again, one of the
29 prophets'. ·'But you,' he asked, 'who do you say I am?'
30 Peter spoke up and said to him, 'You are the Christ'. ·And he gave them strict orders not to tell anyone about him.

8 a. Jr 5:21; Ezk 12:2

First prophecy of the Passion

31   And he began to teach them that the Son of Man was destined to suffer grievously, to be rejected by the elders and the chief priests and the scribes, and to be put to death, and
32 after three days to rise again; ·and he said all this quite openly. Then, taking him aside, Peter started to remonstrate
33 with him. ·But, turning and seeing his disciples, he rebuked Peter and said to him, 'Get behind me, Satan! Because the way you think is not God's way but man's.'

The condition of following Christ

34   He called the people and his disciples to him and said, 'If anyone wants to be a follower of mine, let him renounce
35 himself and take up his cross and follow me. ·For anyone who wants to save his life will lose it; but anyone who loses his life for my sake, and for the sake of the gospel, will save
36 it. ·What gain, then, is it for a man to win the whole world
37 and ruin his life? ·And indeed what can a man offer in
38 exchange for his life? ·For if anyone in this adulterous and sinful generation is ashamed of me and of my words, the Son of Man will also be ashamed of him when he comes in the glory of his Father with the holy angels.'
9   And he said to them, 'I tell you solemnly, there are some standing here who will not taste death before they see the kingdom of God come with power'.

The transfiguration

2   Six days later, Jesus took with him Peter and James and John and led them up a high mountain where they could be alone by themselves. There in their presence he was trans-
3 figured: ·his clothes became dazzlingly white, whiter than any
4 earthly bleacher could make them. ·Elijah appeared to them
5 with Moses; and they were talking with Jesus. ·Then Peter spoke to Jesus: 'Rabbi,' he said 'it is wonderful for us to be here; so let us make three tents, one for you, one for Moses
6 and one for Elijah'. ·He did not know what to say; they were
7 so frightened. ·And a cloud came, covering them in shadow; and there came a voice from the cloud, 'This is my Son, the
8 Beloved. Listen to him.' ·Then suddenly, when they looked round, they saw no one with them any more but only Jesus.

The question about Elijah

9   As they came down from the mountain he warned them to tell no one what they had seen, until after the Son of Man had

10 risen from the dead. ·They observed the warning faithfully, though among themselves they discussed what 'rising from
11 the dead' could mean. ·And they put this question to him, 'Why do the scribes say that Elijah has to come first?'
12 'True,' he said 'Elijah is to come first and to see that everything is as it should be; yet how is it that the scriptures say about the Son of Man that he is to suffer grievously and be
13 treated with contempt? ·However, I tell you that Elijah has come and they have treated him as they pleased, just as the scriptures say about him.'

The epileptic demoniac

14 When they rejoined the disciples they saw a large crowd
15 round them and some scribes arguing with them. ·The moment they saw him the whole crowd were struck with
16 amazement and ran to greet him. ·'What are you arguing
17 about with them?' he asked. ·A man answered him from the crowd, 'Master, I have brought my son to you; there is a
18 spirit of dumbness in him, ·and when it takes hold of him it throws him to the ground, and he foams at the mouth and grinds his teeth and goes rigid. And I asked your disciples to
19 cast it out and they were unable to.' ·'You faithless generation' he said to them in reply. 'How much longer must I be with you? How much longer must I put up with you?.Bring
20 him to me.' ·They brought the boy to him, and as soon as the spirit saw Jesus it threw the boy into convulsions, and he fell to the ground and lay writhing there, foaming at the mouth.
21 Jesus asked the father, 'How long has this been happening
22 to him?' 'From childhood,' he replied, ·'and it has often thrown him into the fire and into the water, in order to destroy him. But if you can do anything, have pity on us and
23 help us.' ·'If you can?' retorted Jesus. 'Everything is possible
24 for anyone who has faith.' ·Immediately the father of the boy
25 cried out, 'I do have faith. Help the little faith I have!' ·And when Jesus saw how many people were pressing round him, he rebuked the unclean spirit. 'Deaf and dumb spirit,' he said 'I command you: come out of him and never enter him
26 again.' ·Then throwing the boy into violent convulsions it came out shouting, and the boy lay there so like a corpse that
27 most of them said, 'He is dead'. ·But Jesus took him by the
28 hand and helped him up, and he was able to stand. ·When he had gone indoors his disciples asked him privately, 'Why
29 were we unable to cast it out?' ·'This is the kind' he answered 'that can only be driven out by prayer.'

Second prophecy of the Passion

30   After leaving that place they made their way through
31 Galilee; and he did not want anyone to know, ·because he
was instructing his disciples; he was telling them, 'The Son of
Man will be delivered into the hands of men; they will put
him to death; and three days after he has been put to death he
32 will rise again'. ·But they did not understand what he said and
were afraid to ask him.

Who is the greatest?

33   They came to Capernaum, and when he was in the house
he asked them, 'What were you arguing about on the road?'
34 They said nothing because they had been arguing which of
35 them was the greatest. ·So he sat down, called the Twelve to
him and said, 'If anyone wants to be first, he must make
36 himself last of all and servant of all'. ·He then took a little
child, set him in front of them, put his arms round him, and
37 said to them, ·'Anyone who welcomes one of these little
children in my name, welcomes me; and anyone who welcomes me welcomes not me but the one who sent me'.

On using the name of Jesus

38   John said to him, 'Master, we saw a man who is not one of
us casting out devils in your name; and because he was not
39 one of us we tried to stop him'. ·But Jesus said, 'You must
not stop him: no one who works a miracle in my name is
40 likely to speak evil of me. ·Anyone who is not against us is
for us.

Charity shown to Christ's disciples

41   'If anyone gives you a cup of water to drink just because
you belong to Christ, then I tell you solemnly, he will most
certainly not lose his reward.

On leading others astray

42   'But anyone who is an obstacle to bring down one of these
little ones who have faith, would be better thrown into the sea
43 with a great millstone round his neck. ·And if your hand
should cause you to sin, cut it off; it is better for you to enter
into life crippled, than to have two hands and go to hell, into
45 the fire that cannot be put out. ·And if your foot should cause
you to sin, cut it off; it is better for you to enter into life lame,
47 than to have two feet and be thrown into hell. ·And if your
eye should cause you to sin, tear it out; it is better for you to

enter into the kingdom of God with one eye, than to have
48 two eyes and be thrown into hell ·where *their worm does not*
49 *die nor their fire go out*.*a* ·For everyone will be salted with fire.
50 Salt is a good thing, but if salt has become insipid, how can
you season it again? Have salt in yourselves and be at peace
with one another.'

The question about divorce

10   Leaving there, he came to the district of Judaea and the far
side of the Jordan. And again crowds gathered round him,
2 and again he taught them, as his custom was. ·Some Pharisees approached him and asked, 'Is it against the law for a
3 man to divorce his wife?' They were testing him. ·He
4 answered them, 'What did Moses command you?' ·'Moses
allowed us' they said 'to draw up a writ of dismissal and so to
5 divorce.' ·Then Jesus said to them, 'It was because you were
so unteachable that he wrote this commandment for you.
6 But from the beginning of creation *God made them male and*
7 *female*. ·*This is why a man must leave father and mother,*
8 *and the two become one body*.*a* They are no longer two, there-
9 fore, but one body. ·So then, what God has united, man must
10 not divide.' ·Back in the house the disciples questioned him
11 again about this, ·and he said to them, 'The man who divorces
his wife and marries another is guilty of adultery against her.
12 And if a woman divorces her husband and marries another
she is guilty of adultery too.'

Jesus and the children

13   People were bringing little children to him, for him to
14 touch them. The disciples turned them away, ·but when Jesus
saw this he was indignant and said to them, 'Let the little
children come to me; do not stop them; for it is to such as
15 these that the kingdom of God belongs. ·I tell you solemnly,
anyone who does not welcome the kingdom of God like a
16 little child will never enter it.' ·Then he put his arms round
them, laid his hands on them and gave them his blessing.

The rich young man

17   He was setting out on a journey when a man ran up, knelt
before him and put this question to him, 'Good master, what
18 must I do to inherit eternal life?' ·Jesus said to him, 'Why do
19 you call me good? No one is good but God alone. ·You know

9 a. Is 66:24
10 a. Gn 1:27; 2:24

the commandments: *You must not kill; You must not commit adultery; You must not steal; You must not bring false witness;* You must not defraud; *Honour your father and*
20 *mother.'* ·And he said to him, 'Master, I have kept all these
21 from my earliest days'. ·Jesus looked steadily at him and loved him, and he said, 'There is one thing you lack. Go and sell everything you own and give the money to the poor, and you will have treasure in heaven; then come, follow me.'
22 But his face fell at these words and he went away sad, for he was a man of great wealth.

The danger of riches

23   Jesus looked round and said to his disciples, 'How hard it is for those who have riches to enter the kingdom of God!'
24 The disciples were astounded by these words, but Jesus insisted, 'My children,' he said to them, 'how hard it is to
25 enter the kingdom of God!' ·It is easier for a camel to pass through the eye of a needle than for a rich man to enter the
26 kingdom of God.' ·They were more astonished than ever. 'In
27 that case' they said to one another 'who can be saved?' ·Jesus gazed at them. 'For men' he said 'it is impossible, but not for God: because everything is possible for God.'

The reward of renunciation

28   Peter took this up. 'What about us?' he asked him. 'We
29 have left everything and followed you.' ·Jesus said, 'I tell you solemnly, there is no one who has left house, brothers, sisters, father, children or land for my sake and for the sake of the
30 gospel ·who will not be repaid a hundred times over, houses, brothers, sisters, mothers, children and land—not without persecutions—now in this present time and, in the world to come, eternal life.
31   'Many who are first will be last, and the last first.'

Third prophecy of the Passion

32   They were on the road, going up to Jerusalem; Jesus was walking on ahead of them; they were in a daze, and those who followed were apprehensive. Once more taking the Twelve aside he began to tell them what was going to happen
33 to him: ·'Now we are going up to Jerusalem, and the Son of Man is about to be handed over to the chief priests and the scribes. They will condemn him to death and will hand him
34 over to the pagans, ·who will mock him and spit at him and scourge him and put him to death; and after three days he will rise again.'

The sons of Zebedee make their request

35 James and John, the sons of Zebedee, approached him.
·   'Master,' they said to him 'we want you to do us a favour.'
36 He said to them, 'What is it you want me to do for you?'
37 They said to him, 'Allow us to sit one at your right hand and
38 the other at your left in your glory'. ·'You do not know what
    you are asking' Jesus said to them. 'Can you drink the cup
    that I must drink, or be baptised with the baptism with which
39 I must be baptised?' ·They replied, 'We can'. Jesus said to
    them, 'The cup that I must drink you shall drink, and with
    the baptism with which I must be baptised you shall be
40 baptised, ·but as for seats at my right hand or my left, these
    are not mine to grant; they belong to those to whom they
    have been allotted'.

Leadership with service

41 When the other ten heard this they began to feel indignant
42 with James and John, ·so Jesus called them to him and said
    to them, 'You know that among the pagans their so-called
    rulers lord it over them, and their great men make their
43 authority felt. ·This is not to happen among you. No; anyone
    who wants to become great among you must be your servant,
44 and anyone who wants to be first among you must be slave to
45 all. ·For the Son of Man himself did not come to be served
    but to serve, and to give his life as a ransom for many.'

The blind man of Jericho

46 They reached Jericho; and as he left Jericho with his
    disciples and a large crowd, Bartimaeus (that is, the son of
    Timaeus), a blind beggar, was sitting at the side of the road.
47 When he heard that it was Jesus of Nazareth, he began to
    shout and to say, 'Son of David, Jesus, have pity on me'.
48 And many of them scolded him and told him to keep quiet,
    but he only shouted all the louder, 'Son of David, have pity
49 on me'. ·Jesus stopped and said, 'Call him here'. So they
    called the blind man. 'Courage,' they said, 'get up; he is
50 calling you.' ·So throwing off his cloak, he jumped up and
51 went to Jesus. ·Then Jesus spoke, 'What do you want me to
    do for you?' 'Rabbuni,'[b] the blind man said to him 'Master,
52 let me see again.' ·Jesus said to him, 'Go; your faith has
    saved you'. And immediately his sight returned and he
    followed him along the road.

b. Aramaic: 'My master'.

IV. THE JERUSALEM MINISTRY

The Messiah enters Jerusalem

11   When they were approaching Jerusalem, in sight of Bethphage and Bethany, close by the Mount of Olives, he sent
2 two of his disciples ·and said to them, 'Go off to the village facing you, and as soon as you enter it you will find a tethered colt that no one has yet ridden. Untie it and bring it
3 here. ·If anyone says to you, "What are you doing?" say, "The Master needs it and will send it back here directly".'
4 They went off and found a colt tethered near a door in the
5 open street. As they untied it, ·some men standing there said,
6 'What are you doing, untying that colt?' ·They gave the
7 answer Jesus had told them, and the men let them go. ·Then they took the colt to Jesus and threw their cloaks on its back,
8 and he sat on it. ·Many people spread their cloaks on the
9 road, others greenery which they had cut in the fields. ·And those who went in front and those who followed were all shouting, '*Hosanna! Blessings on him who comes in the name*
10 *of the Lord!*[a] ·Blessings on the coming kingdom of our father
11 David! *Hosanna* in the highest heavens!' ·He entered Jerusalem and went into the Temple. He looked all round him, but as it was now late, he went out to Bethany with the Twelve.

The barren fig tree

12   Next day as they were leaving Bethany, he felt hungry.
13 Seeing a fig tree in leaf some distance away, he went to see if he could find any fruit on it, but when he came up to it he found nothing but leaves; for it was not the season for figs.
14 And he addressed the fig tree. 'May no one ever eat fruit from you again' he said. And his disciples heard him say this.

The expulsion of the dealers from the Temple

15   So they reached Jerusalem and he went into the Temple and began driving out those who were selling and buying there; he upset the tables of the money changers and the
16 chairs of those who were selling pigeons. ·Nor would he
17 allow anyone to carry anything through the Temple. ·And he taught them and said, 'Does not scripture say: *My house will be called a house of prayer for all the peoples?*[b] But you have
18 turned it into *a robbers' den.*[c] ·This came to the ears of the chief priests and the scribes, and they tried to find some way of doing away with him; they were afraid of him because the

19 people were carried away by his teaching. ·And when evening
came he went out of the city.

The fig tree withered. Faith and prayer

20 Next morning, as they passed by, they saw the fig
21 tree withered to the roots. ·Peter remembered. 'Look,
Rabbi,' he said to Jesus 'the fig tree you cursed has withered
22 away.' ·Jesus answered, 'Have faith in God. ·I tell you
23 solemnly, if anyone says to this mountain, "Get up and
throw yourself into the sea", with no hesitation in his heart
but believing that what he says will happen, it will be done for
24 him. ·I tell you therefore: everything you ask and pray for,
25 believe that you have it already, and it will be yours. ·And
when you stand in prayer, forgive whatever you have against
anybody, so that your Father in heaven may forgive your
failings too.'

The authority of Jesus is questioned

27 They came to Jerusalem again, and as Jesus was walking in
the Temple, the chief priests and the scribes and the elders
28 came to him, ·and they said to him, 'What authority have you
for acting like this? Or who gave you authority to do these
29 things?' ·Jesus said to them, 'I will ask you a question, only
one; answer me and I will tell you my authority for acting like
30 this. ·John's baptism: did it come from heaven, or from
31 man? Answer me that.' ·And they argued it out this way
among themselves: 'If we say from heaven, he will say, "Then
32 why did you refuse to believe him?" ·But dare we say from
man?'—they had the people to fear, for everyone held that
33 John was a real prophet. ·So their reply to Jesus was, 'We do
not know'. And Jesus said to them, 'Nor will I tell you my
authority for acting like this'.

Parable of the wicked husbandmen

12 He went on to speak to them in parables, 'A man planted a
vineyard; he fenced it round, dug out a trough for the winepress and built a tower; then he leased it to tenants and went
2 abroad. ·When the time came, he sent a servant to the
tenants to collect from them his share of the produce from
3 the vineyard. ·But they seized the man, thrashed him and sent
4 him away empty-handed. ·Next he sent another servant to
them; him they beat about the head and treated shamefully.
5 And he sent another and him they killed; then a number of
6 others, and they thrashed some and killed the rest. ·He had

11 a. Ps 118:25–26 **b.** Is 56:7 **c.** Jr 7:11

still someone left: his beloved son. He sent him to them last
7 of all. "They will respect my son" he said. ·But those tenants
said to each other, "This is the heir. Come on, let us kill
8 him, and the inheritance will be ours." ·So they seized him
9 and killed him and threw him out of the vineyard. ·Now what
will the owner of the vineyard do? He will come and make an
10 end of the tenants and give the vineyard to others. ·Have you
not read this text of scripture:

> *It was the stone rejected by the builders*
> *that became the keystone.*
11 > *This was the Lord's doing*
> *and it is wonderful to see?*[a]

12 And they would have liked to arrest him, because they
realised that the parable was aimed at them, but they were
afraid of the crowds. So they left him alone and went away.

On tribute to Caesar

13 Next day they sent to him some Pharisees and some Hero-
14 dians to catch him out in what he said. ·These came and said
to him, 'Master, we know you are an honest man, that you
are not afraid of anyone, because a man's rank means
nothing to you, and that you teach the way of God in all
honesty. Is it permissible to pay taxes to Caesar or not?
15 Should we pay, yes or no?' ·Seeing through their hypocrisy he
said to them, 'Why do you set this trap for me? Hand me a
16 denarius and let me see it.' ·They handed him one and he
said, 'Whose head is this? Whose name?' 'Caesar's' they
17 told him. ·Jesus said to them, 'Give back to Caesar what
belongs to Caesar—and to God what belongs to God'. This
reply took them completely by surprise.

The resurrection of the dead

18 Then some Sadducees—who deny that there is a resurrec-
19 tion—came to him and they put this question to him, ·'Master,
we have it from Moses in writing, if a man's brother dies
leaving a wife but no child, the man must marry the widow to
20 raise up children for his brother. ·Now there were seven
brothers. The first married a wife and then died leaving no chil-
21 dren. ·The second married the widow, and he too died leaving
22 no children; with the third it was the same, ·and none of the
seven left any children. Last of all the woman herself died.
23 Now at the resurrection, when they rise again, whose wife
will she be, since she had been married to all seven?'
24 Jesus said to them, 'Is not the reason why you go wrong,

that you understand neither the scriptures nor the power of
25 God? ·For when they rise from the dead, men and women do
26 not marry; no, they are like the angels in heaven. ·Now about
the dead rising again, have you never read in the Book of
Moses, in the passage about the Bush, how God spoke to
him and said: *I am the God of Abraham, the God of Isaac and*
27 *the God of Jacob*?[b] ·He is God, not of the dead, but of the
living. You are very much mistaken.'

The greatest commandment of all

28 One of the scribes who had listened to them debating and
had observed how well Jesus had answered them, now came
up and put a question to him, 'Which is the first of all the
29 commandments?' ·Jesus replied, 'This is the first: *Listen,*
30 *Israel, the Lord our God is the one Lord,* ·*and you must love the*
Lord your God with all your heart, with all your soul, with all
31 your mind and *with all your strength.*[c] ·The second is this:
You must love your neighbour as yourself.[d] There is no com-
32 mandment greater than these.' ·The scribe said to him, 'Well
spoken, Master; what you have said is true: that he is one
33 and there is no other. ·To love him with all your heart, with
all your understanding and strength, and to love your neighbour as yourself, this is far more important than any holo-
34 caust or sacrifice.' ·Jesus, seeing how wisely he had spoken,
said, 'You are not far from the kingdom of God'. And after
that no one dared to question him any more.

Christ not only son but also Lord of David

35 Later, while teaching in the Temple, Jesus said, 'How can
the scribes maintain that the Christ is the son of David?
36 David himself, moved by the Holy Spirit, said:

> *The Lord said to my Lord:*
> *Sit at my right hand*
> *and I will put your enemies*
> *under your feet.*[e]

37 David himself calls him Lord, in what way then can he be his
son?' And the great majority of the people heard this with
delight.

The scribes condemned by Jesus

38 In his teaching he said, 'Beware of the scribes who like to
walk about in long robes, to be greeted obsequiously in the
39 market squares, ·to take the front seats in the synagogues and

12 a. Ps 118:22–23 **b.** Ex 3:6 **c.** Dt 6:4–5 **d.** Lv 19:18 **e.** Ps 110:1

40 the places of honour at banquets; ·these are the men who
swallow the property of widows, while making a show of
lengthy prayers. The more severe will be the sentence they
receive.'

The widow's mite

41 He sat down opposite the treasury and watched the people
putting money into the treasury, and many of the rich put in
42 a great deal. ·A poor widow came and put in two small coins,
43 the equivalent of a penny. ·Then he called his disciples and
said to them, 'I tell you solemnly, this poor widow has put
44 more in than all who have contributed to the treasury; ·for
they have all put in money they had over, but she from the
little she had has put in everything she possessed, all she had
to live on'.

The eschatological discourse: introduction

13 As he was leaving the Temple one of his disciples said to
him, 'Look at the size of those stones, Master! Look at the
2 size of those great buildings!' ·And Jesus said to him, 'You see
these great buildings? Not a single stone will be left on
another: everything will be destroyed.'
3 And while he was sitting facing the Temple, on the Mount
of Olives, Peter, James, John and Andrew questioned him
4 privately, ·'Tell us, when is this going to happen, and what
sign will there be that all this is about to be fulfilled?'

The beginning of sorrows

5 Then Jesus began to tell them, 'Take care that no one
6 deceives you. ·Many will come using my name and saying,
7 "I am he", and they will deceive many. ·When you hear of
wars and rumours of wars, do not be alarmed, this is
8 something that must happen, but the end will not be yet. ·For
nation will fight against nation, and kingdom against kingdom. There will be earthquakes here and there; there will be
famines. This is the beginning of the birthpangs.
9 'Be on your guard: they will hand you over to sanhedrins;
you will be beaten in synagogues; and you will stand before
governors and kings for my sake, to bear witness before
10 them, ·since the Good News must first be proclaimed to all
the nations.
11 'And when they lead you away to hand you over, do not
worry beforehand about what to say; no, say whatever is
given to you when the time comes, because it is not you who
12 will be speaking: it will be the Holy Spirit. ·Brother will

betray brother to death, and the father his child; children
13 will rise against their parents and have them put to death. ·You
will be hated by all men on account of my name; but the man
who stands firm to the end will be saved.

The great tribulation of Jerusalem

14 'When you see *the disastrous abomination*[a] set up where it
ought not to be (let the reader understand), then those in
15 Judaea must escape to the mountains; ·if a man is on the
housetop, he must not come down to go into the house to
16 collect any of his belongings; ·if a man is in the fields, he
17 must not turn back to fetch his cloak. ·Alas for those with
child, or with babies at the breast, when those days come!
18
19 Pray that this may not be in winter. ·For in those days there
will be *such distress as, until now, has not been*[b] equalled since
the beginning when God created the world, nor ever will be
20 again. ·And if the Lord had not shortened that time, no one
would have survived; but he did shorten the time, for the
sake of the elect whom he chose.
21 'And if anyone says to you then, "Look, here is the Christ"
22 or, "Look, he is there", do not believe it; ·for false Christs
and false prophets will arise and produce signs and portents
23 to deceive the elect, if that were possible. ·You therefore
must be on your guard. I have forewarned you of everything.

The coming of the Son of Man

24 'But in those days, after that time of distress, the sun will
25 be darkened, the moon will lose its brightness, ·the stars will
come falling from heaven and the powers in the heavens will
26 be shaken. ·And then they will see the Son of Man coming in
27 the clouds with great power and glory; ·then too he will send
the angels to gather his chosen from the four winds, from the
ends of the world to the ends of heaven.

The time of this coming

28 'Take the fig tree as a parable: as soon as its twigs grow
supple and its leaves come out, you know that summer is
29 near. ·So with you when you see these things happening:
30 know that he is near, at the very gates. ·I tell you solemnly,
before this generation has passed away all these things will
31 have taken place. ·Heaven and earth will pass away, but my
words will not pass away.
32 'But as for that day or hour, nobody knows it, neither the
angels of heaven, nor the Son; no one but the Father.

13 a. Dn 9:27, and ch. 11, 12 **b.** Dn 12:1

Be on the alert

33 'Be on your guard, stay awake, because you never know
34 when the time will come. ·It is like a man travelling abroad:
he has gone from home, and left his servants in charge, each
with his own task; and he has told the doorkeeper to stay
35 awake. ·So stay awake, because you do not know when the
master of the house is coming, evening, midnight, cockcrow,
36 dawn; ·if he comes unexpectedly, he must not find you asleep.
37 And what I say to you I say to all: Stay awake!'

V. PASSION AND RESURRECTION

The conspiracy against Jesus

14 It was two days before the Passover and the feast of
Unleavened Bread, and the chief priests and the scribes were
looking for a way to arrest Jesus by some trick and have him
2 put to death. ·For they said, 'It must not be during the festivities, or there will be a disturbance among the people'.

The anointing at Bethany

3 Jesus was at Bethany in the house of Simon the leper; he
was at dinner when a woman came in with an alabaster jar of
very costly ointment, pure nard. She broke the jar and
4 poured the ointment on his head. ·Some who were there said
to one another indignantly, 'Why this waste of ointment?
5 Ointment like this could have been sold for over three
hundred denarii and the money given to the poor'; and they
6 were angry with her. ·But Jesus said, 'Leave her alone. Why
are you upsetting her? What she has done for me is one of
7 the good works. ·You have the poor with you always, and
you can be kind to them whenever you wish, but you will not
8 always have me. ·She has done what was in her power to do:
9 she has anointed my body beforehand for its burial. ·I tell
you solemnly, wherever throughout all the world the Good
News is proclaimed, what she has done will be told also, in
remembrance of her.'

Judas betrays Jesus

10 Judas Iscariot, one of the Twelve, approached the chief
11 priests with an offer to hand Jesus over to them. ·They were
delighted to hear it, and promised to give him money; and he
looked for a way of betraying him when the opportunity
should occur.

Preparations for the Passover supper

12 On the first day of Unleavened Bread, when the Passover lamb was sacrificed, his disciples said to him, 'Where do you want us to go and make the preparations for you to eat the
13 passover?' ·So he sent two of his disciples, saying to them, 'Go into the city and you will meet a man carrying a pitcher
14 of water. Follow him, ·and say to the owner of the house which he enters, "The Master says: Where is my dining room
15 in which I can eat the passover with my disciples?" ·He will show you a large upper room furnished with couches, all
16 prepared. Make the preparations for us there.' ·The disciples set out and went to the city and found everything as he had told them, and prepared the Passover.

The treachery of Judas foretold

17
18 When evening came he arrived with the Twelve. ·And while they were at table eating, Jesus said, 'I tell you solemnly, one of you is about to betray me, one of you eating with me'.
19 They were distressed and asked him, one after another, 'Not
20 I, surely?' ·He said to them, 'It is one of the Twelve, one who
21 is dipping into the same dish with me. ·Yes, the Son of Man is going to his fate, as the scriptures say he will, but alas for that man by whom the Son of Man is betrayed! Better for that man if he had never been born!'

The institution of the Eucharist

22 And as they were eating he took some bread, and when he had said the blessing he broke it and gave it to them. 'Take
23 it,' he said 'this is my body.' ·Then he took a cup, and when he had returned thanks he gave it to them, and all drank from
24 it, ·and he said to them, 'This is my blood, the blood of the
25 covenant, which is to be poured out for many. ·I tell you solemnly, I shall not drink any more wine until the day I drink the new wine in the kingdom of God.'

Peter's denial foretold

26 After psalms had been sung they left for the Mount of
27 Olives. ·And Jesus said to them, 'You will all lose faith, for the scripture says: *I shall strike the shepherd and the sheep*
28 *will be scattered,*[a] ·however after my resurrection I shall go
29 before you to Galilee'. ·Peter said, 'Even if all lose faith,
30 I will not'. ·And Jesus said to him, 'I tell you solemnly, this

14 a. Zc 13:7

day, this very night, before the cock crows twice, you will
31 have disowned me three times'. ·But he repeated still more
earnestly, 'If I have to die with you, I will never disown you'.
And they all said the same.

Gethsemane

32   They came to a small estate called Gethsemane, and Jesus
33 said to his disciples, 'Stay here while I pray'. ·Then he took
Peter and James and John with him. And a sudden fear
34 came over him, and great distress. ·And he said to them, 'My
soul is sorrowful to the point of death. Wait here, and keep
35 awake.' ·And going on a little further he threw himself on the
ground and prayed that, if it were possible, this hour might
36 pass him by. ·'Abba (Father)!' he said 'Everything is possible
for you. Take this cup away from me. But let it be as you, not
37 I, would have it.' ·He came back and found them sleeping,
and he said to Peter, 'Simon, are you asleep? Had you not
38 the strength to keep awake one hour? ·You should be awake,
and praying not to be put to the test. The spirit is willing, but
39 the flesh is weak.' ·Again he went away and prayed, saying
40 the same words. ·And once more he came back and found
them sleeping, their eyes were so heavy; and they could find
41 no answer for him. ·He came back a third time and said to
them, 'You can sleep on now and take your rest. It is all over.
The hour has come. Now the Son of Man is to be betrayed
42 into the hands of sinners. ·Get up! Let us go! My betrayer is
close at hand already.'

The arrest

43   Even while he was still speaking, Judas, one of the Twelve,
came up with a number of men armed with swords and
clubs, sent by the chief priests and the scribes and the elders.
44 Now the traitor had arranged a signal with them. 'The one I
kiss,' he had said 'he is the man. Take him in charge, and see
45 he is well guarded when you lead him away.' ·So when the
traitor came, he went straight up to Jesus and said, 'Rabbi!'
46 and kissed him. ·The others seized him and took him in
47 charge. ·Then one of the bystanders drew his sword and
struck out at the high priest's servant, and cut off his ear.
48   Then Jesus spoke, 'Am I a brigand' he said 'that you had
49 to set out to capture me with swords and clubs? ·I was
among you teaching in the Temple day after day and you
never laid hands on me. But this is to fulfil the scriptures.'
50
51 And they all deserted him and ran away. ·A young man who
‒ followed him had nothing on but a linen cloth. They caught

52 hold of him, ·but he left the cloth in their hands and ran
away naked.

Jesus before the Sanhedrin

53   They led Jesus off to the high priest; and all the chief
54 priests and the elders and the scribes assembled here. ·Peter
had followed him at a distance, right into the high priest's
palace, and was sitting with the attendants warming himself
at the fire.
55   The chief priests and the whole Sanhedrin were looking for
evidence against Jesus on which they might pass the death-
56 sentence. But they could not find any. ·Several, indeed,
brought false evidence against him, but their evidence was
57 conflicting. ·Some stood up and submitted this false evidence
58 against him, ·'We heard him say, "I am going to destroy this
Temple made by human hands, and in three days build
59 another, not made by human hands"'. ·But even on this
60 point their evidence was conflicting. ·The high priest then
stood up before the whole assembly and put this question to
Jesus, 'Have you no answer to that? What is this evidence
61 these men are bringing against you?' ·But he was silent and
made no answer at all. The high priest put a second question
to him, 'Are you the Christ,' he said 'the Son of the Blessed
62 One?' ·'I am,' said Jesus 'and you will see *the Son of Man
seated at the right hand of the Power* and *coming with the
63 clouds of heaven.*'[b] ·The high priest tore his robes, 'What need
64 of witnesses have we now?' he said. ·'You heard the blasphemy. What is your finding?' And they all gave their
verdict: he deserved to die.
65   Some of them started spitting at him and, blindfolding
him, began hitting him with their fists and shouting, 'Play the
prophet!' And the attendants rained blows on him.

Peter's denials

66   While Peter was down below in the courtyard, one of the
67 high priest's servant-girls came up. ·She saw Peter warming
himself there, stared at him and said, 'You too were with
68 Jesus, the man from Nazareth'. ·But he denied it. 'I do not
know, I do not understand, what you are talking about' he
69 said. And he went out into the forecourt. ·The servant-girl
saw him and again started telling the bystanders, 'This
70 fellow is one of them'. ·But again he denied it. A little later
the bystanders themselves said to Peter, 'You are one of them

b. Dn 7:13; Ps 110:1

71 for sure! Why, you are a Galilean.' ·But he started calling
down curses on himself and swearing, 'I do not know the
72 man you speak of'. ·At that moment the cock crew for the
second time, and Peter recalled how Jesus had said to him,
'Before the cock crows twice, you will have disowned me
three times'. And he burst into tears.

Jesus before Pilate

15 First thing in the morning, the chief priests together with
the elders and scribes, in short the whole Sanhedrin, had
their plan ready. They had Jesus bound and took him away
and handed him over to Pilate.
2 Pilate questioned him, 'Are you the king of the Jews?' 'It is
3 you who say it' he answered. ·And the chief priests brought
4 many accusations against him. ·Pilate questioned him again,
'Have you no reply at all? See how many accusations they
5 are bringing against you!' ·But, to Pilate's amazement, Jesus
made no further reply.
6 At festival time Pilate used to release a prisoner for them,
7 anyone they asked for. ·Now a man called Barabbas was then
in prison with the rioters who had committed murder during
8 the uprising. ·When the crowd went up and began to ask
9 Pilate the customary favour, ·Pilate answered them, 'Do you
10 want me to release for you the king of the Jews?' ·For he
realised it was out of jealousy that the chief priests had
11 handed Jesus over. ·The chief priests, however, had incited
the crowd to demand that he should release Barabbas for
12 them instead. ·Then Pilate spoke again. 'But in that case,' he
said to them 'what am I to do with the man you call king of
13
14 the Jews?' ·They shouted back, 'Crucify him!' ·'Why?'
Pilate asked them 'What harm has he done?' But they
15 shouted all the louder, 'Crucify him!' ·So Pilate, anxious to
placate the crowd, released Barabbas for them and, having
ordered Jesus to be scourged, handed him over to be crucified.

Jesus crowned with thorns

16 The soldiers led him away to the inner part of the palace,
that is, the Praetorium, and called the whole cohort to-
17 gether. ·They dressed him up in purple, twisted some thorns
18 into a crown and put it on him. ·And they began saluting
19 him, 'Hail, king of the Jews!' ·They struck his head with a
reed and spat on him; and they went down on their knees to
20 do him homage. ·And when they had finished making fun of
him, they took off the purple and dressed him in his own
clothes.

The way of the cross

21　They led him out to crucify him. ·They enlisted a passer-by, Simon of Cyrene, father of Alexander and Rufus,[a] who was
22　coming in from the country, to carry his cross. ·They brought Jesus to the place called Golgotha, which means the place of the skull.

The crucifixion

23　They offered him wine mixed with myrrh, but he refused it.
24　Then they crucified him, and shared out his clothing, casting
25　lots to decide what each should get. ·It was the third hour[b]
26　when they crucified him. ·The inscription giving the charge
27　against him read: 'The King of the Jews'. ·And they crucified two robbers with him, one on his right and one on his left.

The crucified Christ is mocked

29　The passers-by jeered at him; they shook their heads and said, 'Aha! So you would destroy the Temple and rebuild it
30　in three days! ·Then save yourself: come down from the
31　cross!' ·The chief priests and the scribes mocked him among themselves in the same way. 'He saved others,' they said 'he
32　cannot save himself. ·Let the Christ, the king of Israel, come down from the cross now, for us to see it and believe.' Even those who were crucified with him taunted him.

The death of Jesus

33　When the sixth hour came there was darkness over the
34　whole land until the ninth hour. ·And at the ninth hour Jesus cried out in a loud voice, 'Eloi, Eloi, lama sabachthani?' which means, *'My God, my God, why have you deserted me?'*[c]
35　When some of those who stood by heard this, they said,
36　'Listen, he is calling on Elijah'. ·Someone ran and soaked a sponge in vinegar and, putting it on a reed, gave it him to drink saying, 'Wait and see if Elijah will come to take him
37　down'. ·But Jesus gave a loud cry and breathed his last.
38　And the veil of the Temple was torn in two from top to
39　bottom. ·The centurion, who was standing in front of him, had seen how he had died, and he said, 'In truth this man was a son of God'.

15 a. Alexander and Rufus were doubtless known to the Roman circle in which Mark wrote his gospel. Cf. Rm 16:13. **b.** 9 a.m. **c.** Ps 22:1

The women on Calvary

40   There were some women watching from a distance. Among
them were Mary of Magdala, Mary who was the mother of
41 James the younger and Joset, and Salome. ·These used to
follow him and look after him when he was in Galilee. And
there were many other women there who had come up to
Jerusalem with him.

The burial

42   It was now evening, and since it was Preparation Day (that
43 is, the vigil of the sabbath), ·there came Joseph of Arimathaea, a prominent member of the Council, who himself lived
in the hope of seeing the kingdom of God, and he boldly went
44 to Pilate and asked for the body of Jesus. ·Pilate, astonished
that he should have died so soon, summoned the centurion
45 and enquired if he was already dead. ·Having been assured of
46 this by the centurion, he granted the corpse to Joseph ·who
bought a shroud, took Jesus down from the cross,
wrapped him in the shroud and laid him in a tomb which had
been hewn out of the rock. He then rolled a stone against the
47 entrance to the tomb. ·Mary of Magdala and Mary the
mother of Joset were watching and took note of where he
was laid.

The empty tomb. The angel's message

16   When the sabbath was over, Mary of Magdala, Mary the
mother of James, and Salome, bought spices with which to
2 go and anoint him. ·And very early in the morning on the first
day of the week they went to the tomb, just as the sun was
rising.
3   They had been saying to one another, 'Who will roll away
4 the stone for us from the entrance to the tomb?' ·But when
they looked they could see that the stone—which was very
5 big—had already been rolled back. ·On entering the tomb
they saw a young man in a white robe seated on the right-
6 hand side, and they were struck with amazement. ·But he
said to them, 'There is no need for alarm. You are looking for
Jesus of Nazareth, who was crucified: he has risen, he is not
7 here. See, here is the place where they laid him. ·But you
must go and tell his disciples and Peter, "He is going before
you to Galilee; it is there you will see him, just as he told
8 you".' ·And the women came out and ran away from the
tomb because they were frightened out of their wits; and they
said nothing to a soul, for they were afraid . . .

Appearances of the risen Christ[a]

9　　Having risen in the morning on the first day of the week,
he appeared first to Mary of Magdala from whom he had
10　cast out seven devils. ·She then went to those who had been
his companions, and who were mourning and in tears, and
11　told them. ·But they did not believe her when they heard her
say that he was alive and that she had seen him.

12　　After this, he showed himself under another form to two
13　of them as they were on their way into the country. ·These
went back and told the others, who did not believe them
either.

14　　Lastly, he showed himself to the Eleven themselves while
they were at table. He reproached them for their incredulity
and obstinacy, because they had refused to believe those who
15　had seen him after he had risen. ·And he said to them, Go
out to the whole world; proclaim the Good News to all
16　creation. ·He who believes and is baptised will be saved; he
17　who does not believe will be condemned. ·These are the signs
that will be associated with believers: in my name they will
18　cast out devils; they will have the gift of tongues; ·they will
pick up snakes in their hands, and be unharmed should they
drink deadly poison; they will lay their hands on the sick,
who will recover.'

19　　And so the Lord Jesus, after he had spoken to them, was
taken up into heaven: there at the right hand of God he took
20　his place, ·while they, going out, preached everywhere, the
Lord working with them and confirming the word by the
signs that accompanied it.

16 a. Many MSS omit vv. 9–20 and this ending to the gospel may not
have been written by Mark, though it is old enough.

THE GOSPEL
ACCORDING TO
SAINT LUKE

Prologue

1 Seeing that many others have undertaken to draw up ac-
2 counts of the events that have taken place among us, ·exactly
as these were handed down to us by those who from the
3 outset were eyewitnesses and ministers of the word,·I in my
turn, after carefully going over the whole story from the
beginning, have decided to write an ordered account for you,
4 Theophilus, ·so that your Excellency may learn how well
founded the teaching is that you have received.

I. THE BIRTH AND HIDDEN LIFE
OF JOHN THE BAPTIST AND OF JESUS

The birth of John the Baptist foretold

5 In the days of King Herod of Judaea there lived a priest
called Zechariah who belonged to the Abijah section of the
priesthood, and he had a wife, Elizabeth by name, who was
6 a descendant of Aaron. ·Both were worthy in the sight of
God, and scrupulously observed all the commandments and
7 observances of the Lord. ·But they were childless: Elizabeth
was barren and they were both getting on in years.

8 Now it was the turn of Zechariah's section[a] to serve, and
9 he was exercising his priestly office before God ·when it fell
to him by lot, as the ritual custom was, to enter the Lord's
10 sanctuary and burn incense there.[b] ·And at the hour of incense the whole congregation was outside, praying.

11 Then there appeared to him the angel of the Lord, stand-
12 ing on the right of the altar of incense. ·The sight disturbed
13 Zechariah and he was overcome with fear. ·But the angel
said to him, 'Zechariah, do not be afraid, your prayer has
been heard. Your wife Elizabeth is to bear you a son and you
14 must name him John.[c] ·He will be your joy and delight and
15 many will rejoice at his birth, ·for he will be great in the sight

of the Lord; he must drink no wine, no strong drink.[d] Even
from his mother's womb he will be filled with the Holy
16 Spirit, ·and he will bring back many of the sons of Israel to
17 the Lord their God. ·With the spirit and power of Elijah,
he will go before him *to turn the hearts of fathers towards
their children*[e] and the disobedient back to the wisdom
that the virtuous have, preparing for the Lord a people
18 fit for him.' ·Zechariah said to the angel, '*How can I
be sure of this?*[f] I am an old man and my wife is getting on
19 in years.' ·The angel replied, 'I am Gabriel who stand in
God's presence, and I have been sent to speak to you and
20 bring you this good news. ·Listen! Since you have not believed my words, which will come true at their appointed
time, you will be silenced and have no power of speech until
21 this has happened.' ·Meanwhile the people were waiting for
Zechariah and were surprised that he stayed in the sanctuary
22 so long. ·When he came out he could not speak to them, and
they realised that he had received a vision in the sanctuary.
But he could only make signs to them, and remained dumb.
23   When his time of service came to an end he returned home.
24 Some time later his wife Elizabeth conceived, and for five
25 months she kept to herself. ·'The Lord has done this for me'
she said 'now that it has pleased him to take away the
humiliation I suffered among men.'

The annunciation

26   In the sixth month the angel Gabriel was sent by God to a
27 town in Galilee called Nazareth, ·to a virgin betrothed to a
man named Joseph, of the House of David; and the virgin's
28 name was Mary. ·He went in and said to her, 'Rejoice, so
29 highly favoured! The Lord is with you.' ·She was deeply disturbed by these words and asked herself what this greeting
30 could mean, ·but the angel said to her, 'Mary, do not be
31 afraid; you have won God's favour. ·Listen! You are to con-
32 ceive and bear a son, and you must name him Jesus. ·He will
be great and will be called Son of the Most High. The Lord
33 God will give him the throne of his ancestor David; ·he will
rule over the House of Jacob for ever and his reign will have
34 no end.' ·Mary said to the angel, 'But how can this come

1 a. The 24 families of the 'sons of Aaron' were responsible in rotation
for service in the Temple, and in each class or family the individual
was chosen by lot. See 1 Ch 24. **b.** The priest tended the brazier on the
altar of incense in front of the Most Holy Place. **c.** The meaning of the
name is 'Yahweh is gracious'. **d.** See Nb 6:1, where this abstinence is
required in anyone performing a vow to the Lord. **e.** Ml 3:23–24
f. Zechariah asks for a sign in a way reminiscent of Abram, Gn 15:8.

35 about, since I am a virgin?'*ᵍ* ·'The Holy Spirit will come upon
you' the angel answered 'and the power of the Most High
will cover you with its shadow. And so the child will be holy
36 and will be called Son of God. ·Know this too: your kins-
woman Elizabeth has, in her old age, herself conceived a son,
and she whom people called barren is now in her sixth month,
37
38 *for nothing is impossible to God.'ʰ* ·'I am the handmaid of the
Lord,' said Mary 'let what you have said be done to me.'
And the angel left her.

The visitation

39   Mary set out at that time and went as quickly as she could
40 to a town in the hill country of Judah. ·She went into
41 Zechariah's house and greeted Elizabeth. ·Now as soon as
Elizabeth heard Mary's greeting, the child leapt in her womb
42 and Elizabeth was filled with the Holy Spirit. ·She gave a
loud cry and said, 'Of all women you are the most blessed,
43 and blessed is the fruit of your womb. ·Why should I be
44 honoured with a visit from the mother of my Lord? ·For the
moment your greeting reached my ears, the child in my womb
45 leapt for joy. ·Yes, blessed is she who believed that the
promise made her by the Lord would be fulfilled.'

The Magnificat

46   And Mary*ⁱ* said:
'My soul proclaims the greatness of the Lord
47 and my spirit *exults in God my saviour;*
48 because *he has looked upon his lowly handmaid.*
Yes, from this day forward all generations will call me
blessed,
49 for the Almighty has done great things for me.
Holy is his name,
50 and *his mercy reaches from age to age for those who fear him.*
51 He has shown the power of his arm,
he has routed the proud of heart.
52 *He has pulled down princes* from their thrones *and exalted the
lowly.*
53 *The hungry he has filled with good things,* the rich sent empty
away.
54 *He has come to the help of Israel his servant, mindful of his
mercy*
55 —according to the promise he made to our ancestors—
of his mercy to Abraham and to his descendants for ever.'

56   Mary stayed with Elizabeth about three months and then
went back home.

The birth of John the Baptist and visit of the neighbours

57 Meanwhile the time came for Elizabeth to have her child,
58 and she gave birth to a son; ·and when her neighbours and
relations heard that the Lord had shown her so great a kindness, they shared her joy.

The circumcision of John the Baptist

59 Now on the eighth day they came to circumcise the child;
they were going to call*ʲ* him Zechariah after his father,
60 but his mother spoke up. 'No,' she said 'he is to be called
61 John.' ·They said to her, 'But no one in your family has that
62 name', ·and made signs to his father to find out what he
63 wanted him called. ·The father asked for a writing-tablet and
wrote, 'His name is John'. And they were all astonished.
64 At that instant his power of speech returned and he spoke
65 and praised God. ·All their neighbours were filled with awe
and the whole affair was talked about throughout the hill
66 country of Judaea. ·All those who heard of it treasured it in
their hearts. 'What will this child turn out to be?' they
wondered. And indeed the hand of the Lord was with him.

The Benedictus

67 His father Zechariah was filled with the Holy Spirit and
spoke his prophecy:

68   '*Blessed be the Lord, the God of Israel,*ᵏ
     for he has visited his people, he has come to their rescue
69   and he has raised up for us a power for salvation
     in the House of his servant David,
70   even as he proclaimed,
     by the mouth of his holy prophets from ancient times,
71   that he would save us from our enemies
     and from the hands of all who hate us.
72   Thus he shows mercy to our ancestors,
     thus *he remembers* his holy *covenant,*ˡ
73   the oath he swore
     to our father Abraham
74   that he would grant us, free from fear,
     to be delivered from the hands of our enemies,
75   to serve him in holiness and virtue

g. Lit. 'since I do not know man'. h. Gn 18:14 i. Mary's canticle is
reminiscent of Hannah's, 1 S 2:1–10. Other quotations and allusions
in the Magnificat are: 1 S 1:11; Ps 103:17; Ps 111:9; Jb 5:11 and
12:19; Ps 98:3; Ps 107:9; Is 41:8–9. j. The name was normally given
at the time of circumcision. k. Ps 41:13 l. Lv 26:42

in his presence, all our days.

76 And you, little child,
you shall be called Prophet of the Most High,
for you will go before the Lord
to prepare the way for him.

77 To give his people knowledge of salvation
through the forgiveness of their sins;

78 this by the tender mercy of our God
who from on high will bring the rising Sun to visit us,

79 to give light to *those who live
in darkness and the shadow of death,*[m]
and to guide our feet
into the way of peace.'

The hidden life of John the Baptist

80   Meanwhile the child grew up and his spirit matured. And
he lived out in the wilderness until the day he appeared
openly to Israel.

The birth of Jesus and visit of the shepherds

2   Now at this time Caesar Augustus[a] issued a decree for a
2 census of the whole world to be taken. ·This census—the
first[b]—took place while Quirinius was governor of Syria,
3/4 and everyone went to his own town to be registered. ·So
Joseph set out from the town of Nazareth in Galilee and
travelled up to Judaea, to the town of David called Bethle-
5 hem, since he was of David's House and line, ·in order to be
registered together with Mary, his betrothed, who was with
6 child. ·While they were there the time came for her to have
7 her child, ·and she gave birth to a son, her first-born.[c] She
wrapped him in swaddling clothes, and laid him in a manger
8 because there was no room for them at the inn. ·In the
countryside close by there were shepherds who lived in the
fields and took it in turns to watch their flocks during the
9 night. ·The angel of the Lord appeared to them and the glory
10 of the Lord shone round them. They were terrified, ·but the
angel said, 'Do not be afraid. Listen, I bring you news of
11 great joy, a joy to be shared by the whole people. ·Today in
the town of David a saviour has been born to you; he is
12 Christ the Lord. ·And here is a sign for you: you will find a
baby wrapped in swaddling clothes and lying in a manger.'
13 And suddenly with the angel there was a great throng of the
heavenly host, praising God and singing:

14   'Glory to God in the highest heaven,
and peace to men who enjoy his favour'.

15   Now when the angels had gone from them into heaven, the shepherds said to one another, 'Let us go to Bethlehem and see this thing that has happened which the Lord has
16 made known to us'. ·So they hurried away and found Mary
17 and Joseph, and the baby lying in the manger. ·When they saw the child they repeated what they had been told about
18 him, ·and everyone who heard it was astonished at what the
19 shepherds had to say. ·As for Mary, she treasured all these
20 things and pondered them in her heart. ·And the shepherds went back glorifying and praising God for all they had heard and seen; it was exactly as they had been told.

The circumcision of Jesus

21   When the eighth day came and the child was to be circumcised, they gave him the name Jesus, the name the angel had given him before his conception.

Jesus is presented in the Temple

22   And when the day came for them to be purified[d] as laid down by the Law of Moses, they took him up to Jerusalem
23 to present him to the Lord—·observing what stands written in the Law of the Lord: *Every first-born male must be con-*
24 *secrated to the Lord*[e]—·and also to offer in sacrifice, in accordance with what is said in the Law of the Lord, *a pair*
25 *of turtledoves or two young pigeons.*[f] ·Now in Jerusalem there was a man named Simeon. He was an upright and devout man; he looked forward to Israel's comforting and the Holy
26 Spirit rested on him. ·It had been revealed to him by the Holy Spirit that he would not see death until he had set eyes
27 on the Christ of the Lord.[g] ·Prompted by the Spirit he came to the Temple: and when the parents brought in the child
28 Jesus to do for him what the Law required, ·he took him into his arms and blessed God; and he said:

The Nunc Dimittis

29   'Now, Master, you can let your servant go in peace,
      just as you promised;
30   because my eyes have seen the salvation
31   which you have prepared for all the nations to see,
32   a light to enlighten the pagans
      and the glory of your people Israel'.

m. Is 9:1
2 a. Emperor of Rome 30 B.C. to 14 A.D. **b.** About 8–6 B.C. **c.** The term does not necessarily imply younger brothers. **d.** The mother needed to be 'purified'; the child had to be 'redeemed'. **e.** Ex 13:2 **f.** The offering of the poor, Lv 5:7. **g.** 'The anointed one of God'.

The prophecy of Simeon

33 As the child's father and mother stood there wondering at
34 the things that were being said about him, ·Simeon blessed
them and said to Mary his mother, 'You see this child: he is
destined for the fall and for the rising of many in Israel,
35 destined to be a sign that is rejected—·and a sword will pierce
your own soul too—so that the secret thoughts of many may
be laid bare'.

The prophecy of Anna

36 There was a prophetess also, Anna the daughter of
Phanuel, of the tribe of Asher. She was well on in years. Her
days of girlhood over, she had been married for seven years
37 before becoming a widow. She was now eighty-four years
old and never left the Temple, serving God night and day
38 with fasting and prayer. ·She came by just at that moment
and began to praise God; and she spoke of the child to all
who looked forward to the deliverance of Jerusalem.[h]

The hidden life of Jesus at Nazareth

39 When they had done everything the Law of the Lord required, they went back to Galilee, to their own town of
40 Nazareth. ·Meanwhile the child grew to maturity, and he was
filled with wisdom; and God's favour was with him.

Jesus among the doctors of the Law

41 Every year his parents used to go to Jerusalem for the feast
42 of the Passover. ·When he was twelve years old, they went
43 up for the feast as usual. ·When they were on their way home
after the feast, the boy Jesus stayed behind in Jerusalem
44 without his parents knowing it. ·They assumed he was with
the caravan, and it was only after a day's journey that they
went to look for him among their relations and acquaint-
45 ances. ·When they failed to find him they went back to
Jerusalem looking for him everywhere.
46 Three days later, they found him in the Temple, sitting
among the doctors, listening to them, and asking them ques-
47 tions; ·and all those who heard him were astounded at his
48 intelligence and his replies. ·They were overcome when they
saw him, and his mother said to him, 'My child, why have
you done this to us? See how worried your father and I have
49 been, looking for you.' ·'Why were you looking for me?' he
replied 'Did you not know that I must be busy with my

50 Father's affairs?' ·But they did not understand what he meant.

The hidden life at Nazareth resumed

51   He then went down with them and came to Nazareth and lived under their authority. His mother stored up all these
52 things in her heart. ·And Jesus increased in wisdom, in stature, and in favour with God and men.

II. PRELUDE TO THE PUBLIC MINISTRY OF JESUS

The preaching of John the Baptist

3   In the fifteenth year of Tiberius Caesar's reign,[a] when Pontius Pilate[b] was governor of Judaea, Herod[c] tetrarch of Galilee, his brother Philip[d] tetrarch of the lands of Ituraea
2 and Trachonitis, Lysanias tetrarch of Abilene, ·during the pontificate of Annas and Caiaphas,[e] the word of God came
3 to John son of Zechariah, in the wilderness. ·He went through the whole Jordan district proclaiming a baptism of
4 repentance for the forgiveness of sins, ·as it is written in the book of the sayings of the prophet Isaiah:

> *A voice cries in the wilderness:*
> *Prepare a way for the Lord,*
> *make his paths straight.*
5 > *Every valley will be filled in,*
> *every mountain and hill be laid low,*
> *winding ways will be straightened*
> *and rough roads made smooth.*
6 > *And all mankind shall see the salvation of God.[f]*

7   He said, therefore, to the crowds who came to be baptised by him, 'Brood of vipers, who warned you to fly from the
8 retribution that is coming? ·But if you are repentant, produce the appropriate fruits, and do not think of telling your-

---

h. I.e. Israel. Jerusalem is the holy city.
3 a. By Roman dating, the 15th year of Tiberius Caesar's reign was August 28 A.D. to August 29 A.D.; by the Syrian method, it was Sept.–Oct. 27 A.D. to Sept.–Oct. 28 A.D. At that time, Jesus was between 33 and 36 years old. The mistake in calculating 'the Christian era' results from taking Lk 3:23 as an exact statement. **b.** Procurator of Judaea 26–36 A.D. **c.** Herod Antipas, tetrarch of Galilee and Peraea 4 B.C. to 39 A.D. **d.** Tetrarch from 4 B.C. to 34 A.D. **e.** Caiaphas was high priest from 18 to 36 A.D. His father-in-law, Annas, is associated with him here and elsewhere; he had been high priest earlier and presumably still had great influence. **f.** Is 40:3–5

selves, "We have Abraham for our father" because, I tell you, God can raise children for Abraham from these stones.

9 Yes, even now the axe is laid to the roots of the trees, so that any tree which fails to produce good fruit will be cut down and thrown on the fire.'

10 When all the people asked him, 'What must we do, then?'
11 he answered, 'If anyone has two tunics he must share with the man who has none, and the one with something to eat
12 must do the same'. ·There were tax collectors too who came for baptism, and these said to him, 'Master, what must we
13 do?' ·He said to them, 'Exact no more than your rate'.
14 Some soldiers asked him in their turn, 'What about us? What must we do?' He said to them, 'No intimidation! No extortion! Be content with your pay!'

15 A feeling of expectancy had grown among the people, who
16 were beginning to think that John might be the Christ, ·so John declared before them all, 'I baptise you with water, but someone is coming, someone who is more powerful than I am, and I am not fit to undo the strap of his sandals; he will
17 baptise you with the Holy Spirit and fire. ·His winnowing-fan is in his hand to clear his threshing-floor and to gather the wheat into his barn; but the chaff he will burn in a fire
18 that will never go out.' ·As well as this, there were many other things he said to exhort the people and to announce the Good News to them.

John the Baptist imprisoned

19 But Herod the tetrarch, whom he criticised for his relations with his brother's wife Herodias and for all the other crimes
20 Herod had committed, ·added a further crime to all the rest by shutting John up in prison.

Jesus is baptised

21 Now when all the people had been baptised and while Jesus after his own baptism was at prayer, heaven opened
22 and the Holy Spirit descended on him in bodily shape, like a dove. And a voice came from heaven, 'You are my Son, the Beloved; my favour rests on you'.

The ancestry of Jesus

23 When he started to teach, Jesus was about thirty years old, being the son, as it was thought, of Joseph son of Heli,
24 son of Matthat, son of Levi, son of Melchi, son of Jannai,
25 son of Joseph, ·son of Mattathias, son of Amos, son of
26 Nahum, son of Esli, son of Naggai, ·son of Maath, son of

Mattathias, son of Semein, son of Josech, son of Joda,
27 son of Joanan, son of Rhesa, son of Zerubbabel, son of
28 Shealtiel, son of Neri, ·son of Melchi, son of Addi, son of
29 Cosam, son of Elmadam, son of Er, ·son of Joshua, son of
30 Eliezer, son of Jorim, son of Matthat, son of Levi, ·son of
Symeon, son of Judah, son of Joseph, son of Jonam, son of
31 Eliakim, ·son of Melea, son of Menna, son of Mattatha, son
32 of Nathan, son of David, ·son of Jesse, son of Obed, son of
33 Boaz, son of Sala, son of Nahshon, ·son of Amminadab, son
of Admin, son of Arni, son of Hezron, son of Perez, son of
34 Judah, ·son of Jacob, son of Isaac, son of Abraham, son of
35 Terah, son of Nahor, ·son of Serug, son of Reu, son of Peleg,
36 son of Eber, son of Shelah, ·son of Cainan, son of Arphaxad,
37 son of Shem, son of Noah, son of Lamech, ·son of Methuselah,
son of Enoch, son of Jared, son of Mahalaleel, son of Cainan,
38 son of Enos, son of Seth, son of Adam, son of God.

Temptation in the wilderness

4   Filled with the Holy Spirit, Jesus left the Jordan and was
2 led by the Spirit through the wilderness, ·being tempted there
by the devil for forty days. During that time he ate nothing
3 and at the end he was hungry. ·Then the devil said to him,
'If you are the Son of God, tell this stone to turn into a loaf'.
4 But Jesus replied, 'Scripture says: *Man does not live on bread
alone*'.*a*

5   Then leading him to a height, the devil showed him in a
6 moment of time all the kingdoms of the world ·and said to
him, 'I will give you all this power and the glory of these
kingdoms, for it has been committed to me and I give it to
7 anyone I choose. ·Worship me, then, and it shall all be yours.'
8 But Jesus answered him, 'Scripture says:

> *You must worship the Lord your God,
> and serve him alone*'.*b*

9   Then he led him to Jerusalem and made him stand on the
parapet of the Temple. 'If you are the Son of God,' he said to
10 him 'throw yourself down from here, ·for scripture says:

> *He will put his angels in charge of you
> to guard you,*

and again:

11   *They will hold you up on their hands
> in case you hurt your foot against a stone*'.*c*

4 a. Dt 8:3 **b.** Dt 6:13 **c.** Ps 91:11–12

12 But Jesus answered him, 'It has been said:

> You must not put the Lord your God to the test'.ᵈ

13 Having exhausted all these ways of tempting him, the devil left him, to return at the appointed time.

III. THE GALILEAN MINISTRY

Jesus begins to preach

14 Jesus, with the power of the Spirit in him, returned to Galilee; and his reputation spread throughout the country-
15 side. ·He taught in their synagogues and everyone praised him.

Jesus at Nazareth

16 He came to Nazara, where he had been brought up, and went into the synagogue on the sabbath day as he usually did.
17 He stood up to read,ᵉ ·and they handed him the scroll of the prophet Isaiah. Unrolling the scroll he found the place where it is written:

18
> The spirit of the Lord has been given to me,
> for he has anointed me.
> He has sent me to bring the good news to the poor,
> to proclaim liberty to captives
> and to the blind new sight,
> to set the downtrodden free,
19 > to proclaim the Lord's year of favour.ᶠ

20 He then rolled up the scroll, gave it back to the assistant and sat down. And all eyes in the synagogue were fixed on him.
21 Then he began to speak to them, 'This text is being fulfilled
22 today even as you listen'. ·And he won the approval of all, and they were astonished by the gracious words that came from his lips.

23 They said, 'This is Joseph's son, surely?' ·But he replied, 'No doubt you will quote me the saying, "Physician, heal yourself" and tell me, "We have heard all that happened in Capernaum, do the same here in your own countryside" '.
24 And he went on, 'I tell you solemnly, no prophet is ever accepted in his own country.
25 'There were many widows in Israel, I can assure you, in Elijah's day, when heaven remained shut for three years and six months and a great famine raged throughout the land,
26 but Elijah was not sent to any one of these: he was sent *to a*
27 *widow at Zarephath, a Sidonian town.*ᵍ ·And in the prophet

Elisha's time there were many lepers in Israel, but none of these was cured, except the Syrian, Naaman.'

28 When they heard this everyone in the synagogue was
29 enraged. ·They sprang to their feet and hustled him out of the town; and they took him up to the brow of the hill their town was built on, intending to throw him down the cliff,
30 but he slipped through the crowd and walked away.

Jesus teaches in Capernaum and cures a demoniac

31 He went down to Capernaum, a town in Galilee, and
32 taught them on the sabbath. ·And his teaching made a deep impression on them because he spoke with authority.
33 In the synagogue there was a man who was possessed by the spirit of an unclean devil, and it shouted at the top of its
34 voice, ·'Ha! What do you want with us, Jesus of Nazareth? Have you come to destroy us? I know who you are: the
35 Holy One of God.' ·But Jesus said sharply, 'Be quiet! Come out of him!' And the devil, throwing the man down in front of everyone, went out of him without hurting him at all.
36 Astonishment seized them and they were all saying to one another, 'What teaching! He gives orders to unclean spirits
37 with authority and power and they come out.' ·And reports of him went all through the surrounding countryside.

Cure of Simon's mother-in-law

38 Leaving the synagogue he went to Simon's house. Now Simon's mother-in-law was suffering from a high fever and
39 they asked him to do something for her. ·Leaning over her he rebuked the fever and it left her. And she immediately got up and began to wait on them.

A number of cures

40 At sunset all those who had friends suffering from diseases of one kind or another brought them to him, and laying his
41 hands on each he cured them. ·Devils too came out of many people, howling, 'You are the Son of God'. But he rebuked them and would not allow them to speak because they knew that he was the Christ.

Jesus quietly leaves Capernaum and travels through Judaea

42 When daylight came he left the house and made his way to a lonely place. The crowds went to look for him, and when

d. Dt 6:16 **e.** Any adult man could be permitted by the president to read the scriptures. **f.** Is 61:1–2 **g.** 1K 17:9

they had caught up with him they wanted to prevent him
43 leaving them, ·but he answered, 'I must proclaim the Good
News of the kingdom of God to the other towns too, because
44 that is what I was sent to do'. ·And he continued his preaching in the synagogues of Judaea.

The first four disciples are called

5   Now he was standing one day by the Lake of Gennesaret,
with the crowd pressing round him listening to the word of
2 God, ·when he caught sight of two boats close to the bank.
The fishermen had gone out of them and were washing their
3 nets. ·He got into one of the boats—it was Simon's—and
asked him to put out a little from the shore. Then he sat down
and taught the crowds from the boat.
4   When he had finished speaking he said to Simon, 'Put out
5 into deep water and pay out your nets for a catch'. ·'Master,'
Simon replied 'we worked hard all night long and caught
6 nothing, but if you say so, I will pay out the nets.' ·And when
they had done this they netted such a huge number of fish
7 that their nets began to tear, ·so they signalled to their companions in the other boat to come and help them; when these
came, they filled the two boats to sinking point.
8   When Simon Peter saw this he fell at the knees of Jesus
9 saying, 'Leave me, Lord; I am a sinful man'. ·For he and all
his companions were completely overcome by the catch they
10 had made; ·so also were James and John, sons of Zebedee,
who were Simon's partners. But Jesus said to Simon, 'Do
11 not be afraid; from now on it is men you will catch'. ·Then,
bringing their boats back to land, they left everything and
followed him.

Cure of a leper

12   Now Jesus was in one of the towns when a man appeared,
covered with leprosy. Seeing Jesus he fell on his face and
implored him. 'Sir,' he said 'if you want to, you can cure me.'
13 Jesus stretched out his hand, touched him and said, 'Of
course I want to! Be cured!' And the leprosy left him at once.
14 He ordered him to tell no one, 'But go and show yourself to
the priest and make the offering for your healing as Moses
prescribed it, as evidence for them'.
15   His reputation continued to grow, and large crowds would
16 gather to hear him and to have their sickness cured, ·but he
would always go off to some place where he could be alone
and pray.

Cure of a paralytic

17 Now he was teaching one day, and among the audience there were Pharisees and doctors of the Law who had come from every village in Galilee, from Judaea and from Jeru-salem. And the Power of the Lord was behind his works of
18 healing. ·Then some men appeared, carrying on a bed a paralysed man whom they were trying to bring in and lay
19 down in front of him. ·But as the crowd made it impossible to find a way of getting him in, they went up on to the flat roof and lowered him and his stretcher down through the tiles
20 into the middle of the gathering, in front of Jesus. ·Seeing their faith he said, 'My friend, your sins are forgiven you'.
21 The scribes and the Pharisees began to think this over. 'Who is this man talking blasphemy? Who can forgive sins
22 but God alone?' ·But Jesus, aware of their thoughts, made them this reply, 'What are these thoughts you have in your
23 hearts? ·Which of these is easier: to say, "Your sins are for-
24 given you" or to say, "Get up and walk"? ·But to prove to you that the Son of Man has authority on earth to forgive sins,'—he said to the paralysed man—'I order you: get up,
25 and pick up your stretcher and go home.' ·And immediately before their very eyes he got up, picked up what he had been lying on and went home praising God.
26 They were all astounded and praised God, and were filled with awe, saying, 'We have seen strange things today'.

The call of Levi

27 When he went out after this, he noticed a tax collector, Levi by name, sitting by the customs house, and said to him,
28 'Follow me'. ·And leaving everything he got up and followed him.

Eating with sinners in Levi's house

29 In his honour Levi held a great reception in his house, and with them at table was a large gathering of tax collectors
30 and others. ·The Pharisees and their scribes complained to his disciples and said, 'Why do you eat and drink with tax
31 collectors and sinners?' ·Jesus said to them in reply, 'It is not
32 those who are well who need the doctor, but the sick. ·I have not come to call the virtuous, but sinners to repentance.'

Discussion on fasting

33 They then said to him, 'John's disciples are always fasting and saying prayers, and the disciples of the Pharisees too,
34 but yours go on eating and drinking'. ·Jesus replied, 'Surely

you cannot make the bridegroom's attendants fast while the
35 bridegroom is still with them? ·But the time will come, the
time for the bridegroom to be taken away from them; that
will be the time when they will fast.'

36 He also told them this parable, 'No one tears a piece from
a new cloak to put it on an old cloak; if he does, not only
will he have torn the new one, but the piece taken from the
new will not match the old.

37 'And nobody puts new wine into old skins; if he does,
the new wine will burst the skins and then run out, and the
38 skins will be lost. ·No; new wine must be put into fresh skins.
39 And nobody who has been drinking old wine wants new.
"The old is good" he says.'

Picking corn on the sabbath

6   Now one sabbath he happened to be taking a walk through
the cornfields, and his disciples were picking ears of corn,
2 rubbing them in their hands and eating them. ·Some of the
Pharisees said, 'Why are you doing something that is forbid-
3 den on the sabbath day?' ·Jesus answered them, 'So you have
not read what David did when he and his followers were
4 hungry——·how he went into the house of God, took the
loaves of offering and ate them and gave them to his fol-
5 lowers, loaves which only the priests are allowed to eat?' ·And
he said to them, 'The Son of Man is master of the sabbath'.

Cure of the man with a withered hand

6   Now on another sabbath he went into the synagogue and
began to teach, and a man was there whose right hand was
7 withered. ·The scribes and the Pharisees were watching him
to see if he would cure a man on the sabbath, hoping to find
8 something to use against him. ·But he knew their thoughts;
and he said to the man with the withered hand, 'Stand up!
Come out into the middle.' And he came out and stood
9 there. ·Then Jesus said to them, 'I put it to you: is it against
the law on the sabbath to do good, or to do evil; to save life,
10 or to destroy it?' ·Then he looked round at them all and said
to the man 'Stretch out your hand'. He did so, and his hand
11 was better. ·But they were furious, and began to discuss the
best way of dealing with Jesus.

The choice of the Twelve

12   Now it was about this time that he went out into the hills
to pray; and he spent the whole night in prayer to God.
13 When day came he summoned his disciples and picked out

14 twelve of them; he called them 'apostles'; ·Simon whom he
called Peter, and his brother Andrew; James, John, Philip,
15 Bartholomew, ·Matthew, Thomas, James son of Alphaeus,
16 Simon called the Zealot, ·Judas son of James,[a] and Judas
Iscariot who became a traitor.

The crowds follow Jesus

17 He then came down with them and stopped at a piece of
level ground where there was a large gathering of his disciples with a great crowd of people from all parts of Judaea
and from Jerusalem and from the coastal region of Tyre and
18 Sidon ·who had come to hear him and to be cured of their
diseases. People tormented by unclean spirits were also
19 cured, ·and everyone in the crowd was trying to touch him
because power came out of him that cured them all.

The inaugural discourse. The Beatitudes

20 Then fixing his eyes on his disciples he said:

'How happy are you who are poor: yours is the kingdom
of God.
21 Happy you who are hungry now: you shall be satisfied.
Happy you who weep now: you shall laugh.

22 'Happy are you when people hate you, drive you out,
abuse you, denounce your name as criminal, on account of
23 the Son of Man. ·Rejoice when that day comes and dance for
joy, for then your reward will be great in heaven. This was
the way their ancestors treated the prophets.

The curses

24 'But alas for you who are rich: you are having your
consolation now.
25 Alas for you who have your fill now: you shall go
hungry.
Alas for you who laugh now: you shall mourn and weep.

26 'Alas for you when the world speaks well of you! This was
the way their ancestors treated the false prophets.

Love of enemies

27 'But I say this to you who are listening: Love your ene-
28 mies, do good to those who hate you, ·bless those who curse
29 you, pray for those who treat you badly. ·To the man who
slaps you on one cheek, present the other cheek too; to the

6 a. Or possibly 'brother of James'.

man who takes your cloak from you, do not refuse your
30 tunic. ·Give to everyone who asks you, and do not ask for
31 your property back from the man who robs you. ·Treat
32 others as you would like them to treat you. ·If you love those
who love you, what thanks can you expect? Even sinners
33 love those who love them. ·And if you do good to those who
do good to you, what thanks can you expect? For even
34 sinners do that much. ·And if you lend to those from whom
you hope to receive, what thanks can you expect? Even
35 sinners lend to sinners to get back the same amount. ·Instead,
love your enemies and do good, and lend without any hope
· of return. You will have a great reward, and you will be sons
of the Most High, for he himself is kind to the ungrateful and
the wicked.

Compassion and generosity

36
37   'Be compassionate as your Father is compassionate. ·Do
not judge, and you will not be judged yourselves; do not
condemn, and you will not be condemned yourselves; grant
38 pardon, and you will be pardoned. ·Give, and there will be
gifts for you: a full measure, pressed down, shaken together,
and running over, will be poured into your lap; because the
amount you measure out is the amount you will be given
back.'

Integrity

39   He also told a parable to them, 'Can one blind man guide
40 another? Surely both will fall into a pit? ·The disciple is not
superior to his teacher; the fully trained disciple will always
41 be like his teacher. ·Why do you observe the splinter in your
42 brother's eye and never notice the plank in your own? ·How
can you say to your brother, "Brother, let me take out the
splinter that is in your eye", when you cannot see the plank
in your own? Hypocrite! Take the plank out of your own
eye first, and then you will see clearly enough to take out the
splinter that is in your brother's eye.
43   'There is no sound tree that produces rotten fruit, nor
44 again a rotten tree that produces sound fruit. ·For every tree
can be told by its own fruit: people do not pick figs from
45 thorns, nor gather grapes from brambles. ·A good man draws
what is good from the store of goodness in his heart; a bad
man draws what is bad from the store of badness. For a
man's words flow out of what fills his heart.

The true disciple

46   'Why do you call me, "Lord, Lord" and not do what I say?
47   'Everyone who comes to me and listens to my words and
48   acts on them—I will show you what he is like. ·He is like the
man who when he built his house dug, and dug deep, and
laid the foundations on rock; when the river was in flood it
bore down on that house but could not shake it, it was so
49   well built. ·But the one who listens and does nothing is like
the man who built his house on soil, with no foundations:
as soon as the river bore down on it, it collapsed; and what a
ruin that house became!'

Cure of the centurion's servant

7   When he had come to the end of all he wanted the people
2   to hear, he went into Capernaum. ·A centurion there had a
3   servant, a favourite of his, who was sick and near death. ·Hav-
ing heard about Jesus he sent some Jewish elders to him to
4   ask him to come and heal his servant. ·When they came to
Jesus they pleaded earnestly with him. 'He deserves this of
5   you' they said ·'because he is friendly towards our people; in
6   fact, he is the one who built the synagogue.' ·So Jesus went
with them, and was not very far from the house when the
centurion sent word to him by some friends: 'Sir,' he said
'do not put yourself to trouble; because I am not worthy to
7   have you under my roof; ·and for this same reason I did not
presume to come to you myself; but give the word and let my
8   servant be cured. ·For I am under authority myself, and have
soldiers under me; and I say to one man: Go, and he goes;
to another: Come here, and he comes; to my servant; Do
9   this, and he does it.' ·When Jesus heard these words he was
astonished at him and, turning round, said to the crowd
following him, 'I tell you, not even in Israel have I found
10   faith like this'. ·And when the messengers got back to the
house they found the servant in perfect health.

The son of the widow of Nain restored to life

11   Now soon afterwards he went to a town called Nain,
accompanied by his disciples and a great number of people.
12   When he was near the gate of the town it happened that a
dead man was being carried out for burial, the only son of
his mother, and she was a widow. And a considerable number
13   of the townspeople were with her. ·When the Lord[a] saw her

7 a. For the first time in the gospel narrative Jesus is given the title
hitherto reserved for God.

14 he felt sorry for her. 'Do not cry' he said. ·Then he went up and put his hand on the bier and the bearers stood still, and
15 he said, 'Young man, I tell you to get up'. ·And the dead man sat up and began to talk, and Jesus *gave him to his mother*.[b]
16 Everyone was filled with awe and praised God saying, 'A great prophet has appeared among us; God has visited his
17 people'. ·And this opinion of him spread throughout Judaea and all over the countryside.

The Baptist's question. Jesus commends him

18   The disciples of John gave him all this news, and John,
19 summoning two of his disciples, ·sent them to the Lord to ask, 'Are you the one who is to come, or must we wait for
20 someone else?' ·When the men reached Jesus they said, 'John the Baptist has sent us to you, to ask, "Are you the one who is to come or have we to wait for someone else?"'
21 It was just then that he cured many people of diseases and afflictions and of evil spirits, and gave the gift of sight to
22 many who were blind. ·Then he gave the messengers their answer, 'Go back and tell John what you have seen and heard: the blind see again, the lame walk, lepers are cleansed, and the deaf hear, the dead are raised to life, the Good News
23 is proclaimed to the poor ·and happy is the man who does not lose faith in me'.

24   When John's messengers had gone he began to talk to the
25 people about John, 'What did you go out into the wilderness to see? A reed swaying in the breeze? No? Then what did you go out to see? A man dressed in fine clothes? Oh no, those who go in for fine clothes and live luxuriously are to be
26 found at court! ·Then what did you go out to see? A pro-
27 phet? Yes, I tell you, and much more than a prophet: ·he is the one of whom scripture says:

> *See, I am going to send my messenger before you;*
> *he will prepare the way before you.*[c]

28   'I tell you, of all the children born of women, there is no one greater than John; yet the least in the kingdom of God
29 is greater than he is'. ·All the people who heard him, and the tax collectors too, acknowledged God's plan by accepting
30 baptism from John; ·but by refusing baptism from him the Pharisees and the lawyers had thwarted what God had in mind for them.

Jesus condemns his contemporaries

31   'What description, then, can I find for the men of this
32 generation? What are they like? ·They are like children

shouting to one another while they sit in the market place:

> "We played the pipes for you,
> and you wouldn't dance;
> we sang dirges,
> and you wouldn't cry".

33 'For John the Baptist comes, not eating bread, not drink-
34 ing wine, and you say, "He is possessed". ·The Son of Man comes, eating and drinking, and you say, "Look, a glutton and a drunkard, a friend of tax collectors and sinners".
35 Yet Wisdom has been proved right by all her children.'

The woman who was a sinner

36 One of the Pharisees invited him to a meal. When he arrived at the Pharisee's house and took his place at table,
37 a woman came in, who had a bad name in the town. She had heard he was dining with the Pharisee and had brought with
38 her an alabaster jar of ointment. ·She waited behind him at his feet, weeping, and her tears fell on his feet, and she wiped them away with her hair; then she covered his feet with kisses and anointed them with the ointment.
39 When the Pharisee who had invited him saw this, he said to himself, 'If this man were a prophet, he would know who this woman is that is touching him and what a bad name she has
40 has'. ·Then Jesus took him up and said, 'Simon, I have something to say to you'. 'Speak, Master' was the reply.
41 'There was once a creditor who had two men in his debt;
42 one owed him five hundred denarii, the other fifty. ·They were unable to pay, so he pardoned them both. Which of them will
43 love him more?' ·'The one who was pardoned more, I suppose' answered Simon. Jesus said, 'You are right'.
44 Then he turned to the woman. 'Simon,' he said 'you see this woman? I came into your house, and you poured no water over my feet, but she has poured out her tears over
45 my feet and wiped them away with her hair. ·You gave me no kiss, but she has been covering my feet with kisses ever
46 since I came in. ·You did not anoint my head with oil, but
47 she has anointed my feet with ointment. ·For this reason I tell you that her sins, her many sins, must have been forgiven her, or she would not have shown such great love. It is the
48 man who is forgiven little who shows little love.' ·Then he
49 said to her, 'Your sins are forgiven'. ·Those who were with him at table began to say to themselves, 'Who is this man,

b. 1 K 17:23 **c.** Ml 3:1

50 that he even forgives sins?' ·But he said to the woman, 'Your faith has saved you; go in peace'.

The women accompanying Jesus

8   Now after this he made his way through towns and villages preaching, and proclaiming the Good News of the kingdom
2 of God. With him went the Twelve, ·as well as certain women who had been cured of evil spirits and ailments: Mary surnamed the Magdalene, from whom seven demons had gone
3 out, ·Joanna the wife of Herod's steward Chuza, Susanna, and several others who provided for them out of their own resources.

Parable of the sower

4   With a large crowd gathering and people from every town finding their way to him, he used this parable:
5   'A sower went out to sow his seed. As he sowed, some fell on the edge of the path and was trampled on; and the birds
6 of the air ate it up. ·Some seed fell on rock, and when it came
7 up it withered away, having no moisture. ·Some seed fell amongst thorns and the thorns grew with it and choked it.
8 And some seed fell into rich soil and grew and produced its crop a hundredfold.' Saying this he cried, 'Listen, anyone who has ears to hear!'

Why Jesus speaks in parables

9   His disciples asked him what this parable might mean,
10 and he said, The mysteries of the kingdom of God are revealed to you; for the rest there are only parables, so that

> *they may see but not perceive,*
> *listen but not understand.*[a]

The parable of the sower explained

11   'This, then, is what the parable means: the seed is the word
12 of God. ·Those on the edge of the path are people who have heard it, and then the devil comes and carries away the word from their hearts in case they should believe and be saved.
13 Those on the rock are people who, when they first hear it, welcome the word with joy. But these have no root; they be-
14 lieve for a while, and in time of trial they give up. ·As for the part that fell into thorns, this is people who have heard, but as they go on their way they are choked by the worries and riches and pleasures of life and do not reach maturity.
15 As for the part in the rich soil, this is people with a noble and

generous heart who have heard the word and take it to themselves and yield a harvest through their perseverance.

Parable of the lamp

16 'No one lights a lamp to cover it with a bowl or to put it under a bed. No, he puts it on a lamp-stand so that people
17 may see the light when they come in. ·For nothing is hidden but it will be made clear, nothing secret but it will be known
18 and brought to light. ·So take care how you hear; for anyone who has will be given more; from anyone who has not, even what he thinks he has will be taken away.'

The true kinsmen of Jesus

19 His mother and his brothers came looking for him, but
20 they could not get to him because of the crowd. ·He was told, 'Your mother and brothers are standing outside and want
21 to see you'. ·But he said in answer, 'My mother and my brothers are those who hear the word of God and put it into practice'.

The calming of the storm

22 One day, he got into a boat with his disciples and said to them, 'Let us cross over to the other side of the lake'. So they
23 put to sea, ·and as they sailed he fell asleep. When a squall came down on the lake the boat started taking in water and
24 they found themselves in danger. ·So they went to rouse him saying, 'Master! Master! We are going down!' Then he woke up and rebuked the wind and the rough water; and they sub-
25 sided and it was calm again. ·He said to them, 'Where is your faith?' They were awestruck and astonished and said to one another, 'Who can this be, that gives orders even to winds and waves and they obey him?'

The Gerasene demoniac

26 They came to land in the country of the Gerasenes,[b] which
27 is opposite Galilee. ·He was stepping ashore when a man from the town who was possessed by devils came towards him; for a long time the man had worn no clothes, nor did he live in a house, but in the tombs.
28 Catching sight of Jesus he gave a shout, fell at his feet and cried out at the top of his voice, 'What do you want with me, Jesus, son of the Most High God? I implore you, do not
29 torture me.' ·—For Jesus had been telling the unclean spirit to come out of the man. It was a devil that had seized on him

8 a. Is 6:9 **b.** 'Gadarenes' in some versions.

a great many times, and then they used to secure him with chains and fetters to restrain him, but he would always break the fastenings, and the devil would drive him out into the

30 wilds. ·'What is your name?' Jesus asked. 'Legion' he said—

31 because many devils had gone into him. ·And these pleaded with him not to order them to depart into the Abyss.[c]

32 Now there was a large herd of pigs feeding there on the mountain, and the devils pleaded with him to let them go into

33 these. So he gave them leave. ·The devils came out of the man and went into the pigs, and the herd charged down the cliff into the lake and were drowned.

34 When the swineherds saw what had happened they ran off and told their story in the town and in the country round

35 about; ·and the people went out to see what had happened. When they came to Jesus they found the man from whom the devils had gone out sitting at the feet of Jesus, clothed and in

36 his full senses; and they were afraid. ·Those who had witnessed it told them how the man who had been possessed

37 came to be healed. ·The entire population of the Gerasene territory was in a state of panic and asked Jesus to leave them. So he got into the boat and went back.

38 The man from whom the devils had gone out asked to be allowed to stay with him, but he sent him away. ·'Go back home,' he said 'and report all that God has done for you.' So the man went off and spread throughout the town all that Jesus had done for him.

Cure of the woman with a haemorrhage. Jairus' daughter raised to life

40 On his return Jesus was welcomed by the crowd, for they

41 were all there waiting for him. ·And now there came a man named Jairus, who was an official of the synagogue. He fell at Jesus' feet and pleaded with him to come to his house,

42 because he had an only daughter about twelve years old, who was dying. And the crowds were almost stifling Jesus as he went.

43 Now there was a woman suffering from a haemorrhage for

44 twelve years, whom no one had been able to cure. ·She came up behind him and touched the fringe of his cloak; and the

45 haemorrhage stopped at that instant. ·Jesus said, 'Who touched me?' When they all denied that they had, Peter and his companions said, 'Master, it is the crowds round you,

46 pushing'. ·But Jesus said, 'Somebody touched me. I felt that

47 power had gone out from me.' ·Seeing herself discovered, the woman came forward trembling, and falling at his feet ex-

plained in front of all the people why she had touched him
48 and how she had been cured at that very moment. ·My
daughter,' he said 'your faith has restored you to health; go
in peace.'
49 While he was still speaking, someone arrived from the
house of the synagogue official to say, 'Your daughter has
50 died. Do not trouble the Master any further.' ·But Jesus had
heard this, and he spoke to the man, 'Do not be afraid, only
51 have faith and she will be safe'. ·When he came to the house
he allowed no one to go in with him except Peter and John
52 and James, and the child's father and mother. ·They were all
weeping and mourning for her, but Jesus said, 'Stop crying;
53 she is not dead, but asleep'. ·But they laughed at him, know-
54 ing she was dead. ·But taking her by the hand he called to
55 her, 'Child, get up'. ·And her spirit returned and she got up
56 at once. Then he told them to give her something to eat. ·Her
parents were astonished, but he ordered them not to tell
anyone what had happened.

The mission of the Twelve

9 He called the Twelve together and gave them power and
2 authority over all devils and to cure diseases, ·and he sent
3 them out to proclaim the kingdom of God and to heal. ·He
said to them, 'Take nothing for the journey: neither staff,
nor haversack, nor bread, nor money; and let none of you
4 take a spare tunic. ·Whatever house you enter, stay there;
5 and when you leave, let it be from there. ·As for those who
do not welcome you, when you leave their town shake the
6 dust from your feet as a sign to them.' ·So they set out and
went from village to village proclaiming the Good News and
healing everywhere.

Herod and Jesus

7 Meanwhile Herod the tetrarch had heard about all that
was going on; and he was puzzled, because some people
8 were saying that John had risen from the dead, ·others that
Elijah had reappeared, still others that one of the ancient
9 prophets had come back to life. ·But Herod said, 'John? I
beheaded him. So who is this I hear such reports about?' And
he was anxious to see him.

The return of the apostles. Miracle of the loaves

10 On their return the apostles gave him an account of all they
had done. Then he took them with him and withdrew to a

c. The underworld.

town called Bethsaida where they could be by themselves.
11 But the crowds got to know and they went after him. He made them welcome and talked to them about the kingdom of God; and he cured those who were in need of healing.
12   It was late afternoon when the Twelve came to him and said, 'Send the people away, and they can go to the villages and farms round about to find lodging and food; for we are
13 in a lonely place here'. ·He replied, 'Give them something to eat yourselves'. But they said, 'We have no more than five loaves and two fish, unless we are to go ourselves and buy
14 food for all these people'. ·For there were about five thousand men. But he said to his disciples, 'Get them to sit down in
15 parties of about fifty'. ·They did so and made them all sit
16 down. ·Then he took the five loaves and the two fish, raised his eyes to heaven, and said the blessing over them; then he broke them and handed them to his disciples to distribute
17 among the crowd. ·They all ate as much as they wanted, and when the scraps remaining were collected they filled twelve baskets.

Peter's profession of faith

18   Now one day when he was praying alone in the presence of his disciples he put this question to them, 'Who do the
19 crowds say I am?' ·And they answered, 'John the Baptist; others Elijah; and others say one of the ancient prophets
20 come back to life'. ·'But you,' he said 'who do you say I am?'
21 It was Peter who spoke up. 'The Christ of God' he said. ·But he gave them strict orders not to tell anyone anything about this.

First prophecy of the Passion

22   'The Son of Man' he said 'is destined to suffer grievously, to be rejected by the elders and chief priests and scribes and to be put to death, and to be raised up on the third day.'

The condition of following Christ

23   Then to all he said, 'If anyone wants to be a follower of mine, let him renounce himself and take up his cross every
24 day and follow me. ·For anyone who wants to save his life will lose it; but anyone who loses his life for my sake, that
25 man will save it. ·What gain, then, is it for a man to have won the whole world and to have lost or ruined his very self?
26 For if anyone is ashamed of me and of my words, of him the Son of Man will be ashamed when he comes in his own glory and in the glory of the Father and the holy angels.

The kingdom will come soon

27 'I tell you truly, there are some standing here who will not taste death before they see the kingdom of God.'

The transfiguration

28 Now about eight days after this had been said, he took with him Peter and John and James and went up the mountain to
29 pray. ·As he prayed, the aspect of his face was changed and
30 his clothing became brilliant as lightning. ·Suddenly there were two men there talking to him; they were Moses and
31 Elijah ·appearing in glory, and they were speaking of his
32 passing which he was to accomplish in Jerusalem. ·Peter and his companions were heavy with sleep, but they kept awake and saw his glory and the two men standing with him.
33 As these were leaving him, Peter said to Jesus, 'Master, it is wonderful for us to be here; so let us make three tents, one for you, one for Moses and one for Elijah'.—He did not
34 know what he was saying. ·As he spoke, a cloud came and covered them with shadow; and when they went into the
35 cloud the disciples were afraid. ·And a voice came from the cloud saying, 'This is my Son, the Chosen One. Listen to him.'
36 And after the voice had spoken, Jesus was found alone. The disciples kept silence and, at that time, told no one what they had seen.

The epileptic demoniac

37 Now on the following day when they were coming down
38 from the mountain a large crowd came to meet him. ·Suddenly a man in the crowd cried out. 'Master,' he said 'I implore
39 you to look at my son: he is my only child. ·All at once a spirit will take hold of him, and give a sudden cry and throw the boy into convulsions with foaming at the mouth; it is slow to leave him, but when it does it leaves the boy worn out.
40 I begged your disciples to cast it out, and they could not.'
41 'Faithless and perverse generation!' Jesus said in reply 'How much longer must I be among you and put up with you?
42 Bring your son here.' ·The boy was still moving towards Jesus when the devil threw him to the ground in convulsions. But Jesus rebuked the unclean spirit and cured the boy and
43 gave him back to his father, and everyone was awestruck by the greatness of God.

Second prophecy of the Passion

At a time when everyone was full of admiration for all he
44 did, he said to his disciples, ''For your part, you must have·

these words constantly in your mind: The Son of Man is
45 going to be handed over into the power of men'. ·But they
did not understand him when he said this; it was hidden
from them so that they should not see the meaning of it, and
they were afraid to ask him about what he had just said.

Who is the greatest?

46 An argument started between them about which of them
47 was the greatest. Jesus knew what thoughts were going
through their minds, and he took a little child and set him by
48 his side ·and then said to them, 'Anyone who welcomes this
little child in my name welcomes me; and anyone who welcomes me welcomes the one who sent me. For the least
among you all, that is the one who is great.'

On using the name of Jesus

49 John spoke up. 'Master,' he said 'we saw a man casting
out devils in your name, and because he is not with us we
50 tried to stop him.' ·But Jesus said to him, 'You must not stop
him; anyone who is not against you is for you'.

IV. THE JOURNEY TO JERUSALEM

A Samaritan village is inhospitable

51 Now as the time drew near for him to be taken up to
52 heaven, he resolutely took the road for Jerusalem ·and sent
messengers ahead of him. These set out, and they went into a
53 Samaritan village to make preparations for him, ·but the
people would not receive him because he was making for
54 Jerusalem.*ᵃ* ·Seeing this, the disciples James and John said,
'Lord, do you want us to call down fire from heaven to burn
55
56 them up?' ·But he turned and rebuked them, ·and they went
off to another village.

Hardships of the apostolic calling

57 As they travelled along they met a man on the road who
58 said to him, 'I will follow you wherever you go'. ·Jesus
answered, 'Foxes have holes and the birds of the air have
nests, but the Son of Man has nowhere to lay his head'.
59 Another to whom he said, 'Follow me', replied, 'Let me go
60 and bury my father first'. ·But he answered, 'Leave the dead
to bury their dead; your duty is to go and spread the news of
the kingdom of God'.
61 Another said, 'I will follow you, sir, but first let me go and
62 say good-bye to my people at home'. ·Jesus said to him,

'Once the hand is laid on the plough, no one who looks back is fit for the kingdom of God.'

The Mission of the seventy-two disciples

10 After this the Lord appointed seventy-two others and sent them out ahead of him, in pairs, to all the towns and places
2 he himself was to visit. ·He said to them, 'The harvest is rich but the labourers are few, so ask the Lord of the harvest to
3 send labourers to his harvest. ·Start off now, but remember,
4 I am sending you out like lambs among wolves. ·Carry no purse, no haversack, no sandals. Salute no one on the road.
5 Whatever house you go into, let your first words be, "Peace
6 to this house!" ·And if a man of peace lives there, your peace
7 will go and rest on him; if not, it will come back to you. ·Stay in the same house, taking what food and drink they have to offer, for the labourer deserves his wages; do not move from
8 house to house. ·Whenever you go into a town where they
9 make you welcome, eat what is set before you. ·Cure those in it who are sick, and say, "The kingdom of God is very near
10 to you". ·But whenever you enter a town and they do not
11 make you welcome, go out into its streets and say, '"We wipe off the very dust of your town that clings to our feet, and leave it with you. Yet be sure of this: the kingdom of God is very
12 near." ·I tell you, on that day it will not go as hard with Sodom as with that town.
13 'Alas for you, Chorazin! Alas for you, Bethsaida! For if the miracles done in you had been done in Tyre and Sidon, they would have repented long ago, sitting in sackcloth and
14 ashes. ·And still, it will not go as hard with Tyre and Sidon
15 at the Judgement as with you. ·And as for you, Capernaum, did you want to be exalted high as heaven? *You shall be thrown down to hell.*[a]
16 'Anyone who listens to you listens to me; anyone who rejects you rejects me, and those who reject me reject the one who sent me.'

True cause for the apostles to rejoice

17 The seventy-two came back rejoicing. 'Lord,' they said 'even the devils submit to us when we use your name.'
18 He said to them, 'I watched Satan fall like lightning from
19 heaven. ·Yes, I have given you power to tread underfoot serpents and scorpions and the whole strength of the enemy;

9 a. The hatred of Samaritans for Jews would show itself particularly towards those who were on pilgrimage to Jerusalem.
10 a. See Is 14:13, 15.

20 nothing shall ever hurt you. ·Yet do not rejoice that the spirits submit to you; rejoice rather that your names are written in heaven.'

The Good News revealed to the simple. The Father and the Son

21   It was then that, filled with joy by the Holy Spirit, he said, 'I bless you, Father, Lord of heaven and of earth, for hiding these things from the learned and the clever and revealing them to mere children. Yes, Father, for that is what it pleased 22 you to do. ·Everything has been entrusted to me by my Father; and no one knows who the Son is except the Father, and who the Father is except the Son and those to whom the Son chooses to reveal him.'

The privilege of the disciples

23   Then turning to his disciples he spoke to them in private, 24 'Happy the eyes that see what you see, ·for I tell you that many prophets and kings wanted to see what you see, and never saw it; to hear what you hear, and never heard it'.

The great commandment

25   There was a lawyer who, to disconcert him, stood up and said to him, 'Master, what must I do to inherit eternal life?' 26 He said to him, 'What is written in the Law? What do you 27 read there?' ·He replied, '*You must love the Lord your God with all your heart, with all your soul, with all your strength, and with all your mind, and your neighbour as yourself*'.[b] 28 'You have answered right,' said Jesus 'do this and life is yours.'

Parable of the good Samaritan

29   But the man was anxious to justify himself and said to 30 Jesus, 'And who is my neighbour?' ·Jesus replied, 'A man was once on his way down from Jerusalem to Jericho and fell into the hands of brigands; they took all he had, beat him 31 and then made off, leaving him half dead. ·Now a priest happened to be travelling down the same road, but when he 32 saw the man, he passed by on the other side. ·In the same way a Levite who came to the place saw him, and passed by on the 33 other side. ·But a Samaritan traveller who came upon him 34 was moved with compassion when he saw him. ·He went up and bandaged his wounds, pouring oil and wine on them. He then lifted him on to his own mount, carried him to the inn 35 and looked after him. ·Next day, he took out two denarii and handed them to the innkeeper. "Look after him," he said

"and on my way back I will make good any extra expense you
36 have." ·Which of these three, do you think, proved himself a
neighbour to the man who fell into the brigands' hands?'
37 'The one who took pity on him' he replied. Jesus said to him,
'Go, and do the same yourself'.

Martha and Mary

38   In the course of their journey he came to a village, and
a woman named Martha welcomed him into her house.
39 She had a sister called Mary, who sat down at the Lord's
40 feet and listened to him speaking. ·Now Martha who was
distracted with all the serving said, 'Lord, do you not care
that my sister is leaving me to do the serving all by myself?
41 Please tell her to help me.' ·But the Lord answered: 'Martha,
Martha,' he said 'you worry and fret about so many things,
42 and yet few are needed, indeed only one. It is Mary who has
chosen the better part; it is not to be taken from her.'

The Lord's prayer

11   Now once he was in a certain place praying, and when he
had finished one of his disciples said, 'Lord, teach us to
2 pray, just as John taught his disciples'. ·He said to them,
'Say this when you pray:

"Father, may your name be held holy,
      your kingdom come;
3   give us each day our daily bread,
      and forgive us our sins,
4   for we ourselves forgive each one who is in debt to us.
      And do not put us to the test."'

The importunate friend

5   He also said to them, 'Suppose one of you has a friend and
goes to him in the middle of the night to say, "My friend,
6 lend me three loaves, ·because a friend of mine on his travels
has just arrived at my house and I have nothing to offer
7 him"; ·and the man answers from inside the house, "Do not
bother me. The door is bolted now, and my children and I
8 are in bed; I cannot get up to give it you". ·I tell you, if the
man does not get up and give it him for friendship's sake,
persistence will be enough to make him get up and give his
friend all he wants.

b. Dt 6:5 and Lv 19:18

Effective prayer

9 'So I say to you: Ask, and it will be given to you; search, and you will find; knock, and the door will be opened to you.
10 For the one who asks always receives; the one who searches always finds; the one who knocks will always have the door
11 opened to him. ·What father among you would hand his son a stone when he asked for bread? Or hand him a snake
12 instead of a fish? ·Or hand him a scorpion if he asked for an
13 egg? ·If you then, who are evil, know how to give your children what is good, how much more will the heavenly Father give the Holy Spirit to those who ask him!'

Jesus and Beelzebul

14 He was casting out a devil and it was dumb; but when the devil had gone out the dumb man spoke, and the people were
15 amazed. ·But some of them said, 'It is through Beelzebul, the
16 prince of devils, that he casts out devils'. ·Others asked him,
17 as a test, for a sign from heaven; ·but, knowing what they were thinking, he said to them, 'Every kingdom divided against itself is heading for ruin, and a household divided
18 against itself collapses. ·So too with Satan: if he is divided against himself, how can his kingdom stand?—Since you assert that it is through Beelzebul that I cast out devils.
19 Now if it is through Beelzebul that I cast out devils, through whom do your own experts cast them out? Let them be your
20 judges, then. ·But if it is through the finger of God that I cast out devils, then know that the kingdom of God has
21 overtaken you. ·So long as a strong man fully armed guards
22 his own palace, his goods are undisturbed; ·but when someone stronger than he is attacks and defeats him, the stronger man takes away all the weapons he relied on and shares out his spoil.

No compromise

23 'He who is not with me is against me; and he who does not gather with me scatters.'

Return of the unclean spirit

24 'When an unclean spirit goes out of a man it wanders through waterless country looking for a place to rest, and not finding one it says, "I will go back to the home I came
25
26 from". ·But on arrival, finding it swept and tidied, ·it then goes off and brings seven other spirits more wicked than itself, and they go in and set up house there, so that the man ends up by being worse than he was before.'

The truly happy

27 Now as he was speaking, a woman in the crowd raised her voice and said, 'Happy the womb that bore you and the
28 breasts you sucked!' ·But he replied, 'Still happier those who hear the word of God and keep it!'

The sign of Jonah

29 The crowds got even bigger and he addressed them, 'This is a wicked generation; it is asking for a sign. The only sign
30 it will be given is the sign of Jonah. ·For just as Jonah became a sign to the Ninevites, so will the Son of Man be to
31 this generation. ·On Judgement day the Queen of the South will rise up with the men of this generation and condemn them, because she came from the ends of the earth to hear the wisdom of Solomon; and there is something greater than
32 Solomon here. ·On Judgement day the men of Nineveh will stand up with this generation and condemn it, because when Jonah preached they repented; and there is something greater than Jonah here.

The parable of the lamp repeated

33 'No one lights a lamp and puts it in some hidden place or under a tub, but on the lamp-stand so that people may see
34 the light when they come in. ·The lamp of your body is your eye. When your eye is sound, your whole body too is filled with light; but when it is diseased your body too will be all
35 darkness. ·See to it then that the light inside you is not dark-
36 ness, ·If, therefore, your whole body is filled with light, and no trace of darkness, it will be light entirely, as when the lamp shines on you with its rays.'

The Pharisees and the lawyers attacked

37 He had just finished speaking when a Pharisee invited him to dine at his house. He went in and sat down at the table.
38 The Pharisee saw this and was surprised that he had not first
39 washed before the meal. ·But the Lord said to him, 'Oh, you Pharisees! You clean the outside of cup and plate, while inside yourselves you are filled with extortion and wicked-
40 ness. ·Fools! Did not he who made the outside make the
41 inside too? ·Instead, give alms from what you have and then
42 indeed everything will be clean for you. ·But alas for you Pharisees! You who pay your tithe of mint and rue and all sorts of garden herbs and overlook justice and the love of God! These you should have practised, without leaving the

43 others undone. ·Alas for you Pharisees who like taking the seats of honour in the synagogues and being greeted obse-
44 quiously in the market squares! ·Alas for you, because you are like the unmarked tombs that men walk on without knowing it!*

45 A lawyer then spoke up. 'Master,' he said 'when you speak
46 like this you insult us too.' ·'Alas for you lawyers also,' he replied 'because you load on men burdens that are un-endurable, burdens that you yourselves do not move a finger to lift.

47 'Alas for you who build the tombs of the prophets, the
48 men your ancestors killed! ·In this way you both witness what your ancestors did and approve it; they did the killing, you do the building.

49 'And that is why the Wisdom of God said, "I will send them prophets and apostles; some they will slaughter and
50 persecute, ·so that this generation will have to answer for every prophet's blood that has been shed since the founda-
51 tion of the world, ·from the blood of Abel to the blood of Zechariah, who was murdered between the altar and the sanctuary". Yes, I tell you, this generation will have to answer for it all.

52 'Alas for you lawyers who have taken away the key of knowledge! You have not gone in yourselves, and have prevented others going in who wanted to.'

53 When he left the house, the scribes and the Pharisees began a furious attack on him and tried to force answers from
54 him on innumerable questions, ·setting traps to catch him out in something he might say.

Open and fearless speech

12 Meanwhile the people had gathered in their thousands so that they were treading on one another. And he began to speak, first of all to his disciples. 'Be on your guard against
2 the yeast of the Pharisees—that is, their hypocrisy. ·Every-thing that is now covered will be uncovered, and everything
3 now hidden will be made clear. ·For this reason, whatever you have said in the dark will be heard in the daylight, and what you have whispered in hidden places will be proclaimed on the housetops.

4 'To you my friends I say: Do not be afraid of those who
5 kill the body and after that can do no more. ·I will tell you whom to fear: fear him who, after he has killed, has the
6 power to cast into hell. Yes, I tell you, fear him. ·Can you not buy five sparrows for two pennies? And yet not one is for-

7 gotten in God's sight. ·Why, every hair on your head has been counted. There is no need to be afraid: you are worth more than hundreds of sparrows.

8 'I tell you, if anyone openly declares himself for me in the presence of men, the Son of Man will declare himself for him
9 in the presence of God's angels. ·But the man who disowns me in the presence of men will be disowned in the presence of God's angels.

10 'Everyone who says a word against the Son of Man will be forgiven, but he who blasphemes against the Holy Spirit will not be forgiven.

11 'When they take you before synagogues and magistrates and authorities, do not worry about how to defend your-
12 selves or what to say, ·because when the time comes, the Holy Spirit will teach you what you must say.'

On hoarding possessions

13 A man in the crowd said to him, 'Master, tell my brother
14 to give me a share of our inheritance'. ·'My friend,' he replied 'who appointed me your judge, or the arbitrator of your
15 claims?' ·Then he said to them, 'Watch, and be on your guard against avarice of any kind, for a man's life is not made secure by what he owns, even when he has more than he needs'.

16 Then he told them a parable: 'There was once a rich man
17 who, having had a good harvest from his land, ·thought to himself, "What am I to do? I have not enough room to store
18 my crops." ·Then he said, "This is what I will do: I will pull down my barns and build bigger ones, and store all my grain
19 and my goods in them, ·and I will say to my soul: My soul, you have plenty of good things laid by for many years to
20 come; take things easy, eat, drink, have a good time". ·But God said to him, "Fool! This very night the demand will be made for your soul; and this hoard of yours, whose will it be
21 then?" ·So it is when a man stores up treasure for himself in place of making himself rich in the sight of God.'

Trust in Providence

22 Then he said to his disciples, 'That is why I am telling you not to worry about your life and what you are to eat, nor
23 about your body and how you are to clothe it. ·For life means
24 more than food, and the body more than clothing. ·Think of the ravens. They do not sow or reap; they have no store-houses and no barns; yet God feeds them. And how much

11 a. Thus contracting legal impurity, Nb 19:16.

25 more are you worth than the birds! ·Can any of you, for all
26 his worrying, add a single cubit to his span of life? ·If the
smallest things, therefore, are outside your control, why
27 worry about the rest? ·Think of the flowers; they never have
to spin or weave; yet, I assure you, not even Solomon in all
28 his regalia was robed like one of these. ·Now if that is how
God clothes the grass in the field which is there today and
thrown into the furnace tomorrow, how much more will he
29 look after you, you men of little faith! ·But you, you must
not set your hearts on things to eat and things to drink; nor
30 must you worry. ·It is the pagans of this world who set their
hearts on all these things. Your Father well knows you need
31 them. ·No; set your hearts on his kingdom, and these other
things will be given you as well.
32   'There is no need to be afraid, little flock, for it has pleased
your Father to give you the kingdom.

On almsgiving

33   'Sell your possessions and give alms. Get yourselves purses
that do not wear out, treasure that will not fail you, in heaven
34 where no thief can reach it and no moth destroy it. ·For where
your treasure is, there will your heart be also.

On being ready for the Master's return

35   'See that you are dressed for action and have your lamps
36 lit. ·Be like men waiting for their master to return from the
wedding feast, ready to open the door as soon as he comes and
37 knocks. ·Happy those servants whom the master finds awake
when he comes. I tell you solemnly, he will put on an apron,
38 sit them down at table and wait on them. ·It may be in the
second watch he comes, or in the third, but happy those
39 servants if he finds them ready. ·You may be quite sure of
this, that if the householder had known at what hour the
burglar would come, he would not have let anyone break
40 through the wall of his house. ·You too must stand ready,
because the Son of Man is coming at an hour you do not
expect.'
41   Peter said, 'Lord, do you mean this parable for us, or for
42 everyone?' ·The Lord replied, 'What sort of steward,ᵃ then,
is faithful and wise enough for the master to place him over
his household to give them their allowance of food at the
43 proper time? ·Happy that servant if his master's arrival
44 finds him at this employment. ·I tell you truly, he will place
45 him over everything he owns. ·But as for the servant who
says to himself, "My master is taking his time coming",

and sets about beating the menservants and the maids, and
46 eating and drinking and getting drunk, ·his master will come
on a day he does not expect and at an hour he does not know.
The master will cut him off and send him to the same fate as
the unfaithful.

47 'The servant who knows what his master wants, but has
not even started to carry out those wishes, will receive very
48 many strokes of the lash. ·The one who did not know, but
deserves to be beaten for what he has done, will receive fewer
strokes. When a man has had a great deal given him, a great
deal will be demanded of him; when a man has had a great
deal given him on trust, even more will be expected of him.

Jesus and his Passion

49 'I have come to bring fire to the earth, and how I wish it
50 were blazing already! ·There is a baptism I must still receive,
and how great is my distress till it is over!

Jesus the cause of dissension

51 'Do you suppose that I am here to bring peace on earth?
52 No, I tell you, but rather division. ·For from now on a
household of five will be divided; three against two and two
53 against three; ·the father divided against the son, son against
father, mother against daughter, daughter against mother,
mother-in-law against daughter-in-law, daughter-in-law
against mother-in-law.'

On reading the signs of the times

54 He said again to the crowds, 'When you see a cloud loom-
ing up in the west you say at once that rain is coming, and so
55 it does. ·And when the wind is from the south you say it will
56 be hot, and it is. ·Hypocrites! You know how to interpret the
face of the earth and the sky. How is it you do not know how
to interpret these times?

57
58 'Why not judge for yourselves what is right? ·For example:
when you go to court with your opponent, try to settle with
· him on the way, or he may drag you before the judge and the
judge hand you over to the bailiff and the bailiff have you
59 thrown into prison. ·I tell you, you will not get out till you
have paid the very last penny.'

Examples inviting repentance

13 It was just about this time that some people arrived and
told him about the Galileans whose blood Pilate had mingled

12 a. I.e. a servant or employee with authority to act as his master's
deputy in his absence.

2 with that of their sacrifices.ª ·At this he said to them, 'Do you suppose these Galileans who suffered like that were
3 greater sinners than any other Galileans? ·They were not, I tell you. No; but unless you repent you will all perish as they
4 did. ·Or those eighteen on whom the tower at Siloam fell and killed them? Do you suppose that they were more guilty
5 than all the other people living in Jerusalem? ·They were not, I tell you. No; but unless you repent you will all perish as they did.'

Parable of the barren fig tree

6 He told this parable: 'A man had a fig tree planted in his vineyard, and he came looking for fruit on it but found none.
7 He said to the man who looked after the vineyard, "Look here, for three years now I have been coming to look for fruit on this fig tree and finding none. Cut it down: why
8 should it be taking up the ground?" ·"Sir," the man replied "leave it one more year and give me time to dig round it
9 and manure it: ·it may bear fruit next year; if not, then you can cut it down." '

Healing of the crippled woman on a sabbath

10 One sabbath day he was teaching in one of the synagogues,
11 and a woman was there who for eighteen years had been possessed by a spirit that left her enfeebled; she was bent double
12 and quite unable to stand upright. ·When Jesus saw her he called her over and said, 'Woman, you are rid of your
13 infirmity' ·and he laid his hands on her. And at once she straightened up, and she glorified God.
14 But the synagogue official was indignant because Jesus had healed on the sabbath, and he addressed the people present. 'There are six days' he said 'when work is to be done. Come and be healed on one of those days and not on the
15 sabbath.' ·But the Lord answered him. 'Hypocrites!' he said 'Is there one of you who does not untie his ox or his donkey from the manger on the sabbath and take it out for watering?
16 And this woman, a daughter of Abraham whom Satan has held bound these eighteen years—was it not right to untie her
17 bonds on the sabbath day?' ·When he said this, all his adversaries were covered with confusion, and all the people were overjoyed at all the wonders he worked.

Parable of the mustard seed

18 He went on to say, 'What is the kingdom of God like? What
19 shall I compare it with? ·It is like a mustard seed which a

man took and threw into his garden: it grew and became a tree, and the birds of the air sheltered in its branches.'

Parable of the yeast

20 Another thing he said, 'What shall I compare the kingdom of God with? It is like the yeast a woman took and mixed in with three measures of flour till it was leavened all through.'

The narrow door; rejection of the Jews, call of the gentiles

22 Through towns and villages he went teaching, making his
23 way to Jerusalem. ·Someone said to him, 'Sir, will there be
24 only a few saved?' He said to them, ·"Try your best to enter by the narrow door, because, I tell you, many will try to enter and will not succeed.

25 'Once the master of the house has got up and locked the door, you may find yourself knocking on the door, saying, "Lord, open to us" but he will answer, "I do not know where
26 you come from". ·Then you will find yourself saying, "We once ate and drank in your company; you taught in our
27 streets" ·but he will reply, "I do not know where you come from. *Away from me, all you wicked men?"*[b]
28 'Then there will be weeping and grinding of teeth, when you see Abraham and Isaac and Jacob and all the prophets
29 in the kingdom of God, and yourselves turned outside. ·And men from east and west, from north and south, will come to take their places at the feast in the kingdom of God.
30 'Yes, there are those now last who will be first, and those now first who will be last.'

Herod the fox

31 Just at this time some Pharisees came up. 'Go away' they said. 'Leave this place, because Herod means to kill you.'
32 He replied, 'You may go and give that fox this message: Learn that today and tomorrow I cast out devils and on the
33 third day[c] attain my end. ·But for today and tomorrow and the next day I must go on, since it would not be right for a prophet to die outside Jerusalem.

Jerusalem admonished

34 'Jerusalem, Jerusalem, you that kill the prophets and stone those who are sent to you! How often have I longed to gather your children, as a hen gathers her brood under her wings,

13 a. The author expects this incident, and that mentioned in v. 4, to be known to his readers; no other evidence of them remains. **b.** Ps 6:8 **c.** 'after a short time'.

35 and you refused! ·So be it! Your house will be left to you. Yes, I promise you, you shall not see me till the time comes when you say:

Blessings on him who comes in the name of the Lord?'[d]

Healing of a dropsical man on the sabbath

14 Now on a sabbath day he had gone for a meal to the house of one of the leading Pharisees; and they watched him closely. 2/3 There in front of him was a man with dropsy, ·and Jesus addressed the lawyers and Pharisees. 'Is it against the law' 4 he asked 'to cure a man on the sabbath, or not?' ·But they remained silent, so he took the man and cured him and sent 5 him away. ·Then he said to them, 'Which of you here, if his son falls into a well, or his ox, will not pull him out on a 6 sabbath day without hesitation?' ·And to this they could find no answer.

On choosing places at table

7 He then told the guests a parable, because he had noticed 8 how they picked the places of honour. He said this, ·'When someone invites you to a wedding feast, do not take your seat in the place of honour. A more distinguished person 9 than you may have been invited, ·and the person who invited you both may come and say, "Give up your place to this man". And then, to your embarrassment, you would 10 have to go and take the lowest place. ·No; when you are a guest, make your way to the lowest place and sit there, so that, when your host comes, he may say, "My friend, move up higher". In that way, everyone with you at the table will 11 see you honoured. ·For everyone who exalts himself will be humbled, and the man who humbles himself will be exalted.'

On choosing guests to be invited

12 Then he said to his host, 'When you give a lunch or a dinner, do not ask your friends, brothers, relations or rich neighbours, for fear they repay your courtesy by inviting you 13 in return. ·No; when you have a party, invite the poor, the 14 crippled, the lame, the blind; ·that they cannot pay you back means that you are fortunate, because repayment will be made to you when the virtuous rise again.'

The invited guests who made excuses

15 On hearing this, one of those gathered round the table said to him, 'Happy the man who will be at the feast in the king-

16 dom of God!' ·But he said to him, 'There was a man who gave a great banquet, and he invited a large number of people.
17 When the time for the banquet came, he sent his servant to say to those who had been invited, "Come along: everything
18 is ready now". ·But all alike started to make excuses. The first said, "I have bought a piece of land and must go and see
19 it. Please accept my apologies." ·Another said, "I have bought five yoke of oxen and am on my way to try them out.
20 Please accept my apologies." ·Yet another said, "I have just got married and so am unable to come".
21 'The servant returned and reported this to his master. Then the householder, in a rage, said to his servant, "Go out quickly into the streets and alleys of the town and bring
22 in here the poor, the crippled, the blind and the lame". ·"Sir," said the servant "your orders have been carried out and there
23 is still room." ·Then the master said to his servant, "Go to the open roads and the hedgerows and force people to come
24 in to make sure my house is full; ·because, I tell you, not one of those who were invited shall have a taste of my banquet".'

Renouncing all that one holds dear

25 Great crowds accompanied him on his way and he turned
26 and spoke to them. ·"If any man comes to me without hating*a* his father, mother, wife, children, brothers, sisters,
27 yes and his own life too, he cannot be my disciple. ·Anyone who does not carry his cross and come after me cannot be my disciple.

Renouncing possessions

28 'And indeed, which of you here, intending to build a tower would not first sit down and work out the cost to see if he
29 had enough to complete it? ·Otherwise, if he laid the foundation and then found himself unable to finish the work, the onlookers would all start making fun of him and saying,
30 "Here is a man who started to build and was unable to
31 finish". ·Or again, what king marching to war against another king would not first sit down and consider whether with ten thousand men he could stand up to the other who advanced
32 against him with twenty thousand? ·If not, then while the other king was still a long way off, he would send envoys to
33 sue for peace. ·So in the same way, none of you can be my disciple unless he gives up all his possessions.

d. Ps 118:26
14 a. Hebraism: an emphatic way of expressing a total detachment.

On loss of enthusiasm in a disciple

34 'Salt is a useful thing. But if the salt itself loses its taste,
35 how can it be seasoned again? ·It is good for neither soil
nor manure heap. People throw it out. Listen, anyone who
has ears to hear!

The three parables of God's mercy

15 The tax collectors and the sinners, meanwhile, were all
2 seeking his company to hear what he had to say, ·and the
Pharisees and the scribes complained. 'This man' they said
3 'welcomes sinners and eats with them.' ·So he spoke this
parable to them:

The lost sheep

4 'What man among you with a hundred sheep, losing one,
would not leave the ninety-nine in the wilderness and go after
5 the missing one till he found it? ·And when he found it, would
6 he not joyfully take it on his shoulders ·and then, when he
got home, call together his friends and neighbours? "Rejoice
with me," he would say "I have found my sheep that
7 was lost." ·In the same way, I tell you, there will be more
rejoicing in heaven over one repentant sinner than over
ninety-nine virtuous men who have no need of repentance.

The lost drachma

8 'Or again, what woman with ten drachmas would not, if
she lost one, light a lamp and sweep out the house and search
9 thoroughly till she found it? ·And then, when she had found
it, call together her friends and neighbours? "Rejoice with
me," she would say "I have found the drachma I lost."
10 In the same way, I tell you, there is rejoicing among the
angels of God over one repentant sinner.'

The lost son (the 'prodigal') and the dutiful son

11
12 He also said, 'A man had two sons. ·The younger said to
his father, "Father, let me have the share of the estate that
would come to me". So the father divided the property
13 between them. ·A few days later, the younger son got together
everything he had and left for a distant country where he
squandered his money on a life of debauchery.

14 'When he had spent it all, that country experienced a
15 severe famine, and now he began to feel the pinch, ·so he
hired himself out to one of the local inhabitants who put
16 him on his farm to feed the pigs. ·And he would willingly
have filled his belly with the husks the pigs were eating but

17 no one offered him anything. ·Then he came to his senses and said, "How many of my father's paid servants have more food than they want, and here am I dying of hunger!
18 I will leave this place and go to my father and say: Father, I
19 have sinned against heaven and against you; ·I no longer deserve to be called your son; treat me as one of your paid
20 servants." ·So he left the place and went back to his father.

'While he was still a long way off, his father saw him and was moved with pity. He ran to the boy, clasped him in his
21 arms and kissed him tenderly. ·Then his son said, "Father, I have sinned against heaven and against you. I no longer
22 deserve to be called your son." ·But the father said to his servants, "Quick! Bring out the best robe and put it on him;
23 put a ring on his finger and sandals on his feet. ·Bring the calf we have been fattening, and kill it; we are going to have
24 a feast, a celebration, ·because this son of mine was dead and has come back to life; he was lost and is found." And they began to celebrate.

25 'Now the elder son was out in the fields, and on his way back, as he drew near the house, he could hear music and
26 dancing. ·Calling one of the servants he asked what it was
27 all about. ·"Your brother has come" replied the servant "and your father has killed the calf we had fattened because
28 he has got him back safe and sound." ·He was angry then and refused to go in, and his father came out to plead with
29 him; ·but he answered his father, "Look, all these years I have slaved for you and never once disobeyed your orders, yet you never offered me so much as a kid for me to celebrate
30 with my friends. ·But, for this son of yours, when he comes back after swallowing up your property—he and his women —you kill the calf we had been fattening."
31 'The father said, "My son, you are with me always and all
32 I have is yours. ·But it was only right we should celebrate and rejoice, because your brother here was dead and has come to life; he was lost and is found." '

The crafty steward

16   He also said to his disciples, 'There was a rich man and he had a steward who was denounced to him for being wasteful
2 with his property. ·He called for the man and said, "What is this I hear about you? Draw me up an account of your stewardship because you are not to be my steward any
3 longer." ·Then the steward said to himself, "Now that my master is taking the stewardship from me, what am I to do? Dig? I am not strong enough. Go begging? I should be too

4 ashamed. ·Ah, I know what I will do to make sure that when I am dismissed from office there will be some to welcome me into their homes.''

5 'Then he called his master's debtors one by one. To the
6 first he said, "How much do you owe my master?" ·"One hundred measures of oil" was the reply. The steward said, "Here, take your bond; sit down straight away and write
7 fifty". ·To another he said, "And you, sir, how much do you owe?" "One hundred measures of wheat" was the reply. The steward said, "Here, take your bond and write eighty'.

8 'The master praised the dishonest steward for his astuteness.[a] For the children of this world are more astute in dealing with their own kind than are the children of light.'

The right use of money

9 'And so I tell you this: use money, tainted as it is, to win you friends, and thus make sure that when it fails you, they
10 will welcome you into the tents of eternity. ·The man who can be trusted in little things can be trusted in great; the man who
11 is dishonest in little things will be dishonest in great. ·If then you cannot be trusted with money, that tainted thing, who
12 will trust you with genuine riches? ·And if you cannot be trusted with what is not yours, who will give you what is your very own?

13 'No servant can be the slave of two masters; he will either hate the first and love the second, or treat the first with respect and the second with scorn. You cannot be the slave both of God and of money.'

Against the Pharisees and their love of money

14 The Pharisees, who loved money, heard all this and laughed
15 at him. ·He said to them, 'You are the very ones who pass yourselves off as virtuous in people's sight, but God knows your hearts. For what is thought highly of by men is loathsome in the sight of God.

The kingdom stormed

16 'Up to the time of John it was the Law and the Prophets; since then, the kingdom of God has been preached, and by violence everyone is getting in.

The Law remains

17 'It is easier for heaven and earth to disappear than for one little stroke to drop out of the Law.

Marriage indissoluble

18 'Everyone who divorces his wife and marries another is guilty of adultery, and the man who marries a woman divorced by her husband commits adultery.

The rich man and Lazarus

19 'There was a rich man who used to dress in purple and
20 fine linen and feast magnificently every day. ·And at his gate there lay a poor man called Lazarus, covered with sores,
21 who longed to fill himself with the scraps that fell from the rich man's table. Dogs even came and licked his sores.
22 Now the poor man died and was carried away by the angels to the bosom of Abraham. The rich man also died and was buried.
23 'In his torment in Hades he looked up and saw Abraham
24 a long way off with Lazarus in his bosom. ·So he cried out, "Father Abraham, pity me and send Lazarus to dip the tip of his finger in water and cool my tongue, for I am in agony in
25 these flames". ·"My son," Abraham replied "remember that during your life good things came your way, just as bad things came the way of Lazarus. Now he is being comforted here
26 while you are in agony. ·But that is not all: between us and you a great gulf has been fixed, to stop anyone, if he wanted to, crossing from our side to yours, and to stop any crossing from your side to ours."
27 'The rich man replied, "Father, I beg you then to send
28 Lazarus to my father's house, ·since I have five brothers, to give them warning so that they do not come to this place of
29 torment too". ·"They have Moses and the prophets," said
30 Abraham "let them listen to them." ·"Ah no, father Abraham," said the rich man "but if someone comes to them from
31 the dead, they will repent." ·Then Abraham said to him, "If they will not listen either to Moses or to the prophets, they will not be convinced even if someone should rise from the dead".'

On leading others astray

17 He said to his disciples, 'Obstacles are sure to come, but
2 alas for the one who provides them! ·It would be better for him to be thrown into the sea with a millstone put round his neck than that he should lead astray a single one of these
3 little ones. ·Watch yourselves!

16 a. Not for his dishonesty.

Brotherly correction

'If your brother does something wrong, reprove him and,
4 if he is sorry, forgive him. ·And if he wrongs you seven times
a day and seven times comes back to you and says, "I am
sorry", you must forgive him.'

The power of faith

5
6   The apostles said to the Lord, 'Increase our faith'. ·The
Lord replied, 'Were your faith the size of a mustard seed you
could say to this mulberry tree, "Be uprooted and planted in
the sea", and it would obey you.

Humble service

7   'Which of you, with a servant ploughing or minding sheep,
would say to him when he returned from the fields, "Come
8 and have your meal immediately"? ·Would he not be more
likely to say, "Get my supper laid; make yourself tidy and
wait on me while I eat and drink. You can eat and drink
9 yourself afterwards"? ·Must he be grateful to the servant for
10 doing what he was told? ·So with you: when you have done
all you have been told to do, say, "We are merely servants:
we have done no more than our duty".'

The ten lepers

11   Now on the way to Jerusalem he travelled along the border
12 between Samaria and Galilee.ᵃ ·As he entered one of the
villages, ten lepers came to meet him. They stood some way
13 off ·and called to him, 'Jesus! Master! Take pity on us.'
14 When he saw them he said, 'Go and show yourselves to the
priests'. Now as they were going away they were cleansed.
15 Finding himself cured, one of them turned back praising
16 God at the top of his voice ·and threw himself at the feet of
17 Jesus and thanked him. The man was a Samaritan. ·This
made Jesus say, 'Were not all ten made clean? The other
18 nine, where are they? ·It seems that no one has come back to
19 give praise to God, except this foreigner.' ·And he said to
the man, 'Stand up and go on your way. Your faith has
saved you.'

The coming of the kingdom of God

20   Asked by the Pharisees when the kingdom of God was to
come, he gave them this answer, 'The coming of the kingdom
21 of God does not admit of observation ·and there will be no
one to say, "Look here! Look there!" For, you must know,
the kingdom of God is among you.'

The day of the Son of Man

22 He said to the disciples, 'A time will come when you will long to see one of the days of the Son of Man and will not see
23 it. ·They will say to you, "Look there!" or, "Look here!"
24 Make no move; do not set off in pursuit; ·for as the lightning flashing from one part of heaven lights up the other, so will
25 be the Son of Man when his day comes. ·But first he must suffer grievously and be rejected by this generation.

26 'As it was in Noah's day, so will it also be in the days of
27 the Son of Man. ·People were eating and drinking, marrying wives and husbands, right up to the day Noah went into the
28 ark, and the Flood came and destroyed them all. ·It will be the same as it was in Lot's day: people were eating and drink-
29 ing, buying and selling, planting and building, ·but the day Lot left Sodom, God rained fire and brimstone from heaven
30 and it destroyed them all. ·It will be the same when the day comes for the Son of Man to be revealed.

31 'When that day comes, anyone on the housetop, with his possessions in the house, must not come down to collect
32 them, nor must anyone in the fields turn back either. ·Re-
33 member Lot's wife. ·Anyone who tries to preserve his life
34 will lose it; and anyone who loses it will keep it safe. ·I tell you, on that night two will be in one bed: one will be taken,
35 the other left; ·two women will be grinding corn together:
37 one will be taken, the other left.' ·The disciples interrupted. 'Where, Lord?' they asked. He said, 'Where the body is, there too will the vultures gather'.

The unscrupulous judge and the importunate widow

18 Then he told them a parable about the need to pray con-
2 tinually and never lose heart. ·'There was a judge in a certain town' he said 'who had neither fear of God nor respect for
3 man. ·In the same town there was a widow who kept on coming to him and saying, "I want justice from you against
4 my enemy!" ·For a long time he refused, but at last he said to himself, "Maybe I have neither fear of God nor respect for
5 man, ·but since she keeps pestering me I must give this widow her just rights, or she will persist in coming and worry me to death".'

6 And the Lord said, 'You notice what the unjust judge has to
7 say? ·Now will not God see justice done to his chosen who cry to him day and night even when he delays to help them?

17 **a.** Making for the Jordan valley and Jericho; from there he goes up to Jerusalem.

8 I promise you, he will see justice done to them, and done speedily. But when the Son of Man comes, will he find any faith on earth?'

The Pharisee and the publican

9 He spoke the following parable to some people who prided themselves on being virtuous and despised everyone else,
10 'Two men went up to the Temple to pray, one a Pharisee, the
11 other a tax collector. ·The Pharisee stood there and said this prayer to himself, "I thank you, God, that I am not grasping, unjust, adulterous like the rest of mankind, and particularly
12 that I am not like this tax collector here. ·I fast twice a week; I
13 pay tithes on all I get." ·The tax collector stood some distance away, not daring even to raise his eyes to heaven; but he beat his breast and said, "God, be merciful to me, a sinner".
14 This man, I tell you, went home again at rights with God; the other did not. For everyone who exalts himself will be humbled, but the man who humbles himself will be exalted.'

Jesus and the children

15 People even brought little children to him, for him to touch them; but when the disciples saw this they turned them
16 away. ·But Jesus called the children to him and said, 'Let the little children come to me, and do not stop them; for it
17 is to such as these that the kingdom of God belongs. ·I tell you solemnly, anyone who does not welcome the kingdom of God like a little child will never enter it.'

The rich aristocrat

18 A member of one of the leading families put this question to him, 'Good Master, what have I to do to inherit eternal life?'
19 Jesus said to him, 'Why do you call me good? No one is good
20 but God alone. ·You know the commandments: *You must not commit adultery; You must not kill; You must not steal; You must not bring false witness; Honour your father and*
21 *mother*.' ·He replied, 'I have kept all these from my earliest
22 days till now'. ·And when Jesus heard this he said, 'There is still one thing you lack. Sell all that you own and distribute the money to the poor, and you will have treasure in heaven;
23 then come, follow me.' ·But when he heard this he was filled with sadness, for he was very rich.

The danger of riches

24 Jesus looked at him and said, 'How hard it is for those who have riches to make their way into the kingdom of God!

25 Yes, it is easier for a camel to pass through the eye of a needle
26 than for a rich man to enter the kingdom of God.' ·'In that
27 case' said the listeners 'who can be saved?' ·'Things that are
impossible for men' he replied 'are possible for God.'

The reward of renunciation

28   Then Peter said, 'What about us? We left all we had to
29 follow you.' ·He said to them, 'I tell you solemnly, there is
no one who has left house, wife, brothers, parents or children
30 for the sake of the kingdom of God ·who will not be given
repayment many times over in this present time and, in the
world to come, eternal life'.

Third prophecy of the Passion

31   Then taking the Twelve aside he said to them, 'Now we are
going up to Jerusalem, and everything that is written by the
32 prophets about the Son of Man is to come true. ·For he will
be handed over to the pagans and will be mocked, maltreated
33 and spat on, ·and when they have scourged him they will
put him to death; and on the third day he will rise again.'
34 But they could make nothing of this; what he said was quite
obscure to them, they had no idea what it meant.

Entering Jericho: the blind man

35   Now as he drew near to Jericho there was a blind man
36 sitting at the side of the road begging. ·When he heard the
37 crowd going past he asked what it was all about, ·and they
38 told him that Jesus the Nazarene was passing by. ·So he called
39 out, 'Jesus, Son of David, have pity on me'. ·The people in
front scolded him and told him to keep quiet, but he shouted
40 all the louder, 'Son of David, have pity on me'. ·Jesus stopped
and ordered them to bring the man to him, and when he came
41 up, asked him, ·'What do you want me to do for you?' 'Sir,'
42 he replied 'let me see again.' ·Jesus said to him, 'Receive your
43 sight. Your faith has saved you.' ·And instantly his sight
returned and he followed him praising God, and all the
people who saw it gave praise to God for what had happened.

Zacchaeus

19   He entered Jericho and was going through the town ·when
a man whose name was Zacchaeus made his appearance; he
3 was one of the senior tax collectors and a wealthy man. ·He
was anxious to see what kind of man Jesus was, but he was too
4 short and could not see him for the crowd; ·so he ran ahead
and climbed a sycamore tree to catch a glimpse of Jesus

5 who was to pass that way. ·When Jesus reached the spot he
looked up and spoke to him: 'Zacchaeus, come down. Hurry,
6 because I must stay at your house today.' ·And he hurried
7 down and welcomed him joyfully. ·They all complained when
they saw what was happening. 'He has gone to stay at a
8 sinner's house' they said. ·But Zacchaeus stood his ground
and said to the Lord, 'Look, sir, I am going to give half my
property to the poor, and if I have cheated anybody I will
9 pay him back four times the amount'.*a* ·And Jesus said to him,
'Today salvation has come to this house, because this man
10 too is a son of Abraham;*b* ·for the Son of Man has come to
seek out and save what was lost'.

Parable of the pounds

11   While the people were listening to this he went on to tell a
parable, because he was near Jerusalem and they imagined
that the kingdom of God was going to show itself then and
12 there. ·Accordingly he said, 'A man of noble birth went to a
distant country to be appointed king and afterwards return.*c*
13 He summoned ten of his servants and gave them ten pounds.
"Do business with these" he told them "until I get back."
14 But his compatriots detested him and sent a delegation to
follow him with this message, "We do not want this man to be
our king".

15   'Now on his return, having received his appointment as
king, he sent for those servants to whom he had given the
16 money, to find out what profit each had made. ·The first came
17 in and said, "Sir, your one pound has brought in ten". ·"Well
done, my good servant!" he replied "Since you have proved
yourself faithful in a very small thing, you shall have the
18 government of ten cities." ·Then came the second and said,
19 "Sir, your one pound has made five". ·To this one also he
20 said, "And you shall be in charge of five cities". ·Next came
the other and said, "Sir, here is your pound. I put it away
21 safely in a piece of linen ·because I was afraid of you; for you
are an exacting man: you pick up what you have not put
22 down and reap what you have not sown." ·"You wicked
servant!" he said "Out of your own mouth I condemn you.
So you knew I was an exacting man, picking up what I have
23 not put down and reaping what I have not sown? ·Then why
did you not put my money in the bank? On my return I
24 could have drawn it out with interest." ·And he said to those
standing by, "Take the pound from him and give it to the
25 man who has ten pounds". ·And they said to him, "But, sir,
26 he has ten pounds . . ." ·"I tell you, to everyone who has will

be given more; but from the man who has not, even what he
has will be taken away.
27   "But as for my enemies who did not want me for their
king, bring them here and execute them in my presence." '

V. THE JERUSALEM MINISTRY

The Messiah enters Jerusalem

28   When he had said this he went on ahead, going up to
29 Jerusalem. ·Now when he was near Bethphage and Bethany,
close by the Mount of Olives as it is called, he sent two of the
30 disciples, telling them, ·"Go off to the village opposite, and
as you enter it you will find a tethered colt that no one has
31 yet ridden. Untie it and bring it here. ·If anyone asks you,
"Why are you untying it?" you are to say this, "The Master
32 needs it".' ·The messengers went off and found everything
33 just as he had told them. ·As they were untying the colt, its
34 owner said, 'Why are you untying that colt?' ·and they
answered, 'The Master needs it'.
35   So they took the colt to Jesus, and throwing their garments
36 over its back they helped Jesus on to it. ·As he moved off,
37 people spread their cloaks in the road, ·and now, as he was
approaching the downward slope of the Mount of Olives,
the whole group of disciples joyfully began to praise God at
38 the top of their voices for all the miracles they had seen. ·They
cried out:

> 'Blessings on the King who comes,
>   in the name of the Lord!
> Peace in heaven
>   and glory in the highest heavens!'

Jesus defends his disciples for acclaiming him

39   Some Pharisees in the crowd said to him, 'Master, check
40 your disciples', ·but he answered, 'I tell you, if these keep
silence the stones will cry out'.

Lament for Jerusalem

41   As he drew near and came in sight of the city he shed
42 tears over it ·and said, 'If you in your turn had only understood on this day the message of peace! But, alas, it is hidden

19 a. I.e. at the highest rate known to Jewish law (Ex 21:37) or the
rate imposed by Roman law on convicted thieves. **b.** Although he
belongs to a profession generally ranked with pagans. **c.** Probably
alluding to the journey of Archelaus to Rome in 4 B.C. to have the will
of Herod the Great confirmed in his favour. A deputation of Jews
followed him there to contest his claim.

43 from your eyes! ·Yes, a time is coming when your enemies will raise fortifications all round you, when they will en-
44 circle you and hem you in on every side; ·they will dash you and the children inside your walls to the ground; they will leave not one stone standing on another within you—and all because you did not recognise your opportunity when God offered it!'

The expulsion of the dealers from the Temple

45 Then he went into the Temple and began driving out those
46 who were selling. ·'According to scripture,' he said '*my house will be a house of prayer.*[d] But you have turned it into *a robbers' den.*'[e]

Jesus teaches in the Temple

47 He taught in the Temple every day. The chief priests and the scribes, with the support of the leading citizens, tried to
48 do away with him, ·but they did not see how they could carry this out because the people as a whole hung on his words.

The Jews question the authority of Jesus

20 Now one day while he was teaching the people in the Temple and proclaiming the Good News, the chief priests
2 and the scribes came up, together with the elders, ·and spoke to him. 'Tell us' they said 'what authority have you for acting
3 like this? Or who is it that gave you this authority?' ·'And I'
4 replied Jesus 'will ask you a question. Tell me: ·John's bap-
5 tism: did it come from heaven, or from man?' ·And they argued it out this way among themselves, 'If we say from heaven, he will say, "Why did you refuse to believe him?";
6 and if we say from man, the people will stone us, for they are
7 convinced that John was a prophet'. ·So their reply was that
8 they did not know where it came from. ·And Jesus said to them, 'Nor will I tell you my authority for acting like this'.

Parable of the wicked husbandmen

9 And he went on to tell the people this parable: 'A man planted a vineyard and leased it to tenants, and went abroad
10 for a long while. ·When the time came, he sent a servant to the tenants to get his share of the produce of the vineyard from them. But the tenants thrashed him, and sent him away
11 empty-handed. ·But he persevered and sent a second servant; they thrashed him too and treated him shamefully and sent
12 him away empty-handed. ·He still persevered and sent a third;

13 they wounded this one also, and threw him out. ·Then the
owner of the vineyard said, "What am I to do? I will send
14 them my dear son. Perhaps they will respect him." ·But when
the tenants saw him they put their heads together. "This is the
heir," they said "let us kill him so that the inheritance will be
15 ours." ·So they threw him out of the vineyard and killed
him.

16   'Now what will the owner of the vineyard do to them? ·He
will come and make an end of these tenants and give the
17 vineyard to others.' Hearing this they said, 'God forbid!' ·But
he looked hard at them and said, 'Then what does this text
in the scriptures mean:

> *It was the stone rejected by the builders*
> *that became the keystone?*[a]

18 Anyone who falls on that stone will be dashed to pieces;
anyone it falls on will be crushed.'
19   But for their fear of the people, the scribes and the chief
priests would have liked to lay hands on him that very
moment, because they realised that this parable was aimed at
them.

On tribute to Caesar

20   So they waited their opportunity and sent agents to pose
as men devoted to the Law, and to fasten on something he
might say and so enable them to hand him over to the juris-
21 diction and authority of the governor. ·They put to him this
question, 'Master, we know that you say and teach what is
right; you favour no one, but teach the way of God in all
22 honesty. ·Is it permissible for us to pay taxes to Caesar or
23 not?' ·But he was aware of their cunning and said, ·"Show
24 me a denarius. Whose head and name are on it?' 'Caesar's'
25 they said. ·'Well then,' he said to them 'give back to Caesar
what belongs to Caesar—and to God what belongs to God.'
26   As a result, they were unable to find fault with anything
he had to say in public; his answer took them by surprise and
they were silenced.

The resurrection of the dead

27   Some Sadducees—those who say that there is no resurrection—approached him and they put this question to him,
28 'Master, we have it from Moses in writing, that if a man's
married brother dies childless, the man must marry the widow

d. Is 56:7 e. Jr 7:11
20 a. Ps 118:22

29 to raise up children for his brother. ·Well then, there were
30 seven brothers. The first, having married a wife, died child-
31 less. ·The second ·and then the third married the widow. And
32 the same with all seven, they died leaving no children. ·Finally
33 the woman herself died. ·Now, at the resurrection, to which
of them will she be wife since she has been married to all
seven?'

34   Jesus replied, 'The children of this world take wives and
35 husbands, ·but those who are judged worthy of a place in the
other world and in the resurrection from the dead do not
36 marry ·because they can no longer die, for they are the same
as the angels, and being children of the resurrection they are
37 sons of God. ·And Moses himself implies that the dead rise
again, in the passage about the bush where he calls the Lord
the God of Abraham, the God of Isaac and the God of Jacob.[b]
38 Now he is God, not of the dead, but of the living; for to
him all men are in fact alive.'

39   Some scribes[c] then spoke up. 'Well put, Master' they said
40 —because they would not dare to ask him any more questions.

Christ, not only son but also Lord of David

41   He then said to them, 'How can people maintain that the
42 Christ is son of David? ·Why, David himself says in the
Book of Psalms:

> *The Lord said to my Lord:*
> *Sit at my right hand*
43 > *and I will make your enemies*
> *a footstool for you.*[d]

44 David here calls him Lord; how then can he be his son?'

The scribes condemned by Jesus

45   While all the people were listening he said to the disciples,
46 'Beware of the scribes who like to walk about in long robes
and love to be greeted obsequiously in the market squares,
to take the front seats in the synagogues and the places of
47 honour at banquets, ·who swallow the property of widows,
while making a show of lengthy prayers. The more severe
will be the sentence they receive.'

The widow's mite

21   As he looked up he saw rich people putting their offerings
2 into the treasury; ·then he happened to notice a poverty-
3 stricken widow putting in two small coins, ·and he said, 'I

tell you truly, this poor widow has put in more than any of
4 them; ·for these have all contributed money they had over,
but she from the little she had has put in all she had to live
on'.

Discourse on the destruction of Jerusalem:[a] Introduction

5   When some were talking about the Temple, remarking
how it was adorned with fine stonework and votive offerings,
6 he said, ·"All these things you are staring at now—the time
will come when not a single stone will be left on another:
7 everything will be destroyed'. ·And they put to him this
question: 'Master,' they said 'when will this happen, then,
and what sign will there be that this is about to take place?'

The warning signs

8   'Take care not to be deceived,' he said 'because many will
come using my name and saying, "I am he" and, "The time
9 is near at hand". Refuse to join them. ·And when you hear
of wars and revolutions, do not be frightened, for this is
something that must happen but the end is not so soon.'
10 Then he said to them, 'Nation will fight against nation, and
11 kingdom against kingdom. ·There will be great earthquakes
and plagues and famines here and there; there will be fearful
sights and great signs from heaven.
12   'But before all this happens, men will seize you and persecute you; they will hand you over to the synagogues and to
imprisonment, and bring you before kings and governors
13 because of my name ·—and that will be your opportunity to
14 bear witness. ·Keep this carefully in mind: you are not to
15 prepare your defence, ·because I myself shall give you an
eloquence and a wisdom that none of your opponents will
16 be able to resist or contradict. ·You will be betrayed even by
parents and brothers, relations and friends; and some of you
17 will be put to death. ·You will be hated by all men on account
18
19 of my name, ·but not a hair of your head will be lost. ·Your
endurance will win you your lives.

The siege

20   'When you see Jerusalem surrounded by armies, you must
21 realise that she will soon be laid desolate. ·Then those in
Judaea must escape to the mountains, those inside the city

b. Ex 3:6 **c.** Most scribes were Pharisees and believed in the resurrection of the dead. **d.** Ps 110:1
21 a. This passage on the End Time also includes some elements of a
prophecy of the destruction of Jerusalem.

must leave it, and those in country districts must not take
22 refuge in it. ·For this is the time of vengeance when all that
23 scripture says[b] must be fulfilled. ·Alas for those with child,
or with babies at the breast, when those days come!

The disaster and the age of the pagans

'For great misery will descend on the land and wrath on
24 this people. ·They will fall by the edge of the sword and be
led captive to every pagan country; and Jerusalem will be
trampled down by the pagans until the age of the pagans is
completely over.

Cosmic disasters and the coming of the Son of Man

25   'There will be signs in the sun and moon and stars; on
earth nations in agony, bewildered by the clamour of the
26 ocean and its waves; ·men dying of fear as they await what
menaces the world, for the powers of heaven will be shaken.
27 And then they will see the Son of Man coming in a cloud with
28 power and great glory. ·When these things begin to take place,
stand erect, hold your heads high, because your liberation[c]
is near at hand.'

The time of this coming

29   And he told them a parable, 'Think of the fig tree and in-
30 deed every tree. ·As soon as you see them bud, you know that
31 summer is now near. ·So with you when you see these things
32 happening: know that the kingdom of God is near. ·I tell you
solemnly, before this generation has passed away all will have
33 taken place. ·Heaven and earth will pass away, but my words
will never pass away.

Be on the alert

34   'Watch yourselves, or your hearts will be coarsened with
debauchery and drunkenness and the cares of life, and that
35 day will be sprung on you suddenly, ·like a trap. For it will
36 come down on every living man on the face of the earth. ·Stay
awake, praying at all times for the strength to survive all that
is going to happen, and to stand with confidence before the
Son of Man.'

The last days of Jesus

37   In the daytime he would be in the Temple teaching, but
would spend the night on the hill called the Mount of
38 Olives. ·And from early morning the people would gather
round him in the Temple to listen to him.

VI. THE PASSION

The conspiracy against Jesus: Judas betrays him

22 The feast of Unleavened Bread, called the Passover, was
2 now drawing near, ·and the chief priests and the scribes
were looking for some way of doing away with him, because
they mistrusted the people.
3 Then Satan entered into Judas, surnamed Iscariot, who
4 was numbered among the Twelve. ·He went to the chief
priests and the officers of the guard*ᵃ* to discuss a scheme for
5 handing Jesus over to them. ·They were delighted and agreed
6 to give him money. ·He accepted, and looked for an opportunity to betray him to them without the people knowing.

Preparation for the Passover supper

7 The day of Unleavened Bread came round, the day on
8 which the passover had to be sacrificed, ·and he sent Peter
and John, saying, 'Go and make the preparations for us to
9 eat the passover'. ·'Where do you want us to prepare it?' they
10 asked. ·'Listen,' he said 'as you go into the city you will meet
a man carrying a pitcher of water. Follow him into the house
11 he enters ·and tell the owner of the house, "The Master has
this to say to you: Where is the dining room in which I can
12 eat the passover with my disciples?" ·The man will show you
a large upper room furnished with couches. Make the
13 preparations there.' ·They set off and found everything as he
had told them, and prepared the Passover.

The supper

14 When the hour came he took his place at table, and the
15 apostles with him. ·And he said to them, 'I have longed to eat
16 this passover with you before I suffer; ·because, I tell you,
I shall not eat it again until it is fulfilled in the kingdom of
God'.
17 Then, taking a cup,*ᵇ* he gave thanks and said, 'Take this
18 and share it among you, ·because from now on, I tell you, I
shall not drink wine until the kingdom of God comes'.

The institution of the Eucharist

19 Then he took some bread, and when he had given thanks,
broke it and gave it to them, saying, 'This is my body which
20 will be given for you; do this as a memorial of me'. ·He did

b. Possibly alluding to Dn 9:27. **c.** Or 'redemption'.
22 a. The Temple police, chosen from among the Levites. **b.** Luke dis-
tinguishes the Passover and the cup of vv. 15–18 from the bread and
the cup of vv. 19–20.

the same with the cup after supper, and said, 'This cup is the new covenant in my blood which will be poured out for you.

The treachery of Judas foretold

21 'And yet, here with me on the table is the hand of the man
22 who betrays me. ·The Son of Man does indeed go to his fate even as it has been decreed, but alas for that man by whom
23 he is betrayed!' ·And they began to ask one another which of them it could be who was to do this thing.

Who is the greatest?

24 A dispute arose also between them about which should be
25 reckoned the greatest, ·but he said to them, 'Among pagans it is the kings who lord it over them, and those who have
26 authority over them are given the title Benefactor. ·This must not happen with you. No; the greatest among you must behave as if he were the youngest, the leader as if he were
27 the one who serves. ·For who is the greater: the one at table or the one who serves? The one at table, surely? Yet here am I among you as one who serves!

The reward promised to the apostles

28 'You are the men who have stood by me faithfully in my
29 trials; ·and now I confer a kingdom on you, just as my Father
30 conferred one on me: ·you will eat and drink at my table in my kingdom, and you will sit on thrones to judge the twelve tribes of Israel.

Peter's denial and repentance foretold

31 'Simon, Simon! Satan, you must know, has got his wish to
32 sift you all like wheat; ·but I have prayed for you, Simon, that your faith may not fail, and once you have recovered,
33 you in your turn must strengthen your brothers.' ·'Lord,' he answered 'I would be ready to go to prison with you, and
34 to death.' ·Jesus replied, 'I tell you, Peter, by the time the cock crows today you will have denied three times that you know me'.

A time of crisis

35 He said to them, 'When I sent you out without purse or
36 haversack or sandals, were you short of anything? ·'No' they said. He said to them, 'But now if you have a purse, take it; if you have a haversack, do the same; if you have no sword,
37 sell your cloak and buy one, ·because I tell you these words of scripture have to be fulfilled in me: *He let himself be taken for a criminal.*[c] Yes, what scripture says about me is even now

38 reaching its fulfilment.' ·'Lord,' they said 'there are two swords here now.' He said to them, 'That is enough!'

The Mount of Olives

39 He then left to make his way as usual to the Mount of
40 Olives, with the disciples following. ·When they reached the place he said to them, 'Pray not to be put to the test'.
41 Then he withdrew from them, about a stone's throw away,
42 and knelt down and prayed. ·'Father,' he said 'if you are willing, take this cup away from me. Nevertheless, let your
43 will be done, not mine.' ·Then an angel appeared to him,
44 coming from heaven to give him strength. ·In his anguish he prayed even more earnestly, and his sweat fell to the ground like great drops of blood.
45 When he rose from prayer he went to the disciples and
46 found them sleeping for sheer grief. ·'Why are you asleep?' he said to them. 'Get up and pray not to be put to the test.'

The arrest

47 He was still speaking when a number of men appeared, and at the head of them the man called Judas, one of the
48 Twelve, who went up to Jesus to kiss him. ·Jesus said, 'Judas,
49 are you betraying the Son of man with a kiss?' ·His followers, seeing what was happening, said, 'Lord, shall we use our
50 swords?' ·And one of them struck out at the high priest's
51 servant, and cut off his right ear. ·But at this Jesus spoke. 'Leave off!' he said 'That will do!' And touching the man's ear he healed him.
52 Then Jesus spoke to the chief priests and captains of the Temple guard and elders who had come for him. 'Am I a brigand' he said 'that you had to set out with swords and
53 clubs? ·When I was among you in the Temple day after day you never moved to lay hands on me. But this is your hour; this is the reign of darkness.'

Peter's denials

54 They seized him then and led him away, and they took him to the high priest's house. Peter followed at a distance.
55 They had lit a fire in the middle of the courtyard and Peter
56 sat down among them ·and as he was sitting there by the blaze a servant-girl saw him, peered at him, and said, 'This
57 person was with him too'. ·But he denied it. 'Woman,' he
58 said 'I do not know him.' ·Shortly afterwards someone else saw him and said, 'You are another of them'. But Peter
59 replied, 'I am not, my friend'. ·About an hour later another

c. Is 53:12

man insisted, saying, 'This fellow was certainly with him.
60 Why, he is a Galilean.' ·'My friend,' said Peter 'I do not know
what you are talking about.' At that instant, while he was
61 still speaking, the cock crew, ·and the Lord turned and
looked straight at Peter, and Peter remembered what the
Lord had said to him, 'Before the cock crows today, you will
62 have disowned me three times'. ·And he went outside and
wept bitterly.

Jesus mocked by the guards

63 Meanwhile the men who guarded Jesus were mocking and
64 beating him. ·They blindfolded him and questioned him.
65 'Play the prophet' they said. 'Who hit you then?' ·And they
continued heaping insults on him.

Jesus before the Sanhedrin

66 When day broke there was a meeting of the elders of the
people, attended by the chief priests and scribes. He was
67 brought before their council, ·and they said to him, 'If you
68 are the Christ, tell us'. 'If I tell you,' he replied 'you will not
69 believe me, ·and if I question you, you will not answer. ·But
from now on, the Son of Man will be *seated at the right hand
of the Power of God.'* [d] ·Then they all said, 'So you are the
70 Son of God then?' He answered, 'It is you who say I am'.
71 'What need of witnesses have we now?' they said. 'We have
heard it for ourselves from his own lips.'

23 The whole assembly then rose, and they brought him before Pilate.

Jesus before Pilate

2 They began their accusation by saying, 'We found this man
inciting our people to revolt, opposing payment of the tribute
3 to Caesar, and claiming to be Christ, a king'. ·Pilate put to
him this question, 'Are you the king of the Jews?' 'It is you
4 who say it' he replied. ·Pilate then said to the chief priests and
5 the crowd, 'I find no case against this man'. ·But they persisted, 'He is inflaming the people with his teaching all over
Judaea; it has come all the way from Galilee, where he
6 started, down to here'. ·When Pilate heard this, he asked if
7 the man were a Galilean; ·and finding that he came under
Herod's jurisdiction he passed him over to Herod who was
also in Jerusalem at that time.

Jesus before Herod

8 Herod was delighted to see Jesus; he had heard about him
and had been wanting for a long time to set eyes on him;

moreover, he was hoping to see some miracle worked by him.
9 So he questioned him at some length; but without getting
10 any reply. ·Meanwhile the chief priests and the scribes were
11 there, violently pressing their accusations. ·Then Herod,
together with his guards, treated him with contempt and
made fun of him; he put a rich cloak[a] on him and sent him
12 back to Pilate. ·And though Herod and Pilate had been
enemies before, they were reconciled that same day.

Jesus before Pilate again

13 Pilate then summoned the chief priests and the leading
14 men and the people. ·'You brought this man before me' he
said 'as a political agitator. Now I have gone into the matter
myself in your presence and found no case against the man in
15 respect of all the charges you bring against him. ·Nor has
Herod either, since he has sent him back to us. As you can
16 see, the man has done nothing that deserves death, ·so I shall
18 have him flogged and then let him go.' ·But as one man they
19 howled, 'Away with him! Give us Barabbas!' ·(This man had
been thrown into prison for causing a riot in the city and for
murder.)
20 Pilate was anxious to set Jesus free and addressed them
21 again, ·but they shouted back, 'Crucify him! Crucify him!'
22 And for the third time he spoke to them, 'Why? What harm
has this man done? I have found no case against him that
deserves death, so I shall have him punished and then let him
23 go.' ·But they kept on shouting at the top of their voices,
demanding that he should be crucified. And their shouts were
growing louder.
24 Pilate then gave his verdict: their demand was to be
25 granted. ·He released the man they asked for, who had been
imprisoned for rioting and murder, and handed Jesus over to
them to deal with as they pleased.

The way to Calvary

26 As they were leading him away they seized on a man,
Simon from Cyrene, who was coming in from the country,
and made him shoulder the cross and carry it behind Jesus.
27 Large numbers of people followed him, and of women too,[b]
28 who mourned and lamented for him. ·But Jesus turned to
them and said, 'Daughters of Jerusalem, do not weep for me;
29 weep rather for yourselves and for your children. ·For the

d. Ps 110:1
23 a. Ceremonial dress of a prince. b. The Talmud records that noble-
women of Jerusalem used to give soothing drinks to condemned
·criminals.

days will surely come when people will say, "Happy are those
who are barren, the wombs that have never borne, the breasts
30 that have never suckled!" ·Then they will begin to *say to the*
31 *mountains*, "*Fall on us!*"; *to the hills*, "*Cover us!*"[c] ·For if
men use the green wood like this, what will happen when it is
32 dry?' ·Now with him they were also leading out two other
criminals to be executed.

The crucifixion

33 When they reached the place called The Skull, they crucified him there and the two criminals also, one on the right,
34 the other on the left. ·Jesus said, 'Father forgive them; they
do not know what they are doing'. Then they cast lots to
share out his clothing.

The crucified Christ is mocked

35 The people stayed there watching him. As for the leaders,
they jeered at him. 'He saved others,' they said 'let him save
36 himself if he is the Christ of God, the Chosen One.' ·The
soldiers mocked him too, and when they approached to
37 offer him vinegar ·they said, 'If you are the king of the Jews,
38 save yourself'. ·Above him there was an inscription: 'This is
the King of the Jews'.

The good thief

39 One of the criminals hanging there abused him. 'Are you
40 not the Christ?' he said. 'Save yourself and us as well.' ·But
the other spoke up and rebuked him. 'Have you no fear of
God at all?' he said. 'You got the same sentence as he did,
41 but in our case we deserved it: we are paying for what we did.
42 But this man has done nothing wrong. ·Jesus,' he said 're-
43 member me when you come into your kingdom.' ·'Indeed, I
promise you,' he replied 'today you will be with me in paradise.'

The death of Jesus

44 It was now about the sixth hour and, with the sun eclipsed,
a darkness came over the whole land until the ninth hour.
45 The veil of the Temple was torn right down the middle;
46 and when Jesus had cried out in a loud voice, he said, 'Father,
into your hands I commit my spirit'.[d] With these words he
breathed his last.

After the death

47 When the centurion saw what had taken place, he gave
praise to God and said, 'This was a great and good man'.

48 And when all the people who had gathered for the spectacle saw what had happened, they went home beating their breasts.

49 All his friends stood at a distance; so also did the women who had accompanied him from Galilee, and they saw all this happen.

The burial

50 Then a member of the council arrived, an upright and
51 virtuous man named Joseph. ·He had not consented to what the others had planned and carried out. He came from Arimathaea, a Jewish town, and he lived in the hope of seeing
52 the kingdom of God. ·This man went to Pilate and asked for
53 the body of Jesus. ·He then took it down, wrapped it in a shroud and put him in a tomb which was hewn in stone in
54 which no one had yet been laid. ·It was Preparation Day and the sabbath was imminent.

55 Meanwhile the women who had come from Galilee with Jesus were following behind. They took note of the tomb and of the position of the body.

56 Then they returned and prepared spices and ointments. And on the sabbath day they rested, as the Law required.

VII. AFTER THE RESURRECTION

The empty tomb. The angel's message

24 On the first day of the week, at the first sign of dawn, they
2 went to the tomb with the spices they had prepared. ·They
3 found that the stone had been rolled away from the tomb, ·but on entering discovered that the body of the Lord Jesus was
4 not there. ·As they stood there not knowing what to think, two men in brilliant clothes suddenly appeared at their side.
5 Terrified, the women lowered their eyes. But the two men said to them, 'Why look among the dead for someone who is
6 alive? ·He is not here; he has risen. Remember what he told
7 you when he was still in Galilee: ·that the Son of Man had to be handed over into the power of sinful men and be cruci-
8 fied, and rise again on the third day.' ·And they remembered his words.

The apostles refuse to believe the women

9 When the women returned from the tomb they told all
10 this to the Eleven and to all the others. ·The women were Mary of Magdala, Joanna, and Mary the mother of James. The
11 other women with them also told the apostles, ·but this story of theirs seemed pure nonsense, and they did not believe them.

c. Ho 10:8 **d.** Ps 31:5

Peter at the tomb

12 Peter, however, went running to the tomb. He bent down and saw the binding cloths but nothing else; he then went back home, amazed at what had happened.

The road to Emmaus

13 That very same day, two of them were on their way to a
14 village called Emmaus, seven miles*a* from Jerusalem, ·and they were talking together about all that had happened.
15 Now as they talked this over, Jesus himself came up and
16 walked by their side; ·but something prevented them from
17 recognising him. ·He said to them, 'What matters are you discussing as you walk along?'' They stopped short, their faces downcast.
18 Then one of them, called Cleopas, answered him, 'You must be the only person staying in Jerusalem who does not know the things that have been happening there these last
19 few days'. ·'What things?' he asked. 'All about Jesus of Nazareth' they answered 'who proved he was a great prophet by the things he said and did in the sight of God and of
20 the whole people; ·and how our chief priests and our leaders handed him over to be sentenced to death, and had him
21 crucified. ·Our own hope had been that he would be the one to set Israel free. And this is not all: two whole days have
22 gone by since it all happened; ·and some women from our group have astounded us: they went to the tomb in the early
23 morning, ·and when they did not find the body, they came back to tell us they had seen a vision of angels who declared
24 he was alive. ·Some of our friends went to the tomb and found everything exactly as the women had reported, but of him they saw nothing.'
25 Then he said to them, 'You foolish men! So slow to believe
26 the full message of the prophets! ·Was it not ordained that
27 the Christ should suffer and so enter into his glory?' ·Then, starting with Moses and going through all the prophets, he explained to them the passages throughout the scriptures that were about himself.
28 When they drew near to the village to which they were
29 going, he made as if to go on; ·but they pressed him to stay with them. 'It is nearly evening' they said 'and the day is
30 almost over.' So he went in to stay with them. ·Now while he was with them at table, he took the bread and said the bless-
31 ing; then he broke it and handed it to them. ·And their eyes were opened and they recognised him; but he had vanished

32 from their sight. Then they said to each other, 'Did not our
hearts burn within us as he talked to us on the road and
explained the scriptures to us?'
33   They set out that instant and returned to Jerusalem. There
they found the Eleven assembled together with their com-
34 panions, ·who said to them, 'Yes, it is true. The Lord has
35 risen and has appeared to Simon.' ·Then they told their
story of what had happened on the road and how they had
recognised him at the breaking of bread.

Jesus appears to the apostles

36   They were still talking about all this when he himself stood
37 among them and said to them, 'Peace be with you!' ·In a
state of alarm and fright, they thought they were seeing a
38 ghost. ·But he said, 'Why are you so agitated, and why are
39 these doubts rising in your hearts? ·Look at my hands and
feet; yes, it is I indeed. Touch me and see for yourselves; a
40 ghost has no flesh and bones as you can see I have.' ·And as
41 he said this he showed them his hands and feet. ·Their joy
was so great that they still could not believe it, and they stood
there dumbfounded; so he said to them, 'Have you anything
42 here to eat?' ·And they offered him a piece of grilled fish,
43 which he took and ate before their eyes.

Last instructions to the apostles

44   Then he told them, 'This is what I meant when I said,
while I was still with you, that everything written about me in
the Law of Moses, in the Prophets and in the Psalms, has to
45 be fulfilled'. ·He then opened their minds to understand the
46 scriptures, ·and he said to them, 'So you see how it is written
that the Christ would suffer and on the third day rise from
47 the dead, ·and that, in his name, repentance for the forgiveness of sins would be preached to all the nations, beginning
48 from Jerusalem. ·You are witnesses to this.
49   'And now I am sending down to you what the Father has
promised. Stay in the city then, until you are clothed with the
power from on high.'

The ascension

50   Then he took them out as far as the outskirts of Bethany,
51 and lifting up his hands he blessed them. ·Now as he blessed
them, he withdrew from them and was carried up to heaven.
52 They worshipped him and then went back to Jerusalem full
53 of joy; ·and they were continually in the Temple praising God.
   24 a. The identity of the village is disputed.

INTRODUCTION TO
THE GOSPEL AND LETTERS OF
SAINT JOHN

Date, authorship and form of the gospel

Tradition almost unanimously names John the apostle, the son of Zebedee, as the author. Before A.D. 150 the book was known and used by Ignatius of Antioch, Papias, Justin and the author of the *Odes of Solomon*, and the first explicit testimony is by Irenaeus, c. 180: 'Last of all John, too, the disciple of the Lord who leant against his breast, himself brought out a gospel while he was in Ephesus'. The gospel itself has much supporting evidence, apart from its claim to be the work of an eye-witness who was a beloved disciple of the Lord: its vocabulary and style betray its semitic origin, it is familiar with Jewish customs and with the topography of Palestine, and its author is evidently a close friend of Peter.

It was published not by John himself but by his disciples after his death, and it is possible that in this gospel we have the end-stage of a slow process that has brought together not only component parts of different ages but also corrections, additions and sometimes more than one revision of the same discourse. The arrangement of the gospel is not always easy to explain, but it is clear that the author attaches special importance to the Jewish liturgical feasts which punctuate his narrative; the following analysis can be made:

    Prologue (1:1–18)
   I. *First week* of the messianic ministry, ending with the first miracle at Cana (1:19–2:11)
  II. *First Passover* with accompanying events, ending with the second miracle at Cana (2:12–4:54)
 III. *Sabbath 'of the paralytic'* (5:1–47)
 IV. *The Passover 'of the bread of life'* and its discourse (6:1–71)
  V. *The feast of Tabernacles* and the man born blind (7:1–10:21)
 VI. *The feast of Dedication* and the raising of Lazarus (10:22–11:54)
VII. *Week of the Passion* and the crucifixion Passover (11:55–19:42)

VIII. *The resurrection* and week of appearances (20:1–29)
 IX. *Appendix*: the Church and Christ's return (ch. 21)

This division suggests that Christ not only fulfilled the Jewish liturgy but in doing so brought it to an end.

Special characteristics of the gospel

The fourth gospel is concerned to bring out the significance of all that Christ did and said. The things that he did were 'signs', and the meaning of them, hidden at first, could be understood only after his glorification; the things he said had a deeper meaning not perceived at the time but understood only after the Spirit who spoke in the name of the risen Christ had come to 'lead' his disciples 'into all truth'. The gospel is revelation at this stage of development.

The whole of John's thought is dominated by the mystery of the Incarnation, from the Prologue with which the book opens. Here the revelation of Christ's glory, which in the synoptic gospels is associated primarily with his return at the end of time, has a new interpretation: judgement is working here and now in the soul, and eternal life (John's counterpart to the 'kingdom' of the synoptic gospels) is made to be something actually present, already in the possession of those who have faith. God's victory over evil, his salvation of the world, is already guaranteed by Christ's resurrection in glory.

The letters

The three letters are like the gospel in style and doctrine. The first, an encyclical letter to the Christian communities of 'Asia', summarises the whole content of John's religious experience and develops themes from the gospel, for churches threatened with disintegration under the impact of the early heresies. The second letter was written to a church in answer to some who had denied the reality of the Incarnation. The third, which is probably the earliest in date, was written to settle a dispute on jurisdiction in one of the churches acknowledging John's authority.

THE GOSPEL

ACCORDING TO

SAINT JOHN

PROLOGUE

1 In the beginning was the Word:
the Word was with God
and the Word was God.

2 He was with God in the beginning.

3 Through him all things came to be,
not one thing had its being but through him.

4 All that came to be had life in him
and that life was the light of men,

5 a light that shines in the dark,
a light that darkness could not overpower.[a]

6 A man came, sent by God.
His name was John.

7 He came as a witness,
as a witness to speak for the light,
so that everyone might believe through him.

8 He was not the light,
only a witness to speak for the light.

9 The Word was the true light
that enlightens all men;
and he was coming into the world.

10 He was in the world
that had its being through him,
and the world did not know him.

11 He came to his own domain
and his own people did not accept him.

12 But to all who did accept him
he gave power to become children of God,
to all who believe in the name of him

13 who was born not out of human stock
or urge of the flesh
or will of man

but of God himself.

14 The Word was made flesh,
he lived among us,[b]
and we saw his glory,
the glory that is his as the only Son of the Father,
full of grace and truth.

15 John appears as his witness. He proclaims:
'This is the one of whom I said:
He who comes after me
ranks before me
because he existed before me'.

16 Indeed, from his fulness we have, all of us, received—
yes, grace in return for grace,
17 since, though the Law was given through Moses,
grace and truth have come through Jesus Christ.
18 No one has ever seen God;
it is the only Son, who is nearest to the Father's heart,
who has made him known.

I. THE FIRST PASSOVER

A. THE OPENING WEEK

The witness of John

19 This is how John appeared as a witness. When the Jews[c]
sent priests and Levites from Jerusalem to ask him, 'Who are
20 you?' ·he not only declared, but he declared quite openly, 'I
21 am not the Christ'. ·'Well then,' they asked, 'are you Elijah?'[d]
'I am not' he said. 'Are you the Prophet?'[e] He answered,
22 'No'. ·So they said to him, 'Who are you? We must take
back an answer to those who sent us. What have you to say
23 about yourself?' ·So John said, 'I am, as Isaiah prophesied:

> *a voice that cries in the wilderness:*
> *Make a straight way for the Lord'.*[f]

25
24 Now these men had been sent by the Pharisees, ·and they put
this further question to him, 'Why are you baptising if you
are not the Christ, and not Elijah, and not the prophet?'
26 John replied, 'I baptise with water; but there stands among

1 a. Or 'grasp', in the sense of 'enclose' or 'understand'. **b.** 'pitched
his tent among us'. **c.** In Jn this usually indicates the Jewish religious
authorities who were hostile to Jesus; but occasionally the Jews as a
whole. **d.** Whose return was expected, Ml 3:23–24. **e.** The Prophet
greater than Moses who was expected as Messiah, on an interpretation
of Dt 18:15. **f.** Is 40:3

27 you—unknown to you—·the one who is coming after me;
28 and I am not fit to undo his sandal-strap'. ·This happened at
Bethany, on the far side of the Jordan, where John was
baptising.

29   The next day, seeing Jesus coming towards him, John said,
'Look, there is the lamb of God that takes away the sin of the
30 world. ·This is the one I spoke of when I said: A man is
coming after me who ranks before me because he existed
31 before me. ·I did not know him myself, and yet it was to
32 reveal him to Israel that I came baptising with water.' ·John
also declared, 'I saw the Spirit coming down on him from
33 heaven like a dove and resting on him. ·I did not know him
myself, but he who sent me to baptise with water had said to
me, "The man on whom you see the Spirit come down and
rest is the one who is going to baptise with the Holy Spirit".
34 Yes, I have seen and I am the witness that he is the Chosen
One of God.'

The first disciples

35   On the following day as John stood there again with two of
36 his disciples, ·Jesus passed, and John stared hard at him and
37 said, 'Look, there is the lamb of God'. ·Hearing this, the two
38 disciples followed Jesus. ·Jesus turned round, saw them
following and said, 'What do you want?' They answered,
'Rabbi,'—which means Teacher—'where do you live?'
39 'Come and see' he replied; so they went and saw where he
lived, and stayed with him the rest of that day. It was about
the tenth hour.*g*
40   One of these two who became followers of Jesus after
hearing what John had said was Andrew, the brother of
41 Simon Peter. ·Early next morning, Andrew met his brother
and said to him, 'We have found the Messiah'—which means
42 the Christ—·and he took Simon to Jesus. Jesus looked hard
at him and said, 'You are Simon son of John; you are to be
called Cephas'—meaning Rock.
43   The next day, after Jesus had decided to leave for Galilee,
44 he met Philip and said, 'Follow me'. ·Philip came from the
45 same town, Bethsaida, as Andrew and Peter. ·Philip found
Nathanael*h* and said to him, 'We have found the one Moses
wrote about in the Law, the one about whom the prophets
46 wrote: he is Jesus son of Joseph, from Nazareth'. ·'From
Nazareth?' said Nathanael 'Can anything good come from
47 that place?' 'Come and see' replied Philip. ·When Jesus saw
Nathanael coming he said of him, 'There is an Israelite who
48 deserves the name, incapable of deceit'. ·'How do you know

me?' said Nathanael. 'Before Philip came to call you,' said
49 Jesus 'I saw you under the fig tree.' ·Nathanael answered,
'Rabbi, you are the Son of God, you are the King of Israel'.
50 Jesus replied, 'You believe that just because I said: I saw you
under the fig tree. You will see greater things than that.'
51 And then he added, 'I tell you most solemnly, you will see
heaven laid open and, above the Son of Man, the angels of
God ascending and descending'. .

The wedding at Cana

2   Three days later there was a wedding at Cana in Galilee.
2 The mother of Jesus was there, ·and Jesus and his disciples
3 had also been invited. ·When they ran out of wine, since the
wine provided for the wedding was all finished, the mother of
4 Jesus said to him, 'They have no wine'. ·Jesus said, 'Woman,
5 why turn to me? My hour has not come yet.' ·His mother said
6 to the servants, '*Do whatever he tells you*'.*a* ·There were six
stone water jars standing there, meant for the ablutions that
are customary among the Jews: each could hold twenty or
7 thirty gallons. ·Jesus said to the servants, 'Fill the jars with
8 water', and ·they filled them to the brim. ·'Draw some out
9 now' he told them 'and take it to the steward.' ·They did this;
the steward tasted the water, and it had turned into wine.
Having no idea where it came from—only the servants who
had drawn the water knew—the steward called the bride-
10 groom ·and said, 'People generally serve the best wine first,
and keep the cheaper sort till the guests have had plenty to
drink; but you have kept the best wine till now'.
11   This was the first of the signs given by Jesus: it was given at
Cana in Galilee. He let his glory be seen, and his disciples
12 believed in him. ·After this he went down to Capernaum
with his mother and the brothers, but they stayed there only
a few days.

B. THE PASSOVER

The cleansing of the Temple

13   Just before the Jewish Passover Jesus went up to Jerusalem,
14 and in the Temple he found people selling cattle and sheep
and pigeons, and the money changers sitting at their counters
15 there. ·Making a whip out of some cord, he drove them all
out of the Temple, cattle and sheep as well, scattered the
16 money changers' coins, knocked their tables over ·and said to
the pigeon-sellers, 'Take all this out of here and stop turning

g. 4 p.m. h. Probably the Bartholomew of the other gospels.
2 a. Gn 41:55

17 my Father's house into a market'. ·Then his disciples remembered the words of scripture: *Zeal for your house will devour*
18 *me.*[b] ·The Jews intervened and said, 'What sign can you show
19 us to justify what you have done?' ·Jesus answered, 'Destroy
20 this sanctuary, and in three days I will raise it up'. ·The Jews
replied, 'It has taken forty-six years to build this sanctuary:[c]
21 are you going to raise it up in three days?' ·But he was
22 speaking of the sanctuary that was his body, ·and when Jesus
rose from the dead, his disciples remembered that he had
said this, and they believed the scripture and the words he had
said.

23   During his stay in Jerusalem for the Passover many believed in his name when they saw the signs that he gave,
24 but Jesus knew them all and did not trust himself to them;
25 he never needed evidence about any man; he could tell what
a man had in him.

C. THE MYSTERY OF THE SPIRIT REVEALED
TO A MASTER IN ISRAEL

The conversation with Nicodemus

3   There was one of the Pharisees called Nicodemus, a lead-
2 ing Jew, ·who came to Jesus by night and said, 'Rabbi, we
know that you are a teacher who comes from God; for no
one could perform the signs that you do unless God were
3 with him'. ·Jesus answered:

> 'I tell you most solemnly,
> unless a man is born from above,
> he cannot see the kingdom of God'.

4 Nicodemus said, 'How can a grown man be born? Can he go
5 back into his mother's womb and be born again?' ·Jesus
replied:

> 'I tell you most solemnly,
> unless a man is born through water and the Spirit,
> he cannot enter the kingdom of God:
6 > what is born of the flesh is flesh;
> what is born of the Spirit is spirit.
7 > Do not be surprised when I say:
> You must be born from above.
8 > The wind blows wherever it pleases;
> you hear its sound,
> but you cannot tell where it comes from or where it is
> going.
> That is how it is with all who are born of the Spirit.'

⁹
¹⁰   'How can that be possible?' asked Nicodemus. 'You, a
teacher in Israel, and you do not know these things!' replied
Jesus.

11   'I tell you most solemnly,
we speak only about what we know
and witness only to what we have seen
and yet you people reject our evidence.

12   If you do not believe me
when I speak about things in this world,
how are you going to believe me
when I speak to you about heavenly things?

13   No one has gone up to heaven
except the one who came down from heaven,
the Son of Man who is in heaven;
and the Son of Man must be lifted up

14   as Moses lifted up the serpent in the desert,

15   so that everyone who believes may have eternal life in
        him.

16   Yes, God loved the world so much
that he gave his only Son,
so that everyone who believes in him may not be lost
but may have eternal life.

17   For God sent his Son into the world
not to condemn the world,
but so that through him the world might be saved.

18   No one who believes in him will be condemned;
but whoever refuses to believe is condemned already,
because he has refused to believe
in the name of God's only Son.

19   On these grounds is sentence pronounced:
that though the light has come into the world
men have shown they prefer
darkness to the light
because their deeds were evil.

20   And indeed, everybody who does wrong
hates the light and avoids it,
for fear his actions should be exposed;

21   but the man who lives by the truth
comes out into the light,
so that it may be plainly seen that what he does is done
        in God.'

b. Ps 69:9 **c.** Reconstruction work on the Temple began in 19 B.C.
This is therefore the Passover of 28 A.D.

II. JOURNEYS IN SAMARIA AND GALILEE

John bears witness for the last time

22   After this, Jesus went with his disciples into the Judaean
23 countryside and stayed with them there and baptised. ·At the
same time John was baptising at Aenon*a* near Salim, where
there was plenty of water, and people were going there to be
24 baptised. ·This was before John had been put in prison.
25   Now some of John's disciples had opened a discussion with
26 a Jew about purification, ·so they went to John and said,
'Rabbi, the man who was with you on the far side of the
Jordan, the man to whom you bore witness, is baptising now;
27 and everyone is going to him'. ·John replied:

'A man can lay claim
only to what is given him from heaven.

28 'You yourselves can bear me out: I said: I myself am not the
Christ; I am the one who has been sent in front of him.

29   'The bride is only for the bridegroom;
       and yet the bridegroom's friend,
       who stands there and listens,
       is glad when he hears the bridegroom's voice.
       This same joy I feel, and now it is complete.
30   He must grow greater,
       I must grow smaller.
31   He who comes from above
       is above all others;
       he who is born of the earth
       is earthly himself and speaks in an earthly way.
       He who comes from heaven
32   bears witness to the things he has seen and heard,
       even if his testimony is not accepted;
33   though all who do accept his testimony
       are attesting the truthfulness of God,
       since he whom God has sent
       speaks God's own words:
       God gives him the Spirit without reserve.
       The Father loves the Son
       and has entrusted everything to him.
       Anyone who believes in the Son has eternal life,
       but anyone who refuses to believe in the Son will never
         see life:
       the anger of God stays on him.'

The saviour of the world revealed to the Samaritans

4 When Jesus heard that the Pharisees had found out that he
2 was making and baptising more disciples than John—·though
in fact it was his disciples who baptised, not Jesus himself—
3
4 he left Judaea and went back to Galilee. ·This meant that he
had to cross Samaria.

5 On the way he came to the Samaritan town called Sychar,*ᵃ*
6 near the land that Jacob gave to his son Joseph. ·Jacob's well
is there and Jesus, tired by the journey, sat straight down by
7 the well. It was about the sixth hour.*ᵇ* ·When a Samaritan
woman came to draw water, Jesus said to her, 'Give me a
8 drink'. ·His disciples had gone into the town to buy food.
9 The Samaritan woman said to him, 'What? You are a Jew
and you ask me, a Samaritan, for a drink?'—Jews, in fact, do
10 not associate with Samaritans. ·Jesus replied:

'If you only knew what God is offering
and who it is that is saying to you:
Give me a drink,
you would have been the one to ask,
and he would have given you living water'.

11 'You have no bucket, sir,' she answered 'and the well is
12 deep: how could you get this living water? ·Are you a
greater man than our father Jacob who gave us this well and
13 drank from it himself with his sons and his cattle?' ·Jesus
replied:

'Whoever drinks this water
will get thirsty again;
14 but anyone who drinks the water that I shall give
will never be thirsty again:
the water that I shall give
will turn into a spring inside him, welling up to eternal
life'.

15 'Sir,' said the woman 'give me some of that water, so that
I may never get thirsty and never have to come here again to
16 draw water.' ·'Go and call your husband' said Jesus to her
17 'and come back here.' ·The woman answered, 'I have no
husband'. He said to her, 'You are right to say, "I have no
18 husband"; ·for although you have had five, the one you have

3 a. A tradition locates Aenon ('Springs') in the Jordan valley 7 m.
from Scythopolis.
4 a. Either Shechem (Aramaic: Sichara), or Askar at the foot of Mt
Ebal. 'Jacob's Well' is not mentioned in Gn. b. Noon.

19 now is not your husband. You spoke the truth there.' ·'I see
20 you are a prophet, sir' said the woman. ·'Our fathers worshipped on this mountain,[c] while you say that Jerusalem is
21 the place where one ought to worship.' ·Jesus said:

> 'Believe me, woman, the hour is coming
> when you will worship the Father
> neither on this mountain nor in Jerusalem.
22 You worship what you do not know;
> we worship what we do know;
> for salvation comes from the Jews.
23 But the hour will come—in fact it is here already—
> when true worshippers will worship the Father in spirit
> and truth:
> that is the kind of worshipper
> the Father wants.
24 God is spirit,
> and those who worship
> must worship in spirit and truth.'

25 The woman said to him, 'I know that Messiah—that is,
Christ—is coming; and when he comes he will tell us every-
26 thing'. ·'I who am speaking to you,' said Jesus 'I am he.'
27 At this point his disciples returned, and were surprised to
find him speaking to a woman, though none of them asked,
'What do you want from her?' or, 'Why are you talking to
28 her?' ·The woman put down her water jar and hurried back
29 to the town to tell the people, ·'Come and see a man who has
told me everything I ever did; I wonder if he is the Christ?'
30 This brought people out of the town and they started walking
towards him.
31 Meanwhile, the disciples were urging him, 'Rabbi, do have
32 something to eat'; ·but he said, 'I have food to eat that you
33 do not know about'. ·So the disciples asked one another,
34 'Has someone been bringing him food?' ·But Jesus said:

> 'My food
> is to do the will of the one who sent me,
> and to complete his work.
35 Have you not got a saying:
> Four months and then the harvest?
> Well, I tell you:
> Look around you, look at the fields;
> already they are white, ready for harvest!
36 Already ·the reaper is being paid his wages,
> already he is bringing in the grain for eternal life,

and thus sower and reaper rejoice together.
37 For here the proverb holds good:
one sows, another reaps;
38 I sent you to reap
a harvest you had not worked for.
Others worked for it;
and you have come into the rewards of their trouble.'

39 Many Samaritans of that town had believed in him on the strength of the woman's testimony when she said, 'He told
40 me all I have ever done', ·so, when the Samaritans came up to him, they begged him to stay with them. He stayed for two
41 days, and ·when he spoke to them many more came to
42 believe; ·and they said to the woman, 'Now we no longer believe because of what you told us; we have heard him ourselves and we know that he really is the saviour of the world'.

The cure of the nobleman's son

43 When the two days were over Jesus left for Galilee. ·He
44 himself had declared that there is no respect for a prophet in
45 his own country, ·but on his arrival the Galileans received him well, having seen all that he had done at Jerusalem during the festival which they too had attended.
46 He went again to Cana in Galilee, where he had changed the water into wine. Now there was a court official there
47 whose son was ill at Capernaum ·and, hearing that Jesus had arrived in Galilee from Judaea, he went and asked him to
48 come and cure his son as he was at the point of death. ·Jesus said, 'So you will not believe unless you see signs and por-
49 tents!' ·'Sir,' answered the official 'come down before my
50 child dies.' ·'Go home,' said Jesus 'your son will live.' The man believed what Jesus had said and started on his way;
51 and while he was still on the journey back his servants met
52 him with the news that his boy was alive. ·He asked them when the boy had begun to recover. 'The fever left him
53 yesterday' they said 'at the seventh hour.' ·The father realised that this was exactly the time when Jesus had said, 'Your son will live'; and he and all his household believed.
54 This was the second sign given by Jesus, on his return from Judaea to Galilee.

c. Gerizim, the mountain on which the Samaritans built a rival to the Jerusalem Temple; it was destroyed by Hyrcanus, 129 B.C.

III. THE SECOND FEAST AT JERUSALEM

The cure of a sick man at the Pool of Bethzatha

5 Some time after this there was a Jewish festival, and Jesus
2 went up to Jerusalem. ·Now at the Sheep Pool in Jerusalem
there is a building, called Bethzatha in Hebrew, consisting of
3 five porticos; ·and under these were crowds of sick people—
blind, lame, paralysed—waiting for the water to move;
4 for at intervals the angel of the Lord came down into the
pool, and the water was disturbed, and the first person to
enter the water after this disturbance was cured of any ail-
5 ment he suffered from. ·One man there had an illness which
6 had lasted thirty-eight years, ·and when Jesus saw him lying
there and knew he had been in this condition for a long time,
7 he said, 'Do you want to be well again?' ·'Sir,' replied the
sick man 'I have no one to put me into the pool when the
water is disturbed; and while I am still on the way, someone
8 else gets there before me.' ·Jesus said, 'Get up, pick up your
9 sleeping-mat and walk'. ·The man was cured at once, and he
picked up his mat and walked away.
10 Now that day happened to be the sabbath, ·so the Jews
said to the man who had been cured, 'It is the sabbath; you
11 are not allowed to carry your sleeping-mat'. ·He replied, 'But
the man who cured me told me, "Pick up your mat and
12 walk" '. ·They asked, 'Who is the man who said to you, "Pick
13 up your mat and walk"?' ·The man had no idea who it was,
since Jesus had disappeared into the crowd that filled the
14 place. ·After a while Jesus met him in the Temple and said,
'Now you are well again, be sure not to sin any more, or
15 something worse may happen to you'. ·The man went back
and told the Jews that it was Jesus who had cured him.
16 It was because he did things like this on the sabbath that the
17 Jews began to persecute Jesus. ·His answer to them was, 'My
18 Father goes on working, and so do I'. ·But that only made
the Jews even more intent on killing him, because, not content with breaking the sabbath, he spoke of God as his own
Father, and so made himself God's equal.
19 To this accusation Jesus replied:

'I tell you most solemnly,
the Son can do nothing by himself;
he can do only what he sees the Father doing:
and whatever the Father does the Son does too.
20 For the Father loves the Son
and shows him everything he does himself,

and he will show him even greater things than these,
works that will astonish you.

21 Thus, as the Father raises the dead and gives them life,
so the Son gives life to anyone he chooses;

22 for the Father judges no one;
he has entrusted all judgement to the Son,

23 so that all may honour the Son
as they honour the Father.
Whoever refuses honour to the Son
refuses honour to the Father who sent him.

24 I tell you most solemnly,
whoever listens to my words,
and believes in the one who sent me,
has eternal life;
without being brought to judgement
he has passed from death to life.

25 I tell you most solemnly,
the hour will come—in fact it is here already—
when the dead will hear the voice of the Son of God,
and all who hear it will live.

26 For the Father, who is the source of life,
has made the Son the source of life;

27 and, because he is the Son of Man,
has appointed him supreme judge.

28 Do not be surprised at this,
for the hour is coming
when the dead will leave their graves
at the sound of his voice:

29 those who did good
will rise again to life;
and those who did evil, to condemnation.

30 I can do nothing by myself;
I can only judge as I am told to judge,
and my judging is just,
because my aim is to do not my own will,
but the will of him who sent me.

31 'Were I to testify on my own behalf,
my testimony would not be valid;

32 but there is another witness who can speak on my behalf,
and I know that his testimony is valid.

33 You sent messengers to John,
and he gave his testimony to the truth:

34 not that I depend on human testimony;

no, it is for your salvation that I speak of this.

35 John was a lamp alight and shining
and for a time you were content to enjoy the light that
he gave.

36 But my testimony is greater than John's:
the works my Father has given me to carry out,
these same works of mine
testify that the Father has sent me.

37 Besides, the Father who sent me
bears witness to me himself.
You have never heard his voice,
you have never seen his shape,

38 and his word finds no home in you
because you do not believe
in the one he has sent.

39 'You study the scriptures,
believing that in them you have eternal life;
now these same scriptures testify to me,

40 and yet you refuse to come to me for life!

41 As for human approval, this means nothing to me.

42 Besides, I know you too well:
you have no love of God in you.

43 I have come in the name of my Father
and you refuse to accept me;
if someone else comes in his own name
you will accept him.

44 How can you believe,
since you look to one another for approval
and are not concerned
with the approval that comes from the one God?

45 Do not imagine that I am going to accuse you before
the Father:
you place your hopes on Moses,
and Moses will be your accuser.

46 If you really believed him
you would believe me too,
since it was I that he was writing about;

47 but if you refuse to believe what he wrote,
how can you believe what I say?'

IV. ANOTHER PASSOVER, THE BREAD OF LIFE

The miracle of the loaves

6 Some time after this, Jesus went off to the other side of the
2 Sea of Galilee—or of Tiberias—·and a large crowd followed
him, impressed by the signs he gave by curing the sick.
3 Jesus climbed the ·hillside, and sat down there with his
4 disciples. ·It was shortly before the Jewish feast of Passover.
5 Looking up, Jesus saw the crowds approaching and said to
Philip, 'Where can we buy some bread for these people to
6 eat?' ·He only said this to test Philip; he himself knew
7 exactly what he was going to do. ·Philip answered, 'Two
hundred denarii would only buy enough to give them a small
8 piece each'. ·One of his disciples, Andrew, Simon Peter's
9 brother, said, ·'There is a small boy here with five barley
loaves and two fish; but what is that between so many?
10 Jesus said to them, 'Make the people sit down'. There was
plenty of grass there, and as many as five thousand men sat
11 down. ·Then Jesus took the loaves, gave thanks, and gave
them out to all who were sitting ready; he then did the same
12 with the fish, giving out as much as was wanted. ·When they
had eaten enough he said to the disciples, 'Pick up the pieces
13 left over, so that nothing gets wasted'. ·So they picked them
up, and filled twelve hampers with scraps left over from the
14 meal of five barley loaves. ·The people, seeing this sign that
he had given, said, 'This really is the prophet who is to come
15 into the world'. ·Jesus, who could see they were about to
come and take him by force and make him king, escaped
back to the hills by himself.

Jesus walks on the waters

16 That evening the disciples went down to the shore of the
17 lake and ·got into a boat to make for Capernaum on the
other side of the lake. It was getting dark by now and Jesus
18 had still not rejoined them. ·The wind was strong, and the
19 sea was getting rough. ·They had rowed three or four miles
when they saw Jesus walking on the lake and coming towards
20 the boat. This frightened them, ·but he said, 'It is I. Do not be
21 afraid.' ·They were for taking him into the boat, but in no
time it reached the shore at the place they were making for.

The discourse in the synagogue at Capernaum

22 Next day, the crowd that had stayed on the other side saw
that only one boat had been there, and that Jesus had not got

into the boat with his disciples, but that the disciples had set
23 off by themselves. ·Other boats, however, had put in from
Tiberias, near the place where the bread had been eaten.
24 When the people saw that neither Jesus nor his disciples were
there, they got into those boats and crossed to Capernaum to
25 look for Jesus. ·When they found him on the other side, they
26 said to him, 'Rabbi, when did you come here?' ·Jesus
answered:

> 'I tell you most solemnly,
> you are not looking for me
> because you have seen the signs
> but because you had all the bread you wanted to eat.
>
27 > Do not work for food that cannot last,
> but work for food that endures to eternal life,
> the kind of food the Son of Man is offering you,
> for on him the Father, God himself, has set his seal.'

28 Then they said to him, 'What must we do if we are to do
29 the works that God wants?' ·Jesus gave them this answer,
'This is working for God: you must believe in the one he has
30 sent'. ·So they said, 'What sign will you give to show us that
31 we should believe in you? What work will you do? ·Our
fathers had manna to eat in the desert; as scripture says: *He
gave them bread from heaven to eat.*[a]
32 Jesus answered:

> 'I tell you most solemnly,
> it was not Moses who gave you bread from heaven,
> it is my Father who gives you the bread from heaven,
> the true bread;
>
33 > for the bread of God
> is that which comes down from heaven
> and gives life to the world'.

34
35 'Sir,' they said 'give us that bread always.' ·Jesus answered:

> 'I am the bread of life.
> He who comes to me will never be hungry;
> he who believes in me will never thirst.
>
36 > But, as I have told you,
> you can see me and still you do not believe.
>
37 > All that the Father gives me will come to me,
> and whoever comes to me
> I shall not turn him away;
>
38 > because I have come from heaven,
> not to do my own will,

but to do the will of the one who sent me.

39 Now the will of him who sent me
   is that I should lose nothing
   of all that he has given to me,
   and that I should raise it up on the last day.

40 Yes, it is my Father's will
   that whoever sees the Son and believes in him
   shall have eternal life,
   and that I shall raise him up on the last day.'

41   Meanwhile the Jews were complaining to each other about
him, because he had said, 'I am the bread that came down
42 from heaven'. 'Surely this is Jesus son of Joseph' they said.
'We know his father and mother. How can he now say,
43 "I have come down from heaven"?' ·Jesus said in reply,
'Stop complaining to each other.

44 'No one can come to me
   unless he is drawn by the Father who sent me,
   and I will raise him up at the last day.
45 It is written in the prophets:
   They will all be taught by God,[b]
   and to hear the teaching of the Father,
   and learn from it,
   is to come to me.
46 Not that anybody has seen the Father,
   except the one who comes from God:
   he has seen the Father.
47 I tell you most solemnly,
   everybody who believes has eternal life.
48 I am the bread of life.
49 Your fathers ate the manna in the desert
   and they are dead;
50 but this is the bread that comes down from heaven,
   so that a man may eat it and not die.
51 I am the living bread which has come down from
       heaven.
   Anyone who eats this bread will live for ever;
   and the bread that I shall give
   . is my flesh, for the life of the world.'

52   Then the Jews started arguing with one another: 'How can
53 this man give us his flesh to eat?' they said. ·Jesus replied:

'I tell you most solemnly,
if you do not eat the flesh of the Son of Man

6 a. Ex 16:4f **b.** Is 54:13

> and drink his blood,
> you will not have life in you.

54 Anyone who does eat my flesh and drink my blood
> has eternal life,
> and I shall raise him up on the last day.

55 For my flesh is real food
> and my blood is real drink.

56 He who eats my flesh and drinks my blood
> lives in me
> and I live in him.

57 As I, who am sent by the living Father,
> myself draw life from the Father,
> so whoever eats me will draw life from me.

58 This is the bread come down from heaven;
> not like the bread our ancestors ate:
> they are dead,
> but anyone who eats this bread will live for ever.'

59 He taught this doctrine at Capernaum, in the synagogue.
60 After hearing it, many of his followers said, 'This is in-
61 tolerable language. How could anyone accept it?' ·Jesus was
aware that his followers were complaining about it and said,
62 'Does this upset you? ·What if you should see the Son of
Man ascend to where he was before?

63 'It is the spirit that gives life,
> the flesh has nothing to offer.
> The words I have spoken to you are spirit
> and they are life.

64 'But there are some of you who do not believe.' For Jesus
knew from the outset those who did not believe, and who it
65 was that would betray him. ·He went on, 'This is why I told
you that no one could come to me unless the Father allows
66 him'. ·After this, many of his disciples left him and stopped
going with him.

Peter's profession of faith

67 Then Jesus said to the Twelve, 'What about you, do you
68 want to go away too?' ·Simon Peter answered, 'Lord, who
69 shall we go to? You have the message of eternal life, ·and we
70 believe; we know that you are the Holy One of God.' ·Jesus
replied, 'Have I not chosen you, you Twelve? Yet one of you
71 is a devil.' ·He meant Judas son of Simon Iscariot, since this
was the man, one of the Twelve, who was going to betray
him.

V. THE FEAST OF TABERNACLES

Jesus goes up to Jerusalem for the feast and teaches there

7　　After this Jesus stayed in Galilee; he could not stay in Judaea, because the Jews were out to kill him.

²⁄₃　　As the Jewish feast of Tabernacles drew near, ·his brothers*ᵃ* said to him, 'Why not leave this place and go to Judaea, and
4　let your disciples*ᵇ* see the works you are doing; ·if a man wants to be known he does not do things in secret; since you
5　are doing all this, you should let the whole world see.' ·Not
6　even his brothers, in fact, had faith in him. ·Jesus answered, 'The right time for me has not come yet, but any time is the
7　right time for you. ·The world cannot hate you, but it does hate me, because I give evidence that its ways are evil.
8　Go up to the festival yourselves: I am not going to this
9　festival, because for me the time is not ripe yet.' ·Having said that, he stayed behind in Galilee.

10　 · However, after his brothers had left for the festival, he went up as well, but quite privately, without drawing atten-
11　tion to himself. ·At the festival the Jews were on the look-out
12　for him: 'Where is he?' they said. ·People stood in groups whispering*ᶜ* about him. Some said, 'He is a good man';
13　others, 'No, he is leading the people astray'. ·Yet no one spoke about him openly, for fear of the Jews.

14　　When the festival was half over, Jesus went to the Temple
15　and began to teach. ·The Jews were astonished and said,
16　'How did he learn to read? He has not been taught.' ·Jesus answered them:

　　　'My teaching is not from myself:
　　　　it comes from the one who sent me;
17　　　and if anyone is prepared to do his will,
　　　　he will know whether my teaching is from God
　　　　or whether my doctrine is my own.
18　　　When a man's doctrine is his own
　　　　he is hoping to get honour for himself;
　　　　but when he is working for the honour of one who sent
　　　　　　him,
　　　　then he is sincere
　　　　and by no means an impostor.
19　　　Did not Moses give you the Law?
　　　　And yet not one of you keeps the Law!

7 **a.** In the wide sense, as in Mt 12:46: relations of his own generation. **b.** Those in Jerusalem and Judaea. **c.** Or 'In the crowds there was whispering about him'.

20 'Why do you want to kill me?' ·The crowd replied, 'You are
21 mad! Who wants to kill you?' ·Jesus answered, 'One work I
22 did, and you are all surprised by it. ·Moses ordered you to
    practise circumcision—not that it began with him, it goes
    back to the patriarchs—and you circumcise on the sabbath.
23 Now if a man can be circumcised on the sabbath so that the
    Law of Moses is not broken, why are you angry with me for
24 making a man whole and complete on a sabbath? ·Do not
    keep judging according to appearances; let your judgement
    be according to what is right.'

The people discuss the origin of the Messiah

25 Meanwhile some of the people of Jerusalem were saying,
26 'Isn't this the man they want to kill? ·And here he is, speaking
    freely, and they have nothing to say to him! Can it be true the
    authorities have made up their minds that he is the Christ?
27 Yet we all know where he comes from, but when the Christ
    appears no one will know where he comes from.'[d]
28 Then, as Jesus taught in the Temple, he cried out:

    'Yes, you know me and you know where I came from.
    Yet I have not come of myself:
    no, there is one who sent me and I really come from
        him,
    and you do not know him,
29 but I know him
    because I have come from him
    and it was he who sent me.'

30 They would have arrested him then, but because his time
    had not yet come no one laid a hand on him.

Jesus foretells his approaching departure

31 There were many people in the crowds, however, who
    believed in him; they were saying, 'When the Christ comes,
32 will he give more signs than this man?' ·Hearing that ru-
    mours like this about him were spreading among the people,
    the Pharisees sent the Temple police to arrest him.
33 Then Jesus said:

    'I shall remain with you for only a short time now;
    then I shall go back to the one who sent me.
34 You will look for me and will not find me:
    where I am
    you cannot come.'

35 The Jews then said to one another, 'Where is he going that
    we shan't be able to find him? Is he going abroad to the

people who are dispersed among the Greeks and will he
36 teach the Greeks? ·What does he mean when he says:

> "You will look for me and will not find me:
> where I am,
> you cannot come"?'

The promise of living water

37 On the last day and greatest day of the festival, Jesus stood
there and cried out:

> 'If any man is thirsty, let him come to me!
38 Let the man come and drink ·who believes in me!'

As scripture says, From his breast shall flow fountains of
living water.[e]
39 He was speaking of the Spirit which those who believed in
him were to receive; for there was no Spirit as yet because
Jesus had not yet been glorified.

Fresh discussions on the origin of the Messiah

40 Several people who had been listening said, 'Surely he
41 must be the prophet', ·and some said, 'He is the Christ', but
42 others said, 'Would the Christ be from Galilee? ·Does not
scripture say that the Christ must be descended from David
43 and come from the town of Bethlehem?' ·So the people could
44 not agree about him. ·Some would have liked to arrest him,
but no one actually laid hands on him.

45 The police went back to the chief priests and Pharisees who
46 said to them, 'Why haven't you brought him?' ·The police
replied, 'There has never been anybody who has spoken like
47 him'. ·'So' the Pharisees answered 'you have been led astray
48 as well? ·Have any of the authorities believed in him? Any of
49 the Pharisees? ·This rabble knows nothing about the Law—
50 they are damned.' ·One of them, Nicodemus—the same man
51 who had come to Jesus earlier—said to them, ·'But surely the
Law does not allow us to pass judgement on a man without
52 giving him a hearing and discovering what he is about?' ·To
this they answered, 'Are you a Galilean too? Go into the
matter, and see for yourself: prophets do not come out of
Galilee.'

d. Although the prophecy that the Messiah would be born in Bethlehem was well known, it was commonly believed that he would appear
suddenly from some secret place. **e.** Life-giving water for Zion was a
theme of the readings from scripture on the feast of Tabernacles
(Zc 14:8, Ezk 47:1f); the liturgy included prayers for rain and the
commemoration of the miracle of Moses and the water, Ex 17.

The adulterous woman*

53   They all went home, **8** and Jesus went to the Mount of Olives.

2   At daybreak he appeared in the Temple again; and as all the people came to him, he sat down and began to teach them.

3   The scribes and Pharisees brought a woman along who had been caught committing adultery; and making her stand
4 there in full view of everybody, ·they said to Jesus, 'Master, this woman was caught in the very act of committing adul-
5 tery, ·and Moses has ordered us in the Law to condemn women like this to death by stoning. What have you to say?'
6 They asked him this as a test, looking for something to use against him. But Jesus bent down and started writing on the
7 ground with his finger. ·As they persisted with their question, he looked up and said, 'If there is one of you who has not
8 sinned, let him be the first to throw a stone at her'. ·Then he
9 bent down and wrote on the ground again. ·When they heard this they went away one by one, beginning with the eldest, until Jesus was left alone with the woman, who re-
10 mained standing there. ·He looked up and said, 'Woman,
11 where are they? Has no one condemned you?' ·'No one, sir' she replied. 'Neither do I condemn you,' said Jesus 'go away, and don't sin any more.'

Jesus, the light of the world

12   When Jesus spoke to the people again, he said:

'I am the light of the world;
anyone who follows me will not be walking in the dark;
he will have the light of life.'

A discussion on the testimony of Jesus to himself

13   At this the Pharisees said to him, 'You are testifying on
14 your own behalf; your testimony is not valid'. ·Jesus replied:

'It is true that I am testifying on my own behalf,
but my testimony is still valid,
because I know
where I came from and where I am going;
but you do not know
where I come from or where I am going.
15 You judge by human standards;
I judge no one,
16 but if I judge,
my judgement will be sound,
because I am not alone:

the one who sent me is with me;
17   and in your Law it is written
that the testimony of two witnesses is valid.
18   I may be testifying on my own behalf,
but the Father who sent me is my witness too.'

19   They asked him, 'Where is your Father?' Jesus answered:

'You do not know me, nor do you know my Father;
if you did know me, you would know my Father as
well'.

20   He spoke these words in the Treasury, while teaching in
the Temple. No one arrested him, because his time had not
yet come.

The unbelieving Jews warned

21   Again he said to them:

'I am going away; you will look for me
and you will die in your sin.
Where I am going, you cannot come.'

22   The Jews said to one another, 'Will he kill himself? Is that
what he means by saying, "Where I am going, you cannot
23 come"?' ·Jesus went on:

·'You are from below;
I am from above.
You are of this world;
I am not of this world.
24   I have told you already: You will die in your sins.
Yes, if you do not believe that I am He,
you will die in your sins.'

25   So they said to him, 'Who are you?' Jesus answered:

'What I have told you from the outset.
26   About you I have much to say
and much to condemn;
but the one who sent me is truthful,
and what I have learnt from him
I declare to the world.'

27   They failed to understand that he was talking to them
28 about the Father. ·So Jesus said:

'When you have lifted up the Son of Man,
then you will know that I am He

f. The author of this passage is not John; the oldest MSS do not include it or place it elsewhere. The style is that of the Synoptics.

and that I do nothing of myself:
what the Father has taught me
is what I preach;

29　　he who sent me is with me,
and has not left me to myself,
for I always do what pleases him'.

30　As he was saying this, many came to believe in him.

Jesus and Abraham

31　To the Jews who believed in him Jesus said:

'If you make my word your home
you will indeed be my disciples,

32　　you will learn the truth
and the truth will make you free'.

33　They answered, 'We are descended from Abraham and we
have never been the slaves of anyone; what do you mean,
34　"You will be made free"?' ·Jesus replied:

'I tell you most solemnly,
everyone who commits sin is a slave.

35　　Now the slave's place in the house is not assured,
but the son's place is assured.

36　　So if the Son makes you free,
you will be free indeed.

37　　I know that you are descended from Abraham;
but in spite of that you want to kill me
because nothing I say has penetrated into you.

38　　What I, for my part, speak of
is what I have seen with my Father;
but you, you put into action
the lessons learnt from your father.'

39　They repeated, 'Our father is Abraham'. Jesus said to them:

'If you were Abraham's children,
you would do as Abraham did.

40　　As it is, you want to kill me
when I tell you the truth
as I have learnt it from God;
that is not what Abraham did.

41　　What you are doing is what your father does.'

'We were not born of prostitution,'[a] they went on 'we have
42　one father: God.' ·Jesus answered:

'If God were your father, you would love me,
since I have come here from God; yes, I have come
from him;

not that I came because I chose,
no, I was sent, and by him.

43   Do you know why you cannot take in what I say?
It is because you are unable to understand any language.

44   The devil is your father,
and you prefer to do
what your father wants.
He was a murderer from the start;
he was never grounded in the truth;
there is no truth in him at all:
when he lies
he is drawing on his own store,
because he is a liar, and the father of lies.

45   But as for me, I speak the truth
and for that very reason,
you do not believe me.

46   Can one of you convict me of sin?
If I speak the truth, why do you not believe me?

47   A child of God
listens to the words of God;
if you refuse to listen,
it is because you are not God's children.'

48   The Jews replied, 'Are we not right in saying that you are a
Samaritan and possessed by a devil?' Jesus answered:

49   'I am not possessed;
no, I honour my Father,
but you want to dishonour me.

50   Not that I care for my own glory,
there is someone who takes care of that and is the
judge of it.

51   I tell you most solemnly,
whoever keeps my word
will never see death.'

52   The Jews said, 'Now we know for certain that you are
possessed. Abraham is dead, and the prophets are dead, and
yet you say, "Whoever keeps my word will never know the
53 taste of death". ·Are you greater than our father Abraham,
who is dead? The prophets are dead too. Who are you claim-
54 ing to be?' ·Jesus answered:

'If I were to seek my own glory
that would be no glory at all;

8 a. By 'prostitution' the prophets often mean religious infidelity, cf.
Ho 1:2.

> my glory is conferred by the Father,
> by the one of whom you say, "He is our God"
>
> 55 although you do not know him.
> But I know him,
> and if I were to say: I do not know him,
> I should be a liar, as you are liars yourselves.
> But I do know him, and I faithfully keep his word.
>
> 56 Your father Abraham rejoiced
> to think that he would see my Day;
> he saw it and was glad.'

57 The Jews then said, 'You are not fifty yet, and you have
58 seen Abraham!' ·Jesus replied:

> 'I tell you most solemnly,
> before Abraham ever was,
> I Am'.

59 At this they picked up stones to throw at him;[b] but Jesus hid himself and left the Temple.

The cure of the man born blind

9 As he went along, he saw a man who had been blind from
2 birth. ·His disciples asked him, 'Rabbi, who sinned, this man
3 or his parents, for him to have been born blind?' ·'Neither he nor his parents sinned,' Jesus answered 'he was born blind so that the works of God might be displayed in him.

> 4 'As long as the day lasts
> I must carry out the work of the one who sent me;
> the night will soon be here when no one can work.
> 5 As long as I am in the world
> I am the light of the world.'

6 Having said this, he spat on the ground, made a paste with
7 the spittle, put this over the eyes of the blind man, ·and said to him, 'Go and wash in the Pool of Siloam[a] (a name that means 'sent'). So the blind man went off and washed himself, and came away with his sight restored.

8 His neighbours and people who earlier had seen him beg-
9 ging said, 'Isn't this the man who used to sit and beg?' ·Some said, 'Yes, it is the same one'. Others said, 'No, he only looks
10 like him'. The man himself said, 'I am the man'. ·So they said
11 to him, 'Then how do your eyes come to be open?' ·'The man called Jesus' he answered, 'made a paste, daubed my eyes with it and said to me, "Go and wash at Siloam"; so I
12 went, and when I washed I could see.' ·They asked, 'Where is he?' 'I don't know' he answered.

13 They brought the man who had been blind to the Phari-

14 sees. ·It had been a sabbath day when Jesus made the paste
15 and opened the man's eyes, ·so when the Pharisees asked
him how he had come to see, he said, 'He put a paste on my
16 eyes, and I washed, and I can see'. ·Then some of the Pharisees said, 'This man cannot be from God: he does not keep
the sabbath'. Others said, 'How could a sinner produce signs
17 like this?' And there was disagreement among them. ·So
they spoke to the blind man again, 'What have you to say
about him yourself, now that he has opened your eyes?' 'He
is a prophet' replied the man.
18   However, the Jews would not believe that the man had
been blind and had gained his sight, without first sending for
19 his parents and ·asking them, 'Is this man really your son
who you say was born blind? If so, how is it that he is now
20 able to see?' ·His parents answered, 'We know he is our son
21 and we know he was born blind, ·but we don't know how it
is that he can see now, or who opened his eyes. He is old
22 enough: let him speak for himself.' ·His parents spoke like
this out of fear of the Jews, who had already agreed to expel
from the synagogue anyone who should acknowledge Jesus
23 as the Christ. ·This was why his parents said, 'He is old
enough; ask him'.
24   So the Jews again sent for the man and said to him, 'Give
glory to God![b] For our part, we know that this man is a
25 sinner.' ·The man answered, 'I don't know if he is a sinner;
26 I only know that I was blind and now I can see'. ·They said to
him, 'What did he do to you? How did he open your eyes?'
27 He replied, 'I have told you once and you wouldn't listen.
Why do you want to hear it all again? Do you want to
28 become his disciples too?' ·At this they hurled abuse at him:
'You can be his disciple,' they said 'we are disciples of Moses:
29 we know that God spoke to Moses, but as for this man, we
30 don't know where he comes from'. ·The man replied, 'Now
here is an astonishing thing! He has opened my eyes, and you
31 don't know where he comes from! ·We know that God
doesn't listen to sinners, but God does listen to men who are
32 devout and do his will. ·Ever since the world began it is
unheard of for anyone to open the eyes of a man who was
33 born blind; ·if this man were not from God, he couldn't do a
34 thing.' ·'Are you trying to teach us,' they replied 'and you a
sinner through and through, since you were born!' And they
drove him away.

b. Stoning was the penalty for blasphemy. Cf. 10:33.
9 a. Water from this pool was drawn during the feast of Tabernacles
to symbolise the waters of blessing. b. I.e. putting the man on oath.

35 Jesus heard they had driven him away, and when he found him he said to him, 'Do you believe in the Son of Man?'
36 'Sir,' the man replied 'tell me who he is so that I may believe
37 in him.' ·Jesus said, 'You are looking at him; he is speaking
38 to you'. ·The man said, 'Lord, I believe', and worshipped him.
39 Jesus said:

'It is for judgement
that I have come into this world,
so that those without sight may see
and those with sight turn blind'.

40 Hearing this, some Pharisees who were present said to him,
41 'We are not blind, surely?' ·Jesus replied:

'Blind? If you were,
you would not be guilty,
but since you say, "We see",
your guilt remains.

The good shepherd

10 'I tell you most solemnly, anyone who does not enter the sheepfold through the gate, but gets in some other way is a
2   thief and a brigand. ·The one who enters through the gate is
3   the shepherd of the flock; ·the gatekeeper lets him in, the sheep hear his voice, one by one he calls his own sheep and
4   leads them out. ·When he has brought out his flock, he goes ahead of them, and the sheep follow because they know his
5   voice. ·They never follow a stranger but run away from him: they do not recognise the voice of strangers.'
6   Jesus told them[a] this parable but they failed to understand what he meant by telling it to them.

7   So Jesus spoke to them again:

'I tell you most solemnly,
I am the gate of the sheepfold.
8   All others who have come
are thieves and brigands;
but the sheep took no notice of them.
9   I am the gate.
Anyone who enters through me will be safe:
he will go freely in and out
and be sure of finding pasture.
10 The thief comes
only to steal and kill and destroy.
I have come
so that they may have life

and have it to the full.

11   I am the good shepherd:
the good shepherd is one who lays down his life for
his sheep.

12   The hired man, since he is not the shepherd
and the sheep do not belong to him,
abandons the sheep and runs away
as soon as he sees a wolf coming,
and then the wolf attacks and scatters the sheep;

13   this is because he is only a hired man
and has no concern for the sheep.

14   I am the good shepherd;
I know my own
and my own know me,

15   just as the Father knows me
and I know the Father;
and I lay down my life for my sheep.

16   And there are other sheep I have
that are not of this fold,
and these I have to lead as well.
They too will listen to my voice,
and there will be only one flock,
and one shepherd.

17   The Father loves me,
because I lay down my life
in order to take it up again.

18   No one takes it from me;
I lay it down of my own free will,
and as it is in my power to lay it down,
so it is in my power to take it up again;
and this is the command I have been given by my
Father.'

19
20   These words caused disagreement among the Jews. ·Many
said, 'He is possessed, he is raving; why bother to listen to
21 him?' ·Others said, 'These are not the words of a man
possessed by a devil: could a devil open the eyes of the
blind?'

VI. THE FEAST OF DEDICATION

Jesus claims to be the Son of God

22   It was the time when the feast of Dedication was being
23 celebrated in Jerusalem. It was winter, ·and Jesus was in the
Temple walking up and down in the Portico of Solomon.

10 a. The Pharisees.

24 The Jews gathered round him and said, 'How much longer
are you going to keep us in suspense? If you are the Christ,
25 tell us plainly.' ·Jesus replied:

> 'I have told you, but you do not believe.
> The works I do in my Father's name are my witness;
26 but you do not believe,
> because you are no sheep of mine.
27 The sheep that belong to me listen to my voice;
> I know them and they follow me.
28 I give them eternal life;
> they will never be lost
> and no one will ever steal them from me.
29 The Father who gave them to me is greater than any-
> one,
> and no one can steal from the Father.
30 The Father and I are one.'

$^{31}_{32}$　　The Jews fetched stones to stone him, ·so Jesus said to
them, 'I have done many good works for you to see, works
from my Father; for which of these are you stoning me?'
33 The Jews answered him, 'We are not stoning you for doing a
good work but for blasphemy: you are only a man and you
34 claim to be God'. ·Jesus answered:

> 'Is it not written in your Law:
> *I said, you are gods*?[b]

35 So the Law uses the word gods
> of those to whom the word of God was addressed,
> and scripture cannot be rejected.
36 Yet you say to someone the Father has consecrated
> and sent into the world,
> "You are blaspheming",
> because he says, "I am the Son of God".
37 If I am not doing my Father's work,
> there is no need to believe me;
38 but if I am doing it,
> then even if you refuse to believe in me,
> at least believe in the work I do;
> then you will know for sure
> that the Father is in me and I am in the Father.'

39 They wanted to arrest him then, but he eluded them.

Jesus withdraws to the other side of the Jordan

40 He went back again to the far side of the Jordan to stay in
41 the district where John had once been baptising. ·Many

people who came to him there said, 'John gave no signs, but
42 all he said about this man was true'; ·and many of them
believed in him.

The resurrection of Lazarus

11   There was a man named Lazarus who lived in the village of
Bethany with the two sisters, Mary and Martha, and he was
2 ill.—·It was the same Mary, the sister of the sick man Lazarus, who anointed the Lord with ointment and wiped his feet
3 with her hair. ·The sisters sent this message to Jesus, 'Lord,
4 the man you love is ill'. ·On receiving the message, Jesus said,
'This sickness will end not in death but in God's glory, and
through it the Son of God will be glorified'.
5
6   Jesus loved Martha and her sister and Lazarus, ·yet when
he heard that Lazarus was ill he stayed where he was for two
7 more days ·before saying to the disciples, 'Let us go to
8 Judaea'. ·The disciples said, 'Rabbi, it is not long since the
9 Jews wanted to stone you; are you going back again?' ·Jesus
replied:

'Are there not twelve hours in the day?
A man can walk in the daytime without stumbling
because he has the light of this world to see by;
10   but if he walks at night he stumbles,
because there is no light to guide him.'

11   He said that and then added, 'Our friend Lazarus is resting,
12 I am going to wake him'. ·The disciples said to him, 'Lord, if
13 he is able to rest he is sure to get better'. ·The phrase Jesus
used referred to the death of Lazarus, but they thought that
14 by 'rest' he meant 'sleep', so ·Jesus put it plainly, 'Lazarus is
15 dead; ·and for your sake I am glad I was not there because
16 now you will believe. But let us go to him.' ·Then Thomas—
known as the Twin—said to the other disciples, 'Let us go
too, and die with him'.
17   On arriving, Jesus found that Lazarus had been in the tomb
18 for four days already. ·Bethany is only about two miles from
19 Jerusalem, ·and many Jews had come to Martha and Mary to
20 sympathise with them over their brother. ·When Martha
heard that Jesus had come she went to meet him. Mary
21 remained sitting in the house. ·Martha said to Jesus, 'If you
22 had been here, my brother would not have died, ·but I know
that, even now, whatever you ask of God, he will grant you'.
23
24 'Your brother' said Jesus to her 'will rise again.'. ·Martha

b. Ps 82:6

said, 'I know he will rise again at the resurrection on the last
25 day'. ·Jesus said:

> 'I am the resurrection.
> If anyone believes in me, even though he dies he will
>   live,
26 and whoever lives and believes in me
> will never die.
> Do you believe this?'

27 'Yes, Lord,' she said 'I believe that you are the Christ, the
Son of God, the one who was to come into this world.'
28   When she had said this, she went and called her sister
Mary, saying in a low voice, 'The Master is here and wants to
29 see you'. ·Hearing this, Mary got up quickly and went to
30 him. ·Jesus had not yet come into the village; he was still at
31 the place where Martha had met him. ·When the Jews who
were in the house sympathising with Mary saw her get up so
quickly and go out, they followed her, thinking that she was
going to the tomb to weep there.
32   Mary went to Jesus, and as soon as she saw him she threw
herself at his feet, saying, 'Lord, if you had been here, my
33 brother would not have died'. ·At the sight of her tears, and
those of the Jews who followed her, Jesus said in great
distress, with a sigh that came straight from the heart,
34 'Where have you put him?' They said, 'Lord, come and see'.
35 Jesus wept; ·and the Jews said, 'See how much he loved him!'
36
37 But there were some who remarked, 'He opened the eyes of
the blind man, could he not have prevented this man's
38 death?' ·Still sighing, Jesus reached the tomb: it was a cave
39 with a stone to close the opening. ·Jesus said, 'Take the stone
away'. Martha said to him, 'Lord, by now he will smell; this
40 is the fourth day'. ·Jesus replied, 'Have I not told you that if
41 you believe you will see the glory of God?' ·So they took
away the stone. Then Jesus lifted up his eyes and said:

> 'Father, I thank you for hearing my prayer.
42 I knew indeed that you always hear me,
> but I speak
> for the sake of all these who stand round me,
> so that they may believe it was you who sent me.'

43   When he had said this, he cried in a loud voice, 'Lazarus,
44 here! Come out!' ·The dead man came out, his feet and hands
bound with bands of stuff and a cloth round his face. Jesus
said to them, 'Unbind him, let him go free'.

The Jewish leaders decide on the death of Jesus

45 Many of the Jews who had come to visit Mary and had
46 seen what he did believed in him, ·but some of them went to
47 tell the Pharisees what Jesus had done. ·Then the chief priests
and Pharisees called a meeting. ·Here is this man working all
48 these signs' they said 'and what action are we taking? ·If we
let him go on in this way everybody will believe in him, and
the Romans will come and destroy the Holy Place and our
49 nation.' ·One of them, Caiaphas, the high priest that year,
said, 'You don't seem to have grasped the situation at all;
50 you fail to see that it is better for one man to die for the
51 people, than for the whole nation to be destroyed'. ·He did
not speak in his own person, it was as high priest that he
52 made this prophecy that Jesus was to die for the nation—·and
not for the nation only, but to gather together in unity the
53 scattered children of God. ·From that day they were deter-
54 mined to kill him. ·So Jesus no longer went about openly
among the Jews, but left the district for a town called
Ephraim, in the country bordering on the desert, and stayed
there with his disciples.

VII. THE LAST PASSOVER

A. BEFORE THE PASSION

The Passover draws near

55 The Jewish Passover drew near, and many of the country
people who had gone up to Jerusalem to purify themselves
56 looked out for Jesus, saying to one another as they stood
about in the Temple, 'What do you think? Will he come to
57 the festival or not?' ·The chief priests and Pharisees had by
now given their orders: anyone who knew where he was
must inform them so that they could arrest him.

The anointing at Bethany

12 Six days before the Passover, Jesus went to Bethany, where
2 Lazarus was, whom he had raised from the dead. ·They gave
a dinner for him there; Martha waited on them and Lazarus
3 was among those at table. ·Mary brought in a pound of very
costly ointment, pure nard, and with it anointed the feet of
Jesus, wiping them with her hair; the house was full of the
4 scent of the ointment. ·Then Judas Iscariot—one of his
5 disciples, the man who was to betray him—said, ·"Why wasn't
this ointment sold for three hundred denarii, and the money

6 given to the poor?' ·He said this, not because he cared about
the poor, but because he was a thief; he was in charge of the
common fund and used to help himself to the contributions.
7 So Jesus said, 'Leave her alone; she had to keep this scent for
8 the day of my burial. ·You have the poor with you always,
you will not always have me.'

9 Meanwhile a large number of Jews heard that he was there
and came not only on account of Jesus but also to see
10 Lazarus whom he had raised from the dead. ·Then the chief
11 priests decided to kill Lazarus as well, ·since it was on his
account that many of the Jews were leaving them and believing in Jesus.

The Messiah enters Jerusalem

12 The next day the crowds who had come up for the festival
13 heard that Jesus was on his way to Jerusalem. ·They took
branches of palm and went out to meet him, shouting,
'*Hosanna! Blessings on* the King of Israel, *who comes in the*
14 *name of the Lord.*'*[a]* ·Jesus found a young donkey and mounted
15 it—as scripture says: ·*Do not be afraid, daughter of Zion; see,*
16 *your king is coming, mounted on the colt of a donkey.[b]* ·At the
time his disciples did not understand this, but later, after
Jesus had been glorified, they remembered that this had been
written about him and that this was in fact how they had
17 received him. ·All who had been with him when he called
Lazarus out of the tomb and raised him from the dead were
18 telling how they had witnessed it; ·it was because of this, too,
that the crowd came out to meet him: they had heard that he
19 had given this sign. ·Then the Pharisees said to one another,
'You see, there is nothing you can do; look, the whole world
is running after him!'

Jesus foretells his death and subsequent glorification

20 Among those who went up to worship at the festival were
21 some Greeks.*[c]* ·These approached Philip, who came from
Bethsaida in Galilee, and put this request to him, 'Sir, we
22 should like to see Jesus'. ·Philip went to tell Andrew, and
Andrew and Philip together went to tell Jesus.
23 Jesus replied to them:

'Now the hour has come
for the Son of Man to be glorified.
24 I tell you, most solemnly,
unless a wheat grain falls on the ground and dies,
it remains only a single grain;
but if it dies,

it yields a rich harvest.
25 Anyone who loves his life loses it;
anyone who hates his life in this world
will keep it for the eternal life.
26 If a man serves me, he must follow me,
wherever I am, my servant will be there too.
If anyone serves me, my Father will honour him.
27 Now my soul is troubled.
What shall I say:
Father, save me from this hour?
But it was for this very reason that I have come to this
hour.
28 Father, glorify your name!'

A voice came from heaven, 'I have glorified it, and I will
glorify it again'.
29 People standing by, who heard this, said it was a clap of
thunder; others said, 'It was an angel speaking to him'.
30 Jesus answered, 'It was not for my sake that this voice came,
but for yours.
31 'Now sentence is being passed on this world;
now the prince of this world is to be overthrown.[d]
32 And when I am lifted up from the earth,
I shall draw all men to myself.'

33 By these words he indicated the kind of death he would die.
34 The crowd answered, 'The Law has taught us that the Christ
will remain for ever. How can you say, "The Son of Man
35 must be lifted up"? Who is this Son of Man?' ·Jesus then
said:

'The light will be with you only a little longer now.
Walk while you have the light,
or the dark will overtake you;
he who walks in the dark does not know where he is
going.
36 While you still have the light,
believe in the light
and you will become sons of light.'

Having said this, Jesus left them and kept himself hidden.

Conclusion: the unbelief of the Jews

37 Though they had been present when he gave so many signs,
38 they did not believe in him; ·this was to fulfil the words of the

12 a. Ps 118:26 b. Zc 9:9f c. The 'God-fearing men' of Ac 10:2:
converts who observed certain specific Mosaic observances. d. Satan.

prophet Isaiah: *Lord, who could believe what we have heard said, and to whom has the power of the Lord been revealed?*[e]

39 Indeed, they were unable to believe because, as Isaiah says

40 again: ·*He has blinded their eyes, he has hardened their heart, for fear they should see with their eyes and understand with their heart, and turn to me for healing.*[f]

41 Isaiah said this when he saw his glory,[g] and his words referred to Jesus.

42 And yet there were many who did believe in him, even among the leading men, but they did not admit it, through fear of the Pharisees and fear of being expelled from the

43 synagogue: ·they put honour from men before the honour that comes from God.

44 Jesus declared publicly:

'Whoever believes in me
believes not in me
but in the one who sent me,

45 and whoever sees me,
sees the one who sent me.

46 I, the light, have come into the world,
so that whoever believes in me
need not stay in the dark any more.

47 If anyone hears my words and does not keep them faithfully,
it is not I who shall condemn him,
since I have come not to condemn the world,
but to save the world:

48 he who rejects me and refuses my words
has his judge already:
the word itself that I have spoken
will be his judge on the last day.

49 For what I have spoken does not come from myself;
no, what I was to say, what I had to speak,
was commanded by the Father who sent me,

50 and I know that his commands mean eternal life.
And therefore what the Father has told me
is what I speak.'

B. THE LAST SUPPER

Jesus washes his disciples' feet

13 It was before the festival of the Passover, and Jesus knew that the hour had come for him to pass from this world to the Father. He had always loved those who were his in the world, but now he showed how perfect his love was.

2 They were at supper, and the devil had already put it into
the mind of Judas Iscariot son of Simon, to betray him.
3 Jesus knew that the Father had put everything into his hands,
and that he had come from God and was returning to God,
4 and he got up from table, removed his outer garment and,
5 taking a towel, wrapped it round his waist; ·he then poured
water into a basin and began to wash the disciples' feet*a* and
to wipe them with the towel he was wearing.
6 He came to Simon Peter, who said to him, 'Lord, are you
7 going to wash my feet?' ·Jesus answered, 'At the moment you
do not know what I am doing, but later you will understand'.
8 'Never!' said Peter 'You shall never wash my feet.' Jesus
replied, 'If I do not wash you, you can have nothing in
9 common with me'. ·'Then, Lord,' said Simon Peter 'not only
10 my feet, but my hands and my head as well!' ·Jesus said, 'No
one who has taken a bath needs washing, he is clean all over.
11 You too are clean, though not all of you are.' ·He knew who
was going to betray him, that was why he said, 'though not
all of you are'.
12 When he had washed their feet and put on his clothes again
he went back to the table. 'Do you understand' he said 'what
13 I have done to you? ·You call me Master and Lord, and
14 rightly; so I am. ·If I, then, the Lord and Master, have
15 washed your feet, your should wash each other's feet. ·I have
given you an example so that you may copy what I have done
to you.

16   'I tell you most solemnly,
           no servant is greater than his master,
           no messenger is greater than the man who sent him.

17   'Now that you know this, happiness will be yours if you
18 behave accordingly. ·I am not speaking about all of you:
I know the ones I have chosen; but what scripture says must
be fulfilled: *Someone who shares my table rebels against me.*[b]

19   'I tell you this now, before it happens,
           so that when it does happen
           you may believe that I am He.
20   I tell you most solemnly,
           whoever welcomes the one I send welcomes me,
           and whoever welcomes me welcomes the one who sent
           me.'

e. Is 53:1 f. Is 6:9f g. Isaiah's vision in the Temple, Is 6:4, interpreted
as a prophetic vision of Christ's glory.
13 a. The dress and the duty are those of a slave. b Ps. 41:9

The treachery of Judas foretold

21 Having said this, Jesus was troubled in spirit and declared,
22 'I tell you most solemnly, one of you will betray me.' ·The
   disciples looked at one another, wondering which he meant.
23
24 The disciple Jesus loved was reclining next to Jesus; ·Simon
25 Peter signed to him and said, 'Ask who it is he means', ·so
26 leaning back on Jesus' breast he said, 'Who is it, Lord?' ·It is
   the one' replied Jesus 'to whom I give the piece of bread that
   I shall dip in the dish.' He dipped the piece of bread and gave
27 it to Judas son of Simon Iscariot. ·At that instant, after Judas
   had taken the bread, Satan entered him. Jesus then said,
28 'What you are going to do, do quickly'. ·None of the others
29 at table understood the reason he said this. ·Since Judas had
   charge of the common fund, some of them thought Jesus was
   telling him, 'Buy what we need for the festival', or telling him
30 to give something to the poor. ·As soon as Judas had taken
   the piece of bread he went out. Night had fallen.
31 When he had gone Jesus said:

> 'Now has the Son of Man been glorified,
> and in him God has been glorified.
32 If God has been glorified in him,
> God will in turn glorify him in himself,*c*
> and will glorify him very soon.

Farewell discourses

33 'My little children,
> I shall not be with you much longer.
> You will look for me,
> and, as I told the Jews,
> where I am going,
> you cannot come.
34 I give you a new commandment:
> love one another;
> just as I have loved you,
> you also must love one another.
35 By this love you have for one another,
> everyone will know that you are my disciples.'

36 Simon Peter said, 'Lord, where are you going?' Jesus replied, 'Where I am going you cannot follow me now; you
37 will follow me later'. ·Peter said to him, 'Why can't I follow
38 you now? I will lay down my life for you.' ·'Lay down your
   life for me?' answered Jesus. 'I tell you most solemnly,
   before the cock crows you will have disowned me three times.

14   'Do not let your hearts be troubled.
            Trust in God still, and trust in me.
2   There are many rooms in my Father's house;
            if there were not, I should have told you.
            I am going now to prepare a place for you,
3   and after I have gone and prepared you a place,
            I shall return to take you with me;
            so that where I am
            you may be too.
4   You know the way to the place where I am going.'

5   Thomas said, 'Lord, we do not know where you are going,
6   so how can we know the way?' ·Jesus said:

            'I am the Way, the Truth and the Life.
            No one can come to the Father except through me.
7   If you know me, you know my Father too.
            From this moment you know him and have seen him.'

8   Philip said, 'Lord, let us see the Father and then we shall
9   be satisfied'. ·'Have I been with you all this time, Philip,' said
    Jesus to him 'and you still do not know me?

            'To have seen me is to have seen the Father,
            so how can you say, "Let us see the Father"?
10   Do you not believe
            that I am in the Father and the Father is in me?
            The words I say to you I do not speak as from myself:
            it is the Father, living in me, who is doing this work.
11   You must believe me when I say
            that I am in the Father and the Father is in me;
            believe it on the evidence of this work, if for no other
                reason.
12   I tell you most solemnly,
            whoever believes in me
            will perform the same works as I do myself,
            he will perform even greater works,
            because I am going to the Father.
13   Whatever you ask for in my name I will do,
            so that the Father may be glorified in the Son.
14   If you ask for anything in my name,
            I will do it.
15   If you love me you will keep my commandments.
16   I shall ask the Father,
            and he will give you another Advocate[a]

c. I.e. the Father will take the Son of Man to himself in glory.
14 a. Greek *parakletos*: advocate or counsellor or protector.

to be with you for ever,
17 that Spirit of truth
whom the world can never receive
since it neither sees nor knows him;
but you know him,
because he is with you, he is in you.
18 I will not leave you orphans;
I will come back to you.
19 In a short time the world will no longer see me;
but you will see me,
because I live and you will live.
20 On that day
you will understand that I am in my Father
and you in me and I in you.
21 Anybody who receives my commandments and keeps
them
will be one who loves me;
and anybody who loves me will be loved by my Father,
and I shall love him and show myself to him.'

22 Judas[b]—this was not Judas Iscariot—said to him, 'Lord,
what is all this about? Do you intend to show yourself to us
23 and not to the world?' ·Jesus replied:

'If anyone loves me he will keep my word,
and my Father will love him,
and we shall come to him
and make our home with him.
24 Those who do not love me do not keep my words.
And my word is not my own:
it is the word of the one who sent me.
25 I have said these things to you
while still with you;
26 but the Advocate, the Holy Spirit,
whom the Father will send in my name,
will teach you everything
and remind you of all I have said to you.
27 Peace[c] I bequeath to you,
my own peace I give you,
a peace the world cannot give, this is my gift to you.
Do not let your hearts be troubled or afraid.
28 You heard me say:
I am going away, and shall return.
If you loved me you would have been glad to know
that I am going to the Father,
for the Father is greater than I.

29   I have told you this now before it happens,
so that when it does happen you may believe.

30   I shall not talk with you any longer,
because the prince of this world is on his way.
He has no power over me,

31   but the world must be brought to know that I love the Father
and that I am doing exactly what the Father told me.
Come now, let us go.

The true vine

15   'I am the true vine,
and my Father is the vinedresser.

2   Every branch in me that bears no fruit
he cuts away,
and every branch that does bear fruit he prunes
to make it bear even more.

3   You are pruned already,
by means of the word that I have spoken to you.

4   Make your home in me, as I make mine in you.
As a branch cannot bear fruit all by itself,
but must remain part of the vine,
neither can you unless you remain in me.

5   I am the vine,
you are the branches.
Whoever remains in me, with me in him,
bears fruit in plenty;
for cut off from me you can do nothing.

6   Anyone who does not remain in me
is like a branch that has been thrown away
—he withers;
these branches are collected and thrown on the fire,
and they are burnt.

7   If you remain in me
and my words remain in you,
you may ask what you will
and you shall get it.

8   It is to the glory of my Father that you should bear much fruit,
and then you will be my disciples.

9   As the Father has loved me,
so I have loved you.
Remain in my love.

b. 'Judas, brother of James' in Lk 6:16 and Ac 1:13; the Thaddaeus of Mt 10:3 and Mk 3:18. c. The customary Jewish farewell.

10   If you keep my commandments
           you will remain in my love,
           just as I have kept my Father's commandments
           and remain in his love.

11   I have told you this
           so that my own joy may be in you
           and your joy be complete.

12   This is my commandment:
           love one another,
           as I have loved you.

13   A man can have no greater love
           than to lay down his life for his friends.

14   You are my friends,
           if you do what I command you.

15   I shall not call you servants any more,
           because a servant does not know
           his master's business;
           I call you friends,
           because I have made known to you
           everything I have learnt from my Father.

16   You did not choose me,
           no, I chose you;
           and I commissioned you
           to go out and to bear fruit,
           fruit that will last;
           and then the Father will give you
           anything you ask him in my name.

17   What I command you
           is to love one another.

The hostile world

18   'If the world hates you,
           remember that it hated me before you.

19   If you belonged to the world,
           the world would love you as its own;
           but because you do not belong to the world,
           because my choice withdrew you from the world,
           therefore the world hates you.

20   Remember the words I said to you:
           A servant is not greater than his master.
           If they persecuted me,
           they will persecute you too;
           if they kept my word,
           they will keep yours as well.

21   But it will be on my account that they will do all this,

because they do not know the one who sent me.
22 If I had not come,
if I had not spoken to them,
they would have been blameless;
but as it is they have no excuse for their sin.
23 Anyone who hates me hates my Father.
24 If I had not performed such works among them
as no one else has ever done,
they would be blameless;
but as it is, they have seen all this,
and still they hate both me and my Father.
25 But all this was only to fulfil the words written in their
Law:
They hated me for no reason.[a]
26 When the Advocate comes,
whom I shall send to you from the Father,
the Spirit of truth who issues from the Father,
he will be my witness.
27 And you too will be witnesses,
because you have been with me from the outset.

16 'I have told you all this
so that your faith may not be shaken.
2 They will expel you from the synagogues,
and indeed the hour is coming
when anyone who kills you will think he is doing a holy
duty for God.
3 They will do these things
because they have never known either the Father or myself.
4 But I have told you all this,
so that when the time for it comes
you may remember that I told you.

The coming of the Advocate

'I did not tell you this from the outset,
because I was with you;
5 but now I am going to the one who sent me.
Not one of you has asked, "Where are you going?"
6 Yet you are sad at heart because I have told you this.
7 Still, I must tell you the truth:
it is for your own good that I am going
because unless I go,
the Advocate will not come to you;

15 a. Ps 35:19

but if I do go,
I will send him to you.
And when he comes,

8   he will show the world how wrong it was,
about sin,
and about who was in the right,
and about judgement:

9   about sin:
proved by their refusal to believe in me;

10   about who was in the right:
proved by my going to the Father
and your seeing me no more;

11   about judgement:
proved by the prince of this world being already condemned.

12   I still have many things to say to you
but they would be too much for you now.

13   But when the Spirit of truth comes
he will lead you to the complete truth,
since he will not be speaking as from himself
but will say only what he has learnt;
and he will tell you of the things to come.

14   He will glorify me,
since all he tells you
will be taken from what is mine.

15   Everything the Father has is mine;
that is why I said:
All he tells you
will be taken from what is mine.

Jesus to return very soon

16   'In a short time you will no longer see me,
and then a short time later you will see me again.'

17   Then some of his disciples said to one another, 'What does
he mean, "In a short time you will no longer see me, and then
a short time later you will see me again" and, "I am going to

18 the Father"? ·What is this "short time"? We don't know

19 what he means.' ·Jesus knew that they wanted to question
him, so he said, 'You are asking one another what I meant by
saying: In a short time you will no longer see me, and then a
short time later you will see me again.

20   'I tell you most solemnly,
you will be weeping and wailing
while the world will rejoice;

you will be sorrowful,
but your sorrow will turn to joy.

21 A woman in childbirth suffers,
because her time has come;
but when she has given birth to the child she forgets the
 suffering
in her joy that a man has been born into the world.

22 So it is with you: you are sad now,
but I shall see you again, and your hearts will be full
 of joy,
and that joy no one shall take from you.

23 When that day comes,
you will not ask me any questions.
I tell you most solemnly,
anything you ask for from the Father
he will grant in my name.

24 Until now you have not asked for anything in my
 name.
Ask and you will receive,
and so your joy will be complete.

25 I have been telling you all this in metaphors,
the hour is coming
when I shall no longer speak to you in metaphors;
but tell you about the Father in plain words.

26 When that day comes
you will ask in my name;
and I do not say that I shall pray to the Father for you,

27 because the Father himself loves you
for loving me
and believing that I came from God.

28 I came from the Father and have come into the world
and now I leave the world to go to the Father.'

29 His disciples said, 'Now you are speaking plainly and not
30 using metaphors! ·Now we see that you know everything,
and do not have to wait for questions to be put into words;
31 because of this we believe that you came from God.' ·Jesus
answered them:

'Do you believe at last?
32 Listen; the time will come—in fact it has come already—
when you will be scattered, each going his own way
and leaving me alone.
And yet I am not alone,
because the Father is with me.

33   I have told you all this
so that you may find peace in me.
In the world you will have trouble,
but be brave:
I have conquered the world.'

The priestly prayer of Christ

17   After saying this, Jesus raised his eyes to heaven and said:

1   'Father, the hour has come:
glorify your Son
so that your Son may glorify you

2   and, through the power over all mankind*a* that you
        have given him,
let him give eternal life to all those you have entrusted
        to him.

3   And eternal life is this:
to know you,
the only true God,
and Jesus Christ whom you have sent.

4   I have glorified you on earth
and finished the work
that you gave me to do.

5   Now, Father, it is time for you to glorify me
with that glory I had with you
before ever the world was.

6   I have made your name known
to the men you took from the world to give me.
They were yours and you gave them to me,
and they have kept your word.

7   Now at last they know
that all you have given me comes indeed from you;

8   for I have given them
the teaching you gave to me,
and they have truly accepted this, that I came from
        you,
and have believed that it was you who sent me.

9   I pray for them;
I am not praying for the world
but for those you have given me,
because they belong to you:

10   all I have is yours
and all you have is mine,
and in them I am glorified.

11   I am not in the world any longer,
but they are in the world,

and I am coming to you.
Holy Father,
keep those you have given me true to your name,
so that they may be one like us.

12   While I was with them,
I kept those you had given me true to your name.
I have watched over them and not one is lost
except the one who chose to be lost,*b*
and this was to fulfil the scriptures.

13   But now I am coming to you
and while still in the world I say these things
to share my joy with them to the full.

14   I passed your word on to them,
and the world hated them,
because they belong to the world
no more than I belong to the world.

15   I am not asking you to remove them from the world,
but to protect them from the evil one.

16   They do not belong to the world
any more than I belong to the world.

17   Consecrate them in the truth;
your word is truth.

18   As you sent me into the world,
I have sent them into the world,

19   and for their sake I consecrate myself
so that they too may be consecrated in truth.

20   I pray not only for these,
but for those also
who through their words will believe in me.

21   May they all be one.
Father, may they be one in us,
as you are in me and I am in you,
so that the world may believe it was you who sent me.

22   I have given them the glory you gave to me,
that they may be one as we are one.

23   With me in them and you in me,
may they be so completely one
that the world will realise that it was you who sent me
and that I have loved them as much as you loved me.

24   Father,
I want those you have given me
to be with me where I am,
so that they may always see the glory
you have given me

17 **a.** Lit. 'all flesh'. **b.** Lit. 'the son of perdition'.

because you loved me
before the foundation of the world.

25   Father, Righteous One,
the world has not known you,
but I have known you,
and these have known
that you have sent me.

26   I have made your name known to them
and will continue to make it known,
so that the love with which you loved me may be in
    them,
and so that I may be in them.'

C. THE PASSION

The arrest of Jesus

18   After he had said all this Jesus left with his disciples and
crossed the Kedron valley. There was a garden there, and he
2 went into it with his disciples. ·Judas the traitor knew the
3 place well, since Jesus had often met his disciples there, ·and
he brought the cohort[a] to this place together with a detachment of guards sent by the chief priests and the Pharisees, all
4 with lanterns and torches and weapons. ·Knowing everything
that was going to happen to him, Jesus then came forward
5 and said, 'Who are you looking for?' ·They answered, 'Jesus
the Nazarene'. He said, 'I am he'. Now Judas the traitor was
6 standing among them. ·When Jesus said, 'I am he', they
7 moved back and fell to the ground. ·He asked them a second
time, 'Who are you looking for?' They said, 'Jesus, the
8 Nazarene'. ·'I have told you that I am he' replied Jesus. 'If I
9 am the one you are looking for, let these others go.' ·This was
to fulfil the words he had spoken, 'Not one of those you gave
me have I lost'.

10   Simon Peter, who carried a sword, drew it and wounded
the high priest's servant, cutting off his right ear. The ser-
11 vant's name was Malchus. ·Jesus said to Peter, 'Put your
sword back in its scabbard; am I not to drink the cup that the
Father has given me?'

Jesus before Annas and Caiaphas. Peter disowns him

12   The cohort and its captain and the Jewish guards seized
13 Jesus and bound him. ·They took him first to Annas, because
Annas was the father-in-law of Caiaphas, who was high priest
14 that year. ·It was Caiaphas who had suggested to the Jews,
'It is better for one man to die for the people'.

15 Simon Peter, with another disciple, followed Jesus. This
disciple, who was known to the high priest, went with Jesus
16 into the high priest's palace, ·but Peter stayed outside the
door. So the other disciple, the one known to the high priest,
went out, spoke to the woman who was keeping the door and
17 brought Peter in. ·The maid on duty at the door said to
Peter, 'Aren't you another of that man's disciples?' He
18 answered, 'I am not'. ·Now it was cold, and the servants and
guards had lit a charcoal fire and were standing there warming themselves; so Peter stood there too, warming himself
with the others.
19 The high priest questioned Jesus about his disciples and his
20 teaching. ·Jesus answered, 'I have spoken openly for all the
world to hear; I have always taught in the synagogue and in
the Temple where all the Jews meet together: I have said
21 nothing in secret. ·But why ask me? Ask my hearers what I
22 taught: they know what I said.' ·At these words one of the
guards standing by gave Jesus a slap in the face, saying, 'Is
23 that the way to answer the high priest?' ·Jesus replied, 'If
there is something wrong in what I said, point it out; but if
24 there is no offence in it, why do you strike me?' ·Then Annas
sent him, still bound, to Caiaphas the high priest.
25 As Simon Peter stood there warming himself, someone said
to him, 'Aren't you another of his disciples?' He denied it
26 saying, 'I am not'. ·One of the high priest's servants, a relation of the man whose ear Peter had cut off, said, 'Didn't
27 I see you in the garden with him?' ·Again Peter denied it;
and at once a cock crew.

Jesus before Pilate

28 They then led Jesus from the house of Caiaphas to the
Praetorium.[b] It was now morning. They did not go into the
Praetorium themselves or they would be defiled[c] and unable
29 to eat the passover. ·So Pilate came outside to them and said,
'What charge do you bring against this man?' They replied,
30 'If he were not a criminal, we should not be handing him
31 over to you'. ·Pilate said, 'Take him yourselves, and try him
by your own Law'. The Jews answered, 'We are not allowed
32 to put a man to death'. ·This was to fulfil the words Jesus
had spoken indicating the way he was going to die.
33 So Pilate went back into the Praetorium and called Jesus
34 to him, 'Are you the king of the Jews?' he asked. ·Jesus

18 a. A detachment from the Roman garrison in Jerusalem. **b.** The
judicial court of the Roman procurator. **c.** By entering the house of
a pagan. Cf. Lk 7:6.

replied, 'Do you ask this of your own accord, or have others
35 spoken to you about me?' ·Pilate answered, 'Am I a Jew?
It is your own people and the chief priests who have handed
36 you over to me: what have you done?' ·Jesus replied, 'Mine is
not a kingdom of this world; if my kingdom were of this
world, my men would have fought to prevent my being
surrendered to the Jews. But my kingdom is not of this
37 kind.' ·'So you are a king then?' said Pilate. 'It is you who
say it' answered Jesus. 'Yes, I am a king. I was born for this,
I came into the world for this: to bear witness to the truth;
and all who are on the side of truth listen to my voice.
38 'Truth?' said Pilate 'What is that?'; and with that he went
out again to the Jews and said, 'I find no case against him.
39 But according to a custom of yours I should release one
prisoner at the Passover; would you like me, then, to release
40 the king of the Jews?' ·At this they shouted: 'Not this man,'
they said 'but Barabbas'. Barabbas was a brigand.

19 Pilate then had Jesus taken away and scourged; ·and after
this, the soldiers twisted some thorns into a crown and put it
3 on his head, and dressed him in a purple robe. ·They kept
coming up to him and saying, 'Hail, king of the Jews!'; and
they slapped him in the face.
4 Pilate came outside again and said to them, 'Look, I am
going to bring him out to you to let you see that I find no
5 case'. ·Jesus then came out wearing the crown of thorns and
6 the purple robe. Pilate said, 'Here is the man'. ·When they
saw him the chief priests and the guards shouted, 'Crucify
him! Crucify him!' Pilate said, 'Take him yourselves and
7 crucify him: I can find no case against him'. ·'We have a
Law,' the Jews replied 'and according to that Law he ought
to die, because he has claimed to be the Son of God.'
8 When Pilate heard them say this his fears increased.
9 Re-entering the Praetorium, he said to Jesus, 'Where do you
10 come from?' But Jesus made no answer. ·Pilate then said to
him, 'Are you refusing to speak to me? Surely you know I
have power to release you and I have power to crucify you?'
11 'You would have no power over me' replied Jesus 'if it had
not been given you from above; that is why the one who
handed me over to you has the greater guilt.'

Jesus is condemned to death

12 From that moment Pilate was anxious to set him free, but
the Jews shouted, 'If you set him free you are no friend of
Caesar's; anyone who makes himself king is defying Caesar'.
13 Hearing these words, Pilate had Jesus brought out, and

seated himself on the chair of judgement at a place called the
14 Pavement, in Hebrew Gabbatha. ·It was Passover Preparation Day, about the sixth hour.*ᵃ* 'Here is your king' said
15 Pilate to the Jews. ·'Take him away, take him away!' they
said. 'Crucify him!' 'Do you want me to crucify your king?'
said Pilate. The chief priests answered, 'We have no king
16 except Caesar'. ·So in the end Pilate handed him over to them
to be crucified.

The crucifixion

17 They then took charge of Jesus, ·and carrying his own
cross he went out of the city to the place of the skull or, as it
18 was called in Hebrew, Golgotha, ·where they crucified him
with two others, one on either side with Jesus in the middle.
19 Pilate wrote out a notice and had it fixed to the cross; it ran:
20 Jesus the Nazarene, King of the Jews'. ·This notice was read
by many of the Jews, because the place where Jesus was
crucified was not far from the city, and the writing was in
21 Hebrew, Latin and Greek. ·So the Jewish chief priests said to
Pilate, 'You should not write "King of the Jews", but "This
22 man said: I am King of the Jews" '. ·Pilate answered, 'What
I have written, I have written'.

Christ's garments divided

23 When the soldiers had finished crucifying Jesus they took
his clothing and divided it into four shares, one for each
soldier. His undergarment was seamless, woven in one piece
24 from neck to hem; ·so they said to one another, 'Instead of
tearing it, let's throw dice to decide who is to have it'. In this
way the words of scripture were fulfilled:

> They shared out my clothing among them.
> They cast lots for my clothes.*ᵇ*

This is exactly what the soldiers did.

Jesus and his mother

25 Near the cross of Jesus stood his mother and his mother's
sister, Mary the wife of Clopas, and Mary of Magdala.
26 Seeing his mother and the disciple he loved standing near her,
27 Jesus said to his mother, 'Woman, this is your son'. ·Then to
the disciple he said, 'This is your mother'. And from that
moment the disciple made a place for her in his home.

19 a. On Preparation Day, the Passover supper was made ready for
eating after sunset. The sixth hour is midday, by which time all leaven
had to be removed from the house; during the feast only unleavened
bread was eaten. **b.** Ps 22:18

The death of Jesus

28 After this, Jesus knew that everything had now been completed, and to fulfil the scripture perfectly he said:

'*I am thirsty*'.[c]

29 A jar full of vinegar stood there, so putting a sponge soaked in the vinegar on a hyssop stick they held it up to his
30 mouth. ·After Jesus had taken the vinegar he said, 'It is accomplished'; and bowing his head he gave up his spirit.

The pierced Christ

31 It was Preparation Day, and to prevent the bodies remaining on the cross during the sabbath—since that sabbath was a day of special solemnity—the Jews asked Pilate to have
32 the legs broken[d] and the bodies taken away. ·Consequently the soldiers came and broke the legs of the first man who had
33 been crucified with him and then of the other. ·When they came to Jesus, they found he was already dead, and so in-
34 stead of breaking his legs ·one of the soldiers pierced his side with a lance; and immediately there came out blood and
35 water. ·This is the evidence of one who saw it—trustworthy evidence, and he knows he speaks the truth—and he gives it
36 so that you may believe as well. ·Because all this happened to fulfil the words of scripture:

Not one bone of his will be broken;[e]

37 and again, in another place scripture says:

They will look on the one whom they have pierced.[f]

The burial

38 After this, Joseph of Arimathaea, who was a disciple of Jesus—though a secret one because he was afraid of the Jews —asked Pilate to let him remove the body of Jesus. Pilate
39 gave permission, so they came and took it away. ·Nicodemus came as well—the same one who had first come to Jesus at night-time—and he brought a mixture of myrrh and aloes,
40 weighing about a hundred pounds. ·They took the body of Jesus and wrapped it with the spices in linen cloths, following
41 the Jewish burial custom. ·At the place where he had been crucified there was a garden, and in this garden a new tomb
42 in which no one had yet been buried. ·Since it was the Jewish Day of Preparation and the tomb was near at hand, they laid Jesus there.

VIII. THE DAY OF CHRIST'S RESURRECTION

The empty tomb

20 It was very early on the first day of the week and still dark, when Mary of Magdala came to the tomb. She saw that the
2 stone had been moved away from the tomb ·and came running to Simon Peter and the other disciple, the one Jesus loved. 'They have taken the Lord out of the tomb' she said 'and we don't know where they have put him.'

3 So Peter set out with the other disciple to go to the tomb.
4 They ran together, but the other disciple, running faster than
5 Peter, reached the tomb first; ·he bent down and saw the
6 linen cloths lying on the ground, but did not go in. ·Simon Peter who was following now came up, went right into the
7 tomb, saw the linen cloths on the ground, ·and also the cloth that had been over his head; this was not with the linen
8 cloths but rolled up in a place by itself. ·Then the other disciple who had reached the tomb first also went in; he saw
9 and he believed. ·Till this moment they had failed to understand the teaching of scripture, that he must rise from the
10 dead. ·The disciples then went home again.

The appearance to Mary of Magdala

11 Meanwhile Mary stayed outside near the tomb, weeping.
12 Then, still weeping, she stooped to look inside, ·and saw two angels in white sitting where the body of Jesus had been, one
13 at the head, the other at the feet. ·They said, 'Woman, why are you weeping?' 'They have taken my Lord away' she
14 replied 'and I don't know where they have put him.' ·As she said this she turned round and saw Jesus standing there,
15 though she did not recognise him. ·Jesus said, 'Woman, why are you weeping? Who are you looking for?' Supposing him to be the gardener, she said, 'Sir, if you have taken him away, tell me where you have put him, and I will go and remove
16 him'. ·Jesus said, 'Mary!' She knew him then and said to
17 him in Hebrew, 'Rabbuni!'—which means Master. ·Jesus said to her, 'Do not cling to me, because I have not yet ascended to the Father. But go and find the brothers, and tell them: I am ascending to my Father and your Father, to my

c. Ps 22:15 d. To hasten death. e. Two texts are here combined: Ps 34:20 and Ex 12:46. The allusion is both to God protecting the good man, and to the ritual for preparing the Passover lamb. f. Zc 12:10

18 God and your God.' ·So Mary of Magdala went and told the
    disciples that she had seen the Lord and that he had said
    these things to her.

Appearances to the disciples

19   In the evening of that same day, the first day of the week,
    the doors were closed in the room where the disciples were,
    for fear of the Jews. Jesus came and stood among them. He
20 said to them, 'Peace be with you', ·and showed them his
    hands and his side. The disciples were filled with joy when
21 they saw the Lord, ·and he said to them again, 'Peace be
    with you.

        'As the Father sent me,
        so am I sending you.'

22 After saying this he breathed on them and said:

        'Receive the Holy Spirit.
23   For those whose sins you forgive,
        they are forgiven;
        for those whose sins you retain,
        they are retained.'

24   Thomas, called the Twin, who was one of the Twelve, was
25 not with them when Jesus came. ·When the disciples said,
    'We have seen the Lord', he answered, 'Unless I see the holes
    that the nails made in his hands and can put my finger into
    the holes they made, and unless I can put my hand into his
26 side, I refuse to believe'. ·Eight days later the disciples were
    in the house again and Thomas was with them. The doors
    were closed, but Jesus came in and stood among them.
27 'Peace be with you' he said. ·Then he spoke to Thomas, 'Put
    your finger here; look, here are my hands. Give me your
    hand; put it into my side. Doubt no longer but believe.'
28
29 Thomas replied, 'My Lord and my God!' ·Jesus said to him:

        'You believe because you can see me.
        Happy are those who have not seen and yet believe.'

CONCLUSION[a]

30   There were many other signs that Jesus worked and the
31 disciples saw, but they are not recorded in this book. ·These
    are recorded so that you may believe that Jesus is the Christ,

the Son of God, and that believing this you may have life through his name.

APPENDIX[a]

The appearance on the shore of Tiberias

21 Later on, Jesus showed himself again to the disciples. It
2 was by the Sea of Tiberias, and it happened like this: ·Simon Peter, Thomas called the Twin, Nathanael from Cana in Galilee, the sons of Zebedee and two more of his disciples
3 were together. ·Simon Peter said, 'I'm going fishing'. They replied, 'We'll come with you'. They went out and got into the boat but caught nothing that night.
4 It was light by now and there stood Jesus on the shore,
5 though the disciples did not realise that it was Jesus. ·Jesus called out, 'Have you caught anything, friends?' And when
6 they answered, 'No', ·he said, 'Throw the net out to starboard and you'll find something'. So they dropped the net, and there were so many fish that they could not haul it in.
7 The disciple Jesus loved said to Peter, 'It is the Lord'. At these words 'It is the Lord', Simon Peter, who had practically nothing on, wrapped his cloak round him and jumped into
8 the water. ·The other disciples came on in the boat, towing the net and the fish; they were only about a hundred yards from land.
9 As soon as they came ashore they saw that there was some
10 bread there, and a charcoal fire with fish cooking on it. ·Jesus
11 said, 'Bring some of the fish you have just caught'. ·Simon Peter went aboard and dragged the net to the shore, full of big fish, one hundred and fifty-three of them; and in spite of
12 there being so many the net was not broken. ·Jesus said to them, 'Come and have breakfast'. None of the disciples was bold enough to ask, 'Who are you?'; they knew quite well it
13 was the Lord. ·Jesus then stepped forward, took the bread
14 and gave it to them, and the same with the fish. ·This was the third time that Jesus showed himself to the disciples after rising from the dead.
15 After the meal Jesus said to Simon Peter, 'Simon son of John, do you love me more than these others do?' He answered, 'Yes Lord, you know I love you'. Jesus said to
16 him, 'Feed my lambs'. ·A second time he said to him, 'Simon son of John, do you love me?' He replied, 'Yes, Lord, you know I love you'. Jesus said to him, 'Look after my sheep'.
17 Then he said to him a third time, 'Simon son of John, do you

21 a. Added either by the evangelist or by a disciple of his.

love me?' Peter was upset that he asked him the third time, 'Do you love me?' and said, 'Lord, you know everything; you know I love you'. Jesus said to him, 'Feed my sheep.

18   'I tell you most solemnly,
       when you were young
       you put on your own belt
       and walked where you liked;
       but when you grow old
       you will stretch out your hands,
       and somebody else will put a belt round you
       and take you where you would rather not go.'

19 In these words he indicated the kind of death by which Peter would give glory to God. After this he said, 'Follow me'.

20   Peter turned and saw the disciple Jesus loved following them—the one who had leaned on his breast at the supper and had said to him, 'Lord, who is it that will betray you?'

21 Seeing him, Peter said to Jesus, 'What about him, Lord?'

22 Jesus answered, 'If I want him to stay behind till I come,

23 what does it matter to you? You are to follow me.' ·The rumour then went out among the brothers that this disciple would not die. Yet Jesus had not said to Peter, 'He will not die', but, 'If I want him to stay behind till I come'.

Conclusion

24   This disciple is the one who vouches for these things and has written them down, and we know that his testimony is true.

25   There were many other things that Jesus did; if all were written down, the world itself, I suppose, would not hold all the books that would have to be written.

INTRODUCTION TO

THE ACTS OF THE APOSTLES

St Luke's Gospel and The Acts of the Apostles are the two volumes of a single work that today we should call 'a history of the rise of Christianity'. The two books are inseparably linked by their Prologues and by their style. From the text of Acts it is evident that the author was a Christian of the apostolic age, either a thoroughly hellenised Jew or more probably a well-educated 'Greek' with a thorough knowledge of the Septuagint and of Jewish culture and traditions. No other name has ever been suggested than that of Luke, the close friend of Paul, who according to an ancient tradition was a Syrian from Antioch, a doctor and a convert from paganism.

Acts is in the form of a single continuous narrative. It begins with the birth and growth of the primitive Christian community in Jerusalem and tells of the founding of the community in Antioch by hellenist Jews and the conversion of St Paul; it goes on to show the spread of the Church outside Palestine through the missionary travels of Paul and ends with his captivity in Rome in A.D. 61–63. The narrative can be seen to be made up of separate episodes of varying lengths, all containing a great deal of circumstantial detail and commonly joined to each other by editorial formulae.

For the later journeys of Paul, Luke appears to have his own notes; the rest of the book confirms the claim made in the Prologue of the first volume (Lk 1:1–4) that the author collected a large quantity of evidence from a variety of sources. In the editing of this, and the chronological arranging of it, a certain amount of repetition, fusion and anomalies in the order of incidents was unavoidable, but the basic reliability of the work may be seen by checking Luke's account of Paul's missionary activities with Paul's own letters, which were not among his sources. The historical worth of Acts is high, since it not only includes a major section which is an eye-witness account of the events described, but gives much detailed factual information which we should otherwise lack. Although Luke, like any other classical historian, took the freedom to reconstruct speeches which he had not himself heard, there is every evidence that he went back to true sources and treated them with respect: notice, for instance, the archaisms and semitisms left in the reported speeches of Peter and Stephen, and the remarkable distinction between the simple theological background of the earliest Christian sermons and that of Paul's later teaching. It is also to be noticed that he can include a speech which failed to convince its hearers.

Thus Acts is a principal source for much of our knowledge of life in the earliest Christian communities, of the first impact made by the Christian faith on pagan nations, of the primitive beginnings of church organisation, of the early developments of Christology, of the personalities of the apostolic age. Luke is, however, not interested in presenting a formal history of the spread of Christianity. What he is interested in is: 1. The spiritual energy inside Christianity that motivates its expansion, and 2. the spiritual doctrine that he can show by object lessons with the facts at his disposal.

THE ACTS

OF THE APOSTLES

Prologue

1 In my earlier work,[a] Theophilus, I dealt with everything
2 Jesus had done and taught from the beginning ·until the day
he gave his instructions to the apostles he had chosen through
3 the Holy Spirit, and was taken up to heaven. ·He had shown
himself alive to them after his Passion by many demonstra-
tions: for forty days he had continued to appear to them and
4 tell them about the kingdom of God. ·When he had been at
table with them, he had told them not to leave Jerusalem, but
to wait there for what the Father had promised. 'It is' he had
5 said 'what you have heard me speak about: ·John baptised
with water but you, not many days from now, will be baptised with the Holy Spirit.'

The ascension

6 Now having met together,[b] they asked him, 'Lord, has the
time come? Are you going to restore the kingdom to Israel?'
7 He replied, 'It is not for you to know times or dates that the
8 Father has decided by his own authority, ·but you will
receive power when the Holy Spirit comes on you, and then
you will be my witnesses not only in Jerusalem but throughout Judaea and Samaria, and indeed to the ends of the earth'.
9 As he said this he was lifted up while they looked on, and a
10 cloud took him from their sight. ·They were still staring into
the sky when suddenly two men in white were standing near
11 them ·and they said, 'Why are you men from Galilee standing here looking into the sky? Jesus who has been taken up
from you into heaven, this same Jesus will come back in the
same way as you have seen him go there.'

I. THE JERUSALEM CHURCH

The group of apostles

12 So from the Mount of Olives, as it is called, they went
back to Jerusalem, a short distance away, no more than a

1 a. The gospel according to Luke. b. This verse takes up the narrative
broken off in Lk 24:49.

13 sabbath walk; ·and when they reached the city they went to the upper room where they were staying; there were Peter and John, James and Andrew, Philip and Thomas, Bartholomew and Matthew, James son of Alphaeus and Simon the
14 Zealot, and Jude son of James.^c ·All these joined in continuous prayer, together with several women, including Mary the mother of Jesus, and with his brothers.^d

The election of Matthias

15 One day Peter stood up to speak to the brothers^e—there were about a hundred and twenty persons in the congrega-
16 tion: ·'Brothers, the passage of scripture had to be fulfilled in which the Holy Spirit, speaking through David, foretells the fate of Judas, who offered himself as a guide to the men who
17 arrested Jesus—·after having been one of our number and
18 actually sharing this ministry of ours. ·As you know, he bought a field with the money he was paid for his crime. He fell headlong and burst open, and all his entrails poured out.
19 Everybody in Jerusalem heard about it and the field came to be called the Bloody Acre, in their language Hakeldama.
20 Now in the Book of Psalms it says:

> Let his camp be reduced to ruin,
> Let there be no one to live in it.^f

And again:

> Let someone else take his office.^g

21 'We must therefore choose someone who has been with us the whole time that the Lord Jesus was travelling round
22 with us, ·someone who was with us right from the time when John was baptising until the day when he was taken up from us—and he can act with us as a witness to his resurrection.'
23 Having nominated two candidates, Joseph known as
24 Barsabbas, whose surname was Justus, and Matthias, ·they prayed, 'Lord, you can read everyone's heart; show us there-
25 fore which of these two you have chosen ·to take over this ministry and apostolate, which Judas abandoned to go to his
26 proper place'. ·They then drew lots for them, and as the lot fell to Matthias, he was listed as one of the twelve apostles.

Pentecost

2 When Pentecost day came round, they had all met in one
2 room, ·when suddenly they heard what sounded like a powerful wind from heaven, the noise of which filled the entire
3 house in which they were sitting; ·and something appeared

to them that seemed like tongues of fire; these separated and
4 came to rest on the head of each of them. ·They were all filled
with the Holy Spirit, and began to speak foreign languages
as the Spirit gave them the gift of speech.

5   Now there were devout men living in Jerusalem from every
6 nation under heaven, ·and at this sound they all assembled,
each one bewildered to hear these men speaking his own
7 language. ·They were amazed and astonished. 'Surely' they
8 said 'all these men speaking are Galileans? ·How does it
happen that each of us hears them in his own native language?
9 Parthians, Medes and Elamites; people from Mesopotamia,
10 Judaea and Cappadocia, Pontus and Asia, ·Phrygia and
Pamphylia, Egypt and the parts of Libya round Cyrene; as
11 well as visitors from Rome—·Jews and proselytes*a* alike—
Cretans and Arabs; we hear them preaching in our own
12 language about the marvels of God.' ·Everyone was amazed
and unable to explain it; they asked one another what it all
13 meant. ·Some, however, laughed it off. 'They have been drinking too much new wine' they said.

Peter's address to the crowd

14   Then Peter stood up with the Eleven and addressed them
in a loud voice:
'Men of Judaea, and all you who live in Jerusalem, make
no mistake about this, but listen carefully to what I say.
15 These men are not drunk, as you imagine; why, it is only the
16 third hour of the day.*b* ·On the contrary, this is what the
prophet*c* spoke of:

17   In the days to come—it is the Lord who speaks—
        I will pour out my spirit on all mankind.
        Their sons and daughters shall prophesy,
        your young men shall see visions,
        your old men shall dream dreams.
18   Even on my slaves, men and women,
        in those days, I will pour out my spirit.
19   I will display portents in heaven *above*
        and *signs* on earth *below*.
20   The sun will be turned into darkness

c. 'Son' (of Alphaeus, of James) is not in the Greek. This Jude is not
the Jude 'brother' of Jesus, Mt 13:55 and Mk 6:3, and brother of
James (Jude 1). Nor is it likely that 'James of Alphaeus' was James
brother of the Lord. d. Cousins, as in the gospels. e. The term for
Christians, usually the laity as distinct from apostles and elders.
f. Ps 69:25 g. Ps 109:8
2 a. Converts from paganism. b. About 9 a.m. c. Joel. See Jl 3:1–5.

and the moon into blood
before the great Day of the Lord dawns.

21   All who call on the name of the Lord will be saved.

22   'Men of Israel, listen to what I am going to say: Jesus the
Nazarene was a man commended to you by God by the
miracles and portents and signs that God worked through

23 him when he was among you, as you all know. ·This man,
who was put into your power by the deliberate intention and
foreknowledge of God, you took and had crucified by men

24 outside the Law.ᵈ You killed him, ·but God raised him to
life, freeing him from the pangs of Hades; for it was impos-

25 sible for him to be held in its power since, ·as David says of
him:

> I saw the Lord before me always,
> for with him at my right hand nothing can shake me.
26 > So my heart was glad
> and my tongue cried out with joy;
> my body, too, will rest in the hope
27 > that you will not abandon my soul to Hades
> nor allow your holy one to experience corruption.
28 > You have made known the way of life to me,
> you will fill me with gladness through your presence.ᵉ

29   'Brothers, no one can deny that the patriarch David him-
30 self is dead and buried: his tomb is still with us. ·But since
he was a prophet, and knew that God *had sworn him* an oath
*to make one of his descendants succeed him on the throne,*ᶠ

31 what he foresaw and spoke about was the resurrection of the
Christ: he is the one who was *not abandoned to Hades*, and

32 whose body did not *experience corruption*. ·God raised this

33 man Jesus to life, and all of us are witnesses to that. ·Now
raised to the heights by God's right hand, he has received
from the Father the Holy Spirit, who was promised, and

34 what you see and hear is the outpouring of that Spirit. ·For
David himself never went up to heaven; and yet these words
are his.

> The Lord said to my Lord:
> Sit at my right hand
35 > until I make your enemies
> a footstool for you.ᵍ

36   'For this reason the whole House of Israel can be certain
that God has made this Jesus whom you crucified both Lord
and Christ.'

The first conversions

37   Hearing this, they were cut to the heart and said to Peter
38 and the apostles, 'What must we do, brothers?' ·'You must
repent,' Peter answered 'and every one of you must be baptised in the name of Jesus Christ for the forgiveness of your
39 sins, and you will receive the gift of the Holy Spirit. ·The
promise that was made is for you and your children, and for
all *those who are far away, for all those whom the Lord* our
40 God *will call to himself.*[h] ·He spoke to them for a long time
using many arguments, and he urged them, 'Save yourselves
41 from this perverse generation'. ·They were convinced by his
arguments, and they accepted what he said and were baptised. That very day about three thousand were added to
their number.

The early Christian community

42   These remained faithful to the teaching of the apostles, to
the brotherhood, to the breaking of bread and to the prayers.
43   The many miracles and signs worked through the apostles
made a deep impression on everyone.
44   The faithful all lived together and owned everything in
45 common; ·they sold their goods and possessions and shared
out the proceeds among themselves according to what each
one needed.
46   They went as a body to the Temple every day but met in
their houses for the breaking of bread; they shared their
47 food gladly and generously; ·they praised God and were
looked up to by everyone. Day by day the Lord added to
their community those destined to be saved.

The cure of a lame man

3   Once, when Peter and John were going up to the Temple
2 for the prayers at the ninth hour,[a] ·it happened that there was
a man being carried past. He was a cripple from birth; and
they used to put him down every day near the Temple
entrance called the Beautiful Gate so that he could beg from
3 the people going in. ·When this man saw Peter and John on
4 their way into the Temple he begged from them. ·Both Peter
5 and John looked straight at him and said, 'Look at us'. ·He
turned to them expectantly, hoping to get something from
6 them, ·but Peter said, 'I have neither silver nor gold, but I

d. The Romans. e. Ps 16:8–11; quoted according to the LXX. f. 2 S
7:12 and Ps 132:11 g. Ps 110:1 h. Is 57:19
3 a. The time of evening sacrifice.

will give you what I have: in the name of Jesus Christ the
7 Nazarene, walk!' ·Peter then took him by the hand and helped
8 him to stand up. Instantly his feet and ankles became firm, ·he
jumped up, stood, and began to walk, and he went with them
into the Temple, walking and jumping and praising God.
9
10 Everyone could see him walking and praising God, ·and they
recognised him as the man who used to sit begging at the
Beautiful Gate of the Temple. They were all astonished and
unable to explain what had happened to him.

Peter's address to the people

11   Everyone came running towards them in great excitement,
to the Portico of Solomon, as it is called, where the man was
12 still clinging to Peter and John. ·When Peter saw the people
he addressed them, 'Why are you so surprised at this?
Why are you staring at us as though we had made this man
13 walk by our own power or holiness? ·You are Israelites, and
it is *the God of Abraham, Isaac and Jacob, the God of our
ancestors, who has glorified his servant*[b] Jesus, the same Jesus
you handed over and then disowned in the presence of Pilate
14 after Pilate had decided to release him. ·It was you who accused the Holy One, the Just One, you who demanded the
15 reprieve of a murderer ·while you killed the prince of life.
God, however, raised him from the dead, and to that fact we
16 are the witnesses; ·and it is the name of Jesus which, through
our faith in it, has brought back the strength of this man
whom you see here and who is well known to you. It is
faith in that name that has restored this man to health, as
you can all see.

17   'Now I know, brothers, that neither you nor your leaders
18 had any idea what you were really doing; ·this was the way
God carried out what he had foretold, when he said through
19 all his prophets that his Christ would suffer. ·Now you must
repent and turn to God, so that your sins may be wiped out,
20 and so that the Lord may send the time of comfort. Then he
will send you the Christ he has predestined, that is Jesus,
21 whom heaven must keep till the universal restoration comes
which God proclaimed, speaking through his holy prophets.
22 Moses, for example, said: *The Lord God will raise up a prophet like myself for you, from among your own brothers; you
23 must listen to whatever he tells you.* ·*The man who does not
24 listen to that prophet is to be cut off from the people.*[c] ·In fact,
all the prophets that have ever spoken, from Samuel onwards,
have predicted these days.

25   'You are the heirs of the prophets, the heirs of the covenant

God made with our ancestors when he told Abraham: *in your*
26 *offspring all the families of the earth will be blessed.*[d] ·It was
for you in the first place that God raised up his servant and
sent him to bless you by turning every one of you from your
wicked ways.'

Peter and John before the Sanhedrin

4   While they were still talking to the people the priests came
up to them, accompanied by the captain of the Temple and the
2 Sadducees.[a] ·They were extremely annoyed at their teaching
the people the doctrine of the resurrection from the dead by
3 proclaiming the resurrection of Jesus. ·They arrested them,
but as it was already late, they held them till the next day.
4 But many of those who had listened to their message became
believers, the total number of whom had now risen to something like five thousand.
5   The next day the rulers, elders and scribes[b] had a meeting
6 in Jerusalem ·with Annas the high priest, Caiaphas, Jona-
than, Alexander and all the members of the high-priestly
7 families. ·They made the prisoners stand in the middle and
began to interrogate them, 'By what power, and by whose
8 name have you men done this?' ·Then Peter, filled with the
Holy Spirit, addressed them, 'Rulers of the people, and
9 elders! ·If you are questioning us today about an act of
kindness to a cripple, and asking us how he was healed,
10 then I am glad to tell you all, and would indeed be glad to
tell the whole people of Israel, that it was by the name of
Jesus Christ the Nazarene, the one you crucified, whom God
raised from the dead, by this name and by no other that this
man is able to stand up perfectly healthy, here in your pre-
11 sence, today. ·This is *the stone rejected by you the builders*,
12 *but which has proved to be the keystone.*[c] ·For of all the names
in the world given to men, this is the only one by which we
can be saved.'
13   They were astonished at the assurance shown by Peter
and John, considering they were uneducated laymen; and
14 they recognised them as associates of Jesus; but when they
saw the man who had been cured standing by their side, they
15 could find no answer. ·So they ordered them to stand outside
16 while the Sanhedrin had a private discussion. ·'What are
we going to do with these men?' they asked. 'It is obvious to

b. Ex 3:6, 15 and Is 52:13 **c.** Dt 18:18, 19 **d.** Gn 12:3
4 a. The Sadducees (see note on Mt 3:7) are always represented as
denying the doctrine of the resurrection, e.g. Ac 23. **b.** I.e. the Sanhedrin, explained for the non-Jewish reader. **c.** Ps 118:22

everybody in Jerusalem that a miracle has been worked
17 through them in public, and we cannot deny it. ·But to stop
the whole thing spreading any further among the people, let us
caution them never to speak to anyone in this name again.'
18 So they called them in and gave them a warning on no
account to make statements or to teach in the name of Jesus.
19 But Peter and John retorted, 'You must judge whether in
20 God's eyes it is right to listen to you and not to God. ·We
cannot promise to stop proclaiming what we have seen and
21 heard.' ·The court repeated the warnings and then released
them; they could not think of any way to punish them, since
all the people were giving glory to God for what had hap-
22 pened. ·The man who had been miraculously cured was over
forty years old.

The apostles' prayer under persecution

23 As soon as they were released they went to the community
and told them everything the chief priests and elders had said
24 to them. ·When they heard it they lifted up their voice to God
all together. 'Master,' they prayed 'it is you who made
25 heaven and earth and sea, and everything in them; ·you it is
who said through the Holy Spirit and speaking through our
ancestor David, your servant:

> *Why this arrogance among the nations,*
> *these futile plots among the peoples?*
26 > *Kings on earth setting out to war,*
> *princes making an alliance,*
> *against the Lord and against his Anointed.*[d]

27 'This is what has come true: in this very city Herod and
Pontius Pilate *made an alliance* with the pagan *nations* and
the *peoples* of Israel, against your holy servant Jesus whom
28 you *anointed,*[e] ·but only to bring about the very thing that
you in your strength and your wisdom had predetermined
29 should happen. ·And now, Lord, take note of their threats
and help your servants to proclaim your message with all
30 boldness, ·by stretching out your hand to heal and to work
miracles and marvels through the name of your holy servant
31 Jesus.' ·As they prayed, the house where they were assembled
rocked; they were all filled with the Holy Spirit and began to
proclaim the word of God boldly.

The early Christian community

32 The whole group of believers was united, heart and soul;
no one claimed for his own use anything that he had, as
everything they owned was held in common.

33 The apostles continued to testify to the resurrection of the Lord Jesus with great power, and they were all given great respect.
34 None of their members was ever in want, as all those who owned land or houses would sell them, and bring the money
35 from them, ·to present it to the apostles; it was then distributed to any members who might be in need.

The generosity of Barnabas

36 There was a Levite of Cypriot origin called Joseph whom the apostles surnamed Barnabas (which means 'son of
37 encouragement'). ·He owned a piece of land and he sold it and brought the money, and presented it to the apostles.

The fraud of Ananias and Sapphira

5 There was another man, however, called Ananias. He and
2 his wife, Sapphira, agreed to sell a property; ·but with his wife's connivance he kept back part of the proceeds, and
3 brought the rest and presented it to the apostles. ·'Ananias,' Peter said 'how can Satan have so possessed you that you should lie to the Holy Spirit and keep back part of the money
4 from the land? ·While you still owned the land, wasn't it yours to keep, and after you had sold it wasn't the money yours to do with as you liked? What put this scheme into your mind? It is not to men that you have lied, but to God.'
5 When he heard this Ananias fell down dead. This made a
6 profound impression on everyone present. ·The younger men got up, wrapped the body in a sheet, carried it out and buried it.
7 About three hours later his wife came in, not knowing what
8 had taken place. ·Peter challenged her, 'Tell me, was this the price you sold the land for?' 'Yes,' she said 'that was the
9 price.' ·Peter then said, 'So you and your husband have agreed to put the Spirit of the Lord to the test! What made you do it? You hear those footsteps? They have just been to
10 bury your husband; they will carry you out, too.' ·Instantly she dropped dead at his feet. When the young men came in they found she was dead, and they carried her out and
11 buried her by the side of her husband. ·This made a profound impression on the whole Church and on all who heard it.

The general situation

12b They all used to meet by common consent in the Portico
13 of Solomon. ·No one else ever dared to join them, but the

d. Ps 2:1–2 e. I.e. made the Christ, the anointed Messiah.

14 people were loud in their praise ·and the numbers of men and women who came to believe in the Lord increased steadily.
12a So many signs and wonders were worked among the people
15 at the hands of the apostles ·that the sick were even taken out into the streets and laid on beds and sleeping-mats in the hope that at least the shadow of Peter might fall across some
16 of them as he went past. ·People even came crowding in from the towns round about Jerusalem, bringing with them their sick and those tormented by unclean spirits, and all of them were cured.

The apostles' arrest and miraculous deliverance

17 Then the high priest intervened with all his supporters
18 from the party of the Sadducees. Prompted by jealousy, ·they arrested the apostles and had them put in the common gaol.
19 But at night the angel of the Lord opened the prison gates
20 and said as he led them out, ·'Go and stand in the Temple,
21 and tell the people all about this new Life'. ·They did as they were told; they went into the Temple at dawn and began to preach.

A summons to appear before the Sanhedrin

When the high priest arrived, he and his supporters convened the Sanhedrin—this was the full Senate of Israel—and
22 sent to the gaol for them to be brought. ·But when the officials arrived at the prison they found they were not inside, so
23 they went back and reported, ·'We found the gaol securely locked and the warders on duty at the gates, but when we
24 unlocked the door we found no one inside'. ·When the captain of the Temple and the chief priests heard this news they
25 wondered what this could mean. ·Then a man arrived with fresh news. 'At this very moment' he said 'the men you imprisoned are in the Temple. They are standing there preach-
26 ing to the people.' ·The captain went with his men and fetched them. They were afraid to use force in case the people stoned them.
27 When they had brought them in to face the Sanhedrin, the
28 high priest demanded an explanation. ·'We gave you a formal warning' he said 'not to preach in this name, and what have you done? You have filled Jerusalem with your teaching, and seem determined to fix the guilt of this man's death on us.'
29 In reply Peter and the apostles said, 'Obedience to God
30 comes before obedience to men; ·it was the God of our ancestors who raised up Jesus, but it was you who had him
31 executed by hanging on a tree.[a] ·By his own right hand God

has now raised him up to be leader and saviour, to give
repentance and forgiveness of sins through him to Israel.
32 We are witnesses to all this, we and the Holy Spirit whom
33 God has given to those who obey him.' ·This so infuriated
them that they wanted to put them to death.

Gamaliel's intervention

34   One member of the Sanhedrin, however, a Pharisee called
Gamaliel, who was a doctor of the Law and respected by the
whole people,[b] stood up and asked to have the men taken out-
35 side for a time. ·Then he addressed the Sanhedrin, 'Men of
36 Israel, be careful how you deal with these people. ·There was
Theudas who became notorious not so long ago. He claimed
to be someone important, and he even collected about four
hundred followers; but when he was killed, all his followers
37 scattered and that was the end of them. ·And then there was
Judas the Galilean, at the time of the census, who attracted
crowds of supporters; but he got killed too, and all his fol-
38 lowers dispersed. ·What I suggest, therefore, is that you
leave these men alone and let them go. If this enterprise, this
movement of theirs, is of human origin it will break up of its
39 own accord; ·but if it does in fact come from God you will
not only be unable to destroy them, but you might find
yourselves fighting against God.'
40   His advice was accepted; ·and they had the apostles called
in, gave orders for them to be flogged, warned them not to
41 speak in the name of Jesus and released them. ·And so they
left the presence of the Sanhedrin glad to have had the
honour of suffering humiliation for the sake of the name.
42   They preached every day both in the Temple and in private
houses, and their proclamation of the Good News of Christ
Jesus was never interrupted.

II. THE EARLIEST MISSIONS

The institution of the Seven

6   About this time, when the number of disciples was increasing, the Hellenists made a complaint against the
Hebrews:[a] in the daily distribution their own widows were
2 being overlooked. ·So the Twelve called a full meeting of the

5 a. The phrase recalls Dt 21:23. b. Gamaliel I, a Pharisee of the
school of Hillel; he was Paul's teacher.
6 a. 'Hellenists': Jews from outside Palestine; they had their own
synagogues in Jerusalem, where the scriptures were read in Greek.
The 'Hebrews' were Palestinian Jews and in their synagogues scriptures were read in Hebrew.

disciples and addressed them, 'It would not be right for us
3 to neglect the word of God so as to give out food; ·you,
brothers, must select from among yourselves seven men of
good reputation, filled with the Spirit and with wisdom; we
4 will hand over this duty to them, ·and continue to devote
5 ourselves to prayer and to the service of the word'. ·The
whole assembly approved of this proposal and elected
Stephen, a man full of faith and of the Holy Spirit, together
with Philip, Prochorus, Nicanor, Timon, Parmenas, and
6 Nicolaus of Antioch, a convert to Judaism. ·They presented
these to the apostles, who prayed and laid their hands on
them.[b]
7 The word of the Lord continued to spread: the number of
disciples in Jerusalem was greatly increased, and a large
group of priests made their submission to the faith.

Stephen's arrest

8 Stephen was filled with grace and power and began to
9 work miracles and great signs among the people. ·But then
certain people came forward to debate with Stephen, some
from Cyrene and Alexandria who were members of the
synagogue called the Synagogue of Freedmen,[c] and others
10 from Cilicia and Asia. ·They found they could not get the
better of him because of his wisdom, and because it was the
11 Spirit that prompted what he said. ·So they procured some
men to say, 'We heard him using blasphemous language
12 against Moses and against God'. ·Having in this way turned
the people against him as well as the elders and scribes, they
took Stephen by surprise, and arrested him and brought him
13 before the Sanhedrin. ·There they put up false witnesses to
say, 'This man is always making speeches against this Holy
14 Place and the Law. ·We have heard him say that Jesus the
Nazarene is going to destroy this Place and alter the tradi-
15 tions that Moses handed down to us.' ·The members of the
Sanhedrin all looked intently at Stephen, and his face appeared to them like the face of an angel.

Stephen's speech

7 The high priest asked, 'Is this true?' ·He replied, 'My
brothers, my fathers, listen to what I have to say. The God of
glory appeared to our ancestor Abraham, while he was in
3 Mesopotamia before settling in Haran, ·*and said to him,
"Leave your country and your family and go to the land I will*
4 *show you"*.[a] ·So he left Chaldaea and settled in Haran; and

after his father died God made him leave Haran and come
5 to this land where you are living today. ·God did not give
him a single square foot of this land to call his own, yet he
promised to *give it to him and after him to his descendants,*
6 *childless*[b] though he was. ·The actual words God used when
he spoke to him are that *his descendants would be exiles in a*
foreign land, where they would be slaves and oppressed for four
7 *hundred years.* ·*"But I will pass judgement on the nation that*
enslaves them." God said "*and after this they will leave, and*
8 *worship me in this* place."[c] ·Then he made the covenant of
circumcision: so when his son Isaac was born he circumcised
him on the eighth day. Isaac did the same for Jacob, and
Jacob for the twelve patriarchs.
9   'The patriarchs were *jealous of Joseph and sold him into*
10 *slavery in Egypt.*[d] But *God was with him,*[e] ·and rescued him
from all his miseries by making him wise enough to attract
the attention of Pharaoh king of Egypt, who *made him gover-*
nor of Egypt[f] and put him in charge of the royal household.
11 *Then a famine came* that caused much suffering *throughout*
Egypt and Canaan, and our ancestors could find nothing to
12 eat. ·When Jacob *heard that there was grain for sale in Egypt,*
13 he sent our ancestors there on a first visit, ·but it was on the
second that *Joseph made himself known to his brothers,* and
14 told Pharaoh about his family. ·Joseph then sent for his
father Jacob and his whole family, a total of *seventy-five*
15 *people.* ·Jacob went down into Egypt and after he and our
16 ancestors had died there, their bodies were brought back to
Shechem and buried in the tomb that Abraham had bought
and paid for from the sons of Hamor, the father of Shechem.
17   'As the time drew near for God to fulfil the promise he had
solemnly made to Abraham, our nation in Egypt *grew larger*
18 *and larger,* ·*until a new king came to power in Egypt who knew*
19 *nothing of*[g] Joseph. ·*He exploited* our race, and ill-treated our
ancestors, forcing them to expose their babies to prevent their
20 surviving. ·It was at this period that Moses was born, *a fine*
child and favoured by God. He was looked after for three
21 months in his father's house, ·and after he had been exposed,
Pharaoh's daughter adopted him and *brought him up as her*
22 *own son.* ·So Moses was taught all the wisdom of the Egyp-

b. 'and they prayed and laid their hands on them'; probably meaning
the apostles, handing over their duties as in v. 3. c. Probably the descendants of Jews carried off to Rome, 63 B.C. and sold as slaves but
later released.
7 a. Gn 12:1 b. Gn 15:2 c. Gn 15:2, 13, 14; Ex 3:12 d. Gn 37 e. Gn 39
f. Gn 41. Other direct quotations and allusions in this paragraph are
from Gn 42–50. g. O.T. quotations from here to v. 35 are from Ex 1–3.

tians and became a man with power both in his speech and his actions.

23 'At the age of forty he decided to visit *his countrymen, the*
24 *sons of Israel.* ·When he saw one of them being ill-treated he went to his defence and rescued the man by *killing the Egyp-*
25 *tian.* ·He thought his brothers realised that through him
26 God would liberate them, but they did not. ·The next day, when he came across some of them fighting, he tried to reconcile them. 'Friends,' he said 'you are brothers; why are
27 you hurting each other?' ·But *the man who was attacking his fellow countryman* pushed him aside. '*And who appointed you*'
28 he said '*to be our leader and judge? ·Do you intend to kill me*
29 *as you killed the Egyptian yesterday?*' ·Moses fled when he heard this[h] and *he went to stay in the land of Midian,* where he became the father of two sons.

30 'Forty years later, *in the wilderness* near Mount Sinai, *an angel appeared to him in the flames of a bush* that was on fire.
31 Moses was amazed by what he saw. *As he went nearer to look*
32 *at it the voice of the Lord was heard, "I am the God of your ancestors, the God of Abraham, Isaác and Jacob".* Moses
33 trembled and *did not dare to look any more.* ·The Lord said to him, "*Take off your shoes; the place where you are standing is holy ground. ·I have seen the way my people are ill-treated in Egypt, I have heard their groans, and I have come down to liberate them. So come here and let me send you into Egypt.*"

35 'It was the same Moses that they had disowned when they said, "*Who appointed you to be our leader and judge?*" who was now sent to be both leader and redeemer through the
36 angel who had appeared to him in the bush. ·It was Moses who, after performing *miracles and signs in Egypt,* led them out across the Red Sea and *through the wilderness for forty*
37 *years.[i]* ·It was Moses who told the sons of Israel, "*God will raise up a prophet like myself for you from among your own*
38 *brothers*".[j] ·When they held the assembly in the wilderness it was only through Moses that our ancestors could communicate with the angel who had spoken to him on Mount Sinai; it was he who was entrusted with words of life to hand
39 on to us. ·This is the man that our ancestors refused to listen to: they pushed him aside, *turned back to Egypt* in their
40 thoughts, ·*and said to Aaron, "Make some gods to be our leaders; we do not understand what has come over this Moses*
41 *who led us out of Egypt*".[k] ·It was then that *they made a bull calf and offered sacrifice* to the idol. They were perfectly
42 happy with something they had made for themselves. ·God

turned away from them and abandoned them to the worship of the army of heaven,[l] as scripture says in the book of the prophets:

> *Did you bring me victims and sacrifices in the wilderness*
> *for all those forty years, you House of Israel?*
> 43 *No, you carried the tent of Moloch on your shoulders*
> *and the star of the god Rephan,*
> *those idols that you had made to adore.*
> *So now I will exile you even further than Babylon.*[m]

44 'While they were in the desert our ancestors possessed the Tent of Testimony that had been constructed according to the instructions God gave Moses, telling him to *make an* 45 *exact copy of the pattern*[n] he had been shown. ·It was handed down from one ancestor of ours to another until Joshua brought it into the country we had conquered from the nations which were driven out by God as we advanced. Here 46 it stayed until the time of David. ·He won God's favour and asked permission *to have a temple built for* the House of 47 *Jacob*, ·though it was Ṣolomon who actually *built God's* 48 *house*[o] for him. ·Even so the Most High does not live in a house that human hands have built: for as the prophet says:

> 49　　　*With heaven my throne*
> 　　　*and earth my footstool,*
> 　　　*what house could you build me,*
> 　　　*what place could you make for my rest?*
> 50　　　*Was not all this made by my hand?*[p]

51 'You stubborn people, with your pagan hearts and pagan ears. You are always resisting the Holy Spirit, just as your 52 ancestors used to do. ·Can you name a single prophet your ancestors never persecuted? In the past they killed those who foretold the coming of the Just One, and now you have 53 become his betrayers, his murderers. ·You who had the Law brought to you by angels are the very ones who have not kept it.'

54 They were infuriated when they heard this, and ground their teeth at him.

The stoning of Stephen. Saul as persecutor

55 But Stephen, filled with the Holy Spirit, gazed into heaven and saw the glory of God, and Jesus standing at God's right

h. In Ex 2:15 Moses runs away because he is afraid of Pharaoh. **i.** Nb 14:33 **j.** Dt 18:15, 18 **k.** Ex 32:1, 23 and 32:4, 6 **l.** The stars and planets. **m.** Am 5:25-27 (LXX) **n.** Ex 25:40 **o.** 1 K 6:2 **p.** Is 66:1-2.

56 hand. ·'I can see heaven thrown open' he said 'and the Son
57 of Man standing at the right hand of God.' ·At this all the
   members of the council shouted out and stopped their ears
58 with their hands; then they all rushed at him, ·sent him out
   of the city and stoned him. The witnesses*a* put down their
59 clothes at the feet of a young man called Saul. ·As they were
   stoning him, Stephen said in invocation, 'Lord Jesus, receive
60 my spirit'. ·Then he knelt down and said aloud, 'Lord, do not
   hold this sin against them'; and with these words he fell
1 asleep. **8** Saul entirely approved of the killing.

   That day a bitter persecution started against the church in
   Jerusalem, and everyone*a* except the apostles fled to the
   country districts of Judaea and Samaria.
2 There were some devout people, however, who buried
   Stephen and made great mourning for him.
3 Saul then worked for the total destruction of the Church;
   he went from house to house arresting both men and women
   and sending them to prison.

Philip in Samaria

4 Those who had escaped went from place to place preach-
5 ing the Good News. ·One of them was Philip who went to a
6 Samaritan town and proclaimed the Christ to them. ·The
   people united in welcoming the message Philip preached,
   either because they had heard of the miracles he worked or
7 because they saw them for themselves. ·There were, for
   example, unclean spirits that came shrieking out of many who
   were possessed, and several paralytics and cripples were
8 cured. ·As a result there was great rejoicing in that town.

Simon the magician

9 Now a man called Simon had already practised magic
   arts in the town and astounded the Samaritan people. He had
10 given it out that he was someone momentous, ·and everyone
   believed what he said; eminent citizens and ordinary people
   alike had declared, 'He is the divine power that is called
11 Great'. ·They had only been won over to him because of the
12 long time he had spent working on them with his magic. ·But
   when they believed Philip's preaching of the Good News
   about the kingdom of God and the name of Jesus Christ, they
13 were baptised, both men and women, ·and even Simon himself became a believer. After his baptism Simon, who went
   round constantly with Philip, was astonished when he saw
   the wonders and great miracles that took place.
14 When the apostles in Jerusalem heard that Samaria had

accepted the word of God, they sent Peter and John to them,
15 and they went down there, and prayed for the Samaritans to
16 receive the Holy Spirit, ·for as yet he had not come down on
any of them: they had only been baptised in the name of the
17 Lord Jesus. ·Then they laid hands on them, and they received
the Holy Spirit.

18 When Simon saw that the Spirit was given through the
imposition of hands by the apostles, he offered them some
19 money. ·'Give me the same power' he said 'so that anyone I
20 lay my hands on will receive the Holy Spirit.' ·Peter answered,
'May your silver be lost forever, and you with it, for thinking
that money could buy what God has given for nothing!
21 You have no share, no rights, in this: God can see how your
22 heart is warped. ·Repent of this wickedness of yours, and
pray to the Lord; you may still be forgiven for thinking as
23 you did; ·it is plain to me that you are trapped in the bitter-
24 ness of gall and the chains of sin.' ·'Pray to the Lord for me
yourselves' Simon replied 'so that none of the things you
have spoken about may happen to me.'

25 Having given their testimony and proclaimed the word of
the Lord, they went back to Jerusalem, preaching the Good
News to a number of Samaritan villages.

Philip baptises a eunuch

26 The angel of the Lord spoke to Philip saying, 'Be ready to
set out at noon along the road that goes from Jerusalem
27 down to Gaza, the desert road'. ·So he set off on his journey.
Now it happened that an Ethiopian had been on pilgrimage to
Jerusalem; he was a eunuch and an officer at the court of the
kandake, or queen, of Ethiopia, and was in fact her chief
28 treasurer. ·He was now on his way home; and as he sat in his
29 chariot he was reading the prophet Isaiah. ·The Spirit said to
30 Philip, 'Go up and meet that chariot'. ·When Philip ran up,
he heard him reading Isaiah the prophet and asked, 'Do you
31 understand what you are reading?' ·'How can I' he replied
'unless I have someone to guide me?' So he invited Philip
32 to get in and sit by his side. ·Now the passage of scripture he
was reading was this:

> *Like a sheep that is led to the slaughter-house,*
> *like a lamb that is dumb in front of its shearers,*
> *like these he never opens his mouth.*
33 > *He has been humiliated and has no one to defend him.*

q. By the Law, the accusers had to begin the execution of the sentence.
8 a. The persecution seems to have been directed principally against
the Hellenists.

Who will ever talk about his descendants,
since his life on earth has been cut short![b]

34 The eunuch turned to Philip and said, 'Tell me, is the pro-
35 phet referring to himself or someone else?' ·Starting, therefore, with this text of scripture Philip proceeded to explain
the Good News of Jesus to him.

36 Further along the road they came to some water, and the
eunuch said, 'Look, there is some water here; is there any-
38 thing to stop me being baptised?'[c] ·He ordered the chariot to
stop, then Philip and the eunuch both went down into the
39 water and Philip baptised him. ·But after they had come up
out of the water again Philip was taken away by the Spirit of
the Lord, and the eunuch never saw him again but went on
40 his way rejoicing. ·Philip found that he had reached Azotus
and continued his journey proclaiming the Good News in
every town as far as Caesarea.

The conversion of Saul

9 Meanwhile Saul was still breathing threats to slaughter
2 the Lord's disciples. He had gone to the high priest ·and asked
for letters addressed to the synagogues in Damascus, that
would authorise him to arrest and take to Jerusalem any
followers of the Way, men or women, that he could find.

3 Suddenly, while he was travelling to Damascus and just
before he reached the city, there came a light from heaven all
4 round him. ·He fell to the ground, and then he heard a voice
5 saying, 'Saul, Saul, why are you persecuting me?' ·'Who are
you, Lord?' he asked, and the voice answered, 'I am Jesus,
6 and you are persecuting me. ·Get up now and go into the
7 city, and you will be told what you have to do.' ·The men
travelling with Saul stood there speechless, for though they
8 heard the voice they could see no one. ·Saul got up from the
ground, but even with his eyes wide open he could see nothing
at all, and they had to lead him into Damascus by the hand.
9 For three days he was without his sight, and took neither
food nor drink.

10 A disciple called Ananias who lived in Damascus had a
vision in which he heard the Lord say to him, 'Ananias!'
11 When he replied, 'Here I am, Lord', ·the Lord said, 'You
must go to Straight Street and ask at the house of Judas for
someone called Saul, who comes from Tarsus. At this mo-
12 ment he is praying, ·having had a vision of a man called
Ananias coming in and laying hands on him to give him back
his sight.'

13 When he heard that, Ananias said, 'Lord, several people
have told me about this man and all the harm he has been
14 doing to your saints in Jerusalem. ·He has only come here
because he holds a warrant from the chief priests to arrest
15 everybody who invokes your name.' ·The Lord replied, 'You
must go all the same, because this man is my chosen instrument to bring my name before pagans and pagan kings and
16 before the people of Israel; ·I myself will show him how much
17 he himself must suffer for my name'. ·Then Ananias went. He
entered the house, and at once laid his hands on Saul and
said, 'Brother Saul, I have been sent by the Lord Jesus who
appeared to you on your way here so that you may recover
18 your sight and be filled with the Holy Spirit'. ·Immediately
it was as though scales fell away from Saul's eyes and he
19 could see again. So he was baptised there and then, ·and after
taking some food he regained his strength.

Saul's preaching at Damascus

After he had spent only a few days with the disciples in
20 Damascus, ·he began preaching in the synagogues, 'Jesus is
21 the Son of God'. ·All his hearers were amazed. 'Surely' they
said 'this is the man who organised the attack in Jerusalem
against the people who invoke this name, and who came here
for the sole purpose of arresting them to have them tried by
22 the chief priests?' ·Saul's power increased steadily, and he
was able to throw the Jewish colony at Damascus into complete confusion by the way he demonstrated that Jesus was
the Christ.
23 Some time passed,[a] and the Jews worked out a plot to kill
24 him, ·but news of it reached Saul. To make sure of killing
25 him they kept watch on the gates day and night, ·but when it
was dark the disciples took him and let him down from the
top of the wall, lowering him in a basket.

Saul's visit to Jerusalem

26 When he got to Jerusalem he tried to join the disciples,
but they were all afraid of him: they could not believe he was
27 really a disciple. ·Barnabas, however, took charge of him,
introduced him to the apostles, and explained how the Lord
had appeared to Saul and spoken to him on his journey, and
how he had preached boldly at Damascus in the name of

b. Is 53:7–8, quoted from the LXX version. **c.** At the time when verse
numbers were introduced, there was a gloss, numbered v. 37, at this
point.
9 a. Three years, according to Ga 1:17–18.

28 Jesus. ·Saul now started to go round with them in Jerusalem,
29 preaching fearlessly in the name of the Lord. ·But after he
   had spoken to the Hellenists, and argued with them, they
30 became determined to kill him. ·When the brothers knew,
   they took him to Caesarea, and sent him off from there to
   Tarsus.

A lull

31 The churches throughout Judaea, Galilee and Samaria
   were now left in peace, building themselves up, living in the
   fear of the Lord, and filled with the consolation of the Holy
   Spirit.

Peter cures a paralytic at Lydda

32 Peter visited one place after another and eventually came
33 to the saints living down in Lydda. ·There he found a man
   called Aeneas, a paralytic who had been bedridden for eight
34 years. ·Peter said to him, 'Aeneas, Jesus Christ cures you:
   get up and fold up your sleeping mat'. Aeneas got up im-
35 mediately; ·everybody who lived in Lydda and Sharon saw
   him, and they were all converted to the Lord.

Peter raises a woman to life at Jaffa

36 At Jaffa there was a woman disciple called Tabitha, or
   Dorcas in Greek,[b] who never tired of doing good or giving in
37 charity. ·But the time came when she got ill and died, and
38 they washed her and laid her out in a room upstairs. ·Lydda
   is not far from Jaffa, so when the disciples heard that Peter
   was there, they sent two men with an urgent message for him,
   'Come and visit us as soon as possible'.
39 Peter went back with them straightaway, and on his arrival
   they took him to the upstairs room, where all the widows
   stood round him in tears, showing him tunics and other
40 clothes Dorcas had made when she was with them. ·Peter
   sent them all out of the room and knelt down and prayed.
   Then he turned to the dead woman and said, 'Tabitha, stand
41 up'. She opened her eyes, looked at Peter and sat up. ·Peter
   helped her to her feet, then he called in the saints and widows
42 and showed them she was alive. ·The whole of Jaffa heard
   about it and many believed in the Lord.
43 Peter stayed on some time in Jaffa, lodging with a leather-
   tanner called Simon.

Peter visits a Roman centurion

10 One of the centurions of the Italica cohort stationed in
 2 Caesarea was called Cornelius. ·He and the whole of his

household were devout and God-fearing, and he gave generously to Jewish causes and prayed constantly to God.

3 One day at about the ninth hour he had a vision in which he distinctly saw the angel of God come into his house and
4 call out to him, 'Cornelius!' ·He stared at the vision in terror and exclaimed, 'What is it, Lord?' 'Your offering of prayers and alms' the angel answered 'has been accepted by God.
5 Now you must send someone to Jaffa and fetch a man called
6 Simon, known as Peter, ·who is lodging with Simon the
7 tanner whose house is by the sea.' ·When the angel who said this had gone, Cornelius called two of the slaves and a devout
8 soldier of his staff, told them what had happened, and sent them off to Jaffa.

9 Next day, while they were still on their journey and had only a short distance to go before reaching Jaffa, Peter went to
10 the housetop at about the sixth hour to pray. ·He felt hungry and was looking forward to his meal, but before it was ready
11 he fell into a trance ·and saw heaven thrown open and something like a big sheet being let down to earth by its four cor-
12 ners; ·it contained every possible sort of animal and bird,
13 walking, crawling or flying ones. ·A voice then said to him,
14 'Now, Peter; kill and eat!' ·But Peter answered, 'Certainly not, Lord; I have never yet eaten anything profane or un-
15 clean'. ·Again, a second time, the voice spoke to him, 'What God has made clean, you have no right to call profane'.
16 This was repeated three times, and then suddenly the container was drawn up to heaven again.

17 Peter was still worrying over the meaning of the vision he had seen, when the men sent by Cornelius arrived. They had asked where Simon's house was and they were now standing
18 at the door, ·calling out to know if the Simon known as
19 Peter was lodging there. ·Peter's mind was still on the vision and the Spirit had to tell him, 'Some men have come to see
20 you. ·Hurry down, and do not hesitate about going back
21 with them; it was I who told them to come.' ·Peter went down and said to them, 'I am the man you are looking for; why
22 have you come?' ·They said, 'The centurion Cornelius, who is an upright and God-fearing man, highly regarded by the entire Jewish people, was directed by a holy angel to send for you and bring you to his house and to listen to what you
23 have to say'. ·So Peter asked them in and gave them lodging.

Next day, he was ready to go off with them, accompanied
24 by some of the brothers from Jaffa. ·They reached Caesarea the following day, and Cornelius was waiting for them. He

b. I.e. 'Gazelle'.

25 had asked his relations and close friends to be there, ·and as Peter reached the house Cornelius went out to meet him,
26 knelt at his feet and prostrated himself. ·But Peter helped him
27 up. 'Stand up,' he said 'I am only a man after all!' ·Talking together they went in to meet all the people assembled there,
28 and Peter said to them, 'You know it is forbidden for Jews to mix with people of another race and visit them, but God has made it clear to me that I must not call anyone profane
29 or unclean. ·That is why I made no objection to coming when I was sent for; but I should like to know exactly why
30 you sent for me.' ·Cornelius replied, 'Three days ago I was praying in my house at the ninth hour, when I suddenly saw
31 a man in front of me in shining robes. ·He said, "Cornelius, your prayer has been heard and your alms have been ac-
32 cepted as a sacrifice in the sight of God; ·so now you must send to Jaffa and fetch Simon known as Peter who is lodging
33 in the house of Simon the tanner, by the sea". ·So I sent for you at once, and you have been kind enough to come. Here we all are, assembled in front of you to hear what message God has given you for us.'

Peter's address in the house of Cornelius

34 Then Peter addressed them: 'The truth I have now come to
35 realise' he said 'is that God does not have favourites, ·but that anybody of any nationality who fears God and does what is right is acceptable to him.
36 'It is true, God sent his word to the people of Israel, and it was to them that *the good news of peace was brought*[a] by Jesus
37 Christ—but Jesus Christ is Lord of all men. ·You must have heard about the recent happenings in Judaea; about Jesus of Nazareth and how he began in Galilee, after John had
38 been preaching baptism. ·*God had anointed him with the Holy Spirit*[b] and with power, and because God was with him, Jesus went about doing good and curing all who had fallen into
39 the power of the devil. ·Now I, and those with me, can witness to everything he did throughout the countryside of Judaea and in Jerusalem itself; and also to the fact that they
40 killed him by hanging him on a tree, ·yet three days after-
41 wards God raised him to life and allowed him to be seen, ·not by the whole people but only by certain witnesses God had chosen beforehand. Now we are those witnesses—we have eaten and drunk with him after his resurrection from the
42 dead—·and he has ordered us to proclaim this to his people and to tell them that God has appointed him to judge every-
43 one, alive or dead. ·It is to him that all the prophets bear this

witness: that all who believe in Jesus will have their sins forgiven through his name.'

Baptism of the first pagans

44 While Peter was still speaking the Holy Spirit came down
45 on all the listeners. ·Jewish believers who had accompanied Peter were all astonished that the gift of the Holy Spirit
46 should be poured out on the pagans too, ·since they could hear them speaking strange languages and proclaiming the
47 greatness of God. Peter himself then said, ·"Could anyone refuse the water of baptism to these people, now they have
48 received the Holy Spirit just as much as we have?' ·He then gave orders for them to be baptised in the name of Jesus Christ. Afterwards they begged him to stay on for some days.

Jerusalem: Peter justifies his conduct

11 The apostles and the brothers in Judaea heard that the
2 pagans too had accepted the word of God, ·and when Peter
3 came up to Jerusalem the Jews criticised him ·and said, 'So you have been visiting the uncircumcised and eating with
4 them, have you?' ·Peter in reply gave them the details point
5 by point: ·"One day, when I was in the town of Jaffa,' he began 'I fell into a trance as I was praying and had a vision of something like a big sheet being let down from heaven by its four corners. This sheet reached the ground quite close
6 to me. ·I watched it intently and saw all sorts of animals and wild beasts—everything possible that could walk, crawl or
7 fly. ·Then I heard a voice that said to me, "Now, Peter; kill
8 and eat!" ·But I answered: Certainly not, Lord; nothing pro-
9 fane or unclean has ever crossed my lips. ·And a second time the voice spoke from heaven, "What God has made clean,
10 you have no right to call profane". ·This was repeated three times, before the whole of it was drawn up to heaven again.
11 'Just at that moment, three men stopped outside the house where we were staying; they had been sent from Caesarea to
12 fetch me, ·and the Spirit told me to have no hesitation about going back with them. The six brothers here came with me as
13 well, and we entered the man's house. ·He told us he had seen an angel standing in his house who said, "Send to
14 Jaffa and fetch Simon known as Peter; he has a message for you that will save you and your entire household".
15 'I had scarcely begun to speak when the Holy Spirit came down on them in the same way as it came on us at the be-
16 ginning, ·and I remembered that the Lord had said, "John

10 a. Is 52:7 **b.** Is 61:1

baptised with water, but you will be baptised with the Holy
17 Spirit''. ·I realised then that God was giving them the identical thing he gave to us when we believed in the Lord Jesus Christ; and who was I to stand in God's way?'
18   This account satisfied them, and they gave glory to God. 'God' they said 'can evidently grant even the pagans the repentance that leads to life.'

Foundation of the church of Antioch

19   Those who had escaped during the persecution that happened because of Stephen travelled as far as Phoenicia and Cyprus and Antioch,[a] but they usually proclaimed the mes-
20 sage only to Jews. ·Some of them, however, who came from Cyprus and Cyrene, went to Antioch where they started preaching to the Greeks, proclaiming the Good News of the
21 Lord Jesus to them as well. ·The Lord helped them, and a great number believed and were converted to the Lord.
22   The church in Jerusalem heard about this and they sent
23 Barnabas to Antioch. ·There he could see for himself that God had given grace, and this pleased him, and he urged them all to remain faithful to the Lord with heartfelt devo-
24 tion; ·for he was a good man, filled with the Holy Spirit and with faith. And a large number of people were won over to the Lord.
25
26   Barnabas then left for Tarsus to look for Saul, ·and when he found him he brought him to Antioch. As things turned out they were to live together in that church a whole year, instructing a large number of people. It was at Antioch that the disciples were first called 'Christians'.

Barnabas and Saul sent as deputies to Jerusalem

27   While they were there some prophets[b] came down to An-
28 tioch from Jerusalem, ·and one of them whose name was Agabus, seized by the Spirit, stood up and predicted that a famine would spread over the whole empire. This in fact happened before the reign of Claudius came to an end.[c]
29 The disciples decided to send relief, each to contribute what
30 he could afford, to the brothers living in Judaea. ·They did this and delivered their contributions to the elders in the care of Barnabas and Saul.

Peter's arrest and miraculous deliverance[a]

12   It was about this time that King Herod started persecuting
2 certain members of the Church. ·He beheaded James the

3 brother of John, ·and when he saw that this pleased the Jews
4 he decided to arrest Peter as well. ·This was during the days
of Unleavened Bread, and he put Peter in prison, assigning
four squads of four soldiers each to guard him in turns.
Herod meant to try Peter in public after the end of Passover
5 week. ·All the time Peter was under guard the Church prayed
to God for him unremittingly.

6   On the night before Herod was to try him, Peter was
sleeping between two soldiers, fastened with double chains,
while guards kept watch at the main entrance to the prison.
7 Then suddenly the angel of the Lord stood there, and the
cell was filled with light. He tapped Peter on the side and
woke him. 'Get up!' he said 'Hurry!'—and the chains fell
8 from his hands. ·The angel then said, 'Put on your belt and
sandals'. After he had done this, the angel next said, 'Wrap
9 your cloak round you and follow me'. ·Peter followed him,
but had no idea that what the angel did was all happening
10 in reality; he thought he was seeing a vision. ·They passed
through two guard posts one after the other, and reached the
iron gate leading to the city. This opened of its own accord;
they went through it and had walked the whole length of one
11 street when suddenly the angel left him. ·It was only then
that Peter came to himself. 'Now I know it is all true' he said.
'The Lord really did send his angel and has saved me from
Herod and from all that the Jewish people were so certain
would happen to me.'

12   As soon as he realised this he went straight to the house of
Mary the mother of John Mark,[b] where a number of people
13 had assembled and were praying. ·He knocked at the outside
14 door and a servant called Rhoda came to answer it. ·She
recognised Peter's voice and was so overcome with joy that,
instead of opening the door, she ran inside with the news that
15 Peter was standing at the main entrance. ·They said to her,
'You are out of your mind', but she insisted that it was true.
16 Then they said, 'It must be his angel!' ·Peter, meanwhile, was
still knocking, so they opened the door and were amazed to
17 see that it really was Peter himself. ·With a gesture of his hand
he stopped them talking, and described to them how the

11 a. Antioch on the Orontes, capital of Syria. **b.** Christian prophets,
inspired speakers, generally ranked second to the apostles in the lists of
the persons 'gifted by the Spirit'. **c.** Claudius reigned until 54 A.D.
12 a. Herod Agrippa I was king of Judaea and Samaria, 41–44 A.D.
This episode, though fitted in the book between 11:30 and 12:25, must
have taken place before Barnabas and Saul visited Jerusalem. **b.** Mark
is mentioned in ch. 12, 13 and 15: also in Col 4 and Phm 24 and 2 Tim
4. Tradition names him as author of the second gospel.

Lord had led him out of prison. He added, 'Tell James and the brothers'. Then he left and went to another place.

18 When daylight came there was a great commotion among the soldiers, who could not imagine what had become of
19 Peter. ·Herod put out an unsuccessful search for him; he had the guards questioned, and before leaving Judaea to take up residence in Caesarea he gave orders for their execution.

The death of the persecutor

20 Now Herod was on bad terms with the Tyrians and Sidonians. However, they sent a joint deputation which managed to enlist the support of Blastus, the king's chamberlain, and through him negotiated a treaty, since their country de-
21 pended for its food supply on King Herod's territory. ·A day was fixed, and Herod, wearing his robes of state and en-
22 throned on a dais, made a speech to them. ·The people ac-
23 claimed him with, 'It is a god speaking, not a man!', ·and at that moment the angel of the Lord struck him down, because he had not given the glory to God. He was eaten away with worms and died.

Barnabas and Saul return to Antioch

24 The word of God continued to spread and to gain fol-
25 lowers. ·Barnabas and Saul completed their task and came back from Jerusalem, bringing John Mark with them.

III. THE MISSION OF BARNABAS AND PAUL
THE COUNCIL OF JERUSALEM

The mission sent out

13 In the church at Antioch the following were prophets and teachers: Barnabas, Simeon called Niger, and Lucius of Cyrene, Manaen, who had been brought up with Herod the
2 tetrarch, and Saul. ·One day while they were offering worship to the Lord and keeping a fast, the Holy Spirit said, 'I want Barnabas and Saul set apart for the work to which I have
3 called them'. ·So it was that after fasting and prayer they laid their hands on them and sent them off.

Cyprus: the magician Elymas

4 So these two, sent on their mission by the Holy Spirit,
5 went down to Seleucia and from there sailed to Cyprus. ·They landed at Salamis and proclaimed the word of God in the synagogues of the Jews; John acted as their assistant.

6   They travelled the whole length of the island, and at
    Paphos they came in contact with a Jewish magician called
7   Bar-jesus. ·This false prophet was one of the attendants of the
    proconsul Sergius Paulus who was an extremely intelligent
    man. The proconsul summoned Barnabas and Saul and asked
8   to hear the word of God, ·but Elymas Magos—as he was
    called in Greek—tried to stop them so as to prevent the pro-
9   consul's conversion to the faith. ·Then Saul, whose other
10 name is Paul, looked him full in the face ·and said, 'You utter
    fraud, you impostor, you son of the devil, you enemy of all
    true religion, why don't you stop twisting the straight-
11 forward ways of the Lord? ·Now watch how the hand of the
    Lord will strike you: you will be blind, and for a time you
    will not see the sun.' That instant, everything went misty and
    dark for him, and he groped about to find someone to lead
12 him by the hand. ·The proconsul, who had watched every-
    thing, became a believer, being astonished by what he had
    learnt about the Lord.

They arrive at Antioch in Pisidia

13   Paul and his friends went by sea from Paphos to Perga in
     Pamphylia where John left them to go back to Jerusalem.
14 The others carried on from Perga till they reached Antioch
    in Pisidia. Here they went to synagogue on the sabbath and
15 took their seats. ·After the lessons from the Law and the
    Prophets had been read, the presidents of the synagogue sent
    them a message: 'Brothers, if you would like to address some
    words of encouragement to the congregation, please do so'.
16 Paul stood up, held up a hand for silence and began to speak:

Paul's preaching before the Jews

17   'Men of Israel, and fearers of God, listen! ·The God of our
     nation Israel chose our ancestors, and made our people great
     when they were living as foreigners in Egypt; then by divine
18 power he led them out, ·and for about forty years *took care*
19 *of them in the wilderness. ·When he had destroyed seven na-*
20 *tions in Canaan, he put them in possession*[a] of their land ·for
    about four hundred and fifty years. After this he gave them
21 judges, down to the prophet Samuel. ·Then they demanded a
    king, and God gave them Saul son of Kish, a man of the tribe
22 of Benjamin. After forty years, ·he deposed him and made
    David their king, of whom he approved in these words, "*I
    have selected David son of Jesse, a man after my own heart,
23 who will carry out my whole purpose*".[b] ·To keep his promise,

13 a. Dt 1:31; 7:1 **b.** 1 S 13:14

God has raised up for Israel one of David's descendants,
24 Jesus, as Saviour, ·whose coming was heralded by John
when he proclaimed a baptism of repentance for the whole
25 people of Israel. ·Before John ended his career he said, "I
am not the one you imagine me to be; that one is coming
after me and I am not fit to undo his sandal".

26 'My brothers, sons of Abraham's race, and all you who
27 fear God, this message of salvation is meant for you. ·What
the people of Jerusalem and their rulers did, though they did
not realise it, was in fact to fulfil the prophecies read on every
28 sabbath. ·Though they found nothing to justify his death,
they condemned him and asked Pilate to have him executed.
29 When they had carried out everything that scripture foretells
about him they took him down from the tree and buried him
30
31 in a tomb. ·But God raised him from the dead, ·and for many
days he appeared to those who had accompanied him from
Galilee to Jerusalem: and it is these same companions of his
who are now his witnesses before our people.

32 'We have come here to tell you the Good News. It was to
33 our ancestors that God made the promise but ·it is to us,
their children, that he has fulfilled it, by raising Jesus from
the dead. As scripture says in the first psalm: *You are my*
34 *son: today I have become your father.* ·The fact that God raised
him from the dead, never to return to corruption, is no more
than what he had declared: *To you I shall give the sure and*
35 *holy things promised to David.*[c] ·This is explained by another
text: *You will not allow your holy one to experience corrup-*
36 *tion.*[d] ·Now when David in his own time had served God's
purposes he died; he was buried with his ancestors and has
37 certainly *experienced corruption.* ·The one whom God has
raised up, however, has not *experienced corruption.*

38 'My brothers, I want you to realise that it is through him
that forgiveness of your sins is proclaimed. Through him
justification from all sins which the Law of Moses was unable
39 to justify ·is offered to every believer.
40 'So be careful—or what the prophets say will happen to
you.

41   *Cast your eyes around you, mockers;*
        be amazed, and perish!
        For I am doing something in your own days
        that you would not believe if you were to be told of it.'[e]

42 As they left they were asked to preach on the same
43 theme the following sabbath. ·When the meeting broke up
many Jews and devout converts joined Paul and Barnabas,

and in their talks with them Paul and Barnabas urged them
to remain faithful to the grace God had given them.

Paul and Barnabas preach to the pagans

44 The next sabbath almost the whole town assembled to hear
45 the word of God. ·When they saw the crowds, the Jews,
prompted by jealousy, used blasphemies and contradicted
46 everything Paul said. ·Then Paul and Barnabas spoke out
boldly. 'We had to proclaim the word of God to you first,
but since you have rejected it, since you do not think yourselves worthy of eternal life, we must turn to the pagans.
47 For this is what the Lord commanded us to do when he
said:

I have made you a light for the nations,
so that my salvation may reach the ends of the earth.'ᶠ

48 It made the pagans very happy to hear this and they
thanked the Lord for his message; all who were destined for
49 eternal life became believers. ·Thus the word of the Lord
spread through the whole countryside.
50 But the Jews worked upon some of the devout women of
the upper classes and the leading men of the city and persuaded them to turn against Paul and Barnabas and expel
51 them from their territory. ·So they shook the dust from their
52 feet in defiance and went off to Iconium; ·but the disciples
were filled with joy and the Holy Spirit.

Iconium evangelised

14 At Iconium they went to the Jewish synagogue, as they
had at Antioch, and they spoke so effectively that a great
many Jews and Greeks became believers.
2 Some of the Jews, however, refused to believe, and they
poisoned the minds of the pagans against the brothers.ᵃ
3 Accordingly Paul and Barnabas stayed on for some time,
preaching fearlessly for the Lord; and the Lord supported
all they said about his gift of grace, allowing signs and wonders to be performed by them.
4 The people in the city were divided, some supported the
5 Jews, others the apostles, ·but eventually with the connivance of the authorities a move was made by pagans as well
6 as Jews to make attacks on them and to stone them. ·When
the apostles came to hear of this, they went off for safety to

c. Is 55:3 d. Ps 16:9 e. Hab 1:5 f. Is 49:6, quoted freely from the LXX.
14 a. This sentence is a parenthesis. V. 3 continues from v. 1.

Lycaonia where, in the towns of Lystra and Derbe and in the
7 surrounding country, ·they preached the Good News.

Healing of a cripple

8   A man sat there[b] who had never walked in his life, because
9 his feet were crippled from birth; ·and as he listened to Paul
preaching, he managed to catch his eye. Seeing that the man
10 had the faith to be cured, ·Paul said in a loud voice, 'Get to
your feet—stand up', and the cripple jumped up and began
to walk.
11   When the crowd saw what Paul had done they shouted in
the language of Lycaonia, 'These people are gods who have
12 come down to us disguised as men'. ·They addressed Barnabas as Zeus, and since Paul was the principal speaker they
13 called him Hermes.[c] ·The priests of Zeus-outside-the-Gate,
proposing that all the people should offer sacrifice with them,
14 brought garlanded oxen to the gates. ·When the apostles
Barnabas and Paul heard what was happening they tore their
15 clothes,[d] and rushed into the crowd, shouting, ·'Friends,
what do you think you are doing? We are only human beings
like you. We have come with good news to make you turn
from these empty idols to the living God who made heaven
16 and earth and the sea and all that these hold. ·In the past he
17 allowed each nation to go its own way; ·but even then he did
not leave you without evidence of himself in the good things
he does for you: he sends you rain from heaven, he makes
your crops grow when they should, he gives you food and
18 makes you happy.' ·Even this speech, however, was scarcely
enough to stop the crowd offering them sacrifice.

The mission is disrupted

19   Then some Jews arrived from Antioch and Iconium, and
turned the people against the apostles. They stoned Paul and
20 dragged him outside the town, thinking he was dead. ·The
disciples came crowding round him but, as they did so, he
stood up and went back to the town. The next day he and
Barnabas went off to Derbe.
21   Having preached the Good News in that town and made a
considerable number of disciples, they went back through
22 Lystra and Iconium to Antioch. ·They put fresh heart into
the disciples, encouraging them to persevere in the faith. 'We
all have to experience many hardships' they said 'before we
23 enter the kingdom of God.' ·In each of these churches they
appointed elders, and with prayer and fasting they commended them to the Lord in whom they had come to believe.

24
25   They passed through Pisidia and reached Pamphylia. ·Then
after proclaiming the word at Perga they went down to
26 Attalia ·and from there sailed for Antioch, where they had
originally been commended to the grace of God for the work
they had now completed.
27   On their arrival they assembled the church and gave an
account of all that God had done with them, and how he had
28 opened the door of faith to the pagans. ·They stayed there
with the disciples for some time.

Controversy at Antioch

15   Then some men came down from Judaea[a] and taught the
brothers, 'Unless you have yourselves circumcised in the
2 tradition of Moses you cannot be saved'. ·This led to disagreement, and after Paul and Barnabas had had a long
argument with these men it was arranged that Paul and
Barnabas and others of the church should go up to Jerusalem
and discuss the problem with the apostles and elders.
3   All the members of the church saw them off, and as they
passed through Phoenicia and Samaria they told how the
pagans had been converted, and this news was received with
4 the greatest satisfaction by the brothers. ·When they arrived
in Jerusalem they were welcomed by the church and by the
apostles and elders, and gave an account of all that God had
done with them.

Controversy at Jerusalem

5   But certain members of the Pharisees' party who had become believers objected, insisting that the pagans should be
6 circumcised and instructed to keep the Law of Moses. ·The
7 apostles and elders met to look into the matter, ·and after
the discussion had gone on a long time, Peter stood up and
addressed them.

Peter's speech

'My brothers,' he said 'you know perfectly well that in the
early days God made his choice among you: the pagans were
8 to learn the Good News from me and so become believers. ·In
fact God, who can read everyone's heart, showed his approval of them by giving the Holy Spirit to them just as he
9 had to us. ·God made no distinction between them and us,

b. In Lystra. c. Mercury, the messenger or herald of the gods. d. Conventional sign of despair.
15 a. In the allusion to this incident in Ga, they are said to have come
'from James', Ga 2:12.

10 since he purified their hearts by faith. ·It would only provoke God's anger now, surely, if you imposed on the disciples the very burden that neither we nor our ancestors were strong

11 enough to support? ·Remember, we believe that we are saved in the same way as they are: through the grace of the Lord Jesus.'

12   This silenced the entire assembly, and they listened to Barnabas and Paul describing all the signs and wonders God had worked through them among the pagans.

James' speech

13   When they had finished it was James who spoke. 'My
14 brothers,' he said 'listen to me. ·Simeon[b] has described how God first arranged to enlist a people for his name out of the
15 pagans. ·This is entirely in harmony with the words of the prophets, since the scriptures say:

16   *After that I shall return*
    and rebuild the fallen House of David;
    I shall rebuild it from its ruins
    and restore it.
17   *Then the rest of mankind,*
    all the pagans who are consecrated to my name,
    will look for the Lord,
18   *says the Lord who made this ·known so long ago.[c]*

19 'I rule, then, that instead of making things more difficult
20 for pagans who turn to God, ·we send them a letter telling them merely to abstain from anything polluted by idols,[d] from fornication,[e] from the meat of strangled animals and
21 from blood. ·For Moses has always had his preachers in every town, and is read aloud in the synagogues every sabbath.'

The apostolic letter

22   Then the apostles and elders decided to choose delégates to send to Antioch with Paul and Barnabas; the whole church concurred with this. They chose Judas known as Barsabbas and Silas,[f] both leading men in the brotherhood,
23 and gave them this letter to take with them:
    'The apostles and elders, your brothers, send greetings to the brothers of pagan birth in Antioch, Syria and Cilicia.
24 We hear that some of our members have disturbed you with their demands and have unsettled your minds. They acted
25 without any authority from us, ·and so we have decided unanimously to elect delegates and to send them to you
26 with Barnabas and Paul, men we highly respect ·who have

dedicated their lives to the name of our Lord Jesus Christ.
27 Accordingly we are sending you Judas and Silas, ·who will
confirm by word of mouth what we have written in this letter.
28 It has been decided by the Holy Spirit and by ourselves not
29 to saddle you with any burden beyond these essentials: ·you
are to abstain from food sacrificed to idols, from blood, from
the meat of strangled animals and from fornication. Avoid
these, and you will do what is right. Farewell.'

The delegates at Antioch

30 The party left and went down to Antioch, where they
summoned the whole community and delivered the letter.
31 The community read it and were delighted with the en-
32 couragement it gave them. ·Judas and Silas, being themselves
prophets, spoke for a long time, encouraging and strengthen-
33 ing the brothers. ·These two spent some time there, and then
the brothers wished them peace and they went back to those
35 who had sent them. ·Paul and Barnabas, however, stayed on
in Antioch, and there with many others they taught and proclaimed the Good News, the word of the Lord.

IV. PAUL'S MISSIONS

Paul separates from Barnabas and recruits Silas

36 On a later occasion Paul said to Barnabas, 'Let us go back
and visit all the towns where we preached the word of the
Lord, so that we can see how the brothers are doing'.
37
38 Barnabas suggested taking John Mark, ·but Paul was not in
favour of taking along the very man who had deserted them
in Pamphylia and had refused to share in their work.
39 After a violent quarrel they parted company, and Barnabas
40 sailed off with Mark to Cyprus. ·Before Paul left, he chose
Silas to accompany him and was commended by the brothers
to the grace of God.

Lycaonia: Paul recruits Timothy

41 He travelled through Syria and Cilicia, consolidating the
churches.
16 From there he went to Derbe, and then on to Lystra. Here
there was a disciple called Timothy, whose mother was a
Jewess who had become a believer; but his father was a

b. Semitic form of Simon Peter's name. **c.** Am 9:11, 12, quoted according to the LXX. **d.** I.e. which has been offered in sacrifice to false gods.
e. Perhaps all the irregular marriages listed in Lv 18. **f.** Silas, also
mentioned in Ac 18; 1 Th, 2 Th, 2 Co, 1 P.

2 Greek. ·The brothers at Lystra and Iconium spoke well of
3 Timothy, ·and Paul, who wanted to have him as a travelling
companion, had him circumcised. This was on account of the
Jews in the locality where everyone knew his father was a
Greek.

4 As they visited one town after another, they passed on the
decisions reached by the apostles and elders in Jerusalem,
with instructions to respect them.

5 So the churches grew strong in the faith, as well as growing
daily in numbers.

The crossing into Asia Minor

6 They travelled through Phrygia and the Galatian country,
having been told by the Holy Spirit not to preach the word in
7 Asia. ·When they reached the frontier of Mysia they thought
to cross it into Bithynia, but as the Spirit of Jesus would not
8 allow them, ·they went through Mysia and came down to
Troas.

9 One night Paul had a vision: a Macedonian appeared and
appealed to him in these words, 'Come across to Macedonia
10 and help us'. ·Once he had seen this vision we lost no time in
arranging a passage to Macedonia, convinced that God had
called us to bring them the Good News.

Arrival at Philippi

11 Sailing from Troas we made a straight run for Samothrace;
12 the next day for Neapolis, ·and from there for Philippi, a
Roman colony and the principal city of that particular dis-
13 trict of Macedonia. After a few days in this city ·we went
along the river outside the gates as it was the sabbath and
this was a customary place for prayer.[a] We sat down and
14 preached to the women who had come to the meeting. ·One
of these women was called Lydia, a devout woman from the
town of Thyatira who was in the purple-dye trade. She
listened to us, and the Lord opened her heart to accept what
15 Paul was saying. ·After she and her household had been
baptised she sent us an invitation: 'If you really think me a
true believer in the Lord,' she said 'come and stay with us';
and she would take no refusal.

Imprisonment of Paul and Silas

16 One day as we were going to prayer, we met a slave-girl
who was a soothsayer and made a lot of money for her
17 masters by telling fortunes. ·This girl started following Paul
and the rest of us and shouting, 'Here are the servants of the

Most High God; they have come to tell you how to be saved!'
18 She did this every day afterwards until Paul lost his temper
one day and turned round and said to the spirit, 'I order you
in the name of Jesus Christ to leave that woman'. The spirit
went out of her then and there.

19   When her masters saw that there was no hope of making
any more money out of her, they seized Paul and Silas and
20 dragged them to the law courts in the market place ·where
they charged them before the magistrates and said, 'These
people are causing a disturbance in our city. They are Jews
21 and are advocating practices which it is unlawful for us as
22 Romans to accept or follow.'[b] ·The crowd joined in and
showed its hostility to them, so the magistrates had them
23 stripped and ordered them to be flogged. ·They were given
many lashes and then thrown into prison, and the gaoler
24 was told to keep a close watch on them ·So, following his
instructions, he threw them into the inner prison and fastened
their feet in the stocks.

The miraculous deliverance of Paul and Silas

25   Late that night Paul and Silas were praying and singing
26 God's praises, while the other prisoners listened. ·Suddenly
there was an earthquake that shook the prison to its foundations. All the doors flew open and the chains fell from all the
27 prisoners. ·When the gaoler woke and saw the doors wide
open he drew his sword and was about to commit suicide,
28 presuming that the prisoners had escaped. ·But Paul shouted
at the top of his voice, 'Don't do yourself any harm; we are
all here'.

29   The gaoler called for lights, then rushed in, threw himself
30 trembling at the feet of Paul and Silas, ·and escorted them
31 out, saying, 'Sirs, what must I do to be saved?' ·They told
him, 'Become a believer in the Lord Jesus, and you will be
32 saved, and your household too'. ·Then they preached the
33 word of the Lord to him and to all his family. ·Late as it was,
he took them to wash their wounds, and was baptised then
34 and there with all his household. ·Afterwards he took them
home and gave them a meal, and the whole family celebrated
their conversion to belief in God.

35   When it was daylight the magistrates sent the officers with
36 the order: 'Release those men'. ·The gaoler reported the
message to Paul, 'The magistrates have sent an order for your

16 a. There was no synagogue in this Latin city; the Jews met by the
river for ritual ablutions. **b.** The Jews had no right to proselytise
Romans.

37 release; you can go now and be on your way'. ·'What!'
Paul replied 'They flog Roman citizens in public and without
trial and throw us into prison, and then think they can push
us out on the quiet! Oh no! They must come and escort us out
themselves.'

38 The officers reported this to the magistrates, who were
39 horrified to hear the men were Roman citizens. ·They came
40 and begged them to leave the town. ·From the prison they
went to Lydia's house where they saw all the brothers and
gave them some encouragement; then they left.

Thessalonika: difficulties with the Jews

17 Passing through Amphipolis and Apollonia, they eventually reached Thessalonika, where there was a Jewish syna-
2 gogue. ·Paul as usual introduced himself and for three con-
secutive sabbaths developed the arguments from scripture
3 for them, ·explaining and proving how it was ordained that
the Christ should suffer and rise from the dead. 'And the
Christ' he said 'is this Jesus whom I am proclaiming to
4 you.' ·Some of them were convinced and joined Paul and
Silas, and so did a great many God-fearing people and
Greeks, as well as a number of rich women.

5 The Jews, full of resentment, enlisted the help of a gang
from the market place, stirred up a crowd, and soon had the
city in an uproar. They made for Jason's house, hoping to
find them there and drag them off to the People's Assembly;
6 however, they only found Jason and some of the brothers,
and these they dragged before the city council, shouting, 'The
people who have been turning the whole world upside down
7 have come here now; ·they have been staying at Jason's. They
have broken every one of Caesar's edicts by claiming that
8 there is another emperor, Jesus.' ·This accusation alarmed
9 the citizens and the city councillors ·and they made Jason
and the rest give security before setting them free.

Fresh difficulties at Beroea

10 When it was dark the brothers immediately sent Paul and
Silas away to Beroea, where they visited the Jewish synagogue
11 as soon as they arrived. ·Here the Jews were more open-
minded than those in Thessalonika, and they welcomed the
word very readily; every day they studied the scriptures to
12 check whether it was true. ·Many Jews became believers,
and so did many Greek women from the upper classes and a
number of the men.

13 When the Jews of Thessalonika heard that the word of

God was being preached by Paul in Beroea as well, they went
14 there to make trouble and stir up the people. ·So the brothers
arranged for Paul to go immediately as far as the coast,
15 leaving Silas and Timothy behind. ·Paul's escort took him
as far as Athens, and went back with instructions for Silas
and Timothy to rejoin Paul as soon as they could.

Paul in Athens

16 Paul waited for them in Athens and there his whole soul
17 was revolted at the sight of a city given over to idolatry. ·In
the synagogue he held debates with the Jews and the God-
fearing, but in the market place he had debates every day
18 with anyone who would face him. ·Even a few Epicurean and
Stoic philosophers argued with him. Some said, 'Does this
parrot know what he's talking about?' And, because he was
preaching about Jesus and the resurrection, others said,
'He sounds like a propagandist for some outlandish gods'.[a]
19 They invited him to accompany them to the Council of the
Areopagus, where they said to him, 'How much of this new
teaching you were speaking about are we allowed to know?
20 Some of the things you said seemed startling to us and we
21 would like to find out what they mean.' ·The one amusement
the Athenians and the foreigners living there seem to have,
apart from discussing the latest ideas, is listening to lectures
about them.
22 So Paul stood before the whole Council of the Areopagus
and made this speech:

Paul's speech before the Council of the Areopagus

'Men of Athens, I have seen for myself how extremely
23 scrupulous you are in all religious matters, ·because I noticed,
as I strolled round admiring your sacred monuments, that
you had an altar inscribed: To An Unknown God. Well,
the God whom I proclaim is in fact the one whom you already
worship without knowing it.
24 'Since the God who made the world and everything in it is
himself Lord of heaven and earth, he does not make his home
25 in shrines made by human hands. ·Nor is he dependent on
anything that human hands can do for him, since he can
never be in need of anything; on the contrary, it is he who
gives everything—including life and breath—to everyone.
26 From one single stock he not only created the whole human
race so that they could occupy the entire earth, but he decreed

17 a. They assumed that *Anastasis* ('Resurrection') was the name of a
goddess.

how long each nation should flourish and what the boun-
27 daries of its territory should be. ·And he did this so that all
nations might seek the deity and, by feeling their way towards
him, succeed in finding him. Yet in fact he is not far from any
28 of us, ·since it is in him that we live, and move, and exist,[b]
as indeed some of your own writers have said:

"We are all his children".[c]

29   'Since we are the children of God, we have no excuse for
thinking that the deity looks like anything in gold, silver or
stone that has been carved and designed by a man.
30   'God overlooked that sort of thing when men were ignorant, but now he is telling everyone everywhere that they must
31 repent, ·because he has fixed a day when the whole world will
be judged, and judged in righteousness, and he has appointed
a man to be the judge. And God has publicly proved this by
raising this man from the dead.'
32   At this mention of rising from the dead, some of them burst
out laughing; others said, 'We would like to hear you talk
33 about this again'. ·After that Paul left them, ·but there were
34 some who attached themselves to him and became believers,
among them Dionysius the Areopagite and a woman called
Damaris, and others besides.

Foundation of the church of Corinth

18   After this Paul left Athens and went to Corinth, ·where he
met a Jew called Aquila whose family came from Pontus. He
and his wife Priscilla[a] had recently left Italy because an edict
of Claudius had expelled all the Jews from Rome.[b] Paul went
3 to visit them, ·and when he found they were tentmakers, of
the same trade as himself, he lodged with them, and they
4 worked together. ·Every sabbath he used to hold debates in
the synagogues, trying to convert Jews as well as Greeks.
5   After Silas and Timothy had arrived from Macedonia,
Paul devoted all his time to preaching, declaring to the Jews
6 that Jesus was the Christ. ·When they turned against him and
started to insult him, he took his cloak and shook it out in
front of them, saying, 'Your blood be on your own heads;
from now on I can go to the pagans with a clear conscience'.
7 Then he left the synagogue and moved to the house next door
8 that belonged to a worshipper of God called Justus. ·Crispus,
president of the synagogue, and his whole household, all
became believers in the Lord. A great many Corinthians who
9 had heard him became believers and were baptised. ·One
night the Lord spoke to Paul in a vision, 'Do not be afraid

10 to speak out, nor allow yourself to be silenced: ·I am with you. I have so many people on my side in this city that no
11 one will even attempt to hurt you.' ·So Paul stayed there preaching the word of God among them for eighteen months.

The Jews take Paul to court

12   But while Gallio was proconsul of Achaia,[c] the Jews made a concerted attack on Paul and brought him before the tri-
13 bunal. ·'We accuse this man' they said 'of persuading people
14 to worship God in a way that breaks the Law.' ·Before Paul could open his mouth, Gallio said to the Jews, 'Listen, you Jews. If this were a misdemeanour or a crime, I would not
15 hesitate to attend to you; ·but if it is only quibbles about words and names, and about your own Law, then you must deal with it yourselves—I have no intention of making legal
16 decisions about things like that.' ·Then he sent them out of
17 the court, ·and at once they all turned on Sosthenes, the synagogue president, and beat him in front of the court house. Gallio refused to take any notice at all.

Return to Antioch and departure for the third journey

18   After staying on for some time, Paul took leave of the brothers and sailed for Syria,[d] accompanied by Priscilla and Aquila. At Cenchreae he had his hair cut off, because of a vow he had made.
19   When they reached Ephesus, he left them, but first he went
20 alone to the synagogue to debate with the Jews. ·They asked
21 him to stay longer but he declined, ·though when he left he said, 'I will come back another time, God willing'. Then he sailed from Ephesus.
22   He landed at Caesarea, and went up to greet the church.
23 Then he came down to Antioch ·where he spent a short time before continuing his journey through the Galatian country and then through Phrygia, encouraging all the followers.

Apollos

24   An Alexandrian Jew named Apollos now arrived in Ephesus. He was an eloquent man, with a sound knowledge
25 of the scriptures, and yet, ·though he had been given instruction in the Way of the Lord and preached with great spiritual

b. Expression suggested by the Poet Epimenides. c. From the *Phaino-mena* of Aratus.
18 a. Also called Prisca, Rm 16:3; 1 Co 16:19; 2 Tm 4:19. b. This edict was issued in 49 or 50. c. In 52, according to an inscription from Delphi. d. To Antioch.

earnestness and was accurate in all the details he taught about
26 Jesus, he had only experienced the baptism of John. ·When
Priscilla and Aquila heard him speak boldly in the synagogue,
they took an interest in him and gave him further instruction
about the Way.
27 When Apollos thought of crossing over to Achaia, the
brothers encouraged him and wrote asking the disciples to
welcome him. When he arrived there he was able by God's
28 grace to help the believers considerably ·by the energetic
way he refuted the Jews in public and demonstrated from the
scriptures that Jesus was the Christ.

The disciples of John at Ephesus

19 While Apollos was in Corinth, Paul made his way over-
land as far as Ephesus, where he found a number of disciples.
2 When he asked, 'Did you receive the Holy Spirit when you
became believers?' they answered, 'No, we were never even
3 told there was such a thing as a Holy Spirit'. ·'Then how were
you baptised?' he asked. 'With John's baptism' they replied.
4 'John's baptism' said Paul 'was a baptism of repentance; but
he insisted that the people should believe in the one who was
5 to come after him—in other words Jesus.' ·When they heard
6 this, they were baptised in the name of the Lord Jesus, ·and
the moment Paul had laid hands on them the Holy Spirit
came down on them, and they began to speak with tongues
7 and to prophesy. ·There were about twelve of these men.

Foundation of the church of Ephesus

8 He began by going to the synagogue, where he spoke out
boldly and argued persuasively about the kingdom of God.
9 He did this for three months, ·till the attitude of some of the
congregation hardened into unbelief. As soon as they began
attacking the Way in front of the others, he broke with them
and took his disciples apart to hold daily discussions in the
10 lecture room of Tyrannus. ·This went on for two years, with
the result that people from all over Asia,[a] both Jews and
Greeks, were able to hear the word of the Lord.

The Jewish exorcists

11 So remarkable were the miracles worked by God at Paul's
12 hands ·that handkerchiefs or aprons which had touched him
were taken to the sick, and they were cured of their illnesses,
and the evil spirits came out of them.
13 But some itinerant Jewish exorcists tried pronouncing the
name of the Lord Jesus over people who were possessed by

evil spirits; they used to say, 'I command you by the Jesus
14 whose spokesman is Paul'. ·Among those who did this
15 were seven sons of Sceva, a Jewish chief priest. ·The evil
spirit replied, 'Jesus I recognise, and know who Paul is, but
16 who are you?' ·and the man with the evil spirit hurled himself at them and overpowered first one and then another,
and handled them so violently that they fled from that house
17 naked and badly mauled. ·Everybody in Ephesus, both Jews
and Greeks, heard about this episode; they were all greatly
impressed, and the name of the Lord Jesus came to be held
in great honour.
18 Some believers, too, came forward to admit in detail how
19 they had used spells ·and a number of them who had practised
magic collected their books and made a bonfire of them in
public. The value of these was calculated to be fifty thousand
silver pieces.
20 In this impressive way the word of the Lord spread more
and more widely and successfully.

V. A PRISONER FOR CHRIST

Paul's plans

21 When all this was over Paul made up his mind to go back
to Jerusalem through Macedonia and Achaia. 'After I have
been there' he said 'I must go on to see Rome as well.'
22 So he sent two of his helpers, Timothy and Erastus, ahead of
him to Macedonia, while he remained for a time in Asia.

Ephesus: the silversmiths' riot

23 It was during this time that a rather serious disturbance
24 broke out in connection with the Way. ·A silversmith called
Demetrius, who employed a large number of craftsmen mak-
25 ing silver shrines of Diana, ·called a general meeting of his
own men with others in the same trade. 'As you men know,'
he said 'it is on this industry that we depend for our pros-
26 perity. ·Now you must have seen and heard how, not just in
Ephesus but nearly everywhere in Asia, this man Paul has
persuaded and converted a great number of people with his
27 argument that gods made by hand are not gods at all. ·This
threatens not only to discredit our trade, but also to reduce
the sanctuary of the great goddess Diana to unimportance. It
could end up by taking away all the prestige of a goddess
venerated all over Asia, yes, and everywhere in the civilised

19 a. I.e. the region round Ephesus, including the seven towns of
Rv 1:11.

28 world.' ·This speech roused them to fury, and they started
29 to shout, 'Great is Diana of the Ephesians!' ·The whole
town was in an uproar and the mob rushed to the theatre
dragging along two of Paul's Macedonian travelling com-
30 panions, Gaius and Aristarchus. ·Paul wanted to make an
31 appeal to the people, but the disciples refused to let him; ·in
fact, some of the Asiarchs,[b] who were friends of his, sent
messages imploring him not to take the risk of going into the
theatre.
32   By now everybody was shouting different things till the
assembly itself had no idea what was going on; most of them
33 did not even know why they had been summoned. ·The
Jews pushed Alexander to the front, and when some of the
crowd shouted encouragement he raised his hand for silence
in the hope of being able to explain things to the people.
34 When they realised he was a Jew, they all started shouting in
unison, 'Great is Diana of the Ephesians!' and they kept this
35 up for two hours. ·When the town clerk eventually succeeded
in calming the crowd, he said, 'Citizens of Ephesus! Is there
anybody alive who does not know that the city of the Ephesians is the guardian of the temple of great Diana and of her
36 statue that fell from heaven? ·Nobody can contradict this
and there is no need for you to get excited or do anything
37 rash. ·These men you have brought here are not guilty of any
38 sacrilege or blasphemy against our goddess. ·If Demetrius
and the craftsmen he has with him want to complain about
anyone, there are the assizes and the proconsuls; let them
39 take the case to court. ·And if you want to ask any more
40 questions you must raise them in the regular assembly. ·We
could easily be charged with rioting for today's happenings:
there was no ground for it all, and we can give no reason for
41 this gathering.' ·When he had finished this speech he dismissed
the assembly.

Paul leaves Ephesus

20   When the disturbance was over, Paul sent for the disciples
and, after speaking words of encouragement to them, said
2 good-bye and set out for Macedonia. ·On his way through
those areas he said many words of encouragement to them
3 and then made his way into Greece, ·where he spent three
months. He was leaving by ship for Syria[a] when a plot
organised against him by the Jews made him decide to go
4 back by way of Macedonia. ·He was accompanied by
Sopater, son of Pyrrhus, who came from Beroea; Aristarchus and Secundus who came from Thessalonika; Gaius from

Doberus, and Timothy, as well as Tychicus and Trophimus
5 who were from Asia. ·They all went on to Troas where they
6 waited for us. ·We ourselves left Philippi by ship after the
days of Unleavened Bread and met them five days later at
Troas, where we stopped for a week.

Troas: Paul raises a dead man to life

7   On the first day of the week[b] we met to break bread. Paul
was due to leave the next day, and he preached a sermon that
8 went on till the middle of the night. ·A number of lamps were
9 lit in the upstairs room where we were assembled, ·and as
Paul went on and on, a young man called Eutychus who was
sitting on the window-sill grew drowsy and was overcome by
sleep and fell to the ground three floors below. He was picked
10 up dead. ·Paul went down and stooped to clasp the boy to
him. 'There is no need to worry,' he said 'there is still life in
11 him.' ·Then he went back upstairs where he broke bread and
12 ate and carried on talking till he left at daybreak. ·They took
the boy away alive, and were greatly encouraged.

From Troas to Miletus

13   We were now to go on ahead by sea, so we set sail for
Assos, where we were to take Paul on board; this was what
14 he had arranged, for he wanted to go by road. ·When he
rejoined us at Assos we took him aboard and went on to
15 Mitylene. ·The next day we sailed from there and arrived
opposite Chios. The second day we touched at Samos and,
after stopping at Trogyllium, made Miletus the next day.
16 Paul had decided to pass wide of Ephesus so as to avoid
spending time in Asia, since he was anxious to be in Jerusalem, if possible, for the day of Pentecost.

Farewell to the elders of Ephesus

17   From Miletus he sent for the elders of the church of
18 Ephesus. ·When they arrived he addressed these words to
them:
     'You know what my way of life has been ever since the
19 first day I set foot among you in Asia, ·how I have served
the Lord in all humility, with all the sorrows and trials that
20 came to me through the plots of the Jews. ·I have not hesi-
tated to do anything that would be helpful to you; I have

b. Local leaders of the official state worship.
20 a. Taking to Jerusalem the proceeds of the collection, Rm 15:25.
b. The day was reckoned in the Jewish fashion; the Lord's day began
on the evening of Saturday and it was then that this meeting was held.

preached to you, and instructed you both in public and in
21 your homes, ·urging both Jews and Greeks to turn to God
and to believe in our Lord Jesus.

22 'And now you see me a prisoner already in spirit; I am on
my way to Jerusalem, but have no idea what will happen to
23 me there, ·except that the Holy Spirit, in town after town,
has made it clear enough that imprisonment and persecution
24 await me. ·But life to me is not a thing to waste words on,
provided that when I finish my race I have carried out the
mission the Lord Jesus gave me—and that was to bear witness
to the Good News of God's grace.

25 'I now feel sure that none of you among whom I have gone
about proclaiming the kingdom will ever see my face again.
26 And so here and now I swear that my conscience is clear as
27 far as all of you are concerned, ·for I have without faltering
put before you the whole of God's purpose.

28 'Be on your guard for yourselves and for all the flock of
which the Holy Spirit has made you the overseers, to feed the
29 Church of God which he bought with his own blood.· I
know quite well that when I have gone fierce wolves will
30 invade you and will have no mercy on the flock. ·Even from
your own ranks there will be men coming forward with a
travesty of the truth on their lips to induce the disciples to
31 follow them. ·So be on your guard, remembering how night
and day for three years I never failed to keep you right,
32 shedding tears over each one of you. ·And now I commend
you to God, and to the word of his grace that has power to
build you up and to give you your inheritance among all the
sanctified.

33
34 'I have never asked anyone for money or clothes; ·you
know for yourselves that the work I did earned enough to
35 meet my needs and those of my companions. ·I did this to
show you that this is how we must exert ourselves to support
the weak, remembering the words of the Lord Jesus, who
himself said, "There is more happiness in giving than in
receiving".'

36 When he had finished speaking he knelt down with them
37 all and prayed. ·By now they were all in tears; they put their
38 arms round Paul's neck and kissed him; ·what saddened them
most was his saying they would never see his face again. Then
they escorted him to the ship.

The journey to Jerusalem

21 When we had at last torn ourselves away from them and
put to sea, we set a straight course and arrived at Cos; the

next day we reached Rhodes, and from there went on to
2 Patara. ·Here we found a ship bound for Phoenicia, so we
3 went on board and sailed in her. ·After sighting Cyprus and
leaving it to port, we sailed to Syria and put in at Tyre, since
4 the ship was to unload her cargo there. ·We sought out the
disciples and stayed there a week. Speaking in the Spirit,
5 they kept telling Paul not to go on to Jerusalem, ·but when
our time was up we set off. Together with the women and
children they all escorted us on our way till we were out of
the town. When we reached the beach, we knelt down and
6 prayed; ·then, after saying good-bye to each other, we went
aboard and they returned home.
7 The end of our voyage from Tyre came when we landed at
Ptolemais, where we greeted the brothers and stayed one day
8 with them. ·The next day we left and came to Caesarea. Here
we called on Philip the evangelist, one of the Seven, and
9 stayed with him. ·He had four virgin daughters who were
10 prophets. ·When we had been there several days a prophet
11 called Agabus arrived from Judaea ·to see us. He took
Paul's girdle, and tied up his own feet and hands, and said,
'This is what the Holy Spirit says, "The man this girdle
belongs to will be bound like this by the Jews in Jerusalem,
12 and handed over to the pagans" '. ·When we heard this, we
and everybody there implored Paul not to go on to Jerusalem.
13 To this he replied, 'What are you trying to do—weaken my
resolution by your tears? For my part, I am ready not only
to be tied up but even to die in Jerusalem for the name of the
14 Lord Jesus.' ·And so, as he would not be persuaded, we gave
up the attempt, saying, 'The Lord's will be done'.

Paul's arrival in Jerusalem

15 After this we packed and went on up to Jerusalem.
16 Some of the disciples from Caesarea accompanied us and
took us to the house of a Cypriot with whom we were to
lodge; he was called Mnason and had been one of the
earliest disciples.
17 On our arrival in Jerusalem the brothers gave us a very
18 warm welcome. ·The next day Paul went with us to visit
19 James, and all the elders were present. ·After greeting them
he gave a detailed account of all that God had done among
20 the pagans through his ministry. ·They gave glory to God
when they heard this. 'But you see, brother,' they said 'how
thousands of Jews have now become believers, all of them
21 staunch upholders of the Law, and ·they have heard that you
instruct all Jews living among the pagans to break away from

Moses, authorising them not to circumcise their children or
22 to follow the customary practices. ·What is to be done?
Inevitably there will be a meeting of the whole body, since
23 they are bound to hear that you have come. ·So do as we
suggest. We have four men here who are under a vow;
24 take these men along and be purified with them and pay all
the expenses connected with the shaving of their heads.[a]
This will let everyone know there is no truth in the reports
they have heard about you and that you still regularly observe
25 the Law. ·The pagans who have become believers, as we
wrote when we told them our decisions, must abstain from
things sacrificed to idols, from blood, from the meat of
strangled animals and from fornication.'
26 So the next day Paul took the men along and was purified
with them, and he visited the Temple to give notice of the
time when the period of purification would be over and the
offering would have to be presented on behalf of each of
them.

Paul's arrest

27 The seven days were nearly over when some Jews from
Asia caught sight of him in the Temple and stirred up the
28 crowd and seized him, ·shouting, 'Men of Israel, help! This
is the man who preaches to everyone everywhere against our
people, against the Law and against this place. Now he has
profaned this Holy Place by bringing Greeks into the
29 Temple.' ·They had, in fact, previously seen Trophimus the
Ephesian in the city with him, and thought that Paul had
brought him into the Temple.
30 This roused the whole city; people came running from all
sides; they seized Paul and dragged him out of the Temple,
31 and the gates were closed behind them. ·They would have
killed him if a report had not reached the tribune of the
32 cohort[b] that there was rioting all over Jerusalem. ·He immediately called out soldiers and centurions, and charged
down on the crowd, who stopped beating Paul when they
33 saw the tribune and the soldiers. ·When the tribune came up
he arrested Paul, had him bound with two chains and
34 enquired who he was and what he had done. ·People in the
crowd called out different things, and since the noise made it
impossible for him to get any positive information, the
35 tribune ordered Paul to be taken into the fortress. ·When
Paul reached the steps, the crowd became so violent that he
36 had to be carried by the soldiers; ·and indeed the whole
mob was after them, shouting, 'Kill him!'

37 Just as Paul was being taken into the fortress, he asked the tribune if he could have a word with him. The tribune said,
38 'You speak Greek, then? ·So you are not the Egyptian who started the recent revolt and led those four thousand cut-
39 throats[c] out into the desert?' ·'I?' said Paul 'I am a Jew and a citizen of the well-known city of Tarsus in Cilicia. Please
40 give me permission to speak to the people.' ·The man gave his consent and Paul, standing at the top of the steps, gestured to the people with his hand. When all was quiet again he spoke to them in Hebrew.[d]

Paul's address to the Jews of Jerusalem

22 'My brothers, my fathers, listen to what I have to say to
2 you in my defence.' ·When they realised he was speaking in
3 Hebrew, the silence was even greater than before. ·'I am a Jew,' Paul said 'and was born at Tarsus in Cilicia. I was brought up here in this city. I studied under Gamaliel and was taught the exact observance of the Law of our ancestors.
4 In fact, I was as full of duty towards God as you are today. ·I even persecuted this Way to the death, and sent women as
5 well as men to prison in chains ·as the high priest and the whole council of elders can testify, since they even sent me with letters to their brothers in Damascus. When I set off it was with the intention of bringing prisoners back from there to Jerusalem for punishment.
6 'I was on that journey and nearly at Damascus when about midday a bright light from heaven suddenly shone round me.
7 I fell to the ground and heard a voice saying, "Saul, Saul,
8 why are you persecuting me?" ·I answered: Who are you, Lord? and he said to me, "I am Jesus the Nazarene, and you
9 are persecuting me". ·The people with me saw the light but
10 did not hear his voice as he spoke to me. ·I said: What am I to do, Lord? The Lord answered, "Stand up and go into Damascus, and there you will be told what you have been
11 appointed to do". ·The light had been so dazzling that I was blind and my companions had to take me by the hand; and so I came to Damascus.
12 'Someone called Ananias, a devout follower of the Law
13 and highly thought of by all the Jews living there, ·came to see me; he stood beside me and said, "Brother Saul, receive your sight". Instantly my sight came back and I was able to

21 a. For the duration of a nazirite vow, the hair was not to be cut. Discharge from the vow, on fulfilment, had to be celebrated with expensive sacrifices. b. Commanding officer of the Roman garrison. c. Nationalist extremists. d. I.e. Aramaic.

14 see him. ·Then he said, "The God of our ancestors has chosen you to know his will, to see the Just One and hear his own
15 voice speaking, ·because you are to be his witness before all mankind, testifying to what you have seen and heard.
16 And now why delay? It is time you were baptised and had your sins washed away while invoking his name."

17 'Once, after I had got back to Jerusalem, when I was
18 praying in the Temple, I fell into a trance ·and then I saw him. "Hurry," he said "leave Jerusalem at once; they will
19 not accept the testimony you are giving about me." ·Lord, I answered, it is because they know that I used to go from synagogue to synagogue, imprisoning and flogging those
20 who believed in you; ·and that when the blood of your witness[a] Stephen was being shed, I was standing by in full agreement with his murderers, and minding their clothes.
21 Then he said to me, "Go! I am sending you out to the pagans far away." '

Paul the Roman citizen

22 So far they had listened to him, but at these words they began to shout, 'Rid the earth of the man! He is not fit to
23 live!' ·They were yelling, waving their cloaks and throwing
24 dust into the air, ·and so the tribune had him brought into the fortress and ordered him to be examined under the lash,
25 to find out the reason for the outcry against him ·But when they had strapped him down Paul said to the centurion on duty, 'Is it legal for you to flog a man who is a Roman citizen
26 and has not been brought to trial?' ·When he heard this the centurion went and told the tribune; 'Do you realise what you are doing?' he said 'This man is a Roman citizen'.
27 So the tribune came and asked him, 'Tell me, are you a
28 Roman citizen?' 'I am' Paul said. ·The tribune replied, 'It cost me a large sum to acquire this citizenship'. 'But I was
29 born to it' said Paul. ·Then those who were about to examine him hurriedly withdrew, and the tribune himself was alarmed when he realised that he had put a Roman citizen in chains.

His appearance before the Sanhedrin

30 The next day, since he wanted to know what precise charge the Jews were bringing, he freed Paul and gave orders for a meeting of the chief priests and the entire Sanhedrin; then he brought Paul down and stood him in front of them.
23 Paul looked steadily at the Sanhedrin and began to speak, 'My brothers, to this day I have conducted myself before God
2 with a perfectly clear conscience'. ·At this the high priest

Ananias ordered his attendants to strike him on the mouth.
3 Then Paul said to him, 'God will surely strike you, you white-washed wall! How can you sit there to judge me according to the Law, and then break the Law by ordering a man to strike
4 me?' ·The attendants said, 'It is God's high priest you are
5 insulting!' ·Paul answered, 'Brothers, I did not realise it was the high priest, for scripture says: *You must not curse a ruler of your people'.*[a]

6   Now Paul was well aware that one section was made up of Sadducees and the other of Pharisees, so he called out in the Sanhedrin, 'Brothers, I am a Pharisee and the son of Phari-sees. It is for our hope in the resurrection of the dead that I
7 am on trial.' ·As soon as he said this a dispute broke out between the Pharisees and Sadducees, and the assembly was
8 split between the two parties. ·For the Sadducees say there is neither resurrection, nor angel, nor spirit, while the Pharisees
9 accept all three. ·The shouting grew louder, and some of the scribes from the Pharisees' party stood up and protested strongly, 'We find nothing wrong with this man. Suppose a
10 spirit has spoken to him, or an angel?' ·Feeling was running high, and the tribune, afraid that they would tear Paul to pieces, ordered his troops to go down and haul him out and bring him into the fortress.

11   Next night, the Lord appeared to him and said, 'Courage! You have borne witness for me in Jerusalem, now you must do the same in Rome.'

The conspiracy of the Jews against Paul

12   When it was day, the Jews held a secret meeting at which they made a vow not to eat or drink until they had killed
13 Paul. ·There were more than forty who took part in this
14 conspiracy, ·and they went to the chief priests and elders, and told them, 'We have made a solemn vow to let nothing pass
15 our lips until we have killed Paul. ·Now it is up to you and the Sanhedrin together to apply to the tribune to bring him down to you, as though you meant to examine his case more closely; we, on our side, are prepared to dispose of him before he reaches you.'

16   But the son of Paul's sister heard of the ambush they were laying and made his way into the fortress and told Paul,
17 who called one of the centurions and said, 'Take this young
18 man to the tribune; he has something to tell him'. ·So the man took him to the tribune, and reported, 'The prisoner

22 **a.** *Martyr:* the word had not yet acquired its restricted meaning.
23 **a.** Ex 22:27

Paul summoned me and requested me to bring this young
19 man to you; he has something to tell you'. ·Then the tribune
took him by the hand and drew him aside and asked, 'What
20 is it you have to tell me?' ·He replied, 'The Jews have made a
plan to ask you to take Paul down to the Sanhedrin tomorrow, as though they meant to inquire more closely into his
21 case. ·Do not let them persuade you. There are more than
forty of them lying in wait for him, and they have vowed not
to eat or drink until they have got rid of him. They are
ready now and only waiting for your order to be given.'
22 The tribune let the young man go with this caution, 'Tell no
one that you have given me this information'.

Paul transferred to Caesarea

23   Then he summoned two of the centurions and said, 'Get
two hundred soldiers ready to leave for Caesarea by the
third hour of the night with seventy cavalry and two hundred
24 auxiliaries; ·provide horses for Paul, and deliver him un-
25 harmed to Felix the governor'.[b] ·He also wrote a letter in
26 these terms: ·'Claudius Lysias to his Excellency the governor
27 Felix, greetings. ·This man had been seized by the Jews and
would have been murdered by them but I came on the scene
with my troops and got him away, having discovered that he
28 was a Roman citizen. ·Wanting to find out what charge they
were making against him, I brought him before their Sanhe-
29 drin. ·I found that the accusation concerned disputed points
of their Law, but that there was no charge deserving death or
30 imprisonment. ·My information is that there is a conspiracy
against the man, so I hasten to send him to you, and have
notified his accusers that they must state their case against
him in your presence.'

31   The soldiers carried out their orders; they took Paul and
32 escorted him by night to Antipatris. ·Next day they left the
mounted escort to go on with him and returned to the
33 fortress. ·On arriving at Caesarea the escort delivered the
34 letter to the governor and handed Paul over to him. ·The
governor read the letter and asked him what province he
35 he came from. Learning that he was from Cilicia he said, ·'I
will hear your case as soon as your accusers are here too'.
Then he ordered him to be held in Herod's praetorium.

The case before Felix

24   Five days later the high priest Ananias came down with
some of the elders and an advocate named Tertullus, and
2 they laid information against Paul before the governor. ·Paul

was called, and Tertullus opened for the prosecution, 'Your Excellency, Felix, the unbroken peace we enjoy and the
3 reforms this nation owes to your foresight ·are matters we
4 accept, always and everywhere, with all gratitude. ·I do not want to take up too much of your time, but I beg you to give
5 us a brief hearing. ·The plain truth is that we find this man a perfect pest; he stirs up trouble among Jews the world over,
6 and is a ringleader of the Nazarene sect. ·He has even attempted to profane the Temple. We placed him under
7 arrest, intending to judge him according to our Law, ·but the tribune Lysias intervened and took him out of our hands
8 by force, ·ordering his accusers to appear before you; if you ask him[a] you can find out for yourself the truth of all our
9 accusations against this man.' ·The Jews supported him, asserting that these were the facts.

10 When the governor motioned him to speak, Paul answered:

Paul's speech before the Roman governor

'I know that you have administered justice over this nation for many years, and I can therefore speak with confi-
11 dence in my defence. ·As you can verify for yourself, it is no more than twelve days since I went up to Jerusalem on pil-
12 grimage, ·and it is not true that they ever found me arguing with anyone or stirring up the mob, either in the Temple, in
13 the synagogues, or about the town; ·neither can they prove any of the accusations they are making against me now.

14 'What I do admit to you is this: it is according to the Way which they describe as a sect that I worship the God of my ancestors, retaining my belief in all points of the Law and in
15 what is written in the prophets; ·and I hold the same hope in God as they do that there will be a resurrection of good
16 men and bad men alike. ·In these things, I, as much as they, do my best to keep a clear conscience at all times before God and man.

17 'After several years I came to bring alms to my nation and
18 to make offerings; ·it was in connection with these that they found me in the Temple; I had been purified, and there was
19 no crowd involved, and no disturbance. ·But some Jews from Asia . . .—these are the ones who should have appeared before you and accused me of whatever they had against me.
20 At least let those who are present say what crime they found
21 me guilty of when I stood before the Sanhedrin, ·unless it were to do with this single outburst, when I stood up among them

b. Antoninus Felix, procurator of Judaea from 52 to 59–60.
24 a. Lysias.

and called out: It is about the resurrection of the dead that I am on trial before you today.'

Paul's captivity at Caesarea

22 At this, Felix, who knew more about the Way than most people, adjourned the case, saying, 'When Lysias the tribune
23 has come down I will go into your case'. ·He then gave orders to the centurion that Paul should be kept under arrest but free from restriction, and that none of his own people should be prevented from seeing to his needs.

24 Some days later Felix came with his wife Drusilla who was a Jewess.[b] He sent for Paul and gave him a hearing on the
25 subject of faith in Christ Jesus. ·But when he began to treat of righteousness, self-control and the coming Judgement, Felix took fright and said, 'You may go for the present; I
26 will send for you when I find it convenient'. ·At the same time he had hopes of receiving money from Paul, and for this reason he sent for him frequently and had talks with him.

27 When the two years[c] came to an end, Felix was succeeded by Porcius Festus and, being anxious to gain favour with the Jews, Felix left Paul in custody.

Paul appeals to Caesar

25 Three days after his arrival in the province, Festus went up
2 to Jerusalem from Caesarea. ·The chief priests and leaders of the Jews informed him of the case against Paul, urgently
3 asking him to support them rather than Paul, and to have him transferred to Jerusalem. They were, in fact, preparing an
4 ambush to murder him on the way. ·But Festus replied that Paul would remain in custody in Caesarea, and that he would
5 be going back there shortly himself. ·'Let your authorities come down with me' he said 'and if there is anything wrong about the man, they can bring a charge against him.'

6 After staying with them for eight or ten days at the most, he went down to Caesarea and the next day he took his seat
7 on the tribunal and had Paul brought in. ·As soon as Paul appeared, the Jews who had come down from Jerusalem surrounded him, making many serious accusations which
8 they were unable to substantiate. ·Paul's defence was this, 'I have committed no offence whatever against either Jewish
9 law, or the Temple, or Caesar'. ·Festus was anxious to gain favour with the Jews, so he said to Paul ,'Are you willing to go up to Jerusalem and be tried on these charges before me
10 there?' ·But Paul replied, 'I am standing before the tribunal of Caesar and this is where I should be tried. I have done the

11 Jews no wrong, as you very well know. ·If I am guilty of committing any capital crime, I do not ask to be spared the death penalty. But if there is no substance in the accusations these persons bring against me, no one has a right to sur-
12 render me to them. I appeal to Caesar.' ·Then Festus conferred with his advisers and replied, 'You have appealed to Caesar; to Caesar you shall go'.

Paul appears before King Agrippa

13 Some days later King Agrippa and Bernice*a* arrived in
14 Caesarea and paid their respects to Festus. ·Their visit lasted several days, and Festus put Paul's case before the king. 'There is a man here' he said 'whom Felix left behind in
15 custody, ·and while I was in Jerusalem the chief priests and elders of the Jews laid information against him, demanding
16 his condemnation. ·But I told them that Romans are not in the habit of surrendering any man, until the accused confronts his accusers and is given an opportunity to defend him-
17 self against the charge. ·So they came here with me, and I wasted no time but took my seat on the tribunal the very
18 next day and had the man brought in. ·When confronted with him, his accusers did not charge him with any of the
19 crimes I had expected; but they had some argument or other with him about their own religion and about a dead man
20 called Jesus whom Paul alleged to be alive. ·Not feeling qualified to deal with questions of this sort, I asked him if he would be willing to go to Jerusalem to be tried there on this
21 issue. ·But Paul put in an appeal for his case to be reserved for the judgement of the august emperor, so I ordered him to
22 be remanded until I could send him to Caesar.' ·Agrippa said to Festus, 'I should like to hear the man myself'. 'Tomorrow' he answered 'you shall hear him.'

23 So the next day Agrippa and Bernice arrived in great state and entered the audience chamber attended by the tribunes and the city notables; and Festus ordered Paul to be brought
24 in. ·Then Festus said, 'King Agrippa, and all here present with us, you see before you the man about whom the whole Jewish community has petitioned me, both in Jerusalem and here, loudly protesting that he ought not to be allowed to
25 remain alive. ·For my own part I am satisfied that he has

b. Youngest daughter of Herod Agrippa. **c.** The maximum length of protective custody; Felix was breaking the law by continuing to detain Paul.
25 a. Agrippa, Bernice and Drusilla (24:24) were children of Herod Agrippa I.

committed no capital crime, but when he himself appealed
26 to the august emperor I decided to send him. ·But I have
nothing definite that I can write to his Imperial Majesty about
him; that is why I have produced him before you all, and
before you in particular, King Agrippa, so that after the
27 examination I may have something to write. ·It seems to me
pointless to send a prisoner without indicating the charges
against him.'

26 Then Agrippa said to Paul, 'You have leave to speak on
your own behalf'. And Paul held up his hand and began his
defence:

Paul's speech before King Agrippa

2 'I consider myself fortunate, King Agrippa, in that it is
before you I am to answer today all the charges made against
3 me by the Jews, ·the more so because you are an expert in
matters of custom and controversy among the Jews. So I beg
you to listen to me patiently.
4 'My manner of life from my youth, a life spent from the
beginning among my own people and in Jerusalem, is com-
5 mon knowledge among the Jews. ·They have known me for
a long time and could testify, if they would, that I followed
6 the strictest party in our religion and lived as a Pharisee. ·And
now it is for my hope in the promise made by God to our
7 ancestors that I am on trial, ·the promise that our twelve
tribes, constant in worship night and day, hope to attain.
For that hope, Sire, I am actually put on trial by Jews!
8 Why does it seem incredible to you that God should raise the
dead?
9 'As for me, I once thought it was my duty to use every
10 means to oppose the name of Jesus the Nazarene. ·This I did
in Jerusalem; I myself threw many of the saints into prison,
acting on authority from the chief priests, and when they
11 were sentenced to death I cast my vote against them. ·I
often went round the synagogues inflicting penalties, trying
in this way to force them to renounce their faith; my fury
against them was so extreme that I even pursued them into
foreign cities.
12 'On one such expedition I was going to Damascus, armed
13 with full powers and a commission from the chief priests, ·and
at midday as I was on my way, your Majesty, I saw a light
brighter than the sun come down from heaven. It shone
14 brilliantly round me and my fellow travellers. ·We all fell to
the ground, and I heard a voice saying to me in Hebrew, "Saul,
Saul, why are you persecuting me? It is hard for you, kicking

15 like this against the goad."[a] ·Then I said: Who are you,
   Lord? And the Lord answered, "I am Jesus, and you are
16 persecuting me. ·But get up and stand on your feet, for I
   have appeared to you for this reason: to appoint you as my
   servant and as witness of this vision in which you have seen
17 me, and of others in which I shall appear to you. ·*I shall
   deliver you* from the people and *from the pagans, to whom I*
18 *am sending you* ·*to open their eyes*, so that they may turn
   from darkness to light,[b] from the dominion of Satan to God,
   and receive, through faith in me, forgiveness of their sins and
   a share in the inheritance of the sanctified."

19   'After that, King Agrippa, I could not disobey the heaven-
20 ly vision. ·On the contrary I started preaching, first to the
   people of Damascus, then to those of Jerusalem and all the
   countryside of Judaea, and also to the pagans, urging them
   to repent and turn to God, proving their change of heart by
21 their deeds. ·This was why the Jews laid hands on me in the
22 Temple and tried to do away with me. ·But I was blessed
   with God's help, and so I have stood firm to this day, testifying to great and small alike, saying nothing more than what
23 the prophets and Moses himself said would happen: ·that
   the Christ was to suffer and that, as the first to rise from the
   dead, he was to proclaim that light now shone for our people
   and for the pagans too.'

His hearers' reactions

24   He had reached this point in his defence when Festus
   shouted out, 'Paul, you are out of your mind; all that learning
25 of yours is driving you mad'. ·'Festus, your Excellency,'
   answered Paul 'I am not mad: I am speaking nothing but the
26 sober truth. ·The king understands these matters, and to him
   I now speak with assurance, confident that nothing of all this
   is lost on him; after all, these things were not done in a
27 corner. ·King Agrippa, do you believe in the prophets? I
28 know you do.' ·At this Agrippa said to Paul, 'A little more,
   and your arguments would make a Christian of me'.
29 'Little or more,' Paul replied 'I wish before God that not
   only you but all who have heard me today would come to be
   as I am—except for these chains.'

30   At this the king rose to his feet, with the governor and
31 Bernice and those who sat there with them. ·When they had
   retired they talked together and agreed, 'This man is doing
32 nothing that deserves death or imprisonment'. ·And Agrippa

26 a. Greek proverbial expression for useless resistance. **b.** Quotations
from Jr 1; Is 42; Is 9.

remarked to Festus, 'The man could have been set free if he had not appealed to Caesar'.

The departure for Rome

27 When it had been decided that we should sail for Italy, Paul and some other prisoners were handed over to a cen-
2 turion called Julius, of the Augustan cohort. ·We boarded a vessel from Adramyttium bound for ports on the Asiatic coast, and put to sea; we had Aristarchus with us, a Mace-
3 donian of Thessalonika. ·Next day we put in at Sidon, and Julius was considerate enough to allow Paul to go to his friends to be looked after.

4 From there we put to sea again, but as the winds were
5 against us we sailed under the lee of Cyprus, ·then across the open sea off Cilicia and Pamphylia, taking a fortnight
6 to reach Myra in Lycia. ·There the centurion found an Alex- andrian ship leaving for Italy and put us aboard.

7 For some days we made little headway, and we had diffi- culty in making Cnidus. The wind would not allow us to touch there, so we sailed under the lee of Crete off Cape
8 Salmone ·and struggled along the coast until we came to a place called Fair Havens, near the town of Lasea.

Storm and shipwreck

9 A great deal of time had been lost, and navigation was already hazardous since it was now well after the time of the
10 Fast,*a* so Paul gave them this warning, ·'Friends, I can see this voyage will be dangerous and that we run the risk of losing not only the cargo and the ship but also our lives as
11 well'. ·But the centurion took more notice of the captain and
12 ship's owner than of what Paul was saying; ·and since the harbour was unsuitable for wintering, the majority were for putting out from there in the hope of wintering at Phoenix— a harbour in Crete, facing south-west and north-west.

13 A southerly breeze sprang up and, thinking their objective as good as reached, they weighed anchor and began to sail
14 past Crete, close inshore. ·But it was not long before a hurricane, the 'north-easter' as they call it, burst on them
15 from across the island. ·The ship was caught and could not be turned head-on to the wind, so we had to give way to it
16 and let ourselves be driven. ·We ran under the lee of a small island called Cauda and managed with some difficulty to
17 bring the ship's boat under control. ·They hoisted it aboard and with the help of tackle bound cables round the ship; then, afraid of running aground on the Syrtis banks, they

18 floated out the sea-anchor and so let themselves drift. ·As
we were making very heavy weather of it, the next day they
19 began to jettison the cargo, ·and the third day they threw
20 the ship's gear overboard with their own hands. ·For a
number of days both the sun and the stars were invisible and
the storm raged unabated until at last we gave up all hope of
surviving.

21   Then, when they had been without food for a long time,
Paul stood up among the men. 'Friends,' he said 'if you had
listened to me and not put out from Crete, you would have
22 spared yourselves all this damage and loss. ·But now I ask
you not to give way to despair. There will be no loss of life at
23 all, only of the ship. ·Last night there was standing beside me
an angel of the God to whom I belong and whom I serve,
24 and he said, "Do not be afraid, Paul. You are destined to
appear before Caesar, and for this reason God grants you
25 the safety of all who are sailing with you." ·So take courage,
friends; I trust in God that things will turn out just as I was
26 told; ·but we are to be stranded on some island.'

27   On the fourteenth night we were being driven one way and
another in the Adriatic,[b] when about midnight the crew
28 sensed that land of some sort was near. ·They took soundings
and found twenty fathoms; after a short interval they
29 sounded again and found fifteen fathoms. ·Then, afraid that
we might run aground somewhere on a reef, they dropped
30 four anchors from the stern and prayed for daylight. ·When
some of the crew tried to escape from the ship and lowered
the ship's boat into the sea as though to lay out anchors from
31 the bows, ·Paul said to the centurion and his men, 'Unless
32 those men stay on board you cannot hope to be saved'. ·So
the soldiers cut the boat's ropes and let it drop away.

33   Just before daybreak Paul urged them all to have something to eat. 'For fourteen days' he said 'you have been in
34 suspense, going hungry and eating nothing. ·Let me persuade you to have something to eat; your safety is not in
35 doubt. Not a hair of your heads will be lost.' ·With these
words he took some bread, gave thanks to God in front of
36 them all, broke it and began to eat. ·Then they all plucked up
37 courage and took something to eat themselves. ·We were in
all two hundred and seventy-six souls on board that ship.
38 When they had eaten what they wanted they lightened the
ship by throwing the corn overboard into the sea.

27 a. 'the Fast', the feast of Atonement, was kept about the time of
the autumn equinox; winter was coming on. **b.** The term includes the
seas between Greece, Italy and Africa.

39   · When day came they did not recognise the land, but they could make out a kind of bay with a beach; they planned to
40 run the ship aground on this if they could. ·They slipped the anchors and left them to the sea, and at the same time loosened the lashings of the rudders; then, hoisting the fore-
41 sail to the wind, they headed for the beach. ·But the cross-currents carried them into a shoal and the vessel ran aground. The bows were wedged in and stuck fast, while the stern began to break up with the pounding of the waves.
42   The soldiers planned to kill the prisoners for fear that any
43 should swim off and escape. ·But the centurion was deter-mined to bring Paul safely through, and would not let them do what they intended. He gave orders that those who could
44 swim should jump overboard first and so get ashore, ·and the rest follow either on planks or on pieces of wreckage. In this way all came safe and sound to land.

Waiting in Malta

28   Once we had come safely through, we discovered that the
2 island was called Malta. ·The inhabitants treated us with unusual kindness. They made us all welcome, and they lit a huge fire because it had started to rain and the weather
3 was cold. ·Paul had collected a bundle of sticks and was putting them on the fire when a viper brought out by the
4 heat attached itself to his hand. ·When the natives saw the creature hanging from his hand they said to one another, 'That man must be a murderer; he may have escaped the sea,
5 but divine vengeance would not let him live'. ·However, he shook the creature off into the fire and came to no harm,
6 although they were expecting him at any moment to swell up or drop dead on the spot. After they had waited a long time without seeing anything out of the ordinary happen to him, they changed their minds and began to say he was a god.
7   In that neighbourhood there were estates belonging to the prefect of the island, whose name was Publius. He received
8 us and entertained us hospitably for three days. ·It so hap-pened that Publius' father was in bed, suffering from feverish attacks and dysentery. Paul went in to see him, and after a
9 prayer he laid his hands on the man and healed him. ·When this happened, the other sick people on the island came as
10 well and were cured; ·they honoured us with many marks of respect, and when we sailed they put on board the provisions we needed.

From Malta to Rome

11 At the end of three months we set sail in a ship that had wintered in the island; she came from Alexandria and her
12 figurehead was the Twins. ·We put in at Syracuse and spent
13 three days there; ·from there we followed the coast up to Rhegium. After one day there a south wind sprang up and on
14 the second day we made Puteoli,[a] ·where we found some brothers and were much rewarded by staying a week with them. And so we came to Rome.
15 When the brothers there heard of our arrival they came to meet us, as far as the Forum of Appius and the Three Taverns. When Paul saw them he thanked God and took
16 courage. ·On our arrival in Rome Paul was allowed to stay in lodgings of his own with the soldier who guarded him.

Paul makes contact with the Roman Jews

17 After three days he called together the leading Jews. When they had assembled, he said to them, 'Brothers, although I have done nothing against our people or the customs of our ancestors, I was arrested in Jerusalem and handed over to
18 the Romans. ·They examined me and would have set me free, since they found me guilty of nothing involving the
19 death penalty; ·but the Jews lodged an objection, and I was forced to appeal to Caesar, not that I had any accusation to
20 make against my own nation. ·That is why I have asked to see you and talk to you, for it is on account of the hope of Israel that I wear this chain.'
21 They answered, 'We have received no letters from Judaea about you, nor has any countryman of yours arrived here with any report or story of anything to your discredit.
22 We think it would be as well to hear your own account of your position; all we know about this sect is that opinion everywhere condemns it.'

Paul's declaration to the Roman Jews

23 So they arranged a day with him and a large number of them visited him at his lodgings. He put his case to them, testifying to the kingdom of God and trying to persuade them about Jesus, arguing from the Law of Moses and the prophets. This went on from early morning until evening,
24 and some were convinced by what he said, while the rest
25 were sceptical. ·So they disagreed among themselves and, as

28 a. Pozzuoli, on the Gulf of Naples.

they went away, Paul had one last thing to say to them, 'How aptly the Holy Spirit spoke when he told your ancestors through the prophet Isaiah:

26　　*Go to this nation and say:*
　　　　You will hear and hear again but not understand,
　　　　see and see again, but not perceive.
27　　*For the heart of this nation has grown coarse,*
　　　　their ears are dull of hearing and they have shut their eyes,
　　　　for fear they should see with their eyes,
　　　　hear with their ears,
　　　　understand with their heart,
　　　　and be converted
　　　　and be healed by me.[b]

28　　'Understand, then, that this salvation of God has been sent to the pagans; they will listen to it.'

Epilogue

30　　Paul spent the whole of the two years[c] in his own rented
31　　lodging. He welcomed all who came to visit him, ·proclaiming the kingdom of God and teaching the truth about the Lord Jesus Christ with complete freedom and without hindrance from anyone.

b. Is 6:9–10 **c.** See note on 24:27

INTRODUCTION TO

THE LETTERS OF SAINT PAUL

Paul was born about A.D. 10, of a Jewish family living among 'the Greeks' at Tarsus, a Roman municipality in Cilicia. He was educated as a Pharisee in Jerusalem. He was converted to belief in Christ about A.D. 34, and many particulars of his life as an apostle can be found in his letters and in Acts. The letters may be dated from A.D. 50–65. Paul was imprisoned in Rome, A.D. 61–63, and set free for want of evidence; a second imprisonment in Rome ended, according to a very ancient tradition, in martyrdom by execution, probably in the year 67.

Paul's letters show him as a man of sensitive temperament and warm emotions, completely dedicated to the spreading of the 'Good News' that Christ by his death and resurrection was proved to be the one universal saviour of Jew and 'Greek' alike. Crises and controversies led him to explain the message of the gospel in ways adapted to the needs of his readers and so to bring into play his remarkable powers of theological analysis and his grasp of profundities. His letters, in a fluent Greek which was his second mother-tongue, were generally a response to a particular situation in a particular church, and although some passages in them were obviously written after long and careful thought, more often the style suggests spontaneity and urgency. The letters were usually dictated, and then signed by Paul with a short personal greeting.

The order in which the letters are printed in this Bible is the traditional one which arranges them in order of diminishing length. If they are read in the order in which they were written, the development in Paul's theological thinking can be seen as he finds expression for further depths and implications in the gospel.

1 and 2 Thessalonians. A.D. 50–51

1 Thessalonians was written from Corinth, when Paul's companion Timothy had come back from a second visit to Thessalonika and reported to Paul on the state of the church there. Besides a series of practical recommendations, it includes Paul's teaching on

death and the 'second coming' of Christ, expressed in the terms of contemporary apocalyptic writing.

2 Thessalonians, written about a year later, shows that Paul's thought on the same subject had deepened. Parts of the two letters show some close correspondences, and some critics have doubted the authenticity of 2 Thessalonians. However, the earliest authorities accepted them as both by Paul.

1 and 2 Corinthians. A.D. 57

Corinth, a great and populous port, was a magnet to every sort of philosophy and religion and was also a notorious centre of immorality. Paul's converts in the city were particularly in need of instruction and guidance, both about the Good News itself and about the Christian life which it implied. Paul appears to have written four letters to the church in Corinth, of which we now have only two.

His first letter to Corinth has not survived, and the earliest we have was written from Ephesus sometime near Easter, 57. Shortly afterwards, Paul had to pay a brief visit to Corinth in which he had to take painful disciplinary measures, and when later he sent a representative to Corinth instead of going himself, the Corinthians did not accept his authority, and Paul wrote a third letter which was very severe. In Macedonia, towards the end of 57, Paul heard from Titus that the 'severe letter' had had the desired effect, and then he wrote the letter which we know as 2 Corinthians.

However, 2 Corinthians is not a single consistent letter; it has been suggested that it includes part of the lost first letter (2 Co 6:14–7:1) and part of the 'severe letter' (2 Co 10–13).

The two letters to the Corinthians contain much information about urgent problems that faced the church and the important decisions which were made to meet them: questions of morality, about the liturgy and the holding of assemblies, the recognition of spiritual gifts and the avoidance of contamination from pagan religions. It was Paul's religious genius to turn what might have remained textbook cases of conscience into the means of exploring the profound doctrines of Christian liberty, the sanctification of the body, the supremacy of love, and union with Christ.

Galatians. Romans. A.D. 57–58

These two letters analyse the same problem, but while Galatians is Paul's immediate response to a particular situation, Romans is more like a systematic treatise and gives a methodical arrangement to all the new ideas that had emerged from the argument.

Paul had not himself founded the church at Rome. It was a mixed community in which there was a danger that Jewish and non-Jewish converts might look down on each other, and Paul, before visiting the church, sent this considered examination of how Judaism and Christianity were related to one another, using the ideas which he had developed in the Galatian crisis and further refining them. In both these letters we can see Paul correcting the unbalance of the Greek outlook which relied too exclusively on human reason, just as in earlier letters he had corrected the unbalance of the Jewish outlook which relied too heavily on the Law.

Philippians. A.D. 56–57

This is a letter without a lot of doctrinal exposition in it, giving some news to his converts at Philippi and warning them of some enemies who had worked against Paul elsewhere and might turn to them next. At the time of writing, Paul was under arrest, but it is unlikely that this letter was written from Rome during his imprisonment there in 61–63 and it may have been written from Ephesus.

Ephesians. Colossians. Philemon. A.D. 61–63

All three letters are closely related and were written while Paul was under arrest in Rome. It appears that the relation between Ephesians and Colossians is like that between Romans and Galatians. The news of a crisis at Colossae led Paul to write a letter to the Christians there against the growing belief and trust in celestial and cosmic powers. Paul accepts these powers as the angels of Jewish tradition, but he shows that in the great scheme of salvation they have only a preparatory and subordinate part and now there is a new order in which Christ is all. About the same time, he wrote a fuller and more systematic treatment of the same ideas and this is the letter that we know as 'Ephesians' though it was probably written for circulation through all the churches.

Some critics have questioned the authorship of both these letters, and particularly of Ephesians, since it seems to borrow ideas from Colossians and not always to digest them smoothly. But we know nothing of any other person capable of writing them; in parts of them, Paul is at his most personal and characteristic, and they represent a further reconsideration of themes which he had already explored in his earlier letters.

The short letter to Philemon is a personal message which was written in Paul's own handwriting.

1 Timothy. Titus. 2 Timothy. A.D. 65

These are letters of advice and instruction to two of Paul's most loyal followers in their work of organising and leading the communities to which he had sent them. It is possible that 1 Timothy and Titus were written from Macedonia about A.D. 65, but by the time he wrote 2 Timothy, Paul was a prisoner in Rome awaiting death. From the details of his recent movements given in this letter, this must have been a second imprisonment, and not that of 61–63.

Hebrews. A.D. 67

The question who wrote this letter to Jewish Christians has been a subject of debate from the earliest times. It is ranked with Paul's letters in importance, its doctrine has Pauline overtones, and it was written from Italy, perhaps from Rome; but while there may be a strong presumption that its author had come under the influence of Paul, the letter can hardly be attributed to Paul himself.

It is a sustained argument from Old Testament texts, to keep its readers firm under persecution. The theme is that the ineffectual sacrifices of the levitical priests are replaced by the one uniquely efficacious sacrifice of Christ, and that his priesthood is of an altogether higher order than that of the Jewish priests, derived from Aaron.

ROMANS

THE LETTER OF PAUL

TO THE CHURCH OF ROME

Address

1 From Paul, a servant of Christ Jesus who has been called to be an apostle, and specially chosen to preach the Good
2 News that God ·promised long ago through his prophets in the scriptures.
3 This news is about the Son of God who, according to the
4 human nature he took, was a descendant of David: ·it is about Jesus Christ our Lord who, in the order of the spirit, the spirit of holiness that was in him, was proclaimed Son of God in all his power through his resurrection from the dead.
5 Through him we received grace and our apostolic mission to preach the obedience of faith to all pagan nations in honour
6 of his name. ·You are one of these nations, and by his call
7 belong to Jesus Christ. ·To you all, then, who are God's beloved in Rome, called to be saints, may God our Father and the Lord Jesus Christ send grace and peace.·

Thanksgiving and prayer

8 First I thank my God through Jesus Christ for all of you and for the way in which your faith is spoken of all over the
9 world. ·The God I worship spiritually by preaching the Good News of his Son knows that I never fail to mention you in
10 my prayers, ·and to ask to be allowed at long last the oppor-
11 tunity to visit you, if he so wills. ·For I am longing to see you either to strengthen you by sharing a spiritual gift with you,
12 or what is better, to find encouragement among you from our
13 common faith. ·I want you to know, brothers, that I have often planned to visit you—though until now I have always been prevented—in the hope that I might work as fruitfully
14 among you as I have done among the other pagans. ·I owe a duty to Greeks[a] just as much as to barbarians, to the educated

1 a. When contrasted with 'barbarians' (as here), 'Greeks' means the inhabitants of the hellenic world, including the Romans; when contrasted with 'Jews', it means the pagans in general.

15 just as much as to the uneducated, ·and it is this that makes me want to bring the Good News to you too in Rome.

SALVATION BY FAITH

I. JUSTIFICATION

The theme stated

16   For I am not ashamed of the Good News: it is the power of God saving all who have faith—Jews first, but Greeks as well

17 ·—since this is what reveals the justice of God to us: it shows how faith leads to faith, or as scripture says: *The upright man finds life through faith.*[b]

A. GOD'S ANGER AGAINST PAGAN AND JEW

God's anger against the pagans

18   The anger of God is being revealed from heaven against all the impiety and depravity of men who keep truth im-

19 prisoned in their wickedness. ·For what can be known about God is perfectly plain to them since God himself has made it

20 plain. ·Ever since God created the world his everlasting power and deity—however invisible—have been there for the mind to see in the things he has made. That is why such people

21 are without excuse: ·they knew God and yet refused to honour him as God or to thank him; instead, they made nonsense out of logic and their empty minds were darkened.

22 The more they called themselves philosophers, the more

23 stupid they grew, ·until *they exchanged the glory*[c] of the immortal God for a worthless imitation, *for the image* of

24 mortal man, of birds, of quadrupeds and reptiles. ·That is why God left them to their filthy enjoyments and the prac-

25 tices with which they dishonour their own bodies, since they have given up divine truth for a lie and have worshipped and served creatures instead of the creator, who is blessed for ever. Amen!

26   That is why God has abandoned them to degrading passions: why their women have turned from natural inter-

27 course to unnatural practices ·and why their menfolk have given up natural intercourse to be consumed with passion for each other, men doing shameless things with men and getting an appropriate reward for their perversion.

28   In other words, since they refused to see it was rational to

acknowledge God, God has left them to their own irrational
29 ideas and to their monstrous behaviour. ·And so they are
steeped in all sorts of depravity, rottenness, greed and
malice, and addicted to envy, murder, wrangling, treachery
30 and spite. ·Libellers, slanderers, enemies of God, rude, arrogant and boastful, enterprising in sin, rebellious to parents,
31 without brains, honour, love or pity. ·They know what God's
32 verdict is: that those who behave like this deserve to die—
and yet they do it; and what is worse, encourage others to do
the same.

The Jews are not exempt from God's anger

2   So no matter who you are, if you pass judgement you have
no excuse. In judging others you condemn yourself, since you
2 behave no differently from those you judge. ·We know that
3 God condemns that sort of behaviour impartially: ·and when
you judge those who behave like this while you are doing
exactly the same, do you think you will escape God's judge-
4 ment? ·Or are you abusing his abundant goodness, patience
and toleration, not realising that this goodness of God is
5 meant to lead you to repentance? ·Your stubborn refusal to
repent is only adding to the anger God will have towards you
on that day of anger when his just judgements will be made
6 known. ·*He will repay each one as his works deserve.*[a]
7 For those who sought renown and honour and immortality
8 by always doing good there will be eternal life; ·for the
unsubmissive who refused to take truth for their guide and
9 took depravity instead, there will be anger and fury. ·Pain
and suffering will come to every human being who employs
10 himself in evil—Jews first, but Greeks as well; ·renown,
honour and peace will come to everyone who does good—
11 Jews first, but Greeks as well. ·God has no favourites.

The Law will not save them

12   Sinners who were not subject to the Law will perish all the
same, without that Law; sinners who were under the Law will
13 have that Law to judge them. ·It is not listening to the Law
but keeping it that will make people holy in the sight of God.
14 For instance, pagans who never heard of the Law but are led
by reason to do what the Law commands, may not actually
'possess' the Law, but they can be said to 'be' the Law.
15 They can point to the substance of the Law engraved on their
hearts—they can call a witness, that is, their own conscience

b. Hab 2:4 c. Ps 106:20
2 a. Ps 62:12

—they have accusation and defence, that is, their own inner
16 mental dialogue.[b] ·... on the day when, according to the
Good News I preach, God, through Jesus Christ, judges the
secrets of mankind.

17   If you call yourself a Jew, if you really trust in the Law and
18 are proud of your God, ·if you know God's will through the
19 Law and can tell what is right, ·if you are convinced you can
20 guide the blind and be a beacon to those in the dark, ·if you
can teach the ignorant and instruct the unlearned because
21 your Law embodies all knowledge and truth, ·then why not
teach yourself as well as the others? You preach against steal-
22 ing, yet you steal; ·you forbid adultery, yet you commit adult-
23 ery; you despise idols, yet you rob their temples. ·By boasting
about the Law and then disobeying it, you bring God into
24 contempt. ·As scripture says: *It is your fault that the name
of God is blasphemed among the pagans*.

Circumcision will not save them

25   It is a good thing to be circumcised if you keep the Law;
but if you break the Law, you might as well have stayed
26 uncircumcised. ·If a man who is not circumcised obeys the
commandments of the Law, surely that makes up for not
27 being circumcised? ·More than that, the man who keeps the
Law, even though he has not been physically circumcised, is a
living condemnation of the way you disobey the Law in spite
28 of being circumcised and having it all written down. ·To be a
Jew is not just to look like a Jew, and circumcision is more
29 than a physical operation. ·The real Jew is the one who is
inwardly a Jew, and the real circumcision is in the heart—
something not of the letter but of the spirit. A Jew like that
may not be praised by man, but he will be praised by God.

God's promises will not save them

3   Well then, is a Jew any better off? Is there any advantage
2 in being circumcised? ·A great advantage in every way. First,
the Jews are the people to whom God's message was en-
3 trusted. ·What if some of them were unfaithful? Will their
4 lack of fidelity cancel God's fidelity? ·That would be absurd.
God will always be true even though *everyone* proves to be
false;[a] so scripture says: *In all you say your justice shows, and
5 when you are judged you win your case.*[b] ·But if our lack of
holiness makes God demonstrate his integrity, how can we
say God is unjust when—to use a human analogy—he gets
6 angry with us in return? ·That would be absurd, it would
7 mean God could never judge the world. ·You might as well

say that since my untruthfulness makes God demonstrate his truthfulness and thus gives him glory, I should not be judged
8 a sinner at all. ·That would be the same as saying: Do evil as a means to good. Some slanderers have accused us of teaching this, but they are justly condemned.

All are guilty

9   Well: are we any better off? Not at all: as we said before,
10 Jews and Greeks are all under sin's dominion. ·As scripture says:

> *There is not a good man left, no, not one;*
11   *there is not one who understands,*
> *not one who looks for God.*
12   *All have turned aside, tainted all alike;*
> *there is not one good man left, not a single one.*
13   *Their throats are yawning graves;*
> *their tongues are full of deceit.*
> *Vipers' venom is on their lips,*
14   *bitter curses fill their mouths.*
15   *Their feet are swift when blood is to be shed,*
16   *wherever they go there is havoc and ruin.*
17   *They know nothing of the way of peace,*
18   *there is no fear of God before their eyes.*[c]

19   Now all this that the Law says is said, as we know, for the benefit of those who are subject to the Law, but it is meant to silence everyone and to lay the whole world open to God's
20 judgement. ·and this is because *no one can be justified in the sight of*[d] *God by keeping the Law*: all that law does is to tell us what is sinful.

B. FAITH AND THE JUSTICE OF GOD

The revelation of God's justice

21   God's justice that was made known through the Law and
22 the Prophets has now been revealed outside the Law, ·since it is the same justice of God that comes through faith to everyone, Jew and pagan alike, who believes in Jesus Christ.
23 Both Jew and pagan sinned and forfeited God's glory,
24 and both are justified through the free gift of his grace by
25 being redeemed in Christ Jesus ·who was appointed by God to sacrifice his life so as to win reconciliation through faith.

b. This verse follows on from v. 13.
3 a. Ps 116:11 b. Ps 51:4 (LXX) c. Quotations from Ps 14, Ps 5, Ps 140, Ps 10, Is 59, Ps 36. d. Ps 143:2

In this way God makes his justice known; first, for the past,
26 when sins went unpunished because he held his hand, ·then
for the present age, by showing positively that he is just, and
that he justifies everyone who believes in Jesus.

What faith does

27 So what becomes of our boasts? There is no room for
them. What sort of law excludes them? The sort of law that
tells us what to do? On the contrary, it is the law of faith,
28 since, as we see it, a man is justified by faith and not by doing
29 something the Law tells him to do. ·Is God the God of Jews
alone and not of the pagans too? Of the pagans too, most
30 certainly, ·since there is only one God, and he is the one who
will justify the circumcised because of their faith and justify
31 the uncircumcised through their faith. ·Do we mean that
faith makes the Law pointless? Not at all: we are giving the
Law its true value.

C. THE EXAMPLE OF ABRAHAM

Abraham justified by faith

4 Apply this to Abraham, the ancestor from whom we are all
2 descended. ·If Abraham was justified as a reward for doing
something, he would really have had something to boast
3 about, though not in God's sight ·because scripture says:
Abraham put his faith in God, and this faith was considered as
4 *justifying him.*[a] ·If a man has work to show, his wages are not
5 considered as a favour but as his due; ·but when a man has
nothing to show except faith in the one who justifies sinners,
6 then his faith is considered as justifying him. ·And David says
the same: a man is happy if God considers him righteous,
irrespective of good deeds:

7 *Happy those whose crimes are forgiven,*
whose sins are blotted out;
8 *happy the man whom the Lord considers sinless.*[b]

Justified before circumcision

9 Is this happiness meant only for the circumcised, or is it
meant for others as well? Think of Abraham again: *his faith,*
10 we say, *was considered as justifying him,* ·but when was this
done? When he was already circumcised or before he had
been circumcised? It was before he had been circumcised,
11 not after; ·and when he was *circumcised* later it was only *as a*
sign and guarantee that the faith he had before his circum-

cision justified him. In this way Abraham became the ancestor
of all uncircumcised believers, so that they too might be
12 considered righteous; ·and ancestor, also, of those who
though circumcised do not rely on that fact alone, but follow
our ancestor Abraham along the path of faith he trod before
he had been circumcised.

Not justified by obedience to the Law

13   The promise of inheriting the world was not made to
Abraham and his descendants on account of any law but on
14 account of the righteousness which consists in faith . ·If the
world is only to be inherited by those who submit to the Law,
15 then faith is pointless and the promise worth nothing. ·Law
involves the possibility of punishment for breaking the law—
16 only where there is no law can that be avoided. ·That is why
what fulfils the promise depends on faith, so that it may be a
free gift and be available to all of Abraham's descendants,
not only those who belong to the Law but also those who
belong to the faith of Abraham who is the father of all of us.
17 As scripture says: *I have made you the ancestor of many
nations*[c]—Abraham is our father in the eyes of God, in whom
he put his faith, and who brings the dead to life and calls
into being what does not exist.

Abraham's faith, a model of Christian faith

18   Though it seemed Abraham's hope could not be fulfilled,
he hoped and he believed, and through doing so he did
become *the father of many nations* exactly as he had been
promised: *Your descendants will be as many as the stars.*[d]
19 Even the thought that his body was past fatherhood—he was
about a hundred years old—and Sarah too old to become a
20 mother, did not shake his belief. ·Since God had promised it,
Abraham refused either to deny it or even to doubt it, but
21 drew strength from faith, and gave glory to God, ·convinced
22 that God had power to do what he had promised. ·This is the
23 faith that was '*considered as justifying him*'. ·Scripture however does not refer only to him but to us as well when it says
24 that his faith was thus 'considered'; ·our faith too will be
'considered' if we believe in him who raised Jesus our Lord
25 from the dead, ·Jesus who was *put to death for our sins*[e] and
raised to life to justify us.

4 a. Gn 15:6 **b.** Ps 32:1–2 **c.** Gn 17:5 (the same chapter to which
allusion is made in v. 11, above). **d.** Gn 15:5 **e.** Is 53:5, 6

II. SALVATION

Faith guarantees salvation

5 So far then we have seen that, through our Lord Jesus Christ, by faith we are judged righteous and at peace with **2** God, ·since it is by faith and through Jesus that we have entered this state of grace in which we can boast about **3** looking forward to God's glory. ·But that is not all we can boast about; we can boast about our sufferings. These **4** sufferings bring patience, as we know, ·and patience brings **5** perseverance, and perseverance brings hope, ·and this hope is not deceptive, because the love of God has been poured into **6** our hearts by the Holy Spirit which has been given us. ·We were still helpless when at his appointed moment Christ died **7** for sinful men. ·It is not easy to die even for a good man— though of course for someone really worthy, a man might be **8** prepared to die—·but what proves that God loves us is that **9** Christ died for us while we were still sinners. ·Having died to make us righteous, is it likely that he would now fail to save **10** us from God's anger? ·When we were reconciled to God by the death of his Son, we were still enemies; now that we have been reconciled, surely we may count on being saved by the **11** life of his Son? ·Not merely because we have been reconciled but because we are filled with joyful trust in God, through our Lord Jesus Christ, through whom we have already gained our reconciliation.

A. DELIVERANCE FROM SIN AND DEATH AND LAW

Adam and Jesus Christ

12 Well then, sin *entered the world* through one man, and through sin death, and thus death has spread through the **13** whole human race because everyone has sinned. ·Sin existed in the world long before the Law was given. There was no law and so no one could be accused of the sin of 'law-break- **14** ing', ·yet death reigned over all from Adam to Moses, even though their sin, unlike that of Adam, was not a matter of breaking a law.

15 Adam prefigured the One to come, ·but the gift itself considerably outweighed the fall. If it is certain that through one man's fall so many died, it is even more certain that divine grace, coming through the one man, Jesus Christ, **16** came to so many as an abundant free gift. ·The results of the gift also outweigh the results of one man's sin: for after one

single fall came judgement with a verdict of condemnation,
now after many falls comes grace with its verdict of acquittal.
17 If it is certain that death reigned over everyone as the consequence of one man's fall, it is even more certain that one man,
Jesus Christ, will cause everyone to reign in life who receives
the free gift that he does not deserve, of being made right-
18 eous. ·Again, as one man's fall brought condemnation on
everyone, so the good act of one man brings everyone life
19 and makes them justified. ·As by one man's disobedience
many were made sinners, so by one man's obedience many
20 will be made righteous. ·When law came, it was to multiply
the opportunities of falling, but however great the number of
21 sins committed, grace was even greater; ·and so, just as sin
reigned wherever there was death, so grace will reign to bring
eternal life thanks to the righteousness that comes through
Jesus Christ our Lord.

Baptism

6 Does it follow that we should remain in sin so as to let
2 grace have greater scope? ·Of course not. We are dead to sin,
3 so how can we continue to live in it? ·You have been taught
that when we were baptised in Christ Jesus we were baptised
4 in his death; ·in other words, when we were baptised we went
into the tomb with him and joined him in death, so that as
Christ was raised from the dead by the Father's glory, we too
might live a new life.
5 If in union with Christ we have imitated his death, we shall
6 also imitate him in his resurrection. ·We must realise that our
former selves have been crucified with him to destroy this
7 sinful body and to free us from the slavery of sin. ·When a
man dies, of course, he has finished with sin.
8 But we believe that having died with Christ we shall return
9 to life with him: ·Christ, as we know, having been raised from
the dead will never die again. Death has no power over him
10 any more. ·When he died, he died, once for all, to sin, so his life
11 now is life with God; ·and in that way, you too must consider
yourselves to be dead to sin but alive for God in Christ Jesus.

Holiness, not sin, to be the master

12 That is why you must not let sin reign in your mortal
13 bodies or command your obedience to bodily passions, ·why
you must not let any part of your body turn into an unholy
weapon fighting on the side of sin; you should, instead, offer
yourselves to God, and consider yourselves dead men brought
back to life; you should make every part of your body into a

14 weapon fighting on the side of God; ·and then sin will no
longer dominate your life, since you are living by grace and
not by law.

The Christian is freed from the slavery of sin

15 Does the fact that we are living by grace and not by law
16 mean that we are free to sin? Of course not. ·You know that
if you agree to serve and obey a master you become his slaves.
You cannot be slaves of sin that leads to death and at the
same time slaves of obedience that leads to righteousness.
17 You were once slaves of sin, but thank God you submitted
18 without reservation to the creed you were taught. ·You may
have been freed from the slavery of sin, but only to become
19 'slaves' of righteousness. ·If I may use human terms to help
your natural weakness: as once you put your bodies at the
service of vice and immorality, so now you must put them at
the service of righteousness for your sanctification.

The reward of sin and the reward of holiness

20 When you were slaves of sin, you felt no obligation to
21 righteousness, ·and what did you get from this? Nothing but
experiences that now make you blush, since that sort of
22 behaviour ends in death. ·Now, however, you have been set
free from sin, you have been made slaves of God, and you get
a reward leading to your sanctification and ending in eternal
23 life. ·For the wage paid by sin is death; the present given by
God is eternal life in Christ Jesus our Lord.

The Christian is not bound by the Law

7 Brothers, those of you who have studied law will know that
2 laws affect a person only during his lifetime. ·A married
woman, for instance, has legal obligations to her husband
while he is alive, but all these obligations come to an end if
3 the husband dies. ·So if she gives herself to another man while
her husband is still alive, she is legally an adulteress; but after
her husband is dead her legal obligations come to an end, and
she can marry someone else without becoming an adulteress.
4 That is why you, my brothers, who through the body of
Christ, are now dead to the Law, can now give yourselves to
another husband, to him who rose from the dead to make us
5 productive for God. ·Before our conversion[a] our sinful
passions, quite unsubdued by the Law, fertilised our bodies
6 to make them give birth to death. ·But now we are rid of the
Law, freed by death from our imprisonment, free to serve in
the new spiritual way and not the old way of a written law.

The function of the Law

7　Does it follow that the Law itself is sin? Of course not.
What I mean is that I should not have known what sin was
except for the Law. I should not for instance have known
what it means to covet if the Law had not said *You shall not*
8　*covet*. ·But it was this commandment that sin took advantage
of to produce all kinds of covetousness in me, for when there
is no Law, sin is dead.

9　Once, when there was no Law, I[b] was alive; but when the
10　commandment came, sin came to life ·and I died: the commandment was meant to lead me to life but it turned out to
11　mean death for me, ·because sin took advantage of the
commandment to mislead me, and so sin, through that
commandment, killed me.

12　The Law is sacred, and what it commands is sacred, just
13　and good. ·Does that mean that something good killed me?
Of course not. But sin, to show itself in its true colours, used
that good thing to kill me; and thus sin, thanks to the
commandment, was able to exercise all its sinful power.

The inward struggle

14　The Law, of course, as we all know, is spiritual; but I am
15　unspiritual; I have been sold as a slave to sin. ·I cannot
understand my own behaviour. I fail to carry out the things I
want to do, and I find myself doing the very things I hate.
16　When I act against my own will, that means I have a self that
17　acknowledges that the Law is good, ·and so the thing be-
18　having in that way is not my self but sin living in me. ·The
fact is, I know of nothing good living in me—living, that is,
in my unspiritual self—for though the will to do what is good
19　is in me, the performance is not, ·with the result that instead
of doing the good things I want to do, I carry out the sinful
20　things I do not want. ·When I act against my will, then, it is
not my true self doing it, but sin which lives in me.

21　In fact, this seems to be the rule, that every single time I
22　want to do good it is something evil that comes to hand. ·In
23　my inmost self I dearly love God's Law, but ·I can see that
my body follows a different law that battles against the law
which my reason dictates. This is what makes me a prisoner
of that law of sin which lives inside my body.

24　What a wretched man I am! Who will rescue me from this

7 a. 'While we were in the flesh'. b. Rhetorical figure; Paul speaks
in the person of mankind.

25 body doomed to death? ·Thanks be to God through Jesus Christ our Lord!

In short, it is I who with my reason serve the Law of God, and no less I who serve in my unspiritual self the law of sin.

B. THE CHRISTIAN'S SPIRITUAL LIFE

The life of the spirit

8 The reason, therefore, why those who are in Christ Jesus
2 are not condemned, ·is that the law of the spirit of life in Christ Jesus has set you free from the law of sin and death.
3 God has done what the Law, because of our unspiritual nature,[a] was unable to do. God dealt with sin by sending his own Son in a body as physical as any sinful body, and in that
4 body God condemned sin. ·He did this in order that the Law's just demands might be satisfied in us, who behave not as our unspiritual nature but as the spirit dictates.
5 The unspiritual are interested only in what is unspiritual,
6 but the spiritual are interested in spiritual things. ·It is death to limit oneself to what is unspiritual; life and peace can only·
7 come with concern for the spiritual. ·That is because to limit oneself to what is unspiritual is to be at enmity with God: such a limitation never could and never does submit to God's
8 law. ·People who are interested only in unspiritual things can
9 never be pleasing to God. ·Your interests, however, are not in the unspiritual, but in the spiritual, since the Spirit of God has made his home in you. In fact, unless you possessed the
10 Spirit of Christ you would not belong to him. ·Though your body may be dead it is because of sin, but if Christ is in you then your spirit is life itself because you have been justified;
11 and if the Spirit of him who raised Jesus from the dead is living in you, then he who raised Jesus from the dead will give life to your own mortal bodies through his Spirit living in you.
12 So then, my brothers, there is no necessity for us to obey
13 our unspiritual selves or to live unspiritual lives. ·If you do live in that way, you are doomed to die; but if by the Spirit you put an end to the misdeeds of the body you will live.

Children of God

14
15 Everyone moved by the Spirit is a son of God. ·The spirit you received is not the spirit of slaves bringing fear into your lives again; it is the spirit of sons, and it makes us cry out,
16 'Abba, Father!'[b] ·The Spirit himself and our spirit bear
17 united witness that we are children of God. ·And if we are

children we are heirs as well: heirs of God and coheirs with Christ, sharing his sufferings so as to share his glory.

Glory as our destiny

18 I think that what we suffer in this life can never be compared to the glory, as yet unrevealed, which is waiting for us.
19 The whole creation is eagerly waiting for God to reveal his
20 sons. ·It was not for any fault on the part of creation that it was made unable to attain its purpose, it was made so by God;
21 but creation still retains the hope ·of being freed, like us, from its slavery to decadence, to enjoy the same freedom and glory
22 as the children of God. ·From the beginning till now the entire creation, as we know, has been groaning in one great act of
23 giving birth; ·and not only creation, but all of us who possess the first-fruits of the Spirit, we too groan inwardly as we wait
24 for our bodies to be set free. ·For we must be content to hope that we shall be saved—our salvation is not in sight, we
25 should not have to be hoping for it if it were—·but, as I say, we must hope to be saved since we are not saved yet—it is something we must wait for with patience.
26 The Spirit too comes to help us in our weakness. For when we cannot choose words in order to pray properly, the Spirit himself expresses our plea in a way that could never be put
27 into words, ·and God who knows everything in our hearts knows perfectly well what he means, and that the pleas of the saints expressed by the Spirit are according to the mind of God.

God has called us to share his glory

28 We know that by turning everything to their good God co-operates with all those who love him, with all those that he
29 has called according to his purpose. ·They are the ones he chose specially long ago and intended to become true images of his Son, so that his Son might be the eldest of many
30 brothers. ·He called those he intended for this; those he called he justified, and with those he justified he shared his glory.

A hymn to God's love

31 After saying this, what can we add? With God on our side
32 who can be against us? ·Since God did not spare his own Son, but gave him up to benefit us all, we may be certain, after such a gift, that he will not refuse anything he can give.
33 Could anyone accuse those that God has chosen? When
34 God acquits, ·could anyone condemn? Could Christ Jesus?

8 **a.** 'flesh'. **b.** The prayer of Christ in Gethsemane.

No! He not only died for us—he rose from the dead, and there at God's right hand he stands and pleads for us.

35   Nothing therefore can come between us and the love of Christ, even if we are troubled or worried, or being persecuted, or lacking food or clothes, or being threatened or 36 even attacked. ·As scripture promised: *For your sake we are being massacred daily, and reckoned as sheep for the slaugh-* 37 *ter.*[c] ·These are the trials through which we triumph, by the power of him who loved us.

38   For I am certain of this: neither death nor life, no angel, no prince, nothing that exists, nothing still to come, not any 39 power, ·or height or depth,[d] nor any created thing, can ever come between us and the love of God made visible in Christ Jesus our Lord.

C. THE PLACE OF ISRAEL

The privileges of Israel

9   What I want to say now is no pretence; I say it in union with Christ—it is the truth—my conscience in union with the 2 Holy Spirit assures me of it too. ·What I want to say is this: 3 my sorrow is so great, my mental anguish so endless, ·I would willingly be condemned[a] and be cut off from Christ if it could 4 help my brothers of Israel, my own flesh and blood. ·They were adopted as sons, they were given the glory and the covenants; the Law and the ritual were drawn up for them, 5 and the promises were made to them. ·They are descended from the patriarchs and from their flesh and blood came Christ who is above all, God for ever blessed! Amen.

God has kept his promise

6   Does this mean that God has failed to keep his promise? Of course not. Not all those who descend from Israel are 7 Israel; ·not all the descendants of Abraham are his true children. Remember: *It is through Isaac that your name will be* 8 *carried on,*[b] ·which means that it is not physical descent that decides who are the children of God; it is only the children of 9 the promise who will count as the true descendants. ·The actual words in which the promise was made were: *I shall visit you* at such and such a time, *and Sarah will have a son.*[c] 10 Even more to the point is what was said to Rebecca when she 11 was pregnant by our ancestor Isaac, ·but before her twin children were born and before either had done good or evil. 12 In order to stress that God's choice is free, ·since it depends on the one who calls, not on human merit, Rebecca was told:

13 *the elder shall serve the younger*,[d] ·or as scripture says elsewhere: *I showed my love for Jacob and my hatred for Esau*.[e]

God is not unjust

14
15   Does it follow that God is unjust? Of course not. ·Take
what God said to Moses: *I have mercy on whom I will, and I*
16 *show pity to whom I please*.[f] ·In other words, the only thing
that counts is not what human beings want or try to do, but
17 the mercy of God. ·For in scripture he says to Pharaoh: *It
was for this I raised you up, to use you as a means of showing
my power and to make my name known throughout the world*.[g]
18 In other words, when God wants to show mercy he does, and
when he wants to harden someone's heart he does so.
19   You will ask me, 'In that case, how can God ever blame
20 anyone, since no one can oppose his will?' ·But what right
have you, a human being, to cross-examine God? *The pot has
no right to say to the potter: Why did you make me this shape?*[h]
21 Surely a potter can do what he likes with the clay? It is surely
for him to decide whether he will use a particular lump of
clay to make a special pot or an ordinary one?
22   Or else imagine that although God is ready to show his
anger and display his power, yet he patiently puts up with the
people who make him angry, however much they deserve to
23 be destroyed. ·He puts up with them for the sake of those
other people, to whom he wants to be merciful, to whom he
wants to reveal the richness of his glory, people he had
24 prepared for this glory long ago. ·Well, we are those people;
whether we were Jews or pagans we are the ones he has
called.

All has been foretold in the Old Testament

25   That is exactly what God says in Hosea: *I shall say to a
people that was not mine, 'You are my people', and to a
26 nation I never loved, 'I love you'*. ·*Instead of being told, 'You
are no people of mine', they will now be called the sons of the
27 living God*.[i] ·Referring to Israel Isaiah had this to say:
*Though Israel should have as many descendants as there are
28 grains of sand on the seashore, only a remnant will be saved, ·for
without hesitation or delay the Lord will execute his sentence
29 on the earth*.[j] ·As Isaiah foretold: *Had the Lord of hosts not*

c. Ps 44:11 d. 'powers', 'heights' and 'depths' are probably cosmic
forces hostile to mankind.
9 a. *Anathema*, cursed and excommunicated. **b.** Gn 21:12 **c.** Gn 18:10
d. Gn 25:23 **e.** Ml 1:2–3 **f.** Ex 33:19 **g.** Ex 9:16 **h.** Is 29:16 **i.** Ho
2:25 and 2:1 **j.** Is 10:22:23

left us some descendants we should now be like Sodom, we should be like Gomorrah.[k]

30 From this it follows that the pagans who were not looking for righteousness found it all the same, a righteousness that
31 comes of faith, ·while Israel, looking for a righteousness
32 derived from law failed to do what that law required. ·Why did they fail? Because they relied on good deeds instead of trusting in faith. In other words, they *stumbled over the*
33 *stumbling-stone*[l] ·mentioned in scripture: *See how I lay in Zion a stone to stumble over, a rock to trip men up—only those who believe in him will have no cause for shame.*[m]

Israel fails to see that it is God who makes us holy

10 Brothers, I have the very warmest love for the Jews, and I
2 pray to God for them to be saved. ·I can swear to their fer-
3 vour for God, but their zeal is misguided. ·Failing to recognise the righteousness that comes from God, they try to promote their own idea of it, instead of submitting to the
4 righteousness of God. ·But now the Law has come to an end with Christ, and everyone who has faith may be justified.

The testimony of Moses

5 When Moses refers to being justified by the Law, he writes:
6 *those who keep the Law will draw life from it.*[a] ·But the righteousness that comes from faith says this: Do not tell yourself you have to bring Christ down—as in the text: *Who*
7 *will go up to heaven?*[b] ·or that you have to bring Christ back from the dead—as in the text: *Who will go down to the*
8 *underworld?* ·On the positive side it says: *The word,* that is the faith we proclaim, *is very near to you, it is on your lips and in*
9 *your heart.* ·If your lips confess that Jesus is Lord and if you believe in your heart that God raised him from the dead,
10 then you will be saved. ·By believing from the heart you are made righteous; by confessing with your lips you are saved.
11 When scripture says: *those who believe in him will have no*
12 *cause for shame,*[c] it makes no distinction between Jew and Greek: all belong to the same Lord who is rich enough,
13 however many ask his help, ·*for everyone who calls on the name of the Lord will be saved.*[d]

Israel has no excuse

14 But they will not ask his help unless they believe in him, and they will not believe in him unless they have heard of him, and they will not hear of him unless they get a preacher,
15 and they will never have a preacher unless one is sent, but as

scripture says: *The footsteps of those who bring good news is a*
16 *welcome sound.*[e] ·Not everyone, of course, listens to the Good
News. As Isaiah says: *Lord, how many believed what we pro-*
17 *claimed?*[f] ·So faith comes from what is preached, and what is
preached comes from the word of Christ.

18 Let me put the question: is it possible that they did not
hear? Indeed they did; in the words of the psalm, *their voice
has gone out through all the earth, and their message to the*
19 *ends of the world.*[g] ·A second question: is it possible that
Israel did not understand? Moses answered this long ago: *I
will make you jealous of people who are not even a nation;*
20 *I will make you angry with an irreligious people.*[h] ·Isaiah said
more clearly: *I have been found by those who did not seek me,*
21 *and have revealed myself to those who did not consult me;*[i] ·and
referring to Israel he goes on: *Each day I stretched out my
hand to a disobedient and rebellious people.*

The remnant of Israel

11 Let me put a further question then: is it possible that *God
has rejected his people?*[a] Of course not. I, an Israelite, de-
2 scended from Abraham through the tribe of Benjamin, ·could
never agree that God had rejected his people, the people he
chose specially long ago. Do you remember what scripture
says of Elijah—how he complained to God about Israel's
3 behaviour? ·*Lord, they have killed your prophets and broken
down your altars. I, and I only, remain, and they want to kill
4 me.*[b] ·What did God say to that? *I have kept for myself seven
5 thousand men who have not bent the knee to Baal.*[c] ·Today the
same thing has happened: there is a remnant, chosen by
6 grace. ·By grace, you notice, nothing therefore to do with
good deeds, or grace would not be grace at all!

7 What follows? It was not Israel as a whole that found
what it was seeking, but only the chosen few. The rest were
8 not allowed to see the truth; ·as scripture says: *God has given
them a sluggish spirit, unseeing eyes and inattentive ears, and
9 they are still like that today.*[d] ·And David says: *May their own
table prove a trap for them, a snare and a pitfall—let that be
10 their punishment; ·may their eyes be struck incurably blind,
their backs bend for ever.*[e]

k. Is 1:9 l. Is 8:14 m. Is 28:16
10 a. Lv 18:5 b. This quotation, and the two following, are a free
rendering of Dt 30:12–14. c. Is 28:16 d. Jl 3:5 e. Is 52:7 f. Is 53:1
g. Ps 19:4 h. Dt 32:21 i. Is 65:1, 2
11 a. Ps 94:14 b. 1 K 19:10, 14 c. 1 K 19:18 d. Is 29:10 e. Ps 69:22f

The Jews to be restored in the future

11   Let me put another question then: have the Jews fallen for ever, or have they just stumbled? Obviously they have not fallen for ever: their fall, though, has saved the pagans in a
12 way the Jews may now well emulate. ·Think of the extent to which the world, the pagan world, has benefited from their fall and defection—then think how much more it will benefit
13 from the conversion of them all. ·Let me tell you pagans^f this: I have been sent to the pagans as their apostle, and I am
14 proud of being sent, ·but the purpose of it is to make my own people envious of you, and in this way save some of them.
15 Since their rejection meant the reconciliation of the world, do you know what their admission will mean? Nothing less than a resurrection from the dead!

The Jews are still the chosen people

16   A whole batch of bread is made holy if the first handful of dough is made holy; all the branches are holy if the root is
17 holy. ·No doubt some of the branches have been cut off, and, like shoots of wild olive, you have been grafted among the rest to share with them the rich sap provided by the olive tree
18 itself, ·but still, even if you think yourself superior to the other branches, remember that you do not support the root;
19 it is the root that supports you. ·You will say, 'Those branches were cut off on purpose to let me be grafted in!'
20 True, ·they were cut off, but through their unbelief; if you still hold firm, it is only thanks to your faith. Rather than
21 making you proud, that should make you afraid. ·God did not spare the natural branches, and he is not likely to spare you.
22 Do not forget that God can be severe as well as kind: he is severe to those who fell, and he is kind to you, but only for as long as he chooses to be, otherwise you will find yourself cut
23 off too, ·and the Jews, if they give up their unbelief, grafted back in your place. God is perfectly able to graft them back
24 again; ·after all, if you were cut from your natural wild olive to be grafted unnaturally on to a cultivated olive, it will be much easier for them, the natural branches, to be grafted back on the tree they came from.

The conversion of the Jews

25   There is a hidden reason for all this, brothers, of which I do not want you to be ignorant, in case you think you know more than you do. One section of Israel has become blind, but this will last only until the whole pagan world has

26 entered, ·and then after this the rest of Israel will be saved as well. As scripture says: *The liberator will come from Zion,*
27 *he will banish godlessness from Jacob.* ·*And this is the covenant I will make with them when I take their sins away.*[g]

28 The Jews are enemies of God only with regard to the Good News, and enemies only for your sake; but as the chosen people, they are still loved by God, loved for the sake of their
29 ancestors. ·God never takes back his gifts or revokes his choice.

30 Just as you changed from being disobedient to God, and
31 now enjoy mercy because of their disobedience, ·so those who are disobedient now—and only because of the mercy
32 shown to you—will also enjoy mercy eventually. ·God has imprisoned all men in their own disobedience only to show mercy to all mankind.

A hymn to God's mercy and wisdom

33 How rich are the depths of God—how deep his wisdom and knowledge—and how impossible to penetrate his mo-
34 tives or understand his methods! ·*Who could ever know the*
35 *mind of the Lord? Who could ever be his counsellor?* ·*Who*
36 *could ever give him anything or lend him anything?*[h] ·All that exists comes from him; all is by him and for him. To him be glory for ever! Amen.

EXHORTATION

Spiritual worship

12 Think of God's mercy, my brothers, and worship him, I beg you, in a way that is worthy of thinking beings, by offering your living bodies as a holy sacrifice, truly pleasing
2 to God. ·Do not model yourselves on the behaviour of the world around you, but let your behaviour change, modelled by your new mind. This is the only way to discover the will of God and know what is good, what it is that God wants, what is the perfect thing to do.

Humility and charity

3 In the light of the grace I have received I want to urge each one among you not to exaggerate his real importance. Each of you must judge himself soberly by the standard of the faith
4 God has given him. ·Just as each of our bodies has several
5 parts and each part has a separate function, ·so all of us, in union with Christ, form one body, and as parts of it we

f. Converts from paganism. **g.** Is 27:9 **h.** Is 40:13

6 belong to each other. ·Our gifts differ according to the grace given us. If your gift is prophecy, then use it as your faith
7 suggests; ·if administration, then use it for administration; if
8 teaching, then use it for teaching. ·Let the preachers deliver sermons, the almsgivers give freely, the officials be diligent, and those who do works of mercy do them cheerfully.
9 Do not let your love be a pretence, but sincerely prefer
10 good to evil. ·Love each other as much as brothers should,
11 and have a profound respect for each other. ·Work for the Lord with untiring effort and with great earnestness of spirit.
12 If you have hope, this will make you cheerful. Do not give up
13 if trials come; and keep on praying. ·If any of the saints are in need you must share with them; and you should make hospitality your special care.

Charity to everyone, including enemies

14 Bless those who persecute you: never curse them, bless
15 them. ·Rejoice with those who rejoice and be sad with those
16 in sorrow. ·Treat everyone with equal kindness; never be condescending but make real friends with the poor. Do not
17 allow yourself to become self-satisfied. ·Never repay evil with evil but let everyone see that you are interested only in the
18 highest ideals. ·Do all you can to live at peace with everyone.
19 Never try to get revenge; leave that, my friends, to God's anger. As scripture says: *vengeance is mine—I will pay them*
20 *back*,[a] the Lord promises. ·But there is more: *If your enemy is hungry, you should give him food, and if he is thirsty, let him*
21 *drink. Thus you heap red-hot coals on his head.*[b] ·Resist evil and conquer it with good.

Submission to civil authority

13 You must all obey the governing authorities. Since all government comes from God, the civil authorities were
2 appointed by God, ·and so anyone who resists authority is rebelling against God's decision, and such an act is bound to
3 be punished. ·Good behaviour is not afraid of magistrates; only criminals have anything to fear. If you want to live without being afraid of authority, you must live honestly and
4 authority may even honour you. ·The state is there to serve God for your benefit. If you break the law, however, you may well have fear: the bearing of the sword has its significance. The authorities are there to serve God: they carry out God's
5 revenge by punishing wrongdoers. ·You must obey, therefore, not only because you are afraid of being punished, but
6 also for conscience' sake. ·This is also the reason why you

must pay taxes, since all government officials are God's
7 officers. They serve God by collecting taxes. ·Pay every
government official what he has a right to ask—whether it be
direct tax or indirect, fear or honour.

Love and law

8 Avoid getting into debt, except the debt of mutual love. If
you love your fellow men you have carried out your obliga-
9 tions. ·All the commandments: *You shall not commit adultery, you shall not kill, you shall not steal, you shall not covet,*[a]
and so on, are summed up in this single command: *You must
10 love your neighbour as yourself.*[b] ·Love is the one thing that
cannot hurt your neighbour; that is why it is the answer to
every one of the commandments.

Children of the light

11 Besides, you know 'the time' has come: you must wake up
now: our salvation is even nearer than it was when we were
12 converted. ·The night is almost over, it will be daylight soon
—let us give up all the things we prefer to do under cover of
the dark; let us arm ourselves and appear in the light.
13 Let us live decently as people do in the daytime: no drunken
orgies, no promiscuity or licentiousness, and no wrangling or
14 jealousy. ·Let your armour be the Lord Jesus Christ; forget
about satisfying your bodies with all their cravings.

Charity towards the scrupulous

14 If a person's faith is not strong enough, welcome him all
2 the same without starting an argument. ·People range from
those who believe they may eat any sort of meat to those
whose faith is so weak they dare not eat anything except
3 vegetables. ·Meat-eaters must not despise the scrupulous. On
the other hand, the scrupulous must not condemn those who
feel free to eat anything they choose, since God has welcomed
4 them. ·It is not for you to condemn someone else's servant:
whether he stands or falls it is his own master's business; he
will stand, you may be sure, because the Lord has power to
5 make him stand. ·If one man keeps certain days as holier than
others, and another considers all days to be equally holy, each
6 must be left free to hold his own opinion. ·The one who
observes special days does so in honour of the Lord. The one
who eats meat also does so in honour of the Lord, since he
gives thanks to God; but then the man who abstains does

12 **a.** Dt 32:35 **b.** Pr 25:21–22
13 **a.** From the Commandments in Ex 20 and Dt 5: 17–21. **b.** Lv 19:18

that too in honour of the Lord, and so he also gives God
7 thanks. ·The life and death of each of us has its influence on
8 others; ·if we live, we live for the Lord; and if we die, we die
for the Lord, so that alive or dead we belong to the Lord.
9 This explains why Christ both died and came to life, it was so
10 that he might be Lord both of the dead and of the living. ·This
is also why you should never pass judgement on a brother or
treat him with contempt, as some of you have done. We shall
11 all have to stand before the judgement seat of God; ·as
scripture says: *By my life—it is the Lord who speaks—every*
12 *knee shall bend before me, and every tongue shall praise God.*ᵃ ·It
is to God, therefore, that each of us must give an account of
himself.

13   Far from passing judgement on each other, therefore, you
should make up your mind never to be the cause of your
14 brother tripping or falling. ·Now I am perfectly well aware,
of course, and I speak for the Lord Jesus, that no food is
unclean in itself; however, if someone thinks that a particular
15 food is unclean, then it is unclean for him. ·And indeed if your
attitude to food is upsetting your brother, then you are hardly
being guided by charity. You are certainly not free to eat
what you like if that means the downfall of someone for
whom Christ died.
16   In short, you must not compromise your privilege,
17 because the kingdom of God does not mean eating or drinking this or that, it means righteousness and peace and joy
18 brought by the Holy Spirit. ·If you serve Christ in this way
19 you will please God and be respected by men. ·So let us
adopt any custom that leads to peace and our mutual im-
20 provement; ·do not wreck God's work over a question of
food. Of course all food is clean, but it becomes evil if by
21 eating it you make somebody else fall away. ·In such cases
the best course is to abstain from meat and wine and anything else that would make your brother trip or fall or weaken
in any way.
22   Hold on to your own belief, as between yourself and God
—and consider the man fortunate who can make his decision
23 without going against his conscience. ·But anybody who eats
in a state of doubt is condemned, because he is not in good
faith; and every act done in bad faith is a sin.

15   We who are strong have a duty to put up with the qualms
2 of the weak without thinking of ourselves. ·Each of us should
think of his neighbours and help them to become stronger
3 Christians. ·Christ did not think of himself: the words of
scripture—*the insults of those who insult you fall on me*ᵃ—

4 apply to him. ·And indeed everything that was written long ago in the scriptures was meant to teach us something about hope from the examples scripture gives of how people who
5 did not give up were helped by God. ·And may he who helps us when we refuse to give up, help you all to be tolerant with
6 each other, following the example of Christ Jesus, ·so that united in mind and voice you may give glory to the God and Father of our Lord Jesus Christ.

An appeal for unity

7 It can only be to God's glory, then, for you to treat each
8 other in the same friendly way as Christ treated you. ·The reason Christ became the servant of circumcised Jews was not only so that God could faithfully carry out the promises
9 made to the patriarchs, ·it was also to get the pagans to give glory to God for his mercy, as scripture says in one place: *For this I shall praise you among the pagans and sing to your*
10 *name.*[b] ·And in another place: *Rejoice, pagans, with his*
11 *people,*[c] ·and in a third place: *Let all the pagans praise the*
12 *Lord, let all the peoples sing his praises.*[d] ·Isaiah too has this to say: *The root of Jesse will appear, rising up to rule the pagans, and in him the pagans will put their hope.*[e]
13 May the God of hope bring you such joy and peace in your faith that the power of the Holy Spirit will remove all bounds to hope.

EPILOGUE

Paul's ministry

14 It is not because I have any doubts about you, my brothers; on the contrary I am quite certain that you are full of good intentions, perfectly well instructed and able to advise each
15 other. ·The reason why I have written to you, and put some things rather strongly, is to refresh your memories, since God
16 has given me this special position. ·He has appointed me as a priest of Jesus Christ, and I am to carry out my priestly duty by bringing the Good News from God to the pagans, and so make them acceptable as an offering, made holy by the Holy Spirit.
17 I think I have some reason to be proud of what I, in union
18 with Christ Jesus, have been able to do for God. ·What I am presuming to speak of, of course, is only what Christ himself

14 a. Is 45:23
15 a. Ps 69:9 b. Ps 18:50 c. Dt 32:43 (LXX) d. Ps 117:1 e. Is 11:10; 11:1

has done to win the allegiance of the pagans, using what I
19 have said and done ·by the power of signs and wonders, by
the power of the Holy Spirit. Thus, all the way along, from
Jerusalem to Illyricum,*ᶠ* I have preached Christ's Good News
20 to the utmost of my capacity. ·I have always, however, made
it an unbroken rule never to preach where Christ's name has
already been heard. The reason for that was that I had no
21 wish to build on other men's foundations; ·on the contrary,
my chief concern has been to fulfil the text: *Those who have
never been told about him will see him, and those who have
never heard about him will understand.*ᵍ

Paul's plans

22   That is the reason why I have been kept from visiting you
23 so long, ·though for many years I have been longing to pay
you a visit. Now, however, having no more work to do here,
24 I hope to see you on my way to Spain and, after enjoying a
little of your company, to complete the rest of the journey
25 with your good wishes. ·First, however, I must take a present
26 of money to the saints in Jerusalem, ·since Macedonia and
Achaia have decided to send a generous contribution to the
27 poor among the saints at Jerusalem. ·A generous contribution
as it should be, since it is really repaying a debt: the pagans
who share the spiritual possessions of these poor people have
28 a duty to help them with temporal possessions. ·So when I
have done this and officially handed over what has been
29 raised, I shall set out for Spain and visit you on the way. ·I
know that when I reach you I shall arrive with rich blessings
from Christ.
30   But I beg you, brothers, by our Lord Jesus Christ and the
love of the Spirit, to help me through my dangers by praying
31 to God for me. ·Pray that I may escape the unbelievers in
Judaea, and that the aid I carry to Jerusalem may be accepted
32 by the saints. ·Then, if God wills, I shall be feeling very happy
33 when I come to enjoy a period of rest among you. ·May the
God of peace be with you all! Amen.

Greetings and good wishes

16   I commend to you our sister Phoebe,*ᵃ* a deaconess of the
2 church at Cenchreae. ·Give her, in union with the Lord, a
welcome worthy of saints, and help her with anything she
needs: she has looked after a great many people, myself
included.
3   My greetings to Prisca and Aquila, my fellow workers in
4 Christ Jesus, ·who risked death to save my life:*ᵇ* I am not the

only one to owe them a debt of gratitude, all the churches
5 among the pagans do as well. ·My greetings also to the church
that meets at their house.

6   Greetings to my friend Epaenetus, the first of Asia's gifts
7 to Christ; greetings to Mary who worked so hard for you; ·to
those outstanding apostles Andronicus and Junias, my com-
8 patriots and fellow prisoners who became Christians before
9 me; ·to Ampliatus, my friend in the Lord; ·to Urban, my
10 fellow worker in Christ; to my friend Stachys; ·to Apelles
who has gone through so much for Christ; to everyone who
11 belongs to the household of Aristobulus; ·to my compatriot
Herodion; to those in the household of Narcissus who belong
12 to the Lord; ·to Tryphaena and Tryphosa, who work hard for
the Lord; to my friend Persis who has done so much for the
13 Lord; ·to Rufus, a chosen servant of the Lord, and to his
14 mother who has been a mother to me too. ·Greetings to
Asyncritus, Phlegon, Hermes, Patrobas, Hermas, and all the
15 brothers who are with them; ·to Philologus and Julia, Nereus
and his sister, and Olympas and all the saints who are with
16 them. ·Greet each other with a holy kiss. All the churches of
Christ send greetings.

A warning and first postscript

17   I implore you, brothers, be on your guard against anybody
who encourages trouble or puts difficulties in the way of the
18 doctrine you have been taught. Avoid them. ·People like that
are not slaves of Jesus Christ, they are slaves of their own
appetites, confusing the simple-minded with their pious and
19 persuasive arguments. ·Your fidelity to Christ, anyway, is
famous everywhere, and that makes me very happy about
you. I only hope that you are also wise in what is good, and
20 innocent of what is bad. ·The God of peace will soon crush
Satan beneath your feet. The grace of our Lord Jesus Christ
be with you.

Last greetings and second postscript

21   Timothy, who is working with me, sends his greetings; so
22 do my compatriots, Jason and Sosipater. ·I, Tertius, who
23 wrote out this letter, greet you in the Lord. ·Greetings from
Gaius, who is entertaining me and from the whole church

f. The two extremes of Paul's missionary journeys. g. Is 52:15
16 a. Probably the bearer of the letter. **b.** Probably in Ephesus, either
at the time of the riot described in Ac 19 or during Paul's imprisonment there.

that meets in his house. Erastus, the city treasurer, sends his greetings; so does our brother Quartus.

Doxology

25   Glory to him who is able to give you the strength to live according to the Good News I preach, and in which I proclaim Jesus Christ, the revelation of a mystery, kept secret for
26 endless ages, ·but now so clear that it must be broadcast to pagans everywhere to bring them to the obedience of faith. This is only what scripture has predicted, and it is all part of
27 the way the eternal God wants things to be. ·He alone is wisdom; give glory therefore to him through Jesus Christ for ever and ever. Amen.

1 CORINTHIANS

THE FIRST LETTER OF PAUL

TO THE CHURCH AT CORINTH

INTRODUCTION

Address and greetings. Thanksgiving

1 I, Paul, appointed by God to be an apostle, together with
2 brother Sosthenes, send greetings ·to the church of God in
Corinth, to the holy people of Jesus Christ, who are called to
take their place among all the saints everywhere who pray to
our Lord Jesus Christ; for he is their Lord no less than ours.
3 May God our Father and the Lord Jesus Christ send you
grace and peace.
4 I never stop thanking God for all the graces you have
5 received through Jesus Christ. ·I thank him that you have
been enriched in so many ways, especially in your teachers
6 and preachers; ·the witness to Christ has indeed been strong
7 among you ·so that you will not be without any of the gifts of
the Spirit while you are waiting for our Lord Jesus Christ to
8 be revealed; ·and he will keep you steady and without blame
9 until the last day, the day of our Lord Jesus Christ, ·because
God by calling you has joined you to his Son, Jesus Christ;
and God is faithful.

I. DIVISIONS AND SCANDALS

A. FACTIONS IN THE CORINTHIAN CHURCH

Dissensions among the faithful

10 All the same, I do appeal to you, brothers, for the sake of
our Lord Jesus Christ, to make up the differences between
you, and instead of disagreeing among yourselves, to be

11 united again in your belief and practice. ·From what Chloe's people have been telling me, my dear brothers, it is clear that

12 there are serious differences among you. ·What I mean are all these slogans that you have, like: 'I am for Paul', 'I am for

13 Apollos', 'I am for Cephas',[a] 'I am for Christ'. ·Has Christ been parcelled out? Was it Paul that was crucified for you?

14 Were you baptised in the name of Paul? ·I am thankful that

15 I never baptised any of you after Crispus and Gaius ·so none

16 of you can say he was baptised in my name. ·Then there is the family of Stephanas, of course, that I baptised too, but no one else as far as I can remember.

The true wisdom and the false

17 For Christ did not send me to baptise, but to preach the Good News, and not to preach that in the terms of philosophy[b] in which the crucifixion of Christ cannot be expressed.

18 The language of the cross may be illogical to those who are not on the way to salvation, but those of us who are on the

19 way see it as God's power to save. ·As scripture says: *I shall destroy the wisdom of the wise and bring to nothing all the*

20 *learning of the learned.* ·*Where are the philosophers now? Where are the scribes?*[c] Where are any of our thinkers today? Do you see now how God has shown up the foolishness of

21 human wisdom? ·If it was God's wisdom that human wisdom should not know God, it was because God wanted to save those who have faith through the foolishness of the message

22 that we preach. ·And so, while the Jews demand miracles and

23 the Greeks look for wisdom, ·here are we preaching a crucified Christ; to the Jews an obstacle that they cannot get over,

24 to the pagans madness, ·but to those who have been called, whether they are Jews or Greeks, a Christ who is the power

25 and the wisdom of God. ·For God's foolishness is wiser than human wisdom, and God's weakness is stronger than human strength.

26 Take yourselves for instance, brothers, at the time when you were called: how many of you were wise in the ordinary sense of the word, how many were influential people, or came

27 from noble families? ·No, it was to shame the wise that God chose what is foolish by human reckoning, and to shame what is strong that he chose what is weak by human reckoning;

28 those whom the world thinks common and contemptible are the ones that God has chosen—those who are nothing at all

29 to show up those who are everything. ·The human race has

30 nothing to boast about to God, ·but you God has made members of Christ Jesus and by God's doing he has become

our wisdom, and our virtue, and our holiness, and our free-
31 dom. ·As scripture says: *if anyone wants to boast, let him
boast about the Lord.*[d]

2 As for me, brothers, when I came to you, it was not with
any show of oratory or philosophy, but simply to tell you
2 what God had guaranteed. ·During my stay with you, the
only knowledge I claimed to have was about Jesus, and only
3 about him as the crucified Christ. ·Far from relying on any
power of my own, I came among you in great 'fear and
4 trembling'[a] ·and in my speeches and the sermons that I gave,
there were none of the arguments that belong to philosophy;
5 only a demonstration of the power of the Spirit. ·And I did
this so that your faith should not depend on human philosophy but on the power of God.
6 But still we have a wisdom to offer those who have reached
maturity: not a philosophy of our age, it is true, still less of
7 the masters of our age, which are coming to their end. ·The
hidden wisdom of God which we teach in our mysteries is the
wisdom that God predestined to be for our glory before the
8 ages began. ·It is a wisdom that none of the masters of this
age have ever known, or they would not have crucified the
9 Lord of Glory; ·we teach what scripture calls: *the things that
no eye has seen and no ear has heard, things beyond the mind of
man, all that God has prepared for those who love him.*[b]
10 These are the very things that God has revealed to us
through the Spirit, for the Spirit reaches the depths of every-
11 thing, even the depths of God. ·After all, the depths of a man
can only be known by his own spirit, not by any other man,
and in the same way the depths of God can only be known by
12 the Spirit of God. ·Now instead of the spirit of the world, we
have received the Spirit that comes from God, to teach us to
13 understand the gifts that he has given us. ·Therefore we
teach, not in the way in which philosophy is taught, but in the
way that the Spirit teaches us: we teach spiritual things spiri-
14 tually. ·An unspiritual person is one who does not accept
anything of the Spirit of God: he sees it all as nonsense; it is
beyond his understanding because it can only be understood
15 by means of the Spirit. ·A spiritual man, on the other hand, is
able to judge the value of everything, and his own value is not
16 to be judged by other men. ·As scripture says: *Who can know*

1 a. Peter. **b.** 'wisdom', the term used by Paul for the human wisdom
of philosophy and rhetoric. **c.** Quotations from Is 29:14, Ps 33:10 and
Is 33:18 (LXX). **d.** Jr 9:22–23
2 a. A scriptural cliché frequently used by Paul. **b.** A free combination
of Is 64:3 and Jr 3:16.

the mind of the Lord, so who can teach him?[c] But we are those who have the mind of Christ.

3 Brothers, I myself was unable to speak to you as people of the Spirit: I treated you as sensual men, still infants in Christ.
2 What I fed you with was milk, not solid food, for you were not ready for it; and indeed, you are still not ready for it
3 since you are still unspiritual. Isn't that obvious from all the jealousy and wrangling that there is among you, from the
4 way that you go on behaving like ordinary people? ·What could be more unspiritual than your slogans, 'I am for Paul' and 'I am for Apollos'?

The place of the Christian preacher

5 After all, what is Apollos and what is Paul? They are servants who brought the faith to you. Even the different ways in which they brought it were assigned to them by the
6 Lord. ·I did the planting, Apollos did the watering, but God
7 made things grow. ·Neither the planter nor the waterer
8 matters: only God, who makes things grow. ·It is all one who does the planting and who does the watering, and each will
9 duly be paid according to his share in the work. ·We are fellow workers with God; you are God's farm, God's building.
10 By the grace God gave me, I succeeded as an architect and laid the foundations, on which someone else is doing the building. Everyone doing the building must work carefully.
11 For the foundation, nobody can lay any other than the one
12 which has already been laid, that is Jesus Christ. ·On this foundation you can build in gold, silver and jewels, or in
13 wood, grass and straw, ·but whatever the material, the work of each builder is going to be clearly revealed when the day comes. That day will begin with fire, and the fire will test the
14 quality of each man's work. ·If his structure stands up to it,
15 he will get his wages; ·if it is burnt down, he will be the loser, and though he is saved himself, it will be as one who has gone through fire.
16 Didn't you realise that you were God's temple and that the
17 Spirit of God was living among you? ·If anybody should destroy the temple of God, God will destroy him, because the temple of God is sacred; and you are that temple.

Conclusions

18 Make no mistake about it: if any one of you thinks of himself as wise, in the ordinary sense of the word, then he
19 must learn to be a fool before he really can be wise. ·Why? Because the wisdom of this world is foolishness to God. As

scripture says: *The Lord knows wise men's thoughts: he knows*
20 *how useless they are:*[a] ·or again: *God is not convinced by the*
21 *arguments of the wise.*[b] ·So there is nothing to boast about in
22 anything human: ·Paul, Apollos, Cephas, the world, life and
23 death, the present and the future, are all your servants; ·but
you belong to Christ and Christ belongs to God.

4 People must think of us as Christ's servants, stewards
2 entrusted with the mysteries of God. ·What is expected of
stewards is that each one should be found worthy of his
3 trust. ·Not that it makes the slightest difference to me whether
you, or indeed any human tribunal, find me worthy or not.
4 I will not even pass judgement on myself. ·True, my conscience does not reproach me at all, but that does not prove
5 that I am acquitted: the Lord alone is my judge. ·There must
be no passing of premature judgement. Leave that until the
Lord comes: he will light up all that is hidden in the dark and
reveal the secret intentions of men's hearts. Then will be the
time for each one to have whatever praise he deserves, from
God.

6 Now in everything I have said here, brothers, I have taken
Apollos and myself as an example (remember the maxim:
'Keep to what is written'); it is not for you, so full of your
own importance, to go taking sides for one man against
7 another. ·In any case, brother, has anybody given you some
special right? What do you have that was not given to you?
And if it was given, how can you boast as though it were not?
8 Is it that you have everything you want—that you are rich
already, in possession of your kingdom, with us left outside?
Indeed I wish you were really kings, and we could be kings
9 with you! ·But instead, it seems to me, God has put us
apostles at the end of his parade, with the men sentenced to
death; it is true—we have been put on show in front of the
10 whole universe, angels as well as men. ·Here we are, fools
for the sake of Christ, while you are the learned men in
Christ; we have no power, but you are influential; you are
11 celebrities, we are nobodies. ·To this day, we go without
food and drink and clothes; we are beaten and have no
12 homes; ·we work for our living with our own hands. When
we are cursed, we answer with a blessing; when we are
13 hounded, we put up with it; ·we are insulted and we answer
politely. We are treated as the offal of the world, still to this
day, the scum of the·earth.

c. Is 40:13
3 a. Jb 5:13 b. Ps 94:11

An appeal

14 I am saying all this not just to make you ashamed but to
15 bring you, as my dearest children, to your senses. ·You
might have thousands of guardians in Christ, but not more
than one father and it was I who begot you in Christ Jesus
16 by preaching the Good News. ·That is why I beg you to copy
17 me ·and why I have sent you Timothy, my dear and faithful
son in the Lord: he will remind you of the way that I live in
Christ, as I teach it everywhere in all the churches.

18 When it seemed that I was not coming to visit you, some of
19 you became self-important, ·but I will be visiting you soon,
the Lord willing, and then I shall want to know not what
these self-important people have to say, but what they can do,
20 since the kingdom of God is not just words, it is power.
21 It is for you to decide: do I come with a stick in my hand or
in a spirit of love and goodwill?

B. INCEST IN CORINTH

5 I have been told as an undoubted fact that one of you is
living with his father's wife.[a] This is a case of sexual immorality among you that must be unparalleled even among
2 pagans. ·How can you be so proud of yourselves? You
should be in mourning. A man who does a thing like that
3 ought to have been expelled from the community. ·Though I
am far away in body, I am with you in spirit, and have
already condemned the man who did this thing as if I were
4 actually present. ·When you are assembled together in the
name of the Lord Jesus, and I am spiritually present with you,
5 then with the power of our Lord Jesus ·he is to be handed
over to Satan so that his sensual body may be destroyed and
his spirit saved on the day of the Lord.

6 The pride that you take in yourselves is hardly to your
credit. You must know how even a small amount of yeast is
7 enough to leaven all the dough, ·so get rid of all the old yeast,
and make yourselves into a completely new batch of bread,
unleavened as you are meant to be. Christ, our passover, has
8 been sacrificed; ·let us celebrate the feast, then, by getting rid
of all the old yeast of evil and wickedness, having only the
unleavened bread of sincerity and truth.[b]

9 When I wrote in my letter to you not to associate with
10 people living immoral lives, ·I was not meaning to include all
the people in the world who are sexually immoral, any more
than I meant to include all usurers and swindlers or idol-

worshippers. To do that, you would have to withdraw from
11 the world altogether. ·What I wrote was that you should not
associate with a brother Christian who is leading an immoral life, or is a usurer, or idolatrous, or a slanderer, or a
drunkard, or is dishonest; you should not even eat a meal
12 with people like that. ·It is not my business to pass judgement
on those outside. Of those who are inside, you can surely be
13 the judges. ·But of those who are outside, God is the judge.
You must drive out this evil-doer from among you.[c]

C. RECOURSE TO THE PAGAN COURTS

6   How dare one of your members take up a complaint against
another in the lawcourts of the unjust[a] instead of before the
2 saints? ·As you know, it is the saints who are to 'judge the
world'; and if the world is to be judged by you, how can you
3 be unfit to judge trifling cases? ·Since we are also to judge
angels, it follows that we can judge matters of everyday life;
4 but when you have had cases of that kind, the people you
appointed to try them were not even respected in the Church.
5 You should be ashamed: is there really not one reliable man
6 among you to settle differences between brothers ·and so one
brother brings a court case against another in front of un-
7 believers? ·It is bad enough for you to have lawsuits at all
against one another: oughtn't you to let yourselves be
8 wronged, and let yourselves be cheated? ·But you are doing
the wronging and the cheating, and to your own brothers.
9   You know perfectly well that people who do wrong will
not inherit the kingdom of God: people of immoral lives,
10 idolaters, adulterers, catamites, sodomites, ·thieves, usurers,
drunkards, slanderers and swindlers will never inherit the
11 kingdom of God. ·These are the sort of people some of you
were once, but now you have been washed clean, and sanctified, and justified through the name of the Lord Jesus Christ
and through the Spirit of our God.

D. FORNICATION

12   'For me there are no forbidden things';[b] maybe, but not
everything does good. I agree there are no forbidden things

5 a. Stepmother. Lv 18:8 forbids sexual relations with 'your father's
wife'. b. See note *a* to Jn 19, on the Passover practice. c. Dt 13:6
6 a. The pagan magistrates of Corinth. b. Probably one of Paul's own
sayings which has been misapplied by false teachers: this section of the
letter is directed against the libertines, who had been teaching that
sexual intercourse was as necessary for the body as food and drink.

for me, but I am not going to let anything dominate me.
13 Food is only meant for the stomach, and the stomach for
food; yes, and God is going to do away with both of them.
But the body—this is not meant for fornication; it is for the
14 Lord, and the Lord for the body. ·God, who raised the Lord
from the dead, will by his power raise us up too.

15   You know, surely, that your bodies are members making
up the body of Christ; do you think I can take parts of
Christ's body and join them to the body of a prostitute?
16 Never! ·As you know, a man who goes with a prostitute is
one body with her, since *the two*, as it is said, *become one*
17 *flesh.* ·But anyone who is joined to the Lord is one spirit
with him.

18   Keep away from fornication. All the other sins are committed outside the body; but to fornicate is to sin against
19 your own body. ·Your body, you know, is the temple of the
Holy Spirit, who is in you since you received him from God.
20 You are not your own property; ·you have been bought and
paid for. That is why you should use your body for the glory
of God.

II. ANSWERS TO VARIOUS QUESTIONS

A. MARRIAGE AND VIRGINITY

7   Now for the questions about which you wrote. Yes, it is a
2 good thing for a man not to touch a woman; ·but since sex is
always a danger, let each man have his own wife and each
3 woman her own husband. ·The husband must give his wife
what she has the right to expect, and so too the wife to the
4 husband. ·The wife has no rights over her own body; it is the
husband who has them. In the same way, the husband has no
5 rights over his body; the wife has them. ·Do not refuse each
other except by mutual consent, and then only for an agreed
time, to leave yourselves free for prayer; then come together
again in case Satan should take advantage of your weakness
6 to tempt you. ·This is a suggestion, not a rule: ·I should like
7 everyone to be like me, but everybody has his own particular
gifts from God, one with a gift for one thing and another
with a gift for the opposite.

8   There is something I want to add for the sake of widows
and those who are not married: it is a good thing for them to
9 stay as they are, like me, ·but if they cannot control the sexual
urges, they should get married, since it is better to be married
than to be tortured.

10 For the married I have something to say, and this is not from me but from the Lord: a wife must not leave her hus-
11 band—or if she does leave him, she must either remain unmarried or else make it up with her husband—nor must a husband send his wife away.
12 The rest is from me and not from the Lord. If a brother has a wife who is an unbeliever, and she is content to live with
13 him, he must not send her away; and if a woman has an unbeliever for her husband, and he is content to live with her,
14 she must not leave him. ·This is because the unbelieving husband is made one with the saints through his wife, and the unbelieving wife is made one with the saints through her husband. If this were not so, your children would be unclean,
15 whereas in fact they are holy. ·However, if the unbelieving partner does not consent, they may separate; in these circum-stances, the brother or sister is not tied: God has called you
16 to a life of peace. ·If you are a wife, it may be your part to save your husband, for all you know; if a husband, for all you know, it may be your part to save your wife.
17 For the rest, what each one has is what the Lord has given him and he should continue as he was when God's call reached him. This is the ruling that I give in all the churches.
18 If anyone had already been circumcised at the time of his call, he need not disguise it, and anyone who was uncircumcised
19 at the time of his call need not be circumcised; ·because to be circumcised or uncircumcised means nothing: what does
20 matter is to keep the commandments of God. ·Let everyone
21 stay as he was at the time of his call. ·If, when you were called, you were a slave, do not let this bother you; but if you should
22 have the chance of being free, accept it. ·A slave, when he is called in the Lord, becomes the Lord's freedman, and a
23 freeman called in the Lord becomes Christ's slave. ·You have all been bought and paid for; do not be slaves of other men.
24 Each one of you, my brothers, should stay as he was before God at the time of his call.
25 About remaining celibate, I have no directions from the Lord but give my own opinion as one who, by the Lord's
26 mercy, has stayed faithful. ·Well then, I believe that in these present times of stress this is right: that it is good for a man
27 to stay as he is. ·If you are tied to a wife, do not look for freedom; if you are free of a wife, then do not look for one.
28 But if you marry, it is no sin, and it is not a sin for a young girl to get married. They will have their troubles, though, in their married life, and I should like to spare you that.
29 Brothers, this is what I mean: our time is growing short.

Those who have wives should live as though they had none,
30 and those who mourn should live as though they had nothing
to mourn for; those who are enjoying life should live as
though there were nothing to laugh about; those whose life
is buying things should live as though they had nothing of
31 their own; ·and those who have to deal with the world
should not become engrossed in it. I say this because the
world as we know it is passing away.
32 I would like to see you free from all worry. An unmarried
man can devote himself to the Lord's affairs, all he need
33 worry about is pleasing the Lord; ·but a married man has to
bother about the world's affairs and devote himself to
34 pleasing his wife: ·he is torn two ways. In the same way an
unmarried woman, like a young girl, can devote herself to the
Lord's affairs; all she need worry about is being holy in body
and spirit. The married woman, on the other hand, has to
worry about the world's affairs and devote herself to pleasing
35 her husband. ·I say this only to help you, not to put a halter
round your necks, but simply to make sure that everything is
as it should be, and that you give your undivided attention to
the Lord.
36 Still, if there is anyone who feels that it would not be fair
to his daughter to let her grow too old for marriage, and that
he should do something about it, he is free to do as he likes:
37 he is not sinning if there is a marriage. ·On the other hand, if
someone has firmly made his mind up, without any compul-
sion and in complete freedom of choice, to keep his daughter
38 as she is, he will be doing a good thing. ·In other words, the
man who sees that his daughter is married has done a good
thing but the man who keeps his daughter unmarried has
done something even better.[a]
39 A wife is tied as long as her husband is alive. But if the
husband dies, she is free to marry anybody she likes, only it
40 must be in the Lord. ·She would be happier, in my opinion, if
she stayed as she is—and I too have the Spirit of God, I think.

B. FOOD OFFERED TO IDOLS

General principles

8 Now about food sacrificed to idols. 'We all have knowledge'; yes, that is so, but knowledge gives self-importance—
2 it is love that makes the building grow. ·A man may imagine
he understands something, but still not understand anything
3 in the way that he ought to. ·But any man who loves God is
4 known by him. ·Well then, about eating food sacrificed to

idols:[a] we know that idols do not really exist in the world and
5 that there is no god but the One. ·And even if there were
things called gods, either in the sky or on earth—where there
6 certainly seem to be 'gods' and 'lords' in plenty—·still for us
there is one God, the Father, from whom all things come and
for whom we exist; and there is one Lord, Jesus Christ,
through whom all things come and through whom we exist.

The claims of love

7 Some people, however, do not have this knowledge. There
are some who have been so long used to idols that they eat
this food as though it really had been sacrificed to the idol,
8 and their conscience, being weak, is defiled by it. ·Food, of
course, cannot bring us in touch with God: we lose nothing
9 if we refuse to eat, we gain nothing if we eat. ·Only be careful
that you do not make use of this freedom in a way that proves
10 a pitfall for the weak. ·Suppose someone sees you, a man who
understands, eating in some temple of an idol; his own conscience, even if it is weak, may encourage him to eat food
11 which has been offered to idols. ·In this way your knowledge
could become the ruin of someone weak, of a brother for
12 whom Christ died. ·By sinning in this way against your
brothers, and injuring their weak consciences, it would be
13 Christ against whom you sinned. ·That is why, since food can
be the occasion of my brother's downfall, I shall never eat
meat again in case I am the cause of a brother's downfall.

Paul invokes his own example

9 I, personally, am free: I am an apostle and I have seen
2 Jesus our Lord. You are all my work in the Lord. ·Even if I
were not an apostle to others, I should still be an apostle to
3 you who are the seal of my apostolate in the Lord. ·My
4 answer to those who want to interrogate me is this: ·Have we
5 not every right to eat and drink?[a] ·And the right to take a
Christian woman round with us, like all the other apostles
6 and the brothers of the Lord and Cephas? ·Are Barnabas
and I the only ones who are not allowed to stop working?

7 a. 'daughter' is not the only possible word; this passage has been
read as alluding to the practice of a man and a woman living together
under the vows of chastity; a practice for which there is evidence of a
later date.
8 a. At feasts and public ceremonies, portions of the food were 'sacrificed' and went to the gods, the priests and the donors; the whole of the
food was regarded as dedicated, whether it was eaten at a ceremonial
meal or part of it sold in the markets.
9 a. At the expense of the Christian congregations.

7 Nobody ever paid money to stay in the army, and nobody ever planted a vineyard and refused to eat the fruit of it. Who has there ever been that kept a flock and did not feed on the milk from his flock?

8 These may be only human comparisons, but does not the
9 Law itself say the same thing? ·It is written in the Law of Moses: *You must not put a muzzle on the ox when it is treading*
10 *out the corn.*[b] Is it about oxen that God is concerned, ·or is there not an obvious reference to ourselves? Clearly this was written for our sake to show that the ploughman ought to plough in expectation, and the thresher to thresh in the
11 expectation of getting his share. ·If we have sown spiritual things for you, why should you be surprised if we harvest
12 your material things? ·Others are allowed these rights over you and our right is surely greater? In fact we have never exercised this right. On the contrary we have put up with anything rather than obstruct the Good News of Christ in
13 any way. ·Remember that the ministers serving in the Temple get their food from the Temple and those serving at the altar
14 can claim their share from the altar itself. ·In the same sort of way the Lord directed that those who preach the gospel should get their living from the gospel.

15 However, I have not exercised any of these rights, and I am not writing all this to secure this treatment for myself. I would rather die than let anyone take away something that
16 I can boast of. ·Not that I do boast of preaching the gospel, since it is a duty which has been laid on me; I should be
17 punished if I did not preach it! ·If I had chosen this work myself, I might have been paid for it, but as I have not, it is a
18 responsibility which has been put into my hands. ·Do you know what my reward is? It is this: in my preaching, to be able to offer the Good News free, and not insist on the rights which the gospel gives me.

19 So though I am not a slave of any man I have made myself
20 the slave of everyone so as to win as many as I could. ·I made myself a Jew to the Jews, to win the Jews; that is, I who am not a subject of the Law made myself a subject of the Law to those who are the subjects of the Law, to win those who are
21 subject to the Law. ·To those who have no Law, I was free of the Law myself (though not free from God's law, being under
22 the law of Christ) to win those who have no Law. ·For the weak I made myself weak. I made myself all things to all men
23 in order to save some at any cost; ·and I still do this, for the sake of the gospel, to have a share in its blessings.
24 All the runners at the stadium are trying to win, but only

one of them gets the prize. You must run in the same way,
25 meaning to win. ·All the fighters at the games go into strict
training; they do this just to win a wreath that will wither
26 away, but we do it for a wreath that will never wither. ·That
is how I run, intent on winning; that is how I fight, not beat-
27 ing the air. ·I treat my body hard and make it obey me, for,
having been an announcer myself, I should not want to be
disqualified.

A warning, and the lessons of Israel's history

10   I want to remind you, brothers, how our fathers were all
guided by a cloud above them and how they all passed
2 through the sea. ·They were all baptised into Moses in this
3 4 cloud and in this sea; ·all ate the same spiritual food ·and
all drank the same spiritual drink, since they all drank from
the spiritual rock that followed them as they went, and that
5 rock was Christ. ·In spite of this, most of them failed to please
God and their corpses littered the desert.

6   These things all happened as warnings*a* for us, not to have
7 the wicked lusts for forbidden things that they had. ·Do not
become idolaters as some of them did, for scripture says:
After sitting down to eat and drink, the people got up to amuse
8 *themselves.b* ·We must never fall into sexual immorality:
some of them did, and twenty-three thousand met their
9 downfall in one day. ·We are not to put the Lord to the test:
10 some of them did, and they were killed by snakes. ·You must
never complain: some of them did, and they were killed by
the Destroyer.

11   All this happened to them as a warning, and it was written
down to be a lesson for us who are living at the end of the age.
12 The man who thinks he is safe must be careful that he does
13 not fall. ·The trials that you have had to bear are no more
than people normally have. You can trust God not to let you
be tried beyond your strength, and with any trial he will give
you a way out of it and the strength to bear it.

Sacrificial feasts. No compromise with idolatry

14   This is the reason, my dear brothers, why you must keep
15 clear of idolatry. ·I say to you as sensible people: judge for
16 yourselves what I am saying. ·The blessing-cup that we bless
is a communion with the blood of Christ, and the bread that
17 we break is a communion with the body of Christ. ·The fact ·

b. Dt 25:4
10 a. Lit. 'types'; events prefiguring in the history of Israel the spiritual
realities of the messianic age. **b**. Ex 32:6

that there is only one loaf means that, though there are many of us, we form a single body because we all have a share in
18 this one loaf. ·Look at the other Israel, the race, where those
19 who eat the sacrifices are in communion with the altar. ·Does this mean that the food sacrificed to idols has a real value, or
20 that the idol itself is real? ·Not at all. It simply means that the sacrifices that they offer *they sacrifice to demons who are not God.*^c^ I have no desire to see you in communion with demons.
21 You cannot drink the cup of the Lord and the cup of demons. You cannot take your share at the table of the Lord and at
22 the table of demons. ·Do we want to make the Lord angry; are we stronger than he is?

Food sacrificed to idols. Practical solutions

23 'For me there are no forbidden things', but not everything does good. True, there are no forbidden things, but it is not
24 everything that helps the building to grow. ·Nobody should be looking for his own advantage, but everybody for the
25 other man's. ·Do not hesitate to eat anything that is sold in butchers' shops: there is no need to raise questions of con-
26 science; ·for *the earth and everything that is in it belong to the*
27 *Lord.*^d^ ·If an unbeliever invites you to his house, go if you want to, and eat whatever is put in front of you, without
28 asking questions just to satisfy conscience. ·But if someone says to you, 'This food was offered in sacrifice', then, out of consideration for the man that told you, you should not eat
29 it, for the sake of his scruples; ·his scruples, you see, not your own. Why should my freedom depend on somebody
30 else's conscience? ·If I take my share with thankfulness, why should I be blamed for food for which I have thanked God?

Conclusion

31 Whatever you eat, whatever you drink, whatever you do at
32 all, do it for the glory of God. ·Never do anything offensive
33 to anyone—to Jews or Greeks or to the Church of God; ·just as I try to be helpful to everyone at all times, not anxious for my own advantage but for the advantage of everybody else, so that they may be saved.
11 Take me for your model, as I take Christ.

C. DECORUM IN PUBLIC WORSHIP

Women's behaviour at services

2 You have done well in remembering me so constantly and in maintaining the traditions just as I passed them on to you.

3 However, what I want you to understand is that Christ is the
head of every man, man is the head of woman, and God is the
4 head of Christ. ·For a man to pray or prophesy with his head
5 covered is a sign of disrespect to his head.[a] ·For a woman,
however, it is a sign of disrespect to her head[b] if she prays or
prophesies unveiled; she might as well have her hair shaved
6 off. ·In fact, a woman who will not wear a veil ought to have
her hair cut off. If a woman is ashamed to have her hair cut
off or shaved, she ought to wear a veil.
7 A man should certainly not cover his head, since he is the
image of God and reflects God's glory; but woman is the
8 reflection of man's glory. ·For man did not come from
9 woman; no, woman came from man; ·and man was not
created for the sake of woman, but woman was created for
10 the sake of man. ·That is the argument for women's covering
their heads with a symbol of the authority over them, out of
11 respect for the angels.[c] ·However, though woman cannot do
without man, neither can man do without woman, in the
12 Lord; ·woman may come from man, but man is born of
woman—both come from God.
13 Ask yourselves if it is fitting for a woman to pray to God
14 without a veil; ·and whether nature itself does not tell you
15 that long hair on a man is nothing to be admired, ·while
a woman, who was given her hair as a covering, thinks long
hair her glory?
16 To anyone who might still want to argue: it is not the
custom with us, nor in the churches of God.

The Lord's Supper

17 Now that I am on the subject of instructions, I cannot say
that you have done well in holding meetings that do you more
18 harm than good. ·In the first place, I hear that when you all
come together as a community, there are separate factions
19 among you, and I half believe it—·since there must no doubt
be separate groups among you, to distinguish those who are
20 to be trusted. ·The point is, when you hold these meetings, it
21 is not the Lord's Supper[d] that you are eating, ·since when the
time comes to eat, everyone is in such a hurry to start his own
supper that one person goes hungry while another is getting
22 drunk. ·Surely you have homes for eating and drinking in?
Surely you have enough respect for the community of God

c. Dt 32:17 d. Ps 24:1
11 a. His leader, a Greek pun. **b.** Her husband, who is her head; she
is claiming equality. **c.** The guardians of due order in public worship.
d. The *agapē*, or love feast, preceding the liturgical meal.

not to make poor people embarrassed? What am I to say to you? Congratulate you? I cannot congratulate you on this.

23 For this is what I received from the Lord, and in turn passed on to you: that on the same night that he was be-
24 trayed, the Lord Jesus took some bread, ·and thanked God for it and broke it, and he said, 'This is my body, which is for
25 you; do this as a memorial of me'. ·In the same way he took the cup after supper, and said, 'This cup is the new covenant in my blood. Whenever you drink it, do this as a memorial of
26 me.' ·Until the Lord comes, therefore, every time you eat this bread and drink this cup, you are proclaiming his death,
27 and so anyone who eats the bread or drinks the cup of the Lord unworthily will be behaving unworthily towards the body and blood of the Lord.

28 Everyone is to recollect himself before eating this bread
29 and drinking this cup; ·because a person who eats and drinks without recognising the Body is eating and drinking his own
30 condemnation. ·In fact that is why many of you are weak and
31 ill and some of you have died. ·If only we recollected our-
32 selves, we should not be punished like that. ·But when the Lord does punish us like that, it is to correct us and stop us from being condemned with the world.

33 So to sum up, my dear brothers, when you meet for the
34 Meal, wait for one another. ·Anyone who is hungry should eat at home, and then your meeting will not bring your condemnation. The other matters I shall adjust when I come.

Spiritual gifts

12 Now my dear brothers, I want to clear up a wrong im-
2 pression about spiritual gifts. ·You remember that, when you were pagans, whenever you felt irresistibly drawn, it was
3 towards dumb idols? ·It is for that reason that I want you to understand that on the one hand no one can be speaking under the influence of the Holy Spirit and say, 'Curse Jesus', and on the other hand, no one can say, 'Jesus is Lord' unless he is under the influence of the Holy Spirit.

The variety and the unity of gifts

4
5 There is a variety of gifts but always the same Spirit; ·there are all sorts of service to be done, but always to the same
6 Lord; ·working in all sorts of different ways in different
7 people, it is the same God who is working in all of them. ·The particular way in which the Spirit is given to each person is
8 for a good purpose. ·One may have the gift of preaching with wisdom given him by the Spirit; another may have the gift of

9 preaching instruction given him by the same Spirit; ·and another the gift of faith given by the same Spirit; another
10 again the gift of healing, through this one Spirit; ·one, the power of miracles; another, prophecy; another the gift of recognising spirits; another the gift of tongues and another
11 the ability to interpret them. ·All these are the work of one and the same Spirit, who distributes different gifts to different people just as he chooses.

The analogy of the body

12 Just as a human body, though it is made up of many parts, is a single unit because all these parts, though many, make
13 one body, so it is with Christ. ·In the one Spirit we were all baptised, Jews as well as Greeks, slaves as well as citizens, and one Spirit was given to us all to drink.
14 Nor is the body to be identified with any one of its many
15 parts. ·If the foot were to say, 'I am not a hand and so I do not belong to the body', would that mean that it stopped
16 being part of the body? ·If the ear were to say, 'I am not an eye, and so I do not belong to the body', would that mean
17 that it was not a part of the body? ·If your whole body was just one eye, how would you hear anything? If it was just one ear, how would you smell anything?
18 Instead of that, God put all the separate parts into the
19 body on purpose. ·If all the parts were the same, how could it
20 be a body? ·As it is, the parts are many but the body is one.
21 The eye cannot say to the hand, 'I do not need you', nor can the head say to the feet, 'I do not need you'.
22 What is more, it is precisely the parts of the body that seem
23 to be the weakest which are the indispensable ones; ·and it is the least honourable parts of the body that we clothe with the
24 greatest care. So our more improper parts get decorated ·in a way that our more proper parts do not need. God has arranged the body so that more dignity is given to the parts
25 which are without it, ·and so that there may not be disagreements inside the body, but that each part may be
26 equally concerned for all the others. ·If one part is hurt, all parts are hurt with it. If one part is given special honour, all parts enjoy it.
27 Now you together are Christ's body; but each of you is a
28 different part of it. ·In the Church, God has given the first place to apostles, the second to prophets, the third to teachers; after them, miracles, and after them the gift of healing; helpers, good leaders, those with many languages.
29 Are all of them apostles, or all of them prophets, or all of

30 them teachers? Do they all have the gift of miracles, ·or all have the gift of healing? Do all speak strange languages, and all interpret them?

The order of importance in spiritual gifts. Love

31 Be ambitious for the higher gifts. And I am going to show you a way that is better than any of them.

13 If I have all the eloquence of men or of angels, but speak without love, I am simply a gong booming or a cymbal
2 clashing. ·If I have the gift of prophecy, understanding all the mysteries there are, and knowing everything, and if I have faith in all its fulness, to move mountains, but without love,
3 then I am nothing at all. ·If I give away all that I possess, piece by piece, and if I even let them take my body to burn it, but am without love, it will do me no good whatever.

4 Love is always patient and kind; it is never jealous; love is
5 never boastful or conceited; ·it is never rude or selfish; it
6 does not take offence, and is not resentful. ·Love takes no pleasure in other people's sins but delights in the truth; it is
7 always ready to excuse, to trust, to hope, and to endure whatever comes.

8 Love does not come to an end. But if there are gifts of prophecy, the time will come when they must fail; or the gift of languages, it will not continue for ever; and knowledge—
9 for this, too, the time will come when it must fail. ·For our
10 knowledge is imperfect and our prophesying is imperfect; ·but once perfection comes, all imperfect things will disappear.
11 When I was a child, I used to talk like a child, and think like a child, and argue like a child, but now I am a man, all childish
12 ways are put behind me. ·Now we are seeing a dim reflection in a mirror; but then we shall be seeing face to face. The knowledge that I have now is imperfect; but then I shall know as fully as I am known.

13 In short, there are three things that last: faith, hope and love; and the greatest of these is love.

Spiritual gifts: their respective importance in the community

14 You must want love more than anything else; but still hope
2 for the spiritual gifts as well, especially prophecy. ·Anybody with the gift of tongues speaks to God, but not to other people; because nobody understands him when he talks in
3 the spirit about mysterious things. ·On the other hand, the man who prophesies does talk to other people, to their improvement, their encouragement and their consolation.
4 The one with the gift of tongues talks for his own benefit, but

the man who prophesies does so for the benefit of the com-
5 munity. ·While I should like you all to have the gift of
tongues, I would much rather you could prophesy, since the
man who prophesies is of greater importance than the man
with the gift of tongues, unless of course the latter offers an
interpretation so that the church may get some benefit.

6 Now suppose, my dear brothers, I am someone with the
gift of tongues, and I come to visit you, what use shall I be if
all my talking reveals nothing new, tells you nothing, and
7 neither inspires you nor instructs you? ·Think of a musical
instrument, a flute or a harp: if one note on it cannot be
distinguished from another, how can you tell what tune is
8 being played? ·Or if no one can be sure which call the trum-
9 pet has sounded, who will be ready for the attack? ·It is the
same with you: if your tongue does not produce intelligible
speech, how can anyone know what you are saying? You will
10 be talking to the air. ·There are any number of different
languages in the world, and not one of them is meaningless,
11 but if I am ignorant of what the sounds mean, I am a savage
12 to the man who is speaking, and he is a savage to me. ·It is
the same in your own case: since you aspire to spiritual gifts,
concentrate on those which will grow to benefit the community.

13 That is why anybody who has the gift of tongues must pray
14 for the power of interpreting them. ·For if I use this gift in
my prayers, my spirit may be praying but my mind is left
15 barren. ·What is the answer to that? Surely I should pray not
only with the spirit but with the mind as well? And sing
praises not only with the spirit but with the mind as well?
16 Any uninitiated person will never be able to say Amen to your
thanksgiving, if you only bless God with the spirit, for he will
17 have no idea what you are saying. ·However well you make
18 your thanksgiving, the other gets no benefit from it. ·I thank
God that I have a greater gift of tongues than all of you,
19 but when I am in the presence of the community I would
rather say five words that mean something than ten thousand
words in a tongue.

20 Brothers, you are not to be childish in your outlook. You
can be babies as far as wickedness is concerned, but mentally
21 you must be adult. ·In the written Law it says: *Through men
speaking strange languages and through the lips of foreigners,
I shall talk to the nation, and still they will not listen to me,*
22 *says the Lord.*[a] ·You see then, that the strange languages are
meant to be a sign not for believers but for unbelievers, while

14 a. A free version of Is 28:11–12.

on the other hand, prophecy is a sign not for unbelievers but
23 for believers. ·So that any uninitiated people or unbelievers, coming into a meeting of the whole church where everybody
24 was speaking in tongues, would say you were all mad; ·but if you were all prophesying and an unbeliever or uninitiated person came in, he would find himself analysed and judged
25 by everyone speaking; ·he would find his secret thoughts laid bare, and then fall on his face and worship God, declaring that *God is among you indeed.*[b]

Regulating spiritual gifts

26 So, my dear brothers, what conclusion is to be drawn? At all your meetings, let everyone be ready with a psalm or a sermon or a revelation, or ready to use his gift of tongues or to give an interpretation; but it must always be for the
27 common good. ·If there are people present with the gift of tongues, let only two or three, at the most, be allowed to use it, and only one at a time, and there must be someone to
28 interpret. ·If there is no interpreter present, they must keep quiet in church and speak only to themselves and to God.
29 As for prophets, let two or three of them speak, and the
30 others attend to them. ·If one of the listeners receives a revelation, then the man who is already speaking should
31 stop. ·For you can all prophesy in turn, so that everybody
32 will learn something and everybody will be encouraged. ·Pro-
33 phets can always control their prophetic spirits, ·since God is not a God of disorder but of peace.
34 As in all the churches of the saints, ·women are to remain quiet at meetings since they have no permission to speak; they must keep in the background as the Law itself lays it
35 down. ·If they have any questions to ask, they should ask their husbands at home: it does not seem right for a woman to raise her voice at meetings.
36 Do you think the word of God came out of yourselves? Or
37 that it has come only to you? ·Anyone who claims to be a prophet or inspired ought to recognise that what I am writing
38 to you is a command from the Lord. ·Unless he recognises this, you should not recognise him.
39 And so, my dear brothers, by all means be ambitious to
40 prophesy, do not suppress the gift of tongues, ·but let everything be done with propriety and in order.

III. THE RESURRECTION OF THE DEAD

The fact of the resurrection

15 Brothers, I want to remind you of the gospel I preached to you, the gospel that you received and in which you are firmly
2 established; ·because the gospel will save you only if you keep believing exactly what I preached to you—believing anything else will not lead to anything.
3 Well then, in the first place, I taught you what I had been taught myself, namely that Christ died for our sins, in
4 accordance with the scriptures; ·that he was buried; and that he was raised to life on the third day, in accordance with the
5 scriptures; ·that he appeared first to Cephas and secondly to
6 the Twelve. ·Next he appeared to more than five hundred of the brothers at the same time, most of whom are still alive,
7 though some have died; ·then he appeared to James, and
8 then to all the apostles; ·and last of all he appeared to me too; it was as though I was born when no one expected it.
9 I am the least of the apostles; in fact, since I persecuted the
10 Church of God, I hardly deserve the name apostle; ·but by God's grace that is what I am, and the grace that he gave me has not been fruitless. On the contrary, I, or rather the grace of God that is with me, have worked harder than any of the
11 others; ·but what matters is that I preach what they preach, and this is what you all believed.
12 Now if Christ raised from the dead is what has been preached, how can some of you be saying that there is no
13 resurrection of the dead? ·If there is no resurrection of the
14 dead, Christ himself cannot have been raised, ·and if Christ has not been raised then our preaching is useless and your
15 believing it is useless; ·indeed, we are shown up as witnesses who have committed perjury before God, because we swore
16 in evidence before God that he had raised Christ to life. ·For
17 if the dead are not raised, Christ has not been raised, ·and if
18 Christ has not been raised, you are still in your sins. ·And what is more serious, all who have died in Christ have
19 perished. ·If our hope in Christ has been for this life only, we are the most unfortunate of all people.
20 But Christ has in fact been raised from the dead, the first-
21 fruits of all who have fallen asleep. ·Death came through one man and in the same way the resurrection of the dead has
22 come through one man. ·Just as all men die in Adam, so all
23 men will be brought to life in Christ; ·but all of them in their

b. Is 45:14

proper order: Christ as the first-fruits and then, after the
24 coming of Christ, those who belong to him. ·After that will
come the end, when he hands over the kingdom to God the
Father, having done away with every sovereignty, authority
25 and power. ·For he must be king *until he has put all his*
26 *enemies under his feet*[a] ·and the last of the enemies to be
destroyed is death, for everything is to be *put under his feet*.
27 —Though when it is said that *everything is subjected*, this
clearly cannot include the One who subjected everything to
28 him. ·And when everything is subjected to him, then the Son
himself will be subject in his turn to the One who subjected all
things to him, so that God may be all in all.

29   If this were not true, what do people hope to gain by being
baptised for the dead? If the dead are not ever going to be
30 raised, why be baptised on their behalf? ·What about our-
31 selves? Why are we living under a constant threat? ·I face
death every day, brothers, and I can swear it by the pride that
32 I take in you in Christ Jesus our Lord. ·If my motives were
only human ones, what good would it do me to fight the wild
33 animals at Ephesus? ·You say: *Let us eat and drink today;*
tomorrow we shall be dead.[b] You must stop being led astray:
34 'Bad friends ruin the noblest people'.[c] ·Come to your senses,
behave properly, and leave sin alone; there are some of you
who seem not to know God at all; you should be ashamed.

The manner of the resurrection

35   Someone may ask, 'How are dead people raised, and what
36 sort of body do they have when they come back?' ·They are
stupid questions. Whatever you sow in the ground has to die
37 before it is given new life ·and the thing that you sow is not
what is going to come; you sow a bare grain, say of wheat or
38 something like that, and then God gives it the sort of body
that he has chosen: each sort of seed gets its own sort of
body.
39   Everything that is flesh is not the same flesh: there is
human flesh, animals' flesh, the flesh of birds and the flesh of
40 fish. ·Then there are heavenly bodies and there are earthly
bodies; but the heavenly bodies have a beauty of their own
41 and the earthly bodies a different one. ·The sun has its
brightness, the moon a different brightness, and the stars a
different brightness, and the stars differ from each other in
42 brightness. ·It is the same with the resurrection of the dead:
the thing that is sown is perishable but what is raised is
43 imperishable; ·the thing that is sown is contemptible but
what is raised is glorious; the thing that is sown is weak but

44 what is raised is powerful; ·when it is sown it embodies the soul, when it is raised it embodies the spirit.

If the soul has its own embodiment, so does the spirit have
45 its own embodiment. ·The first *man*, Adam, as scripture says, *became a living soul*; but the last Adam has become a life-
46 giving spirit. ·That is, first the one with the soul, not the
47 spirit, and after that, the one with the spirit. ·The first man, being from the earth, is earthly by nature; the second man is
48 from heaven. ·As this earthly man was, so are we on earth;
49 and as the heavenly man is, so are we in heaven. ·And we, who have been modelled on the earthly man, will be modelled on the heavenly man.

50 Or else, brothers, put it this way: flesh and blood cannot inherit the kingdom of God: and the perishable cannot
51 inherit what lasts for ever. ·I will tell you something that has been secret: that we are not all going to die, but we shall all
52 be changed. ·This will be instantaneous, in the twinkling of an eye, when the last trumpet sounds. It will sound, and the dead will be raised, imperishable, and we shall be changed as well,
53 because our present perishable nature must put on imperishability and this moral nature must put on immortality.

A hymn of triumph. Conclusion

54 When this perishable nature has put on imperishability, and when this mortal nature has put on immortality, then the words of scripture will come true: *Death is swallowed up in*
55 *victory*. ·*Death, where is your* victory? *Death, where is your*
56 *sting?*[d] ·Now the sting of death is sin, and sin gets its power
57 from the Law. ·So let us thank God for giving us the victory through our Lord Jesus Christ.

58 Never give in then, my dear brothers, never admit defeat; keep on working at the Lord's work always, knowing that, in the Lord, you cannot be labouring in vain.

CONCLUSION

Commendations. Greetings

16 Now about the collection made for the saints: you are to
2 do as I told the churches in Galatia to do. ·Every Sunday, each one of you must put aside what he can afford, so that
3 collections need not be made after I have come. ·When I am with you, I will send your offering to Jerusalem by the hand of

15 a. Ps 110:1 **b.** Is 22:13 **c.** This quotation from Menander's *Thais* may have become a proverb. **d.** A free version; see Ho 13:14.

4 whatever men you give letters of reference to; ·if it seems worth while for me to go too, they can travel with me.

5 I shall be coming to you after I have passed through Macedonia—and I am doing no more than pass through Mace-
6 donia—·and I may be staying with you, perhaps even passing the winter, to make sure that it is you who send me on my
7 way wherever my travels take me. ·As you see, I do not want to make it only a passing visit to you and I hope to spend
8 some time with you, the Lord permitting. ·In any case I shall
9 be staying at Ephesus until Pentecost ·because a big and important door has opened for my work and there is a great deal of opposition.

10 If Timothy comes, show him that he has nothing to be
11 afraid of in you: like me, he is doing the Lord's work, ·and nobody is to be scornful of him. Send him happily on his way to come back to me; the brothers and I are waiting for
12 him. ·As for our brother Apollos, I begged him to come to you with the brothers but he was quite firm that he did not want to go yet and he will come as soon as he can.

13 Be awake to all the dangers; stay firm in the faith; be brave
14 and be strong. ·Let everything you do be done in love.

15 There is something else to ask you, brothers. You know how the Stephanas family, who were the first-fruits of
16 Achaia, have really worked hard to help the saints. ·Well, I want you in your turn to put yourselves at the service of people like this, and anyone who helps and works with them.
17 I am delighted that Stephanas, Fortunatus and Achaicus
18 have arrived; they make up for your absence. ·They have settled my mind, and yours too; I hope you appreciate men like this.

19 All the churches of Asia send you greetings. Aquila and Prisca, with the church that meets at their house, send you
20 their warmest wishes, in the Lord. ·All the brothers send you their greetings. Greet one another with a holy kiss.

21 This greeting is in my own hand—Paul.

22 If anyone does not love the Lord, a curse on him. 'Maran atha.'[a]

23 The grace of the Lord Jesus be with you.

24 My love is with you all in Christ Jesus.

16 a. Aramaic. 'The Lord is coming', or 'Lord, come'.

2 CORINTHIANS

THE SECOND LETTER OF PAUL

TO THE CHURCH AT CORINTH

INTRODUCTION

Address of greetings. Thanksgiving

1 From Paul, appointed by God to be an apostle of Christ Jesus, and from Timothy, one of the brothers, to the church of God at Corinth and to all the saints in the whole of
2 Achaia. ·Grace and peace to you from God our Father and the Lord Jesus Christ.

3 Blessed be the God and Father of our Lord Jesus Christ, a
4 gentle Father and the God of all consolation, ·who comforts us in all our sorrows, so that we can offer others, in their sorrows, the consolation that we have received from God
5 ourselves. ·Indeed, as the sufferings of Christ overflow to us,
6 so, through Christ, does our consolation overflow. ·When we are made to suffer, it is for your consolation and salvation. When, instead, we are comforted, this should be a consolation to you, supporting you in patiently bearing the same
7 sufferings as we bear. ·And our hope for you is confident, since we know that, sharing our sufferings, you will also share our consolations.

8 For we should like you to realise, brothers, that the things we had to undergo in Asia were more of a burden than we could carry, so that we despaired of coming through alive.
9 Yes, we were carrying our own death warrant with us, and it has taught us not to rely on ourselves but only on God, who
10 raises the dead to life. ·And he saved us from dying, as he will save us again; yes, that is our firm hope in him, that in
11 the future he will save us again. ·You must all join in the prayers for us: the more people there are asking for help for us, the more will be giving thanks when it is granted to us.

I. SOME RECENT EVENTS REVIEWED

Why Paul changed his plans

12   There is one thing we are proud of, and our conscience tells us it is true: that we have always treated everybody, and especially you, with the reverence and sincerity which come from God, and by the grace of God we have done this with-
13   out ulterior motives. ·There are no hidden meanings in our letters besides what you can read for yourselves and under-
14   stand. ·And I hope that, although you do not know us very well yet, you will have come to recognise, when the day of our Lord Jesus comes, that you can be as proud of us as we are of you.

15   Because I was so sure of this, I had meant to come to you
16   first, so that you would benefit doubly; ·staying with you before going to Macedonia and coming back to you again on the way back from Macedonia, for you to see me on my way
17   to Judaea. ·Do you think I was not sure of my own intentions when I planned this? Do you really think that when I am making my plans, my motives are ordinary human ones, and
18   that I say Yes, yes, and No, no, at the same time? ·I swear by God's truth, there is no Yes and No about what we say to
19   you. ·The Son of God, the Christ Jesus that we proclaimed among you—I mean Silvanus and Timothy and I—was
20   never Yes and No: with him it was always Yes, ·and however many the promises God made, the Yes to them all is in him. That is why it is 'through him' that we answer Amen to the
21   praise of God. ·Remember it is God himself who assures us all, and you, of our standing in Christ, and has anointed us,
22   marking us with his seal and giving us the pledge, the Spirit, that we carry in our hearts.

23   By my life, I call God to witness that the reason why I did
24   not come to Corinth after all was to spare your feelings. ·We are not dictators over your faith, but are fellow workers with you for your happiness; in the faith you are steady enough.

2   Well then, I made up my mind not to pay you a second
2   distressing visit. ·I may have hurt you, but if so I have hurt
3   the only people who could give me any pleasure. ·I wrote as I did to make sure that, when I came, I should not be distressed by the very people who should have made me happy. I am sure you all know that I could never be happy unless
4   you were. ·When I wrote to you, in deep distress and anguish of mind, and in tears, it was not to make you feel hurt but to let you know how much love I have for you.

5 Someone has been the cause of pain; and the cause of pain not to me, but to some degree—not to overstate it—to all of
6 you. ·The punishment already imposed by the majority on
7 the man in question is enough; ·and the best thing now is to give him your forgiveness and encouragement, or he might
8 break down from so much misery. ·So I am asking you to
9 give some definite proof of your love for him. ·What I really wrote for, after all, was to test you and see whether you are
10 completely obedient. ·Anybody that you forgive, I forgive; and as for my forgiving anything—if there has been anything to be forgiven, I have forgiven it for your sake in the presence
11 of Christ. ·And so we will not be outwitted by Satan—we know well enough what his intentions are.

From Troas to Macedonia. The apostolate: its importance

12 When I went up to Troas to preach the Good News of Christ, and the door was wide open for my work there in the
13 Lord, ·I was so continually uneasy in mind at not meeting brother Titus there, I said good-bye to them and went on to Macedonia.
14 Thanks be to God who, wherever he goes, makes us, in Christ, partners of his triumph,[a] and through us is spreading
15 the knowledge of himself, like a sweet smell, everywhere. ·We are Christ's incense to God for those who are being saved and
16 for those who are not; ·for the last, the smell of death that leads to death, for the first the sweet smell of life that leads to
17 life. And who could be qualified for work like this? ·At least we do not go round offering the word of God for sale, as many other people do. In Christ, we speak as men of sincerity, as envoys of God and in God's presence.
3 Does this sound like a new attempt to commend ourselves to you? Unlike other people, we need no letters of recom-
2 mendation either to you or from you, ·because you are yourselves our letter, written in our hearts, that anybody can see
3 and read, ·and it is plain that you are a letter from Christ, drawn up by us, and written not with ink but with the Spirit of the living God, not on stone tablets but on the tablets of your living hearts.
4 Before God, we are confident of this through Christ:
5 not that we are qualified in ourselves to claim anything as
6 our own work: all our qualifications come from God. ·He is the one who has given us the qualifications to be the administrators of this new covenant, which is not a covenant of written letters but of the Spirit: the written letters bring death,

2 a. Like a victorious general making his ceremonial entry into Rome.

7 but the Spirit gives life. ·Now if the administering of death, in the written letters engraved on stones, was accompanied by such a brightness that the Israelites could not bear looking at
8 the face of Moses, though it was a brightness that faded, ·then how much greater will be the brightness that surrounds the
9 administering of the Spirit! ·For if there was any splendour in administering condemnation, there must be very much
10 greater splendour in administering justification. ·In fact, compared with this greater splendour, the thing that used to
11 have such splendour now seems to have none; ·and if what was so temporary had any splendour, there must be much more in what is going to last for ever.

12
13   Having this hope, we can be quite confident; ·not like Moses, who put a veil over his face so that the Israelites
14 would not notice the ending of what had to fade.[a] ·And anyway, their minds had been dulled; indeed, to this very day, that same veil is still there when the old covenant is being read, a veil never lifted, since Christ alone can remove it.
15 Yes, even today, whenever Moses is read, the veil is over
16 their minds. ·It will not be removed until they turn to the
17 Lord. ·Now this Lord is the Spirit, and where the Spirit of the
18 Lord is, there is freedom. ·And we, with our unveiled faces reflecting like mirrors the brightness of the Lord, all grow brighter and brighter as we are turned into the image that we reflect; this is the work of the Lord who is Spirit.

4   Since we have by an act of mercy been entrusted with this work of administration, there is no weakening on our part.
2 On the contrary, we will have none of the reticence of those who are ashamed, no deceitfulness or watering down the word of God; but the way we commend ourselves to every human being with a conscience is by stating the truth openly
3 in the sight of God. ·If our gospel does not penetrate the veil, then the veil is on those who are not on the way to salvation;
4 the unbelievers whose minds the god of this world has blinded, to stop them seeing the light shed by the Good
5 News of the glory of Christ, who is the image of God. ·For it is not ourselves that we are preaching, but Christ Jesus as the
6 Lord, and ourselves as your servants for Jesus' sake. ·It is the same God that said, 'Let there be light shining out of darkness', who has shone in our minds to radiate the light of the knowledge of God's glory, the glory on the face of Christ.

The trials and hopes of the apostolate

7   We are only the earthenware jars that hold this treasure, to make it clear that such an overwhelming power comes from

8 God and not from us. ·We are in difficulties on all sides, but
never cornered; we see no answer to our problems, but never
9 despair; ·we have been persecuted, but never deserted;
10 knocked down, but never killed; ·always, wherever we may
be, we carry with us in our body the death of Jesus, so that
11 the life of Jesus, too, may always be seen in our body. ·In-
deed, while we are still alive, we are consigned to our death
every day, for the sake of Jesus, so that in our mortal flesh
12 the life of Jesus, too, may be openly shown. ·So death is at
work in us, but life in you.

13   But as we have the same spirit of faith that is mentioned in
scripture—*I believed, and therefore I spoke*[a]—we too believe
14 and therefore we too speak, ·knowing that he who raised the
Lord Jesus to life will raise us with Jesus in our turn, and put
15 us by his side and you with us. ·You see, all this is for your
benefit, so that the more grace is multiplied among people,
the more thanksgiving there will be, to the glory of God.

16   That is why there is no weakening on our part, and instead,
though this outer man of ours may be falling into decay, the
17 inner man is renewed day by day. ·Yes, the troubles which
are soon over, though they weigh little, train us for the
carrying of a weight of eternal glory which is out of all
18 proportion to them. ·And so we have no eyes for things that
are visible, but only for things that are invisible; for visible
things last only for a time, and the invisible things are
eternal.

5   For we know that when the tent that we live in on earth is
folded up, there is a house built by God for us, an everlasting
2 home not made by human hands, in the heavens. ·In this
present state, it is true, we groan as we wait with longing to
3 put on our heavenly home over the other; ·we should like to
4 be found wearing clothes and not without them. ·Yes, we
groan and find it a burden being still in this tent, not that we
want to strip it off, but to put the second garment over it and
5 to have what must die taken up into life. ·This is the purpose
for which God made us, and he has given us the pledge of the
Spirit.

6   We are always full of confidence, then, when we remember
that to live in the body means to be exiled from the Lord,
7
8 going as we do by faith and not by sight—·we are full of
confidence, I say, and actually want to be exiled from the
9 body and make our home with the Lord. ·Whether we are
living in the body or exiled from it, we are intent on pleasing

3 **a.** See Ex 34:33.
4 **a.** Ps 116:10

10 him. ·For all the truth about us will be brought out in the law court of Christ, and each of us will get what he deserves for the things he did in the body, good or bad.

The apostolate in action

11 And so it is with the fear of the Lord in mind that we try to win people over. God knows us for what we really are, and I
12 hope that in your consciences you know us too. ·This is not another attempt to commend ourselves to you: we are simply giving you reasons to be proud of us, so that you will have an answer ready for the people who can boast more about what
13 they seem than what they are. ·If we seemed out of our senses, it was for God; but if we are being reasonable now, it is for
14 your sake. ·And this is because the love of Christ overwhelms us when we reflect that if one man has died for all, then all
15 men should be dead; ·and the reason he died for all was so that living men should live no longer for themselves, but for him who died and was raised to life for them.
16 From now onwards, therefore, we do not judge anyone by the standards of the flesh. Even if we did once know Christ in
17 the flesh, that is not how we know him now. ·And for anyone who is in Christ, there is a new creation; the old creation has
18 gone, and now the new one is here. ·It is all God's work. It was God who reconciled us to himself through Christ and
19 gave us the work of handing on this reconciliation. ·In other words, God in Christ was reconciling the world to himself, not holding men's faults against them, and he has entrusted
20 to us the news that they are reconciled. ·So we are ambassadors for Christ; it is as though God were appealing through us, and the appeal that we make in Christ's name is: be re-
21 conciled to God. ·For our sake God made the sinless one into sin, so that in him we might become the goodness of God.

6   As his fellow workers, we beg you once again not to neglect
2   the grace of God that you have received. ·For he says: *At the favourable time, I have listened to you; on the day of salvation I came to your help.*[a] Well, now is the favourable time; this is the day of salvation.
3   We do nothing that people might object to, so as not to
4   bring discredit on our function as God's servants. ·Instead, we prove we are servants of God by great fortitude in times
5   of suffering: in times of hardship and distress; ·when we are flogged, or sent to prison, or mobbed; labouring, sleepless,
6   starving. ·We prove we are God's servants by our purity, knowledge, patience and kindness; by a spirit of holiness, by
7   a love free from affectation; ·by the word of truth and by the

power of God; by being armed with the weapons of right-
8 eousness in the right hand and in the left, ·prepared for
honour or disgrace, for blame or praise; taken for impostors
9 while we are genuine; ·obscure yet famous; said to be dying
and here are we alive; rumoured to be executed before we are
10 sentenced; ·thought most miserable and yet we are always
rejoicing; taken for paupers though we make others rich, for
people having nothing though we have everything.

Paul opens his heart. A warning

11   Corinthians, we have spoken to you very frankly; our
12 mind has been opened in front of you. ·Any constraint that
you feel is not on our side; the constraint is in your own
13 selves. ·I speak as if to children of mine: as a fair exchange,
open your minds in the same way.

14   Do not harness yourselves in an uneven team with unbelievers. Virtue is no companion for crime. Light and
15 darkness have nothing in common. ·Christ is not the ally of
Beliar, nor has a believer anything to share with an un-
16 believer. ·The temple of God has no common ground with
idols, and that is what we are—the temple of the living God.
We have God's word for it: *I will make my home among
them and live with them; I will be their God and they shall be*
17 *my people.*[b] ·Then *come away from them and keep aloof, says
the Lord. Touch nothing that is unclean,*[c] *and I will welcome
18 you ·and be your father, and you shall be my sons and daughters, says the Almighty Lord.*[d]

7   With promises like these made to us, dear brothers, let us
wash off all that can soil either body or spirit, to reach perfection of holiness in the fear of God.

2   Keep a place for us in your hearts. We have not injured
3 anyone, or ruined anyone, or exploited anyone. ·I am not
saying this to put any blame on you; as I have already told
you, you are in our hearts—together we live or together we
4 die. ·I have the very greatest confidence in you, and I am so
proud of you that in all our trouble I am filled with consolation and my joy is overflowing.

Paul in Macedonia; he is joined by Titus

5   Even after we had come to Macedonia, however, there was
no rest for this body of ours. Far from it; we found trouble
6 on all sides: quarrels outside, misgivings inside. ·But God
comforts the miserable, and he comforted us, by the arrival
7 of Titus, ·and not only by his arrival but also by the comfort

6 **a.** Is 49:8 **b.** Lv 26:11–12 **c.** Is 52:11 **d.** Is 43:6

which he had gained from you. He has told us all about how you want to see me, how sorry you were, and how concerned for me, and so I am happier now than I was before.

8 But to tell the truth, even if I distressed you by my letter, I do not regret it. I did regret it before, and I see that that 9 letter did distress you, at least for a time; but I am happy now—not because I made you suffer, but because your suffering led to your repentance. Yours has been a kind of suffering that God approves, and so you have come to no 10 kind of harm from us. ·To suffer in God's way means changing for the better and leaves no regrets, but to suffer as 11 the world knows suffering brings death. ·Just look at what suffering in God's way has brought you: what keenness, what explanations, what indignation, what alarm! Yes, and what aching to see me, what concern for me, and what justice done! In every way you have shown yourselves blameless in this 12 affair. ·So then, though I wrote the letter to you, it was not written for the sake either of the offender or of the one offended; it was to make you realise, in the sight of God, your 13 own concern for us. ·That is what we have found so encouraging.

With this encouragement, too, we had the even greater happiness of finding Titus so happy; thanks to you all, he 14 has no more worries; ·I had rather boasted to him about you, and now I have not been made to look foolish; in fact, our boasting to Titus has proved to be as true as anything that we 15 ever said to you. ·His own personal affection for you is all the greater when he remembers how willing you have all been, 16 and with what deep respect you welcomed him. ·I am very happy knowing that I can rely on you so completely.

II. ORGANISATION OF THE COLLECTION

Why the Corinthians should be generous

8 Now here, brothers, is the news of the grace of God which 2 was given in the churches in Macedonia; ·and of how, throughout great trials by suffering, their constant cheerfulness and their intense poverty have overflowed in a wealth 3 of generosity. ·I can swear that they gave not only as much as they could afford, but far more, and quite spontaneously, 4 begging and begging us for the favour of sharing in this 5 service to the saints ·and, what was quite unexpected, they offered their own selves first to God and, under God, to us.

6 Because of this, we have asked Titus, since he has already

made a beginning, to bring this work of mercy to the same
7 point of success among you. ·You always have the most of
everything—of faith, of eloquence, of understanding, of
keenness for any cause, and the biggest share of our affection
—so we expect you to put the most into this work of mercy
8 too. ·It is not an order that I am giving you; I am just testing
the genuineness of your love against the keenness of others.
9 Remember how generous the Lord Jesus was: he was rich,
but he became poor for your sake, to make you rich out of
10 his poverty. ·As I say, I am only making a suggestion; it is
only fair to you, since you were the first, a year ago, not only
11 in taking action but even in deciding to. ·So now finish the
work and let the results be worthy, as far as you can afford it,
12 of the decision you made so promptly. ·As long as the
readiness is there, a man is acceptable with whatever he can
13 afford; never mind what is beyond his means. ·This does not
mean that to give relief to others you ought to make things
14 difficult for yourselves: it is a question of balancing ·what
happens to be your surplus now against their present need,
and one day they may have something to spare that will
15 supply your own need. That is how we strike a balance: ·as
scripture says: *The man who gathered much had none too
much, the man who gathered little did not go short.*[a]

The delegates recommended to the Corinthians

16 I thank God for putting into Titus' heart the same concern
17 for you that I have myself. ·He did what we asked him;
indeed he is more concerned than ever, and is visiting you on
18 his own initiative. ·As his companion we are sending the
brother who is famous in all the churches for spreading the
19 gospel. ·More than that, he happens to be the same brother
who has been elected by the churches to be our companion
on this errand of mercy that, for the glory of God, we have
20 undertaken to satisfy our impatience to help. ·We hope that
in this way there will be no accusations made about our
21 administering such a large fund; ·for *we are trying to do right*
22 not only *in the sight of God* but *also* in the sight of *men.*[b] ·To
accompany these, we are sending a third brother, of whose
keenness we have often had proof in many different ways,
and who is particularly keen about this, because he has great
23 confidence in you. ·Titus, perhaps I should add, is my own
colleague and fellow worker in your interests; the other two
brothers, who are delegates of the churches, are a real glory
24 to Christ. ·So then, in front of all the churches, give them a

8 a. Ex 16:18 **b.** Pr 3:4 (LXX)

proof of your love, and prove to them that we are right to be proud of you.

9 There is really no need for me to write to you on the
2 subject of offering your services to the saints, ·since I know how anxious you are to help; in fact, I boast about you to the Macedonians, telling them, 'Achaia has been ready since last
3 year'. So your zeal has been a spur to many more. ·I am sending the brothers all the same, to make sure that our boasting about you does not prove to have been empty this time, and that you really are ready as I said you would be.
4 If some of the Macedonians who are coming with me found you unprepared, we should be humiliated—to say nothing of
5 yourselves—after being so confident. ·That is why I have thought it necessary to ask these brothers to go on to you ahead of us, and make sure in advance that the gift you promised is all ready, and that it all comes as a gift out of your generosity and not by being extorted from you.

Blessings to be expected from the collection

6 Do not forget: thin sowing means thin reaping; the more
7 you sow, the more you reap. ·Each one should give what he has decided in his own mind, not grudgingly or because he is
8 made to, for *God loves a cheerful giver.*[a] ·And there is no limit to the blessings which God can send you—he will make sure that you will always have all you need for yourselves in every possible circumstance, and still have something to spare for
9 all sorts of good works. ·As scripture says: *He was free in almsgiving, and gave to the poor: his good deeds will never be forgotten.*[b]
10 The one who provides *seed for the sower and bread for food* will provide you with all the seed you want and make *the*
11 *harvest of your good deeds* a larger one, ·and, made richer in every way, you will be able to do all the generous things which, through us, are the cause of thanksgiving to God.
12 For doing this holy service is not only supplying all the needs of the saints, but it is also increasing the amount of thanks-
13 giving that God receives. ·By offering this service, you show them what you are, and that makes them give glory to God for the way you accept and profess the gospel of Christ, and
14 for your sympathetic generosity to them and to all. ·And their prayers for you, too, show how they are drawn to you
15 on account of all the grace that God has given you. ·Thanks be to God for his inexpressible gift!

III. PAUL'S APOLOGIA

Paul's reply to accusations of weakness

10   This is a personal matter; this is Paul himself appealing to you by the gentleness and patience of Christ—I, the man who is so humble when he is facing you, but bullies you when he is

2 at a distance. ·I only ask that I do not have to bully you when I come, with all the confident assurance I mean to show when I come face to face with people I could name who think we go

3 by ordinary human motives. ·We live in the flesh, of course,

4 but the muscles that we fight with are not flesh. ·Our war is not fought with weapons of flesh, yet they are strong enough, in God's cause, to demolish fortresses. We demolish sophis-

5 tries, ·and the arrogance that tries to resist the knowledge of God; every thought is our prisoner, captured to be brought

6 into obedience to Christ. ·Once you have given your complete obedience, we are prepared to punish any disobedience.

7   Face plain facts. Anybody who is convinced that he belongs to Christ must go on to reflect that we all belong to Christ no

8 less than he does. ·Maybe I do boast rather too much about our authority, but the Lord gave it to me for building you up and not for pulling you down, and I shall not be ashamed of

9 it. ·I do not want you to think of me as someone who only

10 frightens you by letter. ·Someone said, 'He writes powerful and strongly-worded letters but when he is with you you see

11 only half a man and no preacher at all'. ·The man who said that can remember this: whatever we are like in the words of our letters when we are absent, that is what we shall be like in our actions when we are present.

His reply to the accusation of ambition

12   We are not being so bold as to rank ourselves, or invite comparison, with certain people who write their own references. Measuring themselves against themselves, and comparing themselves to themselves, they are simply foolish.

13 We, on the other hand, are not going to boast without a standard to measure against: taking for our measure the yardstick which God gave us to measure with, which is long

14 enough to reach to you. ·We are not stretching further than we ought; otherwise we should not have reached you, as we

15 did come all the way to you with the gospel of Christ. ·So we are not boasting without any measure, about work that was done by other people; in fact, we trust that, as your faith

9 a. Pr 22:8 (LXX) **b.** Ps 112:9

grows, we shall get taller and taller, when judged by our own

16 standard. ·I mean, we shall be carrying the gospel to places far beyond you, without encroaching on anyone else's field,

17 not boasting of the work already done. ·*If anyone wants to*

18 *boast, let him boast of the Lord.*ᵃ ·It is not the man who commends himself that can be accepted, but the man who is commended by the Lord.

Paul is driven to sound his own praises

11   I only wish you were able to tolerate a little foolishness

2 from me. But of course: you are tolerant towards me. ·You see, the jealousy that I feel for you is God's own jealousy: I arranged for you to marry Christ so that I might give you

3 away as a chaste virgin to this one husband. ·But the serpent, with his cunning, seduced Eve, and I am afraid that in the same way your ideas may get corrupted and turned away

4 from simple devotion to Christ. ·Because any newcomer has only to proclaim a new Jesus, different from the one that we preached, or you have only to receive a new spirit, different from the one you have already received, or a new gospel, different from the one you have already accepted—and you

5 welcome it with open arms. ·As far as I can tell, these arch-

6 apostles have nothing more than I have. ·I may not be a polished speechmaker, but as for knowledge, that is a different matter; surely we have made this plain, speaking on every subject in front of all of you.

7   Or was I wrong, lowering myself so as to lift you high, by preaching the gospel of God to you and taking no fee for it?

8 I was robbing other churches living on them so that I could

9 serve you. ·When I was with you and ran out of money, I was no burden to anyone; the brothers who came from Macedonia provided me with everything I wanted. I was very careful, and I always shall be, not to be a burden to you in any way,

10 and by Christ's truth in me, this cause of boasting will never

11 be taken from me in the regions of Achaia. ·Would I do that

12 if I did not love you? God knows I do. ·I intend to go on doing what I am doing now—leaving no opportunity for those people who are looking for an opportunity to claim

13 equality with us in what they boast of. ·These people are counterfeit apostles, they are dishonest workmen disguised

14 as apostles of Christ. ·There is nothing unexpected about that;

15 if Satan himself goes disguised as an angel of light, ·there is no need to be surprised when his servants, too, disguise themselves as the servants of righteousness. They will come to the end that they deserve.

16 As I said before, let no one take me for a fool; but if you must, then treat me as a fool and let me do a little boasting of 17 my own. ·What I am going to say now is not prompted by the Lord, but said as if in a fit of folly, in the certainty that I have 18 something to boast about. ·So many others have been boasting of their worldly achievements, that I will boast myself. 19 You are all wise men and can cheerfully tolerate fools, 20 yes, even to tolerating somebody who makes slaves of you, makes you feed him, imposes on you, orders you about and 21 slaps you in the face. ·I hope you are ashamed of us for being weak with you instead!

But if anyone wants some brazen speaking—I am still talking as a fool—then I can be as brazen as any of them, and 22 about the same things. ·Hebrews, are they? So am I. Israel- 23 ites? So am I. Descendants of Abraham? So am I. ·The servants of Christ? I must be mad to say this, but so am I, and more than they: more, because I have worked harder, I have been sent to prison more often, and whipped so many 24 times more, often almost to death. ·Five times I had the 25 thirty-nine lashes from the Jews; ·three times I have been beaten with sticks; once I was stoned; three times I have been shipwrecked and once adrift in the open sea for a night 26 and a day. ·Constantly travelling, I have been in danger from rivers and in danger from brigands, in danger from my own people and in danger from pagans; in danger in the towns, in danger in the open country, danger at sea and danger from 27 so-called brothers. ·I have worked and laboured, often without sleep; I have been hungry and thirsty and often 28 starving; I have been in the cold without clothes. ·And, to leave out much more, there is my daily preoccupation: my 29 anxiety for all the churches. ·When any man has had scruples, I have had scruples with him; when any man is made to fall, I am tortured.

30 If I am to boast, then let me boast of my own feebleness. 31 The God and Father of the Lord Jesus—bless him for ever— 32 knows that I am not lying. ·When I was in Damascus, the ethnarch of King Aretas put guards round the city to catch 33 me, ·and I had to be let down over the wall in a hamper, through a window, in order to escape.

12 Must I go on boasting, though there is nothing to be gained by it? But I will move on to the visions and revela- 2 tions I have had from the Lord. ·I know a man in Christ who, fourteen years ago, was caught up—whether still in the body or out of the body, I do not know; God knows—right into

10 a. Jr 9:23

3 the third heaven.ᵃ ·I do know, however, that this same person—whether in the body or out of the body, I do not know;
4 God knows—·was caught up into paradise and heard things
5 which must not and cannot be put into human language. ·I will boast about a man like that, but not about anything of
6 my own except my weaknesses. ·If I should decide to boast, I should not be made to look foolish, because I should only be speaking the truth; but I am not going to, in case anyone should begin to think I am better than he can actually see and hear me to be.

7 In view of the extraordinary nature of these revelations, to stop me from getting too proud I was given a thorn in the flesh, an angel of Satan to beat me and stop me from getting
8 too proud! ·About this thing, I have pleaded with the Lord
9 three times for it to leave me, ·but he has said, 'My grace is enough for you: my power is at its best in weakness'. So I shall be very happy to make my weaknesses my special boast
10 so that the power of Christ may stay over me, ·and that is why I am quite content with my weaknesses, and with insults, hardships, persecutions, and the agonies I go through for Christ's sake. For it is when I am weak that I am strong.

11 I have been talking like a fool, but you forced me to do it: you are the ones who should have been commending me. Though I am a nobody, there is not a thing these arch-
12 apostles have that I do not have as well. ·You have seen done among you all the things that mark the true apostle, un-
13 failingly produced: the signs, the marvels, the miracles. ·Is there anything of which you have had less than the other churches have had, except that I have not myself been a
14 burden on you? For this unfairness, please forgive me. ·I am all prepared now to come to you for the third time, and I am not going to be a burden on you: it is you I want, not your possessions. Children are not expected to save up for their
15 parents, but parents for children. ·I am perfectly willing to spend what I have, and to be expended, in the interests of your souls. Because I love you more, must I be loved the less?

16 All very well, you say: I personally put no pressure on you, but like the cunning fellow that I am, I took you in by a
17 trick. ·So we exploited you, did we, through one of the men
18 that I have sent to you? ·Well, Titus went at my urging, and I sent the brother that came with him. Can Titus have exploited you? You know that he and I have always been guided by the same spirit and trodden in the same tracks.

Paul's fears and anxieties

19 All this time you have been thinking that our defence is addressed to you, but it is before God that we, in Christ, are speaking; and it is all, my dear brothers, for your benefit.
20 What I am afraid of is that when I come I may find you different from what I want you to be, and you may find that I am not as you would like me to be; and then there will be wrangling, jealousy, and tempers roused, intrigues and back-
21 biting and gossip, obstinacies and disorder. ·I am afraid that on my next visit, my God may make me ashamed on your account and I shall be grieving over all those who sinned before and have still not repented of the impurities, fornication and debauchery they committed.

13 This will be the third time I have come to you. *The evidence of three, or at least two, witnesses is necessary to sustain the*
2 *charge.*[a] ·I gave warning when I was with you the second time and I give warning now, too, before I come, to those who sinned before and to any others, that when I come again,
3 I shall have no mercy. ·You want proof, you say, that it is Christ speaking in me: you have known him not as a weak-
4 ling, but as a power among you? ·Yes, but he was crucified through weakness, and still he lives now through the power of God. So then, we are weak, as he was, but we shall live with him, through the power of God, for your benefit.

5 Examine yourselves to make sure you are in the faith; test yourselves. Do you acknowledge that Jesus Christ is really in
6 you? If not, you have failed the test, ·but we, as I hope you
7 will come to see, have not failed it. ·We pray to God that you will do nothing wrong: not that we want to appear as the ones who have been successful—we would rather that you
8 did well even though we failed. ·We have no power to resist
9 the truth; only to further it. ·We are only too glad to be weak provided you are strong. What we ask in our prayers is for
10 you to be made perfect. ·That is why I am writing this from a distance, so that when I am with you I shall not need to be strict, with the authority which the Lord gave me for building up and not for destroying.

12 a. I.e. the highest heaven.
13 a. Dt 19:15

CONCLUSION

Recommendations. Greetings. Final good wishes

11   In the meantime, brothers, we wish you happiness; try to grow perfect; help one another. Be united; live in peace, and the God of love and peace will be with you.

12   Greet one another with the holy kiss. All the saints send you greetings.

13   The grace of the Lord Jesus Christ, the love of God and the fellowship of the Holy Spirit be with you all.

GALATIANS

THE LETTER OF PAUL

TO THE CHURCH OF GALATIA

Address

1 From Paul to the churches of Galatia, and from all the brothers who are here with me, an apostle who does not owe his authority to men or his appointment to any human being but who has been appointed by Jesus Christ and by God the **3** Father who raised Jesus from the dead. ·We wish you the grace and peace of God our Father and of the Lord Jesus **4** Christ, ·who in order to rescue us from this present wicked world sacrificed himself for our sins, in accordance with the **5** will of God our Father, ·to whom be glory for ever and ever. Amen.

A warning

6 I am astonished at the promptness with which you have turned away from the one who called you and have decided to **7** follow a different version of the Good News. ·Not that there can be more than one Good News; it is merely that some troublemakers among you want to change the Good News of **8** Christ; ·and let me warn you that if anyone preaches a version of the Good News different from the one we have already preached to you, whether it be ourselves or an angel from **9** heaven, he is to be condemned. ·I am only repeating what we told you before: if anyone preaches a version of the Good News different from the one you have already heard, he is to **10** be condemned. ·So now whom am I trying to please—man, or God? Would you say it is men's approval I am looking for?[a] If I still wanted that, I should not be what I am—a servant of Christ.

1 a. Probably a rejoinder to an accusation by the judaisers that Paul was trying to make the pagans' conversion easy by not insisting on circumcision.

I. PAUL'S APOLOGIA

God's call

11 The fact is, brothers, and I want you to realise this, the
12 Good News I preached is not a human message ·that I was
given by men, it is something I learnt only through a revela-
13 tion of Jesus Christ. ·You must have heard of my career as a
practising Jew, how merciless I was in persecuting the Church
14 of God, how much damage I did to it, ·how I stood out
among other Jews of my generation, and how enthusiastic
I was for the traditions of my ancestors.
15 Then God, who had specially *chosen* me while I was *still in*
16 *my mother's womb*,[b] called me through his grace and chose ·to
reveal his Son in me, so that I might preach the Good News
about him to the pagans. I did not stop to discuss this with
17 any human being, ·nor did I go up to Jerusalem to see those
who were already apostles before me, but I went off to
Arabia[c] at once and later went straight back from there to
18 Damascus. ·Even when after three years I went up to Jeru-
19 salem to visit Cephas and stayed with him for fifteen days, ·I
did not see any of the other apostles; I only saw James, the
20 brother of the Lord, ·and I swear before God that what I
21 have just written is the literal truth. ·After that I went to
22 Syria and Cilicia, ·and was still not known by sight to the
23 churches of Christ in Judaea, ·who had heard nothing except
that their one-time persecutor was now preaching the faith
24 he had previously tried to destroy; ·and they gave glory to
God for me.

The meeting at Jerusalem

2 It was not till fourteen years had passed that I went up to
Jerusalem again. I went with Barnabas and took Titus with
2 me. ·I went there as the result of a revelation, and privately I
laid before the leading men the Good News as I proclaim it
among the pagans; I did so for fear the course I was adopting
3 or had already adopted would not be allowed. ·And what
happened? Even though Titus who had come with me is a
4 Greek, he was not obliged to be circumcised. ·The question
came up only because some who do not really belong to the
brotherhood have furtively crept in to spy on the liberty we
5 enjoy in Christ Jesus, and want to reduce us all to slavery. ·I
was so determined to safeguard for you the true meaning of
the Good News, that I refused even out of deference to yield
6 to such people for one moment. ·As a result, these people

who are acknowledged leaders—not that their importance
matters to me, since God has no favourites—these leaders, as
I say, had nothing to add to the Good News as I preach it.
7 On the contrary, they recognised that I had been commissioned to preach the Good News to the uncircumcised
just as Peter had been commissioned to preach it to the
8 circumcised. ·The same person whose action had made Peter
the apostle of the circumcised had given me a similar mission
9 to the pagans. ·So, James, Cephas and John, these leaders,
these pillars, shook hands with Barnabas and me as a sign of
partnership: we were to go to the pagans and they to the
10 circumcised.ᵃ ·The only thing they insisted on was that we
should remember to help the poor, as indeed I was anxious
to do.

Peter and Paul at Antioch

11 When Cephas came to Antioch, however, I opposed him
12 to his face, since he was manifestly in the wrong. ·His
custom had been to eat with the pagans,ᵇ but after certain
friends of James arrived he stopped doing this and kept away
from them altogether for fear of the group that insisted on
13 circumcision. ·The other Jews joined him in this pretence,
and even Barnabas felt himself obliged to copy their behaviour.
14 When I saw they were not respecting the true meaning of
the Good News, I said to Cephas in front of everyone, 'In
spite of being a Jew, you live like the pagans and not like the
Jews, so you have no right to make the pagans copy Jewish
ways'.

The Good News as proclaimed by Paul

15
16 'Though we were born Jews and not pagan sinners, ·we
acknowledge that what makes a man righteous is not
obedience to the Law, but faith in Jesus Christ. We had to
become believers in Christ Jesus no less than you had, and
now we hold that faith in Christ rather than fidelity to the
Law is what justifies us, and that *no one can be justified*ᶜ by
17 keeping the Law. ·Now if we were to admit that the result of
looking to Christ to justify us is to make us sinners like the
rest, it would follow that Christ had induced us to sin, which

b. Is. 49:1 c. Probably the kingdom of the Nabataean Arabs, to the
S. of Damascus.
2 a. The distinction is geographical rather than racial; when Paul went
among the Gentiles the resident Jews were his first concern. b. Converts
from paganism. c. Ps 143:2

18 would be absurd. ·If I were to return to a position I had already abandoned, I should be admitting I had done some-
19 thing wrong. ·In other words, through the Law I am dead to the Law, so that now I can live for God. I have been crucified
20 with Christ, ·and I live now not with my own life but with the life of Christ who lives in me. The life I now live in this body I live in faith: faith in the Son of God who loved me and who
21 sacrificed himself for my sake. ·I cannot bring myself to give up God's gift: if the Law can justify us, there is no point in the death of Christ.'

II. DOCTRINAL MATTERS

Justification by faith

3   Are you people in Galatia mad? Has someone put a spell on you, in spite of the plain explanation you have had of the
2 crucifixion of Jesus Christ? ·Let me ask you one question: was it because you practised the Law that you received the Spirit, or because you believed what was preached to you?
3 Are you foolish enough to end in outward observances what
4 you began in the Spirit? ·Have all the favours you received been wasted? And if this were so, they would most certainly
5 have been wasted. ·Does God give you the Spirit so freely and work miracles among you because you practise the Law, or because you believed what was preached to you?
6   Take Abraham for example: *he put his faith in God, and*
7 *this faith was considered as justifying him.*[a] ·Don't you see that it is those who rely on faith who are the sons of Abra-
8 ham? ·Scripture foresaw that God was going to use faith to justify the pagans, and proclaimed the Good News long ago when Abraham was told: *In you all the pagans will be blessed.*[b]
9 Those therefore who rely on faith receive the same blessing as Abraham, the man of faith.

The curse brought by the Law

10   On the other hand, those who rely on the keeping of the Law are under a curse, since scripture says: *Cursed be every-one who does not persevere in observing everything prescribed*
11 *in the book of the Law.*[c] ·The Law will not justify anyone in the sight of God, because we are told: *the righteous man finds*
12 *life through faith.*[d] ·The Law is not even based on faith, since we are told: *The man who practises these precepts finds life*
13 *through practising them.*[e] ·Christ redeemed us from the curse of the Law by being cursed for our sake, since scripture says:
14 *Cursed be everyone who is hanged on a tree.*[f] ·This was done

so that in Christ Jesus the blessing of Abraham might include the pagans, and so that through faith we might receive the promised Spirit.

The Law did not cancel the promise

15 Compare this, brothers, with what happens in ordinary life. If a will has been drawn up in due form, no one is
16 allowed to disregard it or add to it. ·Now the promises were addressed to Abraham *and to his descendants*—notice, in passing, that scripture does not use a plural word as if there were several descendants, it uses the singular: to his posterity,
17 which is Christ. ·But my point is this: once God had expressed his will in due form, no law that came four hundred and thirty years later could cancel that and make the promise
18 meaningless. ·If you inherit something as a legal right, it does not come to you as the result of a promise, and it was precisely in the form of a promise that God made his gift to Abraham.

The purpose of the Law

19 What then was the purpose of adding the Law? This was done to specify crimes, until the posterity came to whom the promise was addressed. The Law was promulgated by
20 angels,[g] assisted by an intermediary. ·Now there can only be
21 an intermediary between two parties, yet God is one. ·Does this mean that there is opposition between the Law and the promises of God? Of course not. We could have been justified by the Law if we were given had been capable of
22 giving life, ·but it is not: scripture makes no exceptions when it says that sin is master everywhere. In this way the promise can only be given through faith in Jesus Christ and can only be given to those who have this faith.

The coming of faith

23 Before faith came, we were allowed no freedom by the
24 Law; we were being looked after till faith was revealed. ·The Law was to be our guardian until the Christ came and we
25 could be justified by faith. ·Now that that time has come we
26 are no longer under that guardian, ·and you are, all of you,
27 sons of God through faith in Christ Jesus. ·All baptised in
28 Christ, you have all clothed yourselves in Christ, ·and there are no more distinctions between Jew and Greek, slave and

3 a. Gn 15:6 b. Gn 12:3 c. Dt 27:26 d. Hab 2:4 e. Lv 18:5 f. Dt 21:23 g. In Jewish tradition angels were present at Sinai; the 'intermediary' is Moses.

free, male and female, but all of you are one in Christ Jesus.
29 Merely by belonging to Christ you are the posterity of Abraham, the heirs he was promised.

Sons of God

4 Let me put this another way: an heir, even if he has actually inherited everything, is no different from a slave for as long
2 as he remains a child. ·He is under the control of guardians and administrators until he reaches the age fixed by his
3 father. ·Now before we came of age we were as good as slaves
4 to the elemental principles of this world,*ª* ·but when the appointed time came, God sent his Son, born of a woman,
5 born a subject of the Law, ·to redeem the subjects of the Law
6 and to enable us to be adopted as sons. ·The proof that you are sons is that God has sent the Spirit of his Son into our
7 hearts: the Spirit that cries, 'Abba, Father', ·and it is this that makes you a son, you are not a slave any more; and if God has made you son, then he has made you heir.
8 Once you were ignorant of God, and enslaved to 'gods'
9 who are not really gods at all; ·but now that you have come to acknowledge God—or rather, now that God has acknowledged you—how can you want to go back to elemental things like these, that can do nothing and give nothing, and
10 be their slaves? ·You and your special days and months and
11 seasons and years! ·You make me feel I have wasted my time with you.

A personal appeal

12 Brothers, all I ask is that you should copy me as I copied you. You have never treated me in an unfriendly way before;
13 even at the beginning, when that illness gave me the oppor-
14 tunity to preach the Good News to you, ·you never showed the least sign of being revolted or disgusted by my disease that was such a trial to you; instead you welcomed me as an
15 angel of God, as if I were Christ Jesus himself. ·What has become of this enthusiasm you had? I swear that you would even have gone so far as to pluck out your eyes and give
16 them to me. ·Is it telling you the truth that has made me
17 your enemy? ·The blame lies in the way they have tried to win you over: by separating you from me, they want to win
18 you over to themselves. ·It is always a good thing to win people over—and I do not have to be there with you—but it
19 must be for a good purpose, ·my children! I must go through the pain of giving birth to you all over again, until Christ is
20 formed in you. ·I wish I were with you now so that I could

know exactly what to say; as it is, I have no idea what to do
for the best.

The two covenants: Hagar and Sarah

21 You want to be subject to the Law? Then listen to what the
22 Law says. ·It says, if you remember, that Abraham had two
    sons, one by the slave-girl, and one by his free-born wife.
23 The child of the slave-girl was born in the ordinary way; the
    child of the free woman was born as the result of a promise.
24 This can be regarded as an allegory: the women stand for the
    two covenants. The first who comes from Mount Sinai, and
25 whose children are slaves, is Hagar—·since Sinai is in Arabia
    —and she corresponds to the present Jerusalem that is a slave
26 like her children. ·The Jerusalem above, however, is free and
27 is our mother, ·since scripture says: *Shout for joy, you barren
    women who bore no children! Break into shouts of joy and
    gladness, you who were never in labour. For there are more*
28 *sons of the forsaken one than sons of the wedded wife.*[b] ·Now
29 you, my brothers, like Isaac, are children of the promise, ·and
    as at that time the child born in the ordinary way persecuted
30 the child born in the Spirit's way, so also now. ·Does not
    scripture say: *Drive away that slave-girl and her son; this
    slave-girl's son is not to share the inheritance with the son*[c] of
31 the free woman? ·So, my brothers, we are the children, not of
    the slave-girl, but of the free-born wife.

III. EXHORTATION

Christian liberty

5 When Christ freed us, he meant us to remain free. Stand
   firm, therefore, and do not submit again to the yoke of
2 slavery. ·It is I, Paul, who tell you this: if you allow yourselves
   to be circumcised, Christ will be of no benefit to you at all.
3 With all solemnity I repeat my warning: Everyone who
4 accepts circumcision is obliged to keep the whole Law. ·But
   if you do look to the Law to make you justified, then you
   have separated yourselves from Christ, and have fallen from
5 grace. ·Christians are told by the Spirit to look to faith for
6 those rewards that righteousness hopes for, ·since in Christ
   Jesus whether you are circumcised or not makes no difference—what matters is faith that makes its power felt through
   love.
7 You began your race well: who made you less anxious to

---

4 a. The principles that make up the physical universe; Paul has related the Law to 'outward observances', 3:3. **b.** Is 54:1 **c.** Gn 21:10

8 obey the truth? ·You were not prompted by him who called
9 you! ·The yeast seems to be spreading through the whole
10 batch of you. ·I feel sure that, united in the Lord, you will
agree with me, and anybody who troubles you in future will
11 be condemned, no matter who he is. ·As for me, my brothers,
if I still preach circumcision,[a] why am I still persecuted? If I
12 did that now, would there be any scandal of the cross? ·Tell
those who are disturbing you I would like to see the knife
slip.

Liberty and charity

13 My brothers, you were called, as you know, to liberty; but
be careful, or this liberty will provide an opening for self-
indulgence. Serve one another, rather, in works of love,
14 since the whole of the Law is summarised in a single com-
15 mand: *Love your neighbour as yourself*.[b] ·If you go snapping
at each other and tearing each other to pieces, you had better
watch or you will destroy the whole community.
16 Let me put it like this: if you are guided by the Spirit you
17 will be in no danger of yielding to self-indulgence, ·since self-
indulgence is the opposite of the Spirit, the Spirit is totally
against such a thing, and it is precisely because the two are so
opposed that you do not always carry out your good inten-
18 tions. ·If you are led by the Spirit, no law can touch you.
19 When self-indulgence is at work the results are obvious:
fornication, gross indecency and sexual irresponsibility;
20 idolatry and sorcery; feuds and wrangling, jealousy, bad
21 temper and quarrels; disagreements, factions, ·envy; drunkenness, orgies and similar things. I warn you now, as I
warned you before: those who behave like this will not in-
22 herit the kingdom of God. ·What the Spirit brings is very
different: love, joy, peace, patience, kindness, goodness,
23 trustfulness, ·gentleness and self-control. There can be no
24 law against things like that, of course. ·You cannot belong to
Christ Jesus unless you crucify all self-indulgent passions and
desires.
25 Since the Spirit is our life, let us be directed by the Spirit.
26 We must stop being conceited, provocative and envious.

On kindness and perseverance

6 Brothers, if one of you misbehaves, the more spiritual of
you who set him right should do so in a spirit of gentleness,
2 not forgetting that you may be tempted yourselves. ·You
should carry each other's troubles and fulfil the law of
3 Christ. ·It is the people who are not important who often

4 make the mistake of thinking that they are. ·Let each of you examine his own conduct; if you find anything to boast about, it will at least be something of your own, not just
5 something better than your neighbour has. ·Everyone has his own burden to carry.

6 People under instruction should always contribute something to the support of the man who is instructing them.

7 Don't delude yourself into thinking God can be cheated:
8 where a man sows, there he reaps: ·if he sows in the field of self-indulgence he will get a harvest of corruption out of it; if he sows in the field of the Spirit he will get from it a harvest
9 of eternal life. ·We must never get tired of doing good because if we don't give up the struggle we shall get our harvest
10 at the proper time. ·While we have the chance, we must do good to all, and especially to our brothers in the faith.

Epilogue

11 Take good note of what I am adding in my own hand-
12 writing and in large letters. ·It is only self-interest that makes them want to force circumcision on you—they want to
13 escape persecution for the cross of Christ—·they accept circumcision but do not keep the Law themselves; they only want you to be circumcised so that they can boast of the fact.
14 As for me, the only thing I can boast about is the cross of our Lord Jesus Christ, through whom the world is crucified to
15 me, and I to the world. ·It does not matter if a person is circumcised or not; what matters is for him to become an
16 altogether new creature. ·Peace and mercy to all who follow this rule, who form the Israel of God.
17 I want no more trouble from anybody after this; the marks
18 on my body are those of Jesus. ·The grace of our Lord Jesus Christ be with your spirit, my brothers. Amen.

5 a. As Paul's enemies were apparently claiming. **b.** Lv 19:18

EPHESIANS

THE LETTER OF PAUL

TO THE CHURCH AT EPHESUS

Address and Greetings

1 From Paul, appointed by God to be an apostle of Christ
2 Jesus, to the saints who are faithful to Christ Jesus: ·Grace
and peace to you from God our Father and from the Lord
Jesus Christ.

I. THE MYSTERY OF SALVATION AND OF THE CHURCH

God's plan of salvation

3   Blessed be God the Father of our Lord Jesus Christ,
    who has blessed us with all the spiritual blessings of
       heaven in Christ.
4   Before the world was made, he chose us, chose us in
       Christ,
    to be holy and spotless, and to live through love in his
       presence,
5   determining that we should become his adopted sons,
       through Jesus Christ
    for his own kind purposes,
6   to make us praise the glory of his grace,
    his free gift to us in the Beloved,
7   in whom, through his blood, we gain our freedom, the
       forgiveness of our sins.
    Such is the richness of the grace
8   which he has showered on us
    in all wisdom and insight.
9   He has let us know the mystery of his purpose,
    the hidden plan he so kindly made in Christ from the
       beginning
10   to act upon when the times had run their course to the
       end:

that he would bring everything together under Christ,
as head,
everything in the heavens and everything on earth.

11 And it is in him that we were claimed as God's own,
chosen from the beginning,
under the predetermined plan of the one who guides all
things
as he decides by his own will;

12 chosen to be,
for his greater glory,
the people who would put their hopes in Christ before
he came.

13 Now you too, in him,
have heard the message of the truth and the good news
of your salvation,
and have believed it;
and you too have been stamped with the seal of the
Holy Spirit of the Promise,

14 the pledge of our inheritance
which brings freedom for those whom God has taken
for his own,
to make his glory praised.

The triumph and the supremacy of Christ

15 That will explain why I, having once heard about your
faith in the Lord Jesus, and the love that you show towards
16 all the saints, ·have never failed to remember you in my
17 prayers and to thank God for you. ·May the God of our Lord
Jesus Christ, the Father of glory, give you a spirit of wisdom
and perception of what is revealed, to bring you to full
18 knowledge of him. ·May he enlighten the eyes of your mind
so that you can see what hope his call holds for you, what
19 rich glories he has promised the saints will inherit ·and how
infinitely great is the power that he has exercised for us
believers. This you can tell from the strength of his power
20 at work in Christ, when he used it to raise him from the dead
21 and to make him sit at his right hand, in heaven, ·far above
Sovereignty, Authority, Power, or Domination,*ᵃ* or any
other name that can be named, not only in this age but also
22 in the age to come. ·*He has put all things under his feet,*ᵇ and
made him, as the ruler of everything, the head of the Church;
23 which is his body, the fullness of him who fills the whole
creation.

1 a. Orders of the angelic hierarchy in Jewish literature. b. Ps 8:6

Salvation in Christ a free gift

2 And you were dead, through the crimes and the sins ·in which you used to live when you were following the way of this world, obeying the ruler who governs the air,[a] the spirit

3 who is at work in the rebellious. ·We all were among them too in the past, living sensual lives, ruled entirely by our own physical desires and our own ideas; so that by nature we

4 were as much under God's anger as the rest of the world. ·But God loved us with so much love that he was generous with

5 his mercy: ·when we were dead through our sins, he brought us to life with Christ—it is through grace that you have been

6 saved—·and raised us up with him and gave us a place with him in heaven, in Christ Jesus.

7 This was to show for all ages to come, through his goodness towards us in Christ Jesus, how infinitely rich he is in

8 grace. ·Because it is by grace that you have been saved, through faith; not by anything of your own, but by a gift

9 from God; ·not by anything that you have done, so that

10 nobody can claim the credit. ·We are God's work of art, created in Christ Jesus to live the good life as from the beginning he had meant us to live it.

Reconciliation of the Jews and the pagans with each other and with God

11 Do not forget, then, that there was a time when you who were pagans physically, termed the Uncircumcised by those who speak of themselves as the Circumcision by reason of a

12 physical operation, ·do not forget, I say, that you had no Christ and were excluded from membership of Israel, aliens with no part in the covenants with their Promise; you were immersed in this world, without hope and without God.

13 But now in Christ Jesus, you that used to be so far apart from us have been brought very close, by the blood of Christ.

14 For he is the peace between us, and has made the two into one and broken down the barrier which used to keep them apart, actually destroying in his own person the hostility

15 caused by the rules and decrees of the Law. This was to create one single New Man in himself out of the two of them

16 and by restoring peace ·through the cross, to unite them both in a single Body and reconcile them with God. In his own

17 person he killed the hostility. ·Later he came to bring the good news of peace, *peace to you who were far away and peace*

18 *to those who were near at hand.*[b] ·Through him, both of us have in the one Spirit our way to come to the Father.

19 So you are no longer aliens or foreign visitors: you are
20 citizens like all the saints, and part of God's household. ·You
are part of a building that has the apostles and prophets*c* for
its foundations, and Christ Jesus himself for its main corner-
21 stone. ·As every structure is aligned on him, all grow into one
22 holy temple in the Lord; ·and you too, in him, are being built
into a house where God lives, in the Spirit.

Paul, a servant of the mystery

3 So I, Paul, a prisoner of Christ Jesus for the sake of you
2 pagans ... ·You have probably heard how I have been
3 entrusted by God with the grace he meant for you, ·and that
it was by a revelation that I was given the knowledge of the
4 mystery, as I have just described it very shortly. ·If you read
my words, you will have some idea of the depths that I see in
5 the mystery of Christ. ·This mystery that has now been
revealed through the Spirit to his holy apostles and prophets
6 was unknown to any men in past generations; ·it means that
pagans now share the same inheritance, that they are parts of
the same body, and that the same promise has been made to
7 them, in Christ Jesus, through the gospel. ·I have been made
the servant of that gospel by a gift of grace from God who
8 gave it to me by his own power. ·I, who am less than the least
of all the saints, have been entrusted with this special grace,
not only of proclaiming to the pagans the infinite treasure of
9 Christ ·but also of explaining how the mystery is to be
dispensed. Through all the ages, this has been kept hidden in
10 God, the creator of everything. Why? ·So that the Sovereignties and Powers should learn only now, through the Church,
11 how comprehensive God's wisdom really is, ·exactly according to the plan which he had had from all eternity in Christ
12 Jesus our Lord. ·This is why we are bold enough to approach
13 God in complete confidence, through our faith in him; ·so,
I beg you, never lose confidence just because of the trials that
I go through on your account: they are your glory.

Paul's prayer

14 This, then, is what I pray, kneeling before the Father,
15 from whom every family,*a* whether spiritual or natural, takes
its name:
16 Out of his infinite glory, may he give you the power through
17 his Spirit for your hidden self to grow strong, ·so that Christ

2 a. Satan. b. Is 57:19 c. The N.T. prophets.
3 a. A pun on the words 'Father' and 'family' (clan or tribe) is lost in
translation; traces of it survive in *paternity* and *patriotism*.

may live in your hearts through faith, and then, planted in
18 love and built on love, ·you will with all the saints have
strength to grasp the breadth and the length, the height and
19 the depth; ·until, knowing the love of Christ, which is beyond
all knowledge, you are filled with the utter fullness of God.

20 Glory be to him whose power, working in us, can do
21 infinitely more than we can ask or imagine; ·glory be to him
from generation to generation in the Church and in Christ
Jesus for ever and ever. Amen.

II. EXHORTATION

A call to unity

4 I, the prisoner in the Lord, implore you therefore to lead a
2 life worthy of your vocation. ·Bear with one another charit-
3 ably, in complete selflessness, gentleness and patience. ·Do all
you can to preserve the unity of the Spirit by the peace that
4 binds you together. ·There is one Body, one Spirit, just as
you were all called into one and the same hope when you
5 were called. ·There is one Lord, one faith, one baptism, ·and
6 one God who is Father of all, over all, through all and within
all.

7 Each one of us, however, has been given his own share of
8 grace, given as Christ allotted it. ·It was said that he would:

When he ascended to the height, he captured prisoners,
he gave gifts to men.ᵃ

9 When it says, 'he ascended', what can it mean if not that he
10 descended right down to the lower regions of the earth? ·The
one who rose higher than all the heavens to fill all things is
11 none other than the one who descended. ·And to some, his
gift was that they should be apostles; to some, prophets; to
12 some, evangelists; to some, pastors and teachers; ·so that the
saints together make a unity in the work of service, building
13 up the body of Christ. ·In this way we are all to come to
unity in our faith and in our knowledge of the Son of God,
until we become the perfect Man, fully mature with the fullness of Christ himself.

14 Then we shall not be children any longer, or tossed one
way and another and carried along by every wind of doctrine,
at the mercy of all the tricks men play and their cleverness in
15 practising deceit. ·If we live by the truth and in love, we shall
16 grow in all ways into Christ, who is the head ·by whom the
whole body is fitted and joined together, every joint adding
its own strength, for each separate part to work according to

its function. So the body grows until it has built itself up, in love.

The new life in Christ

17 In particular, I want to urge you in the name of the Lord, not to go on living the aimless kind of life that pagans live.
18 Intellectually they are in the dark, and they are estranged from the life of God, without knowledge because they have
19 shut their hearts to it. ·Their sense of right and wrong once dulled, they have abandoned themselves to sexuality and
20 eagerly pursue a career of indecency of every kind. ·Now that
21 is hardly the way you have learnt from Christ, ·unless you failed to hear him properly when you were taught what the
22 truth is in Jesus. ·You must give up your old way of life; you must put aside your old self, which gets corrupted by follow-
23 ing illusory desires. ·Your mind must be renewed by a spiritual
24 revolution ·so that you can put on the new self that has been created in God's way, in the goodness and holiness of the truth.

25 So from now on, there must be no more lies: *You must speak the truth to one another*,[b] since we are all parts of one
26 another. ·*Even if you are angry, you must not sin:*[c] never let
27 the sun set on your anger ·or else you will give the devil a
28 foothold. ·Anyone who was a thief must stop stealing; he should try to find some useful manual work instead, and be able to do some good by helping others that are in need.
29 Guard against foul talk; let your words be for the improve-ment of others, as occasion offers, and do good to your
30 listeners, ·otherwise you will only be grieving the Holy Spirit of God who has marked you with his seal for you to be set
31 free when the day comes. ·Never have grudges against others, or lose your temper, or raise your voice to anybody, or call
32 each other names, or allow any sort of spitefulness. ·Be friends with one another, and kind, forgiving each other as readily as God forgave you in Christ.

5 Try, then, to imitate God, as children of his that he loves,
2 and follow Christ by loving as he loved you, giving himself up in our place *as a fragrant offering and a sacrifice to God.*[a]
3 Among you there must be not even a mention of fornication or impurity in any of its forms, or promiscuity: this would
4 hardly become the saints! ·There must be no coarseness, or salacious talk and jokes—all this is wrong for you; raise your
5 voices in thanksgiving instead. ·For you can be quite certain

4 a. Ps 68:18 b. Zc 8:16 c. Ps 4:4 (LXX)
5 a. Ex 29:18

that nobody who actually indulges in fornication or impurity
or promiscuity—which is worshipping a false god—can
6 inherit anything of the kingdom of God. ·Do not let anyone
deceive you with empty arguments: it is for this loose living
that God's anger comes down on those who rebel against
7 him. ·Make sure that you are not included with them.
8 You were darkness once, but now you are light in the Lord;
9 be like children of light, ·for the effects of the light are seen in
10 complete goodness and right living and truth. ·Try to dis-
11 cover what the Lord wants of you, ·having nothing to do
with the futile works of darkness but exposing them by
12 contrast. ·The things which are done in secret are things that
13 people are ashamed even to speak of; ·but anything exposed
14 by the light will be illuminated ·and anything illuminated
turns into light. That is why it is said:[b]

> Wake up from your sleep,
> rise from the dead,
> and Christ will shine on you.

15 So be very careful about the sort of lives you lead, like intelli-
16 gent and not like senseless people. ·This may be a wicked age,
17 but your lives should redeem it. ·And do not be thoughtless
18 but recognise what is the will of the Lord. ·Do not drug
yourselves with wine, this is simply dissipation; be filled with
19 the Spirit. ·Sing the words and tunes of the psalms and hymns
when you are together, and go on singing and chanting to the
20 Lord in your hearts, ·so that always and everywhere you are
giving thanks to God who is our Father in the name of our
Lord Jesus Christ.

The morals of the home

21
22　　Give way to one another in obedience to Christ. ·Wives
should regard their husbands as they regard the Lord,
23 since as Christ is head of the Church and saves the whole
24 body, so is a husband the head of his wife; ·and as the
Church submits to Christ, so should wives to their husbands,
25 in everything. ·Husbands should love their wives just as
26 Christ loved the Church and sacrificed himself for her ·to
make her holy. He made her clean by washing her in water
27 with a form of words, ·so that when he took her to himself
she would be glorious, with no speck or wrinkle or anything
28 like that, but holy and faultless. ·In the same way, husbands
must love their wives as they love their own bodies; for a man
29 to love his wife is for him to love himself. ·A man never hates
his own body, but he feeds it and looks after it; and that is

30 the way Christ treats the Church, ·because it is his body—
31 and we are its living parts. ·*For this reason, a man must leave
his father and mother and be joined to his wife, and the two will*
32 *become one body.*[c] ·This mystery has many implications; but
33 I am saying it applies to Christ and the Church. ·To sum up;
you too, each one of you, must love his wife as he loves
himself; and let every wife respect her husband.

6   Children, be obedient to your parents in the Lord—that is
2 your duty. ·The first commandment that has a promise
3 attached to it is: *Honour your father and mother,* ·and the
promise is: *and you will prosper and have a long life in the*
4 *land.*[a] ·And parents, never drive your children to resentment
but in bringing them up correct them and guide them as the
Lord does.

5   Slaves, be obedient to the men who are called your masters
in this world, with deep respect and sincere loyalty, as you
6 are obedient to Christ: ·not only when you are under their
eye, as if you had only to please men, but because you are
slaves of Christ and wholeheartedly do the will of God.
7 Work hard and willingly, but do it for the sake of the Lord
8 and not for the sake of men. ·You can be sure that everyone,
whether a slave or a free man, will be properly rewarded by
9 the Lord for whatever work he has done well. ·And those of
you who are employers, treat your slaves in the same spirit;
do without threats, remembering that they and you have the
same Master in heaven and he is not impressed by one person
more than by another.

The spiritual war

10   Finally, grow strong in the Lord, with the strength of his
11 power. ·Put God's armour on so as to be able to resist the
12 devil's tactics. ·For it is not against human enemies that we
have to struggle, but against the Sovereignties and the Powers
who originate the darkness in this world, the spiritual army
13 of evil in the heavens. ·That is why you must rely on God's
armour, or you will not be able to put up any resistance when
the worst happens, or have enough resources to hold your
ground.

14   So stand your ground, with *truth buckled round your waist,*
15 and *integrity for a breastplate,*[b] ·wearing for shoes on your
16 feet *the eagerness to spread the gospel of peace*[c] ·and always
carrying the shield of faith so that you can use it to put out
17 the burning arrows of the evil one. ·And then you must

b. Presumably a quotation from a Christian hymn. **c.** Gn 2:24
6 a. Ex 20:12 **b.** Is 59:17 **c.** Is 40:9

accept *salvation from God to be your helmet* and receive the word of God from the Spirit to use as a sword.

18   Pray all the time, asking for what you need, praying in the Spirit on every possible occasion. Never get tired of staying

19 awake to pray for all the saints; ·and pray for me to be given an opportunity to open my mouth and speak without fear

20 and give out the mystery of the gospel ·of which I am an ambassador in chains; pray that in proclaiming it I may speak as boldly as I ought to.

Personal news and final salutation

21   I should like you to know, as well, what is happening to me and what I am doing; my dear brother Tychicus, my loyal

22 helper in the Lord, will tell you everything. ·I am sending him to you precisely for this purpose, to give you news about us and reassure you.

23   May God the Father and the Lord Jesus Christ grant

24 peace, love and faith to all the brothers. ·May grace and eternal life be with all who love our Lord Jesus Christ.

PHILIPPIANS

THE LETTER OF PAUL

TO THE CHURCH AT PHILIPPI

Address

1   From Paul and Timothy, servants of Christ Jesus, to all
the saints in Christ Jesus, together with their presiding elders
2 and deacons. ·We wish you the grace and peace of God our
Father and of the Lord Jesus Christ.

Thanksgiving and prayer

3
4   I thank my God whenever I think of you; and ·every time
5 I pray for all of you, I pray with joy, ·remembering how you
have helped to spread the Good News from the day you first
6 heard it right up to the present. ·I am quite certain that the
One who began this good work in you will see that it is
7 finished when the Day of Christ Jesus comes. ·It is only
natural that I should feel like this towards you all, since you
have shared the privileges which have been mine: both my
chains and my work defending and establishing the gospel.
8 You have a permanent place in my heart, ·and God knows
how much I miss you all, loving you as Christ Jesus loves
9 you. ·My prayer is that your love for each other may increase
more and more and never stop improving your knowledge
10 and deepening your perception ·so that you can always
recognise what is best. This will help you to become pure and
11 blameless, and prepare you for the Day of Christ, ·when you
will reach the perfect goodness which Jesus Christ produces
in us for the glory and praise of God.

Paul's own circumstances

12   I am glad to tell you, brothers, that the things that happened to me have actually been a help to the Good News.
13   My chains, in Christ, have become famous not only all
14 over the Praetorium but everywhere, ·and most of the
brothers have taken courage in the Lord from these chains of
mine and are getting more and more daring in announcing

15 the Message without any fear. ·It is true that some of them are doing it just out of rivalry and competition, but the rest

16 preach Christ with the right intention, ·out of nothing but love, as they know that this is my invariable way of defending

17 the gospel. ·The others, who proclaim Christ for jealous or selfish motives, do not mind if they make my chains heavier

18 to bear. ·But does it matter? Whether from dishonest motives or in sincerity, Christ is proclaimed; and that makes

19 me happy; ·and I shall continue being happy, because I know *this will help to save me,*[a] thanks to your prayers and to the

20 help which will be given to me by the Spirit of Jesus. ·My one hope and trust is that I shall never have to admit defeat, but that now as always I shall have the courage for Christ to be glorified in my body, whether by my life or by my death.

21 Life to me, of course, is Christ, but then death would bring

22 me something more; ·but then again, if living in this body means doing work which is having good results—I do not

23 know what I should choose. ·I am caught in this dilemma: I want to be gone and be with Christ, which would be very

24 much the better, ·but for me to stay alive in this body is a

25 more urgent need for your sake. ·This weighs with me so much that I feel sure I shall survive and stay with you all, and help you to progress in the faith and even increase your joy

26 in it; ·and so you will have another reason to give praise to Christ Jesus on my account when I am with you again.

Fight for the faith

27 Avoid anything in your everyday lives that would be unworthy of the gospel of Christ, so that, whether I come to you and see for myself, or stay at a distance and only hear about you, I shall know that you are unanimous in meeting the attack with firm resistance, united by your love for the

28 faith of the gospel ·and quite unshaken by your enemies. This would be the sure sign that they will lose and you will be

29 saved. It would be a sign from God ·that he has given you the privilege not only of believing in Christ, but of suffering for

30 him as well. ·You and I are together in the same fight as you saw me fighting before and, as you will have heard, I am fighting still.

Preserve unity in humility

2 If our life in Christ means anything to you, if love can persuade at all, or the Spirit that we have in common, or any

2 tenderness and sympathy, ·then be united in your convictions and united in your love, with a common purpose and a

common mind. That is the one thing which would make me
3 completely happy. ·There must be no competition among
you, no conceit; but everybody is to be self-effacing. Always
4 consider the other person to be better than yourself, ·so that
nobody thinks of his own interests first but everybody thinks
5 of other people's interests instead. ·In your minds you must
be the same as Christ Jesus:[a]

6   His state was divine,
         yet he did not cling
         to his equality with God
7   but emptied himself
         to assume the condition of a slave,
         and became as men are;
         and being as all men are,
8   he was humbler yet,
         even to accepting death,
         death on a cross.
9   But God raised him high
         and gave him the name
         which is above all other names
10   so that *all beings*
         in the heavens, on earth and in the underworld,
         should bend the knee[b] at the name of Jesus
11   and that every tongue should acclaim
         Jesus Christ as Lord,
         to the glory of God the Father.

Work for salvation

12   So then, my dear friends, continue to do as I tell you, as
you always have; not only as you did when I was there with
you, but even more now that I am no longer there; and work
13 for your salvation 'in fear and trembling'. ·It is God, for his
own loving purpose, who puts both the will and the action
14 into you. ·Do all that has to be done without complaining or
15 arguing ·and then you will be innocent and genuine, *perfect
children of God among a deceitful and underhand brood,*[c] and
16 you will shine in the world like bright stars ·because you are
offering it the word of life. This would give me something
to be proud of for the Day of Christ, and would mean that I
had not run in the race and exhausted myself for nothing.
17 And then, if my blood has to be shed as part of your own

1 a. Jb 13:16 (LXX)
2 a. Vv. 6–11 are a hymn, though whether composed or only quoted
by Paul is uncertain. **b.** Is 45:23 **c.** Dt 32:5

sacrifice and offering—which is your faith[d]—I shall still be
18 happy and rejoice with all of you, ·and you must be just as
happy and rejoice with me.

The mission of Timothy and Epaphroditus

19 I hope, in the Lord Jesus, to send Timothy to you soon, and
20 I shall be reassured by having news of you. ·I have nobody
else like him here, as wholeheartedly concerned for your
21 welfare: ·all the rest seem more interested in themselves than
22 in Jesus Christ. ·But you know how he has proved himself by
working with me on behalf of the Good News like a son
23 helping his father. ·That is why he is the one that I am hoping
to send you, as soon as I know something definite about my
24 fate. ·But I continue to trust, in the Lord, that I shall be
coming soon myself.

25 It is essential, I think, to send brother Epaphroditus back
to you. He was sent as your representative to help me when I
needed someone to be my companion in working and
26 battling, ·but he misses you all and is worried because you
27 heard about his illness. ·It is true that he has been ill, and
almost died, but God took pity on him, and on me as well as
him, and spared me what would have been one grief on top of
28 another. ·So I shall send him back as promptly as I can; you
will be happy to see him again, and that will make me less
29 sorry. ·Give him a most hearty welcome, in the Lord;
30 people like him are to be honoured. ·It was for Christ's work
that he came so near to dying, and he risked his life to give me
the help that you were not able to give me yourselves.

3 Finally, my brothers, rejoice in the Lord.[a]

The true way of Christian salvation

It is no trouble to me to repeat what I have already written
to you, and as far as you are concerned, it will make for
2 safety. ·Beware of dogs! Watch out for the people who are
3 making mischief. Watch out for the cutters.[b] ·We are the real
people of the circumcision, we who worship in accordance
with the Spirit of God; we have our own glory from Christ
4 Jesus without having to rely on a physical operation. ·If it
came to relying on physical evidence, I should be fully
qualified myself. Take any man who thinks he can rely on
5 what is physical: I am even better qualified. ·I was born of the
race of Israel and of the tribe of Benjamin, a Hebrew born of
Hebrew parents, and I was circumcised when I was eight days
6 old. As for the Law, I was a Pharisee; ·as for working for
religion, I was a persecutor of the Church; as far as the Law

7 can make you perfect, I was faultless. ·But because of Christ, I have come to consider all these advantages that I had as
8 disadvantages. ·Not only that, but I believe nothing can happen that will outweigh the supreme advantage of knowing Christ Jesus my Lord. For him I have accepted the loss of everything, and I look on everything as so much rubbish if
9 only I can have Christ ·and be given a place in him. I am no longer trying for perfection by my own efforts, the perfection that comes from the Law, but I want only the perfection that comes through faith in Christ, and is from God and based on
10 faith. ·All I want is to know Christ and the power of his resurrection and to share his sufferings by reproducing the
11 pattern of his death. ·That is the way I can hope to take my
12 place in the resurrection of the dead. ·Not that I have become perfect yet: I have not yet won, but I am still running, trying
13 to capture the prize for which Christ Jesus captured me. ·I can assure you my brothers, I am far from thinking that I have already won. All I can say is that I forget the past and I strain
14 ahead for what is still to come; ·I am racing for the finish, for the prize to which God calls us upwards to receive in Christ
15 Jesus. ·We who are called 'perfect' must all think in this way. If there is some point on which you see things differently,
16 God will make it clear to you; ·meanwhile, let us go forward on the road that has brought us to where we are.

17   My brothers, be united in following my rule of life. Take as your models everybody who is already doing this and study
18 them as you used to study us. ·I have told you often, and I repeat it today with tears, there are many who are behaving
19 as the enemies of the cross of Christ. ·They are destined to be lost. They make foods into their god and they are proudest of something they ought to think shameful; the things they
20 think important are earthly things. ·For us, our homeland is in heaven, and from heaven comes the saviour we are waiting
21 for, the Lord Jesus Christ, ·and he will transfigure these wretched bodies of ours into copies of his glorious body. He will do that by the same power with which he can subdue the whole universe.

4   So then, my brothers and dear friends, do not give way but remain faithful in the Lord. I miss you very much, dear friends; you are my joy and my crown.

d. Libations were common to Greek and Jewish sacrifices.
3 a. Paul's conclusion is interrupted by a long postscript. b. A contemptuous reference to the circumcisers comparing circumcision with self-inflicted gashes in pagan cults.

Last advice

2 I appeal to Evodia and I appeal to Syntyche to come to
3 agreement with each other, in the Lord; ·and I ask you,
Syzygus,[a] to be truly a 'companion' and to help them in this.
These women were a help to me when I was fighting to defend
the Good News—and so, at the same time, were Clement and
the others who worked with me. Their names are written in
the book of life.
4 I want you to be happy, always happy in the Lord; I
5 repeat, what I want is your happiness. ·Let your tolerance be
6 evident to everyone: the Lord is very near. ·There is no need
to worry; but if there is anything you need, pray for it,
7 asking God for it with prayer and thanksgiving, ·and that
peace of God, which is so much greater than we can understand, will guard your hearts and your thoughts, in Christ
8 Jesus. ·Finally, brothers, fill your minds with everything that
is true, everything that is noble, everything that is good and
pure, everything that we love and honour, and everything
9 that can be thought virtuous or worthy of praise. ·Keep doing
all the things that you learnt from me and have been taught
by me and have heard or seen that I do. Then the God of
peace will be with you.

Thanks for help received

10 It is a great joy to me, in the Lord, that at last you have
shown some concern for me again; though of course you were
11 concerned before, and only lacked an opportunity. ·I am not
talking about shortage of money: I have learnt to manage on
12 whatever I have, ·I know how to be poor and I know how to
be rich too. I have been through my initiation and now I am
ready for anything anywhere: full stomach or empty stomach,
13 poverty or plenty. ·There is nothing I cannot master with the
14 help of the One who gives me strength. ·All the same, it was
15 good of you to share with me in my hardships. ·In the early
days of the Good News, as you people of Philippi well know,
when I left Macedonia, no other church helped me with gifts
16 of money. You were the only ones; ·and twice since my stay
17 in Thessalonika you have sent me what I needed. ·It is not
your gift that I value; what is valuable to me is the interest
18 that is mounting up in your account. ·Now for the time
being I have everything that I need and more: I am fully
provided now that I have received from Epaphroditus the
offering that you sent, *a sweet fragrance*—the sacrifice that
19 God accepts and finds pleasing. ·In return my God will fulfil

all your needs, in Christ Jesus, as lavishly as only God can.
20 Glory to God, our Father, for ever and ever. Amen.

Greetings and final wish

21   My greetings to every one of the saints in Christ Jesus. The
22 brothers who are with me send their greetings. ·All the saints
   send their greetings, especially those of the imperial house-
23 hold.[b] ·May the grace of the Lord Jesus Christ be with your
   spirit.

4 a. 'Companion' is the meaning of the proper name Syzygus. **b.** I.e.
in the service of the emperor.

COLOSSIANS

THE LETTER OF PAUL

TO THE CHURCH AT COLOSSAE

PREFACE

Address

1 From Paul, appointed by God to be an apostle of Christ
2 Jesus, and from our brother Timothy ·to the saints in
Colossae, our faithful brothers in Christ: Grace and peace to
you from God our Father.

Thanksgiving and prayer

3 We have never failed to remember you in our prayers and
to give thanks for you to God, the Father of our Lord Jesus
4 Christ ·ever since we heard about your faith in Christ Jesus
5 and the love that you show towards all the saints ·because of
the hope which is stored up for you in heaven. It is only
recently that you heard of this, when it was announced in the
6 message of the truth. The Good News ·which has reached
you is spreading all over the world and producing the same
results as it has among you ever since the day when you heard
7 about God's grace and understood what this really is. ·Epa-
phras, who taught you, is one of our closest fellow workers
8 and a faithful deputy for us as Christ's servant, ·and it was he
who told us all about your love in the Spirit.
9 That will explain why, ever since the day he told us, we
have never failed to pray for you, and what we ask God is
that through perfect wisdom and spiritual understanding you
10 should reach the fullest knowledge of his will. ·So you will be
able to lead the kind of life which the Lord expects of you, a
life acceptable to him in all its aspects; showing the results in
all the good actions you do and increasing your knowledge of
11 God. ·You will have in you the strength, based on his own
glorious power, never to give in, but to bear anything
12 joyfully, ·thanking the Father who has made it possible for
you to join the saints and with them to inherit the light.

13 Because that is what he has done: he has taken us out of the power of darkness and created a place for us in the king-
14 dom of the Son that he loves, ·and in him, we gain our freedom, the forgiveness of our sins.

I. FORMAL INSTRUCTION

Christ is the head of all creation

15 He is the image of the unseen God
and the first-born of all creation,
16 for in him were created
all things in heaven and on earth:
everything visible and everything invisible,
Thrones, Dominations, Sovereignties, Powers—
all things were created through him and for him.
17 Before anything was created, he existed,
and he holds all things in unity.
18 Now the Church is his body,
he is its head.

As he is the Beginning,
he was first to be born from the dead,
so that he should be first in every way;
19 because God wanted all perfection
to be found in him
20 and all things to be reconciled through him and for him,
everything in heaven and everything on earth,
when he made peace
by his death on the cross.

The Colossians have their share in salvation

21 Not long ago, you were foreigners and enemies, in the way
22 that you used to think and the evil things that you did; ·but now he has reconciled you, by his death and in that mortal body. Now you are able to appear before him holy, pure and
23 blameless—·as long as you persevere and stand firm on the solid base of the faith, never letting yourselves drift away from the hope promised by the Good News, which you have heard, which has been preached to the whole human race, and of which I, Paul, have become the servant.

Paul's labours in the service of the pagans

24 It makes me happy to suffer for you, as I am suffering now, and in my own body to do what I can to make up all that has still to be undergone by Christ for the sake of his body, the

25 Church. ·I became the servant of the Church when God made
26 me responsible for delivering God's message to you, ·the
message which was a mystery hidden for generations and
27 centuries and has now been revealed to his saints. ·It was God's
purpose to reveal it to them and to show all the rich glory of
this mystery to pagans. The mystery is Christ among you,
28 your hope of glory: ·this is the Christ we proclaim, this is the
wisdom in which we thoroughly train everyone and instruct
29 everyone, to make them all perfect in Christ. ·It is for this I
struggle wearily on, helped only by his power driving me
irresistibly.

Paul's concern for the Colossians' faith

2   Yes, I want you to know that I do have to struggle hard for
you, and for those in Laodicea, and for so many others who
2 have never seen me face to face. ·It is all to bind you together
in love and to stir your minds, so that your understanding
may come to full development, until you really know God's
3 secret ·in which all the jewels of wisdom and knowledge are
hidden.
4   I say this to make sure that no one deceives you with
5 specious arguments. ·I may be absent in body, but in spirit
I am there among you, delighted to find you all in harmony
and to see how firm your faith in Christ is.

II. A WARNING AGAINST SOME ERRORS

Live according to the true faith in Christ, not according to false teaching

6   You must live your whole life according to the Christ you
7 have received—Jesus the Lord; ·you must be rooted in him
and built on him and held firm by the faith you have been
taught, and full of thanksgiving.
8   Make sure that no one traps you and deprives you of your
freedom by some secondhand, empty, rational philosophy
based on the principles of this world instead of on Christ.

Christ alone is the true head of men and angels

9   In his body lives the fullness of divinity, and in him you too
10 often find your own fulfilment, ·in the one who is the head of
every Sovereignty and Power.[a]
11   In him you have been circumcised, with a circumcision not
performed by human hand, but by the complete stripping of
your body of flesh. This is circumcision according to Christ.
12 You have been buried with him, when you were baptised;

and by baptism, too, you have been raised up with him
through your belief in the power of God who raised him
13 from the dead. ·You were dead, because you were sinners
and had not been circumcised: he[b] has brought you to life
with him, he has forgiven us all our sins.

14   He has overridden the Law, and cancelled every record of
the debt that we had to pay; he has done away with it by
15 nailing it to the cross;[c] ·and so he got rid of the Sovereignties
and the Powers, and paraded them in public, behind him in
his triumphal procession.[d]

Against the false asceticism based on 'the principles of this world'

16   From now onwards, never let anyone else decide what you
should eat or drink, or whether you are to observe annual
17 festivals, New Moons or sabbaths. ·These were only pale
18 reflections of what was coming: the reality is Christ. ·Do not
be taken in by people who like grovelling to angels and
worshipping them; people like that are always going on
about some vision they have had, inflating themselves to a
19 false importance with their worldly outlook. ·A man of this
sort is not united to the head, and it is the head that adds
strength and holds the whole body together, with all its joints
and sinews—and this is the only way in which it can reach its
full growth in God.

20   If you have really died with Christ to the principles of this
world, why do you still let rules dictate to you, as though you
21 were still living in the world? ·"It is forbidden to pick up this,
it is forbidden to taste that, it is forbidden to touch something
22 else'; ·all these prohibitions are only concerned with things
that perish by their very use—an example of *human doctrines*
23 *and regulations*![e] ·It may be argued that true wisdom is to be
found in these, with their self-imposed devotions, their self-
abasement, and their severe treatment of the body; but once
the flesh starts to protest, they are no use at all.

Live-giving union with the glorified Christ

3   Since you have been brought back to true life with Christ,
you must look for the things that are in heaven, where Christ
2 is, sitting at God's right hand. ·Let your thoughts be on
heavenly things, not on the things that are on the earth,
3 because you have died, and now the life you have is hidden

2 a. I.e. over the highest orders of angels. b. God the Father.
c. Destroying our death warrant. d. The tradition was that the Law
was brought down to Moses by angels. e. Is 29:13

4 with Christ in God. ·But when Christ is revealed—and he is your life—you too will be revealed in all your glory with him.

III. EXHORTATION

General rules of Christian behaviour

5 That is why you must kill everything in you that belongs only to earthly life: fornication, impurity, guilty passion, evil desires and especially greed, which is the same thing as
6 worshipping a false god; ·all this is the sort of behaviour that
7 makes God angry. ·And it is the way in which you used to live when you were surrounded by people doing the same thing,
8 but now you, of all people, must give all these things up: getting angry, being bad-tempered, spitefulness, abusive
9 language and dirty talk; ·and never tell each other lies. You
10 have stripped off your old behaviour with your old self, ·and you have put on a new self which will progress towards true knowledge the more it is renewed in the image of its creator;
11 and in that image there is no room for distinction between Greek and Jew, between the circumcised or the uncircumcised, or between barbarian and Scythian, slave and free man. There is only Christ: he is everything and he is in everything.
12 You are God's chosen race, his saints; he loves you, and you should be clothed in sincere compassion, in kindness and
13 humility, gentleness and patience. ·Bear with one another; forgive each other as soon as a quarrel begins. The Lord has
14 forgiven you; now you must do the same. ·Over all these clothes, to keep them together and complete them, put on
15 love. ·And may the peace of Christ reign in your hearts, because it is for this that you were called together as parts of one body. Always be thankful.
16 Let the message of Christ, in all its richness, find a home with you. Teach each other, and advise each other, in all wisdom. With gratitude in your hearts sing psalms and hymns
17 and inspired songs to God; ·and never say or do anything except in the name of the Lord Jesus, giving thanks to God the Father through him.

The morals of the home and household

18 Wives, give way to your husbands, as you should in the
19 Lord. ·Husbands, love your wives and treat them with
20 gentleness. ·Children, be obedient to your parents always,
21 because that is what will please the Lord. ·Parents, never

drive your children to resentment or you will make them feel frustrated.

22 Slaves, be obedient to the men who are called your masters in this world; not only when you are under their eye, as if you had only to please men, but wholeheartedly, out of
23 respect for the Master. ·Whatever your work is, put your heart into it as if it were for the Lord and not for men,
24 knowing that the Lord will repay you by making you his
25 heirs. It is Christ the Lord that you are serving; ·anyone who does wrong will be repaid in kind and he does not favour one
1 person more than another. 4 Masters, make sure that your slaves are given what is just and fair, knowing that you too have a Master in heaven.

The apostolic spirit

2 Be persevering in your prayers and be thankful as you stay
3 awake to pray. ·Pray for us especially, asking God to show us opportunities for announcing the message and proclaiming the mystery of Christ, for the sake of which I am in chains;
4 pray that I may proclaim it as clearly as I ought.
5 Be tactful with those who are not Christians and be sure
6 you make the best use of your time with them. ·Talk to them agreeably and with a flavour of wit, and try to fit your answers to the needs of each one.

Personal news

7 Tychicus will tell you all the news about me. He is a brother I love very much, and a loyal helper and companion
8 in the service of the Lord. ·I am sending him to you precisely for this purpose: to give you news about us and to reassure
9 you. ·With him I am sending Onesimus, that dear and faithful brother who is a fellow citizen of yours. They will tell you everything that is happening here.

Greetings and final wishes

10 Aristarchus, who is here in prison with me, sends his greetings, and so does Mark, the cousin of Barnabas—you were sent some instructions about him; if he comes to you,
11 give him a warm welcome—·and Jesus Justus adds his greetings. Of all those who have come over from the Circumcision, these are the only ones actually working with me for the kingdom of God. They have been a great comfort to me.
12 Epaphras, your fellow citizen, sends his greetings; this servant of Christ Jesus never stops battling for you, praying that you will never lapse but always hold perfectly and securely to

13 the will of God. ·I can testify for him that he works hard for
14 you, as well as for those at Laodicea and Hierapolis. ·Greet-
ings from my dear friend Luke, the doctor, and also from
Demas.

15 Please give my greetings to the brothers at Laodicea and to
16 Nympha and the church which meets in her house. ·After this
letter has been read among you, send it on to be read in the
church of the Laodiceans; and get the letter from Laodicea
17 for you to read yourselves. ·Give Archippus this message,
'Remember the service that the Lord wants you to do, and
try to carry it out'.

18 Here is a greeting in my own handwriting—PAUL. Remember the chains I wear. Grace be with you.

1 THESSALONIANS

THE FIRST LETTER OF PAUL

TO THE CHURCH IN THESSALONIKA

Address

1   From Paul, Silvanus and Timothy, to the Church in Thessalonika which is in God the Father and the Lord Jesus Christ; wishing you grace and peace.

Thanksgiving and congratulations

2   We always mention you in our prayers and thank God for
3   you all, ·and constantly remember before God our Father how you have shown your faith in action, worked for love and persevered through hope, in our Lord Jesus Christ.
4   We know, brothers, that God loves you and that you have
5   been chosen, ·because when we brought the Good News to you, it came to you not only as words, but as power and as the Holy Spirit and as utter conviction. And you observed the sort of life we lived when we were with you, which was for
6   your instruction, ·and you were led to become imitators of us, and of the Lord; and it was with the joy of the Holy Spirit that you took to the gospel, in spite of the great opposition
7   all round you. ·This has made you the great example to all
8   believers in Macedonia and Achaia ·since it was from you that the word of the Lord started to spread—and not only throughout Macedonia and Achaia, for the news of your faith in God has spread everywhere. We do not need to tell
9   other people about it: ·other people tell us how we started the work among you, how you broke with idolatry when you were converted to God and became servants of the real,
10   living God; ·and how you are now waiting for Jesus, his Son, whom he raised from the dead, to come from heaven to save us from the retribution which is coming.

Paul's example in Thessalonika

2   You know yourselves, my brothers, that our visit to you has not proved ineffectual.

2 We had, as you know, been given rough treatment and been grossly insulted at Philippi, and it was our God who gave us the courage to proclaim his Good News to you in the
3 face of great opposition. ·We have not taken to preaching because we are deluded, or immoral, or trying to deceive
4 anyone; ·it was God who decided that we were fit to be entrusted with the Good News, and when we are speaking, we are not trying to please men but God, *who can read* our
5 *inmost thoughts.*[a] ·You know very well, and we can swear it before God, that never at any time have our speeches been
6 simply flattery, or a cover for trying to get money; ·nor have we ever looked for any special honour from men, either from
7 you or anybody else, ·when we could have imposed ourselves on you with full weight, as apostles of Christ.

Instead, we were unassuming. Like a mother feeding and
8 looking after her own children, ·we felt so devoted and protective towards you, and had come to love you so much, that we were eager to hand over to you not only the Good News
9 but our whole lives as well. ·Let me remind you, brothers, how hard we used to work, slaving night and day so as not to be a burden on any one of you while we were proclaiming
10 God's Good News to you. ·You are witnesses, and so is God, that our treatment of you, since you became believers, has
11 been impeccably right and fair. ·You can remember how we treated every one of you as a father treats his children,
12 teaching you what was right, encouraging you and appealing to you to live a life worthy of God, who is calling you to share the glory of his kingdom.

The faith and the patience of the Thessalonians

13 Another reason why we constantly thank God for you is that as soon as you heard the message that we brought you as God's message, you accepted it for what it really is, God's message and not some human thinking; and it is still a living
14 power among you who believe it. ·For you, my brothers, have been like the churches of God in Christ Jesus which are in Judaea, in suffering the same treatment from your own
15 countrymen as they have suffered from the Jews, ·the people who put the Lord Jesus to death, and the prophets too. And now they have been persecuting us, and acting in a way that cannot please God and makes them the enemies of the whole
16 human race, ·because they are hindering us from preaching to the pagans and trying to save them. They never stop trying *to finish off the sins they have begun,*[b] but retribution is overtaking them at last.

Paul's anxiety

17 A short time after we had been separated from you—in body but never in thought, brothers—we had an especially
18 strong desire and longing to see you face to face again, ·and we tried hard to come and visit you; I, Paul, tried more than
19 once, but Satan prevented us. ·What do you think is our pride and our joy? You are; and you will be *the crown* of which we shall be *proudest* in the presence of our Lord Jesus
20 when he comes; ·you are our pride and our joy.

Timothy's mission to Thessalonika

3 When we could not bear the waiting any longer, we decided it would be best to be left without a companion at Athens,
2 and ·sent our brother Timothy, who is God's helper in spreading the Good News of Christ, to keep you firm and
3 strong in the faith ·and prevent any of you from being un-settled by the present troubles. As you know, these are bound
4 to come our way: ·when we were with you, we warned you that we must expect to have persecutions to bear, and that is
5 what has happened now, as you have found out. ·That is why, when I could not stand waiting any longer, I sent to assure myself of your faith: I was afraid the Tempter[a] might have tried you too hard, and all our work might have been wasted.

Paul thanks God for good reports of the Thessalonians

6 However, Timothy is now back from you and he has given us good news of your faith and your love, telling us that you always remember us with pleasure and want to see us quite
7 as much as we want to see you. ·And so, brothers, your faith has been a great comfort to us in the middle of our own
8 troubles and sorrows; ·now we can breathe again, as you are
9 still holding firm in the Lord. ·How can we thank God enough for you, for all the joy we feel before our God on your ac-
10 count? ·We are earnestly praying night and day to be able to see you face to face again and make up any shortcomings in your faith.

11 May God our Father himself, and our Lord Jesus Christ,
12 make it easy for us to come to you. ·May the Lord be generous in increasing your love and make you love one another and the whole human race as much as we love you.
13 And may he so confirm your hearts in holiness that you may

2 a. Jr 11:20 **b.** 2 M 6:14
3 a. I.e. 'the one who puts you to the test'.

be blameless in the sight of our God and Father when our Lord Jesus Christ comes *with all his saints.*

Live in holiness and charity

4 Finally, brothers, we urge you and appeal to you in the Lord Jesus to make more and more progress in the kind of life that you are meant to live: the life that God wants, as
2 you learnt from us, and as you are already living it. ·You have not forgotten the instructions we gave you on the authority of the Lord Jesus.
3 What God wants is for you all to be holy. He wants you to
4 keep away from fornication, ·and each one of you to know how to use the body that belongs to him*a* in a way that is holy
5 and honourable, ·not giving way to selfish lust like *the pagans*
6 *who do not know God.b* ·He wants nobody at all ever to sin by taking advantage of a brother in these matters; the Lord always punishes sins of that sort, as we told you before and
7 assured you. ·We have been called by God to be holy, not to
8 be immoral; ·in other words, anyone who objects is not objecting to a human authority, but to God, *who gives you his Holy Spirit.c*
9 As for loving our brothers, there is no need for anyone to write to you about that, since you have learnt from God
10 yourselves to love one another, ·and in fact this is what you are doing with all the brothers throughout the whole of Macedonia. However, we do urge you, brothers, to go on
11 making even greater progress ·and to make a point of living quietly, attending to your own business and earning your
12 living, just as we told you to, ·so that you are seen to be respectable by those outside the Church, though you do not have to depend on them.

The dead and the living at the time of the Lord's coming

13 We want you to be quite certain, brothers, about those who have died,*d* to make sure that you do not grieve about them,
14 like the other people who have no hope. ·We believe that Jesus died and rose again, and that it will be the same for those who have died in Jesus; God will bring them with him.
15 We can tell you this from the Lord's own teaching, that any of us who are left alive until the Lord's coming will not have
16 any advantage over those who have died. ·At the trumpet of God, the voice of the archangel will call out the command and the Lord himself will come down from heaven; those
17 who have died in Christ will be the first to rise, ·and then those of us who are still alive will be taken up in the clouds,

together with them, to meet the Lord in the air. So we shall
18 stay with the Lord for ever. ·With such thoughts as these you
should comfort one another.

Watchfulness while awaiting the coming of the Lord

5   You will not be expecting us to write anything to you,
2 brothers, about 'times and seasons', ·since you know very
well that the Day of the Lord is going to come like a thief in
3 the night. ·It is when people are saying, 'How quiet and
peaceful it is' that the worst suddenly happens, as suddenly as
labour pains come on a pregnant woman; and there will be
no way for anybody to evade it.
4   But it is not as if you live in the dark, my brothers, for that
5 Day to overtake you like a thief. ·No, you are all sons of light
and sons of the day: we do not belong to the night or to
6 darkness, ·so we should not go on sleeping, as everyone else
7 does, but stay wide awake and sober. ·Night is the time for
8 sleepers to sleep and drunkards to be drunk, ·but we belong
to the day and we should be sober; let us put on faith and
love for a *breastplate*, and the hope of *salvation* for a *helmet*.
9 God never meant us to experience the Retribution, but to
10 win salvation through our Lord Jesus Christ, ·who died for
11 us so that, alive or dead, we should still live united to him. ·So
give encouragement to each other, and keep strengthening
one another, as you do already.

Some demands made by life in community

12   We appeal to you, my brothers, to be considerate to those
who are working amongst you and are above you in the Lord
13 as your teachers. ·Have the greatest respect and affection for
them because of their work.
14   Be at peace among yourselves. ·And this is what we ask
you to do, brothers: warn the idlers, give courage to those
who are apprehensive, care for the weak and be patient with
15 everyone. ·Make sure that people do not try to take revenge;
16 you must all think of what is best for each other and for the
17 community. ·Be happy at all times; ·pray constantly;
18 and for all things give thanks to God, because this is what
God expects you to do in Christ Jesus.
19
20   Never try to suppress the Spirit ·or treat the gift of pro-
21 phecy with contempt; ·think before you do anything—hold
22 on to what is good ·and *avoid every* form of *evil*.

4 **a.** Lit. 'the vessel that is his': either his own body or his wife's. **b.** Jr
10:25; Ps 79:6 **c.** Ezk 37:14 **d.** Lit. 'those who are sleeping'.

Closing prayer and farewell

23   May the God of peace make you perfect and holy; and
may you all be kept safe and blameless, spirit, soul and body,
24 for the coming of our Lord Jesus Christ. ·God has called you
and he will not fail you.

25   Pray for us, my brothers.

26
27   Greet all the brothers with the holy kiss. ·My orders, in the
Lord's name, are that this letter is to be read to all the
brothers.

28   The grace of our Lord Jesus Christ be with you.

2 THESSALONIANS

THE SECOND LETTER OF PAUL

TO THE CHURCH IN THESSALONIKA

Address

1 From Paul, Silvanus and Timothy, to the Church in Thessalonika which is in God our Father and the Lord Jesus 2 Christ; ·wishing you grace and peace from God the Father and the Lord Jesus Christ.

Thanksgiving and encouragement. The Last Judgement

3 We feel we must be continually thanking God for you, brothers; quite rightly, because your faith is growing so wonderfully and the love that you have for one another never 4 stops increasing; ·and among the churches of God we can take special pride in you for your constancy and faith under 5 all the persecutions and troubles you have to bear. ·It all shows that God's judgement is just, and the purpose of it is that you may be found worthy of the kingdom of God; it is for the sake of this that you are suffering now.

6 God will very rightly repay with injury those who are 7 injuring you, ·and reward you, who are suffering now, with the same peace as he will give us, when the Lord Jesus 8 appears from heaven with the angels of his power. ·He will come *in flaming fire* to impose the penalty on *all who do not acknowledge God*[a] and *refuse to accept* the Good News of our 9 Lord Jesus. ·It will be their punishment to be lost eternally, excluded *from the presence of the Lord and from the glory of* 10 *his strength* ·*on that day* when he comes *to be glorified among his saints* and *seen in his glory*[b] by all who believe in him; and you are believers, through our witness.

11 Knowing this, we pray continually that our God will make you worthy of his call, and by his power fulfil all your desires

---

1 a. God's *coming in fire* is quoted from Is 66:15; the penalty on *those who do not acknowledge him* is a quotation from Jr 10:25. b. Quotations from Is 2:10–17; 49:3; 66:5.

for goodness and complete all that you have been doing
12 through faith; ·because in this way *the name* of our Lord
Jesus Christ *will be glorified* in you and you in him, by the
grace of our God and the Lord Jesus Christ.

The coming of the Lord and the prelude to it

2   To turn now, brothers, to the coming of our Lord Jesus
2 Christ and how we shall all be gathered round him: ·please
do not get excited too soon or alarmed by any prediction or
rumour or any letter claiming to come from us, implying
3 that the Day of the Lord has already arrived. ·Never let
anyone deceive you in this way.
   It cannot happen until the Great Revolt has taken place
4 and the Rebel, the Lost One, has appeared. ·This is the
Enemy, the one who claims to be so much *greater than all*
that men call 'god', so much greater than anything that is
worshipped, that *he enthrones himself* in *God's* sanctuary and
5 claims that he is God. ·Surely you remember me telling you
6 about this when I was with you? ·And you know, too, what is
still holding him back from appearing before his appointed
7 time. ·Rebellion is at its work already, but in secret, and the
8 one who is holding it back has first to be removed ·before the
Rebel appears openly. The Lord *will kill him with the breath
of his mouth*[a] and will annihilate him with his glorious
appearance at his coming.
9   But when the Rebel comes, Satan will set to work: there
will be all kinds of miracles and a deceptive show of signs
10 and portents, ·and everything evil that can deceive those who
are bound for destruction because they would not grasp the
11 love of the truth which could have saved them. ·The reason
why God is sending a power to delude them and make them
12 believe what is untrue ·is to condemn all who refused to
believe in the truth and chose wickedness instead.

Encouragement to persevere

13   But we feel that we must be continually thanking God for
you, brothers whom the Lord loves, because God chose you
from the beginning to be saved by the sanctifying Spirit and
14 by faith in the truth. ·Through the Good News that we
brought he called you to this so that you should share the
15 glory of our Lord Jesus Christ. ·Stand firm, then, brothers,
and keep the traditions that we taught you, whether by word
16 of mouth or by letter. ·May our Lord Jesus Christ himself,

and God our Father who has given us his love and, through his grace, such inexhaustible comfort and such sure hope,

17 comfort you and strengthen you in everything good that you do or say.

3 Finally, brothers, pray for us; pray that the Lord's message may spread quickly, and be received with honour as it was

2 among you; ·and pray that we may be preserved from the interference of bigoted and evil people, for faith is not given

3 to everyone. ·But the Lord is faithful, and he will give you

4 strength and guard you from the evil one, ·and we, in the Lord, have every confidence that you are doing and will go

5 on doing all that we tell you. ·May the Lord turn your hearts towards the love of God and the fortitude of Christ.

Against idleness and disunity

6 In the name of the Lord Jesus Christ, we urge you, brothers, to keep away from any of the brothers who refuses to work or to live according to the tradition we passed on to you.

7 You know how you are supposed to imitate us: now we

8 were not idle when we were with you, ·nor did we ever have our meals at anyone's table without paying for them; no, we worked night and day, slaving and straining, so as not to be a

9 burden on any of you. ·This was not because we had no right to be, but in order to make ourselves an example for you to follow.

10 We gave you a rule when we were with you: not to let

11 anyone have any food if he refused to do any work. ·Now we hear that there are some of you who are living in idleness, doing no work themselves but interfering with everyone

12 else's. ·In the Lord Jesus Christ, we order and call on people of this kind to go on quietly working and earning the food that they eat.

13 My brothers, never grow tired of doing what is right.

14 If anyone refuses to obey what I have written in this letter, take note of him and have nothing to do with him, so that he

15 will feel that he is in the wrong; ·though you are not to regard him as an enemy but as a brother in need of correction.

Prayer and farewell wishes

16 May the Lord of peace himself give you peace all the time and in every way. The Lord be with you all.

2 a. Is 11:4

17 From me, PAUL, these greetings in my own handwriting,
which is the mark of genuineness in every letter; this is my
18 own writing. ·May the grace of our Lord Jesus Christ be with
you all.

1 TIMOTHY

THE FIRST LETTER

FROM PAUL TO TIMOTHY

Address

1 From Paul, apostle of Christ Jesus appointed by the command of God our saviour and of Christ Jesus our hope,
2 to Timothy, true child of mine in the faith; wishing you grace, mercy and peace from God the Father and from Christ Jesus our Lord.

Suppress the false teachers

3 As I asked you when I was leaving for Macedonia, please stay at Ephesus, to insist that certain people stop teaching
4 strange doctrines ·and taking notice of myths and endless genealogies; these things are only likely to raise irrelevant doubts instead of furthering the designs of God which are
5 revealed in faith. ·The only purpose of this instruction is that there should be love, coming out of a pure heart, a clear
6 conscience and a sincere faith. ·There are some people who have gone off the straight course and taken a road that leads
7 to empty speculation; ·they claim to be doctors of the Law but they understand neither the arguments they are using nor the opinions they are upholding.

The purpose of the Law

8 We know, of course, that the Law is good, but only pro-
9 vided it is treated like any law, ·in the understanding that laws are not framed for people who are good. On the contrary, they are for criminals and revolutionaries, for the irreligious and the wicked, for the sacrilegious and the irreverent; they are for people who kill their fathers or mothers
10 and for murderers, ·for those who are immoral with women or with boys or with men, for liars and for perjurers—and for
11 everything else that is contrary to the sound teaching ·that goes with the Good News of the glory of the blessed God, the gospel that was entrusted to me.

Paul on his own calling

12 I thank Christ Jesus our Lord, who has given me strength, and who judged me faithful enough to call me into his service
13 even though I used to be a blasphemer and did all I could to injure and discredit the faith. Mercy, however, was shown me, because until I became a believer I had been acting in
14 ignorance; ·and the grace of our Lord filled me with faith and
15 with the love that is in Christ Jesus. ·Here is a saying that you can rely on and nobody should doubt: that Christ Jesus came into the world to save sinners. I myself am the greatest
16 of them; ·and if mercy has been shown to me, it is because Jesus Christ meant to make me the greatest evidence of his inexhaustible patience for all the other people who would
17 later have to trust in him to come to eternal life. ·To the eternal King, the undying, invisible and only God, be honour and glory for ever and ever. Amen.

Timothy's responsibility

18 Timothy, my son, these are the instructions that I am giving you: I ask you to remember the words once spoken over you by the prophets, and taking them to heart to fight
19 like a good soldier ·with faith and a good conscience for your weapons. Some people have put conscience aside and
20 wrecked their faith in consequence. ·I mean men like Hymenaeus and Alexander, whom I have handed over to Satan to teach them not to be blasphemous.

Liturgical prayer

2 My advice is that, first of all, there should be prayers offered for everyone—petitions, intercessions and thanks-
2 giving—·and especially for kings and others in authority, so that we may be able to live religious and reverent lives in
3 peace and quiet. ·To do this is right, and will please God our
4 saviour: ·he wants everyone to be saved and reach full
5 knowledge of the truth. ·For there is only one God, and there is only one mediator between God and mankind, himself a
6 man, Christ Jesus, ·who sacrificed himself as a ransom for them all. He is the evidence of this, sent at the appointed
7 time, and ·I have been named a herald and apostle of it and— I am telling the truth and no lie—a teacher of the faith and the truth to the pagans.
8 In every place, then, I want the men to lift their hands up reverently in prayer, with no anger or argument.

Women in the assembly

9   Similarly, I direct that women are to wear suitable clothes
and to be dressed quietly and modestly, without braided hair
or gold and jewellery or expensive clothes; their adornment
10   is ·to do the sort of good works that are proper for women
11   who profess to be religious. ·During instruction, a woman
12   should be quiet and respectful. ·I am not giving permission
for a woman to teach or to tell a man what to do. A woman
13   ought not to speak, ·because Adam was formed first and Eve
14   afterwards, ·and it was not Adam who was led astray but the
15   woman who was led astray and fell into sin. ·Nevertheless,
she will be saved by childbearing, provided she lives a modest
life and is constant in faith and love and holiness.

The elder-in-charge

3   Here is a saying that you can rely on: To want to be a
2 . presiding elder[a] is to want to do a noble work. ·That is why
the president must have an impeccable character. He must
not have been married more than once, and he must be
temperate, discreet and courteous, hospitable and a good
3   teacher; ·not a heavy drinker, nor hot-tempered, but kind
4   and peaceable. He must not be a lover of money. ·He must be
a man who manages his own family well and brings his
5   children up to obey him and be well-behaved: ·how can any
man who does not understand how to manage his own family
6   have responsibility for the church of God? ·He should not be
a new convert, in case pride might turn his head and then he
7   might be condemned as the devil was condemned. ·It is also
necessary that people outside the Church should speak well
of him, so that he never gets a bad reputation and falls into
the devil's trap.

Deacons

8   In the same way, deacons must be respectable men whose
word can be trusted, moderate in the amount of wine they
9   drink and with no squalid greed for money. ·They must be
10   conscientious believers in the mystery of the faith. ·They are
to be examined first, and only admitted to serve as deacons if
11   there is nothing against them. ·In the same way, the women
must be respectable, not gossips but sober and quite reliable.
12   Deacons must not have been married more than once, and
must be men who manage their children and families well.

3 a. The word *episcopos* used here by Paul had not yet acquired the
same meaning as 'bishop'.

13 Those of them who carry out their duties well as deacons will earn a high standing for themselves and be rewarded with great assurance in their work for the faith in Christ Jesus.

The Church and the mystery of the spiritual life

14 At the moment of writing to you, I am hoping that I may
15 be with you soon; ·but in case I should be delayed, I wanted you to know how people ought to behave in God's family— that is, in the Church of the living God, which upholds the
16 truth and keeps it safe. ·Without any doubt, the mystery of our religion is very deep indeed:

> He was made visible in the flesh,
> attested by the Spirit,
> seen by angels,
> proclaimed to the pagans,
> believed in by the world,
> taken up in glory.

False teachers

4 The Spirit has explicitly said that during the last times there will be some who will desert the faith and choose to listen to deceitful spirits and doctrines that come from the
2 devils; ·and the cause of this is the lies told by hypocrites whose consciences are branded as though with a red-hot
3 iron:[a] ·they will say marriage is forbidden, and lay down rules about abstaining from foods which God created to be accepted with thanksgiving by all who believe and who know
4 the truth.[b] ·Everything God has created is good, and no food
5 is to be rejected, provided grace is said for it: ·the word of
6 God and the prayer make it holy. ·If you put all this to the brothers, you will be a good servant of Christ Jesus and show that you have really digested the teaching of the faith and the
7 good doctrine which you have always followed. ·Have nothing to do with godless myths and old wives' tales. Train
8 yourself spiritually. ·'Physical exercises are useful enough, but the usefulness of spirituality is unlimited, since it holds out the reward of life here and now and of the future life as
9 well'; ·that is a saying that you can rely on and nobody should
10 doubt it. ·I mean that the point of all our toiling and battling is that we have put our trust in the living God and he is the saviour of the whole human race but particularly of all
11 believers. ·This is what you are to enforce in your teaching.
12 Do not let people disregard you because you are young, but be an example to all the believers in the way you speak

and behave, and in your love, your faith and your purity.
13 Make use of the time until I arrive by reading to the people,
14 preaching and teaching. ·You have in you a spiritual gift
which was given to you when the prophets spoke and the
body of elders laid their hands on you; do not let it lie
15 unused. ·Think hard about all this, and put it into practice,
and everyone will be able to see how you are advancing.
16 Take great care about what you do and what you teach;
always do this, and in this way you will save both yourself
and those who listen to you.

Pastoral practice

5   Do not speak harshly to a man older than yourself, but
·   advise him as you would your own father; treat the younger
2 men as brothers ·and older women as you would your mother.
Always treat young women with propriety, as if they were
sisters.

Widows

3   Be considerate to widows; I mean those who are truly
4 widows. ·If a widow has children or grandchildren, they are
to learn first of all to do their duty to their own families and
repay their debt to their parents, because this is what pleases
5 God. ·But a woman who is really widowed and left without
anybody can give herself up to God and consecrate all her
6 days and nights to petitions and prayer. ·The one who thinks
7 only of pleasure is already dead while she is still alive: ·re-
mind them of all this, too, so that their lives may be blame-
8 less. ·Anyone who does not look after his own relations,
especially if they are living with him, has rejected the faith
and is worse than an unbeliever.
9   Enrolment as a widow is permissible only for a woman at
10 least sixty years old who has had only one husband. ·She
must be a woman known for her good works and for the way
in which she has brought up her children, shown hospitality
to strangers and washed the saints' feet, helped people who
11 are in trouble and been active in all kinds of good work. ·Do
not accept young widows because if their natural desires get
stronger than their dedication to Christ, they want to marry
12 again, ·and then people condemn them for being unfaithful to
13 their original promise. ·Besides, they learn how to be idle and
go round from house to house; and then, not merely idle,

4 a. Like runaway slaves. **b.** The rejection of marriage was to be one
of the hallmarks of Gnosticism; dietary regulations were more
specifically Jewish.

they learn to be gossips and meddlers in other people's affairs, and to chatter when they would be better keeping
14 quiet. ·I think it is best for young widows to marry again and have children and a home to look after, and not give the
15 enemy any chance to raise a scandal about them; ·there are
16 already some who have left us to follow Satan. ·If a Christian woman has widowed relatives, she should support them and not make the Church bear the expense but enable it to support those who are genuinely widows.

The elders

17 The elders who do their work well while they are in charge are to be given double consideration, especially those who are
18 assiduous in preaching and teaching. ·As scripture says: *You must not muzzle an ox when it is treading out the corn;*[a] and
19 again: *The worker deserves his pay.*[b] ·Never accept any accusation brought against an elder unless it is supported *by two*
20 *or three witnesses.* ·If any of them are at fault, reprimand
21 them publicly, as a warning to the rest. ·Before God, and before Jesus Christ and the angels he has chosen, I put it to you as a duty to keep these rules impartially and never to be
22 influenced by favouritism. ·Do not be too quick to lay hands on any man, and never make yourself an accomplice in anybody else's sin; keep yourself pure.
23 You should give up drinking only water and have a little wine for the sake of your digestion and the frequent bouts of illness that you have.
24 The faults of some people are obvious long before anyone makes any complaint about them, while others have faults
25 that are not discovered until afterwards. ·In the same way, the good that people do can be obvious; but even when it is not, it cannot be hidden for ever.

Slaves

6 All slaves 'under the yoke' must have unqualified respect for their masters, so that the name of God and our teaching
2 are not brought into disrepute. ·Slaves whose masters are believers are not to think any the less of them because they are brothers; on the contrary, they should serve them all the better, since those who have the benefit of their services are believers and dear to God.

The true teacher and the false teacher

This is what you are to teach them to believe and persuade
3 them to do. ·Anyone who teaches anything different, and

does not keep to the sound teaching which is that of our Lord
Jesus Christ, the doctrine which is in accordance with true
4 religion, ·is simply ignorant and must be full of self-conceit—
with a craze for questioning everything and arguing about
words. All that can come of this is jealousy, contention,
5 abuse and wicked mistrust of one another; ·and unending
disputes by people who are neither rational nor informed and
6 imagine that religion is a way of making a profit. ·Religion, of
course, does bring large profits, but only to those who are
7 content with what they have. ·We brought nothing into the
8 world, and we can take nothing out of it; ·but as long as we
9 have food and clothing, let us be content with that. ·People
who long to be rich are a prey to temptation; they get trapped
into all sorts of foolish and dangerous ambitions which even-
10 tually plunge them into ruin and destruction. ·'The love of
money is the root of all evils' and there are some who, pur-
suing it, have wandered away from the faith, and so given
their souls any number of fatal wounds.

Timothy's vocation recalled

11 But, as a man dedicated to God, you must avoid all that.
You must aim to be saintly and religious, filled with faith and
12 love, patient and gentle. ·Fight the good fight of the faith and
win for yourself the eternal life to which you were called
when you made your profession and spoke up for the truth
13 in front of many witnesses. ·Now, before God the source of
all life and before Jesus Christ, who spoke up as a witness for
14 the truth in front of Pontius Pilate, I put to you the duty ·of
doing all that you have been told, with no faults or failures,
until the Appearing of our Lord Jesus Christ,

15 who at the due time will be revealed
by God, the blessed and only Ruler of all,
the King of kings and the Lord of lords,
16 who alone is immortal,
whose home is in inaccessible light,
whom no man has seen and no man is able to see:
to him be honour and everlasting power. Amen.

Rich Christians

17 Warn those who are rich in this world's goods that they are
not to look down on other people; and not to set their hopes
on money, which is untrustworthy, but on God who, out of

5 a. Dt 25:4 b. Not traceable in the O.T.; but this is also to be found
in Lk 10:7 where, again, it may be a quotation.

18 his riches, gives us all that we need for our happiness. ·Tell
them that they are to do good, and be rich in good works, to
19 be generous and willing to share—·this is the way they can
save up a good capital sum for the future if they want to
make sure of the only life that is real.

Final warning and conclusion

20 My dear Timothy, take great care of all that has been
entrusted to you. Have nothing to do with the pointless
philosophical discussions and antagonistic beliefs of the
21 'knowledge' which is not knowledge at all; ·by adopting this,
some have gone right away from the faith. Grace be with you.

2 TIMOTHY

THE SECOND LETTER

FROM PAUL TO TIMOTHY

Greeting and thanksgiving

1 From Paul, appointed by God to be an apostle of Christ
2 Jesus in his design to promise life in Christ Jesus; ·to Timothy,
dear child of mine, wishing you grace, mercy and peace from
God the Father and from Christ Jesus our Lord.

3 Night and day I thank God, keeping my conscience clear
and remembering my duty to him as my ancestors did, and
always I remember you in my prayers; I remember your
4 tears ·and long to see you again to complete my happiness.
5 Then I am reminded of the sincere faith which you have; it
came first to live in your grandmother Lois, and your mother
Eunice, and I have no doubt that it is the same faith in you as
well.

The gifts that Timothy has received

6 That is why I am reminding you now to fan into a flame the
7 gift that God gave you when I laid my hands on you. ·God's
gift was not a spirit of timidity, but the Spirit of power, and
8 love, and self-control. ·So you are never to be ashamed of
witnessing to the Lord, or ashamed of me for being his
prisoner; but with me, bear the hardships for the sake of the
9 Good News, relying on the power of God ·who has saved us
and called us to be holy—not because of anything we ourselves have done but for his own purpose and by his own
grace. This grace had already been granted to us, in Christ
10 Jesus, before the beginning of time, ·but it has only been
revealed by the Appearing of our saviour Christ Jesus. He
abolished death, and he has proclaimed life and immortality
11 through the Good News; ·and I have been named its herald,
its apostle and its teacher.
12 It is only on account of this that I am experiencing fresh
hardships here now;[a] but I have not lost confidence, because

1 a. The second imprisonment at Rome.

I know who it is that I have put my trust in, and I have no doubt at all that he is able to take care of all that I have entrusted to him until that Day.

13 Keep as your pattern the sound teaching you have heard
14 from me, in the faith and love that are in Christ Jesus. ·You have been trusted to look after something precious; guard it with the help of the Holy Spirit who lives in us.

15 As you know, Phygelus and Hermogenes and all the others
16 from Asia refuse to have anything more to do with me. ·I hope the Lord will be kind to all the family of Onesiphorus, because he has often been a comfort to me and has never
17 been ashamed of my chains. ·On the contrary, as soon as he reached Rome, he really searched hard for me and found out
18 where I was. ·May it be the Lord's will that he shall find the Lord's mercy on that Day. You know better than anyone else how much he helped me at Ephesus.

How Timothy should face hardships

2 Accept the strength, my dear son, that comes from the
2 grace of Christ Jesus. ·You have heard everything that I teach in public; hand it on to reliable people so that they in turn will be able to teach others.

3 Put up with your share of difficulties, like a good soldier of
4 Christ Jesus. ·In the army, no soldier gets himself mixed up in civilian life, because he must be at the disposal of the man
5 who enlisted him; ·or take an athlete—he cannot win any
6 crown unless he has kept all the rules of the contest; ·and again, it is the working farmer who has the first claim on any
7 crop that is harvested. ·Think over what I have said, and the Lord will show you how to understand it all.

8 Remember the Good News that I carry, 'Jesus Christ risen
9 from the dead, sprung from the race of David'; ·it is on account of this that I have my own hardships to bear, even to being chained like a criminal—but they cannot chain up
10 God's news. ·So I bear it all for the sake of those who are chosen, so that in the end they may have the salvation that is in Christ Jesus and the eternal glory that comes with it.

11 Here is a saying that you can rely on:

If we have died with him, then we shall live with him.
12 If we hold firm, then we shall reign with him.
If we disown him, then he will disown us.
13 We may be unfaithful, but he is always faithful,
for he cannot disown his own self.

The struggle against the immediate danger from false teachers

14 Remind them of this; and tell them in the name of God that there is to be no wrangling about words: all that this ever achieves is the destruction of those who are listening.
15 Do all you can to present yourself in front of God as a man who has come through his trials, and a man who has no cause to be ashamed of his life's work and has kept a
16 straight course with the message of the truth. ·Have nothing to do with pointless philosophical discussions—they only
17 lead further and further away from true religion. ·Talk of this kind corrodes like gangrene, as in the case of Hymenaeus
18 and Philetus, ·the men who have gone right away from the truth and claim that the resurrection has already taken place. Some people's faith cannot stand up to them.
19 However, God's solid foundation stone is still in position, and this is the inscription on it: '*The Lord knows those who are his own*'[a] and 'All who *call on the name of the Lord*[b] must avoid sin'.
20 Not all the dishes in a large house are made of gold and silver; some are made of wood or earthenware: some are kept for special occasions and others are for ordinary purposes.
21 Now, to avoid these faults that I am speaking about is the way for anyone to become a vessel for special occasions, fit for the Master himself to use, and kept ready for any good work.
22 Instead of giving in to your impulses like a young man, fasten your attention on holiness, faith, love and peace, in union with all those who call on the Lord with pure minds.
23 Avoid these futile and silly speculations, understanding that
24 they only give rise to quarrels; ·and a servant of the Lord is not to engage in quarrels, but has to be kind to everyone, a
25 good teacher, and patient. ·He has to be gentle when he corrects people who dispute what he says, never forgetting that God may give them a change of mind so that they
26 recognise the truth and ·come to their senses, once out of the trap where the devil caught them and kept them enslaved.

The dangers of the last days

3 You may be quite sure that in the last days there are going
2 to be some difficult times. ·People will be self-centred and grasping; boastful, arrogant and rude; disobedient to their
3 parents, ungrateful, irreligious; ·heartless and unappeasable;

2 a. Nb 16:5, 26 b. Is 26:13

they will be slanderers, profligates, savages and enemies of
4 everything that is good; ·they will be treacherous and reck-
less and demented by pride, preferring their own pleasure to
5 God. ·They will keep up the outward appearance of religion
but will have rejected the inner power of it. Have nothing to
do with people like that.

6　　Of the same kind, too, are those men who insinuate themselves into families in order to get influence over silly women
who are obsessed with their sins and follow one craze after
7 another ·in the attempt to educate themselves, but can never
8 come to knowledge of the truth. ·Men like this defy the truth
just as Jannes and Jambres defied Moses:[a] their minds are
9 corrupt and their faith spurious. ·But they will not be able to
go on any longer: their foolishness, like that of the other two,
must become obvious to everybody.

10　　You know, though, what I have taught, how I have lived,
what I have aimed at; you know my faith, my patience and
11 my love; my constancy ·and the persecutions and hardships
that came to me in places like Antioch, Iconium and Lystra—
all the persecutions I have endured; and the Lord has rescued
12 me from every one of them. ·You are well aware, then, that
anybody who tries to live in devotion to Christ is certain to
13 be attacked; ·while these wicked impostors will go from bad
to worse, deceiving others and deceived themselves.

14　　You must keep to what you have been taught and know to
15 be true; remember who your teachers were, ·and how, ever
since you were a child, you have known the holy scriptures—
from these you can learn the wisdom that leads to salvation
16 through faith in Christ Jesus. ·All scripture is inspired by
God and can profitably be used for teaching, for refuting
error, for guiding people's lives and teaching them to be
17 holy. ·This is how the man who is dedicated to God becomes
fully equipped and ready for any good work.

A solemn charge

4　　Before God and before Christ Jesus who is to be judge of
the living and the dead, I put this duty to you, in the name of
2 his Appearing and of his kingdom: ·proclaim the message
and, welcome or unwelcome, insist on it. Refute falsehood,
correct error, call to obedience—but do all with patience and
3 with the intention of teaching. ·The time is sure to come
when, far from being content with sound teaching, people
will be avid for the latest novelty and collect themselves a
4 whole series of teachers according to their own tastes; ·and
then, instead of listening to the truth, they will turn to

5 myths. ·Be careful always to choose the right course; be brave under trials; make the preaching of the Good News your life's work, in thoroughgoing service.

Paul in the evening of his life

6 As for me, my life is already being poured away as a liba-
7 tion, and the time has come for me to be gone. ·I have fought the good fight to the end; I have run the race to the finish;
8 I have kept the faith; ·all there is to come now is the crown of righteousness reserved for me, which the Lord, the righteous judge, will give to me on that Day; and not only to me but to all those who have longed for his Appearing.

Final advice

9 Do your best to come and see me as soon as you can.
10 As it is, Demas has deserted me for love of this life and gone to Thessalonika, Crescens has gone to Galatia and Titus to
11 Dalmatia; ·only Luke is with me. Get Mark to come and bring him with you; I find him a useful helper in my work.
12 I have sent Tychicus to Ephesus. ·When you come, bring the
13 cloak I left with Carpus in Troas, and the scrolls, especially
14 the parchment ones. ·Alexander the coppersmith has done me a lot of harm; *the Lord will repay him for what he has*
15 *done.*[a] ·Be on your guard against him yourself, because he has been bitterly contesting everything that we say.
16 The first time I had to present my defence, there was not a single witness to support me. Every one of them deserted me
17 —may they not be held accountable for it. ·But the Lord stood by me and gave me power, so that through me the whole message might be proclaimed for all the pagans to
18 hear; and so I was *rescued from the lion's mouth.*[b] ·The Lord will rescue me from all evil attempts on me, and bring me safely to his heavenly kingdom. To him be glory for ever and ever. Amen.

Farewells and final good wishes

19 Greetings to Prisca and Aquila, and the family of Onesi-
20 phorus. ·Erastus remained at Corinth, and I left Trophimus
21 ill at Miletus. ·Do your best to come before the winter.

Greetings to you from Eubulus, Pudens, Linus, Claudia and all the brothers.

22 The Lord be with your spirit. Grace be with you.

3 a. In Jewish tradition, the leaders of the Egyptian magicians and disciples of Balaam.
4 a. Ps 28:4 and 62:12; Pr 24:12 **b.** Ps 22:21

TITUS

THE LETTER FROM PAUL TO TITUS

Address

1   From Paul, servant of God, an apostle of Jesus Christ to
bring those whom God has chosen to faith and to the know-
2 ledge of the truth that leads to true religion; ·and to give
them the hope of the eternal life that was promised so long
3 ago by God. He does not lie ·and so, at the appointed time,
he revealed his decision, and, by the command of God our
4 saviour, I have been commissioned to proclaim it. ·To Titus,
true child of mine in the faith that we share, wishing you
grace and peace from God the Father and from Christ Jesus
our saviour.

The appointment of elders

5   The reason I left you behind in Crete was for you to get
everything organised there and appoint elders in every town,
6 in the way that I told you: ·that is, each of them must be a
man of irreproachable character; he must not have been
married more than once, and his children must be believers
and not uncontrollable or liable to be charged with disorderly
7 conduct. ·Since, as president, he will be God's representative,
he must be irreproachable: never an arrogant or hot-
tempered man, nor a heavy drinker or violent, nor out to
8 make money; ·but a man who is hospitable and a friend of all
9 that is good; sensible, moral, devout and self-controlled; ·and
he must have a firm grasp of the unchanging message of the
tradition, so that he can be counted on for both expounding
the sound doctrine and refuting those who argue against it.

Opposing the false teachers

10   And in fact you have there a great many people who need
to be disciplined, who talk nonsense and try to make others
believe it, particularly among those of the Circumcision.
11 They have got to be silenced: men of this kind ruin whole
families, by teaching things that they ought not to, and doing
12 it with the vile motive of making money. ·It was one of
themselves, one of their own prophets, who said,ᵃ 'Cretans

were never anything but liars, dangerous animals and lazy';
13 and that is a true statement. So you will have to be severe in
14 correcting them, and make them sound in the faith ·so that
they stop taking notice of Jewish myths and doing what they
are told to do by people who are no longer interested in the
truth.

15   To all who are pure themselves, everything is pure; but to
those who have been corrupted and lack faith, nothing can
be pure—the corruption is both in their minds and in their
16 consciences. ·They claim to have knowledge of God but the
things they do are nothing but a denial of him; they are
outrageously rebellious and quite incapable of doing good.

Some specific moral instruction

2   It is for you, then, to preach the behaviour which goes with
2 healthy doctrine. ·The older men should be reserved, digni-
fied, moderate, sound in faith and love and constancy.
3 Similarly, the older women should behave as though they
were religious, with no scandalmongering and no habitual
wine-drinking—they are to be the teachers of the right
4 behaviour ·and show the younger women how they should
5 love their husbands and love their children, ·how they are to
be sensible and chaste, and how to work in their homes, and
be gentle, and do as their husbands tell them, so that the
6 message of God is never disgraced. ·In the same way, you
7 have got to persuade the younger men to be moderate ·and in
everything you do make yourself an example to them of
working for good: when you are teaching, be an example to
8 them in your sincerity and earnestness ·and in keeping all
that you say so wholesome that nobody can make objections
to it; and then any opponent will be at a loss, with no accusa-
9 tions to make against us. ·Tell the slaves that they are to be
obedient to their masters and always do what they want
10 without any argument; ·and there must be no petty thieving—
they must show complete honesty at all times, so that they
are in every way a credit to the teaching of God our saviour.

The basis of the Christian moral life

11   You see, God's grace has been revealed, and it has made
12 salvation possible for the whole human race ·and taught us
that what we have to do is to give up everything that does not
lead to God, and all our worldly ambitions; we must be self-
restrained and live good and religious lives here in this present
13 world, ·while we are waiting in hope for the blessing which

1 a. Attributed to the Cretan poet Epimenides of Knossos.

will come with the Appearing of the glory of our great God
14 and saviour Christ Jesus.*a* ·He sacrificed himself for us in
order to *set us free from all wickedness*b and *to purify a people
so that it could be his very own*c and would have no ambition
except to do good.

15 Now this is what you are to say, whether you are giving
instruction or correcting errors; you can do so with full
authority, and no one is to question it.

General instruction for believers

3 Remind them that it is their duty to be obedient to the
officials and representatives of the government; to be ready
2 to do good at every opportunity; ·not to go slandering other
people or picking quarrels, but to be courteous and always
3 polite to all kinds of people. ·Remember, there was a time
when we too were ignorant, disobedient and misled and
enslaved by different passions and luxuries; we lived then in
wickedness and ill-will; hating each other and hateful ourselves.

4 But when the kindness and love of God our saviour for
5 mankind were revealed, ·it was not because he was concerned
with any righteous actions we might have done ourselves; it
was for no reason except his own compassion that he saved
us, by means of the cleansing water of rebirth and by renew-
6 ing us with the Holy Spirit ·which he has so generously
7 poured over us through Jesus Christ our saviour. ·He did
this so that we should be justified by his grace, to become
8 heirs looking forward to inheriting eternal life. ·This is
doctrine that you can rely on.

Personal advice to Titus

I want you to be quite uncompromising in teaching all this,
so that those who now believe in God may keep their minds
constantly occupied in doing good works. All this is good,
9 and will do nothing but good to everybody. ·But avoid
pointless speculations, and those genealogies, and the
quibbles and disputes about the Law—these are useless and
10 can do no good to anyone. ·If a man disputes what you
teach, then after a first and a second warning, have no more
11 to do with him: ·you will know that any man of that sort has
already lapsed and condemned himself as a sinner.

Practical recommendations, farewells and good wishes

12 As soon as I have sent Artemas or Tychicus to you, lose no
time in joining me at Nicopolis, where I have decided to

13 spend the winter. ·See to all the travelling arrangements for Zenas the lawyer and Apollos, and make sure they have
14 everything they need. ·All our people are to learn to occupy themselves in doing good works for their practical needs as well, and not to be entirely unproductive.
15   All those who are with me send their greetings. Greetings to those who love us in the faith. Grace be with you all.

PHILEMON

THE LETTER FROM PAUL TO

PHILEMON

Address

1 From Paul, a prisoner of Christ Jesus and from our
2 brother Timothy; to our dear fellow worker Philemon, ·our
sister Apphia, our fellow soldier Archippus and the church
3 that meets in your house; ·wishing you the grace and the
peace of God our Father and the Lord Jesus Christ.

Thanksgiving and prayer

4 I always mention you in my prayers and thank God for
5 you, ·because I hear of the love and the faith which you have
6 for the Lord Jesus and for all the saints. ·I pray that this faith
will give rise to a sense of fellowship that will show you all the
7 good things that we are able to do for Christ. ·I am so
delighted, and comforted, to know of your love; they tell me,
brother, how you have put new heart into the saints.

The request about Onesimus

8 Now, although in Christ I can have no diffidence about
9 telling you to do whatever is your duty, ·I am appealing to
your love instead, reminding you that this is Paul writing, an
old man now and, what is more, still a prisoner of Christ
10 Jesus. ·I am appealing to you for a child of mine, whose
father I became while wearing these chains: I mean Onesi-
11 mus. ·He was of no use to you before, but he will be useful[a]
12 to you now, as he has been to me. ·I am sending him back to
you, and with him—I could say—a part of my own self.
13 I should have liked to keep him with me; he could have been
a substitute for you, to help me while I am in the chains that
14 the Good News has brought me. ·However, I did not want to
do anything without your consent; it would have been forc-
15 ing your act of kindness, which should be spontaneous. ·I
know you have been deprived of Onesimus for a time, but it
16 was only so that you could have him back for ever, ·not as a

slave any more, but something much better than a slave, a dear brother; especially dear to me, but how much more to you, as a blood-brother as well as a brother in the Lord.

17 So if all that we have in common means anything to you,
18 welcome him as you would me; ·but if he has wronged you in any way or owes you anything, then let me pay for it.
19 I am writing this in my own handwriting: I, Paul, shall pay it back—I will not add any mention of your own debt to me,
20 which is yourself. ·Well then, brother, I am counting on you,
21 in the Lord; put new heart into me, in Christ. ·I am writing with complete confidence in your compliance, sure that you will do even more than I ask.

A personal request. Good wishes

22 There is another thing: will you get a place ready for me to stay in? I am hoping through your prayers to be restored to you.
23 Epaphras, a prisoner with me in Christ Jesus, sends his
24 greetings; ·so do my colleagues Mark, Aristarchus, Demas and Luke.
25 May the grace of our Lord Jesus Christ be with your spirit.

a. A pun—'Onesimus' means 'useful'.

THE LETTER TO THE

HEBREWS

A LETTER ADDRESSED
TO A JEWISH-CHRISTIAN COMMUNITY

PROLOGUE

The greatness of the incarnate Son of God

1   At various times in the past and in various different ways,
God spoke to our ancestors through the prophets; but
2 in our own time, the last days, he has spoken to us through his
Son, the Son that he has appointed to inherit everything and
3 through whom he made everything there is. ·He is the radiant
light of God's glory and the perfect copy of his nature,
sustaining the universe by his powerful command; and now
that he has destroyed the defilement of sin, he has gone to
take his place in heaven at the right hand of divine Majesty.
4 So he is now as far above the angels as the title which he has
inherited is higher than their own name.

I. THE SON IS GREATER THAN
THE ANGELS

Proof from the scriptures

5   God has never said to any angel: *You are my Son, today I
have become your father;*[a] or: *I will be a father to him and he a
6 son to me.*[b] ·Again, when he brings the First-born into the
7 world, he says: *Let all the angels of God worship him.*[c] ·About
the angels, he says: *He makes his angels winds and his servants
8 flames of fire,*[d] ·but to his Son he says: *God, your throne shall last
for ever and ever;* and: *his royal sceptre is the sceptre of virtue;
9 virtue you love as much as you hate wickedness. This is why
God, your God, has anointed you with the oil of gladness, above
10 all your rivals.*[e] ·And again: *It is you, Lord, who laid earth's
foundations in the beginning, the heavens are the work of your
11 hands; ·all will vanish, though you remain, all wear out like a*

12 *garment; ·you will roll them up like a cloak, and like a garment
   they will be changed. But yourself, you never change and your*
13 *years are unending.*[f] ·God has never said to any angel: *Sit at
   my right hand and I will make your enemies a footstool for you.*[g]
14 The truth is they are all spirits whose work is service, sent to
   help those who will be the heirs of salvation.

An exhortation

2 We ought, then, to turn our minds more attentively than
   before to what we have been taught, so that we do not drift
2 away. ·If a promise that was made through angels[a] proved to
   be so true that every infringement and disobedience brought
3 its own proper punishment, ·then we shall certainly not go
   unpunished if we neglect this salvation that is promised to us.
   The promise was first announced by the Lord himself, and is
4 guaranteed to· us by those who heard him; ·God himself
   confirmed their witness with signs and marvels and miracles
   of all kinds, and by freely giving the gifts of the Holy Spirit.

Redemption brought by Christ, not by angels

5 He did not appoint angels to be rulers of the world to come,
6 and that world is what we are talking about. ·Somewhere
   there is a passage that shows us this. It runs: *What is man
   that you should spare a thought for him, the son of man that
7 you should care for him? ·For a short while you made him
   lower than the angels; you crowned him with glory and splen-
8 dour. ·You have put him in command of everything.*[b] Well then,
   if he has *put him in command of everything*, he has left nothing
   which is not under his command. At present, it is true, we are
   not able to see that *everything has been put under his com-
9 mand*, ·but we do see in Jesus one who was *for a short while
   made lower than the angels* and is now *crowned with glory and
   splendour* because he submitted to death; by God's grace he
   had to experience death for all mankind.
10 As it was his purpose to bring a great many of his sons into
   glory it was appropriate that God, for whom everything
   exists and through whom everything exists, should make
   perfect, through suffering, the leader who would take them to
11 their salvation. ·For the one who sanctifies, and the ones who
   are sanctified, are of the same stock; that is why he openly
12 calls them *brothers* ·in the text: *I shall announce your name to*

1 a. Ps 2:7 **b.** 2 S 7:14 **c.** Dt 32:43 **d.** Ps 104:4 **e.** Ps 45:6–7
f. Ps 102:25–27 **g.** Ps 110:1
2 a. The Law. **b.** Ps 8:4–6 (LXX)

13 *my brothers, praise you in full assembly;*[c] or the text: *·In him
I hope*; or the text: *Here I am with the children whom God has
given me.*[d]

14   Since all the *children* share the same blood and flesh, he too
shared equally in it, so that by his death he could take away all
15 the power of the devil, who had power over death, ·and set
free all those who had been held in slavery all their lives by
16 the fear of death. ·For it was not the angels that he took to
17 himself; he took to himself *descent from Abraham.*[e] ·It was
essential that he should in this way become completely like
his brothers so that he could be a compassionate and trustworthy high priest of God's religion, able to atone for human
18 sins. ·That is, because he has himself been through temptation he is able to help others who are tempted.

II. JESUS THE FAITHFUL AND MERCIFUL HIGH PRIEST

Christ higher than Moses

3   That is why all you who are holy brothers and have had
the same heavenly call should turn your minds to Jesus, the
2 apostle and the high priest of our religion. ·He was *faithful* to
the one who appointed him, just like *Moses*, who stayed
3 faithful *in all his house;* ·but he has been found to deserve a
greater glory than Moses. It is the difference between the
honour given to the man that built the house and to the house
4 itself. ·Every house is built by someone, of course; but God
5 built everything that exists. ·It is true that Moses was *faithful
in the house* of God, as a servant, acting as witness to the
6 things which were to be divulged later; ·but Christ was faithful as a son, and as the master in the house. And we are his
house, as long as we cling to our hope with the confidence
that we glory in.

How to reach God's land of rest

7   The Holy Spirit says: *If only you would listen to him today;*
8 *do not harden your hearts, as happened in the Rebellion, on the*
9 *Day of Temptation in the wilderness, ·when your ancestors
challenged me and tested me, though they had seen what I
10 could do ·for forty years. That was why I was angry with that
generation and said: How unreliable these people who refuse to
11 grasp my ways! ·And so, in anger, I swore that not one would
12 reach the place of rest I had for them.*[a] ·Take care, brothers,
that there is not in any one of your community a wicked
mind, so unbelieving as to turn away from the living God.
13 Every day, as long as this 'today' lasts, keep encouraging one

another so that none of you is *hardened* by the lure of sin,

14 because we shall remain co-heirs with Christ only if we keep
15 a grasp on our first confidence right to the end. ·In this
saying: *If only you would listen to him today; do not harden*
16 *your hearts, as happened in the Rebellion,* ·those who *rebelled*
after they had *listened* were all the people who were brought
17 out of Egypt by Moses. ·And those who made God *angry for*
forty years were the ones who sinned and whose *dead bodies*
18 *were left lying in the wilderness.*[b] ·Those that he *swore would*
never reach the place of rest he had for them were those who
19 had been disobedient. ·We see, then, that it was because they
were unfaithful that they were not able to reach it.

4 Be careful, then: the promise of *reaching the place of rest*
he had for them still holds good, and none of you must think
2 that he has come too late for it. ·We received the Good News
exactly as they did; but hearing the message did them no good
because they did not share the faith of those who listened.
3 We, however, who have faith, shall reach a place of rest, as in
the text: *And so, in anger, I swore that not one would reach the*
place of rest I had for them. God's work was undoubtedly all
4 finished at the beginning of the world; ·as one text says,
referring to the seventh day: *After all his work God rested on*
5 *the seventh day.*[a] ·The text we are considering says: *They shall*
6 *not reach the place of rest I had for them.* ·It is established,
then, that there would be some people who would reach it,
and since those who first heard the Good News failed to
7 reach it through their disobedience, ·God fixed another day
when, much later, he said 'today' through David in the text
already quoted: *If only you would listen to him today; do not*
8 *harden your hearts.* ·If Joshua had led them into this place of
rest, God would not later on have spoken so much of another
9 day. ·There must still be, therefore, a place of rest reserved for
10 God's people, the seventh-day rest, ·since to *reach the place of*
11 *rest* is to *rest after your work,* as God did after his. ·We must
therefore do everything we can to *reach this place of rest,* or
some of you might copy this example of disobedience and be
lost.

The word of God and Christ the priest

12 The word of God is something alive and active: it cuts like
any double-edged sword but more finely: it can slip through

c. Ps 22:22 d. This, and the previous text, are from Is 8:17–18.
e. Is 41:8–9
3 a. Ps 95 b. Nb 14:29
4 a. Gn 2:2

the place where the soul is divided from the spirit, or joints
from the marrow; it can judge the secret emotions and
13 thoughts. ·No created thing can hide from him; everything is
uncovered and open to the eyes of the one to whom we must
give account of ourselves.

14   Since in Jesus, the Son of God, we have the supreme high
priest who has gone through to the highest heaven, we must
15 never let go of the faith that we have professed. ·For it is not
as if we had a high priest who was incapable of feeling our
weaknesses with us; but we have one who has been tempted
16 in every way that we are, though he is without sin. ·Let us be
confident, then, in approaching the throne of grace, that we
shall have mercy from him and find grace when we are in
need of help.

Jesus the compassionate high priest

5   Every high priest has been taken out of mankind and is
appointed to act for men in their relations with God, to offer
2 gifts and sacrifices for sins; and so ·he can sympathise with
those who are ignorant or uncertain because he too lives
3 in the limitations of weakness. ·That is why he has to make
4 sin offerings for himself as well as for the people. ·No one
takes this honour on himself, but each one is called by God,
5 as Aaron was. ·Nor did Christ give himself the glory of
becoming high priest, but he had it from the one who said to
6 him: *You are my son, today I have become your father,*[a] ·and
in another text: *You are a priest of the order of Melchizedek,*
7 *and for ever.*[b] ·During his life on earth, he offered up prayer
and entreaty, aloud and in silent tears, to the one who had
the power to save him out of death, and he submitted so
8 humbly that his prayer was heard. ·Although he was Son,
9 he learnt to obey through suffering; ·but having been made
perfect, he became for all who obey him the source of eternal
10 salvation ·and was acclaimed by God with the title of high
priest *of the order of Melchizedek.*

III. THE AUTHENTIC PRIESTHOOD OF
JESUS CHRIST

Christian life and theology

11   On this subject we have many things to say, and they are
difficult to explain because you have grown so slow at under-
12 standing. ·Really, when you should by this time have become
masters, you need someone to teach you all over again the

elementary principles of interpreting God's oracles; you
13 have gone back to needing milk, and not solid food. ·Truly,
anyone who is still living on milk cannot digest the doctrine
14 of righteousness because he is still a baby. ·Solid food is for
mature men with minds trained by practice to distingush
between good and bad.

The author explains his intention

6   Let us leave behind us then all the elementary teaching
about Christ and concentrate on its completion, without
going over the fundamental doctrines again: the turning
2 away from dead actions and towards faith in God; ·the
teaching about baptisms and the laying-on of hands; the
teaching about the resurrection of the dead and eternal
3 judgement. ·This, God willing, is what we propose to do.
4   As for those people who were once brought into the light,
and tasted the gift from heaven, and received a share of the
5 Holy Spirit, ·and appreciated the good message of God and
6 the powers of the world to come ·and yet in spite of this have
fallen away—it is impossible for them to be renewed a second
time. They cannot be repentant if they have wilfully crucified
7 the Son of God and openly mocked him. ·A field that has been
well watered by frequent rain, and gives the crops that are
wanted by the owners who grew them, is given God's blessing;
8 but one that grows brambles and thistles is abandoned,
and practically cursed. It will end by being burnt.

Words of hope and encouragement

9   But you, my dear people—in spite of what we have just
said, we are sure you are in a better state and on the way to
10 salvation. ·God would not be so unjust as to forget all you
have done, the love that you have for his name or the services
11 you have done, and are still doing, for the saints.[a] ·Our one
desire is that every one of you should go on showing the same
earnestness to the end, to the perfect fulfilment of our hopes,
12 never growing careless, but imitating those who have the
faith and the perseverance to inherit the promises.
13   When God made the promise to Abraham, he *swore by his
own self*, since it was impossible for him to swear by anyone
14 greater: ·*I will shower blessings on you and give you many
15 descendants.*[b] ·Because of that, Abraham persevered and saw
16 the promise fulfilled. ·Men, of course, swear by an oath by

5 a. Ps 2:7 **b.** Ps 110:4
6 a. The same phrase is used in Rm and 2 Co about a collection of
money made for the church in Jerusalem. **b.** Gn 22

something greater than themselves, and between men, con-
17 firmation by an oath puts an end to all dispute. ·In the same
way, when God wanted to make the heirs to the promise
thoroughly realise that his purpose was unalterable, he con-
18 veyed this by an oath; ·so that there would be two unalterable things in which it was impossible for God to be lying,
and so that we, now we have found safety, should have a
strong encouragement to take a firm grip on the hope that is
19 held out to us. ·Here we have an anchor for our soul, as sure
as it is firm, and reaching right *through beyond the veil*[c]
20 where Jesus has entered before us and on our behalf, to
become a high *priest of the order of Melchizedek, and for
ever.*

A. CHRIST'S PRIESTHOOD HIGHER THAN LEVITICAL PRIESTHOOD

Melchizedek[a]

7   You remember that *Melchizedek, king of Salem, a priest of
God Most High, went to meet Abraham who was on his way*
2 *back after defeating the kings*, and *blessed him;* ·and also that
it was to him that Abraham gave *a tenth of all that he had.* By
the interpretation of his name, he is, first, 'king of righteous-
3 ness' and also *king of Salem*, that is, 'king of peace'; ·he has
no father, mother or ancestry, and his life has no beginning
or ending; he is like the Son of God. He remains a priest for
ever.

Melchizedek accepted tithes from Abraham

4   Now think how great this man must have been, if the
patriarch *Abraham paid him a tenth of the treasure he had
5 captured.*[b] ·We know that any of the descendants of Levi who
are admitted to the priesthood are obliged by the Law to take
tithes from the people, and this is taking them from their own
brothers although they too are descended from Abraham.
6 But this man, who was not of the same descent, took his
tenth from Abraham, and he gave his blessing to the holder
7 of the promises. ·Now it is indisputable that a blessing is
8 given by a superior to an inferior. ·Further, in the one case it
is ordinary mortal men who receive the tithes, and in the
9 other, someone who is declared to be still alive. ·It could be
said that Levi himself, who receives tithes, actually paid
10 them, in the person of Abraham, ·because he was still in the
loins of his ancestor when *Melchizedek came to meet him.*

From levitical priesthood to the priesthood of Melchizedek

11   Now if perfection had been reached through the levitical priesthood because the Law given to the nation rests on it, why was it still necessary for a new priesthood to arise, one *of the same order as Melchizedek*[c] not counted as being 'of
12   the same order as' Aaron? ·But any change in the priesthood must mean a change in the Law as well.
13   So our Lord, of whom these things were said, belonged to a different tribe, the members of which have never done
14   service at the altar; ·everyone knows he came from Judah, a tribe which Moses did not even mention when dealing with priests.

The abrogation of the old Law

15   This[d] becomes even more clearly evident when there
16   appears a second Melchizedek, who is a priest ·not by virtue of a law about physical descent, but by the power of an
17   indestructible life. ·For it was about him that the prophecy was made: *You are a priest of the order of Melchizedek, and*
18   *for ever*. ·The earlier commandment is thus abolished, be-
19   cause it was neither effective nor useful, ·since the Law could not make anyone perfect; but now this commandment is replaced by something better—the hope that brings us nearer to God.

Christ's priesthood is unchanging

20   What is more, this was not done without the taking of an oath. The others, indeed, were made priests without any
21   oath; ·but he with an oath sworn by the one who declared to him: *The Lord has sworn an oath which he will never retract:*
22   *you are a priest, and for ever*.[e] ·And it follows that it is a greater covenant for which Jesus has become our guarantee.
23   Then there used to be a great number of those other priests,
24   because death put an end to each one of them; ·but this one,
25   because he remains *for ever*, can never lose his priesthood. ·It follows, then, that his power to save is utterly certain, since he is living for ever to intercede for all who come to God through him.

c. Lv 16:2
7 a. Gn 14, from which the following quotation is made, is silent about any ancestors or descendants of Melchizedek, and about 'the beginning and ending' of his life. b. The regular tithe paid to levitical priests was a tenth. c. Ps 110:4 d. What has been said in v. 12. e. Ps 110:4

The perfection of the heavenly high priest

26 To suit us, the ideal high priest would have to be holy, innocent and uncontaminated, beyond the influence of
27 sinners, and raised up above the heavens; ·one who would not need to offer sacrifices every day, as the other high priests do for their own sins and then for those of the people, because he has done this once and for all by offering himself.
28 The Law appoints high priests who are men subject to weakness; but the promise on oath, which came after the Law, appointed the Son who is made perfect *for ever*.

B. THE SUPERIORITY OF THE WORSHIP, THE SANCTUARY AND THE MEDIATION PROVIDED BY CHRIST THE PRIEST

The new priesthood and the new sanctuary

8 The great point of all that we have said is that we have a high priest of exactly this kind. He has his place *at the right* of
2 the throne of divine Majesty in the heavens, ·and he is the minister of the sanctuary and of the true *Tent* of Meeting
3 which *the Lord*, and not any man, *set up*.[a] ·It is the duty of every high priest to offer gifts and sacrifices, and so this one
4 too must have something to offer. ·In fact, if he were on earth, he would not be a priest at all, since there are others
5 who make the offerings laid down by the Law ·and these only maintain the service of a model or a reflection of the heavenly realities. For Moses, when he had the Tent to build, was warned by God who said: *See that you make everything according to the pattern shown you on the mountain.*[b]

Christ is the mediator of a greater covenant

6 We have seen that he has been given a ministry of a far higher order, and to the same degree it is a better covenant of
7 which he is the mediator, founded on better promises. ·If that first covenant had been without a fault, there would have
8 been no need for a second one to replace it. ·And in fact God does find fault with them; he says:

See, the days are coming—it is the Lord who speaks—
when I will establish a new covenant
with the House of Israel and the House of Judah,
9 *but not a covenant like the one I made with their ancestors*
on the day I took them by the hand

to bring them out of the land of Egypt.
They abandoned that covenant of mine,
and so I on my side deserted them. It is the Lord who
    speaks.

10 *No, this is the covenant I will make*
with the House of Israel
when those days arrive—it is the Lord who speaks.
I will put my laws into their minds
and write them on their hearts.   ╲
Then I will be their God
and they shall be my people.

11 *There will be no further need for neighbour to try to teach*
    neighbour,
or brother to say to brother,
'Learn to know the Lord'.
No, they will all know me,
the least no less than the greatest,

12 *since I will forgive their iniquities*
and never call their sins to mind.[c]

13 By speaking of a *new* covenant, he implies that the first one is
already old. Now anything old only gets more antiquated
until in the end it disappears.

Christ enters the heavenly sanctuary

9 The first covenant also had its laws governing worship, and
2 its sanctuary, a sanctuary on this earth. ·There was a tent
which comprised two compartments: the first, in which the
lamp-stand, the table and the presentation loaves were kept,
3 was called the Holy Place; ·then beyond the second veil, an
4 innermost part which was called the Holy of Holies ·to which
belonged the gold altar of incense, and the ark of the covenant, plated all over with gold. In this were kept the gold jar
containing the manna, Aaron's branch that grew the buds,
5 and the stone tablets of the covenant. ·On top of it was the
throne of mercy, and outspread over it were the glorious
cherubs. This is not the time to go into greater detail about
this.
6 Under these provisions, priests are constantly going into
7 the outer tent to carry out their acts of worship, ·but the
second tent is entered only once a year, and then only by the
high priest who must go in by himself and take the blood to
8 offer for his own faults and the people's. ·By this, the Holy
Spirit is showing that no one has the right to go into the

8 a. Nb 24:6 (LXX) b. Ex 25:40 c. Jr 31:31–34

9 sanctuary as long as the outer tent remains standing; ·it is a symbol for this present time. None of the gifts and sacrifices offered under these regulations can possibly bring any wor-
10 shipper to perfection in his inner self; ·they are rules about the outward life, connected with foods and drinks and washing at various times, intended to be in force only until it should be time to reform them.

11 But now Christ has come, as the high priest of all the blessings which were to come. He has passed through the greater, the more perfect tent, which is better than the one made by men's hands because it is not of this created order;
12 and he has entered the sanctuary once and for all, taking with him not the blood of goats and bull calves, but his own
13 blood, having won an eternal redemption for us. ·The blood of goats and bulls and the ashes of a heifer are sprinkled on those who have incurred defilement and they restore the
14 holiness of their outward lives; how much more effectively the blood of Christ, who offered himself as the perfect sacrifice to God through the eternal Spirit, can purify our inner self from dead actions so that we do our service to the living God.

Christ seals the new covenant with his blood

15 He brings a new covenant, as the mediator, only so that the people who were called to an eternal inheritance may actually receive what was promised: his death took place to
16 cancel the sins that infringed the earlier covenant. ·Now wherever a will is in question, the death of the testator must
17 be established; ·indeed, it only becomes valid with that death, since it is not meant to have any effect while the
18 testator is still alive. ·That explains why even the earlier covenant needed something to be killed in order to take
19 effect, ·and why, after Moses had announced all the commandments of the Law to the people, he took the calves' blood, the goats' blood and some water, and with these he sprinkled the book itself and all the people, using scarlet
20 wool and hyssop; ·saying as he did so: *This is the blood of the*
21 *covenant that God has laid down for you.*[a] ·After that, he sprinkled the tent and all the liturgical vessels with blood in
22 the same way. ·In fact, according to the Law almost everything has to be purified[b] with blood; and if there is no shed-
23 ding of blood, there is no remission. ·Obviously, only the copies of heavenly things can be purified in this way, and the heavenly things themselves have to be purified by a higher
24 sort of sacrifice than this. ·It is not as though Christ had

entered a man-made sanctuary which was only modelled on the real one; but it was heaven itself, so that he could appear
25 in the actual presence of God on our behalf. ·And he does not have to offer himself again and again, like the high priest going into the sanctuary year after year with the blood that is
26 not his own, ·or else he would have had to suffer over and over again since the world began. Instead of that, he has made his appearance once and for all, now at the end of the last
27 age, to do away with sin by sacrificing himself. ·Since men
28 only die once, and after that comes judgement, ·so Christ, too, offers himself only once *to take the faults of many on himself,*[c] and when he appears a second time, it will not be to deal with sin but to reward with salvation those who are waiting for him.

SUMMARY: CHRIST'S SACRIFICE SUPERIOR TO THE SACRIFICES OF THE MOSAIC LAW

The old sacrifices ineffective

10 So, since the Law has no more than a *reflection* of these realities, and no finished picture of them, it is quite incapable of bringing the worshippers to perfection, with the same
2 sacrifices repeatedly offered year after year. ·Otherwise, the offering of them would have stopped, because the worshippers, when they had been purified once, would have no
3 awareness of sins. ·Instead of that, the sins are recalled year
4 after year in the sacrifices. ·Bulls' blood and goats' blood are
5 useless for taking away sins, ·and this is what he said, on coming into the world:

> *You who wanted no sacrifice or oblation,*
> *prepared a body for me.*
6 > *You took no pleasure in holocausts or sacrifices for sin;*
7 > *then I said,*
> *just as I was commanded in the scroll of the book,*
> *'God, here I am! I am coming to obey your will.'*[a]

8 Notice that he says first: *You did not want* what the Law lays down as the things to be offered, that is: *the sacrifices, the oblations, the holocausts and the sacrifices for sin,* and *you*
9 *took no pleasure* in them; ·and then he says: *Here I am! I am coming to obey your will.* He is abolishing the first sort to

9 a. Ex 24:8 b. Many instances are given in Lv. c. Is 53:12
10 a. Ps 40:6–8 (LXX)

10 replace it with the second. ·And this *will* was for us to be made holy by the *offering* of his *body* made once and for all by Jesus Christ.

The efficacy of Christ's sacrifice

11   All the priests stand at their duties every day, offering over and over again the same sacrifices which are quite incapable
12 of taking sins away. ·He, on the other hand, has offered one single sacrifice for sins, and then taken his place for ever, *at*
13 *the right hand of God*, ·where he is now waiting *until his*
14 *enemies are made into a footstool for him.*[b] ·By virtue of that one single offering, he has achieved the eternal perfection of
15 all whom he is sanctifying. ·The Holy Spirit assures us of this; for he says, first:

16   *This is the covenant I will make with them*
         when those days arrive;[c]

and the Lord then goes on to say:

         I will put my laws into their hearts
         and write them on their minds.
17   *I will never call their sins to mind,*
         or their offences.

18 When all sins have been forgiven, there can be no more sin offerings.

IV. PERSEVERING FAITH

The Christian opportunity

19   In other words, brothers, through the blood of Jesus we
20 have the right to enter the sanctuary, ·by a new way which he has opened for us, a living opening through the curtain, that
21 is to say, his body. ·And we have the *supreme high priest* over
22 all *the house of God*. ·So as we go in, let us be sincere in heart and filled with faith, our minds sprinkled and free from any trace of bad conscience and our bodies washed with pure
23 water. ·Let us keep firm in the hope we profess, because the
24 one who made the promise is faithful. ·Let us be concerned
25 for each other, to stir a response in love and good works. ·Do not stay away from the meetings of the community, as some do, but encourage each other to go; the more so as you see the Day drawing near.

The danger of apostasy

26   If, after we have been given knowledge of the truth, we should deliberately commit any sins, then there is no longer

27 any sacrifice for them. ·There will be left only the dreadful
prospect of judgement and of *the raging fire* that is to *burn*
28 *rebels*.[d] ·Anyone who disregards the Law of Moses is ruth-
29 lessly *put to death on the word of two witnesses or three;*[e] ·and
you may be sure that anyone who tramples on the Son of
God, and who treats *the blood of the covenant* which sanctified him as if it were not holy, and who insults the Spirit of
30 grace, will be condemned to a far severer punishment. ·We
are all aware who it was that said: *Vengeance is mine; I will*
31 *repay*.[f] And again: *The Lord will judge his people.* ·It is a
dreadful thing to fall into the hands of the living God.

Motives for perseverance

32 Remember all the sufferings that you had to meet after you
33 received the light, in earlier days; ·sometimes by being yourselves publicly exposed to insults and violence, and sometimes as associates of others who were treated in the same
34 way. ·For you not only shared in the sufferings of those who
were in prison, but you happily accepted being stripped of
your belongings, knowing that you owned something that
35 was better and lasting. ·Be as confident now, then, since the
36 reward is so great. ·You will need endurance to do God's
will and gain what he has promised.

37 Only *a little while now, a very little while,*
and the one that is coming will have come; he will not delay.[g]
38 *The righteous man will live by faith,*
but if he draws back, my soul will take no pleasure in him.[h]

39 You and I are not the sort of people who *draw back*, and are
lost by it; we are the sort who keep *faithful* until our souls
are saved.

The exemplary faith of our ancestors

11 Only faith can guarantee the blessings that we hope for, or
prove the existence of the realities that at present remain
2 unseen. ·It was for faith that our ancestors were commended.
3 It is by faith that we understand that the world was created
by one word from God, so that no apparent cause can
account for the things we can see.
4 It was because of his faith that Abel offered God a better
sacrifice than Cain, and for that he was declared to be

b. Ps 110 c. From the long quotation from Jr 31 made in ch. 8.
d. Is 26:11 (LXX) e. Dt 17:6 f. Dt 32:35–36 g. Is 26:20 (LXX)
h. Hab 2:3–4 (LXX)

righteous when *God* made acknowledgement of *his offerings.*
Though he is dead, he still speaks by faith.

5   It was because of his faith that Enoch was taken up and
did not have to experience death: *he was not to be found
because God had taken him.*[a] This was because before his

6 assumption it is attested that *he had pleased God.* ·Now it is
impossible to please·God without faith, since anyone who
comes to him must believe that he exists and rewards those
who try to find him.

7   It was through his faith that Noah, when he had been
warned by God of something that had never been seen
before, felt a holy fear and built an ark to save his family. By
his faith the world was convicted, and he was able to claim
the righteousness which is the reward of faith.

8   It was by faith that Abraham obeyed the call to *set out* for
a country that was the inheritance given to him and his
descendants, and that *he set out* without knowing where he

9 was going. ·By faith he arrived, *as a foreigner*, in the Promised Land, and lived there as if in a strange country, with
Isaac and Jacob, who were heirs with him of the same pro-

10 mise. ·They lived there in tents while he looked forward to a
city founded, designed and built by God.

11   It was equally by faith that Sarah, in spite of being past the
age, was made able to conceive, because she believed that he

12 who had made the promise would be faithful to it. ·Because
of this, there came from one man, and one who was already
as good as dead himself, *more descendants than could be
counted, as many as the stars of heaven or the grains of sand on
the seashore.*[b]

13   All these died in faith, before receiving any of the things
that had been promised, but they saw them in the far distance and welcomed them, recognising that they were only

14 *strangers and nomads on earth.* ·People who use such terms
about themselves make it quite plain that they are in search

15 of their real homeland. ·They can hardly have meant the
country they came from, since they had the opportunity to go

16 back to it; ·but in fact they were longing for a better homeland, their heavenly homeland. That is why God is not
ashamed to be called their God, since he has founded the city
for them.

17   It was by faith that Abraham, *when put to the test, offered
up Isaac.*[c] He offered to sacrifice his only son even though the

18 promises had been made to him ·and he had been told: *It is

19 through Isaac that your name will be carried on.*[d] ·He was
confident that God had the power even to raise the dead; and

so, figuratively speaking, he was given back Isaac from the dead.

20 It was by faith that this same Isaac gave his blessing to
21 Jacob and Esau for the still distant future. ·By faith Jacob, when he was dying, blessed each of Joseph's sons, *leaning on*
22 *the end of his stick as though bowing to pray.*[e] ·It was by faith that, when he was about to die, Joseph recalled the Exodus of the Israelites and made the arrangements for his own burial.

23 It was by faith that Moses, when he was born, *was hidden by his parents for three months;* they defied the royal edict
24 when they *saw* he was such a *fine* child. ·It was by faith that, *when he grew to manhood*, Moses refused to be known as the
25 son of Pharaoh's daughter ·and chose to be ill-treated in company with God's people rather than to enjoy for a time
26 the pleasures of sin. ·He considered that the insults offered to the Anointed were something more precious than all the treasures of Egypt, because he had his eyes fixed on the
27 reward. ·It was by faith that he left Egypt and was not afraid of the king's anger; he held to his purpose like a man who
28 could see the Invisible. ·It was by faith that he kept *the Passover* and sprinkled *the blood* to prevent *the Destroyer*
29 from touching any of the first-born sons of Israel. ·It was by faith they crossed the Red Sea as easily as dry land, while the Egyptians, trying to do the same, were drowned.

30 It was through faith that the walls of Jericho fell down
31 when the people had been round them for seven days. ·It was by faith that Rahab the prostitute welcomed the spies and so was not killed with the unbelievers.

32 Is there any need to say more? There is not time for me to give an account of Gideon, Barak, Samson, Jephthah, or of
33 David, Samuel and the prophets. ·These were men who through faith conquered kingdoms, did what is right and earned the promises. They could keep a lion's mouth shut,
34 put out blazing fires and emerge unscathed from battle. They were weak people who were given strength, to be brave in
35 war and drive back foreign invaders. ·Some came back to their wives from the dead, by resurrection; and others submitted to torture, refusing release so that they would rise
36 again to a better life. ·Some had to bear being pilloried and
37 flogged, or even chained up in prison. ·They were stoned, or sawn in half,[f] or beheaded; they were homeless, and dressed

11 a. Gn 5:24 **b.** Gn 22:17, also quoted in Ex 32. **c.** Gn 22:1–14 **d.** Gn 21:12 **e.** Gn 47:31 **f.** Some apocryphal books say that this was how King Manasseh had Isaiah executed.

in the skins of sheep and goats; they were penniless and were
38 given nothing but ill-treatment. ·They were too good for the
world and they went out to live in deserts and mountains and
39 in caves and ravines. ·These are all heroes of faith, but they
40 did not receive what was promised, ·since God had made
provision for us to have something better, and they were not
to reach perfection except with us.

The example of Jesus Christ

12   With so many witnesses in a great cloud on every side of us,
we too, then, should throw off everything that hinders us,
especially the sin that clings so easily, and keep running
2 steadily in the race we have started. ·Let us not lose sight of
Jesus, who leads us in our faith and brings it to perfection:
for the sake of the joy which was still in the future, he endured the cross, disregarding the shamefulness of it, and
from now on has taken his place at the right of God's throne.
3 Think of the way he stood such opposition from sinners and
4 then you will not give up for want of courage. ·In the fight
against sin, you have not yet had to keep fighting to the
point of death.

God's fatherly instruction

5   Have you forgotten that encouraging text in which you are
addressed as sons? *My son, when the Lord corrects you, do not
treat it lightly; but do not get discouraged when he reprimands
6 you.* ·*For the Lord trains the ones that he loves and he punishes
7 all those that he acknowledges as his sons.*[a] ·Suffering is part of
your *training;* God is treating you as his *sons.* Has there ever
8 been any *son* whose father did not *train* him? ·If you were not
getting this training, as all of you are, then you would not be
9 *sons* but bastards. ·Besides, we have all had our human
fathers who punished us, and we respected them for it; we
ought to be even more willing to submit ourselves to our
10 spiritual Father, to be given life. ·Our human fathers were
thinking of this short life when they punished us, and could
only do what they thought best; but he does it all for our own
11 good, so that we may share his own holiness. ·Of course, any
punishment is most painful at the time, and far from
pleasant; but later, in those on whom it has been used, it
12 bears fruit in peace and goodness. ·So *hold up your limp arms
13 and steady your trembling knees*[b] ·and *smooth out the path you
tread;*[c] then the injured limb will not be wrenched, it will
grow strong again.

Unfaithfulness is punished

14 *Always be wanting peace*[a] with all people, and the holiness
15 without which no one can ever see the Lord. ·Be careful that
no one is deprived of the grace of God and that no *root of
bitterness should begin to grow and make trouble;*[e] this can
16 poison a whole community. ·And be careful that there is no
immorality, or that any of you does not degrade religion like
17 Esau, *who sold his birthright* for one single meal. ·As you
know, when he wanted to obtain the blessing afterwards, he
was rejected and, though he pleaded for it with tears, he was
unable to elicit a change of heart.

The two covenants

18 What you have come to is nothing known to the senses:
not a *blazing fire*,[f] or a *gloom* turning to *total darkness*, or a
19 *storm;* ·or *trumpeting thunder* or the *great voice speaking*
which made everyone that heard it beg that no more should
20 be said to them. ·They were appalled at the order that was
given: *If even an animal touches the mountain, it must be*
21 *stoned.* ·The whole scene was so terrible that Moses said: *I am*
22 *afraid*,[g] and was trembling with fright. ·But what you have
come to is Mount Zion and the city of the living God, the
heavenly Jerusalem where the millions of angels have
23 gathered for the festival, ·with the whole Church in which
everyone is a 'first-born son' and a citizen of heaven. You
have come to God himself, the supreme Judge, and been
placed with the spirits of the saints who have been made
24 perfect; ·and to Jesus, the mediator who brings a new covenant and a blood for purification which pleads more insist-
25 ently than Abel's. ·Make sure that you never refuse to listen
when he speaks. The people who refused to listen to the
warning from a voice on earth could not escape their punishment, and how shall we escape if we turn away from a voice
26 that warns us from heaven? ·That time his voice made the
earth shake, but now he has given us this promise: *I shall
make the earth shake once more and* not only the earth but
27 *heaven as well.*[h] ·The words *once more* show that since the
things being shaken are created things, they are going to be
28 changed, so that the unshakeable things will be left. ·We have
been given possession of an unshakeable kingdom. Let us
therefore hold on to the grace that we have been given and

12 a. Ps 3:11–12 (LXX) **b.** Is 35:3 **c.** Pr 4:26 (LXX) **d.** Ps 34:14
e. Dt 29:17 **f.** The quotations in vv. 18–20 are from Ex 19 (recalled in
Dt 4). **g.** Dt 9:19 **h.** Hg 2:6, probably influenced also by Ps 68:8.

use it to worship God in the way that he finds acceptable, in
29 reverence and fear. ·For our *God* is a *consuming fire*.[1]

APPENDIX

Final recommendations

13   Continue to love each other like brothers, ·and remember
always to welcome strangers, for by doing this, some people
3 have entertained angels without knowing it. ·Keep in mind
those who are in prison, as though you were in prison with
them; and those who are being badly treated, since you too
4 are in the one body. ·Marriage is to be honoured by all, and
marriages are to be kept undefiled, because fornicators and
5 adulterers will come under God's judgement. ·Put greed out
of your lives and be content with whatever you have; God
6 himself has said: *I will not fail you or desert you*,[a] ·and so we
can say with confidence: *With the Lord to help me, I fear
nothing: what can man do to me?*[b]

Faithfulness

7   Remember your leaders, who preached the word of God
to you, and as you reflect on the outcome of their lives,
8 imitate their faith. ·Jesus Christ is the same today as he was
9 yesterday and as he will be for ever. ·Do not let yourselves be
led astray by all sorts of strange doctrines: it is better to rely
on grace for inner strength than on dietary laws which have
10 done no good to those who kept them. ·We have our own
altar from which those who serve the tabernacle have no
11 right to eat. ·The bodies of the animals *whose blood is brought
into the sanctuary* by the high priest *for the atonement of sin
12 are burnt outside the camp*,[c] ·and so Jesus too suffered outside
13 the gate to sanctify the people with his own blood. ·Let us go
to him, then, *outside the camp*, and share his degradation.
14 For there is no eternal city for us in this life but we look for
15 one in the life to come. ·Through him, *let us offer God* an
unending *sacrifice of praise*,[d] a verbal sacrifice that is offered
16 every time we acknowledge his name. ·Keep doing good
works and sharing your resources, for these are sacrifices
that please God.

Obedience to religious leaders

17   Obey your leaders and do as they tell you, because they
must give an account of the way they look after your souls;

make this a joy for them to do, and not a grief—you your-
18 selves would be the losers. ·We are sure that our own conscience is clear and we are certainly determined to behave
19 honourably in everything we do; pray for us. ·I ask you very
particularly to pray that I may come back to you all the
sooner.

EPILOGUE

News, good wishes and greetings

20　I pray that the God of peace, *who brought* our Lord Jesus
back[e] from the dead *to become the great Shepherd of the*
21 *sheep*[f] *by the blood that sealed an eternal covenant,*[g] ·may
make you ready to do his will in any kind of good action;
and turn us all into whatever is acceptable to himself through
Jesus Christ, to whom be glory for ever and ever, Amen.
22　I do ask you, brothers, to take these words of advice
kindly; that is why I have written to you so briefly.
23　I want you to know that our brother Timothy has been set
free. If he arrives in time, he will be with me when I see you.
24 Greetings to all your leaders and to all the saints. The saints
25 of Italy send you greetings. ·Grace be with you all.

. Dt 4:24
13 a. Dt 31:6 **b.** Ps 118:6; Ps 27:1 **c.** Lv 16:27 **d.** Ps 50:14 **e.** Is 63:11
f. Ezk 34:23 **g.** Ezk 37:26

INTRODUCTION TO

THE LETTERS TO ALL CHRISTIANS

Seven letters not written by Paul are included in the New Testament and these, because they were addressed to the Church at large, have been known as 'the catholic epistles'. The three of them attributed to John have been briefly introduced in the introductory note to John's Gospel.

James

The traditional attribution of this letter to 'James, the brother of the Lord', is supported by internal evidence. Though it was written in Greek, the letter is full of hebraisms and its style of argument is characteristically semitic, and it was clearly intended for Jewish converts so familiar with the Old Testament that they would understand allusions to it without direct quotation. It is more a sermon than a letter and consists largely of moral exhortations, laying particular stress on the practical 'good works' expected of Christians and re-presenting much of the Jewish Wisdom tradition. It takes a different point of view from Paul's on the problem of relating faith to works, and may either be earlier than Galatians-Romans and written as early as A.D. 49, or it may be a rejoinder to what Paul had written and be placed at 57 or 58.

Jude

This is also a letter to Jewish Christians, probably written between A.D. 70 and 80. It denounces certain false teachers and threatens them with the punishments promised by Jewish tradition, and it quotes from apocryphal Jewish writings.

1 Peter. 2 Peter

1 Peter has from the earliest times been accepted as written by the apostle, though it may not have been first composed as a single letter. It is addressed to Christian churches largely made up of converts from paganism, and is in quite good Greek, perhaps through the help of the disciple Silvanus mentioned in it as secretary. The letter reflects a time of trial through which the

churches were passing and contains much practical teaching under the dominating theme of fortitude in persecution.

2 Peter seems to date from later than Peter's death, though the writer may have had some claim to represent Peter and was possibly a disciple of his. One possibility is that he filled out one of Peter's writings by adopting the letter of Jude to make a chapter (ch. 2).

THE LETTER OF

JAMES

Address and greetings

1   From James, servant of God and of the Lord Jesus Christ. Greetings to the twelve tribes of the Dispersion.*a*

Trials a privilege

2   My brothers, you will always have your trials but, when
3 they come, try to treat them as a happy privilege;*b* ·you understand that your faith is only put to the test to make
4 you patient, ·but patience too is to have its practical results so that you will become fully-developed, complete, with nothing missing.
5   If there is any one of you who needs wisdom, he must ask God, who gives to all freely and ungrudgingly; it will be given
6 to him. ·But he must ask with faith, and no trace of doubt,
7 because a person who has doubts is like the ·waves thrown
8 up in the sea when the wind drives. ·That sort of person, in two minds, wavering between going different ways, must not expect that the Lord will give him anything.
9   It is right for the poor·brother to be proud of his high
10 rank, ·and the rich one to be thankful that he has been humbled, because riches last no longer than *the flowers in the*
11 *grass;* ·the scorching sun comes up, and *the grass withers, the flower falls;*c* what looked so beautiful now disappears. It is the same with the rich man: his business goes on; he himself perishes.
12   *Happy the man who stands firm*d* when trials come. He has proved himself, and will win the prize of life, the crown that the Lord has promised to those who love him.

Temptation

13   Never, when you have been tempted, say, 'God sent the temptation'; God cannot be tempted to do anything wrong,
14 and he does not tempt anybody. ·Everyone who is tempted is
15 attracted and seduced by his own wrong desire. ·Then the desire conceives and gives birth to sin, and when sin is fully grown, it too has a child, and the child is death.

16
17 Make no mistake about this, my dear brothers: ·it is all that is good, everything that is perfect, which is given us from above; it comes down from the Father of all light; with him there is no such thing as alteration, no shadow of a change.

18 By his own choice he made us his children by the message of the truth so that we should be a sort of first-fruits of all that he had created.

True religion

19 Remember this, my dear brothers: be *quick to listen*[e] but
20 *slow* to speak and slow to rouse your temper; ·God's
21 righteousness is never served by man's anger; ·so do away with all the impurities and bad habits that are still left in you—accept and submit to the word which has been planted
22 in you and can save your souls. ·But you must do what the word tells you, and not just listen to it and deceive yourselves.
23 To listen to the word and not obey is like looking at your
24 own features in a mirror and then, ·after a quick look, going
25 off and immediately forgetting what you looked like. ·But the man who looks steadily at the perfect law of freedom and makes that his habit—not listening and then forgetting, but actively putting it into practice—will be happy in all that he does.

26 Nobody must imagine that he is religious while he still goes on deceiving himself and not keeping control over his tongue; anyone who does this has the wrong idea of religion.

27 Pure, unspoilt religion, in the eyes of God our Father is this: coming to the help of orphans and widows when they need it, and keeping oneself uncontaminated by the world.

Respect for the poor

2 My brothers, do not try to combine faith in Jesus Christ, our glorified Lord, with the making of distinctions between
2 classes of people. ·Now suppose a man comes into your synagogue,[a] beautifully dressed and with a gold ring on, and at the same time a poor man comes in, in shabby clothes,
3 and you take notice of the well-dressed man, and say, 'Come this way to the best seats'; then you tell the poor man, 'Stand

1 a. In O.T. days the 'Dispersion' (*diaspora*) meant the Jews who had emigrated from their own country. The writer is using it here to mean the Jewish-Christians, living in the Graeco-Roman world. **b.** 'happy privilege' is a pun on the greeting formula in v. 1. **c.** Is 40:6–7 **d.** Dn 12:12 **e.** Si 5:11
2 a. Jewish Christians may still have been attending synagogues, or the writer may have adopted this word for the Christian assembly.

over there' or 'You can sit on the floor by my foot-rest'.
4 Can't you see that you have used two different standards in
your mind, and turned yourselves into judges, and corrupt
judges at that?

5   Listen, my dear brothers: it was those who are poor
according to the world that God chose, to be rich in faith
and to be the heirs to the kingdom which he promised to
6 those who love him. ·In spite of this, you have no respect
for anybody who is poor. Isn't it always the rich who are
against you? Isn't it always their doing when you are dragged
7 before the court? ·Aren't they the ones who insult the
8 honourable name to which you have been dedicated? ·Well,
the right thing to do is to keep the supreme law of scripture:
9 *you must love your neighbour as yourself;*[b] ·but as soon as you
make distinctions between classes of people, you are committing sin, and under condemnation for breaking the Law.
10   You see, if a man keeps the whole of the Law, except for
one small point at which he fails, he is still guilty of breaking
11 it all. ·It was the same person who said, '*You must not commit adultery*' and '*You must not kill*'.[c] Now if you commit
murder, you do not have to commit adultery as well to be-
12 come a breaker of the Law. ·Talk and behave like people
13 who are going to be judged by the law of freedom, ·because
there will be judgement without mercy for those who have
not been merciful themselves; but the merciful need have no
fear of judgement.

Faith and good works

14   Take the case, my brothers, of someone who has never
done a single good act but claims that he has faith. Will that
15 faith save him? ·If one of the brothers or one of the sisters
16 is in need of clothes and has not enough food to live on, ·and
one of you says to them, 'I wish you well; keep yourself
warm and eat plenty', without giving them these bare neces-
17 sities of life, then what good is that? ·Faith is like that: if
good works do not go with it, it is quite dead.

18   This is the way to talk to people of that kind: 'You say
· you have faith and I have good deeds; I will prove to you
that I have faith by showing you my good deeds—now you
prove to me that you have faith without any good deeds to
19 show. ·You believe in the one God—that is creditable enough,
but the demons have the same belief, and they tremble with
20 fear. ·Do realise, you senseless man, that faith without good
21 deeds is useless. ·You surely know that Abraham our father
was justified by his deed, because he *offered his son Isaac on*

22 *the altar?*[d] ·There you see it: faith and deeds were working
23 together; his faith became perfect by what he did. ·This is
what scripture really means when it says: *Abraham put his
faith in God, and this was counted as making him justified;*[e]
and that is why he was called 'the friend of God'.

24 You see now that it is by doing something good, and not
25 only by believing, that a man is justified. ·There is another
example of the same kind: Rahab the prostitute, justified by
her deeds because she welcomed the messengers and showed
26 them a different way to leave. ·A body dies when it is
separated from the spirit, and in the same way faith is dead
if it is separated from good deeds.

Uncontrolled language

3 Only a few of you, my brothers, should be teachers,
bearing in mind that those of us who teach can expect a
stricter judgement.
2 After all, every one of us does something wrong, over and
over again; the only man who could reach perfection would
be someone who never said anything wrong—he would be
3 able to control every part of himself. ·Once we put a bit into
the horse's mouth, to make it do what we want, we have the
4 whole animal under our control. ·Or think of ships: no matter
how big they are, even if a gale is driving them, the man
at the helm can steer them anywhere he likes by controlling a
5 tiny rudder. ·So is the tongue only a tiny part of the body,
but it can proudly claim that it does great things. Think how
6 small a flame can set fire to a huge forest; ·the tongue is a
flame like that. Among all the parts of the body, the tongue
is a whole wicked world in itself: it infects the whole body;
catching fire itself from hell, it sets fire to the whole wheel of
7 creation. ·Wild animals and birds, reptiles and fish can all
8 be tamed by man, and often are; ·but nobody can tame the
tongue—it is a pest that will not keep still, full of deadly
9 poison. ·We use it to bless the Lord and Father, but we also
10 use it to curse men who are made in God's image: ·the
blessing and the curse come out of the same mouth. My
11 brothers, this must be wrong—·does any water supply give
12 a flow of fresh water and salt ·water out of the same pipe?
Can a fig tree give you olives, my brothers, or a vine give
figs? No more can sea water give you fresh water.

b. Lv 19:18 **c.** Ex 20 **d.** Gn 22:9 **e.** Gn 15:6

Real wisdom and its opposite

13 If there are any wise or learned men among you, let them show it by their good lives, with humility and wisdom in
14 their actions. ·But if at heart you have the bitterness of jealousy, or a self-seeking ambition, never make any claims
15 for yourself or cover up the truth with lies—·principles of this kind are not the wisdom that comes down from above:
16 they are only earthly, animal and devilish. ·Wherever you find jealousy and ambition, you find disharmony, and wicked
17 things of every kind being done; ·whereas the wisdom that comes down from above is essentially something pure; it also makes for peace, and is kindly and considerate; it is full of compassion and shows itself by doing good; nor is there any
18 trace of partiality or hypocrisy in it. ·Peacemakers, when they work for peace, sow the seeds which will bear fruit in holiness.

Disunity among Christians

4 Where do these wars and battles between yourselves first start? Isn't it precisely in the desires fighting inside your
2 own selves? ·You want something and you haven't got it; so you are prepared to kill. You have an ambition that you cannot satisfy; so you fight to get your way by force. Why you don't have what you want is because you don't pray for
3 it; ·when you do pray and don't get it, it is because you have not prayed properly, you have prayed for something to indulge your own desires.
4 You are as unfaithful as adulterous wives; don't you realise that making the world your friend is making God your enemy? Anyone who chooses the world for his friend turns
5 himself into God's enemy. ·Surely you don't think scripture is wrong when it says: the spirit which he sent to live in us
6 wants us for himself alone? ·But he has been even more generous to us, as scripture says: *God opposes the proud but*
7 *he gives generously to the humble.*[a] ·Give in to God, then;
8 resist the devil, and he will run away from you. ·The nearer you go to God, the nearer he will come to you. Clean your hands, you sinners, and clear your minds, you waverers.
9 Look at your wretched condition, and weep for it in misery; be miserable instead of laughing, gloomy instead of happy.
10 Humble yourselves before the Lord and he will lift you up.
11 Brothers, do not slander one another. Anyone who slanders a brother, or condemns him, is speaking against the Law and condemning the Law. But if you condemn the Law, you have stopped keeping it and become a judge over it.

12 There is only one lawgiver and he is the only judge and has the power to acquit or to sentence. Who are you to give a verdict on your neighbour?

A warning for the rich and the self-confident

13   Here is the answer for those of you who talk like this: 'Today or tomorrow, we are off to this or that town; we are going to spend a year there, trading, and make some money'.
14 You never know what will happen tomorrow: you are no more than a mist that is here for a little while and then
15 disappears. ·The most you should ever say is: 'If it is the
16 Lord's will, we shall still be alive to do this or that'. ·But how proud and sure of yourselves you are now! Pride of this
17 kind is always wicked. ·Everyone who knows what is the right thing to do and doesn't do it commits a sin.

5   Now an answer for the rich. Start crying, weep for the
2 miseries that are coming to you. ·Your wealth is all rotting,
3 your clothes are all eaten up by moths. ·All your gold and your silver are corroding away, and the same corrosion will be your own sentence, and eat into your body. It was a burning fire that you stored up as your treasure for the last
4 days. ·Labourers mowed your fields, and you cheated them— listen to the wages that you kept back, calling out; realise that the cries of the reapers have reached the ears of the
5 Lord of hosts. ·On earth you have had a life of comfort and luxury; in the time of slaughter you went on eating to your
6 heart's content. ·It was you who condemned the innocent and killed them; they offered you no resistance.

A final exhortation

7   Now be patient, brothers, until the Lord's coming. Think of a farmer: how patiently he waits for the precious fruit of the ground until it has had the autumn rains and the spring
8 rains! ·You too have to be patient; do not lose heart, because
9 the Lord's coming will be soon. ·Do not make complaints against one another, brothers, so as not to be brought to judgement yourselves; the Judge is already to be seen waiting
10 at the gates. ·For your example, brothers, in submitting with patience, take the prophets who spoke in the name of
11 the Lord; ·remember it is those who had endurance that we say are the blessed ones. You have heard of the patience of Job, and understood the Lord's purpose, realising that *the Lord is kind and compassionate*.[a]

4 a. Pr 3:34 (LXX)
5 a. Ps 103:8

12 Above all, my brothers, do not swear by heaven or by the earth, or use any oaths at all. If you mean 'yes', you must say 'yes'; if you mean 'no', say 'no'. Otherwise you make yourselves liable to judgement.

13 If any one of you is in trouble, he should pray; if anyone
14 is feeling happy, he should sing a psalm. ·If one of you is ill, he should send for the elders of the church, and they must anoint him with oil in the name of the Lord and pray over
15 him. ·The prayer of faith will save the sick man and the Lord will raise him up again; and if he has committed any sins, he
16 will be forgiven. ·So confess your sins to one another, and pray for one another, and this will cure you; the heartfelt
17 prayer of a good man works very powerfully. ·Elijah was a human being like ourselves—he prayed hard for it not to
18 rain, and no rain fell for three-and-a-half years; ·then he prayed again and the sky gave rain and the earth gave crops.

19 My brothers, if one of you strays away from the truth, and
20 another brings him back to it, ·he may be sure that anyone who can bring back a sinner from the wrong way that he has taken will be saving a soul from death and *covering up a great number of sins.*[b]

b. Pr 10:12

1 PETER

THE FIRST LETTER OF PETER

Address. Greetings

1 Peter, apostle of Jesus Christ, sends greetings to all those
living among foreigners in the Dispersion of Pontus, Galatia,
2 Cappadocia, Asia and Bithynia, who have been chosen, ·by
the provident purpose of God the Father, to be made holy
by the Spirit, obedient to Jesus Christ and sprinkled with his
blood. Grace and peace be with you more and more.

Introduction. The salvation of Christians

3 Blessed be God the Father of our Lord Jesus Christ, who
in his great mercy has given us a new birth as his sons, by
raising Jesus Christ from the dead, so that we have a sure
4 hope ·and the promise of an inheritance that can never be
spoilt or soiled and never fade away, because it is being kept
5 for you in the heavens. ·Through your faith, God's power will
guard you until the salvation which has been prepared is
6 revealed at the end of time. ·This is a cause of great joy for
you, even though you may for a short time have to bear
7 being plagued by all sorts of trials; ·so that, when Jesus
Christ is revealed, your faith will have been tested and proved
like gold—only it is more precious than gold, which is corruptible even though it bears testing by fire—and then you
8 will have praise and glory and honour. ·You did not see him,
yet you love him; and still without seeing him, you are already filled with a joy so glorious that it cannot be described,
9 because you believe; ·and you are sure of the end to which
your faith looks forward, that is, the salvation of your souls.

The hope of the prophets

10 It was this salvation that the prophets were looking and
searching so hard for; their prophecies were about the grace
11 which was to come to you. ·The Spirit of Christ which was in
them foretold the sufferings of Christ and the glories that
would come after them, and they tried to find out at what
12 time and in what circumstances all this was to be expected. ·It

was revealed to them that the news they brought of all the things which have now been announced to you, by those who preached to you the Good News through the Holy Spirit sent from heaven, was for you and not for themselves. Even the angels long to catch a glimpse of these things.

A call to sanctity and watchfulness

13 Free your minds, then, of encumbrances; control them, and put your trust in nothing but the grace that will be given

14 you when Jesus Christ is revealed. ·Do not behave in the way that you liked to before you learnt the truth; make a habit

15 of obedience: ·be holy in all you do, since it is the Holy

16 One who has called you, ·and scripture says: *Be holy, for I am holy.*[a]

17 If you are acknowledging as your Father one who has no favourites and judges everyone according to what he has done, you must be scrupulously careful as long as you are

18 living away from your home. ·Remember, the ransom that was *paid to free you*[b] from the useless way of life your ancestors handed down was not paid in anything corruptible,

19 neither in *silver* nor gold, ·but in the precious blood of a

20 lamb without spot or stain, namely Christ; ·who, though known since before the world was made, has been revealed

21 only in our time, the end of the ages, for your sake. ·Through him you now have faith in God, who raised him from the dead and gave him glory for that very reason—so that you would have faith and hope in God.

Love

22 You have been obedient to the truth and purified your souls until you can love like brothers, in sincerity; let your

23 love for each other be real and from the heart—·your new birth was not from any mortal seed but from the everlasting

24 word of the living and eternal God. ·*All flesh is grass and its glory like the wild flower's. The grass withers, the flower falls,*

25 *but the word of the Lord remains for ever.*[c] What is this word? It is the Good News that has been brought to you.

Integrity

2 Be sure, then, you are never spiteful, or deceitful, or

2 hypocritical, or envious and critical of each other. ·You are new born, and, like babies, you should be hungry for nothing but milk—the spiritual honesty which will help you to grow

3 up to salvation—·now that you have *tasted the goodness of the Lord.*[a]

The new priesthood

4 He is the living stone, rejected by men but chosen by God
5 and precious to him; set yourselves close to him ·so that you
too, the holy priesthood that offers the spiritual sacrifices
which Jesus Christ has made acceptable to God, may be
6 living stones making a spiritual house. ·As scripture says:
*See how I lay in Zion a precious cornerstone that I have
chosen* and *the man who rests his trust on it will not be disap-*
7 *pointed.*[b] ·That means that for you who are believers, it is
precious; but for unbelievers, *the stone rejected by the builders
8 has proved to be the keystone,*[c] ·*a stone to stumble over, a rock
to bring men down.*[d] They stumble over it because they do
not believe in the word; it was the fate in store for them.
9 But you are *a chosen race, a royal priesthood, a consecrated
nation, a people set apart*[e] to sing the praises of God who
called you out of the darkness into his wonderful light.
10 Once you were *not a people*[f] at all and now you are the
People of God; once you were *outside the mercy* and now *you
have been given mercy.*

The obligations of Christians: towards pagans

11 I urge you, my dear people, while you are *visitors and
pilgrims*[g] to keep yourselves free from the selfish passions
12 that attack the soul. ·Always behave honourably among
pagans so that they can see your good works for themselves
and, when the day of reckoning comes, give thanks to God
for the things which now make them denounce you as
criminals.

Towards civil authority

13 For the sake of the Lord, accept the authority of every
14 social institution: the emperor, as the supreme authority, ·and
the governors as commissioned by him to punish criminals
15 and praise good citizenship. ·God wants you to be good
citizens, so as to silence what fools are saying in their
16 ignorance. ·You are slaves of no one except God, so behave
like free men, and never use your freedom as an excuse for
17 wickedness. ·Have respect for everyone and love for our
community; fear God and honour the emperor.

1 a. Lv 19:2 b. Is 52:3 e. Is 40:6–8
2 a. Ps 34:8 b. Is 28:16 c. Ps 18:22 d. Is 8:14 e. Is 43:20–21 f. Ho
1:9; the two other quotations in this sentence are allusive references
to Ho 2. g. Ps 39:12

Towards masters

18 Slaves must be respectful and obedient to their masters, not only when they are kind and gentle but also when they
19 are unfair. ·You see, there is some merit in putting up with the pains of unearned punishment if it is done for the sake
20 of God ·but there is nothing meritorious in taking a beating patiently if you have done something wrong to deserve it. The merit, in the sight of God, is in bearing it patiently when you are punished after doing your duty.
21 This, in fact, is what you were called to do, because Christ suffered for you and left an example for you to follow the way
22 he took. ·He had not done anything wrong, and *there had*
23 *been no perjury in his mouth.*[h] ·He was insulted and did not retaliate with insults; when he was tortured he made no
24 threats but he put his trust in the righteous judge. ·He was *bearing our faults* in his own body on the cross, so that we might die to our faults and live for holiness; *through his wounds you have been healed.* You had *gone astray like sheep* but now you have come back to the shepherd and guardian[i] of your souls.

In marriage

3 In the same way, wives should be obedient to their husbands. Then, if there are some husbands who have not yet obeyed the word, they may find themselves won over, with-
2 out a word spoken, by the way their wives behave, ·when they
3 see how faithful and conscientious they are. ·Do not dress up for show: doing up your hair, wearing gold bracelets and
4 fine clothes; ·all this should be inside, in a person's heart, imperishable: the ornament of a sweet and gentle disposition
5 —this is what is precious in the sight of God. ·That was how the holy women of the past dressed themselves attractively— they hoped in God and were tender and obedient to their
6 husbands; ·like Sarah, who was obedient to Abraham, and called him her *lord.* You are now her children, as long as you
· live good lives and do not give way to fear or worry.
7 In the same way, husbands must always treat their wives with consideration in their life together, respecting a woman as one who, though she may be the weaker partner, is equally an heir to the life of grace. This will stop anything from coming in the way of your prayers.

Towards the brothers

8 Finally: you should all agree among yourselves and be sympathetic; love the brothers, have compassion and be self-
9 effacing. ·Never pay back one wrong with another, or an angry word with another one; instead, pay back with a blessing. That is what you are called to do, so that you inherit
10 a blessing yourself. ·Remember: *Anyone who wants to have a happy life and to enjoy prosperity must banish malice from*
11 *his tongue, deceitful conversation from his lips; ·he must never yield to evil but must practise good; he must seek peace and*
12 *pursue it. ·Because the face of the Lord frowns on evil men, but the eyes of the Lord are turned towards the virtuous.*[a]

In persecution

13 No one can hurt you if you are determined to do only what
14 is right; ·if you do have to suffer for being good, you will count it a blessing. *There is no need to be afraid or to worry*
15 *about them.*[b] ·Simply *reverence the Lord*[c] Christ in your hearts, and always have your answer ready for people who ask you
16 the reason for the hope that you all have. ·But give it with courtesy and respect and with a clear conscience, so that those who slander you when you are living a good life in Christ may be proved wrong in the accusations that they
17 bring. ·And if it is the will of God that you should suffer, it is better to suffer for doing right than for doing wrong.

The resurrection and 'the descent into hell'

18 Why, Christ himself, innocent though he was, had died once for sins, died for the guilty, to lead us to God. In the body he was put to death, in the spirit he was raised to life,
19 and, in the spirit, he went to preach to the spirits in prison.
20 Now it was long ago, when Noah was still building that ark which saved only a small group of eight people 'by water', and when God was still waiting patiently, that these spirits
21 refused to believe. ·That water is a type of the baptism which saves you now, and which is not the washing off of physical dirt but a pledge made to God from a good conscience,
22 through the resurrection of Jesus Christ, ·who has entered heaven and is at God's right hand, now that he has made the angels and Dominations and Powers his subjects.

h. This quotation, and the others in this paragraph, are from Is 53.
i. *episcopos.*
3 a. Ps 34:12–16 b. Is 8:12–13 (LXX) c. Pr 3:25

4 Think of what Christ suffered in this life, and then arm
yourselves with the same resolution that he had: anyone
who in this life has bodily suffering has broken with sin,
2 because for the rest of his life on earth he is not ruled by
3 human passions but only by the will of God. ·You spent
quite long enough in the past living the sort of life that pagans
live, behaving indecently, giving way to your passions, drinking all the time, having wild parties and drunken orgies and
4 degrading yourselves by following false gods. ·So people
cannot understand why you no longer hurry off with them
to join this flood which is rushing down to ruin, and then
5 they begin to spread libels about you. ·They will have to
answer for it in front of the judge who is ready to judge the
6 living and the dead. ·And because he is their judge too, the
dead had to be told the Good News as well, so that though,
in their life on earth, they had been through the judgement
that comes to all humanity, they might come to God's life
in the spirit.

The revelation of Christ is close

7 Everything will soon come to an end, so, to pray better,
8 keep a calm and sober mind. ·Above all, never let your
love for each other grow insincere, since *love covers over*
9 *many a sin.*[a] ·Welcome each other into your houses without
10 grumbling. ·Each one of you has received a special grace, so,
like good stewards responsible for all these different graces
11 of God, put yourselves at the service of others. ·If you are a
speaker, speak in words which seem to come from God; if
you are a helper, help as though every action was done at
God's orders; so that in everything God may receive the
glory, through Jesus Christ, since to him alone belong all
glory and power for ever and ever. Amen.

Recapitulation

12 My dear people, you must not think it unaccountable that
you should be tested by fire. There is nothing extraordinary
13 in what has happened to you. ·If you can have some share
in the sufferings of Christ, be glad, because you will enjoy a
14 much greater gladness when his glory is revealed. ·It is a
blessing for you when they insult you for bearing the name
of Christ, because it means that you have the Spirit of glory,
15 the Spirit of God resting on you. ·None of you should ever
deserve to suffer for being a murderer, a thief, a criminal or
16 an informer; ·but if anyone of you should suffer for being a

Christian, then he is not to be ashamed of it; he should
17 thank God that he has been called one. ·The time has come
for the judgement to begin at the household of God; and if
what we know now is only the beginning, what will it be
when it comes down to those who refuse to believe God's
18 Good News? ·*If it is hard for a good man to be saved, what*
19 *will happen to the wicked and to sinners?*[b] ·So even those
whom God allows to suffer must trust themselves to the
constancy of the creator and go on doing good.

Instructions: to the elders

5   Now I have something to tell your elders: I am an elder
myself, and a witness to the sufferings of Christ, and with
2 you I have a share in the glory that is to be revealed. ·Be the
shepherds of the flock of God that is entrusted to you: watch
over it, not simply as a duty but gladly, because God wants
it; not for sordid money, but because you are eager to do
3 it. ·Never be a dictator over any group that is put in your
charge, but be an example that the whole flock can follow.
4 When the chief shepherd appears, you will be given the crown
of unfading glory.

To the faithful

5   To the rest of you I say: do what the elders tell you, and
all wrap yourselves in humility to be servants of each other,
because *God refuses the proud and will always favour the*
6 *humble.*[a] ·Bow down, then, before the power of God now,
7 and he will raise you up on the appointed day; ·*unload* all *your*
8 *worries on to him,*[b] since he is looking after you. ·*Be calm*
but vigilant, because your enemy the devil is prowling round
9 like a roaring lion, looking for someone to eat. ·Stand up to
him, strong in faith and in the knowledge that your brothers
10 all over the world are suffering the same things. ·You will
have to suffer only for a little while: the God of all grace
who called you to eternal glory in Christ will see that all is
well again: he will confirm, strengthen and support you.
11 His power lasts for ever and ever. Amen.

Last words. Greetings

12   I write these few words to you through Silvanus, who is a
brother I know I can trust to encourage you never to let go
this true grace of God to which I bear witness.

4 a. Pr 10:12 **b.** Pr 11:31 (LXX)
5 a. Pr 3:34 (LXX) **b.** Ps 55:22

13   Your sister in Babylon, who is with you among the chosen, sends you greetings; so does my son, Mark.

14   Greet one another with a kiss of love.
Peace to you all who are in Christ.

2 PETER

THE SECOND LETTER OF PETER

Greetings

1 From Simeon Peter, servant and apostle of Jesus Christ;
to all who treasure the same faith as ourselves, given through
2 the righteousness of our God and saviour Jesus Christ. ·May
you have more and more grace and peace as you come to
know our Lord more and more.

A call to Christian living, and its reward

3 By his divine power, he has given us all the things that we
need for life and for true devotion, bringing us to know God
himself, who has called us by his own glory and goodness.
4 In making these gifts, he has given us the guarantee of something very great and wonderful to come: through them
you will be able to share the divine nature and to escape
5 corruption in a world that is sunk in vice. ·But to attain
this, you will have to do your utmost yourselves, adding
goodness to the faith that you have, understanding to your
6 goodness, ·self-control to your understanding, patience to
7 your self-control, true devotion to your patience, ·kindness
towards your fellow men to your devotion, and, to this kind-
8 ness, love. ·If you have a generous supply of these, they will
not leave you ineffectual or unproductive: they will bring you
9 to a real knowledge of our Lord Jesus Christ. ·But without
them a man is blind or else short-sighted; he has forgotten
10 how his past sins were washed away. ·Brothers, you have been
called and chosen: work all the harder to justify it. If you do
all these things there is no danger that you will ever fall away.
11 In this way you will be granted admittance into the eternal
kingdom of our Lord and saviour Jesus Christ.

The apostolic witness

12 That is why I am continually recalling the same truths to
you, even though you already know them and firmly hold
13 them. ·I am sure it is my duty, as long as I am in this tent, to
14 keep stirring you up with reminders, ·since I know the time
for taking off this tent is coming soon, as our Lord Jesus

15 Christ foretold to me. ·And I shall take great care that after
my own departure you will still have a means to recall these
things to memory.

16   It was not any cleverly invented myths that we were repeating when we brought you the knowledge of the power
and the coming of our Lord Jesus Christ; we had seen his
17 majesty for ourselves. ·He was honoured and glorified by
God the Father, when the Sublime Glory itself spoke to him
and said, 'This is my Son, the Beloved; he enjoys my favour'.
18 We heard this ourselves, spoken from heaven, when we were
with him on the holy mountain.[a]

The value of prophecy

19   So we have confirmation of what was said in prophecies;
and you will be right to depend on prophecy and take it as a
lamp for lighting a way through the dark until the dawn
20 comes and the morning star rises in your minds. ·At the same
time, we must be most careful to remember that the interpretation of scriptural prophecy is never a matter for the indi-
21 vidual. ·Why? Because no prophecy ever came from man's
initiative. When men spoke for God it was the Holy Spirit
that moved them.

False teachers

2   As there were false prophets in the past history of our
people, so you too will have your false teachers, who will
insinuate their own disruptive views and disown the Master
who purchased their freedom. They will destroy themselves
2 very quickly; ·but there will be many who copy their shameful behaviour and the Way of Truth will be brought into
3 disrepute on their account. ·They will eagerly try to buy you
for themselves with insidious speeches, but for them the
Condemnation, pronounced so long ago, is at its work
4 already, and Destruction is not asleep. ·When angels sinned,
God did not spare them: he sent them down to the underworld and consigned them to the dark underground caves to
5 be held there till the day of Judgement. ·Nor did he spare
the world in ancient times: it was only Noah he saved, the
preacher of righteousness, along with seven others, when
6 he sent the Flood over a disobedient world. ·The cities of
Sodom and Gomorrah, these too he condemned and reduced
to ashes; he destroyed them completely, as a warning to
7 anybody lacking reverence in the future; ·he rescued Lot,
however, a holy man who had been sickened by the shameless
8 way in which these vile people behaved—·for that holy man,

living among them, was outraged in his good soul by the
9 crimes that he saw and heard of every day. ·These are all
examples of how the Lord can rescue the good from the
ordeal, and hold the wicked for their punishment until the
10 day of Judgement, ·especially those who are governed by
their corrupt bodily desires and have no respect for authority.

The punishment to come

Such self-willed people with no reverence are not afraid
11 of offending against the glorious ones, ·but the angels in their
greater strength and power make no complaint or accusation
12 against them in front of the Lord. ·All the same, these people
who only insult anything that they do not understand are
not reasoning beings, but simply animals born to be caught
and killed, and they will quite certainly destroy themselves
13 by their own work of destruction, ·and get their reward of
evil for the evil that they do. They are unsightly blots on
your society: men whose only object is dissipation all day
long, and they amuse themselves deceiving you even when
14 they are your guests at a meal; ·with their eyes always looking
for adultery; men with an infinite capacity for sinning, they
will seduce any soul which is at all unstable. Greed is the
one lesson their minds have learnt. They are under a curse.
15 They have left the right path and wandered off to follow the
path of Balaam son of Beor, who thought he could profit
16 best by sinning, ·until he was called to order for his faults.
The dumb donkey put a stop to that prophet's madness when
17 it talked like a man. ·People like this are dried-up rivers,
fogs swirling in the wind, and the dark underworld is the
18 place reserved for them. ·With their high-flown talk, which
is all hollow, they tempt back the ones who have only just
escaped from paganism, playing on their bodily desires with
19 debaucheries. ·They may promise freedom but they themselves are slaves, slaves to corruption; because if anyone lets
himself be dominated by anything, then he is a slave to it;
20 and anyone who has escaped the pollution of the world
once by coming to know our Lord and saviour Jesus Christ,
and who then allows himself to be entangled by it a second
time and mastered, will end up in a worse state than he
21 began in. ·It would even have been better for him never to
have learnt the way of holiness, than to know it and after-
22 wards desert the holy rule that was entrusted to him. ·What
he has done is exactly as the proverb rightly says: *The dog*

1 a. At the transfiguration; Mt 17, Mk 9, Lk 9.

goes back to his own vomit^a and: When the sow has been washed, it wallows in the mud.

The Day of the Lord; the prophets and the apostles

3 My friends, this is my second letter to you, and in both of them I have tried to awaken a true understanding in you by
2 giving you a reminder: ·recalling to you what was said in the past by the holy prophets and the commandments of the Lord and saviour which you were given by the apostles.
3 We must be careful to remember that during the last days there are bound to be people who will be scornful, the kind who always please themselves what they do, and they
4 will make fun of the promise ·and ask, 'Well, where is this coming? Everything goes on as it has since the Fathers died,
5 as it has since it began at the creation.' ·They are choosing to forget that there were heavens at the beginning, and that the earth was formed by the word of God out of water and
6 between the waters, ·so that the world of that time was de-
7 stroyed by being flooded by water. ·But by the same word, the present sky and earth are destined for fire, and are only being reserved until Judgement day so that all sinners may be destroyed.
8 But there is one thing, my friends, that you must never forget: that with the Lord, 'a day' can mean a thousand years,
9 and *a thousand years is like a day*.^a ·The Lord is not being slow to carry out his promises, as anybody else might be called slow; but he is being patient with you all, wanting nobody to be lost and everybody to be brought to change his
10 ways. ·The Day of the Lord will come like a thief, and then with a roar the sky will vanish, the elements will catch fire and fall apart, the earth and all that it contains will be burnt up.

Conclusion and doxology

11 Since everything is coming to an end like this, you should
12 be living holy and saintly lives ·while you wait and long for the Day of God to come, when the sky will dissolve in flames
13 and the elements melt in the heat. ·What we are waiting for is what he promised: the new heavens and new earth, the place
14 where righteousness will be at home. ·So then, my friends, while you are waiting, do your best to live lives without spot
15 or stain so that he will find you at peace. ·Think of our Lord's patience as your opportunity to be saved: our brother Paul, who is so dear to us, told you this when he wrote to you
16 with the wisdom that is his special gift. ·He always writes like

this when he deals with this sort of subject, and this makes some points in his letter hard to understand; these are the points that uneducated and unbalanced people distort, in the same way as they distort the rest of scripture—a fatal thing

17 for them to do. ·You have been warned about this, my friends; be careful not to get carried away by the errors of unprincipled people, from the firm ground that you are

18 standing on. ·Instead, go on growing in the grace and in the knowledge of our Lord and saviour Jesus Christ. To him be glory, in time and in eternity. Amen.

2 a. Pr 26:11
3 a. Ps 90:4

1 JOHN

THE FIRST LETTER OF JOHN

INTRODUCTION

The incarnate Word

1 Something which has existed since the beginning,
   that we have heard,
   and we have seen with our own eyes;
   that we have watched
   and touched with our hands:
   the Word, who is life—
   this is our subject.

2 That life was made visible:
   we saw it and we are giving our testimony,
   telling you of the eternal life
   which was with the Father and has been made visible to
      us.

3 What we have seen and heard
   we are telling you
   so that you too may be in union with us,
   as we are in union
   with the Father
   and with his Son Jesus Christ.

4 We are writing this to you to make our own joy com-
      plete.

I. WALK IN THE LIGHT

5 This is what we have heard from him,
   and the message that we are announcing to you:
   God is light; there is no darkness in him at all.

6 If we say that we are in union with God[a]
   while we are living in darkness,
   we are lying because we are not living the truth.

7 But if we live our lives in the light,
   as he is in the light,
   we are in union with one another,

and the blood of Jesus, his Son,
purifies us from all sin.

First condition: break with sin

8   If we say we have no sin in us,
we are deceiving ourselves
and refusing to admit the truth;

9   but if we acknowledge our sins,
then God who is faithful and just
will forgive our sins and purify us
from everything that is wrong.

10   To say that we have never sinned
is to call God a liar
and to show that his word is not in us.

2   I am writing this, my children,
to stop you sinning;
but if anyone should sin,
we have our advocate with the Father,
Jesus Christ, who is just;

2   he is the sacrifice that takes our sins away,
and not only ours,
but the whole world's.

Second condition: keep the commandments, especially the law of love

3   We can be sure that we know God
only by keeping his commandments.

4   Anyone who says, 'I know him',
and does not keep his commandments,
is a liar,
refusing to admit the truth.

5   But when anyone does obey what he has said,
God's love comes to perfection in him.
We can be sure
that we are in God

6   only when the one who claims to be living in him
is living the same kind of life as Christ lived.

7   My dear people,
this is not a new commandment that I am writing to tell
you,

1 a. In the translation, 'God' or 'Christ' has been used in several places, where the Greek has a simple pronoun, in order to make the writer's meaning clear.

but an old commandment
that you were given from the beginning,
the original commandment which was the message
　　brought to you.

8　Yet in another way, what I am writing to you,
and what is being carried out in your lives as it was in
　　his,
is a new commandment;
because the night is over
and the real light is already shining.

9　Anyone who claims to be in the light
but hates his brother
is still in the dark.

10　But anyone who loves his brother is living in the light
and need not be afraid of stumbling;

11　unlike the man who hates his brother and is in the
　　darkness,
not knowing where he is going,
because it is too dark to see.

Third condition: detachment from the world

12　I am writing to you, my own children,
whose sins have already been forgiven through his
　　name;

13　I am writing to you, fathers,
who have come to know the one
who has existed since the beginning;
I am writing to you, young men,
who have already overcome the Evil One;

14　I have written to you, children,
because you already know the Father;
I have written to you, fathers,
because you have come to know the one
who has existed since the beginning;
I have written to you, young men,
because you are strong and God's word has made its
　　home in you,
and you have overcome the Evil One.

15　You must not love this passing world
or anything that is in the world.
The love of the Father cannot be
in any man who loves the world,

16　because nothing the world has to offer
—the sensual body,
the lustful eye,

pride in possessions—
could ever come from the Father
but only from the world;

17   and the world, with all it craves for,
is coming to an end;
but anyone who does the will of God
remains for ever.

Fourth condition: be on guard against the enemies of Christ

18   Children, these are the last days;
you were told that an Antichrist must come,
and now several antichrists have already appeared;
we know from this that these are the last days.

19   These rivals of Christ came out of our own number, but
they had never really belonged;
if they had belonged, they would have stayed with us;
but they left us, to prove that not one of them
ever belonged to us.

20   But you have been anointed by the Holy One,
and have all received the knowledge.

21   It is not because you do not know the truth that I am
writing to you
but rather because you know it already
and know that no lie can come from the truth.

22   The man who denies that Jesus is the Christ—
he is the liar,
he is Antichrist;
and he is denying the Father as well as the Son,

23   because no one who has the Father can deny the Son,
and to acknowledge the Son is to have the Father as well.

24   Keep alive in yourselves what you were taught in the
beginning;
as long as what you were taught in the beginning is
alive in you,
you will live in the Son
and in the Father;

25   and what is promised to you by his own promise
is eternal life.

26   This is all that I am writing to you about the people who
are trying to lead you astray.

27   But you have not lost the anointing that he gave you,
and you do not need anyone to teach you;
the anointing he gave teaches you everything;
you are anointed with truth, not with a lie,
and as it has taught you, so you must stay in him.

28　Live in Christ, then, my children,
　　so that if he appears, we may have full confidence,
　　and not turn from him in shame
　　at his coming.

29　You know that God is righteous—
　　then you must recognise that everyone whose life is
　　　righteous
　　has been begotten by him.

II. LIVE AS GOD'S CHILDREN

3　Think of the love that the Father has lavished on us,
　　by letting us be called God's children;
　　and that is what we are.
　　Because the world refused to acknowledge him,
　　therefore it does not acknowledge us.

2　My dear people, we are already the children of God
　　but what we are to be in the future has not yet been
　　　revealed;
　　all we know is, that when it is revealed
　　we shall be like him
　　because we shall see him as he really is.

First condition: break with sin

3　Surely everyone who entertains this hope
　　must purify himself, must try to be as pure as Christ.

4　Anyone who sins at all
　　breaks the law,
　　because to sin is to break the law.

5　Now you know that he appeared in order to abolish sin,
　　and that in him there is no sin;

6　anyone who lives in God does not sin,
　　and anyone who sins
　　has never seen him or known him.

7　My children, do not let anyone lead you astray;
　　to live a holy life
　　is to be holy just as he is holy;

8　to lead a sinful life is to belong to the devil,
　　since the devil was a sinner from the beginning.
　　It was to undo all that the devil has done
　　that the Son of God appeared.

9　No one who has been begotten by God sins;
　　because God's seed remains inside him,
　　he cannot sin when he has been begotten by God.

Second condition: keep the commandments, especially the law of love

10 In this way we distinguish the children of God
from the children of the devil:
anybody not living a holy life
and not loving his brother
is no child of God's.

11 This is the message
as you heard it from the beginning:
that we are to love one another;

12 not to be like Cain, who belonged to the Evil One
and cut his brother's throat;
cut his brother's throat simply for this reason,
that his own life was evil and his brother lived a good
life.

13 You must not be surprised, brothers, when the world
hates you;

14 we have passed out of death and into life,
and of this we can be sure
because we love our brothers.

15 If you refuse to love, you must remain dead;
to hate your brother is to be a murderer,
and murderers, as you know, do not have eternal life in
them.

16 This has taught us love—
that he gave up his life for us;
and we, too, ought to give up our lives for our brothers.

17 If a man who was rich enough in this world's goods
saw that one of his brothers was in need,
but closed his heart to him,
how could the love of God be living in him?

18 My children,
our love is not to be just words or mere talk,
but something real and active;

19 only by this can we be certain
that we are children of the truth
and be able to quieten our conscience in his presence,

20 whatever accusations it may raise against us,
because God is greater than our conscience and he
knows everything.

21 My dear people,
if we cannot be condemned by our own conscience,
we need not be afraid in God's presence,

22 and whatever we ask him,

we shall receive,
because we keep his commandments
and live the kind of life that he wants.

23 His commandments are these:
that we believe in the name of his Son Jesus Christ
and that we love one another
as he told us to.

24 Whoever keeps his commandments
lives in God and God lives in him.
We know that he lives in us
by the Spirit that he has given us.

Third condition: be on guard against the enemies of Christ and against the world

4 It is not every spirit, my dear people, that you can trust;
test them, to see if they come from God;
there are many false prophets, now, in the world.

2 You can tell the spirits that come from God by this:
every spirit which acknowledges that Jesus the Christ
    has come in the flesh
is from God;

3 but any spirit which will not say this of Jesus
is not from God,
but is the spirit of Antichrist,
whose coming you were warned about.
Well, now he is here, in the world.

4 Children,
you have already overcome these false prophets,
because you are from God and you have in you
one who is greater than anyone in this world;

5 as for them, they are of the world,
and so they speak the language of the world
and the world listens to them.

6 But we are children of God,
and those who know God listen to us;
those who are not of God refuse to listen to us.
This is how we can tell
the spirit of truth from the spirit of falsehood.

III. LOVE AND FAITH

Love

7 My dear people,
let us love one another

since love comes from God
and everyone who loves is begotten by God and knows
     God.

8   Anyone who fails to love can never have known God,
    because God is love.

9   God's love for us was revealed
    when God sent into the world his only Son
    so that we could have life through him;

10 this is the love I mean:
    not our love for God,
    but God's love for us when he sent his Son
    to be the sacrifice that takes our sins away.

11 My dear people,
    since God has loved us so much,
    we too should love one another.

12 No one has ever seen God;
    but as long as we love one another
    God will live in us
    and his love will be complete in us.

13 We can know that we are living in him
    and he is living in us
    because he lets us share his Spirit.

14 We ourselves saw and we testify
    that the Father sent his Son
    as saviour of the world.

15 If anyone acknowledges that Jesus is the Son of God,
    God lives in him, and he in God.

16 We ourselves have known and put our faith in
    God's love towards ourselves.
    God is love
    and anyone who lives in love lives in God,
    and God lives in him.

17 Love will come to its perfection in us
    when we can face the day of Judgement without fear;
    because even in this world
    we have become as he is.

18 In love there can be no fear,
    but fear is driven out by perfect love:
    because to fear is to expect punishment,
    and anyone who is afraid is still imperfect in love.

19 We are to love, then,
    because he loved us first.

20 Anyone who says, 'I love God'.
    and hates his brother,
    is a liar,

since a man who does not love the brother that he can
    see
cannot love God, whom he has never seen.

21   So this is the commandment that he has given us,
that anyone who loves God must also love his brother.

5   Whoever believes that Jesus is the Christ
has been begotten by God;
and whoever loves the Father that begot him
loves the child whom he begets.

2   We can be sure that we love God's children
if we love God himself and do what he has commanded
    us;

3   this is what loving God is—
keeping his commandments;

4   and his commandments are not difficult,
because anyone who has been begotten by God
has already overcome the world;
this is the victory over the world—
our faith.

Faith

5   Who can overcome the world?
Only the man who believes that Jesus is the Son of God:

6   Jesus Christ who came by water and blood,[a]
not with water only,
but with water and blood;
with the Spirit as another witness—
since the Spirit is the truth—

7   so that there are three witnesses,

8   the Spirit, the water and the blood,
and all three of them agree.

9   We accept the testimony of human witnesses,
but God's testimony is much greater,
and this is God's testimony,
given as evidence for his Son.

10   Everybody who believes in the Son of God
has this testimony inside him;
and anyone who will not believe God
is making God out to be a liar,
because he has not trusted
the testimony God has given about his Son.

11   This is the testimony:
God has given us eternal life
and this life is in his Son;

12   anyone who has the Son has life,
      anyone who does not have the Son does not have life.

Conclusion

13   I have written all this to you
      so that you who believe in the name of the Son of God
      may be sure that you have eternal life.

ENDING

Prayer for sinners

14   We are quite confident that if we ask him for anything,
      and it is in accordance with his will,
      he will hear us;

15   and, knowing that whatever we may ask, he hears us,
      we know that we have already been granted what we
         asked of him.

16   If anybody sees his brother commit a sin
      that is not a deadly sin,
      he has only to pray, and God will give life to the sinner
      —not those who commit a deadly sin;
      for there is a sin that is death,
      and I will not say that you must pray about that.

17   Every kind of wrong-doing is sin,
      but not all sin is deadly.

Summary of the letter

18   We know that anyone who has been begotten by God
      does not sin,
      because the begotten Son of God protects him,
      and the Evil One does not touch him.

19   We know that we belong to God,
      but the whole world lies in the power of the Evil One.

20   We know, too, that the Son of God has come,
      and has given us the power
      to know the true God.
      We are in the true God,
      as we are in his Son, Jesus Christ.
      This is the true God,
      this is eternal life.

21   Children, be on your guard against false gods.

5 a. The water and the blood from the side of Jesus, Jn 19:34, are
here used as figures of his 'coming' to all Christians, through the water
of baptism and through his sacrificial death.

2 JOHN

THE SECOND LETTER OF JOHN

1   From the Elder: my greetings to the Lady, the chosen one,[a] and to her children, she whom I love in the truth—and I am not the only one, for so do all who have come to know the
2 truth—·because of the truth that lives in us and will be with
3 us for ever. ·In our life of truth and love, we shall have grace, mercy and peace from God the Father and from Jesus Christ, the Son of the Father.

The law of love

4   It has given me great joy to find that your children have been living the life of truth as we were commanded by the
5 Father. ·I am writing now, dear lady, not to give you any new commandment, but the one which we were given at the beginning, and to plead: let us love one another.
6   To love is to live according to his commandments: this is the commandment which you have heard since the beginning, to live a life of love.

The enemies of Christ

7   There are many deceivers about in the world, refusing to admit that Jesus Christ has come in the flesh. They are the
8 Deceiver; they are the Antichrist. ·Watch yourselves, or all
9 our work will be lost and not get the reward it deserves. ·If anybody does not keep within the teaching of Christ but goes beyond it, he cannot have God with him: only those who keep to what he taught can have the Father and the
10 Son with them. ·If anyone comes to you bringing a different doctrine, you must not receive him in your house or even
11 give him a greeting. ·To greet him would make you a partner in his wicked work.
12   There are several things I have to tell you, but I have thought it best not to trust them to paper and ink. I hope

instead to visit you and talk to you personally, so that our joy may be complete.

13   Greetings to you from the children of your sister,[b] the chosen one.

1 a. The local church to which the letter is addressed. **b.** The local church from which the letter is sent.

3 JOHN

THE THIRD LETTER OF JOHN

1 From the Elder: greetings to my dear friend Gaius, whom
2 I love in the truth. ·My dear friend, I hope everything is going
happily with you and that you are as well physically as you
3 are spiritually. ·It was a great joy to me when some brothers
came and told of your faithfulness to the truth, and of your
4 life in the truth. ·It is always my greatest joy to hear that my
children are living according to the truth.

5 My friend, you have done faithful work in looking after
these brothers, even though they were complete strangers to
6 you. ·They are a proof to the whole Church of your charity
and it would be a very good thing if you could help them on
7 their journey in a way that God would approve. ·It was
entirely for the sake of the name that they set out, without
8 depending on the pagans for anything; ·it is our duty to
welcome men of this sort and contribute our share to their
work for the truth.

Beware of the example of Diotrephes

9 I have written a note for the members of the church, but
Diotrephes, who seems to enjoy being in charge of it, refuses
10 to accept us. ·So if I come I shall tell everyone how he has
behaved, and about the wicked accusations he has been
circulating against us. As if that were not enough, he not only
refuses to welcome our brothers, but prevents the other
people who would have liked to from doing it, and expels
11 them from the church. ·My dear friend, never follow such a
bad example, but keep following the good one; anyone who
does what is right is a child of God, but the person who does
what is wrong has never seen God.

Commendation of Demetrius

12 Demetrius has been approved by everyone, and indeed by
the truth itself. We too will vouch for him and you know that
our testimony is true.

Epilogue

13   There were several things I had to tell you but I would
14 rather not trust them to pen and ink. ·However, I hope to see
15 you soon and talk to you personally. ·Peace be with you;
greetings from your friends; greet each of our friends by
name.

THE LETTER OF

JUDE

Address

1 From Jude, servant of Jesus Christ and brother of James;
to those who are called, to those who are dear to God the
2 Father and kept safe for Jesus Christ, ·wishing you all
mercy and peace and love.

The reason for this letter

3 My dear friends, at a time when I was eagerly looking
forward to writing to you about the salvation that we all
share, I have been forced to write to you now and appeal to
you to fight hard for the faith which has been once and for all
4 entrusted to the saints. ·Certain people have infiltrated
among you, and they are the ones you had a warning about,
in writing, long ago, when they were condemned for denying
all religion, turning the grace of our God into immorality, and
rejecting our only Master and the Lord, Jesus Christ.

The false teachers: the certainty of their punishment

5 I should like to remind you—though you have already
learnt it once and for all—how the Lord rescued the nation
from Egypt, but afterwards he still destroyed the men who
6 did not trust him. ·Next let me remind you of the angels who
had supreme authority but did not keep it and left their
appointed sphere;[a] he has kept them down in the dark, in
7 spiritual chains, to be judged on the great day. ·The fornication of Sodom and Gomorrah and the other nearby towns
was equally unnatural, and it is a warning to us that they are
paying for their crimes in eternal fire.

Their violent language

8 Nevertheless, these people are doing the same: in their
delusions they not only defile their bodies and disregard
9 authority, but abuse the glorious angels as well. ·Not even
the archangel Michael, when he was engaged in argument
with the devil about the corpse of Moses, dared to denounce
him in the language of abuse; ·all he said was, 'Let the Lord

10 correct you'. ·But these people abuse anything they do not understand; and the only things they do understand—just by nature like unreasoning animals—will turn out to be fatal to them.

Their vicious behaviour

11 May they get what they deserve, because they have followed Cain; they have rushed to make the same mistake as Balaam and for the same reward; they have rebelled just as

12 Korah did—and share the same fate. ·They are a dangerous obstacle to your community meals, coming for the food and quite shamelessly only looking after themselves. They are like clouds blown about by the winds and bringing no rain, or like barren trees which are then uprooted in the winter and so

13 are twice dead; ·like wild sea waves capped with shame as if with foam; or like shooting stars bound for an eternity of

14 black darkness. ·It was with them in mind that Enoch, the seventh patriarch from Adam, made his prophecy when he said, 'I tell you, the Lord will come with his saints in their

15 tens of thousands, ·to pronounce judgement on all mankind and to sentence the wicked for all the wicked things they have done, and for all the defiant things said against him by

16 irreligious sinners'. ·They are mischief-makers, grumblers governed only by their own desires, with *mouths full of boastful talk*, ready with flattery for other people when they see some advantage in it.

A warning

17 But remember, my dear friends, what the apostles of our
18 Lord Jesus Christ told you to expect. ·'At the end of time,' they told you 'there are going to be people who sneer at religion and follow nothing but their own desires for wicked-

19 ness.' ·These unspiritual and selfish people are nothing but mischief-makers.

The duties of love

20 But you, my dear friends, must use your holy faith as your foundation and build on that, praying in the Holy Spirit;
21 keep yourselves within the love of God and wait for the mercy of our Lord Jesus Christ to give you eternal life.
22 When there are some who have doubts, reassure them;
23 when there are some to be saved from the fire, pull them out; but there are others to whom you must be kind with great

a. Briefly mentioned in Gn 6 : 1–2, but elaborated in *The Book of Enoch*.

caution, keeping your distance even from outside clothing which is contaminated by vice.

Doxology

24 Glory be to him who can keep you from falling and bring
25 you safe to his glorious presence, innocent and happy. ·To God, the only God, who saves us through Jesus Christ our Lord, be the glory, majesty, authority and power, which he had before time began, now and for ever. Amen.

INTRODUCTION TO

THE BOOK OF REVELATION

A 'Revelation' (called *Apocalypse*, from the Greek term) is a distinct literary form; apocalyptic writing was very popular in some Jewish circles at the beginning of the Christian era. The framework of a Revelation is always a vision of hidden supernatural events; the language in which the vision is described is richly symbolic and so allusive that the message can be interpreted in more ways than one.

Thus the Book of Revelation is not to be accepted simply as an allegory which can be directly translated into other terms. It contains the author's vision of heaven and of the vindication of the Christian martyrs in the world to come, but it must be understood first and foremost as a tract for the times, written to increase the hope and determination of the Church on earth in a period of disturbance and bitter persecution, and prophesying the certain downfall and destruction of the Roman imperial power. The imagery, largely drawn from the Old Testament, especially Daniel, allows the author to allude to the enemy, Rome, under the disguise of the old enemy, Babylon; and to present the happenings of his own day, seen by their reflections in the heavens, as recapitulations or fulfilments of the great events of Israel's past.

The text contains difficulties: there are repetitions and interruptions, and there are passages out of context. One promising hypothesis is that the strictly prophetic part of the book is made up of two different 'apocalypses' written at different times and later conflated. The author cannot be identified with the author of the Gospel according to John, but we can say that the book was written inside the evangelist's immediate circle and is pervaded by his doctrine. Its date is generally estimated as A.D. 95, but there are some who believe that parts, at least, were composed as early as Nero's time, shortly before A.D. 70.

THE BOOK OF

REVELATION

Prologue

1   This is the revelation given by God to Jesus Christ so that
he could tell his servants about the *things which are* now *to
take place*[a] very soon; he sent his angel to make it known to

2 his servant John, ·and John has written down everything he
saw and swears it is the word of God guaranteed by Jesus

3 Christ. ·Happy the man who reads this prophecy, and happy
those who listen to him, if they treasure all that it says,
because the Time is close.

I. THE LETTERS TO THE CHURCHES
OF ASIA

Address and greeting[b]

4   From John, to the seven churches of Asia: grace and peace
to you from him who is, who was, and who is to come, from

5 the seven spirits in his presence before his throne, ·and from
Jesus Christ, *the faithful witness, the First-born* from the
dead, *the Ruler of the kings of the earth.* He loves us and has

6 washed away our sins with his blood, ·and made us a *line of
kings, priests to serve* his God and Father; to him, then, be

7 glory and power for ever and ever. Amen. ·It is he who *is
coming on the clouds;* everyone will see him, even *those who
pierced him,* and *all the races of the earth will mourn over*

8 *him.* This is the truth. Amen. ·'I am the Alpha and the
Omega' says the Lord God, who is, who was, and who is to
come, the Almighty.

The beginning of the vision

9   My name is John, and through our union in Jesus I am
your brother and share your sufferings, your kingdom, and all
you endure. I was on the island of Patmos[c] for having

10 preached God's word and witnessed for Jesus; ·it was the
Lord's day and the Spirit possessed me, and I heard a voice

11 behind me, shouting like a trumpet, ·'Write down all that you

see in a book, and send it to the seven churches of Ephesus,
Smyrna, Pergamum, Thyatira, Sardis, Philadelphia and
12 Laodicea'. ·I turned round to see who had spoken to me, and
13 when I turned I saw seven gold lamp-stands ·and, surrounded
by them, a figure *like a Son of man,*[d] dressed in a long robe
14 tied at the waist with a *golden girdle.* ·*His head* and *his hair*
were *white as white wool* or as snow, *his eyes* like a *burning*
15 *flame,* ·*his feet like burnished bronze* when it has been refined
in a furnace, and *his voice like the sound of the ocean.*[e] ·In his
right hand he was holding seven stars, out of his mouth came
a sharp sword, double-edged, and his face was like the sun
shining with all its force.
17 When I saw him, I fell in a dead faint at his feet, but he
touched me with his right hand and said, 'Do not be afraid; it
18 is I, *the First and the Last;* I am the Living One, ·I was dead
and now I am to live for ever and ever, and I hold the keys of
19 death and of the underworld. ·Now write down all that you
see of present happenings and *things that are still to come.*[f]
20 The secret of the seven stars you have seen in my right hand,
and of the seven golden lamp-stands is this: the seven stars
are the angels of the seven churches, and the seven lamp-
stands are the seven churches themselves.

1. Ephesus

2 'Write to the angel of the church in Ephesus and say, "Here
is the message of the one who holds the seven stars in his
right hand and who lives surrounded by the seven golden
2 lamp-stands: ·I know all about you: how hard you work and
how much you put up with. I know you cannot stand wicked
men, and how you tested the impostors who called them-
3 selves apostles and proved they were liars. ·I know, too, that
you have patience, and have suffered for my name without
4 growing tired. ·Nevertheless, I have this complaint to make;
5 you have less love now than you used to. ·Think where you
were before you fell; repent, and do as you used to at first, or
else, if you will not repent, I shall come to you and take your
6 lamp-stand from its place. ·It is in your favour, nevertheless,
that you loathe as I do what the Nicolaitans are doing.
7 If anyone has ears to hear, let him listen to what the Spirit is

1 a. Dn 2:28 **b.** This section contains many O.T. allusions to the time
of the Messiah. The five direct quotations printed in italic are from:
Ps 89:37, 27; Is 55:4; Ex 19:6; Dn 7:13; and Zc 12:10, 14. **c.** Patmos
(10m. × 5m.) was used by the Romans as a penal colony. **d.** The
messianic figure in Dn; the descriptive quotations which follow are
from Dn 7 and 10. **e.** Ezk 43:2 **f.** Dn 2:28

saying to the churches: those who prove victorious I will feed *from the tree of life set in* God's *paradise*."ᵃ

2. Smyrna

8 'Write to the angel of the church in Smyrna and say, "Here is the message of *the First* and *the Last*, who was dead and
9 has come to life again: ·I know the trials you have had, and how poor you are—though you are rich—and the slanderous accusations that have been made by the people who profess to be Jews but are really members of the synagogue of Satan.
10 Do not be afraid of the sufferings that are coming to you: I tell you, the devil is going to send some of you to prison *to test you*, and you must face an ordeal for *ten days*.ᵇ Even if you have to die, keep faithful, and I will give you the crown of
11 life for your prize. ·If anyone has ears to hear, let him listen to what the Spirit is saying to the churches: for those who prove victorious there is nothing to be afraid of in the second death."

3. Pergamum

12 'Write to the angel of the church in Pergamum and say, "Here is the message of the one who has the sharp sword,
13 double-edged: ·I know where you live, in the place where Satan is enthroned, and that you still hold firmly to my name, and did not disown your faith in me even when my faithful witness, Antipas, was killed in your own town, where Satan lives.ᶜ
14 Nevertheless, I have one or two complaints to make: some of you are followers of Balaam, who taught Balak to set a trap for the Israelites so that they committed adultery by
15 eating food that had been sacrificed to idols; ·and among you, too, there are some as bad who accept what the Nico-
16 laitans teach. ·You must repent, or I shall soon come to you
17 and attack these people with the sword out of my mouth. ·If anyone has ears to hear, let him listen to what the Spirit is saying to the churches: to those who prove victorious I will give the hidden manna and a white stoneᵈ—a stone with *a new name* written on it, known only to the man who receives it."

4. Thyatira

18 'Write to the angel of the church in Thyatira and say, "Here is the message of the Son of God who has eyes like a
19 burning flame and feet like burnished bronze: ·I know all about you and how charitable you are; I know your faith and

devotion and how much you put up with, and I know how
20 you are still making progress. ·Nevertheless, I have a complaint to make: you are encouraging the woman Jezebel[e]
who claims to be a prophetess, and by her teaching she is
luring my servants away to commit the adultery of eating
21 food which has been sacrificed to idols. ·I have given her
time to reform but she is not willing to change her adulter-
22 ous life. ·Now I am consigning her to bed, and all her partners in adultery to troubles that will test them severely,
23 unless they repent of their practices; ·and I will see that her
children die, so that all the churches realise that it is I who
search heart and loins and give each one of you what your
24 *behaviour deserves.*[f] ·But on the rest of you in Thyatira, all of
you who have not accepted this teaching or learnt the secrets
of Satan, as they are called, I am not laying any special duty;
25 but hold firmly on to what you already have until I come.
26 To those who prove victorious, and keep working for me
until the end, *I will give* the authority over *the pagans*[g]
27 which I myself have been given by my Father, *to rule them*
28 *with an iron sceptre and shatter them like earthenware.* ·And
29 I will give him the Morning Star.[h] ·If anyone has ears to hear,
let him listen to what the Spirit is saying to the churches.''

5. Sardis

3   'Write to the angel of the church in Sardis and say, ''Here
is the message of the one who holds the seven spirits of God
and the seven stars: I know all about you: how you are
2 reputed to be alive and yet are dead. ·Wake up; revive what
little you have left: it is dying fast. So far I have failed to
notice anything in the way you live that my God could
3 possibly call perfect, ·and yet do you remember how eager
you were when you first heard the message? Hold on to that.
Repent. If you do not wake up, I shall come to you like a
4 thief, without telling you at what hour to expect me. ·There
are a few in Sardis, it is true, who have kept their robes from
being dirtied, and they are fit to come with me, dressed in
5 white. ·Those who prove victorious will be dressed, like these,
in white robes; I shall not blot their names out of the book of
life, but acknowledge their names in the presence of my

2 **a.** Gn 2:9 **b.** I.e. of short duration. **c.** I.e. 'where emperor-worship
is practised.' **d.** The manna hidden by Jeremiah (2 M 2:4–8), to be the
food of those who are saved in the heavenly kingdom; the white stone
is a badge or token of admittance or membership. **e.** By this name the
writer is indicating a prophetess of the Nicolaitan sect. **f.** Jr 11:20
g. Ps 2:8–9 **h.** Symbol of power and thus of the resurrection.

6 Father and his angels. ·If anyone has ears to hear, let him listen to what the Spirit is saying to the churches.''

6. Philadelphia

7 'Write to the angel of the church in Philadelphia and say, "Here is the message of the holy and faithful one who *has the key of David*, so that *when he opens, nobody can close, and*
8 *when he closes, nobody can open*:[a] ·I know all about you; and now I have opened in front of you a door that nobody will be able to close—and I know that though you are not very strong, you have kept my commandments and not disowned
9 my name. ·Now I am going to make the synagogue of Satan —those who profess to be Jews, but are liars, because they are no such thing—I will make them come and *fall at your*
10 *feet*[b] and admit that *you are* the people *that I love*.[c] ·Because you have kept my commandment to endure trials, I will keep you safe in the time of trial which is going to come for the
11 whole world, to test the people of the world. ·Soon I shall be with you: hold firmly to what you already have, and let
12 nobody take your prize away from you. ·Those who prove victorious I will make into pillars in the sanctuary of my God, and they will stay there for ever; I will inscribe on them the name of my God and the name of the city of my God, the new Jerusalem which comes down from my God in heaven,
13 and my own new name as well. ·If anyone has ears to hear, let him listen to what the Spirit is saying to the churches.''

7. Laodicea

14 'Write to the angel of the church in Laodicea and say, "Here is the message of the Amen, the faithful, the true
15 witness, the ultimate source of God's creation: ·I know all about you: how you are neither cold nor hot. I wish you were
16 one or the other, ·but since you are neither, but only luke-
17 warm, I will spit you out of my mouth. ·You say to yourself, 'I am rich, I have made a fortune, and have everything I want', never realising that you are wretchedly and pitiably
18 poor, and blind and naked too. ·I warn you, buy from me the gold that has been tested in the fire to make you really rich, and white robes to clothe you and cover your shameful nakedness, and eye ointment to put on your eyes so that you
19 are able to see. ·I *am* the one *who reproves and disciplines all*
20 *those he loves*:[d] so repent in real earnest. ·Look, I am standing at the door, knocking. If one of you hears me calling and opens the door, I will come in to share his meal, side by side
21 with him. ·Those who prove victorious I will allow to share

my throne, just as I was victorious myself and took my place
22 with my Father on his throne. ·If anyone has ears to hear, let
him listen to what the Spirit is saying to the churches."'

II. THE PROPHETIC VISIONS

A. THE PRELUDE TO THE GREAT DAY

God entrusts the future of the world to the Lamb

4   Then, in my vision, I saw a door open in heaven and heard
the same voice speaking to me, the voice like a trumpet, saying, 'Come up here: I will show you *what is to come* in the
2 future'. ·With that, the Spirit possessed me and I saw a
throne standing in heaven, and the *One* who was *sitting on the*
3 *throne*, ·and the Person sitting there looked like a diamond
and a ruby. There was a rainbow encircling the throne, and
4 this looked like an emerald.*ᵃ* ·Round the throne in a circle
were twenty-four thrones, and on them I saw twenty-four
elders sitting, dressed in white robes with golden crowns on
5 their heads. ·Flashes of lightning were coming from the
throne, and the sound of peals of thunder, and in front of the
throne there were seven flaming lamps burning, the seven
6 Spirits of God. ·Between the throne and myself was a sea that
seemed to be made of glass, like crystal. *In the centre*,
grouped round the throne itself, were *four animalsᵇ with many*
7 *eyes*, in front and behind. ·*The first* animal was like *a lion, the*
second like *a bull, the third* animal had *a human face*, and *the*
8 *fourth* animal was like a flying *eagle*. ·*Each* of the four animals
had *six wings* and *had eyes all the way round* as well as inside;
and day and night they never stopped singing:

> '*Holy, Holy, Holy*
> *is the Lord God, the Almighty;*
> *he was, he is and he is to come*'.

9 Every time the animals glorified and honoured and gave
thanks to the One sitting on the throne, *who lives for ever and*
10 *ever*, ·the twenty-four elders prostrated themselves before
him to worship the One *who lives for ever and ever*, and
11 threw down their crowns in front of the throne, saying, "You
are our Lord and our God, you are worthy of glory and

3 **a.** Is 22:22 **b.** Is 45:14 **c.** Is 43:4 **d.** Pr 3:12
4 **a.** For many of the descriptive details in this scene the writer draws
on Ezk 1 and 10 and Is 6. **b.** The angels or 'principles' which direct
the physical world. Since Irenaeus, these four creatures have been used
as symbols of the four evangelists.

honour and power, because you made all the universe and it
was only by your will that everything was made and exists'.

5 I saw that in the right hand of the One sitting on the throne
there was *a scroll that had writing on back and front*[a] and was
2 sealed with seven seals. ·Then I saw a powerful angel who
called with a loud voice, 'Is there anyone worthy to open the
3 scroll and break the seals of it?' ·But there was no one, in
heaven or on the earth or under the earth, who was able to
4 open the scroll and read it. ·I wept bitterly because there was
5 nobody fit to open the scroll and read it, ·but one of the
elders said to me, 'There is no need to cry: *the Lion* of the
tribe *of Judah, the Root*[b] of David, has triumphed, and he will
open the scroll and the seven seals of it'.

6 Then I saw, standing between the throne with its four
animals and the circle of the elders, a Lamb that seemed to
have been sacrificed; it had seven horns, and it had seven eyes,
which are the seven Spirits God has *sent out all over the*
7 *world.*[c] ·The Lamb came forward to take the scroll from the
8 right hand of the One sitting on the throne, ·and when he
took it, the four animals prostrated themselves before him
and with them the twenty-four elders; each one of them was
holding a harp and had a golden bowl full of incense made of
9 the prayers of the saints. ·They sang a new hymn:

> 'You are worthy to take the scroll
> and break the seals of it,
> because you were sacrificed, and with your blood
> you bought men for God
> of every race, language, people and nation
> 10   and made them *a line of kings and priests,*[d]
> to serve our God and to rule the world'.

11 In my vision, I heard the sound of an immense number of
angels gathered round the throne and the animals and the
elders; there were *ten thousand times ten thousand of them*[e]
12 and *thousands upon thousands*, ·shouting, 'The Lamb that was
sacrificed is worthy to be given power, riches, wisdom,
13 strength, honour, glory and blessing'. ·Then I heard all the
living things in creation—everything that lives in the air, and
on the ground, and under the ground, and in the sea, crying,
'To the One who is sitting on the throne and to the Lamb, be
14 all praise, honour, glory and power, for ever and ever'. ·And
the four animals said, 'Amen'; and the elders prostrated
themselves to worship.

The Lamb breaks the seven seals

6   Then I saw the Lamb break one of the seven seals, and I
heard one of the four animals shout in a voice like thunder,
2 'Come'. ·Immediately a white horse appeared, and the rider
on it was holding a bow; he was given the victor's crown and
he went away, to go from victory to victory.
3   When he broke the second seal, I heard the second animal
4 shout, 'Come'. ·And out came another horse, bright red, and
its rider was given this duty: to take away peace from the earth
and set people killing each other. He was given a huge sword.
5   When he broke the third seal, I heard the third animal
shout, 'Come'. Immediately a black horse appeared, and its
6 rider was holding a pair of scales; ·and I seemed to hear a
voice shout from among the four animals and say, 'A ration
of corn for a day's wages, and three rations of barley for a
day's wages, but do not tamper with the oil or the wine'.
7   When he broke the fourth seal, I heard the voice of the
8 fourth animal shout, 'Come'. ·Immediately another horse
appeared, deathly pale, and its rider was called Plague, and
·Hades followed at his heels.
    They were given authority over a quarter of the earth, *to
kill by the sword, by famine, by plague and wild beasts.*[a]
9   When he broke the fifth seal, I saw underneath the altar the
souls of all the people who had been killed on account of the
10 word of God, for witnessing to it. ·They shouted aloud,
'Holy, faithful Master, how much longer will you wait before
you pass sentence and take vengeance for our death on the
11 inhabitants of the earth?' ·Each of them was given a white
robe, and they were told to be patient a little longer, until the
roll was complete and their fellow servants and brothers had
been killed just as they had been.
12   In my vision, when he broke the sixth seal, there was a
violent earthquake and the sun went as black as coarse sack-
13 cloth; the moon turned red as blood all over, ·and *the stars of
the sky fell*[b] on to the earth *like figs* dropping from a fig tree
14 when a high wind shakes it; ·the *sky disappeared like a scroll
rolling up* and all the mountains and islands were shaken
15 from their places. ·Then all the earthly rulers, the governors
and the commanders, the rich people and the men of
influence, the whole population, slaves and citizens, took to
16 the mountains *to hide in caves and among the rocks.*[c] ·*They
said to the mountains*[d] and the rocks, '*Fall on us* and hide us

5 a. Ezk 2:9 b. Gn 49:9; Is 11:10 c. Zc 4:10 d. Is 61:6 e. Dn 7:10
6 a. Ezk 14:21 b. Is 34:4 c. Ho 10:8 d. Is 2:10, 18, 19

away from the One who sits on the throne and from the anger
17 of the Lamb. ·For *the Great Day of his anger* has come, *and
who can survive it?'*[e]

God's servants will be preserved

7   Next I saw four angels, standing at *the four corners of the
earth,*[a] holding the four winds of the world back to keep them
2 from blowing over the land or the sea or in the trees. ·Then
I saw another angel rising where the sun rises, carrying the
seal of the living God; he called in a powerful voice to the
3 four angels whose duty was to devastate land and sea. ·'Wait
before you do any damage on land or at sea or to the trees,
until we have put the *seal on the foreheads*[b] of the servants of
4 our God'. ·Then I heard how many were sealed: a hundred
and forty-four thousand,[c] out of all the tribes of Israel.
5   From the tribe of Judah, twelve thousand had been sealed;
from the tribe of Reuben, twelve thousand; from the tribe of
6 Gad, twelve thousand; ·from the tribe of Asher, twelve thousand; from the tribe of Naphtali, twelve thousand; from the
7 tribe of Manasseh, twelve thousand; ·from the tribe of
Simeon, twelve thousand; from the tribe of Levi, twelve
thousand; from the tribe of Issachar, twelve thousand;
8 from the tribe of Zebulun, twelve thousand; from the tribe of
Joseph, twelve thousand; and from the tribe of Benjamin,
twelve thousand were sealed.

The rewarding of the saints

9   After that I saw a huge number, impossible to count, of
people from every nation, race, tribe and language; they
were standing in front of the throne and in front of the Lamb,
dressed in white robes and holding palms in their hands.
10 They shouted aloud, ·'Victory to our God, who sits on the
11 throne, and to the Lamb!' ·And all the angels who were
standing in a circle round the throne, surrounding the elders
and the four animals, prostrated themselves before the
throne, and touched the ground with their foreheads, wor-
12 shipping God ·with these words, 'Amen. Praise and glory
and wisdom and thanksgiving and honour and power and
strength to our God for ever and ever. Amen.'
13   One of the elders then spoke, and asked me, 'Do you know
who these people are, dressed in white robes, and where they
14 have come from?' ·I answered him, 'You can tell me, my lord'.
Then he said, 'These are the people who have been through
the great persecution,[d] and because they have washed their
15 robes white again in the blood of the Lamb, ·they now stand

in front of God's throne and serve him day and night in his
sanctuary; and the One who sits on the throne will spread his
16 tent over them. ·*They will never hunger or thirst* again; *neither*
17 *the sun nor scorching wind will ever plague them*, ·because the
Lamb who is at the throne *will be their shepherd and will lead
them to springs of living water*;[e] and God *will wipe away all
tears from their eyes.*'[f]

The seventh seal

8   The Lamb then broke the seventh seal, and there was
silence in heaven for about half an hour.[a]

The prayers of the saints bring the coming of the Great Day nearer

2   Next I saw seven trumpets being given to the seven angels
3 who stand in the presence of God. ·Another angel, who had a
golden censer,[b] came and stood at the altar.[c] A large quantity
of incense was given to him to offer with the prayers of all the
saints on the golden altar that stood in front of the throne;
4 and so from the angel's hand the smoke of the incense went
up in the presence of God and with it the prayers of the
5 saints. ·Then the angel took the censer and *filled it with the
fire* from the altar, which he then threw down on to the earth;
immediately there came peals of thunder and flashes of
lightning, and the earth shook.

The first four trumpets

6   The seven angels that had the seven trumpets now made
7 ready to sound them. ·The first blew his trumpet and, with
that, hail and fire, mixed with blood, were dropped on the
earth; a third of the earth was burnt up, and a third of all
8 trees, and every blade of grass was burnt. ·The second angel
blew his trumpet, and it was as though a great mountain, all
on fire, had been dropped into the sea: a third of the sea
9 turned into blood, ·a third of all the living things in the sea
10 were killed, and a third of all ships were destroyed. ·The third
angel blew his trumpet, and a huge star fell from the sky,
burning like a ball of fire, and it fell on a third of all rivers

e. Jl 2:11; 3:4
7 a. Ezk 7:2 b. Ezk 9:4 (see also Is 44:5). c. Twelve (the sacred number)
squared and multiplied by a thousand, representing the totality of the
faithful. d. Under Nero. e. Is 49:10 f. Is 25:8
8 a. An awed silence; the 'coming of Yahweh' is preceded by silence
in the prophetic writings. b. In the shape of a shovel: the flat incense-
vessel was also used for carrying live coals from the altar on which
offerings were burnt. c. The altar of incense.

11 and springs; ·this was the star called Wormwood, and a third
 of all water turned to bitter wormwood, so that many people
12 died from drinking it. ·The fourth angel blew his trumpet,
 and a third of the sun and a third of the moon and a third of
 the stars were blasted, so that the light went out of a third of
 them and for a third of the day there was no illumination, and
 the same with the night.

13   In my vision, I heard an eagle, calling aloud as it flew high
 overhead, 'Trouble, trouble, trouble, for all the people on
 earth at the sound of the other three trumpets which the
 three angels are going to blow'.

The fifth trumpet

9   Then the fifth angel blew his trumpet, and I saw a star*a* that
 had fallen from heaven on to the earth, and he was given the
2 key to the shaft leading down to the Abyss.*b* ·When he
 unlocked the shaft of the Abyss, *smoke poured up* out of the
 Abyss *like the smoke from a* huge *furnace*^c so that the sun and
3 the sky were darkened by it, ·and out of the smoke dropped
 locusts which were given the powers that scorpions have on
4 the earth: ·they were forbidden to harm any fields or crops or
 trees and told only to attack any men who were without
5 God's seal on their foreheads. ·They were not to kill them,
 but to give them pain for five months, and the pain was to be
6 the pain of a scorpion's sting. ·When this happens, *men will
 long for death and not find it anywhere*;*d* they will want to die
 and death will evade them.

7   To look at, these locusts were *like horses armoured for
 battle*;*e* they had things that looked like gold crowns on their
8 heads, and faces that seemed human, ·and hair like women's
9 hair, and *teeth like lions' teeth.* ·They had body-armour like
 iron breastplates, and the noise of their wings sounded like a
10 great charge of horses and chariots into battle. ·Their tails
 were like scorpions', with stings, and it was with them that
11 they were able to injure people for five months. ·As their
 leader they had their emperor, the angel of the Abyss, whose
 name in Hebrew is Abaddon, or Apollyon*f* in Greek.

12   That was the first of the troubles; there are still two more
 to come.

The sixth trumpet

13   The sixth angel blew his trumpet, and I heard a voice come
14 out of the four horns of the golden altar in front of God. ·It
 spoke to the sixth angel with the trumpet, and said, 'Release
 the four angels that are chained up at the great river Euph-

15 rates'. ·These four angels had been put there ready for this
hour of this day of this month of this year, and now they were
16 released to destroy a third of the human race. ·I learnt how
many there were in their army: twice ten thousand times ten
17 thousand mounted men. ·In my vision I saw the horses, and
the riders with their breastplates of flame colour, hyacinth-
blue and sulphur-yellow; the horses had lions' heads, and
fire, smoke and sulphur were coming out of their mouths.
18 It was by these three plagues, the fire, the smoke and the
sulphur coming out of their mouths, that the one third of the
19 human race was killed. ·All the horses' power was in their
mouths and their tails: their tails were like snakes, and had
20 heads that were able to wound. ·But the rest of the human
race, who escaped these plagues, refused either to abandon
*the things they had made with their own hands*ᵃ—the *idols*
*made of gold, silver, bronze, stone and wood*ʰ that can neither
21 see nor hear nor move—or to stop worshipping devils. ·Nor
did they give up their murdering, or witchcraft, or fornication
or stealing.

The imminence of the last punishment

10   Then I saw another powerful angel coming down from
heaven, wrapped in a cloud, with a rainbow over his head;
2 his face was like the sun, and his legs were pillars of fire. ·In
his hand he had a small scroll, unrolled; he put his right foot
3 in the sea and his left foot on the land ·and he shouted so
loud, it was *like a lion roaring*. At this, seven claps of thunder
4 made themselves heard ·and when the seven thunderclaps
had spoken, I was preparing to write, when I heard a voice
from heaven say to me, 'Keep the words of the seven thunder-
5 claps secret and do not write them down'. ·Then the angel
that I had seen, standing on the sea and the land, *raised his*
6 *right hand to heaven,*ᵃ ·and *swore by the One who lives for ever*
and ever, *and made heaven and all that is in it,* and *earth and*
all it bears, and *the sea and all it holds,*ᵇ 'The time of waiting
7 is over; ·at the time when the seventh angel is heard sounding
his trumpet, God's secret intention will be fulfilled, just as he
announced in the Good News told to *his servants the*
prophets'.

9 a. A fallen angel. b. Where fallen angels were imprisoned, to be
released only to their final punishment. c. Ex 19:18 d. Jb 3:21 e. The
descriptive details in vv. 7–9 owe much to Jl 1 and 2. f. 'Destruction'.
g. Is 17:8 h. Dn 5:4
10 a. Dt 32:40 b. Ne 9:6

The seer eats the small scroll

8   Then I heard the voice I had heard from heaven speaking to me again. 'Go,' it said 'and take that open scroll out of the
9 hand of the angel standing on sea and land.' ·I went to the angel and asked him to give me the small scroll, and he said, 'Take it and eat it; it will turn your stomach sour, but in
10 your mouth it will taste as sweet as honey'. ·So I took it out of the angel's hand, and swallowed it; it was as sweet as honey in my mouth, but when I had eaten it my stomach
11 turned sour. ·Then I was told, 'You are to prophesy again, this time about many different nations and countries and languages and emperors'.

The two witnesses

11   Then I was given a long cane as a measuring rod, and I was told, 'Go and measure God's sanctuary, and the altar, and
2 the people who worship there; ·but leave out the outer court and do not measure it, because it has been handed over to pagans—they will trample on the holy city for forty-two
3 months.^a ·But I shall send my two witnesses to prophesy for those twelve hundred and sixty days, wearing sackcloth.
4 These are the *two olive trees*^b and the two lamps *that stand*
5 *before the Lord of the world*.^c ·Fire can come from their mouths and consume their enemies if anyone tries to harm them; and if anybody does try to harm them he will cer-
6 tainly be killed in this way. ·They are able to lock up the sky so that it does not rain as long as they are prophesying; they are able to turn water into blood and strike the whole world
7 with any plague as often as they like. ·When they have completed their witnessing, the beast that comes out of the Abyss *is going to make war on them and overcome them*^d and
8 kill them. ·Their corpses will lie in the main street of the Great City known by the symbolic names Sodom and Egypt,
9 in which their Lord was crucified.^e ·Men out of every people, race, language and nation will stare at their corpses, for
10 three-and-a-half days, not letting them be buried, ·and the people of the world will be glad about it and celebrate the event by giving presents to each other, because these two prophets have been a plague to the people of the world.'
11   After the three-and-a-half days, *God breathed life into them and they stood up*,^f and everybody who saw it happen
12 was terrified; ·then they heard a loud voice from heaven say to them, 'Come up here', and while their enemies were
13 watching, they went up to heaven in a cloud. ·Immediately,

there was a violent earthquake, and a tenth of the city collapsed; seven thousand persons[g] were killed in the earthquake, and the survivors, overcome with fear, could only praise the God of heaven.

The seventh trumpet

14   That was the second of the troubles; the third is to come quickly after it.

15   Then the seventh angel blew his trumpet, and voices could be heard shouting in heaven, calling, 'The kingdom of the world has become the kingdom of our Lord and his Christ,

16   and he will reign for ever and ever'. ·The twenty-four elders, enthroned in the presence of God, prostrated themselves and touched the ground with their foreheads worshipping God

17   with these words, 'We give thanks to you, Almighty Lord God, He-Is-and-He-Was, for using your great power and

18   beginning your reign. ·*The nations were seething with rage*[h] and now the time has come for your own anger, and for the dead to be judged, and for your servants the prophets, for the saints and for all who worship you, small or great, to be rewarded. The time has come to destroy those who are destroying the earth.'

19   Then the sanctuary of God in heaven opened, and the ark of the covenant could be seen inside it. Then came flashes of lightning, peals of thunder and an earthquake, and violent hail.

The vision of the woman and the dragon

12   Now a great sign appeared in heaven: a woman, adorned with the sun, standing on the moon, and with the twelve stars

2   on her head for a crown. ·She was pregnant, and in labour,

3   crying aloud in the pangs of childbirth. ·Then a second sign appeared in the sky, a huge red dragon which had seven heads and ten horns, and each of the seven heads crowned

4   with a coronet. ·Its tail dragged a third of *the stars from the sky and dropped them to the earth,*[a] and the dragon stopped in

11 a. This period, taken from Dn, is used as the symbol for any time of persecution. b. Zc 4:3, 14, where they symbolise Joshua and Zerubbabel; here they probably represent Peter and Paul. c. 2 K 1:10 d. Dn 7:21 e. The 'Great City' or 'Babylon' in this book is Rome, whose actions were identified with Sodom's rejection of God's messengers and Egypt's oppression of God's people. The words 'in which their Lord was crucified' may be a gloss, or may be justified by the responsibility of the Roman authority for the crucifixion. f. Ezk 37:5, 10 g. That is, a great number of all classes. h. Ps 2:1, 5
12 a. Dn 8:10

front of the woman as she was having the child, so that he
5 could eat it as soon as it was born from its mother. ·The
woman brought *a male child into the world*, the son who was
to rule all the nations with an iron sceptre,[b] and the child was
6 taken straight up to God and to his throne, ·while the woman
escaped into the desert, where God had made a place of
safety ready, for her to be looked after in the twelve hundred
and sixty days.

7 And now war broke out in heaven, when Michael with
his angels attacked the dragon. The dragon fought back with
8 his angels, ·but they were defeated and driven out of heaven.
9 The great dragon, the primeval serpent, known as the devil or
Satan, who had deceived all the world, was hurled down to
10 the earth and his angels were hurled down with him. ·Then I
heard a voice shout from heaven, 'Victory and power and
empire for ever have been won by our God, and all authority
for his Christ, now that the persecutor, who accused our
brothers day and night before our God, has been brought
11 down. ·They have triumphed over him by the blood of the
Lamb and by the witness of their martyrdom, because even
12 in the face of death they would not cling to life. ·Let the
heavens rejoice and all who live there; but for you, earth and
sea, trouble is coming—because the devil has gone down to
you in a rage, knowing that his days are numbered.'

13 As soon as the devil found himself thrown down to the
earth, he sprang in pursuit of the woman, the mother of the
14 male child, ·but she was given a huge pair of eagle's wings to
fly away from the serpent into the desert, to the place where
she was to be looked after for *a year and twice a year and half*
15 *a year*.[c] ·So the serpent vomited water from his mouth, like a
river, after the woman, to sweep her away in the current,
16 but the earth came to her rescue; it opened its mouth and
17 swallowed the river thrown up by the dragon's jaws. ·Then
the dragon was enraged with the woman and went away to
make war on the rest of her children, that is, all who obey
God's commandments and bear witness for Jesus.

The dragon delegates his power to the beast

18 I was standing on the seashore. **13** Then I saw *a beast
emerge from the sea:*[a] it had seven heads and ten horns, with
a coronet on each of its ten horns, and its heads were marked
2 with blasphemous titles.[b] ·I saw that the beast *was like a
leopard*, with paws like *a bear* and a mouth like *a lion;*[c] the
dragon had handed over to it his own power and his throne
3 and his worldwide authority. ·I saw that one of its heads

seemed to have had a fatal wound but that this deadly injury had healed and, after that, the whole world had marvelled
4 and followed the beast. ·They prostrated themselves in front of the dragon because he had given the beast his authority; and they prostrated themselves in front of the beast, saying, 'Who can compare with the beast?[d] How could anybody
5 defeat him?' ·For forty-two months the beast was allowed *to mouth its boasts*[e] and blasphemies and to do whatever it
6 wanted; ·and it mouthed its blasphemies against God, against his name, his heavenly Tent and all those who are sheltered
7 there. ·It was allowed *to make war against the saints and conquer them, and given power* over every race, people, lan-
8 guage and nation; ·and all people of the world will worship it, that is, everybody whose name has not been written down since the foundation of the world in the book of life of the
9 sacrificial Lamb. ·If anyone has ears to hear, let him listen:
10 *Captivity for those who are destined for captivity; the sword for those who are to die by the sword.*[f] This is why the saints must have constancy and faith.

The false prophet as the slave of the beast

11 Then I saw a second beast;[g] it emerged from the ground; it had two horns like a lamb, but made a noise like a dragon.
12 This second beast was servant to the first beast, and extended its authority everywhere, making the world and all its people worship the first beast, which had had the fatal wound and
13 had been healed. ·And it worked great miracles, even to calling down fire from heaven on to the earth while people
14 watched. ·Through the miracles which it was allowed to do on behalf of the first beast, it was able to win over the people of the world and persuade them to put up a statue in honour of the beast that had been wounded by the sword and still
15 lived. ·It was allowed to breathe life into this statue, so that the statue of the beast was able to speak, and to have *anyone who refused to worship the statue of the beast*[h] put to death.
16 He compelled everyone—small and great, rich and poor, slave and citizen—to be branded on the right hand or on the
17 forehead, ·and made it illegal for anyone to buy or sell anything unless he had been branded with the name of the beast or with the number of *i*ts name.

b. Ps 2:9 **c.** Dn 7:25. Cf. 11:3.
13 a. Dn 7:3 **b.** Seven heads represent a succession of seven Roman emperors; ten crowned horns are ten subject kings. **c.** Dn 7:4–6 **d.** A parody of the name Michael, 'Who-can-compare-with-God?' **e.** Dn 7:8, 11 **f.** Jr 15:2 **g.** Also called 'the false prophet', 16:13; 19:20; 20:10. **h.** Dn 3:5–7, 15

18   There is need for shrewdness here: if anyone is clever
enough he may interpret the number of the beast: it is the
number of a man, the number 666.[i]

The companions of the Lamb

14   Next in my vision I saw Mount Zion, and standing on it a
Lamb who had with him a hundred and forty-four thousand
people, all with his name and his Father's name written on
2   their foreheads. ·I heard a sound coming out of the sky like the
sound of the ocean or the roar of thunder; it seemed to be the
3   sound of harpists playing their harps. ·There in front of the
throne they were singing a new hymn in the presence of the
four animals and the elders, a hymn that could only be learnt
by the hundred and forty-four thousand who had been
4   redeemed from the world. ·These are the ones who have kept
their virginity[a] and not been defiled with women; they *follow*
the Lamb wherever he goes; they have been redeemed from
amongst men to be *the first-fruits for God*[b] and for the Lamb.
5   They never *allowed a lie to pass their lips*[c] and no fault can be
found in them.

Angels announce the day of Judgement

6   Then I saw another angel, flying high overhead, sent to
announce the Good News of eternity to all who live on the
7   earth, every nation, race, language and tribe. ·He was calling,
'Fear God and praise him, because the time has come for him
to sit in judgement; worship *the maker of heaven and earth
and sea*[d] and every water-spring'.
8   A second angel followed him, calling, '*Babylon has fallen,
Babylon the Great has fallen,*[e] Babylon which gave the whole
world *the wine of* God's *anger* to drink'.
9   A third angel followed, shouting aloud, 'All those who
worship the beast and his statue, or have had themselves
10   branded on the hand or forehead, ·will be made to drink the
wine of God's fury which is ready, undiluted, in his cup of
anger; in *fire and brimstone*[f] they will be tortured in the
11   presence of the holy angels and the Lamb ·and *the smoke* of
their torture *will go up for ever*[g] and ever. There will be no
respite, *night or day*, for those who worshipped the beast or its
12   statue or accepted branding with its name.' ·This is why there
must be constancy in the saints who keep the commandments
13   of God and faith in Jesus. ·Then I heard a voice from heaven
say to me, 'Write down: Happy are those who die in the
Lord! Happy indeed, the Spirit says; now they can rest for
ever after their work, since their good deeds go with them.'

The harvest and vintage of the pagans

14 Now in my vision I saw a white *cloud* and, *sitting on it, one like a son of man* with a gold crown on his head and a sharp
15 sickle in his hand. ·Then another angel came out of the sanctuary, and shouted aloud to the one sitting on the cloud, 'Put your sickle in and reap: harvest time has come and *the*
16 *harvest* of the earth *is ripe*'.[h] ·Then the one sitting on the cloud set his sickle to work on the earth, and the earth's harvest was reaped.
17 Another angel, who also carried a sharp sickle, came out of
18 the temple in heaven, ·and the angel in charge of the fire left the altar and shouted aloud to the one with the sharp sickle, 'Put your sickle in and cut all the bunches off the vine of the
19 earth; all its grapes are ripe'. ·So the angel set his sickle to work on the earth and harvested the whole vintage of the earth and put it into a huge winepress, the winepress of
20 God's anger, ·outside the city, where it was trodden until the blood that came out of the winepress was up to the horses' bridles as far away as sixteen hundred furlongs.

The hymn of Moses and the Lamb

15 What I saw next, in heaven, was a great and wonderful sign: seven angels were bringing the seven plagues that are
2 the last of all, because they exhaust the anger of God. ·I seemed to see a glass lake suffused with fire, and standing by the lake of glass, those who had fought against the beast and won, and against his statue and the number which is his
3 name. They all had harps from God, ·and they were singing the hymn of Moses, the servant of God, and of the Lamb:

'How great and wonderful are all your works,
Lord God Almighty;
just and true are all your ways,
King of nations.
4 *Who would not revere* and *praise your name, O Lord?*
You alone are holy,

i. Codes and riddles were made in both Greek and Hebr. by using numbers for letters, according to their order in the alphabet. Some commentators have claimed that 666 is the total of the number-values of 'Nero Caesar'.
14 a. As so often in the O.T., 'virginity' stands for faithfulness, and 'adultery' or 'fornication' for idolatry. b. Jr 2:2–3 c. Zp 3:13 d. Ex 20:11 e. Is 21:9. The *wine of* God's *anger* is a phrase from Is 51:17, also used in Jr 25:15f. f. Gn 19:28 g. Is 34:9–10 h. Jl 4:13; Am 8:2

and all the pagans will come and adore you
for the many acts of justice you have shown.'[a]

The seven bowls of plagues

5 After this, in my vision, the sanctuary, the Tent of the Testi-
6 mony, opened in heaven, ·and out came the seven angels with
the seven plagues, wearing pure white linen, fastened round
7 their waists with golden girdles. ·One of the four animals
gave the seven angels seven golden bowls filled with the anger
8 of God who lives for ever and ever. ·*The smoke from the
glory* and the power *of God filled the temple so that no one
could go into it*[b] until the seven plagues of the seven angels
were completed.

16 Then I heard a voice from the sanctuary shouting to the
seven angels, 'Go, and empty the seven bowls of God's
anger over the earth'.

2 The first angel went and emptied his bowl over the earth;
at once, on all the people who had been branded with the
mark of the beast and had worshipped its statue, there came
disgusting and virulent sores.

3 The second angel emptied his bowl over the sea, and it
turned to blood, like the blood of a corpse, and every living
creature in the sea died.

4 The third angel emptied his bowl into the rivers and water-
5 springs and they turned into blood. ·Then I heard the angel
of water say, 'You are the holy He-Is-and-He-Was, the Just
6 One, and this is a just punishment: ·they spilt the blood of the
saints and the prophets, and blood is what you have given
7 them to drink; it is what they deserve'. ·And I heard the altar
itself say, 'Truly, Lord God Almighty, the punishments you
give are true and just'.

8 The fourth angel emptied his bowl over the sun and it was
9 made to scorch people with its flames; ·but though people
were scorched by the fierce heat of it, they cursed the name of
God who had the power to cause such plagues, and they
would not repent and praise him.

10 The fifth angel emptied his bowl over the throne of the
beast and its whole empire was plunged into darkness. Men
11 were biting their tongues for pain, ·but instead of repenting for
what they had done, they cursed the God of heaven because
of their pains and sores.

12 The sixth angel emptied his bowl over the great river
Euphrates; all the water dried up so that a way was made for
13 the kings of the East[a] to come in. ·Then from the jaws of
dragon and beast and false prophet I saw three foul spirits

14 come; they looked like frogs ·and in fact were demon spirits, able to work miracles, going out to all the kings of the world to call them together for the war of the Great Day of God the
15 Almighty.—·This is how it will be: I shall come like a thief. Happy is the man who has stayed awake and not taken off his clothes so that he does not go out naked and expose his
16 shame.—·They called the kings together at the place called, in Hebrew, Armageddon.[b]
17 The seventh angel emptied his bowl into the air, and a voice
18 shouted from the sanctuary, 'The end has come'. ·Then there were flashes of lightning and peals of thunder and the most violent earthquake *that anyone has ever seen since there have*
19 *been* men *on the earth.*[c] ·The Great City was split into three parts and the cities of the world collapsed; Babylon the Great was not forgotten: God made her drink the full wine-
20 cup of his anger. ·Every island vanished and the mountains
21 disappeared; ·and hail, with great hailstones weighing a talent each, fell from the sky on the people. They cursed God for sending a plague of hail; it was the most terrible plague.

B. THE PUNISHMENT OF BABYLON

The famous prostitute

17 One of the seven angels that had the seven bowls came to speak to me, and said, 'Come here and I will show you the punishment given to the famous prostitute[a] *who* rules
2 *enthroned beside abundant waters,*[b] ·the one with whom all the kings of the earth have committed fornication, and who has made all the population of the world drunk with the wine of
3 her adultery'.[c] ·He took me in spirit to a desert, and there I saw a woman riding a scarlet beast which had seven heads and ten horns and had blasphemous titles written all over it.
4 The woman was dressed in purple and scarlet, and glittered with gold and jewels and pearls, and she was holding a gold
5 winecup filled with the disgusting filth of her fornication; ·on her forehead was written a name, a cryptic name: 'Babylon the Great, the mother of all the prostitutes and all the filthy

15 a. This hymn is nearer to the Psalms than to the Song of Moses in Ex 15. The two direct quotations are from Jr 10 and Ps 86; the opening of it is reminiscent of Ps 92 and 98. b. 1 K 8:10-11
16 a. Of Parthia, the savage enemy dreaded by the Roman world. b. 'Megiddo mountains'; Josiah's defeat at Megiddo, 2 K 23:29f, made this place a symbol of military disaster, cf. Zc 12:11. c. Dn 12:1
17 a. Rome. b. Jr 51:13, a literal description of Babylon, here applied metaphorically, as the author explains in v. 15. c. I.e. the idolatry of emperor-worship.

6 practices on the earth'. ·I saw that she was drunk, drunk with the blood of the saints, and the blood of the martyrs to Jesus;
7 and when I saw her, I was completely mystified. ·The angel said to me, 'Don't you understand? Now I will tell you the meaning of this woman, and of the beast she is riding, with the seven heads and the ten horns.

The symbolism of the beast and the prostitute

8   'The beast you have seen once was and now is not;[a] he is yet to come up from the Abyss, but only to go to his destruction. And the people of the world, whose names have not been written since the beginning of the world in the book of life, will think it miraculous when they see how the beast once
9 was and now is not and is still to come. ·Here there is need for cleverness, for a shrewd mind; the seven heads are the seven hills, and the woman is sitting on them.
10   'The seven heads are also seven emperors. Five of them have already gone, one is here now, and one is yet to come;
11 once here, he must stay for a short while. ·The beast, who once was and now is not, is at the same time the eighth and one of the seven, and he is going to his destruction.
12   '*The ten horns are ten kings*[e] who have not yet been given their royal power but will have royal authority only for a
13 single hour and in association with the beast. ·They are all of one mind in putting their strength and their powers at the
14 beast's disposal, ·and they will go to war against the Lamb; but the Lamb is *the Lord of lords and the King of kings,*[f] and he will defeat them and they will be defeated by his followers, the called, the chosen, the faithful.'
15   The angel continued, 'The waters you saw, beside which the prostitute was sitting, are all the peoples, the populations,
16 the nations and the languages. ·But the time will come when the ten horns and the beast will turn against the prostitute, and *strip off her clothes and leave her naked;*[g] then they will
17 eat her flesh and burn the remains in the fire. ·In fact, God influenced their minds to do what he intended, to agree together to put their royal powers at the beast's disposal until
18 the time when God's words should be fulfilled. ·The woman you saw is the great city which has authority over all the rulers on earth.'

An angel announces the fall of Babylon

18   After this, I saw another angel come down from heaven, with great authority given to him; *the earth was lit up with his*
2 *glory.*[a] ·At the top of his voice he shouted, '*Babylon has*

fallen, Babylon the Great has fallen, and has become *the haunt of devils*[b] and a lodging for every foul spirit and dirty,
3 loathsome bird. ·All the nations have been intoxicated by the wine of her prostitution; every king in the earth has committed fornication with her, and every merchant grown rich through her debauchery.'

The people of God summoned away

4   A new voice spoke from heaven; I heard it say, 'Come out, my people, away from her, so that you do not share in her
5 crimes and have the same plagues to bear. ·*Her sins have reached up to heaven,*[c] and God has her crimes in mind:
6 *she is to be paid in her own coin.*[d] She must be paid double the amount she exacted. She is to have a doubly strong cup of
7 her own mixture. ·Every one of her shows and orgies is to be matched by a torture or a grief. *I am the queen on my throne, she says to herself,*[e] and *I am no widow* and shall never be in
8 mourning. ·For that, *within a single day*, the plagues will fall on her: disease and mourning and famine. She will be burnt right up. The Lord God has condemned her, and he has great power.'

The people of the world mourn for Babylon

9   There will be mourning and weeping for her by the kings of the earth who have fornicated with her and lived with her in
10 luxury. They see the smoke as she burns, ·while they keep at a safe distance from fear of her agony. They will say:

'Mourn, mourn for this great city,
Babylon, so powerful a city,
doomed as you are within a single hour'.

11 There will be weeping and distress over her among all the traders of the earth when there is nobody left to buy their
12 cargoes of goods; ·their stocks of gold and silver, jewels and pearls, linen and purple and silks and scarlet; all the sandal-wood, every piece in ivory or fine wood, in bronze or iron or
13 marble; ·the cinnamon and spices, the myrrh and ointment and incense; wine, oil, flour and corn; their stocks of cattle, sheep, horses and chariots, their slaves, their human cargo.

---

d. The popular belief that Nero would return from the dead at the head of a Parthian army accounts for this parody of the divine title. **e.** Dn 7:24; here they are kings of the satellite nations. **f.** Dn 10:17 **g.** Ezk 16:37f
18 a. Ezk 43:2 **b.** Is 34:11f **c.** Jr 51:9 **d.** Jr 50:15 **e.** Is 47:8

14 'All the fruits you had set your hearts on have failed you; gone for ever, never to return, is your life of magnificence and ease.'

15 The traders who had made a fortune out of her will be standing at a safe distance from fear of her agony, mourning 16 and weeping. ·They will be saying:

'Mourn, mourn for this great city;
for all the linen and purple and scarlet that you wore,
for all your finery of gold and jewels and pearls;
17 your riches are all destroyed within a single hour'.

All the captains and seafaring men, sailors and all those who make a living from the sea will be keeping a safe distance, 18 watching the smoke as she burns, and crying out, 'Has there 19 ever been a city as great as this!' ·They will throw dust on their heads and say, with tears and groans:

'Mourn, mourn for this great city
whose lavish living has made a fortune
for every owner of a sea-going ship;
ruined within a single hour.

20 'Now heaven, celebrate her downfall, and all you saints, apostles and prophets: God has given judgement for you against her.'

21 Then a powerful angel picked up a boulder like a great millstone, and as he hurled it into the sea, he said, 'That is how the great city of Babylon is going to be hurled down, never to be seen again.

22 'Never again in you, Babylon,
will be heard the song of harpists and minstrels,
the music of flute and trumpet;
never again will craftsmen of every skill be found
or *the sound of the mill*[f] be heard;
23 never again will shine *the light of the lamp*,
never again will be heard
the voices of bridegroom and bride.
Your traders were the princes of the earth,
all the nations were under your spell.

24 In her you will find the blood of prophets and saints, and all the blood that was ever shed on earth.'

Songs of victory in heaven

19 After this I seemed to hear the great sound of a huge crowd in heaven, singing, 'Alleluia! Victory and glory and power to

2 our God! ·He judges fairly, he punishes justly, and he has condemned the famous prostitute who corrupted the earth with her fornication; he has avenged his servants that she
3 killed'. ·They sang again, 'Alleluia! *The smoke* of her *will go*
4 *up for ever* and ever.' ·Then the twenty-four elders and the four animals prostrated themselves and worshipped God seated there on his throne, and they cried, 'Amen, Alleluia'.
5 Then a voice came from the throne; it said, 'Praise our God, you servants of his and *all who, great or small, revere*
6 *him*'. ·And I seemed to hear the voices of a huge crowd, like the sound of the ocean or the great roar of thunder, answering, 'Alleluia! The reign of the Lord our God Almighty has
7 begun; ·let us be glad and joyful and give praise to God,
8 because this is the time for the marriage of the Lamb. ·His bride is ready, and she has been able to dress herself in dazzling white linen, because her linen is made of the good
9 deeds of the saints.' ·The angel said, 'Write this: Happy are those who are invited to the wedding feast of the Lamb', and he added, 'All the things you have written are true messages
10 from God'. ·Then I knelt at his feet to worship him, but he said to me, 'Don't do that: I am a servant just like you and all your brothers who are witnesses to Jesus. It is God that you must worship.' The witness Jesus gave is the same as the spirit of prophecy.

C. THE DESTRUCTION OF THE PAGAN NATIONS

The first battle of the End

11 And now I saw heaven open, and a white horse appear; its rider was called Faithful and True; he is *a judge with integ-*
12 *rity,*[a] a warrior for justice. ·His eyes were flames of fire, and his head was crowned with many coronets; the name written
13 on him was known only to himself, ·*his cloak was soaked in blood.*[b] He is known by the name, The Word of God.
14 Behind him, dressed in linen of dazzling white, rode the
15 armies of heaven on white horses. ·From his mouth came a sharp sword to strike the pagans with; he is the one *who will rule them with an iron sceptre,*[c] and tread out the wine of
16 Almighty God's fierce anger. ·On his cloak and on his thigh[d] there was a name written: *The King of kings and the Lord of lords.*
17 I saw an angel standing in the sun, and he shouted aloud to

f. Jr 25:10
19 a. Is 11:4 b. Is 63:1 c. Ps 2:9 d. I.e. the place where he wears his sword; so, perhaps, 'on his sword'.

all the birds that were flying high overhead in the sky, 'Come here, *Gather together at the great feast*[e] that God is giving.
18 *There will be the flesh* of kings for you, and the flesh of great generals and heroes, the flesh of horses and their riders and of all kinds of men, citizens and slaves, small and great.'
19 Then I saw the beast, with all the kings of the earth and their armies, gathered together to fight the rider and his
20 army. ·But the beast was taken prisoner, together with the false prophet who had worked miracles on the beast's behalf and by them had deceived all who had been branded with the mark of the beast and worshipped his statue. These two were thrown alive into the fiery lake of burning sulphur.
21 All the rest were killed by the sword of the rider, which came out of his mouth, and *all the birds were gorged with their flesh.*

The reign of a thousand years

20 Then I saw an angel come down from heaven with the key of the Abyss in his hand and an enormous chain. ·He over-
2 powered the dragon, that primeval serpent which is the devil
3 and Satan, and chained him up for a thousand years. ·He threw him into the Abyss, and shut the entrance and sealed it over him, to make sure he would not deceive the nations again until the thousand years had passed. At the end of that time he must be released, but only for a short while.
4 Then I saw some thrones, and I saw *those who are given the power to be judges*[a] take their seats on them. I saw the souls of all who had been beheaded for having witnessed for Jesus and for having preached God's word, and those who refused to worship the beast or his statue and would not have the brand-mark on their foreheads or hands; they came to life,
5 and reigned with Christ for a thousand years. ·This is the first resurrection; the rest of the dead did not come to life until
6 the thousand years were over. ·Happy and blessed are those who share in the first resurrection; the second death cannot affect them but they will be priests of God and of Christ and reign with him for a thousand years.

The second battle of the End

7 When the thousand years are over, Satan will be released
8 from his prison ·and will come out to deceive all the nations in the four quarters of the earth, *Gog and Magog,*[b] and mobilise them for war. His armies will be as many as the sands of the
9 sea; ·they will come swarming over the entire country and besiege the camp of the saints, which is the city that God loves. But *fire will come down on them from heaven*[c] and

10 consume them. ·Then the devil, who misled them, will be thrown into the lake of fire and sulphur, where the beast and the false prophet are, and their torture will not stop, day or night, for ever and ever.

The punishment of the pagans

11   Then I saw a great white throne and the One who was sitting on it. In his presence, earth and sky vanished, leaving
12 no trace. ·I saw the dead, both great and small, standing in front of his throne, while the book of life was opened, and *other books opened* which were the record of what they had done in their lives, by which the dead were judged.
13
14   The sea gave up all the dead who were in it; ·Death and Hades were emptied of the dead that were in them; and every one was judged according to the way in which he had lived. Then Death and Hades were thrown into the burning lake.
15 This burning lake is the second death; ·and anybody whose name could not be found written in the book of life was thrown into the burning lake.

D. THE JERUSALEM OF THE FUTURE

The heavenly Jerusalem

21   Then I saw *a new heaven and a new earth;*[a] the first heaven and the first earth had disappeared now, and there was no
2 longer any sea. ·I saw the holy city, and the new Jerusalem, coming down from God out of heaven, as beautiful as a
3 bride all dressed for her husband. ·Then I heard a loud voice call from the throne, 'You see this city? Here God lives among men. He will make *his home among them; they shall be his people,*[b] and he will be their God; his name is *God-with-*
4 *them.* ·*He will wipe away all tears from their eyes;*[c] there will be no more death, and no more mourning or sadness. The world of the past has gone.'
5   Then the One sitting on the throne spoke: 'Now I am making the whole of creation new' he said. 'Write this: that
6 what I am saying is sure and will come true.' ·And then he said, 'It is already done. I am the Alpha and the Omega, the Beginning and the End. I will give water from the well of life
7 free to anybody who is thirsty; ·it is the rightful inheritance of the one who proves victorious; and *I will be his God* and *he a*

e. Ezk 39:17
20 a. Dn 7:22 b. Ezk 38:2 c. Ezk 38:22
21 a. Is 65:17 b. Ezk 37:27 c. Is 8:8 and 25:8

8 *son to me.*[d] ·But the legacy for cowards, for those who break their word, or worship obscenities, for murderers and fornicators, and for fortune-tellers, idolaters or any other sort of liars, is the second death in the burning lake of sulphur.'

The messianic Jerusalem

9 One of the seven angels that had the seven bowls full of the seven last plagues came to speak to me, and said, 'Come here

10 and I will show you the bride that the Lamb has married'. ·*In the spirit, he took me to the top of an enormous high mountain*[e] and showed me Jerusalem, the holy city, coming down from

11 God out of heaven. ·It *had all the radiant glory of God*[f] and glittered like some precious jewel of crystal-clear diamond.

12 The walls of it were of a great height, and had twelve gates; at each of the twelve gates there was an angel, and over the

13 gates were written the names *of the twelve tribes of Israel; ·on the east there were three gates, on the north three gates, on the*

14 *south three gates, and on the west three gates.*[g] ·The city walls stood on twelve foundation stones, each one of which bore the name of one of the twelve apostles of the Lamb.

15 The angel that was speaking to me was carrying a gold measuring rod to measure the city and its gates and wall.

16 The plan of the city is perfectly square, its length the same as its breadth. He measured the city with his rod and it was twelve thousand furlongs in length and in breadth, and equal

17 in height. ·He measured its wall, and this was a hundred and forty-four cubits high—the angel was using the ordinary

18 cubit. ·The wall was built of diamond, and the city of pure

19 gold, like polished glass. ·The foundations of the city wall were faced with all kinds of precious stone: the first with diamond, the second lapis lazuli, the third turquoise, the

20 fourth crystal, ·the fifth agate, the sixth ruby, the seventh gold quartz, the eighth malachite, the ninth topaz, the tenth emerald, the eleventh sapphire and the twelfth amethyst.

21 The twelve gates were twelve pearls, each gate being made of a single pearl, and the main street of the city was pure gold,

22 transparent as glass. ·I saw that there was no temple in the city since the Lord God Almighty and the Lamb were them-

23 selves the temple, ·and the city did not need the sun or the moon for light, since it was lit by the radiant glory of God

24 and the Lamb was a lighted torch for it. ·*The pagan nations will live by its light*[h] and the kings of the earth will bring it

25 their treasures. ·*The gates of it will never be shut by day*—and

26 there will be no night there—·and *the nations will come,*

27 *bringing their treasure* and their wealth. ·Nothing unclean

may come into it: no one who does what is loathsome or false,
but only those who are listed in the Lamb's book of life.

22 Then the angel showed me the river of life, rising from the
throne of God and of the Lamb and flowing crystal-clear
2 down the middle of the city street. *On either side of the river
were the trees of life, which bear twelve crops of fruit in a year,
one in each month, and the leaves of which are the cure for the
pagans.*[a]
3 *The ban will be lifted.*[b] The throne of God and of the Lamb
will be in its place in the city; his servants will worship him,
4 they will see him face to face, and his name will be written on
5 their foreheads. ·It will never be night again and they will not
need lamplight or sunlight, because the Lord God will be
shining on them. They will reign for ever and ever.
6 The angel said to me, 'All that you have written is sure and
will come true: the Lord God who gives the spirit to the
prophets has sent his angel to reveal to his servants *what is
7 soon to take place*. ·Very soon now, I shall be with you again.'
Happy are those who treasure the prophetic message of this
book.
8 I, John, am the one who heard and saw these things. When
I had heard and seen them all, I knelt at the feet of the angel
9 who had shown them to me, to worship him; ·but he said,
'Don't do that: I am a servant just like you and like your
brothers the prophets and like those who treasure what you
have written in this book. It is God that you must worship.'
10 This, too, he said to me, 'Do not keep the prophecies in
11 this book a secret, because the Time is close. ·Meanwhile let
the sinner go on sinning, and the unclean continue to be
unclean; let those who do good go on doing good, and those
12 who are holy continue to be holy. ·Very soon now, I shall be
with you again, *bringing the reward to be given to every man
13 according to what he deserves*.[c] ·I am the Alpha and the
Omega, *the First and the Last*, the Beginning and the End.
14 Happy are those who will have washed their robes clean, so
that they will have the right to feed on the tree of life and can
15 come through the gates into the city. ·These others must stay
outside: dogs, fortune-tellers, and fornicators, and murderers,
and idolaters, and everyone of false speech and false life.'

d. 2 S 7:14 **e.** Ezk 40:2 **f.** Is 60:1–2 **g.** Ezk 48:31–35 **h.** Is 60:3
22 a. Ezk 47:12 **b.** Zc 14:11 **c.** Ps 62:12

EPILOGUE

16 I, Jesus, have sent my angel to make these revelations to you for the sake of the churches. I am of David's line, the root of David and the bright star of the morning.

17 The Spirit and the Bride say, 'Come'. Let everyone who listens answer, 'Come'. *Then let all who are thirsty come:*[d] all who want it may *have the water* of life, *and have it free*.

18 This is my solemn warning to all who hear the prophecies in this book: if anyone adds anything to them, God will add

19 to him every plague mentioned in the book; ·if anyone cuts anything out of the prophecies in this book, God will cut off his share of the tree of life and of the holy city, which are described in the book.

20 The one who guarantees these revelations repeats his promise: I shall indeed *be with you* soon. Amen; come, Lord Jesus.

21 May the grace of the Lord Jesus be with you all. Amen.

d. Is 55:1